Pro ADO.NET with VB .NET 1.1

SAHIL MALIK, PAUL DICKINSON, FABIO CLAUDIO FERRACCHIATI,
KEVIN HOFFMAN, BIPIN JOSHI, DONNY MACK, JOHN MCTAINSH,
MATT MILNER, JAN NARKIEWICZ, AND DOUG SEVEN

Pro ADO.NET with VB .NET 1.1

Copyright © 2005 by Sahil Malik, Paul Dickinson, Fabio Claudio Ferracchiati, Kevin Hoffman, Bipin Joshi, Donny Mack, John McTainsh, Matt Milner, Jan Narkiewicz, and Doug Seven

ISBN (pbk): 1-59059-434-7

Printed and bound in the United States of America 9 8 7 6 5 4 3 2 1

Trademarked names may appear in this book. Rather than use a trademark symbol with every occurrence of a trademarked name, we use the names only in an editorial fashion and to the benefit of the trademark owner, with no intention of infringement of the trademark.

Lead Editor: Dominic Shakeshaft

Technical Reviewers: Kapil Apshankar, Martin Beaulieu, Paul Churchill, Michael Cohen, Chris Crane, Slavomir Furman, Dan Green, Jeffrey Hasan, Lauren Hightower, Christian Holm, Mark Horner, Jody Kerr, Don Lee, Alex Lowe, Rob MacDonald, Craig McQueen, Arun Nair, J. Boyd Nolan PE, Phil Powers DeGeorge, Trevor Scott, Donald Xie

Editorial Board: Steve Anglin, Dan Appleman, Ewan Buckingham, Gary Cornell, Tony Davis, John Franklin, Jason Gilmore, Chris Mills, Dominic Shakeshaft, Jim Sumser

Project Manager: Beth Christmas

Copy Edit Manager: Nicole LeClerc

Copy Editor: Linda Marousek

Production Manager: Kari Brooks-Copony

Production Editor: Ellie Fountain

Compositor: Molly Sharp

Proofreader: Linda Seifert

Indexer: Kevin Broccoli, Martin Brooks

Cover Designer: Kurt Krames

Manufacturing Manager: Tom Debolski

Distributed to the book trade in the United States by Springer-Verlag New York, Inc., 233 Spring Street, 6th Floor, New York, NY 10013, and outside the United States by Springer-Verlag GmbH & Co. KG, Tiergartenstr. 17, 69112 Heidelberg, Germany.

In the United States: phone 1-800-SPRINGER, fax 201-348-4505, e-mail orders@springer-ny.com, or visit http://www.springer-ny.com. Outside the United States: fax +49 6221 345229, e-mail orders@springer.de, or visit http://www.springer.de.

For information on translations, please contact Apress directly at 2560 Ninth Street, Suite 219, Berkeley, CA 94710. Phone 510-549-5930, fax 510-549-5939, e-mail info@apress.com, or visit http://www.apress.com.

The information in this book is distributed on an "as is" basis, without warranty. Although every precaution has been taken in the preparation of this work, neither the author(s) nor Apress shall have any liability to any person or entity with respect to any loss or damage caused or alleged to be caused directly or indirectly by the information contained in this work.

The source code for this book is available to readers at http://www.apress.com in the Downloads section.

I would like to dedicate this book to my parents.
Mom, thank you very much for taking care of my every need as I was working both
on the book and my job around the clock, I couldn't do this without you.
Pop, thank you so much for being a never-ending source of inspiration and strength.
I love you both very much.

—*Sahil Malik*

Contents at a Glance

Contents

About the Authors

SAHIL MALIK has been working as an independent consultant in Microsoft technology for most of his adult life. He actually holds the record for being kicked out of his college for spending too much time in the computer center (but finished college anyway). Sahil has worked for many top-notch clients across the globe, including many Fortune 100 companies and government organizations within the United States. Sahil started programming in a DOS world, moved to Win32 API, Borland C++, MFC, VC++/ATL, VB6, and eventually to .NET in both VB.NET and C# worlds. Sahil is currently helping architect one of the 50 highest-traffic Web sites in the world using ASP.NET 2.0.

PAUL DICKINSON was born very early on in life and has continued to age at a reasonable pace. He first discovered his computing prowess with the advent of the Atari ST and Kick Off 2. People came from far and wide only to be humiliated with his crushing one-twos and deadly banana shots. In order to better himself he went off to UMIST (the University of Manchester Institute of Science and Technology) to study Computation. Proving that academia wasn't for Paul, he graduated unspectacularly and spent several years cutting his software development teeth writing software to control mass spectrometers. His most recent resting place involves developing information management systems for laboratories. On the frequent occasions that Paul isn't in front of a computer, he can be found hurtling round country roads in hired sports cars or searching for the perfect doner kebab. He'd like to thank his beautiful wife, Sue, for giving him the will to sit in darkened rooms working all hours. Paul can be reached at http://www.pauldickinson.com.

FABIO CLAUDIO FERRACCHIATI is a software developer and technical writer. In the early years of his ten-year career, he worked with classical languages and old Microsoft tools like Visual Basic and Visual C++. After five years he decided to dedicate his attention to the Internet and all its related technologies. In 1998 he started a parallel career writing technical articles for Italian and international magazines. He works in Rome for CPI Progetti Spa (http://www.cpiprogetti.it), where he develops Internet/intranet solutions using Microsoft technologies. Fabio would like to thank every one of his CPI colleagues. In particular, he would like to thank Angelo for his kindness.

Let me say a few words about my love, Danila, who helps me in my work and gives up her time to stay with me on workdays and weekends. Also, she helps with my diet—it's very hard preparing carrots, salads, and vegetables every day (a little voice inside me says, "It's harder eating them…"). I'm sure that I could never find another girl like her, and I don't want to. Thanks for everything.

KEVIN HOFFMAN is a software technology junkie who is currently eating and breathing anything and everything that has to do with the .NET Framework. He started programming in BASIC on a Commodore VIC-20 that his grandfather had repaired after it was found in the trash, and has been a tech addict ever since, working at everything from nationwide UNIX mainframe support to a software engineer for one of the most popular e-commerce Web sites on the Internet. Recently, he's found that he loves to write about and teach programming as much as he loves doing it himself.

I would like to dedicate my work for this book to my mother, Marie, who has always been a treasured source of infinite love and support. Also, I would like to dedicate my work to my brother, Kurt, and sister-in-law, Nina, who have always been encouraging and supportive.

■**BIPIN JOSHI** is a software developer from Mumbai with skills in Microsoft technologies. Currently, he works on .NET technologies with Mastek Ltd., a global applications outsourcing company with offshore software development centers in India. He runs his personal Web site at `http://www.bipinjoshi.com`, which provides articles, tutorials, and source code on a variety of .NET topics. He also contributes regularly to other popular Web sites. When away from computers, he spends time in deep meditation exploring the Divine. He can be contacted via his Web site.

This work is dedicated to my Baba, Aai, and Bhau (father, mother, and brother). Without their wonderful support and encouragement this would not have been possible.

■**DONNY MACK**, MCP, MCSD, Microsoft .NET MVP, is a native of Washington State, and one of the co-founders of DotNetJunkies.com—an education company solely dedicated to ASP.NET and other web-related .NET technologies. DotNetJunkies.com is a free, online, centralized resource Web site used by .NET developers to feed their .NET passion.

Prior to founding DotNetJunkies.com with Doug Seven, Mack worked at Microsoft Corporation as a Visual Interdev/ASP support professional assisting developers from all over the world in troubleshooting and utilizing new advances in technology to improve application performance and functionality. Mack's need for bleeding edge technology is such that he spends his waking hours (and some of his nonwaking hours) writing code and developing content for DotNetJunkies.com. Mack is an MCP, MCSD, and one of the few Microsoft .NET MVP's in the world. He has worked closely with Doug Seven and the ASP.NET development team throughout the development of the technology.

■**JOHN MCTAINSH** started coding in high school on the Apple II and ZX81 in 1982. In the early days, he worked mostly with the Motorola chipset in assembly language, making simple but fast games, and programming microcontrollers. He completed his engineering degree in 1988, and moved to Asia to work in the offshore oil and gas exploration industry. Starting as a commercial diver, he soon got back into coding, developing control systems for underwater robots in C and C++. Since then, he's written many control systems and various other applications and drivers, mostly for PC hardware. John currently lives in Australia, where he works as a team leader developing public safety software for computer-aided dispatch systems used by police, fire, and ambulance vehicles.

I would like to thank my parents for a great upbringing, and my wife and daughter for putting up with my tap-tap coding late into the night. Thanks Claudia, Rebecca, Dorothy, and Albert.

■**MATT MILNER** works as a Technical Architect for BORN in Minneapolis, where he designs and builds Microsoft solutions for clients in a variety of industries. Matt's primary focus has been using Windows DNA architecture and he is excited about the move to .NET and all the powerful new features. When Matt is not working at the computer, he spends his time in his woodshop, reading, or enjoying the many great natural resources of Minnesota.

■**JAN D. NARKIEWICZ** is Chief Technical Officer at Software Pronto, Inc (jann@softwarepronto.com). Jan began his career as a Microsoft developer thanks to basketball star, Michael Jordan. In the early 90s, Jan noticed that no matter what happened during a game, Michael Jordan's team won. Similarly, no matter what happened in technology, Microsoft always won. (Then again, this strategy is ten years old and may need some revamping.) Clearly there was a bandwagon to be jumped upon.

Over the years, Jan managed to work on an e-mail system that resided on 17 million desktops, helped automate factories that make the blue jeans you have in your closet (trust me, you own this brand), and kept the skies over the Emirate of Abu Dhabi safe from enemy aircraft. All this was achieved using technology such as COM/DCOM, COM+, C++, VB, C#, ADO, SQL Server, Oracle, DB2, ASP.NET, ADO.NET, Java, Linux, and XML. In his spare time, Jan is Academic Coordinator for the Windows curriculum at U.C. Berkeley Extension, teaches at U.C. Santa Cruz Extension, writes for *ASP Today*, and occasionally plays some football (a.k.a. soccer).

■**DOUG SEVEN** is the co-creator of DotNetJunkies.com, a free, online, centralized resource Web site used by developers to learn more about the .NET Framework—specifically, ASP.NET. Seven comes to DotNetJunkies.com by way of technical roles at Nordstrom, Microsoft, and GiftCertificates.com, and as a training specialist at Seattle Coffee Company. At Microsoft, Seven was a technical lead in the developer support group, where he taught classes in Visual Basic and ADO to Technical Routers, the first-tier support group. After leaving Microsoft, Seven worked as a web developer for GiftCertificates.com before leaving to pursue life as a DotNetJunkie.

Seven has authored several resource materials covering the .NET Framework, including *Programming Data-Driven Web Applications with ASP.NET*, and has contributed to *ASP.NET: Tips, Tutorials, and Code* as well as countless magazine and Web site articles.

In his spare time, Seven, a self-proclaimed workaholic, enjoys writing code and answering technical questions. On the rare occasions when he can squeeze in a social life, he likes to learn about fine wines and sit by the pool, in the sun.

My work on this book is a direct credit to the great support I've received from my family and friends. Specifically, I would like to thank Dawniel Giebel for all of her understanding, support, and most of all for sharing her love, life, and wine; Donny Mack for continuing to fight the good fight with me; Mark Anders, Rob Howard, Scott Guthrie, and Susan Warren for answering all my questions so quickly; Dene "Madam D." Holdsworth, Jason Pace, and Tres Henry for being the number one fans of DotNetJunkies.com—someday we'll be as cool as GotDotNet.com; Alex Lowe, Trevor Scott, David Barnes, Claire Brittle, Craig McQueen, and Jeffery Hasan for all the great review work to make this book excellent; Avril Corbin, Alastair Ewins, Chandy Nethansinghe, Charlotte Smith, and Helen Cuthill for everything; Ed Hickey for the best professional advice I ever received: "Write code every day, even if it's just one line."; Jon Serious for letting me play around with SeriousDotNet.com; Lance Hayes for being the greatest country music aficionado in the world; Corinne "Jimi" Gurkey and Willy G. for being so cool all the time; Dave Sceppa for being a great ADO resource while I was at Microsoft, for being generally sarcastic all the time, and for writing great books.

Introduction

ADO.NET is Microsoft's latest data access technology and, as an integral part of the .NET Framework, is far more than just an ADO upgrade. ADO.NET provides an extensive set of .NET classes that facilitate efficient access to data in a large variety of sources, enable sophisticated manipulation and sorting of data, and form an important framework within which to implement interapplication communication.

ADO.NET has already proved itself as a core component of any data-driven .NET application or web service. Understanding its power and flexibility is essential to anyone wanting to use .NET's transport technologies to best effect.

What Does This Book Cover?

This book provides a thorough investigation of the ADO.NET classes, adopting a practical, solution-oriented approach. It looks at how to use the various components of ADO.NET effectively within the field of data-centric application development.

The journey begins in Chapter 1, which looks at the .NET data providers—the sets of classes that provide connectivity to a variety of data stores. Subsequent chapters then begin to delve deeper into the specifics of ADO.NET. Chapter 2 looks at data readers—what they are, why you use them, and also how you can use them in a number of situations. This in-depth look continues in Chapter 3, where you'll learn about the DataSet, while Chapter 4 introduces and explores data adapter classes.

Chapter 5 then takes a closer look at the DataSet, which enables you to work with data while disconnected from the data source. It includes an introduction to how XML schemas can be useful when manipulating DataSets. This leads nicely in to Chapter 6, where you explore the use of XML with DataSets more fully, covering issues such as XPath and data validation, among others.

You round off your coverage of the DataSet in Chapter 7, where you examine constraints, relations, and views, all of which influence the way that data is presented and manipulated. The chapter also introduces the DataView, and includes some examples of its use.

Chapter 8 moves on to look at the topic of *transactions*, a subject of paramount importance in the business world where either all operations on a data source must succeed, or all of them must fail. Among other things, this chapter examines isolation levels and their impact, performance, and some advanced transaction techniques.

The concept of *mapping* is explored in Chapter 9. This is where you can make ADO.NET give different names to the tables and columns in your code from the names they had in the original data source, enabling you to make your applications as intuitive as possible.

Chapter 10 looks at creating your own component for accessing data services, at the benefits of doing so, at deploying it, and at using it once it exists. The chapter also looks at tips for better performance. This leads well in to Chapter 11, where you look at ADO.NET and web services—in particular, at exchanging data, using XML, and security.

In Chapter 12, you revisit the subject of XML, but this time considering it from the point of view of the database, rather than ADO.NET. We show how SQL Server 2000 has native support for XML, allowing you to tailor how much manipulation the server performs, and how much you do in your applications.

Chapter 13 moves in to the more theoretical realms of performance and security. Of course, both of these are important considerations if you're going to be dealing with high levels of demand and/or sensitive data, so this chapter covers many methods of improving both.

The penultimate Chapter 14 discusses integration and migration—in particular, accessing ADO data sources from .NET, and handling the migration process from ADO to ADO.NET.

Finally, Chapter 15 explains how to create your own custom .NET data provider. It takes you through the whole process in case-study fashion—from helping you decide that you might need one, through the architecture and design, to its actual implementation. The chapter also demonstrates a number of ways in which such a provider might be used.

Who Is This Book For?

If you're already developing Visual Basic .NET applications within the .NET Framework, or you have experience in developing data-driven applications with ADO and wish to make the transition to .NET, then this book is for you. It is aimed at fairly experienced programmers, and is not intended for the casual ASP.NET developer or the beginner. It does not cover the basics of Visual Basic.NET or the Microsoft Data Access technologies.

What You Need to Use This Book

To work through and run the samples in this book, you need to have the following:

- Windows 2000 or Windows XP

- The .NET Framework SDK

- Visual Studio .NET (either Standard or Professional, though the latter is preferred)

- Either the Microsoft Data Engine (MSDE) or SQL Server 2000

The complete source code for the samples is available for download from the Apress Web site at http://www.apress.com.

Conventions

We've used a number of different styles of text and layout in this book to help you differentiate between the different kinds of information. Here are examples of the styles we used, and an explanation of what they mean.

Code has several styles. If it's a word that we're talking about in the text – for example, when discussing a For...Next loop, it's in this font. If it's a block of code that can be entered as part of a program and run, then it's also in bold typeface:

```
<?xml version 1.0?>
```

Sometimes, you'll see code in a mixture of styles, like this:

```xml
<?xml version 1.0?>
<Invoice>
   <part>
      <name>Widget</name>
      <price>$10.00</price>
   </part>
</invoice>
```

In cases like this, the code that does not appear in bold typeface is code you're already familiar with; the line in bold is a new addition to the code since you last looked at it.

CHAPTER 1

■ ■ ■

An Overview of ADO.NET

In today's Internet-driven, information-abundant world, applications almost always require access to data of one form or another. In some cases, that data is stored in a database under the control of products such as Microsoft SQL Server or Oracle. In others, it will be stored in a spreadsheet, or an XML file, or in one of countless different proprietary data formats. Regardless of the specifics of the data store in question, however, there must be a technology that allows an application to connect to the data, and to execute commands against it. In the .NET Framework, that technology is ADO.NET.

In the most practical terms, ADO.NET is a library of classes that are defined in and beneath the .NET Framework's System.Data namespace—there are classes that represent connections to databases, the tables in those databases, and the types of data those tables contain. Speaking more broadly, ADO.NET is Microsoft's latest data-access strategy—its best attempt yet at the goal of Universal Data Access.

In this chapter, you're going to take a fairly quick overview of ADO.NET before you start concentrating on key features throughout the book. By design, therefore, you're going to be moving along rapidly, and we won't shy away from showing snippets of code—it really is the best way of getting to grips with the concepts. By the end, you should have a good understanding of the basic workings of ADO.NET, and a taste of some of its more exciting features. With luck, you'll be eager to go further into the book!

ADO.NET Architecture

The ADO.NET object model consists of two fundamental components: the *.NET data provider*, and the *dataset*. Although—as you'll see—these two components have to work together, they represent two very different ways of interacting with data. In a nutshell, data providers (for there are several) are specialized to particular types of data sources, giving the developer an efficient conduit for performing direct operations on the data in those sources. A dataset, on the other hand, can be thought of as a kind of data store in its own right; it is not specialized for working with data from any particular source type, but it has powerful features for manipulating the data it contains.

From these definitions, two data-access strategies emerge. In the first, you use a data provider to connect to a data source, perform some quick operations on that source (including, potentially, a simple read operation), and then disconnect. In the second, you again use the data provider to connect, but then copy data into a dataset, and disconnect. After that, you can use the data in the dataset at your leisure—and if at some stage you need to make changes to the data source, you can reconnect and do that.

Because the .NET data providers are key to both of these strategies, they need to be light-weight and efficient, creating a minimal layer between your application and the data source. In use, a .NET data provider is generally composed of the following four main objects:

- A *connection* object, which provides connectivity to a data source.

- A *command* object, which enables database commands (such as SQL commands or stored procedures) to be executed against the data source.

- A *data reader* object, which provides a forward-only, read-only stream of data from the data source to your application.

- A *data adapter* object, which provides a bridge between a dataset and the data source. The data adapter object uses command objects to execute SELECT, INSERT, UPDATE, and DELETE commands against the data source, and places any requested data into, or reconciles data from, a dataset.

As just explained, a dataset is not a part of any .NET data provider, but it makes sense to include a quick definition here. An ADO.NET *dataset* object is an in-memory, disconnected representation of a data source (or a subset of that source). Putting these facts together with our earlier discussion of data access strategies leads to the diagram in Figure 1-1.

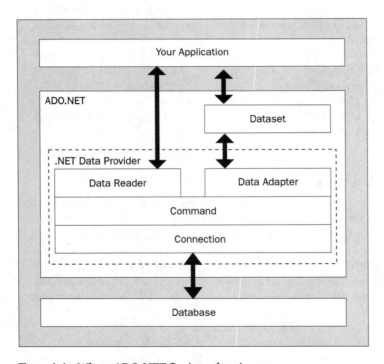

Figure 1-1. *Where ADO.NET fits into the picture*

.NET Data Providers

So, the model followed by ADO.NET is to have different data providers for different data sources, with the aim of optimizing data access for each source type. A .NET data provider can be written for any data source, but the .NET Framework ships with the following four data providers as standard:

- *SQL Server .NET data provider*: This is a .NET data provider designed explicitly for use with SQL Server 7.0 and above. It uses a proprietary protocol to connect directly to the database, without an intervening OLE DB layer. The classes for this data provider can be found in the `System.Data.SqlClient` namespace.

- *OLE DB .NET data provider*: This is a .NET data provider designed for use with all OLE DB–compliant data sources. It uses a data source–specific OLE DB provider (through COM interoperability) to access the data source and execute commands. The classes for this data provider can be found in the `System.Data.OleDb` namespace.

■**Caution** Note that the OLE DB .NET data provider doesn't support OLE DB 2.5 interfaces, such as those required for the OLE DB providers for Exchange and Internet Publishing. Similarly, it doesn't support the `MSDASQL` provider (the OLE DB provider for ODBC). Note also that for applications that use SQL Server 6.5 or earlier, you *must* use the OLE DB .NET data provider.

- *The Oracle data provider*: This is a .NET data provider designed for use with all Oracle data sources (specifically, version 8.1.7 and above). The classes for this data provider can be found in the `System.Data.OracleClient` namespace.

- *The ODBC .NET data provider*: This is a .NET data provider optimized for accessing ODBC data sources. The classes for this data provider can be found in the `System.Data.ODBC` namespace.

And it's not just Microsoft that can create .NET data providers—you can do it too, as you'll see in Chapter 15. In fact, a quick Internet search will reveal a burgeoning set of .NET data providers being written by developers for many different databases and data sources.

The key to this generality and extensibility is that regardless of the data source they target, all .NET data providers implement the same interfaces, and work in the same manner. In this chapter, you'll take a first look at those interfaces and the functionality they encapsulate, and explore the semantics of connecting to and working with a data source through a .NET data provider.

Meet the Players

.NET data providers can contain additional support classes, but their main features are the four classes that we listed at the start of the chapter: the connection, the command, the data reader, and the data adapter. These classes are implementations of four ADO.NET interfaces that can be found in the System.Data namespace. Figure 1-2 shows these classes and interfaces.

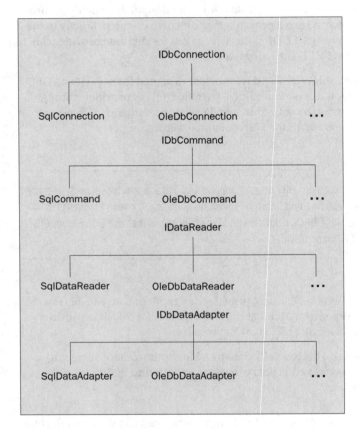

Figure 1-2. *Sample classes and interfaces within ADO.NET*

Connection Classes

An instance of a connection class is used to represent a connection to a specific data source. Such an object stores the information that ADO.NET needs to connect to a data source in the form of a connection string.

The IDbConnection interface's ConnectionString property can hold information such as the name and location of the data source to connect to, the name and password of a user with permission to access the data, and so on. In addition, connection classes have methods for opening and closing connections, and for beginning a transaction; and they have properties for setting the timeout period of the connection, and for returning the current state of the connection (that is, open or closed).

We'll be looking at issues of syntax more closely later on, but one way to create and configure a SqlConnection object (that is, the connection object defined by the SQL Server .NET data provider) is:

```
Dim con As New SqlConnection()
con.ConnectionString = "server=(local);database=Northwind;uid=sa;pwd=;"
```

■**Caution** Unlike previous versions of ADO, connection objects *must* be closed explicitly, using the IDbConnection.Close() method, in order to release the actual connection to the data source. The latter *will not* be implicitly released through garbage collection when the connection object falls out of scope. For this reason, it's a good idea always to wrap your ADO.NET data access code in a Try block, and to ensure that the connection is closed in the Finally block.

Command Classes

ADO.NET command classes implement the IDbCommand interface, and instances are used to execute SQL statements or stored procedures against the data source specified by a connection object. To this end, command classes have a CommandText property that contains the text of the command to be executed, and a CommandType property that indicates whether the command is a SQL statement, the name of a stored procedure, or the name of a table. Given the connection object you created in the previous code, you might create a command object like the following:

```
Dim str As String = "SELECT EmployeeID, FirstName, LastName FROM Employees"
Dim cmd As New SqlCommand(str, con)
```

There are three distinct execute methods: ExecuteReader(), which returns a DataReader object; ExecuteScalar(), which returns a single value; and ExecuteNonQuery(), which is for use when no data will be returned from the query (say, for a SQL UPDATE statement).

To help it do its job, a command object contains a collection of parameter objects that represent the parameters to be passed into a SQL query or a stored procedure. These objects expose the IDataParameter interface, and form part of the .NET data provider—that is, each provider also has its own implementation of the IDataParameter (and IDataParameterCollection) interface.

As you'd expect, .NET data providers are free to implement their own methods over and above those required to implement interfaces like IDbCommand. In the case of the Oracle .NET data provider, for example, the OracleCommand class includes methods called ExecuteOracleScalar() and ExecuteOracleNonQuery() that return and receive Oracle-specific values, rather than generic .NET types.

Data Reader Classes

Data reader classes implement the IDataReader interface, and—as stated previously—a data reader object represents a forward-only, read-only stream of data from the data source. You can't use a data reader to navigate through the data at random, and you can't use it to update the data source. Rather, a data reader allows extremely fast access to data that you want to iterate through just once, and it's recommended that you use one (rather than a DataSet) wherever it's appropriate to do so.

A data reader object can be created *only* by calling the ExecuteReader() method of a command object; you can't instantiate one directly. After that, you can use the data reader's Read() method to iterate through the rows in the returned stream of data, using a programming construct something like this:

```
Try
  con.Open()
  Dim reader As SqlDataReader = cmd.ExecuteReader()
  While reader.Read()

    ' Do something with the value
  End While
  reader.Close()
Finally
  con.Close()
End Try
```

A set of methods for retrieving the values of the fields in a record (row) is defined by the IDataRecord interface, which is inherited by IDataReader, and must therefore also be implemented in a data reader class. Each of these methods takes the zero-based column ordinal as its input argument, and is named after the type of data it specializes in retrieving—typical examples are GetBoolean(), GetChar(), and GetFloat().

These "Get" methods provide the most efficient access to the data when the data type of the column is known, because the amount of type conversion is reduced. When the data type of the column *isn't* known, you can use the ToString() method of the System.Object class to get the value as a string.

```
While reader.Read()
  myInt = reader.GetInt32(0)
  myString = reader.Item(1).ToString()
End While
```

A connection object can support only one data reader at a time, so you *must* explicitly close the data reader when you're done with it. This will free the connection for other uses.

■**Note** If the command that's being executed returns a data reader and one or more output parameters, those parameters are not accessible until the data reader has been closed.

Data Adapter Classes

The fourth and final major class in a .NET data provider is the data adapter, which acts as the bridge between a disconnected DataSet object (more to follow on this soon) and the data source. It implements two interfaces. The first of these, IDataAdapter, defines methods for populating a DataSet with data from the data source (the most significant of which is Fill()) and for updating the data source with changes made to the DataSet on the client. The second interface, IDbDataAdapter, defines four properties, each of type IDbCommand. These properties set or return command objects that specify the commands to be executed when the data source is to be queried or updated.

■**Note** The methods of a data adapter object will always leave a connection in the state in which they found it. In other words, if the connection is already open when you call a data adapter method, it will remain open afterward. If the connection is closed to start with, the method will open it, execute, and then close it again.

The DataSet Class

The other major component of ADO.NET is the DataSet object, which you can think of as being similar to an in-memory relational database. DataSet objects contain DataTable objects, relationships, and constraints, allowing them to replicate an entire data source, or selected parts of it, in a disconnected fashion.

A DataSet object is *always* disconnected from the source whose data it contains, and as a consequence it doesn't care where the data comes from—it can be used to manipulate data from a traditional database or an XML document, or anything in between. In order to connect a DataSet to a data source, you need to use a data adapter as an intermediary between the DataSet and the .NET data provider. For example, to populate a DataSet with data from the Employees table in the Northwind database, you might use code that looks something like this.

```
Imports System
Imports System.Data
Imports System.Data.SqlClient

Module Module1
  Sub Main()

    ' Create the connection
    Dim con As New SqlConnection()
    con.ConnectionString = "server=(local);database=Northwind;uid=sa;pwd=;"
```

```
        ' Create the command object
        Dim str As String = _
                        "SELECT EmployeeID, FirstName, LastName FROM Employees"
        Dim cmd As New SqlCommand(str, con)

        ' Create a new data adapter object, passing in the SELECT command
        Dim da As New SqlDataAdapter(cmd)

        ' Create a new DataSet
        Dim ds As New DataSet()

        ' Fill the DataSet, using the data adapter
        da.Fill(ds, "Employees")
    End Sub
End Module
```

After creating the connection and command objects just as you did previously, there are three steps involved in populating the DataSet:

1. Instantiate a new data adapter object. Before you can fill the DataSet, you need to specify the connection information, and the data you want to fill it with. There are a number of ways of doing that, but probably the easiest way is to pass the command object you created earlier into the data adapter's constructor, as you do in the previous code.

2. Create the new DataSet.

3. Call the data adapter's Fill() method, to which you pass the DataSet that you want to populate, and the name of the table within the DataSet that you want to fill. Calling the Fill() method against a closed connection like this, the connection is automatically opened and then reclosed when the DataSet has been filled.

The DataTable Class

Implicit in the description of filling a DataSet object given previously is that these objects can contain more than one table of data: objects of ADO.NET's DataTable class represent a *single* table within a DataSet. The DataSet class has a property called Tables that returns a collection of these objects; a DataTable object represents data in tabular format, using collections of DataColumn and DataRow objects to represent each column and row in the table, as shown in Figure 1-3.

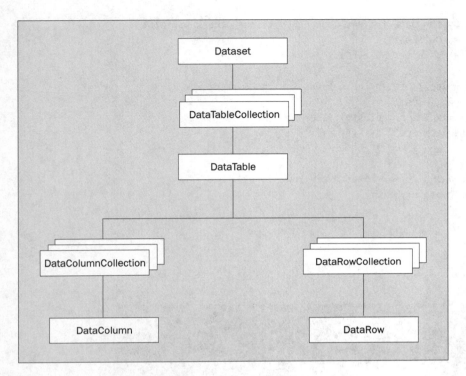

Figure 1-3. DataTable *and its place within ADO.NET*

If you want to access the data in a DataTable, you have to access the appropriate DataRow object, and index into that to get the data for a particular column. The index can be either the numerical index of the column (0 for the first column, and so on), or its name. The following example first iterates through the DataColumnCollection to retrieve the names of the columns in the first table of the DataSet. It then iterates through each row, and each column for the current row, and displays the data in a crude command-line table.

```
' Fill the DataSet, using the data adapter
da.Fill(ds, "Employees")
' Display the column names
Dim dc As DataColumn
For Each dc In ds.Tables(0).Columns
  Console.Write("{0,15}", dc.ColumnName)
Next

' Add a newline after the column headings
Console.Write(vbCrLf)
```

```
    ' Display the data for each row. Loop through the rows first
    Dim dr As DataRow
    For Each dr in ds.Tables(0).Rows

        ' Then loop through the columns for the current row
        Dim i As Integer
        For i = 1 To ds.Tables(0).Columns.Count
            Console.Write("{0,15}", dr(i - 1))
        Next i

        ' Add a line break after every row
        Console.Write(vbCrLf)
    Next
  End Sub
End Module
```

Figure 1-4 shows the result of the previous code.

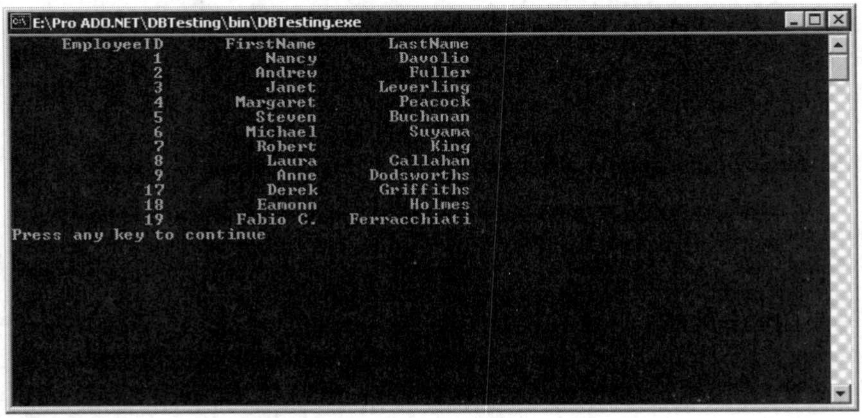

Figure 1-4. *DataTable.vb*

Establishing Connections to Data Sources

In the chapters to come, you'll look closely at the workings of data readers and DataSets. As the preceding sections have described, however, both of these techniques for data access and manipulation are reliant on the creation of connection and command objects. It's these two that you'll be taking a more careful look at now, starting with the former. You're going to examine the different ways to create a connection object, and look at what you can do with them.

As you know, ADO.NET connection classes are used to make a connection between your application and a data source.

- The connection class is instantiated, a connection string is set, and the connection is opened.

- While the connection is open, commands may be executed over the connection in order to retrieve or manipulate data in the data source.

- When you are done with the connection, close it to release the resource.

As previously stated, it's critical that you close the connection explicitly, using the connection object's Close() method. If you fail to do so, the connection will not be released, even if the connection object falls out of scope and is garbage-collected.

Concrete Connection Classes

With the exception of the format of the connection string that's used to connect to a data source, the .NET data providers' connection classes behave in the same way. Let's take the two .NET data providers that ship with the .NET Framework as our examples and see how they work. Given the information in this section, you should feel comfortable about working with any .NET data provider with only the briefest look at its documentation.

Constructing a Connection

The SqlConnection and OleDbConnection classes both expose two constructors for creating instances of these classes in our applications. The first constructor creates a new, "empty" instance of the connection class, while the second creates an instance of the connection class using the connection string as follows:

```
Dim con As New SqlConnection()
con.ConnectionString = "server=(local);database=Northwind;uid=sa;pwd=;"
```

or:

```
Dim con As New SqlConnection( _
               "server=(local);database=Northwind;uid=sa;pwd=;")
```

Because you're creating an instance of the *Sql*Connection class in this example, you're already making it clear that you'll be connecting to a SQL Server database—you're using the SQL Server .NET data provider! The connection string just needs to specify the server and database to be connected. When you're using the *OleDb*Connection class, on the other hand, the name of an OLE DB provider *is* required in the connection string, for example:

- SQLOLEDB: Microsoft OLE DB provider for SQL Server

```
Dim con As New OleDbConnection( _
               "Provider=SQLOLEDB;Data Source=(local);" & _
               "Initial Catalog=Northwind;Integrated Security=SSPI;")
```

- Microsoft.Jet.OLEDB.4.0: OLE DB provider for Microsoft Jet

```
Dim con As New OleDbConnection( _
                 "Provider=Microsoft.Jet.OLEDB.4.0;" & _
                 "Data Source=C:\Program Files\Microsoft Office\" & _
                 "Office\Samples\Northwind.mdb;")
```

Storing Connection Strings in a Configuration File

The .NET Framework uses XML-formatted text files for maintaining configuration information. These configuration files can contain anything from assembly references and versioning information, to authentication information and key-value pairs of application-specific data. Applications may have zero, one, or more configuration files. In web applications, the file must be named Web.config, while for executable applications the filename also ends in .config, but it's prefixed with the application name, such as myApp.exe.config.

The XML structure of the configuration file is similar for both application types. (For more information, see ms-help://MS.VSCC/MS.MSDNVS/cpguide/html/cpconapplicationconfigurationfiles.htm.) In either case, the file may include an element named <appSettings>, and it's here that key-value pairs may be stored. Storing connection strings in a configuration file allows us to maintain them in a single location, making for easy modification without recompilation, should they ever change.

■Note Values in the <appSettings> element of a configuration file are available to any class in the application, whether it's a web form class, a business logic class, or a data access layer class.

To use a .NET configuration file as a store for connection strings, you just need to add a new <add> element as a child of the <appSettings> element for each connection string in the application. The key attribute specifies the name by which you will refer to this connection string, while the value attribute specifies the connection string itself.

```
<?xml version="1.0" encoding="utf-8" ?>
<configuration>
  <appSettings>
    <add key="constring"
        value="server=(local);database=Northwind;uid=sa;pwd=;"/>
  </appSettings>
</configuration>
```

The classes for accessing the configuration file can be found in the System.Configuration namespace. To create a connection using a string stored in the configuration file, you just need to add a reference to the System.Configuration namespace and use the ConfigurationSettings class, like the following:

```
...
Imports System.Configuration
...
Dim con As New SqlConnection( _
                    ConfigurationSettings.AppSettings("constring"))
...
```

Connection Events

Before you leave connection classes alone for the time being, you should note that they all expose three events: Disposed, StateChange, and InfoMessage. Of these, the Disposed event is not specific to ADO.NET connections—it's inherited from the System.ComponentModel.Component class, and is fired when the object is destroyed—and since that is not an ADO.NET specific event, it is out of scope of this book. The other two events are more interesting from our point of view.

StateChange

The StateChange event is fired whenever the state of the connection changes from "open" to "closed," or vice versa. In the following code, you create an event handler for the StateChange event that writes the current state to the screen:

```
Module Module1
  Dim WithEvents con As SqlConnection

  Sub Main()
    con = New SqlConnection(ConfigurationSettings.AppSettings("constring"))

    Dim cmd As New SqlCommand()
    cmd.CommandText = "SELECT TOP 5 * FROM Customers"
    cmd.Connection = con

    Try
      con.Open()

      Dim reader As SqlDataReader = cmd.ExecuteReader()
      While reader.Read()
        Console.WriteLine( _
              "{0} - {1}", reader.GetString(0), reader.GetString(1))
      End While
      reader.Close()
    Finally
      con.Close()
    End Try
  End Sub
```

```
Sub con_StateChange(ByVal Sender As Object, _
            ByVal E As StateChangeEventArgs) Handles con.StateChange
    Console.WriteLine( _
            "{0} - {1}", "ConnectionState", E.CurrentState.ToString())
    End Sub
End Module
```

In the preceding code, you defined a method called con_StateChange() to handle the
StateChange event of the SqlConnection object called con. When the connection is opened,
the StateChange event is fired. The same occurs when the connection is closed (see Figure 1-5).

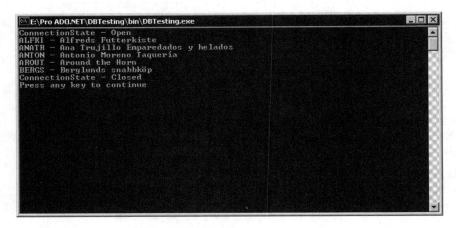

Figure 1-5. *StateChange.vb*

InfoMessage

The InfoMessage event is fired whenever a .NET data provider sends a warning or an informational message to the client. Any handler for this event will receive the sender as its first
argument, and a provider-specific object containing data about the event (with a type called
something like SqlInfoMessageEventArgs or OleDbInfoMessageEventArgs, inherited from
System.EventArgs) as its second.

In the following code, you raise the InfoMessage event by using a SQL PRINT command.
The PRINT argument gets sent to the event handler as an error, and is accessible in the
SqlInfoMessageEventArgs.Errors collection.

```
Module Module1
    Dim WithEvents con As SqlConnection

    Sub Main()
        con = New SqlConnection( _
                ConfigurationSettings.AppSettings("constring"))
```

```
    Dim cmd As New SqlCommand()
    cmd.CommandText = "PRINT('This raises an InfoMessage event')"
    cmd.Connection = con

    Try
      con.Open()
      cmd.ExecuteNonQuery()
    Finally
      con.Close()
    End Try
  End Sub

  Sub con_InfoMessage(ByVal Sender As Object, _
              ByVal E As SqlInfoMessageEventArgs) Handles con.InfoMessage
    Console.WriteLine( _
              "{0} - {1}", "InfoMessage", E.Errors.Item(0).ToString())
  End Sub
End Module
```

When the SqlCommand object (cmd) executes the SQL command, the InfoMessage event is fired, and the con_InfoMessage() method is executed.

Connection Pooling in the Data Providers

Connection pooling is the practice of keeping a permanent set of open database connections to be shared by sessions that use the same data source, thereby avoiding the need to create and destroy connections all the time. The .NET data providers manage connection pooling automatically, so that developers don't have to worry about it. If you need to do so, however, you can gain explicit control over pooling behavior through modifiers that you can place in your connection strings.

The OLE DB .NET data provider, for example, pools connections using OLE DB session pooling, but this can be disabled using a connection string argument. The following connection string disables pooling and automatic transaction enlistment:

```
Dim con As New OleDbConnection("Provider=SQLOLEDB;" & _
        "OLE DB Services=-4;Data Source=(local);Integrated Security=SSPI;")
```

Note For a full list of "OLE DB Services" values, see "Overriding Provider Service Defaults" in the MSDN Library (http://msdn.microsoft.com/library/default.asp?url=/library/en-us/oledb/htm/ oledboverriding_provider_service_defaults.asp).

The SQL Server .NET data provider, on the other hand, relies on Windows 2000 component services to manage connection pooling. In this scheme, each connection pool is associated with a particular connection string. When a connection is opened, the SQL Server .NET data provider looks for an existing pool whose connections use *exactly* the same connection string. If none is found, a new pool is created; if a matching pool is found, a connection from within that pool is used.

```
Dim con As New SqlConnection("server=(local);database=Northwind;" & _
         "uid=sa;pwd=;pooling=true;min pool size=0;max pool size=100;")
```

When a connection pool is created, *multiple* connection objects can be created within that pool, so that the minimum pool size requirement is satisfied. If they're required later on, new connections are added to the pool, up to the maximum pool size. If the maximum pool size has been reached, any further requests are queued until a connection becomes available. (An error is raised if the Connection.Timeout value elapses before a connection becomes available.) To make a used connection available in the pool once again, it must be closed by calling either the Close() or the Dispose() method. When the connection is closed, it is returned to the pool.

Using Commands

Having now gone into some more detail regarding the ADO.NET connection classes, you can switch your attention to our other key topic in this chapter. As you know, the .NET data providers' command classes are used to execute commands on a data source, across a connection. Once a connection has been established, a command can be used to execute a SQL statement or a stored procedure. In this section, you'll look more closely at these features, and see how to take maximum advantage of them.

Concrete Command Classes

The various ADO.NET command classes all implement the System.Data.IDbCommand interface, with the result that they expose similar functionality. As we mentioned earlier, however, the .NET data providers are free to add functionality that's specific to the data sources they support. The result of this is that some providers gain additional methods, such as the following:

- The SqlCommand class exposes a method called ExecuteXmlReader() for returning an XML stream. This is a capability given to the SqlCommand class based on the XML capabilities of SQL Server 7.0 and greater.

- The OracleCommand class exposes two alternative "Execute" methods that are strictly for use with Oracle databases.

Using a Command with a SQL Statement

Two of the most important properties defined by the IDbCommand interface (and therefore exposed by all command classes) are CommandText, which contains a string that's set to the command to be executed, and CommandType, which describes what kind of command is stored in CommandText. Possible values for the CommandType property are:

- CommandType.Text: A SQL statement (this is the default setting)

- CommandType.TableDirect: The name of a table whose columns will all be returned

- CommandType.StoredProcedure: The name of a stored procedure

To create a command that executes a SQL statement, then, you just need to construct it by passing in the statement in question and a connection object, as you've seen. In fact, though, ADO.NET command classes expose four constructors. The following is the SqlCommand class's set:

- Public Sub New(): Creates a new SqlCommand object with all of its properties at their default values, and no associated connection

- Public Sub New(String): Creates a SqlCommand object with the CommandText property set, but no associated connection

- Public Sub New(String, SqlConnection): Creates a SqlCommand object with the CommandText property set, and the specified SqlConnection object stored in its Connection property

- Public Sub New(String, SqlConnection, SqlTransaction): Creates a SqlCommand object with the CommandText property set, the specified SqlConnection object stored in its Connection property, and a SqlTransaction object for the command to execute in

---

■**Tip** We'll have much more to say on the subject of transactions in Chapter 8, which is dedicated to the topic.

Executing the Command

To execute a command and return any results, the IDbCommand interface provides three methods, as follows:

- ExecuteNonQuery()

- ExecuteReader()

- ExecuteScalar()

In addition, individual providers are free to add their own methods to the command class. In this section, you'll also take a quick look at one of the most important of these—ExecuteXmlReader(), which is implemented only by the SqlCommand class.

ExecuteNonQuery

ExecuteNonQuery() is used for executing operations that don't return a result set—generally speaking, these will be UPDATE, INSERT, or DELETE statements. The ExecuteNonQuery() method simply returns an integer that indicates the number of rows in the data source that were affected by the operation. For all other operation types, –1 is returned. In the following code, ExecuteNonQuery() returns the number of rows affected by a DELETE statement:

```
Dim con As New SqlConnection(ConfigurationSettings.AppSettings("constring"))
Dim cmd As New SqlCommand()

cmd.CommandText = "DELETE FROM Employees WHERE FirstName = 'Derek'"
cmd.Connection = con

Try
  con.Open()
  Console.WriteLine("{0} - {1}", _
                    "cmd.ExecuteNonQuery()", cmd.ExecuteNonQuery().ToString())
Finally
  con.Close()
End Try
```

ExecuteReader

As you've already seen, ExecuteReader() returns a data reader object, such as an OleDbReader or a SqlDataReader. It's usually called without arguments, but there are occasions when it's useful to specify one of the members of the CommandBehavior enumeration in order to affect the format in which results are returned. The members of the CommandBehavior enumeration are

- CloseConnection: The connection is closed when the associated data reader is closed.

- KeyInfo: The query returns column and primary key information for the data selected, rather than the data itself. This means that the query can be executed without locking any of the selected rows.

- SchemaOnly: The command returns only column information.

- SequentialAccess: The results of the query are read sequentially, column by column.

- SingleResult: Always returns a single result set, rather than the multiple sets that can be returned in the default setting.

- SingleRow: Always returns a single row of data.

The following code demonstrates how to call the ExecuteReader() method, using the CommandBehavior.SingleRow enumerator to return the first record in the result set:

```
Dim con As New SqlConnection(ConfigurationSettings.AppSettings("constring"))
Dim cmd As New SqlCommand()
```

```
cmd.CommandText = "SELECT * FROM Customers"
cmd.Connection = con

Try
  con.Open()
  Dim reader As SqlDataReader = cmd.ExecuteReader(CommandBehavior.SingleRow)
  While reader.Read()
    Console.WriteLine("{0} - {1}", _
                      reader.GetString(0), reader.GetString(1))
  End While
  reader.Close()
Finally
  con.Close()
End Try
```

Here, you create a SqlDataReader instance called reader. The ExecuteReader() method populates the data reader with the first row in the result set.

ExecuteScalar

The ExecuteScalar() method returns an Object representing the first column of the first row in the result set; all other columns and rows are ignored. It's particularly useful for returning aggregate values, such as the result of a SELECT COUNT(*) SQL statement. Using ExecuteScalar() requires fewer system resources than using ExecuteReader() and then invoking the IDataReader.Read() method to get at the value you want. Unlike ExecuteReader(), ExecuteScalar() doesn't create a data reader stream on the connection.

```
Dim con As New SqlConnection(ConfigurationSettings.AppSettings("constring"))
Dim cmd As New SqlCommand()

cmd.CommandText = "SELECT COUNT(*) FROM Customers"
cmd.Connection = con

Try
  con.Open()
  Console.WriteLine("{0} - {1}", _
                    "cmd.ExecuteScalar()", cmd.ExecuteScalar().ToString())
Finally
  con.Close()
End Try
```

ExecuteXmlReader

The ExecuteXmlReader() method is only available for the SqlCommand object. The CommandText property of a SqlCommand object on which the ExecuteXmlReader() method is being invoked should contain a SQL command with a valid FOR XML clause, or a command that returns ntext data in valid XML format.

■Note You can find more information about using the SQL FOR XML clause in the following article at the Microsoft Web site: "A Survey of Microsoft SQL Server 2000 XML Features" (http://msdn.microsoft.com/library/default.asp?url=/library/en-us/dnexxml/html/xml07162001.asp).

The following code demonstrates how to invoke the ExecuteXmlReader() method using a SELECT FOR XML command against SQL Server 7.0 with XML support, or SQL Server 2000.

```
Dim con As New SqlConnection(ConfigurationSettings.AppSettings("constring"))
Dim cmd As New SqlCommand()

cmd.CommandText = "SELECT * FROM Customers FOR XML AUTO, XMLDATA"
cmd.Connection = con

Try
  con.Open()
  Dim reader As XmlReader = cmd.ExecuteXmlReader()
  While reader.Read()
    Console.WriteLine(reader.ReadOuterXml())
  End While
  reader.Close()
Finally
  con.Close()
End Try
```

Here, you select all of the records from the Customers table of the Northwind database, and return them as an XML stream. Like a data reader, the XmlReader class exposes a Read() method that reads the next node in the XML stream. As you read through the XML stream, you use the ReadOuterXml() method to read the content, including the markup of each node and all of its children, as seen in Figure 1-6.

Figure 1-6. *ExecuteXMLReader.vb*

Using a Command with a Stored Procedure

In fact, according to Microsoft's guidelines, executing SQL statements against a data store is not usually the best way to retrieve data. Where the option exists, it's more efficient to write a stored procedure that produces the same result, and to invoke the stored procedure using ADO.NET.

By constructing your command object with (or by setting the CommandText property to) the name of a stored procedure, you can execute stored procedures. The only other step necessary is to set the CommandType to CommandType.StoredProcedure. This is demonstrated in the following code, where you execute the Northwind database's "Ten Most Expensive Products" stored procedure:

```
Dim con As New SqlConnection(ConfigurationSettings.AppSettings("constring"))
Dim cmd As New SqlCommand("Ten Most Expensive Products", con)
cmd.CommandType = CommandType.StoredProcedure

Try
  con.Open()
  Dim reader As SqlDataReader = cmd.ExecuteReader()
  While reader.Read()
    Console.WriteLine("{0} - {1:C}", _
                      reader.GetString(0), reader.GetDecimal(1))
  End While
  reader.Close()
Finally
  con.Close()
End Try
```

Results of the preceding code are shown in Figure 1-7.

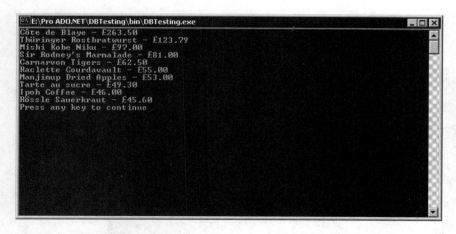

Figure 1-7. *StoredProcedure.vb*

Using Parameters with Command Objects

The .NET data providers include classes for creating *parameter objects* that can be added to a command object's `Parameters` collection. The parameters are created with a name, a data type, a specification of whether they're to be used for input or output, and a value (if applicable). The `SqlParameter` and `OleDbParameter` classes function in the same way, but `SqlParameter` objects are passed to SQL Server as named parameters, and must map to parameters in the stored procedures.

Creating Parameterized SQL Queries

We can create a parameterized SQL query by including one or more parameters in the SQL statement, and then adding the same parameters to the command object's `Parameters` collection. This is demonstrated in the following code:

```
Dim con As New SqlConnection(ConfigurationSettings.AppSettings("constring"))
Dim cmd As New SqlCommand( _
          "SELECT * FROM Customers WHERE Country = @country", con)
cmd.Parameters.Add( _
          New SqlParameter("@country", SqlDbType.VarChar, 50)).Value = "USA"

Try
  con.Open()
  Dim reader As SqlDataReader = cmd.ExecuteReader()
  While reader.Read()
    Console.WriteLine("{0} - {1}", reader.GetString(0), reader.GetString(1))
  End While
  reader.Close()
Finally
  con.Close()
End Try
```

The results of the preceding code are shown in Figure 1-8.

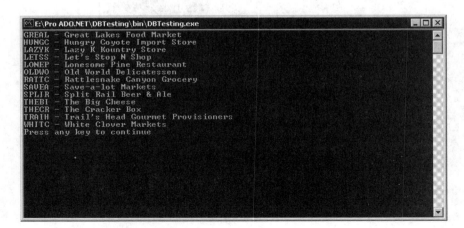

Figure 1-8. *Parameters1.vb*

Here, you create a new SqlCommand object with a SQL statement that uses a parameter in its WHERE clause. Next, you add a new SqlParameter to the SqlCommand.Parameters collection. To the SqlParameter constructor, you pass the parameter's name and data type. (The data types are defined using the values of enumerations named SqlDbType, OleDbType, etc., depending on the .NET data provider being used.)

By default, the Parameter objects are created as input parameters, but setting the Direction property of the Parameter object can configure them as output parameters. The following example adds an output parameter to the preceding code.

```
Dim con As New SqlConnection(ConfigurationSettings.AppSettings("constring"))
Dim cmd As New SqlCommand( _
    "SELECT * FROM Customers WHERE Country = @country;" & _
    "SELECT @count = COUNT(*) FROM Customers WHERE Country = @country", con)

cmd.Parameters.Add( _
    New SqlParameter("@country", SqlDbType.VarChar, 50)).Value = "USA"
cmd.Parameters.Add(New SqlParameter("@count", SqlDbType.Int))
cmd.Parameters("@count").Direction = ParameterDirection.Output

Try
  con.Open()
  Dim reader As SqlDataReader = cmd.ExecuteReader()
  While reader.Read()
    Console.WriteLine("{0} - {1}", reader.GetString(0), reader.GetString(1))
  End While
  reader.Close()
Finally
  con.Close()
End Try

Console.WriteLine("{0} - {1}", _
                "Count", cmd.Parameters("@count").Value.ToString())
```

Here, you add a new SqlParameter—@count—to the Parameters collection, and set its Direction property to ParameterDirection.Output.

Executing Parameterized Stored Procedures

The same steps are used to execute a parameterized stored procedure. In the following code, you'll execute a command that calls a stored procedure that returns a result set and one output parameter. First of all, add the following stored procedure to the Northwind database:

```
CREATE PROCEDURE [GetCountryAndOutputParam]
@country varchar (50),
@count int output
AS
SELECT * FROM Customers WHERE Country = @country
SELECT @count=COUNT(*) FROM Customers WHERE Country = @country
```

This returns the total count of records in the Customers table as an output parameter named @count, as well as a result set of records from the Customers table for which the Country field has the value of the @country input parameter. The code to execute it is almost identical to that from the previous code example, except that you define the SqlCommand as a stored procedure.

```
Dim con As New SqlConnection(ConfigurationSettings.AppSettings("constring"))
Dim cmd As New SqlCommand("GetCountryAndOutputParam", con)
cmd.CommandType = CommandType.StoredProcedure
```

As you'd expect, executing this code will produce exactly the same output as the parameterized query example.

ADO.NET and ADO 2.6

Since ADO.NET is more or less a direct replacement for ADO 2.6 within the .NET world, and because most developers using it will be familiar to some degree with traditional ADO, it's worth taking a moment as you draw to the close of this chapter to consider some of the differences between the two technologies.

There are two chief differences between ADO.NET and ADO 2.6. First, ADO.NET is specifically geared toward two distinct environments: disconnected result sets and read-only, forward-only connected access to the data source. Second, ADO.NET doesn't present a single, unified object model to the developer regardless of the data source. Rather, it uses source-specific classes implemented by the .NET data providers.

Disconnected Data Access

The first of the scenarios for which ADO.NET is optimized is the disconnected result set. As you've seen, this is handled by the DataSet, which is fully malleable and updateable, but doesn't retain a persistent connection to the data source itself. The DataSet is similar in some ways to ADO's disconnected Recordset, but with the DataSet, the disconnection is automatic. Previously, developers had to disconnect the Recordset from the data source and close the connection explicitly (a source of much confusion and many errors). ADO.NET's approach here is far more transparent, and a good deal shorter in code!

Read-Only, Forward-Only Access

The second situation for which ADO.NET is optimized is where you want to iterate through each row in a result set, one row at a time. In this scenario, you don't need to wait for the entire result set to load before you start going through it. For this type of access, it makes sense to keep the connection to the data source open until you've finished iterating through the data—and it's for precisely these situations that the data reader was designed. Again, because you have a class designed specifically for the task, you can write much cleaner code.

Taking these two changes together, the upshot is that where you had a single object (the Recordset) doing all the work in ADO 2.6, you now have specialized classes for the two most common scenarios. This means that a lot of the obscure (and often misunderstood) parameters you used to have when opening a `Recordset` or executing a command can be abolished, and you can be sure that you're getting exactly the type of object you want. The potential disadvantage is if you want a nonstandard way of accessing your data—say, a connected result set that you can navigate through and update—ADO.NET just doesn't provide that.

It's worth remembering, though, that the whole of the .NET Framework was designed with an eye on distributed computing over the Internet, and particularly on exposing functionality through web services. Leaving database connections open for extended periods could seriously impact on the scalability of an application, and it's in keeping with the aims of .NET to prohibit it. If you really do need this functionality, then for the time being at least, you're probably better off using "classic" ADO.

Tip It's still possible to update the data source by executing commands using command objects, of course. Combining these with a data reader can be the most efficient technique of all if you need connected access, but you'll need a good amount of custom code in order to simulate a truly updateable connected `Recordset`.

Provider-Specific Classes

The other big difference between ADO.NET and ADO is that there are specific sets of classes for each of the providers. In ADO, you simply used `Connection`, `Command`, and `Recordset` objects, regardless of the data source you were accessing. If you changed the database system—say, from Access to SQL Server—then (in theory at least) all you needed to change was the connection string. Now you need to create a specific `SqlConnection`, `OleDbConnection`, etc., object, depending on the data source. If you want to change the data source used by your code, you need to change the namespaces imported into the project, and the code for declaring and instantiating any provider-specific classes, as well as the connection string.

On its own, that may be a trivial search-and-replace task, but there's an even greater difference here. As you've seen, the common methods and properties for the .NET provider classes are defined in interfaces in the `System.Data` namespace—but the ADO.NET programmer doesn't need to know whether the methods and properties that they're using are defined in the interface, or are specific to the provider. To clarify this, a quick examination of the `IDbConnection` interface reveals that it defines just four public properties, and five public methods.

- Properties:

    - `ConnectionString`

    - `ConnectionTimeout`

    - `Database`

    - `State`

- Methods:

  - `BeginTransaction()`

  - `ChangeDatabase()`

  - `Close()`

  - `CreateCommand()`

  - `Open()`

Doing the same for the `OleDbConnection` class, however, reveals that as well as implementing `IDbConnection` (and a couple of other interfaces), there are new properties (`DataSource`, `Provider`, `ServerVersion`), methods (`CreateObjRef()`, `GetOleDbSchemaTable()`, `ReleaseObjectPool()`), and even a couple of events that *aren't* implementing any interface. Rather, they're defined afresh in this class. The other providers implement some of these features, but not all of them. Short of checking the documentation, there's no way of knowing for sure whether a method or a property is common to all providers.

This extensibility is potentially both a big advantage and a big disadvantage. On the one hand, it allows developers of .NET data providers an enormous amount of flexibility. It's possible to add not only extra members, but also extra classes and other types (for example, the SQL Server .NET data provider has a `SqlDebugging` class with no equivalent in the other providers). This gives scope for providers to be developed for data sources that don't fit so comfortably into the existing model, in much the same way as the OLE DB 2.5 interfaces allowed the development of the `MSDAIPP` and `ExOLEDB` OLE DB providers. The downside is that if provider developers go their own ways, developers using ADO.NET will need to be familiar with each provider that they have to use. Hopefully, however, the fixing of the core functionality in the ADO.NET interfaces will ensure that differences between the providers remain relatively minor.

Using ADO 2.x in .NET

Although we've stressed that you should use ADO.NET rather than ADO whenever possible, there are still a couple of scenarios where there's really no alternative but to use traditional ADO. We've mentioned these already, but it's worth reiterating them in one place.

- You absolutely *have* to use a connected `Recordset`, and need to be able to update the data source. One reason for this might be the more flexible lock and cursor types available in ADO. If your application has a small enough number of users to permit simultaneous connections, and you need to be able to see changes to the data source as they're made, ADO may be a better choice.

- You need to use the ADO `Record` and `Stream` objects—for example, if you're using the OLE DB provider for Exchange 2000 (`ExOLEDB`) or Internet Publishing (`MSDAIPP`). Until the OLE DB .NET data provider is updated to support the OLE DB 2.5 interfaces (or .NET providers for these data sources become available), you'll need to use ADO.

To use ADO 2.*x* from .NET, you need to create a *runtime callable wrapper* (RCW) for the COM component. You can do this in Visual Studio .NET by selecting the Microsoft ActiveX Data Objects Library from the COM tab of the Add Reference dialog box, as shown in Figure 1-9.

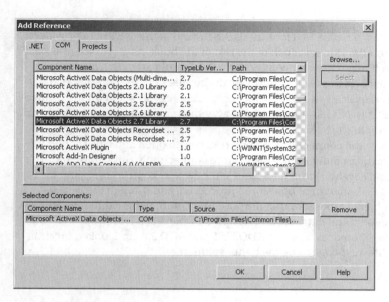

Figure 1-9. *Adding a reference to ADO 2.*x

Alternatively, you can use the command-line tool TlbImp.exe to import the type library into .NET, as shown in Figure 1-10.

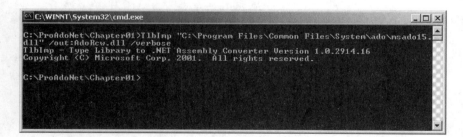

Figure 1-10. *Using* TlbImp.exe *to create a RCW (runtime callable wrapper) for ADO 2.*x

---

■**Tip** Note that this operation doesn't install the assembly into the Global Assembly Cache, so you'll need to make sure that the DLL is in the same directory as the code calling it.

Once you've got your RCW for the ADODB library, using it is similar to using any other type library with Visual Basic 6.

Summary

Your goal in this chapter was to have a first look at ADO.NET, and at the .NET data providers that will be occupying your attention for much of the rest of the book. As discussed, the .NET data providers are the mechanism used for connecting a .NET application to a data source, and they expose four primary classes for that purpose: the connection, the command, the data reader, and the data adapter. Most of your time in this chapter was spent on the connection and command classes; the others—plus the `DataSet`, which you also touched upon—have chapters to themselves, later in the book.

Here, then, you saw how the connection classes work: how to open and close connections, how to use an application configuration file to store connection strings, and how to handle the connection class's events. From there, you saw how to execute a command on a connection, using either a SQL statement or a stored procedure, and through the various methods that command objects expose for that purpose. You compared the different access models implied by data readers and datasets, and described when each is appropriate. Finally, you examined some of the differences between ADO.NET and ADO 2.6, and looked for situations when the latter might—just *might*—be the better solution.

CHAPTER 2

■ ■ ■

Using Data Readers

The RecordSet that you used with ADO was a multitalented beast. In days of yore, when two-tiered, connected applications were the norm, the RecordSet provided us with connected functionality by utilizing server-side cursors. As application architectures evolved and *n*-tiered, disconnected architectures gained favor, the RecordSet also had to evolve to provide for client-side cursors. Although the RecordSet coped admirably with its changing role, it was becoming cumbersome in its attempts to be all things to all people.

With ADO.NET, the RecordSet is no more. Instead, as you've begun to see, you find yourself with a whole host of objects that perform data-related tasks. In ADO.NET, the DataSet is like the RecordSet in a disconnected state: it's a snapshot of some data taken at some point in time that can be manipulated as required and then persisted back to the database. A data reader, on the other hand, is ADO.NET's equivalent of a connected RecordSet: it allows us fast, forward-only, read-only access to a stream of data.

The DataSet object will be the subject of Chapter 3. Here, you'll be looking more closely at data readers, which of course you've already begun to use. In this chapter, you'll be adding to the things you've already seen. In particular, you will cover the following:

- Examining the interfaces implemented by data reader classes

- Accessing data in multiple result sets

- Comparing type-safe and type-unsafe data access

- Creating a simple, real-world application using the DataReader

- Understanding performance issues

Data Reader Basics

Although each data reader is designed to access a specific type of data source, all data readers have the same essential characteristics, as follows:

- Connected access

- High performance

- Small footprint

- Strongly typed data access (if required)

In Chapter 1, you learned that data reader classes must implement both the IDataReader and IDataRecord interfaces. The IDataReader interface provides the methods and properties that allow you to traverse result sets and query the data reader for its state. Meanwhile, the IDataRecord interface provides methods and properties for *accessing* the data in result sets. Let's have a closer look at these in turn.

The IDataReader Interface

The IDataReader interface defines a number of methods and properties that provide a user with a means of traversing result sets and getting details of the result set being dealt with, as shown in Tables 2-1 and 2-2.

Table 2-1. IDataReader *Methods*

Method	Description
Close()	Closes the data reader object
GetSchemaTable()	Returns a DataTable that describes the schema of the data reader's result set
NextResult()	Moves the data reader to the next result set (if one exists)
Read()	Moves the data reader to the next record in the result set

Table 2-2. IDataReader *Properties*

Property	Description
Depth	Gets a value indicating the depth of nesting for the current record.
IsClosed	Returns a Boolean value indicating whether the data reader is closed.
RecordsAffected	Gets the number of records affected by the execution of the SQL statement. A value of –1 indicates that a SELECT statement was executed. Any other value indicates that an UPDATE, DELETE, or INSERT statement was executed.

Let's not dwell too much on these methods and properties now, because you'll be seeing them in use over the course of this chapter. Do notice, though, that none of these methods actually manipulates the contents of a result set—remember, data readers are read-only.

The IDataRecord Interface

Moving around a record set is all very well, but it's not much use if you can't actually access the data in the records. This is where the IDataRecord interface comes into play. Through the methods and properties of this interface, you can access the column values for the current record in the data reader. Table 2-3 shows some of the methods and Table 2-4 shows the properties.

Table 2-3. *A Partial List of* IDataRecord *Methods*

Method	Description
GetBoolean()	Gets a Boolean value for a given column
GetByte()	Gets an 8-bit unsigned integer for a given column
GetInt64()	Gets a 64-bit signed integer for a given column

Table 2-4. IDataRecord *Properties*

Property	Description
FieldCount	Gets the number of columns in the current record (row)
Item	Gets a given column's value in the form of an Object

In fact, the IDataRecord interface defines a total of 22 methods, all but one of which (the exception is IsDBNull()) take the form "GetXxx()", where Xxx is the type of the data to be retrieved. In addition to these, it's quite likely that a particular data reader will provide database-specific data types in its implementation. A case in point is the SqlDataReader, which provides methods for retrieving specific SQL types, such as GetSqlInt64() and GetSqlMoney(). If you were to use an OleDbDataReader, you'd use the GetInt64() and GetDecimal() methods to retrieve similar data.

The point is that through these interfaces, the designers of ADO.NET have defined the *minimum* amount of functionality that data readers should implement in order to meet their users' needs. Now, let's move on and start to increase your knowledge of how that functionality can be employed.

Data Reader Operations

From the work you did in Chapter 1, you'll already be comfortable with creating data readers, and using them to perform a number of fairly simple data access operations. In this chapter, you're going to look at some more advanced possibilities: working with multiple result sets, accessing data in a type-safe manner, and getting hold of a schema for the data in a result set. You'll also put together a short example that places all of the theory in a more realistic setting. First, though, you'd better have a quick recap of the things you've seen so far.

- Data reader objects cannot be created explicitly. They can only be created through a call to the ExecuteReader() method of a suitably configured ADO.NET command object.

- A connection to the data source must be open before the ExecuteReader() method can be called successfully. An exception of type InvalidOperationException will be raised if this has not been done.

- You can traverse the result set represented by a data reader object by calling that object's Read() method repeatedly, until the method returns False. At this point, there are no more records in the result set.

- When a data reader is first created, it is "positioned" *before* the first record in the result set. At least one call to the Read() method must be made before you attempt to use any of the data reader's data-access methods.

- You should always call the data reader's Close() method when you have finished with it. Failing to do so will prevent other objects from using the connection.

As long as you bear these essentials in mind, you shouldn't find it too difficult to extend your work with data readers into more complex territory, as you'll begin to see now.

Navigating Multiple Result Sets

It's generally desirable to avoid making multiple trips to the data layer. The overhead of numerous calls across a network, and the increase in network traffic, can seriously affect the performance of an application. The effects of unnecessary calls become even more apparent when the amount of data being transferred is sizeable. One way to avoid this is by executing multiple statements in one trip to the database. Using the Command object, you can do this quite easily.

The following code demonstrates how to run multiple statements in one call, using the SQL Server .NET data provider. The SELECT statements in use here are therefore being run against SQL Server; you should note that they might not be valid against all databases.

■**Note** You should also note that you're reusing the configuration file that you set up in order to simplify the examples in the Chapter 1. It's the source of the "constring" that you use in the first line of code in the following example.

```
Dim con As New SqlConnection(ConfigurationSettings.AppSettings("constring"))
Dim cmd As New SqlCommand()

cmd.CommandText = "SELECT * FROM Categories; SELECT * FROM Customers"
cmd.Connection = con

Try
  con.Open()
  Dim reader As SqlDataReader = cmd.ExecuteReader()
```

Here, you're selecting data from the Categories and Customers tables, courtesy of the semicolon in the string that's assigned to the Command object's CommandText property. Apart from that, however, this code should look pretty familiar so far.

After the call to ExecuteReader(), the data reader you have at your disposal has two result sets: the first contains the records from the Categories table, and the second has the data for the Customers table. To traverse these results requires a change to your usual practices.

```
Do
  While reader.Read()
```

```
      Console.WriteLine(reader(0) & vbTab & reader(1))
    End While
  Loop While reader.NextResult()
  reader.Close()
Finally
  con.Close()
End Try
```

Now that you have multiple result sets, you need to move through the data in a slightly different way. Getting from one result set to the next requires the NextResult() method, which is defined by the IDataReader interface. It works in a similar way to the Read() method, in that once there are no more result sets to navigate, it returns False. Looking at the code, though, you can see that the Do...Loop While construct is used to perform the operation, rather than the usual While...End While construct.

The reason for the change is that when data readers are returned, they are already positioned on the first result set. If you were to use a While...End While loop, you'd immediately skip to the second set! It's very easy to forget this difference in behavior, so if you seem to be missing your first result set, check that you're not calling NextResult() before you retrieve any data.

Note If you call NextResult() immediately on a newly returned data reader with multiple result sets, then NextResult() skips the first result set.

Accessing the Data in a Type-Safe Manner

Looking closely at the previous example, you may have noticed another change from your usual habits. Rather than using GetInt32() or GetString() to retrieve values from the data reader, you just used its default Item() property and left the Console.WriteLine() method to deal with the rest. Had you chosen to do so (although it wouldn't have worked terribly well in this case), you could also have used the Item() property by passing column names, rather than their ordinals. In another example, you might imagine writing code something like the following:

```
While reader.Read()
  Dim OrderID As Object = reader("OrderID")
  Dim OrderDate As Object = reader("OrderDate")
  Dim OrderFreight As Object = reader("OrderFreight")

  Console.WriteLine(OrderID & vbTab & OrderDate & vbTab & OrderFreight)
End While
```

The trouble with using the Item() property, in either of its forms, is that when you use it to access a column, you have no idea what's actually being returned—you're completely data-type agnostic. If you turn to the GetXxx() methods, however, you regain the data types, but lose the ability to use column names.

```
While reader.Read()
  Dim OrderID As Integer = reader.GetInt32(0)
  Dim OrderDate As DateTime = reader.GetDateTime(1)
  Dim OrderFreight As Decimal = reader.GetDecimal(2)

  Console.WriteLine(OrderID & vbTab & OrderDate & vbTab & OrderFreight)
End While
```

In some ways, this is an improvement—using ordinals and correct data types is faster than using column names and Objects—but the nature of the values you're returning is nowhere near as clear. One possible way around this is to define some constant values in your code to make it clearer what's going on.

```
Const OrderIDIdx As Integer = 0
Const OrderDateIdx As Integer = 1
Const OrderFreightIdx As Integer = 2

While reader.Read()
  Dim OrderID As Integer = reader.GetInt32(OrderIDIdx)
  Dim OrderDate As DateTime = reader.GetDateTime(OrderDateIdx)
  Dim OrderFreight As Decimal = reader.GetDecimal(OrderFreightIdx)

  Console.WriteLine(OrderID & vbTab & OrderDate & vbTab & OrderFreight)
End While
```

But, this introduces the problem of maintainability. If this is a new project and your database schema is constantly "evolving", then keeping these values in sync with the schema could be a nightmare. The data reader's GetOrdinal() method provides a great way to work around this. It takes the column name as a parameter, and returns that column's ordinal position.

```
Dim OrderIDIdx As Integer = reader.GetOrdinal("OrderID")
Dim OrderDateIdx As Integer = reader.GetOrdinal("OrderDate")
Dim OrderFreightIdx As Integer = reader.GetOrdinal("Freight")
```

Now you can use type-safe methods to access the data, without needing to know at design time the order in which the columns will appear. As an added bonus, the process of looking up a column by name is quite a resource-intensive operation—but using GetOrdinal, you do it only once. This is *slightly* slower than using constants from the start, but in many cases it provides the best solution.

SQL Server Types

So far, you've looked at using the Item() property and the type-safe methods that all data readers have, simply by virtue of implementing the IDataReader (and therefore the IDataRecord) interface. As such, the examples you've used would work equally well with the SQL Server and OLE DB .NET data providers. (Of course, you'd have to switch to using objects from the System.Data.OleDb namespace, but the methods and properties being used would be unchanged.)

If you're working with SQL Server 7.0 or later, however, you can use the SQL Server .NET data provider to access the real SQL types, rather than the .NET Framework's closest available matches. In order to do this, the first thing you'll want to do is import a new namespace into your application.

```
Imports System.Data.SqlTypes
```

The System.Data.SqlTypes namespace contains the definitions for the SQL data types you'll use—and once you've got those, the changes to the code itself are not difficult. The following is a complete example that puts their use into context:

```
Dim con As New SqlConnection(ConfigurationSettings.AppSettings("constring"))
Dim cmd As New SqlCommand()
cmd.CommandText = "SELECT OrderID, OrderDate, Freight FROM Orders"
cmd.Connection = con

Try
  con.Open()
  Dim reader As SqlDataReader = cmd.ExecuteReader()

  Dim OrderIDIdx As Integer = reader.GetOrdinal("OrderID")
  Dim OrderDateIdx As Integer = reader.GetOrdinal("OrderDate")
  Dim OrderFreightIdx As Integer = reader.GetOrdinal("Freight")

  While reader.Read()
    Dim OrderID As SqlInt32 = reader.GetSqlInt32(OrderIDIdx)
    Dim OrderDate As SqlDateTime = reader.GetSqlDateTime(OrderDateIdx)
    Dim OrderFreight As SqlMoney = reader.GetSqlMoney(OrderFreightIdx)

    Console.WriteLine(OrderID.ToString() & vbTab & _
                      OrderDate.ToString() & vbTab & OrderFreight.ToString())
  End While
  reader.Close()
Finally
  con.Close()
End Try
```

The changes from what you've seen before are to be found inside the While...End While loop. You're now getting "proper" SQL types rather than generic .NET types, so that (for example) GetInt32() has been replaced with GetSqlInt32(). Most interesting of all, however, is the line where you access the Freight column. Where before you'd have written something like the following:

```
Dim OrderFreight As Decimal = reader.GetDecimal(OrderFreightIdx)
```

you can now write this:

```
Dim OrderFreight As SqlMoney = reader.GetSqlMoney(OrderFreightIdx)
```

In real terms, SqlMoney wraps a Decimal value anyway, but using the former further clarifies what you're dealing with, and protects you against any changes that Microsoft makes to
the SqlMoney type in the future—the changes will be picked up automatically. Having a specific type enables you to define methods for working with money that would not be relevant
for all decimal values, and to force these methods only to accept money types.

Perhaps inevitably, there's a subtle problem involved in using the GetSqlXxx() methods.
By design, they don't convert the SQL Server data types into .NET data types, which results in
slightly better performance. However, if you store the returned values in variables with .NET
data types, the CLR has to perform a conversion between the two formats. Such conversion
operations can nullify any performance gains.

Another issue worth mentioning is that the CLR doesn't automatically convert the SQL
Server data types into strings when the values are used in string concatenation expressions.
Instead, you need to call their ToString() functions explicitly in order to generate a string representation of their value. In the call to the Console.WriteLine() function in the previous code
example, you do just that.

■**Note** If you use the SQL Server .NET data provider, you can retrieve values in their native SQL Server
data types by using any of the GetSqlXxx() methods. Using these functions with the native SQL types
defined in the System.Data.SqlTypes namespace results in slightly more efficient code. To take advantage of it, you must ensure that you don't inadvertently assign the return value of a GetSqlXxx() method
to a .NET CLR data type.

Getting the Result Set's Schema

If you don't know exactly what a particular data source contains, or even if you just want to generate a list of column headings for display purposes, it can be useful to get hold of a result set's
schema. Data reader objects provide a method that does just this. It's called GetSchemaTable(),
and it's defined by the IDataReader interface.

In order to illustrate the power of this method, you'll have a look at a small Windows
application called SqlGetSchemaExample that you'll find in the code download for this book
(the download also includes an OLE DB version of the same example) in the Downloads section of the Apress Web site (http://www.apress.com). The application is pretty simple: the
main form has a DataGrid component called DataGrid1, and a single Button control called
Button1. All of the code is in the button's Click event handler.

```
Private Sub Button1_Click(ByVal sender As System.Object, _
                    ByVal e As System.EventArgs) Handles Button1.Click
  Dim con As New SqlConnection( _
                    "server=(local);database=Northwind;uid=sa;pwd=;")
  Dim cmd As New SqlCommand("SELECT * FROM ORDERS", con)

  Try
    con.Open()
```

```
    Dim reader As SqlDataReader = _
                        cmd.ExecuteReader(CommandBehavior.SchemaOnly)
    DataGrid1.SetDataBinding(reader.GetSchemaTable(), "")
    reader.Close()
  Finally
    con.Close()
  End Try
End Sub
```

The basic outline of this is probably starting to look pretty familiar, but look at the call to ExecuteReader()—and in particular, at the argument you're passing to it. The CommandBehavior.SchemaOnly value tells the command that no result sets are to be returned—you're just interested in the schema that would be generated on executing the SQL statement or stored procedure. If you were to specify SchemaOnly and then call reader.Read(), a value of False would be returned immediately, because there are no results.

After creating the data reader, you call its GetSchemaTable() method. This will return a DataTable that represents the schema for the result set (in this case, the would-be result set) that's returned. You can then bind this DataTable directly to the DataGrid component, which you do in the call to SetDataBinding(). The output from this example can be seen in Figure 2-1.

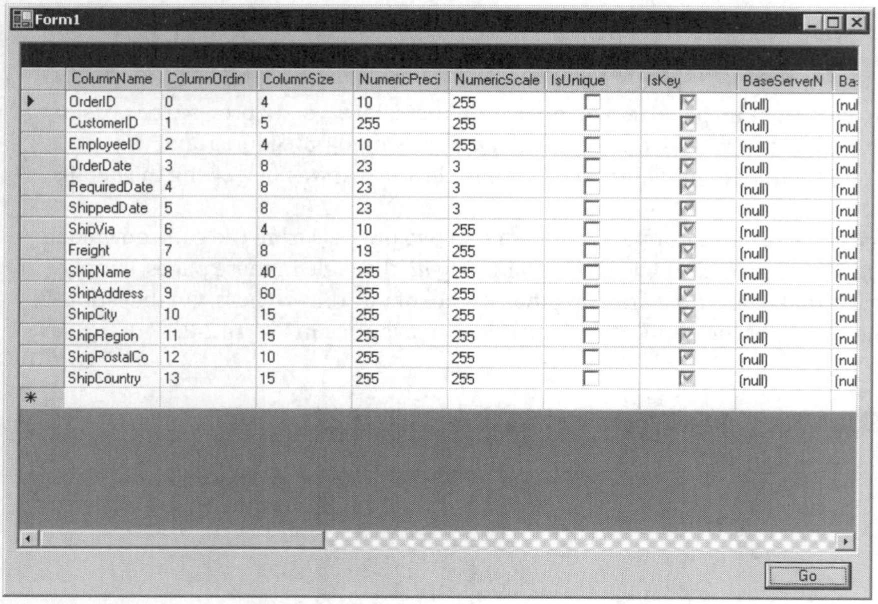

ColumnName	ColumnOrdin	ColumnSize	NumericPreci	NumericScale	IsUnique	IsKey	BaseServerN	Ba:
OrderID	0	4	10	255	☐	☑	(null)	(nul
CustomerID	1	5	255	255	☐	☑	(null)	(nul
EmployeeID	2	4	10	255	☐	☑	(null)	(nul
OrderDate	3	8	23	3	☐	☑	(null)	(nul
RequiredDate	4	8	23	3	☐	☑	(null)	(nul
ShippedDate	5	8	23	3	☐	☑	(null)	(nul
ShipVia	6	4	10	255	☐	☑	(null)	(nul
Freight	7	8	19	255	☐	☑	(null)	(nul
ShipName	8	40	255	255	☐	☑	(null)	(nul
ShipAddress	9	60	255	255	☐	☑	(null)	(nul
ShipCity	10	15	255	255	☐	☑	(null)	(nul
ShipRegion	11	15	255	255	☐	☑	(null)	(nul
ShipPostalCo	12	10	255	255	☐	☑	(null)	(nul
ShipCountry	13	15	255	255	☐	☑	(null)	(nul

Figure 2-1. SqlGetSchemaExample *in action*

If you were to run the example that uses the OLE DB .NET data provider, you'd get some slightly different output: you'd see some columns ordered a little differently, and a couple of them would contain different values. These variations, however, are explained by how the two providers interpret and present the data they receive. For example, the OleDbDataReader will return a column size of 16 for DateTime types, while the SqlDataReader will return a column size of 8.

As well as being a neat facility, as you'll see in the application you're about to create, getting the schema like this is an extremely fast operation—much faster than creating a DataTable, selecting data into it, and then trying to work out the schema by enumerating the DataColumns on the table.

■Tip If you're intrigued as to how such a technique might work, you should refer to the SqlEmulateSchemaTable and OleDbEmulateSchemaTable projects in the code download.

By looking at the sample output, you can work out the structure of the DataTable that's been returned to you by GetSchemaTable(). Each row in the DataTable represents a column from the result set, and each column contains a discrete piece of information about the result set's column schema. Given that it's not possible to see all of the information on this page, you're strongly recommended to run one of the applications to see for yourself the kind of information you can retrieve.

Bringing It All Together

In this section, you're going to look at an application that allows you to browse the orders that are stored in the Northwind database. You'll use SQL, stored procedures, and the GetSchemaTable() method to provide you with a simple and fast way of viewing the details for a particular order.

The source code for this example is contained in two projects from the code download: SqlBrowser and OleDbBrowser. You won't be examining *all* the code in these pages, simply because the parts that deal with generating the GUI are of no concern here. On that subject, though, the main GUI for the application looks like what you see in Figure 2-2.

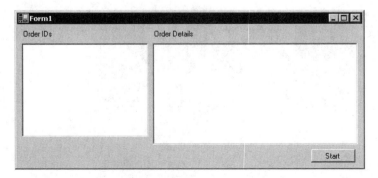

Figure 2-2. *The main GUI for* SqlBrowser

Most of the interesting code is contained in two event handlers: one that's executed when Start is clicked, which populates the OrderIDs column; and one that's executed when the current selection in the OrderIDs column changes. Let's begin by looking at the former.

```
Private con As New SqlConnection( _
  "Data Source=(local);Initial Catalog=Northwind;Integrated Security=SSPI;")


Private Sub Button1_Click(ByVal sender As System.Object, _
                          ByVal e As System.EventArgs) Handles Button1.Click

  Dim cmd As New SqlCommand("SELECT OrderID FROM Orders", con)
  Try
    con.Open()
    Dim reader As SqlDataReader = cmd.ExecuteReader()
    While reader.Read()
      OrderIDsList.Items.Add(reader.GetInt32(0))
    End While
    reader.Close()
  Finally
    con.Close()
  End Try
End Sub
```

This method is pretty straightforward. You create a SqlCommand object that will select the OrderIDs column from the Orders table. As usual, you open the connection and call ExecuteReader(). As you read each record, you add the value from the OrderID column to the OrderIDs list. Because you only selected a single column, using reader.GetInt32(0) in this code is safe—there are no other columns in the data reader.

When you click Start, then, the left-hand list box is populated with all of the Order IDs from the Orders table. In the second handler, you arrange things so that when an Order ID in the list is selected, the order details appear in the ListView on the right (the ListView class is located in the System.Windows.Forms namespace). The code looks like the following:

```
Private ColumnsSet As Boolean = False


Private Sub OrderIDsList_SelectedIndexChanged( _
                ByVal sender As Object, ByVal e As System.EventArgs) _
                Handles OrderIDsList.SelectedIndexChanged
  Dim OrderID As Integer = Convert.ToInt32(OrderIDsList.SelectedItem)
  Dim StoredProcCommand As New SqlCommand("CustOrdersDetail", con)
  With StoredProcCommand
    .CommandType = CommandType.StoredProcedure
    .Parameters.Add("@OrderID", OrderID)
  End With

  Dim RowList As New ArrayList()
```

```
Try
  con.Open()
  Dim reader As SqlDataReader = StoredProcCommand.ExecuteReader()
  While reader.Read()
    Dim Values(reader.FieldCount) As Object
    reader.GetValues(Values)
    RowList.Add(Values)
  End While

  If Not ColumnsSet Then
    Dim schema As DataTable = reader.GetSchemaTable()
    SetColumnHeaders(schema)
  End If
  reader.Close()
Finally
  con.Close()
End Try

PopulateOrderDetails(RowList)
End Sub
```

The first line in this method gets the currently selected item in the OrderIDs list and converts it to an Int32. This value is then used as the Order ID when you add a new parameter to the command object. In the While loop, you then use the data reader's GetValues() method to retrieve the values of all the columns for each record in turn, and add them to an ArrayList.

Now, the next bit of code is something new. You need to add columns to the ListView so that you can view the details of each order in a sensible fashion. You've arranged things here so that if the global ColumnsSet variable is True, then you've already added columns to the ListView, and there's no need to do it again. If it's still False, the columns need to be added.

■Tip In a production application, this would not be a good place for this code. It makes no sense to check the variable every time you select a new order, and you should always try to avoid doing data processing while you're still using the data reader. For the purposes of this chapter, however, it keeps the explanation simple.

Assuming that you haven't already added the columns to the table, you call the SetColumnHeaders() helper method. To it, you pass the DataTable containing the schema for the result set. The method looks like the following:

```
Private Sub SetColumnHeaders(ByVal schema As DataTable)

  OrderDetailsList.View = View.Details

  Dim row As DataRow
  For Each row In schema.Rows
```

```
      OrderDetailsList.Columns.Add( _
                            row("ColumnName"), 100, HorizontalAlignment.Left)
    Next
    ColumnsSet = True
End Sub
```

First, you set the View property of the OrderDetailsList (this is the ListView in your
GUI) to Details, forcing it to display all columns. Next, you iterate over all the columns in the
schema DataTable, and add a new column for each row. You access the "ColumnName" column
in the row to set the name of the column in the ListView. The other two values specify the layout of the columns: the second value (100) is the width of the column, and the third value sets
the alignment of the column. Before the method exits, it sets the global variable ColumnsSet to
True to indicate that the columns were added successfully.

With that done, you can return to the OrderIDs list's second event handler. You close the
data reader and the connection, and finally call a method named PopulateOrderDetails().
Into this method, you pass the ArrayList that contains all the row values that you received
from the data reader. The method will use the following information to populate the ListView:

```
Private Sub PopulateOrderDetails(ByVal RowList As ArrayList)

  OrderDetailsList.Items.Clear()

  Dim row As Object()
  For Each row In RowList
    Dim OrderDetails(row.Length) As String
    Dim col As Object

    Dim ColIdx As Integer
    For ColIdx = 0 To row.Length - 1
      OrderDetails(ColIdx) = Convert.ToString(row(ColIdx))
    Next

    Dim NewItem As New ListViewItem(OrderDetails)
    OrderDetailsList.Items.Add(NewItem)
  Next
End Sub
```

The first thing this method does is to call Clear() on the ListView—this removes any
items that may previously have been added. After that, to add the column values for each row
into the ListView, you need to create a ListViewItem object and add that to the Items collection of the ListView. In order to generate a ListViewItem, you want to create an array of
strings, where each string in the array corresponds to a column in the ListView. Using the
Length property of the row object enables you to allocate enough strings in the array to hold
each column that exists in the row. You then iterate over the columns in the row, convert each
one to a String, and insert it into the string array. Once you've built the String array, you create a new ListViewItem and add it to the ListView.

If you haven't done so already, fire up the application and click Start. In the blink of an eye, you should see the left-hand list fill up with order numbers. Select an order number, and the right-hand list will display the order details. Your results should look something like Figure 2-3.

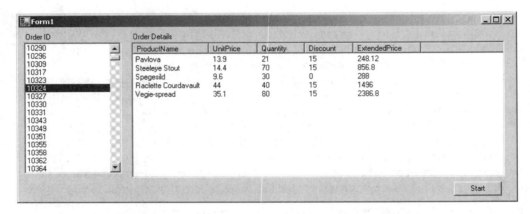

Figure 2-3. *Running the* SqlBrowser

Let's recap. To populate the left-hand list with Order IDs, you used a SqlCommand object to execute a SELECT statement that retrieved the OrderID column from the Orders table. In order to populate the right-hand list, you have to first select an order from the left-hand list; this Order ID is then used as the parameter to be passed to the CustOrdersDetail stored procedure. On executing this stored procedure, you use the GetSchemaTable() method to return a DataTable containing the schema for the result set; this is then used to set the column headers in the right-hand list view. Finally, the order data you cached away is used to populate the right-hand view.

This application is a good example of when data readers are the right choice for accessing the data in a data store. If you take this application a little further, you might use it to generate reports on the orders. You don't need to modify the data in order to create reports, so the read-only aspect of the data reader isn't an issue.

It would be possible to implement this application using DataTables, but doing so would incur more of a performance overhead. For example, consider the code that populates the ListView containing the Order IDs. With the data reader, you only ever have a single Order ID in memory at one time, as you add it to the ListView. In a DataTable implementation, you'd have to select all of the Order IDs in the table, then enumerate over each ID and add it to the ListView. This means that before you could populate the Order ID ListView, you'd have to store the whole table in memory, demanding a much larger memory footprint.

Commonly Encountered Exceptions

To conclude this chapter, you'll have a look at a couple of the exceptions that you might encounter when using data reader objects. They're not meant to be exhaustive; they're just the ones that tend to be raised by common programming errors.

IndexOutOfBoundsException

ADO.NET raises the IndexOutOfBoundsException when an attempt is made to access a column that doesn't exist in the data reader. This will usually be through one of the GetXxx() methods or Item(). Trying to retrieve the fourth column from a data reader that contains only three columns will certainly generate this exception. If the Item() property has been used to find a named column (rather than using an ordinal), the exception message will specify the name of the column it failed to find.

InvalidOperationException

The following four data reader-associated problems are likely to cause an InvalidOperation-Exception:

- This exception is thrown when an attempt is made to do something with an object that conflicts with its internal state. For example, closing a data reader and then calling GetSchemaTable() will throw this exception with the message "Invalid attempt to read data when reader is closed." Closing the connection and then attempting to access any data from the data reader will also raise this exception. The data reader requires an open connection in order to function.

- Care should be taken when calling ExecuteReader() with a CommandBehavior value of SequentialAccess. When this mode is specified, the data reader expects to access the columns in a sequential order. In other words, if you access column four, you can't then access column three—you'll cause the exception to be thrown with the message "Invalid attempt to read from column ordinal '3'." With CommandBehavior.SequentialAccess, you may only read from column ordinal "5" or greater.

- If you close the connection while the data reader is still retrieving data, then an exception will be raised with the message "Invalid attempt to read when reader is closed."

- Another common error resulting in this exception happens when attempting to call ExecuteReader() while the connection is closed. Although, technically, the data reader itself does not throw it in this case, you'll only ever see it when you try to create the data reader. The message for this exception reads "ExecuteReader requires an open and available Connection (state=Closed)."

Data Reader Performance Considerations

Performance is one of the most important reasons for wanting to use a data reader in the first place, but there are ways to improve it still further. In this section, you'll examine how to optimize data access through a DataReader object.

The examples you'll look at here involve a simple table in a SQL Server database. This table has two columns. The first is called ID, which contains the primary key and stores integers. The second is called Name and contains strings up to 255 characters long. One million rows have been added to this table—the IDs are numbered sequentially from 0 to 999999, and to populate the Name column random numbers were generated, converted into strings, and inserted into the column.

All the results shown here are based on the data reader accessing the million rows over ten iterations. In other words, for each test result you see, rows have been accessed ten million times. Maybe the chance of you ever needing to retrieve 10 million rows in a single chunk is slim, but by retrieving so much data you increase the duration of the work being done, hopefully providing more realistic results.

The following is the basic outline for the code that was used for profiling:

```
Dim StartTime As Long = DateTime.Now.Ticks

While reader.Read()
  ' Do your data access here
End While

Dim EndTime As Long = DateTime.Now.Ticks
Dim TimeTaken As New TimeSpan(EndTime - StartTime)
```

The first line of code gets the current time, represented by the number of 100 nanosecond intervals that have elapsed since 12:00 a.m., January 1, 0001. Then you do your data processing in the While loop, as usual. Once you've finished processing the data, you get the current time again. Finally, you subtract the start time from the end time to receive a TimeSpan object. If you use the TotalSeconds property of the TimeSpan object, you get the number of seconds it took to process the data. As you can see, it's not rocket science!

Column Ordinal vs. Column Name

As you know, there are several ways of retrieving data from a data reader, and two that you've looked at already use the column's ordinal or its name with the Item() property. There are quite serious performance implications to consider when deciding which of these techniques to use. To refresh your memory, the following are two quick examples:

```
Dim ID As Object = reader("ID")
Dim ID As Object = reader(0)
```

Table 2-5 shows the results of running tests that read each row in turn. One test used the column ordinal, and the other test used the column name.

Table 2-5. *Ordinal vs. Column Name Comparison*

Provider	Method	Time (for 10 Million Records) in Seconds
SqlClient	reader("ID") reader(0)	48.3995952 64.192304
OleDb	reader("ID") reader(0)	131.1285536 152.5092976

It's pretty clear that, regardless of which provider you use, the column ordinal is significantly faster. Also, as you'd expect, the OleDb provider produces much slower times (you're working against SQL Server 2000 in all of these tests). The results for the OleDb provider are still valid, though: if you were running against another back end, you'd still expect to see the ordinal indexer outperform the column name indexer.

The *reason* for the difference in performance is that when you use the column name, the providers still have to map that name to the appropriate ordinal value. The current providers do this by calling GetOrdinal(), which takes the column name and returns the column's ordinal; using this providers then call GetValue(), which returns the column's value.

In terms of performance, then, there's no contest: using the ordinal is much faster. Problems can start to occur, however, if the schema changes—you might reference the wrong column with an ordinal. At least if a column name is removed, you know that you'll get an exception. Earlier in the chapter, you got around this problem by using GetOrdinal() once, storing the ordinal in a variable, and using the variable thereafter. Nothing you've seen here changes the validity of that technique.

Type-Safe Access vs. Type-Unsafe Access

As you've just seen, accessing data using the default Item() property is very fast, but no consideration is made about the data types it's dealing with. Sometimes this is all right, but at other times it's nice to be able to access data in a type-safe manner (if for no other reason than that it makes you feel good inside!).

The following code shows a couple of examples of how you might access data in a type-safe manner:

```
Dim ID As SqlInt32 = reader.GetSqlInt32(0)
Dim Name As SqlString = reader.GetSqlString(1)

Dim ID As Integer = reader.GetInt32(0)
Dim Name As String = reader.GetString(1)
```

The first two lines make use of the SqlClient's knowledge of SQL Server, and retrieve proper SQL types. The third and fourth lines get the data back in a type-safe manner, but when you use GetString(), you don't really know how that data was being stored in the database. Also, all of these methods use the column ordinal; none of them allows you to retrieve a column based on its name.

So, is there a tradeoff between being able to access data like this, and using the Item() property? Running the tests produced the results found in Table 2-6.

Table 2-6. *Performance Comparison Between .NET Type, DBType, and Type Conversion*

Provider	Method	Time (for 1 Million Records) in Seconds
SqlClient	reader.GetString(1) reader.GetSqlString(1) CStr(reader(1))	65.7545504 65.6844496 46.81732
OleDb	reader.GetString(1) CStr(reader(1))	140.1114704 147.061464

Looking at the `SqlClient` results first, you can see that there's practically no difference in retrieving data from the `Name` column as a `SqlString` or a `String` data type. This is to be expected, because if you were to delve into the intermediate language for the `GetString()` and `GetSqlString()` methods, you'd see that `GetString()` actually calls straight through to `GetSqlString()`! Look at what happens when you use `Item()`, though: in comparison with the type-safe access, it's *much* faster. In fact, this is to be expected too: when you call `GetSqlString()`, the `SqlClient` jumps through lots of hoops to get you a nice, cuddly `SqlString`. When you use `Item()`, you're getting an `Object` back, and leaving it to the runtime to perform the type conversion for you.

Turning your attention to the `OleDb` provider, you find that the typed `GetString()` method is actually faster than the indexer! This is more difficult to explain, but the most likely reason is that the `OleDbDataReader` object accesses all the data in its native format. In other words, when you use the `GetString()` method, the `DataReader` does as little work as possible to coerce the value it has into a `String` object.

When you ask yourself whether you should use the type-safe methods, the answer is, once again, "It depends." If the `SqlDataReader` object is being used, and all-out performance is the order of the day, then the `Item()` property is a lot faster. If the `OleDbDataReader` is being used, the type-safe access methods don't carry the same performance penalty. When considering performance, always try to think of the big picture. Don't take the blinkered approach and assume that just because *a* is faster than *b*, *a* is always better. As the previous scenario illustrates, this isn't necessarily the case.

Summary

In this chapter, you've looked at ADO.NET data reader objects and, in particular, at `SqlDataReader` and `OleDbDataReader`. You've seen how you can traverse one or many result sets using `NextResult()`, and also how you can access data using either the `Item()` property, or type-safe methods.

To consolidate your newfound knowledge, you created a simple application that demonstrated the core functionality of the data readers. To finish with, you also considered the performance implications of accessing data in various ways, and looked at the situations where one method may be better than the next.

Note that although most of the examples presented here used the SQL Server .NET data provider, the code download includes complementary projects that use the OLE DB .NET data provider instead.

CHAPTER 3

■ ■ ■

DataSets

The ADO.NET DataSet object is the centerpiece of a disconnected, data-driven application. It is an in-memory representation of a complete set of data, including tables, relationships, and constraints—it follows the model of a relational database. A DataSet is independent of the format of the original data source, but the data in a DataSet can be accessed, manipulated, updated, or deleted, and then reconciled with the original data. Because of the DataSet's disconnected nature, there is less contention for valuable resources such as database connections, plus less record locking. From our discussions in Chapter 1, you know this much already.

What we didn't express in Chapter 1—at least, not in so many words—is that the DataSet object was designed from the ground up to be highly integrated with XML. DataSets use XML for transmission and persistence, to the extent that DataSet objects and XML documents are almost interchangeable. If an object or application doesn't support ADO.NET but can parse XML, then it can treat the DataSet as an XML file. If the object supports ADO.NET, then the data can be materialized into a DataSet, which will expose all of the properties and methods of the System.Data.DataSet class.

■Tip There will be more to say about the relationship between DataSet objects and XML in Chapters 5 and 6.

The DataSet Object Model

In Chapter 1, we presented an abbreviated picture of the object model that springs from the DataSet object. Here, you can add some flesh to those bones and look at the bigger picture. A more complete idea of the model will help you understand the power and usefulness of DataSets, as shown in Figure 3-1.

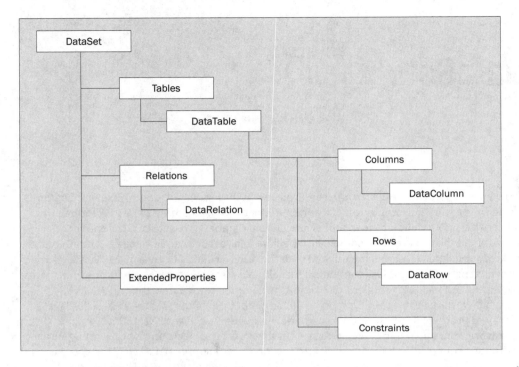

Figure 3-1. *A* DataSet *and its main constituents*

The diagram in Figure 3-1 shows the three collection properties that together make up the relational data structure of the DataSet: Tables, Relations, and ExtendedProperties. Table 3-1 describes each of these properties.

Table 3-1. DataSet *and Its Main Constituents*

Property	Description
Tables	DataSet.Tables is an object of type System.Data.DataTableCollection that can contain zero or more System.Data.DataTable objects. Each DataTable represents a table of data that's been extracted from a data source. In turn, each DataTable has collections called Columns and Rows, which can contain zero or more DataColumn or DataRow objects, respectively.
Relations	The DataSet.Relations property is a System.Data.DataRelation-Collection object that can contain zero or more System.Data.DataRelation objects. A DataRelation object defines a parent-child relationship between two tables, based on foreign key values.
ExtendedProperties	DataSet.ExtendedProperties is a System.Data.PropertyCollection object that can contain zero or more user-defined properties. The ExtendedProperties collection can be used to store custom data related to the DataSet, such as the time when it was constructed.

To understand the `DataSet` fully, then, you first need to understand the `DataTable`. For that reason, you'll spend the first part of this chapter dissecting the `DataTable` class, understanding how it works, and its role in a data-driven application. Once you've dealt with `DataTables`, you'll start using them in `DataSets`, building `DataRelations` between them in the same way that you'd have relationships between two tables in a database. Before you finish, you'll also learn how to cache `DataSets` for increased application performance.

The DataTable

Don't think that the `DataTable` class is in some way subservient to `DataSet`—it's central to the ADO.NET architecture, and `DataTable` objects can be used independently of `DataSets`, if that's what you need. As outlined previously, a `DataTable` contains (among other things) a `Columns` collection, a `Rows` collection, and a `Constraints` collection. The `Columns` and `Constraints` collections together define the schema for the `DataTable` (that is, the rules that govern what data the table can hold), while the `Rows` collection contains the data itself. Table 3-2 describes the functions of each collection.

Table 3-2. *Various Collections in a* `DataTable`

Property	Description
Columns	The `Columns` collection is an instance of the `System.Data.DataColumnCollection` class, and is a container for zero or more `DataColumn` objects. The `DataColumn` objects define the properties of each `DataTable` column, such as their names, the type of data they store, and any primary key or incremental numbering information.
Rows	The `Rows` collection is an instance of the `System.Data.DataRowCollection` class, and is a container for zero or more `DataRow` objects. The `DataRow` objects contain the actual data in the `DataTable`, as defined by the `DataTable.Columns` collection. Each `DataRow` has one item for each `DataColumn` in the `Columns` collection.
Constraints	The `Constraints` collection is an instance of the `System.Data.ConstraintCollection` class, and is a container for zero or more `System.Data.ForeignKeyConstraint` and/or `System.Data.UniqueConstraint` objects. The former define the action to be taken on a column in a primary key/foreign key relationship when a row is updated or deleted, while the latter are used to enforce the rule that all values in a given column should be unique.

DataColumn

As stated, a `DataColumn` can be used to define the name and data type of a column in a `DataTable`. You can create a new `DataColumn` either by using the `DataColumn` constructor, or by invoking the `Add()` method of the `DataTable.Columns` collection property.

```
Dim myColumn As New DataColumn("ID", Type.GetType("System.Int32"))
```

or

```
productsTable.Columns.Add("ID", Type.GetType("System.Int32"))
```

The version of the `DataTable.Columns.Add()` method that you've used here expects two arguments: the name of the new `DataColumn`, and a `Type` object. (For the second of these, you've used the `System.Type` class's convenient `GetType()` method.) In fact, there are four other overloaded versions of this method; here's how you might use them.

- `productsTable.Columns.Add()`: Creates and adds a new `DataColumn` to the `DataColumn-Collection` (and therefore, by implication, a new column to the table). In the absence of anything to specify otherwise, the new `DataColumn` object is given a default name (`Column1`, `Column2`, etc.).

- `productsTable.Columns.Add("ColumnName")`: Creates and adds a `DataColumn` with the specified name to the table. The default data type of any column for which no type is specified is `System.String`.

- `productsTable.Columns.Add(myDataColumn)`: Adds the specified, pre-existing `DataColumn` object to the `DataColumnCollection`.

- `productsTable.Columns.Add("SubTotal", _`
                `Type.GetType("System.Single"), _`
                `"Sum(Price)")`: Creates and adds a `DataColumn` with the specified name, data type, and `Expression` property. The expression can be used to filter rows, to calculate the values in a column, or (as in this case) to create an aggregate column.

In the following code snippet, you create a new `DataTable` object through one of its three constructors (the other two allow for the creation of a table with a default name, and for the synthesis of a table from a stream). Once created, you define the table's schema by creating three new columns in the `Columns` collection.

```
'Create a new DataTable
Dim productsTable As New DataTable("Products")
'Build the Products schema
productsTable.Columns.Add("ID", Type.GetType("System.Int32"))
productsTable.Columns.Add("Name", Type.GetType("System.String"))
productsTable.Columns.Add("Category", Type.GetType("System.Int32"))
```

To build the schema for this new table, you call the `Add()` method of the `DataTable.Columns` collection once for each column that you want to add to the `DataTable`. For each `DataColumn`, you pass in arguments for the `ColumnName` and `DataType` properties. The result is a `DataTable` named `Products` that's made up of three columns named `ID`, `Name`, and `Category`.

DataRow

With the `DataTable` constructed and the columns defined, you can begin populating the `DataTable` with data. This process involves adding new `DataRow` objects to the `DataTable.Rows` collection. To create a new row in the `DataTable`, first you invoke the `DataTable.NewRow()` method, which returns a `DataRow` that conforms to the `DataTable`'s current schema. Second, you set the value of each column in the `DataRow`, before calling the `DataTable.Rows.Add()` method and passing the new `DataRow` object as the only argument.

```
'Create a new DataRow with the same schema as the DataTable
Dim tempRow As DataRow
tempRow = productsTable.NewRow()
'Set the column values
tempRow.Item("ID") = 1
tempRow.Item("Name") = "Caterham Seven de Dion"
tempRow.Item("Category") = 1
'Add the DataRow to the DataTable
productsTable.Rows.Add(tempRow)
```

In this example, you're adding one row to productsTable. First, you create a new DataRow object (tempRow) using the schema from the DataTable by calling the productsTable.NewRow() method. Next, you set the value for each of the columns defined in the productsTable.Columns collection. Last, you invoke the productsTable.Rows.Add() method to add the new DataRow to the productsTable.Rows collection.

Constraints

Relational databases enforce data integrity with *constraints*—rules applied to a column that define what action to take when data in a related column or row is altered. In ADO.NET, there are two types of constraints: ForeignKeyConstraints and UniqueConstraints. You'll take a quick look at constraints here, with one or two fairly straightforward examples, but we'll save deeper coverage for dedicated treatment in Chapter 7.

ForeignKeyConstraint

A ForeignKeyConstraint is intended for use in a primary key/foreign key relationship; when a value in a column of a parent table is changed or deleted, a ForeignKeyConstraint defines how the child table should react. For example, if a parent record is deleted, you could specify that all child records should be deleted too—or you could set the related field in the child records to null or default values, explicitly identifying orphaned records. This is known as a *cascading action*, because an action on the parent has consequences that travel down to affect the child as well.

The action to be taken on the child is defined in the ForeignKeyConstraint.DeleteRule and/or the ForeignKeyConstrint.UpdateRule property, and can be set to one of four possible System.Data.Rule enumerators, as shown in Table 3-3.

Table 3-3. *The* System.Data.Rule *Enumeration*

Value	Description
Cascade	Deletes or updates related rows. This is the default action.
SetNull	Sets values in related rows to DBNull.
SetDefault	Sets values in related rows to the value of their column's DefaultValue property.
None	No action is taken on related rows.

UniqueConstraint

A UniqueConstraint enforces that the values in a column should be unique. This type of constraint is set automatically for primary key columns, which is covered in the following section. If a column has a UniqueConstraint, attempting to set the same value for that column in two different rows throws an exception of type System.Data.ConstraintException.

You can also set a UniqueConstraint over more than one column. In this case, setting the same values for every constrained column in two rows of the same table will throw an exception.

PrimaryKey

Since the DataSet and DataTable objects are designed to support all of the basic concepts of relational databases, a DataTable can and should have a *primary key*. In a DataTable, the primary key is defined as an *array* of DataColumns that together provide a unique identifier for a DataRow within the DataTable. To create a primary key, you need to set the PrimaryKey property of the DataTable to an array of DataColumns. When you define a primary key in this way, a UniqueConstraint is automatically applied to the DataColumn array.

```
'Set up the ID column as the primary key
Dim pk(1) As DataColumn
pk(0) = productsTable.Columns("ID")
productsTable.PrimaryKey = pk
```

Dynamically Constructing a DataTable

Let's start to put together some of the things that you've looked at so far. In the following code example, which is an amalgam of the snippets you've seen so far, you create a DataTable, set the primary key, and then set the AutoIncrement and ReadOnly properties of the DataColumn. In addition, the DataColumn class exposes properties for setting up a read-only, auto-increment column, which you do here for your ID column.

```
'Create the table
Dim productsTable As New DataTable("Products")

'Build the Products schema
productsTable.Columns.Add("ID", Type.GetType("System.Int32"))
productsTable.Columns.Add("Name", Type.GetType("System.String"))
productsTable.Columns.Add("Category", Type.GetType("System.Int32"))

'Set up the ID column as the primary key
Dim pk(1) As DataColumn
pk(0) = productsTable.Columns("ID")
productsTable.PrimaryKey = pk

productsTable.Columns("ID").AutoIncrement = True
productsTable.Columns("ID").AutoIncrementSeed = 1
productsTable.Columns("ID").ReadOnly = True
```

Once the `DataTable` is constructed, you can fill it with `DataRows`. For this example, you'll populate the `DataTable` with alternating values by using the `Math.IEEERemainder()` method. In even-numbered rows, you'll set the `Name` column of the `DataRow` to `Caterham Seven de Dion`, and the `Category` value to 1. For odd-numbered rows, you'll set the `Name` to `Dodge Viper` and the `Category` value to 2.

```
Dim tempRow As DataRow

'Populate the Products table with 10 cars
Dim i As Int32 = 0
For i = 1 To 10
  tempRow = productsTable.NewRow()

  'Make every even row a Caterham Seven de Dion
  If Math.IEEERemainder(i, 2) = 0 Then
    tempRow("Name") = "Caterham Seven de Dion #" & i.ToString()
    tempRow("Category") = 1
  Else
    tempRow("Name") = "Dodge Viper #" & i.ToString()
    tempRow("Category") = 2
  End If

  productsTable.Rows.Add(tempRow)
Next i
```

The interesting thing about this code, compared to what you had earlier, is that you don't need to set a value for the `ID` column—it's a read-only, *auto-increment* column.

DataTable Events

Like many of the objects in the .NET Framework, the `DataTable` exposes a set of events. In this case, the events can be captured and handled in order to update the user interface, or to validate edits or deletes before they are committed. Not including the inherited from `MarshalByValueComponent.Disposed` event, there are six events in all, and they all work in more or less the same way, with similar arguments. Table 3-4 describes the six events.

Table 3-4. `System.Data.DataTable` *Events*

Event	Description
ColumnChanging	Occurs when a value is being changed in the specified `DataColumn` in a `DataRow`.
ColumnChanged	Occurs after a value has been changed in the specified `DataColumn` in a `DataRow`.
RowChanging	Occurs when a `DataRow` is changing. This event will fire each time a change is made to the `DataRow`, after the `ColumnChanging` event has fired.
RowChanged	Occurs after a `DataRow` has been changed successfully.
RowDeleting	Occurs when a `DataRow` is about to be deleted.
RowDeleted	Occurs after a `DataRow` is successfully deleted.

Each of the DataTable events works in the same fashion. Handlers for the ColumnChanging and ColumnChanged events receive a DataColumnChangeEventArgs object, which exposes three properties. These properties are described in Table 3-5.

Table 3-5. DataColumnChangeEventArgs *Properties*

Property	Description
Column	Gets the DataColumn object with the changing value.
ProposedValue	Gets or sets the proposed value—that is, the new value being assigned to the column. In a ColumnChanging event handler, for example, you could evaluate the ProposedValue and make a decision on whether to accept or reject the change. You'll have an example of this in action shortly.
Row	Gets the DataRow object with the changing value.

The handlers for the other events take a DataRowChangeEventArgs object, which exposes just two properties, as shown in Table 3-6.

Table 3-6. DataRowChangeEventArgs *Properties*

Property	Description
Action	Gets the action (added, changed, deleted, etc.) that will occur/has occurred on the DataRow
Row	Gets the DataRow object upon which the action will occur/has occurred

DataTable Events Example

In the following example, you're going to create a DataTable and populate it dynamically, just as you did in the previous sample code. However, you're also going to build an ASP.NET interface that will enable rows in the DataTable to be updated and deleted, causing each of the aforementioned events to be fired, and giving you the opportunity to handle them. To give you an idea of where you're headed, the web form you're building is going to look like what you see in Figure 3-2.

Let's start by building the ASP.NET web form interface. Create a new web application file named DataTableExample.aspx.

```
<%@ Page Inherits="DataTableExample" Src="DataTableExample.aspx.vb" %>
<html>
<body>
<form runat="server">
  <table CellPadding="4" CellSpacing="0" Border="0">
    <tr>
      <td VALIGN="TOP">
        <h3>Products Table</h3>
        <asp:DataGrid runat="server" id="productGrid"
                     CellPadding="4" CellSpacing="0"
                     BorderWidth="1" Gridlines="Horizontal"
                     Font-Names="Verdana, Arial, sans-serif"
                     Font-Size="x-small" HeaderStyle-Font-Bold="True"
```

```
              OnEditCommand="DataGrid_OnEditCommand"
              OnCancelCommand="DataGrid_OnCancelCommand"
              OnUpdateCommand="DataGrid_OnUpdateCommand"
              OnDeleteCommand="DataGrid_OnDeleteCommand">
    <Columns>
        <asp:ButtonColumn Text="Delete" CommandName="Delete" />
        <asp:EditCommandColumn EditText="Edit"
                               CancelText="Cancel"
                               UpdateText="Update" />
    </Columns>
  </asp:DataGrid>
 </td>
 <td VALIGN="TOP">
  <h3>DataTable Events List</h3>
  <asp:Label runat="server" id="eventsList"
          Font-Names="Verdana, Arial, sans-serif"
          Font-Size="x-small" />
 </td>
</tr>
</table>
</form>
</body>
</html>
```

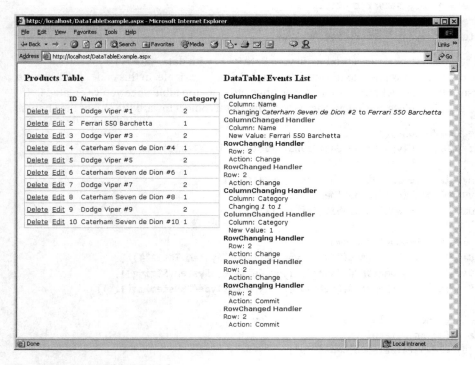

Figure 3-2. *DataTableExample.aspx*

In the web form, you have a DataGrid that specifies methods for the "edit", "cancel", "update", and "delete" commands. These commands will be handled in the code-behind class that's specified in the Page directive at the top of the web form. As it stands, the DataGrid has two columns in its Columns collection: a ButtonColumn that will have a Delete link button, and an EditCommandColumn that will enable editing of the row. Also, you have a Label control that you'll use to display information about the events that are fired.

To build the code-behind class, create a file named DataTableExample.aspx.vb and save it in the same directory as the web form file. At the top of the file, you need to import the necessary namespaces, and declare the class.

```
Imports System
Imports System.Data
Imports System.Web
Imports System.Web.UI
Imports System.Web.UI.WebControls

Public Class DataTableExample
  Inherits Page
```

Next, you need to declare the DataTable object, and the code-behind variables that map to the web form's server controls.

```
'Declare the DataTable object at the class level
Protected WithEvents myDataTable As DataTable

'Map the web form server controls
Protected WithEvents productGrid As DataGrid
Protected WithEvents eventsList As Label
```

Now you need to write a method to fill your DataTable with data. MakeData() creates a DataTable object and assigns it to the class-level myDataTable variable. In this code, you'll also be making use of the ASP.NET application's Cache object to store the table once you've created it. If you haven't used it before, we'll have more to say about this object toward the end of the chapter.

```
Private Sub MakeData()
  myDataTable = CType(Cache.Get("myDataTable"), DataTable)

  'If myDataTable is not in the cache, create it
  If myDataTable Is Nothing Then
    myDataTable = New DataTable("Products")

    'Build the Products schema
    myDataTable.Columns.Add("ID", Type.GetType("System.Int32"))
    myDataTable.Columns.Add("Name", Type.GetType("System.String"))
    myDataTable.Columns.Add("Category", Type.GetType("System.Int32"))

    'Set up the ID column as the PrimaryKey
    Dim pk(1) As DataColumn
    pk(0) = myDataTable.Columns("ID")
```

```
    myDataTable.PrimaryKey = pk

    myDataTable.Columns("ID").AutoIncrement = True
    myDataTable.Columns("ID").AutoIncrementSeed = 1
    myDataTable.Columns("ID").ReadOnly = True

    Dim tempRow As DataRow

    'Populate the Products table with 10 cars
    Dim i As Int32 = 0
    For i = 1 To 10
      tempRow = myDataTable.NewRow()

      'Make every other car a Caterham Seven de Dion
      If Math.IEEERemainder(i, 2) = 0 Then
        tempRow("Name") = "Caterham Seven de Dion #" & i.ToString()
        tempRow("Category") = 1
      Else
        tempRow("Name") = "Dodge Viper #" & i.ToString()
        tempRow("Category") = 2
      End If

      myDataTable.Rows.Add(tempRow)
    Next i

    Cache.Insert("myDataTable", myDataTable)
  End If
End Sub
```

The MakeData() method is nearly identical to your earlier code for creating DataTables dynamically, with one significant difference: at the end of MakeData(), you place the myData-Table object in the cache. This will make sure that the DataTable object remains accessible after postback operations, so that you don't have to re-create it each time.

Next, you have to create a BindData() method that will invoke the MakeData() method and bind the DataGrid server control called productGrid to the myDataTable object. This will be called when the application first loads, and after every change to the table.

```
Private Sub BindData()

  'Get the DataSet
  MakeData()

  'Set the DataGrid.DataSource properties
  productGrid.DataSource = myDataTable

  'Bind the DataGrid
  productGrid.DataBind()
End Sub
```

With these support methods in place, you need to build the event handlers for the
DataTable events. These are similar to one another: they all render event information in the
Label server control called eventList. In the ColumnChanging event handler, for example, you
write that the event was fired, the name of the column that's changing, the original value of
the column, and the proposed value.

```
Private Sub ColumnChangingHandler(ByVal Sender As Object, _
                                  ByVal E As DataColumnChangeEventArgs) _
                                  Handles myDataTable.ColumnChanging

    EventsList.Text &= String.Format("<B>ColumnChanging Handler</B><BR>" & _
                                     "  Column: {0}<BR>", _
                                     E.Column.ColumnName)

    Dim propValue As String = E.ProposedValue.ToString().ToLower()

    'If the user changed the name of the car to anything
    'with the word "pinto" in it, raise an exception.
    If E.Column.ColumnName = "Name" AndAlso _
      propValue.IndexOf("pinto") > -1 Then
      Throw(New System.Exception("Pintos are not allowed on this list."))
    Else
      EventsList.Text &= String.Format("  Changing <I>{0}</I>" & _
                                       " to <I>{1}</I><BR>", _
                                       E.Row(E.Column.ColumnName), _
                                       E.ProposedValue)
    End If
End Sub
```

In this example, you prohibit any user from changing a Name field value to anything
including the word "Pinto" (after all, this is an exotic car list, and the Pinto, while a classic,
is far from exotic). If "Pinto" *is* in the proposed value, you throw a System.Exception containing the string "Pintos are not allowed on this list." By throwing an exception, the change is
rejected, and the original values are restored.

The remaining event handlers are similar to ColumnChangingHandler(), although you don't
throw any more exceptions.

```
Private Sub ColumnChangedHandler(ByVal Sender As Object, _
                                 ByVal E As DataColumnChangeEventArgs) _
                                 Handles myDataTable. ColumnChanged

    EventsList.Text &= String.Format("<FONT COLOR=""RED"">" & _
                       "<B>ColumnChanged Handler</B></FONT><BR>" & _
                       "  Column: {0}<BR>", E.Column.ColumnName)
    EventsList.Text &= String.Format("  New Value: {0}<BR>", _
                                     E.ProposedValue)
End Sub
```

```vb
Private Sub RowChangingHandler(ByVal Sender As Object, _
                            ByVal E As DataRowChangeEventArgs) _
                          . Handles MyDataTable.RowChanging

  EventsList.Text &= String.Format("<B>RowChanging Handler</B><BR>" & _
                          "  Row: {0}<BR>", E.Row("ID"))
  EventsList.Text &= String.Format("  Action: {0}<BR>", _
                          E.Action)
End Sub

Private Sub RowChangedHandler(ByVal Sender As Object, _
                          ByVal E As DataRowChangeEventArgs) _
                          Handles MyDataTable.RowChanged

  EventsList.Text &= String.Format("<FONT COLOR=""RED""><B>" & _
                          "RowChanged Handler</B></FONT><BR>" & _
                          "Row: {0}<BR>", E.Row("ID"))
  EventsList.Text &= String.Format("  Action: {0}<BR>", _
                          E.Action)
End Sub

Private Sub RowDeletingHandler(ByVal Sender As Object, _
                            ByVal E As DataRowChangeEventArgs) _
                            Handles MyDataTable.RowDeleting

  EventsList.Text &= String.Format("<B>RowDeleting Handler</B><BR>" & _
                          "Row: {0}<BR>", E.Row("ID"))
  EventsList.Text &= String.Format("  Action: {0}<BR>", _
                          E.Action)
End Sub

Private Sub RowDeletedHandler(ByVal Sender As Object, _
                          ByVal E As DataRowChangeEventArgs) _
                          Handles MyDataTable.RowDeleted

  EventsList.Text &= "<FONT COLOR=""RED"">" & _
                          "<B>RowDeleted Handler</B></FONT><BR>"
  EventsList.Text &= String.Format("  Action: {0}<BR>", _
                          E.Action)
End Sub
```

Next, you need to create event handlers for the DataGrid's Edit, Update, Cancel, and Delete buttons, which become visible in the web form at various times. In the code for the web form, you stated that the names of the event-handling methods should be DataGrid_OnEditCommand(), DataGrid_OnUpdateCommand(), DataGrid_OnCancelCommand(), and DataGrid_OnDeleteCommand().

In the first of these, start by clearing the Label server control called EventsList (so that you get a list of events for the current postback only), and set the EditItemIndex property of the DataGrid to the index of the row that was clicked on. This puts the DataGrid into edit mode, and renders TextBox server controls in each non–read-only column, with the row values in those TextBoxes.

```
Protected Sub DataGrid_OnEditCommand(ByVal Sender As Object, _
                                     ByVal E As DataGridCommandEventArgs)
    EventsList.Text = ""
    CType(Sender, DataGrid).EditItemIndex = e.Item.ItemIndex
    BindData()
End Sub
```

In the DataGrid_OnCancelCommand() event handler, you simply set the DataGrid's EditItemIndex value to –1, which turns off the DataGrid edit mode.

```
Protected Sub DataGrid_OnCancelCommand(ByVal Sender As Object, _
                                       ByVal E As DataGridCommandEventArgs)
    CType(Sender, DataGrid).EditItemIndex = -1
    BindData()
End Sub
```

The DataGrid_OnUpdateCommand() event handler is a little more complicated.

```
Protected Sub DataGrid_OnUpdateCommand(ByVal Sender As Object, _
                                       ByVal E As DataGridCommandEventArgs)
    EventsList.Text = ""

    'Cast the Sender object to its true type: it's the source DataGrid
    Dim senderGrid As DataGrid = CType(Sender, DataGrid)
```

In this handler, you need to set the class-level myDataTable object to the current instance of the DataTable (the one saved in the cache) by invoking the MakeData() method.

```
    'Invoke MakeData() to create the myDataTable object
    MakeData()
```

Then, you create a new TextBox object and cast the first control in each column as an instance of the TextBox class. These control instances represent the TextBoxes that rendered in the DataGrid edit mode.

```
    'Get the edited item values
    Dim Name As TextBox = CType(E.Item.Cells(3).Controls(0), TextBox)
    Dim Category As TextBox = CType(E.Item.Cells(4).Controls(0), TextBox)
```

Next, you get the primary key value of the row being updated by setting a String object to the value of the text in the third column of the DataGrid (the first column contains the Delete link button, and the second contains the Edit/Update/Cancel link button).

```
'Get the PrimaryKey column text
Dim item As String = E.Item.Cells(2).Text
```

After that, you use the primary key value you just captured to invoke the `DataTable.Rows.Find()` method, which will return the `DataRow` that is being edited.

```
'Get the DataRow from myDataTable
Dim dr As DataRow = myDataTable.Rows.Find(Int32.Parse(item))
```

In a `Try...Catch` block, you then attempt to change the values in the `DataRow` to the values submitted by the user, through a call to the `DataRow` object's `AcceptChanges()` method. If the proposed value includes the word "Pinto", the `ColumnChangingHandler()` method will throw an exception, and the code in the `Catch` block will be executed. If not, the values in the `DataRow` will be changed.

```
'Change DataRow values. This will raise the ColumnChanging event.
Try
   dr(1) = Name.Text
   dr(2) = Int32.Parse(Category.Text)

   'Commit changes to DataRow. This will raise the ColumnChanged event.
   dr.AcceptChanges()
Catch ex As Exception
   EventsList.Text &= "<FONT COLOR=""RED""><B>Error: </FONT>" & _
                      ex.Message & "</B>"
End Try
```

Lastly, you recache the `DataTable`, set the `EditItemIndex` to –1 (to turn off the `DataGrid` edit mode), and invoke the `BindData()` method that you wrote earlier.

```
'Recache the DataTable
Cache.Insert("myDataTable", myDataTable)

'Bind the DataGrid
senderGrid.EditItemIndex = -1
BindData()
End Sub
```

The `DataGrid_OnDeleteCommand()` event handler contains similar functionality to the last one, but instead of updating the row, you use the `DataRowCollection.Remove()` method to delete the specified `DataRow` from the `DataTable.Rows` collection.

```
Protected Sub DataGrid_OnDeleteCommand(ByVal Sender As Object, _
                                ByVal E As DataGridCommandEventArgs)
   EventsList.Text = ""
   'Get hold of the DataGrid object that raised the event
   Dim senderGrid As DataGrid = CType(Sender, DataGrid)
```

```
   'Get the data
   MakeData()

   'Get the PrimaryKey column text
   Dim item As String = E.Item.Cells(2).Text

   'Get the DataRow from myDataTable
   Dim dr As DataRow = myDataTable.Rows.Find(Int32.Parse(item))

   'Use the Remove() method to delete the row
   myDataTable.Rows.Remove(dr)

   'Recache the DataSet
   Cache.Insert("myDataTable", myDataTable)

   'Bind the DataGrid
   senderGrid.EditItemIndex = -1
   BindData()
End Sub
```

Lastly, you create the Page_Load() event handler, which will fire each time the page is loaded—including on a postback. Here, you check for that possibility, and if this is the first request for the page, you use the Cache.Remove() method to make sure there is no cached version of myDataTable.

```
Protected Sub Page_Load(ByVal Sender As Object, _
                        ByVal E As EventArgs)
   If Not Page.IsPostBack Then

      'Start with a fresh DataTable
      Cache.Remove("myDataTable")
   End If
```

Next, you invoke MakeData() to create the myDataTable object. On the first request for this page, the MakeData() method will create the myDataTable object and insert it into the cache. If this is a postback, then MakeData() will cast the cached myDataTable object into the myData-Table class-level object.

```
   'Create a new DataTable by calling the MakeData method
   MakeData()
```

Lastly, if this request is not a postback, you invoke the BindData() method to bind the DataGrid. If this *is* a postback, the BindData() method will be invoked in the event handler that's fired on the postback, such as DataGrid_OnEditCommand().

```
   If Not Page.IsPostBack Then
      BindData()
   End If
 End Sub
End Class
```

With the code all complete, you can test the event handlers by browsing to the page. In the DataGrid, click the Edit link and change a value. When you click Update, notice that the ColumnChanged and ColumnChanging event handlers get fired twice—this is because they're fired once for each column in the row that changed. Also notice that the RowChanging and RowChanged events fire three times: once with each column change, and once when AcceptChanges() is invoked on the DataRow.

If you try to change the Name value of any row to any string containing the word "Pinto", an exception is thrown, as shown in Figure 3-3. As a result, the change fails, and the data is rolled back.

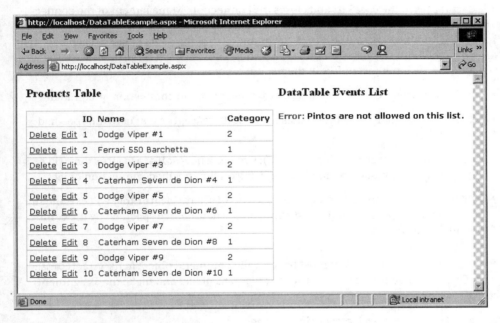

Figure 3-3. *DataTableExample.aspx in action*

Now that you understand how the DataTable class works, let's look at how DataTable objects are used in a DataSet, and how you can build relationships between DataTables.

Populating a DataSet

So far, you've looked at the dynamic creation of DataTable objects, and seen how to populate them with data. Although it was a useful exercise, it wasn't particularly realistic on two counts. First, you'll normally be dealing with DataTable objects that belong to DataSet objects. Second, you'll usually be using data from a data source, rather than generating it for yourself.

The first of these two is quite easy to address: to populate a DataSet with a dynamically created DataTable, you just need to use the DataSet.Tables collection's Add() method. For the second, you need to use a data adapter object, which we touched upon briefly back in Chapter 1. Here, you'll look at the basic operation of data adapters a little more closely, but such is the versatility and power of these objects that they also get Chapter 4 all to themselves.

Constructing a Data Adapter

To use a data adapter, you must specify a connection to a data source, and a command that will be executed. When you execute the command, you specify the DataSet that you want to fill. The data adapter creates connection and command objects (if necessary), opens the connection to the database, executes the command on the connection, places the results into one or more DataTables in the DataSet, and closes the connection. Management of the connection's state is therefore a function of the data adapter, not the DataSet.

In the .NET Framework, the SqlDataAdapter and OleDbDataAdapter classes each have four constructors, and both sets have the same semantics. The following is the quartet for the former; the one for the latter just differs in the parameter types:

- Public Sub New(): Creates a new SqlDataAdapter with no connection or command

- Public Sub New(SqlCommand): Creates a new SqlDataAdapter that uses the specified command object

- Public Sub New(String, SqlConnection): Creates a new SqlDataAdapter that will execute the SQL command specified in the string on the specified connection object

- Public Sub New(String, String): Creates a new SqlDataAdapter that will execute the SQL command specified in the first string on the data source specified by the connection in the second string

For the data adapter to work, it must have a valid command object in its SelectCommand property. One way to do that is to construct a SqlCommand object and make the assignment directly.

```
'Define the SQL command and connection string
Dim mySqlStmt As String = "SELECT * FROM Customers"
Dim myConString As String = "server=(local);database=Northwind;uid=sa;pwd=;"

'Construct a new SqlDataAdapter
Dim myDataAdapter As New SqlDataAdapter()

'Construct the SqlCommand that will be the data adapter's SelectCommand
Dim myConnection As New SqlConnection(myConString)
Dim myCommand As New SqlCommand(mySqlStmt, myConnection)

'Set the SelectCommand property
myDataAdapter.SelectCommand = myCommand
```

Alternatively, if you construct the data adapter using one of the overloaded constructors, a command object will be constructed and assigned to the SelectCommand property automatically.

```
Dim mySqlStmt As String = "SELECT * FROM Customers"
Dim myConString As String = "server=(local);database=Northwind;uid=sa;pwd=;"

Dim myDataAdapter As New SqlDataAdapter(mySqlStmt, myConString)
```

Invoking the Fill Method

To populate a DataSet with a new DataTable, you can use the data adapter's Fill() method and pass in the DataSet as an argument. The Fill() method will create a DataTable in the DataSet and fill it with the results of the SQL command. The sequence of events runs something like the following:

1. The connection to the database is opened (if it wasn't already open).

2. The SQL command is executed.

3. A new DataTable(s) is constructed and added to the DataSet.Tables collection.

4. The DataTable is populated with the results of the command.

5. The connection is closed, unless it was already open before Fill() was called.

Note If a connection is open, the data adapter will leave it open after the command has executed. This is useful if you're using one connection to execute several commands.

When Fill() is invoked, a new DataTable is added to the DataSet.Tables collection. By default, the new DataTable will be given a TableName property value of Table, and additional tables will be given the TableName values Table1, Table2, and so on. If you need to, you can pass a table name of your choosing into the Fill() method. The string value you specify will be assigned to the DataTable.TableName property.

```
myDataAdapter.Fill(myDataSet, "Customers")
```

A DataTable created by this means is accessible either by its DataSet.Tables collection index value

```
'The first table has an index of 0
Dim myDataTable As DataTable = ds.Tables(0)
```

or by its DataTable.TableName property.

```
Dim myDataTable As DataTable = ds.Tables("Customers")
```

Retrieving the Tables Collection's Metadata

The DataSet.Tables collection is an instance of the DataTableCollection class, and like other .NET collections it exposes properties like Count and Item(). However, it's also possible to use the DataSet.Tables collection to discover some interesting information about the tables it contains. Conveniently, you can display the values of some of the tables' properties by binding the collection itself (rather than one of the DataTables it contains) to a DataGrid, as shown in Figure 3-4.

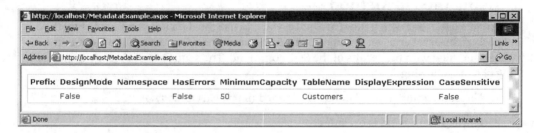

Figure 3-4. *MetadataExample.aspx*

Setting up this example is comparatively uncomplicated. In a new web application file named MetadataExample.aspx, create the following web form, which only contains a single DataGrid:

```
<%@ Page Inherits="MetadataExample" Src="MetadataExample.aspx.vb" %>
<HTML>
  <BODY>
    <FORM runat="server">
      <asp:DataGrid runat="server" id="metadataDataGrid"
                    CellPadding="4" CellSpacing="0"
                    BorderWidth="1" Gridlines="Horizontal"
                    Font-Names="Verdana, Arial, sans-serif"
                    Font-Size="x-small"
                    HeaderStyle-Font-Bold="True" />
    </FORM>
  </BODY>
</HTML>
```

Then, in the code-behind file, pull in a selection of data from the Northwind database, but then bind the metadataDataGrid to the myDataSet.Tables collection itself, rather than to one of the DataTables it contains.

```
Imports System
Imports System.Data
Imports System.Data.SqlClient
Imports System.Web
```

```vb
Imports System.Web.UI
Imports System.Web.UI.WebControls

Public Class MetadataExample
  Inherits Page

  'Map the web form server control
  Protected WithEvents metadataDataGrid As DataGrid

  Protected Sub Page_Load(ByVal Sender As Object, ByVal E As EventArgs)
    If Not Page.IsPostBack Then

      'Create a new DataSet with name "Northwind"
      Dim myDataSet As New DataSet("Northwind")

      'Create the SQL and ConnectionString values
      Dim mySqlStmt As String = "SELECT TOP 10 CustomerID, " & _
                "CompanyName, ContactName, ContactTitle FROM Customers"
      Dim myConString As String = _
                "server=localhost;database=Northwind;uid=sa;pwd=;"

      'Construct a new SqlDataAdapter with the preceding values
      Dim myDataAdapter As New SqlDataAdapter(mySqlStmt, myConString)

      'Invoke the Fill() method to create a new DataTable in the DataSet
      myDataAdapter.Fill(myDataSet, "Customers")

      metadataDataGrid.DataSource = myDataSet.Tables
      Page.DataBind()

    End If
  End Sub
End Class
```

Browsing to the web form renders a table containing some of the properties of the DataTables in the myDataSet.Tables collection. Briefly, these are described in Table 3-7.

Table 3-7. System.Data.DataTable *Properties*

Property	Description
CaseSensitive	A Boolean value indicating whether string comparisons within the table are case-sensitive.
DesignMode	A Boolean value indicating whether the DataTable is currently in design mode in an IDE.
DisplayExpression	The expression that will return a value used to represent this table in the UI.

continues

Table 3-7. *continued*

Property	Description
HasErrors	A Boolean value indicating whether there are errors in any row in any DataTable in the DataSet to which this table belongs.
MinimumCapacity	The initial starting size (number of rows) for this DataTable.
Namespace	The namespace for the XML representation of this DataTable. This is the same as the Prefix value.
Prefix	The namespace for the XML representation of this DataTable. As you'll see in Chapter 5, a DataSet can be represented in XML, and each DataTable in the set can have its own XML namespace.
TableName	The name of the DataTable.

Populating the Tables Collection with Multiple DataTables

Back in Chapter 1, you saw an example of using a data adapter to place a single DataTable in a DataSet, and there's a second example in the preceding section. As you found with the columns in a DataTable, however, the *real* power of the DataSet lies in its ability to hold multiple related tables, and to make data available based on the relationships between DataTables.

You can populate a DataSet with multiple tables in a number of different ways. You can create a DataTable dynamically and use the DataSet.Tables.Add() method to add the DataTable to the DataSet.Tables collection; you can use multiple data adapters to fill the same DataSet; or you can use one data adapter and set its SelectCommand.CommandText property before invoking Fill() for the second time. The code to accomplish this is as follows:

- Using multiple data adapters to fill the same DataSet

```
myDataAdapter.Fill(myDataSet, "Customers")
myOtherDataAdapter.Fill(myDataSet, "Employees")
```

- Using a single data adapter to fill the same DataSet using different SQL commands each time

```
'Set the SelectCommand.CommandText property
myDataAdapter.SelectCommand.CommandText = "SELECT * FROM Customers"

'Invoke the Fill() method
myDataAdapter.Fill(myDataSet, "Customers")

'Reset the SelectCommand.CommandText property
myDataAdapter.SelectCommand.CommandText = "SELECT * FROM Orders"

'Invoke the Fill() method for the second table
myDataAdapter.Fill(myDataSet, "Orders")
```

As stated previously, if no table name is passed into the `Fill()` method, then the newly constructed `DataTable` will be named `Table`, `Table1`, `Table2`, and so on. This naming rule also applies when you use SQL commands that return multiple result sets.

```
myDataAdapter.SelectCommand.CommandText = _
                    "SELECT * FROM Customers; SELECT * FROM Orders"
myDataAdapter.Fill(myDataSet)
```

The preceding code, for example, will populate the `DataSet` with two `DataTables`: `Table` and `Table1`.

The Relations Collection

The `DataSet.Relations` property is an instance of the `DataRelationCollection` class. The `Relations` collection contains `DataRelation` objects, which are used to create parent-child relationships between `DataTables` in the `DataSet`. A primary key/foreign key relationship is an example of this type of relationship.

We can create a relationship between two tables in a `DataSet` by invoking the `DataSet.Relations.Add()` method. There are seven overloaded `Add()` methods, as follows:

- `Public Sub Add(DataRelation)`: Adds the specified `DataRelation` object to the collection.

- `Public Function Add(DataColumn, DataColumn) As DataRelation`: Creates a Data-Relation object in the collection based on the two `DataColumns`. The first argument is the parent column and the second argument is the child column. The `DataRelation` is given a default name.

- `Public Function Add(DataColumn(), DataColumn()) As DataRelation`: Creates a `DataRelation` object in the collection based on the two `DataColumn` arrays. The first argument is the parent column array and the second argument is the child column array. The `DataRelation` is given a default name.

- `Public Function Add(String, DataColumn, DataColumn) As DataRelation`: Creates a `DataRelation` object in the collection with the specified string as the `DataRelation.RelationName` property.

- `Public Function Add(String, DataColumn(), DataColumn()) As DataRelation`: Creates a `DataRelation` object in the collection with the specified string as the `DataRelation.RelationName` property. The `DataRelation` is based on the two `DataColumn` arrays.

- `Public Function Add(String, DataColumn, DataColumn, Boolean) As DataRelation`: Creates a `DataRelation` object in the collection with the specified string as the `DataRelation.RelationName` property. The `DataRelation` is based on the two `DataColumns`. The Boolean argument indicates whether to create constraints (the default setting is `True`).

- `Public Function Add(String, DataColumn(), DataColumn(), Boolean) As DataRelation`: Creates a `DataRelation` object in the collection with the specified string as the `DataRelation.RelationName` property. The `DataRelation` is based on the two `DataColumn` arrays. The Boolean argument indicates whether to create constraints.

You can create a relationship in a `DataSet` using any of these overloaded methods. The following is an example using the method `Public Function Add(String, DataColumn, DataColumn) As DataRelation`:

```
'Create a relationship between Customers and Orders
myDataSet.Relations.Add("CustomersToOrders", _
                myDataSet.Tables("Customers").Columns("CustomerID"), _
                myDataSet.Tables("Orders").Columns("CustomerID"))
```

In this code, you invoke the `Add()` method of the `myDataSet.Relations` object to create a new `DataRelation` object in the `myDataSet.Relations` collection. As a result, a new `UniqueConstraint` is added to the parent `DataTable`, and a `ForeignKeyConstraint` is added to the child `DataTable`. The former ensures that all parent column values are unique in the table, and the latter sets up cascading deletes and updates from parent to child records.

It's also possible to construct the `DataRelation` object explicitly, and then add it to the `Relations` collection.

```
'Create two DataColumns
Dim parentColumn As DataColumn
Dim childColumn As DataColumn
'Set the two columns to instances of the parent and child columns
parentColumn = myDataSet.Tables("Customers").Columns("CustomerID")
childColumn = myDataSet.Tables("Orders").Columns("CustomerID")

'Create a new DataRelation object
Dim customersToOrders As New DataRelation( _
                    "CustomersToOrders", parentColumn, childColumn)

'Add the DataRelation to the DataSet.Relations collection
myDataSet.Relations.Add(customersToOrders)
```

As mentioned previously, a `DataRelation` can be constructed using an *array* of `DataColumns` for both the parent and child columns. Imagine, for example, that there's a table of `Employees` and a table of `Managers`. The `Managers` table contains data about the employees who are also managers (this example assumes that the names of such employees are duplicated in both the `Employees` table and the `Managers` table).

```
'Create arrays of DataColumns for the parent and child columns
Dim parentArray(2) As DataColumn
parentArray(0) = myDataSet.Tables("Employees").Columns("FirstName")
parentArray(1) = myDataSet.Tables("Employees").Columns("LastName")

Dim childArray(2) As DataColumn
childArray(0) = myDataSet.Tables("Managers").Columns("FirstName")
childArray(1) = myDataSet.Tables("Managers").Columns("LastName")

Dim EmpToMngr As New DataRelation( _
                    "EmployeesToManagers", parentArray, childArray)
myDataSet.Relations.Add(EmpToMngr)
```

Here, you're constructing a DataRelation using a DataColumn array for the parent and child columns of the relationship. When the relationship is constructed, a UniqueConstraint is added to the Employees table, enforcing a unique combination of first and last names, and a ForeignKeyConstraint is added to the Managers table, enforcing cascading deletes and updates across the relationship.

DataRelations Example

In the following example, you're going to build a DataSet and populate it with two DataTables: Customers and Orders. You'll then build a DataRelation establishing Customers as the parent and Orders as the child. In the ASP.NET web form, you'll add a Delete ButtonColumn to the Customers DataGrid, which will invoke a DeleteCustomer() method. This method will delete the appropriate row from the Customers DataTable. Because you have a DataRelation, this will cascade the delete to the child table, Orders, and delete all of the orders for the customer you're deleting, as shown in Figure 3-5.

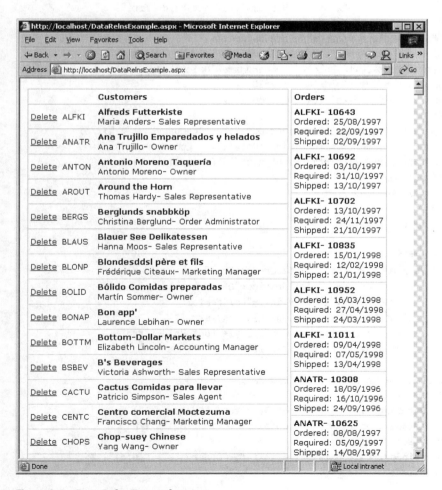

Figure 3-5. *DataRelnsExample.aspx*

Create a new ASP.NET web form named DataRelnsExample.aspx, and add the following code:

```
<%@ Page Inherits="DataRelnsExample" Src="DataRelnsExample.aspx.vb" %>
<%@ Import Namespace="System.Data" %>

<HTML>
<BODY>
 <FORM runat="server">
  <TABLE Border="0" CellPadding="2" CellSpacing="0">
   <TR>
    <TD valign="top">
     <asp:DataGrid runat="server" id="customersDataGrid"
                   CellPadding="4" CellSpacing="0"
                   BorderWidth="1" Gridlines="Horizontal"
                   Font-Names="Verdana, Arial, sans-serif"
                   Font-Size="x-small" HeaderStyle-Font-Bold="True"
                   AutogenerateColumns="False"
                   OnDeleteCommand="DeleteCustomer">
      <Columns>
       <asp:ButtonColumn Text="Delete" CommandName="Delete" />
       <asp:BoundColumn DataField="CustomerID" />
       <asp:TemplateColumn HeaderText="Customers">
        <ItemTemplate>
          <b><%# DataBinder.Eval(Container.DataItem, "CompanyName") %></b>
          <br><%# DataBinder.Eval(Container.DataItem, "ContactName") %>-
          <%# DataBinder.Eval(Container.DataItem, "ContactTitle") %>
        </ItemTemplate>
       </asp:TemplateColumn>
      </Columns>
     </asp:DataGrid>
    </TD>
    <TD valign="top">
     <asp:DataGrid runat="server" id="ordersDataGrid"
                   CellPadding="4" CellSpacing="0"
                   BorderWidth="1" Gridlines="Horizontal"
                   Font-Names="Verdana, Arial, sans-serif"
                   Font-Size="x-small" HeaderStyle-Font-Bold="True"
                   AutogenerateColumns="False">
      <Columns>
       <asp:TemplateColumn HeaderText="Orders">
        <ItemTemplate>
         <b><%# DataBinder.Eval(Container.DataItem, "CustomerID") %>-
         <%# DataBinder.Eval(Container.DataItem, "OrderID") %></b>
         <br>Ordered:
         <%# DataBinder.Eval(Container.DataItem, "OrderDate", "{0:d}") %>
         <br>Required:
```

```
      <%# DataBinder.Eval(Container.DataItem, "RequiredDate", "{0:d}") %>
      <br>Shipped:
      <%# DataBinder.Eval(Container.DataItem, "ShippedDate", "{0:d}") %>
    </ItemTemplate>
   </asp:TemplateColumn>
  </Columns>
 </asp:DataGrid>
</TD>
</TR>
</TABLE>
</FORM>
</BODY>
</HTML>
```

This web form uses BoundColumn and TemplateColumn objects to create a custom layout for your data. In the customersDataGrid, you use the OnDeleteCommand attribute to specify the method that should be invoked when the Delete button is clicked: DeleteCustomer().

Next, create a code-behind file named DataRelnsExample.aspx.vb in the same directory as the web form. Start by building the class definition, which includes some variable definitions for the web form server controls, and a class-level DataSet.

```
Imports System
Imports System.Data
Imports System.Data.SqlClient
Imports System.Web
Imports System.Web.UI
Imports System.Web.UI.WebControls

Public Class DataRelnsExample
  Inherits Page

  'Map the web form server controls
  Protected WithEvents customersDataGrid As DataGrid
  Protected WithEvents ordersDataGrid As DataGrid

  'Declare the DataSet object at the class level
  Protected myDataSet As DataSet
```

Now you need the method that will fill the DataSet. The DataSet contains two DataTables: Customers and Orders.

```
Private Sub MakeData()
  myDataSet = CType(Cache.Get("myDataSet"), DataSet)

  'If myDataSet is not in the cache, create it
  If myDataSet Is Nothing Then
    myDataSet = New DataSet("Northwind")
```

```
'Create the SQL and ConnectionString values
Dim mySqlStmt As String = "SELECT CustomerID, CompanyName, " & _
        "ContactName, ContactTitle FROM Customers ORDER BY CustomerID"
Dim myConString As String = _
        "server=localhost;database=Northwind;uid=sa;pwd=;"

'Construct a new SqlDataAdapter with the preceding values
Dim myDataAdapter As New SqlDataAdapter(mySqlStmt, myConString)

'Invoke the Fill() method to create a new DataTable in the DataSet
myDataAdapter.Fill(myDataSet, "Customers")

'Change the DataAdapter's SelectCommand and fill another table
mySqlStmt = "SELECT OrderID, CustomerID,OrderDate, " & _
            "RequiredDate, ShippedDate FROM Orders " & _
            "ORDER BY CustomerID"
myDataAdapter.SelectCommand.CommandText = mySqlStmt

myDataAdapter.Fill(myDataSet, "Orders")
```

Identify the Customers table's primary key by creating a new DataColumn array containing only the CustomerID DataColumn, and set the Customers table's PrimaryKey property to this new array.

```
Dim pk(1) As DataColumn
pk(0) = myDataSet.Tables("Customers").Columns("CustomerID")
myDataSet.Tables("Customers").PrimaryKey = pk
```

Define the primary key/foreign key relationship between the Customers and Orders tables.

```
'Create a relationship between Customers and Orders
myDataSet.Relations.Add("CustomersToOrders", _
            myDataSet.Tables("Customers").Columns("CustomerID"), _
            myDataSet.Tables("Orders").Columns("CustomerID"))

    Cache.Insert("myDataSet", myDataSet)
  End If
End Sub
```

Create a BindData() method that can be called from anywhere in the class. In it, bind the DataGrid server controls to their respective DataTables in the DataSet.

```
Private Sub BindData()
  customersDataGrid.DataSource = myDataSet.Tables("Customers")
  ordersDataGrid.DataSource = myDataSet.Tables("Orders")
  Page.DataBind()
End Sub
```

Create the DeleteCustomer() method that will be invoked when the Delete button is clicked.

```
Protected Sub DeleteCustomer(ByVal Sender As Object, _
                             ByVal E As DataGridCommandEventArgs)
    MakeData()

    'Find the DataRow based on the primary key value
    Dim myDataRow As DataRow = _
            myDataSet.Tables("Customers").Rows.Find(E.Item.Cells(1).Text)

    'Remove the DataRow from the DataSet and bind the server control
    myDataSet.Tables("Customers").Rows.Remove(myDataRow)
    BindData()
End Sub
```

Finally, create the Page_Load() event handler, which will invoke MakeData() and BindData() only on the first request for the page.

```
Protected Sub Page_Load(ByVal Sender As Object, ByVal E As EventArgs)
    If Not Page.IsPostBack Then

        'Create a new DataSet by invoking the MakeData() method
        MakeData()

        'Bind the data to the server controls
        BindData()
    End If
End Sub
End Class
```

When you browse to this page, you can test the DataRelation by clicking a Delete link for any row. When the form is posted, the DeleteCustomer() method is invoked, and the specified Customer table row is removed. Because you have a parent-child relationship, the delete is cascaded to the child table, Orders, and all of the orders for the specified customer are deleted as well.

Merging DataSets

The DataSet class exposes a Merge() method that's used to merge one DataSet into another, a DataTable into a DataSet, or an array of DataRows into a DataSet. This type of action is useful when you have data for the same purpose coming from two separate sources—say, inventory data coming from multiple remote locations. Each location can pass a DataSet object to a centralized application where the DataSets can be merged.

In a situation like this, the central application may have a DataSet of the most recent inventory data for each remote location, which includes location IDs, product IDs, quantities, and so forth. A remote location can then pass to the central application a DataSet filled with the latest inventory data. This data may include updated inventory quantities, new product IDs and quantities, and possibly a new field that specifies product attributes (such as color) that are not reflected in the product's ID, but are required to specify the product as a different item. The DataSet.Merge() method can be used to merge the two DataSets, and arguments can be chosen to determine how to handle any changes to the data and/or schema.

The DataSet class has the following overloaded Merge() methods:

- Public Sub Merge(DataRow()): Merges an array of DataRow objects into the calling DataSet.

- Public Sub Merge(DataSet): Merges a DataSet into the calling DataSet.

- Public Sub Merge(DataTable): Merges a DataTable into the calling DataSet.

- Public Sub Merge(DataSet, Boolean): Merges a DataSet into the calling DataSet, pre-serving changes according to the Boolean argument. A value of True indicates that any changes to the calling DataSet should be maintained. A value of False indicates that such changes should be discarded.

- Public Sub Merge(DataRow(), Boolean, MissingSchemaAction): Merges an array of DataRow objects into the calling DataSet, preserving changes to the DataSet according to the Boolean argument, and handling an incompatible schema according to the MissingSchemaAction argument.

- Public Sub Merge(DataSet, Boolean, MissingSchemaAction): Merges a DataSet into the calling DataSet, preserving changes to the DataSet according to the Boolean argument, and handling an incompatible schema according to the MissingSchemaAction argument.

- Public Sub Merge(DataTable, Boolean, MissingSchemaAction): Merges a DataTable into the calling DataSet, preserving changes to the DataSet according to the Boolean argument, and handling an incompatible schema according to the MissingSchemaAction argument.

The MissingSchemaAction argument is an enumerator that specifies how to handle the merge operation if the object being merged has a different schema from the calling DataSet. This scenario would occur if, say, a new DataColumn were added to the schema in the merging DataSet. You'll have a closer look at this possibility in a moment.

Merging Two DataSets

The example that we talked about when introducing the Merge() method is quite complex, and demonstrating it would take more space than we have here. Instead, let's walk through some code snippets that demonstrate some of the different ways in which the Merge() method can be used.

To merge two DataSets, you invoke the Merge() method on the DataSet that you want to merge the data into, and pass another DataSet into the method as its sole argument.

MyDataSet.Merge(myOtherDataSet)

The result being this method is a DataSet with all the values from myOtherDataSet merged into myDataSet. If both DataSets have records with the same primary key value, the values from the myOtherDataSet object are set as the values of the myDataSet records (reflecting "updates" to those records). Any records not already in the myDataSet object are added.

Merging Two DataSets and Maintaining Original Values

Alternatively, you can merge two DataSets, but ensure that the values in the target DataSet are preserved in the face of any changes, while new values are added.

MyDataSet.Merge(myOtherDataSet, True)

The second argument to this Merge() call is a Boolean value indicating whether the values in the target DataSet (myDataSet) should be preserved. This allows you to maintain existing values and add new records at the same time.

Merging Two DataSets with Different Schemas

As described previously, you can merge two DataSets with different schemas, and specify how the schema differences should be handled.

MyDataSet.Merge(myOtherDataSet, True, MissingSchemaAction.Add)

The MissingSchemaAction enumeration is used to specify how schema differences should be handled. The possible enumerators are shown in Table 3-8.

Table 3-8. *The* MissingSchemaAction *Enumeration*

Value	Description
Add	Indicates that additional columns defined in the source DataSet (myOther-DataSet) should be added to the schema of the target DataSet (myDataSet)
AddWithKey	Indicates that additional columns defined in the source DataSet should be added to the target DataSet along with any primary key information
Error	Indicates that a System.SystemException will be thrown if the target schema and source schema do not match
Ignore	Indicates that any additional columns in the source DataSet should be ignored when it is merged into the target DataSet

Included in the sample code for this chapter [see the Downloads section of the Apress Web site (http://www.apress.com)] is an ASP.NET web application called DataMergeExample.aspx that demonstrates various Merge() method options. It's quite large, but you should feel free to examine and experiment with it at your leisure. It looks like the example in Figure 3-6.

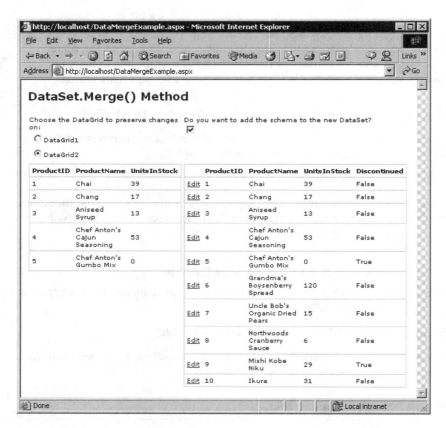

Figure 3-6. *DataMergeExample.aspx*

Caching DataSets for Better Performance

As you've seen in a couple of the ASP.NET web applications that you've developed in this chapter, you can cache a DataSet in order to increase the performance of the application. Rather than going to the database and retrieving the requested data for every request, you can put the DataSet into a cache on the server. Each time a request is made, you can check the cache for the DataSet, and only connect to the database if a cached version of the DataSet is not present. Let's take a closer look at how that mechanism works.

For an example, take an online retailer, who will likely have a catalog that displays all of the products for sale on its Web site. It's unlikely that this data will change very frequently, so it's a perfect candidate for storing in the cache. With a cached `DataSet`, the first Web site visitor who makes a request for the catalog causes the database access to occur, at which point the data retrieved is put into a `DataSet`. The `DataSet` is then cached for the use of all future requests, eliminating the need for additional connections to the database.

■Note Sometimes, it's a better choice to use a `DataReader` object to get data from a database, and stream it into an application (see Chapters 2 and 4). Since the `DataReader` streams one record at a time, there is a performance gain over bringing all of the records into a `DataSet`. However, a `DataReader` cannot be cached, so using it implies going and getting the data on each request. What you're looking at here is the payoff between bringing more data into your application at once, and reducing the network traffic and database connections by caching the `DataSet`. Caching a `DataSet` is not always the best solution.

Items are stored in the cache as key-value pairs, making them easy to work with. An item can be placed in the cache using one of following three techniques, all of which use the `System.Web.Caching.Cache` class:

- `Cache("CachedDataSet") = myDataSet`

- `Cache.Add("CachedDataSet", myDataSet)`

- `Cache.Insert("CachedDataSet", myDataSet)`

In the following web form, you retrieve data from the database on the first request, and then place it in the cache. When you add the `DataSet` to the cache, you set an expiration time of five minutes, so that all requests in the next five minutes will use the cached `DataSet`. On the first request after the cached `DataSet` expires, database access will recur, and a new `DataSet` will be cached.

To help prove your point, when the `DataSet` is first created, you add a key-value pair to the `DataSet.ExtendedProperties` collection. This is a collection that can hold user-defined key-value pairs, and you're going to use it here to store the *time* that the `DataSet` was created, so that you can render it on the page.

On this occasion, the ASP.NET web form you're going to create will have a `Label` server control and a `DataGrid` server control. As usual, you start by creating the web form file. This time, it's called CachedDataSetEx.aspx, and it's straightforward.

```
<%@ Page Inherits="CachedDataSetEx" Src="CachedDataSetEx.aspx.vb" %>
<HTML>
  <BODY>
    <asp:Label runat="server" id="DataLocation" />
    <asp:DataGrid runat="server" id="myDataGrid" />
  </BODY>
</HTML>
```

Now, create a code-behind file named CachedDataSetEx.aspx.vb, where you start by declaring the class and mapping variables to the web form server controls.

```
Imports System
Imports System.Data
Imports System.Data.SqlClient
Imports System.Web
Imports System.Web.UI
Imports System.Web.UI.WebControls

Public Class CachedDataSetExample
  Inherits Page

  Protected WithEvents myDataGrid As DataGrid
  Protected WithEvents DataLocation As Label
```

In the Page_Load() event handler, you construct a new DataSet and set it to the result of the Cache.Get() method, which returns an Object instance matching the specified key name. Since this is an Object data type, you must cast the object to a DataSet.

```
  Protected Sub Page_Load(ByVal Sender As Object, ByVal E As EventArgs)
    Dim myDataSet As DataSet = CType(Cache.Get("CachedDataSet"), DataSet)
```

If the result of this statement is that myDataSet is Nothing, then the DataSet was not in the cache, and must be created by accessing the database. The myDataSet instance will be Nothing on the first request for the page, or if the cached version of the DataSet has expired, as you'll see in a moment.

If myDataSet is not Nothing, then it *did* exist in the cache, and can be used without any database access.

```
    If myDataSet Is Nothing Then
      DataLocation.Text = "<P><B>The data came from a connection " + _
                          "to the database.</B></P>"

      Dim myAdapter As New SqlDataAdapter( _
         "SELECT TOP 10 ProductID, ProductName, UnitPrice FROM Products;", _
         "server=localhost;database=Northwind;uid=sa;pwd=;")
      myDataSet = New DataSet()
      myAdapter.Fill(myDataSet, "Products")

      'Add a key-value pair to the ExtendedProperties
      'specifying what time the DataSet was created.
      myDataSet.ExtendedProperties.Add( _
                          "CreateTime", DateTime.Now.ToLongTimeString())

      'Insert the DataSet object in cache, setting a null file
      'dependency (this object does not depend on file changes)
      'and a five minute expiration interval
```

```
        Cache.Insert("CachedDataSet", myDataSet, Nothing, _
                        DateTime.Now.AddMinutes(5), TimeSpan.Zero)
    Else
        DataLocation.Text = "<P><B>The data came from the cache. " + _
                "It was created at: " + _
                myDataSet.ExtendedProperties("CreateTime").ToString() + _
                "</P><P>The current system time is: " + _
                DateTime.Now.ToLongTimeString() + "</B></P>"
    End If
```

Lastly, you bind the DataSet to a DataGrid.

```
    myDataGrid.DataSource = myDataSet.Tables("Products")
    myDataGrid.DataBind()
  End Sub
End Class
```

You can test the cache by browsing to this web form. On the first request, you see the results shown in Figure 3-7.

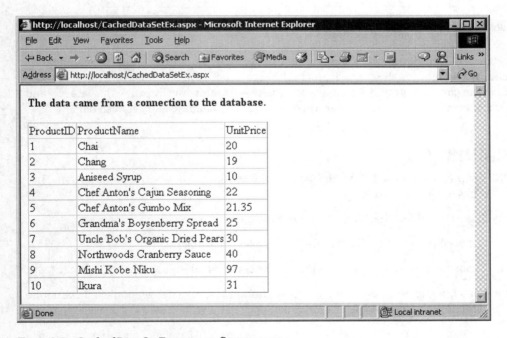

Figure 3-7. *CachedDataSetEx.aspx on first request*

After waiting a few minutes, refresh the page, and you'll see something like what is shown in Figure 3-8.

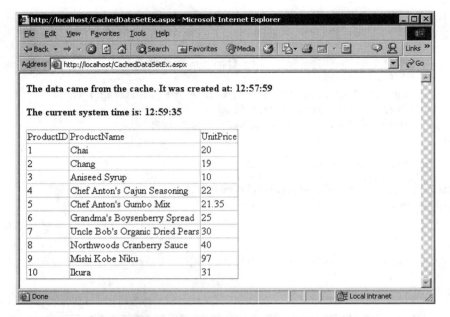

Figure 3-8. *CachedDataSetEx.aspx—results when read from the cache*

Since you specified in the call to Cache.Insert() that the DataSet should remain in the cache for five minutes, the data adapter in the Page_Load() event handler will not try to connect to the database. After five minutes, the cache will automatically expire the DataSet, and on the next request the data adapter will connect to the database and get fresh data.

Summary

In this chapter, you learned about the DataSet and its role in a data-driven application. The DataSet has the following qualities:

- It is a data object that works with the basic concepts of relational databases.

- It can contain multiple DataTable and DataRelation objects.

- It can have constraints, such as UniqueConstraints and ForeignKeyConstraints.

- Data integrity that's enforced by constraints holds true to the relational data structure, with data changes and deletes cascaded to related DataTables.

- It can be merged with other DataSets, DataTables, and DataRows, plus their data and schemas can be consolidated.

Concurrent with learning these qualities, you saw how, in an ASP.NET web application, a DataSet could be put into the cache to reduce connections to the database, and increase application performance.

CHAPTER 4

■ ■ ■

Using Data Adapters

From a purely functional point of view, the main difference between data readers and data adapters is that the latter contain logic for updating the data source as well as reading it, and that's going to be the main thrust of your investigations in this chapter. You're going to examine the different ways that data adapters allow you to change the data in data sources, and the assistance that they can (sometimes) provide you in order to do so. Along the way, you'll also flesh out some of the detail on data adapters that we began to introduce in earlier chapters.

In this chapter, then, you will take a look at all aspects of data adapters, but you'll be focusing your attention on these concepts:

- Filling DataSet and DataTable objects by retrieving data from different databases

- Updating the information in data stores using SQL statements and stored procedures

- Reviewing the abilities and limitations of CommandBuilder objects

- Using data adapter events to deal with issues of concurrency

Data Adapters Up Close

In Chapter 1, we talked about data adapters implementing the IDataAdapter and IDbDataAdapter interfaces, without going into further detail. In fact, it's not the case that the various data adapters simply contain implementations of these interfaces' methods. Though that's effectively the outcome, there are a couple of stages in between.

The .NET Framework class hierarchy contains an abstract class that provider-specific data adapters inherit from called System.Data.Common.DataAdapter. It's the DataAdapter class that implements the IDataAdapter interface. The DataAdapter class provides the basic facilities for constructing a disconnected data-access mechanism to fill a DataSet object and to update a data source.

A second .NET Framework class, System.Data.Common.DbDataAdapter, is derived from the DataAdapter class, and is used to implement more specific functionalities. The DbDataAdapter class implements the IDbDataAdapter interface, so every class inheriting from it provides the capabilities that the interface defines.

Using More Complex Queries

Until now, your work with DataAdapters and DataSets has involved rather simple queries in which data has been retrieved from a single table at a time. In real projects, the SQL SELECT statements tend to be more complex: tables are joined to other tables using primary and foreign keys. What exactly happens to a DataSet object when you specify a more complex query to execute? Starting from the following tables contained in the pubs database (as seen in Figure 4-1), you'll build such a query.

Figure 4-1. *Complex query table structure*

Here, the authors, titleauthor, and titles tables are joined together by their respective primary and foreign keys. Given this information, we can write a SQL SELECT statement to retrieve an author's first and last name, and the related books that he has written.

```
SELECT authors.au_fname, authors.au_lname, titles.title
FROM (authors INNER JOIN titleauthor ON authors.au_id = titleauthor.au_id)
INNER JOIN titles ON titleauthor.title_id = titles.title_id
```

Executing a query like this will produce a single DataTable in the DataSet—the database engine handles the relationships to produce a single result set combining data from three tables. However, you can also use a data adapter to obtain the three tables used in Figure 4-1 and in the previous code, complete with the relationships between them, as separate tables in the DataSet. In order to create a DataSet that has the same table structure and the same relationships as the data source, one option is to use several DataAdapter objects to fill it, and then to add the relations and the constraints to the generated DataSet structure.

```
' Create a connection object
Dim dbConn As New SqlConnection( _
            "server=(local); database=pubs; integrated security=true")
Dim ds As New DataSet("AuthorsAndTitles")

' Create the data adapter object pointing to the authors table
Dim daAuthors As New SqlDataAdapter( _
            "SELECT au_id, au_fname, au_lname FROM authors", dbConn)
```

```
' Fill the DataSet with author
daAuthors.Fill(ds, "Author")
' Create the data adapter object pointing to the titleauthor table
Dim daTitleAuthor As New SqlDataAdapter( _
                "SELECT au_id, title_id FROM titleauthor", dbConn)

' Fill the DataSet with titleauthor
daTitleAuthor.Fill(ds, "TitleAuthor")

' Create the data adapter object pointing to the titles table
Dim daTitle As New SqlDataAdapter( _
                "SELECT title_id, title FROM titles", dbConn)

' Fill the DataSet with titles
daTitle.Fill(ds, "Titles")
```

By following this path, you're maintaining a different DataTable object for each table in the database, creating a more complex structure. As you can see from the following code, after defining DataAdapter objects for each of the authors, titleauthor, and titles tables, and filling the DataSet, you can complete the in-memory data structure by defining primary key and foreign key constraints between the tables. This is similar to what you saw in Chapter 3.

```
' Define a primary key and other properties for each table
ds.Tables("Titles").Columns("title_id").Unique = True
ds.Tables("Titles").Columns("title_id").AllowDBNull = False
ds.Tables("Titles").PrimaryKey = _
        New DataColumn() {ds.Tables("Titles").Columns("title_id")}

ds.Tables("Author").Columns("au_id").Unique = True
ds.Tables("Author").Columns("au_id").AllowDBNull = False
ds.Tables("Author").PrimaryKey = _
        New DataColumn() {ds.Tables("Author").Columns("au_id")}

ds.Tables("TitleAuthor").PrimaryKey = _
        New DataColumn() {ds.Tables("TitleAuthor").Columns("au_id"), _
                          ds.Tables("TitleAuthor").Columns("title_id")}

' Define constraints (primary key/foriegn key relationships)
Dim fk1 As New ForeignKeyConstraint("authorstitleauthor", _
                            ds.Tables("Author").Columns("au_id"), _
                            ds.Tables("TitleAuthor").Columns("au_id"))
ds.Tables("TitleAuthor").Constraints.Add(fk1)

Dim fk2 As New ForeignKeyConstraint("titlestitleauthor", _
                            ds.Tables("Titles").Columns("title_id"), _
                            ds.Tables("TitleAuthor").Columns("title_id"))
ds.Tables("TitleAuthor").Constraints.Add(fk2)
```

Working this way has two main advantages. First, it means that you can easily present the relationship data to users, so that they can see and work with the relationships. Secondly, as you'll see shortly, it makes updating the data source easier. Finding an UPDATE statement that corresponds to a SELECT statement containing JOINs is a complex proposition, but if you have separate, related DataTable objects, each can be updated by its own simple UPDATE statement.

Filling a DataSet Object with Just a Few Records

Not since Chapter 1 have the queries you've seen involved WHERE conditions, raising the possibility that you'll be dealing with tables that contain a lot of records. Each time you refresh the DataSet's content using the Fill() method, a lot of time will be spent retrieving the records and filling the DataSet object. Usually, the solution is simply to use a filtered query that extracts only the records you really need, but for some operations there's a different approach. For example, if you want to be able to show all of the records in a table, but to do so by displaying a "page" of results at a time, then you need to use a variant of the Fill() method that expects the following four arguments:

- The DataSet object to fill

- The numeric position of the record to start with

- The maximum number of records to retrieve

- The name of the table that will be added to the DataSet

Using this version of the Fill() method, you can retrieve exactly the number of records you want by adding to or refreshing the DataSet with new or old records, respectively. Figure 4-2 shows an application that uses this method to browse between records in the authors and titles tables, retrieving just one record at a time.

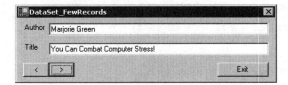

Figure 4-2. DataSet_FewRecords *sample application*

This application is available in the code download for this book (located in the Downloads section of the Apress Web site [http://www.apress.com]); it's called DataSet_FewRecords. Let's examine the code that allows you to create this effect.

```
Private da As SqlDataAdapter
Private iCurr As Integer = 0
Private iMax As Integer = 0
```

First of all, you declare class member variables. The SqlDataAdapter will be used to fill a DataSet object that will be created in the Windows form's load event handler. The iCurr integer represents the current record number to display in the application, while the iMax integer contains the number of records in the table that's retrieved from the data source.

```
Private Sub frmMain_Load(ByVal sender As System.Object, _
            ByVal e As System.EventArgs) Handles MyBase.Load

  ' Create a connection object
  Dim dbConn As New SqlConnection( _
            "server=(local); database=pubs; integrated security=true")

  Try
    ' Retrieve maximum number of records
    dbConn.Open()
    Dim cmd = New SqlCommand("SELECT COUNT(authors.au_fname) " & _
            "FROM (authors INNER JOIN titleauthor ON " & _
            "authors.au_id = titleauthor.au_id) INNER JOIN " & _
            "titles ON titleauthor.title_id = titles.title_id", dbConn)
    iMax = CInt(cmd.ExecuteScalar()) - 1
  Finally
    dbConn.Close()
  End Try
```

The value stored in the iMax variable will be used in a navigation bar to prevent any attempt to read an "out-of-bounds" record. In the preceding code, a SqlCommand object is used to execute a scalar query that retrieves just the first field of the first record resulting from the specified statement.

```
  ' Create the data adapter object pointing to the authors table
  da = New SqlDataAdapter("SELECT authors.au_fname, " & _
            "authors.au_lname, titles.title FROM " & _
            "(authors INNER JOIN titleauthor ON " & _
            "authors.au_id = titleauthor.au_id) INNER JOIN " & _
            "titles ON titleauthor.title_id = titles.title_id", dbConn)

  Dim ds As New DataSet("Authors")

  ' Fill the DataSet
  da.Fill(ds, iCurr, 1, "AuthorAndTitle")

  FillForm(ds)

End Sub
```

In the last part of the event handler code, the global DataAdapter object is created, and the SQL statement is specified in order to retrieve the author's first name, last name, and title. The Fill() method is used to retrieve just the first record, and the resulting DataSet is passed to the FillForm() method for display.

```
Sub FillForm(ByVal ds As DataSet)
  txtAuthor.Text = ds.Tables("AuthorAndTitle").Rows(0)("au_fname") & _
                   " " & ds.Tables("AuthorAndTitle").Rows(0)("au_lname")
  txtTitle.Text = ds.Tables("AuthorAndTitle").Rows(0)("title").ToString()
End Sub
```

Finally, the code behind the navigation buttons will create a new DataSet object that will be filled with either the previous or the next record. The resulting record will be displayed by the FillForm() method, as shown in the following code:

```
Private Sub btnNext_Click(ByVal sender As System.Object, _
                       ByVal e As System.EventArgs) Handles btnNext.Click
  If iCurr < iMax Then
    Dim ds As New DataSet("Authors")
    iCurr = iCurr + 1

    ' Fill the DataSet
    da.Fill(ds, iCurr, 1, "AuthorAndTitle")

    FillForm(ds)
  End If
End Sub

Private Sub btnPrev_Click(ByVal sender As System.Object, _
                       ByVal e As System.EventArgs) Handles btnPrev.Click
  If iCurr > 0 Then
    Dim ds As New DataSet("Authors")

    iCurr = iCurr - 1

    ' Fill the DataSet
    da.Fill(ds, iCurr, 1, "AuthorAndTitle")

    FillForm(ds)
  End If
End Sub
```

Filling a DataSet Using a Stored Procedure

As you've observed before, it's a great idea to use stored procedures in your applications, for at least the following reasons:

- They remove SQL statements from the application's code, making the code more readable and maintainable.

- They run faster, because they are already compiled into the database. If you embed SQL in your applications, the SQL string is passed to the database and re-compiled every time you run it, which is less efficient. However, for repeating SQL queries, the execution plans are cached in SQL Server 2000 onward.

- They reduce the surface area available for hackers to execute SQL injection attacks, etc. on your database. You can now control all application stored procedures with tightened down security settings.

- .NET code could be disassembled (also, see Dotfuscator), but if innate table knowledge resides in stored procedures, the end hacker might never know how the data is actually arranged in your database.

- You can now have a database guru, instead of a .NET developer, maintain the stored procedures and change them without re-compiling the application.

Let's take a look at a simple Microsoft SQL Server stored procedure that retrieves an author specified by her identification column value:

```
CREATE PROCEDURE spRetrieveAuthor
  @au_id integer
AS SELECT * FROM authors WHERE au_id = @au_id
```

Calling a stored procedure from code in order to fill a DataSet is similar to what you've seen previously. The main difference consists of declaring the type of the command you're going to execute.

```
cmd.CommandText = "spRetrieveAuthor"
cmd.CommandType = System.Data.CommandType.StoredProcedure
cmd.Connection = dbConn
cmd.Parameters.Add(New SqlParameter("@au_id", SqlType.Char, 11, "au_id"))
```

The previous code shows that you have to specify the name of the stored procedure in the CommandText property. Moreover, you set the CommandType property to CommandType.Stored-Procedure to inform the data adapter that it has to execute a stored procedure instead of a SQL statement. Finally, the code provides a value for every parameter expected by the stored procedure. In this case, the code declares just the author identification column, au_id.

```
Dim da As New SqlDataAdapter(cmd, dbConn)
Dim ds As New DataSet("Author")
da.SelectCommand.Parameters(0).Value = "172-32-1176"
da.Fill(ds)

If Not ds Is Nothing Then
  MessageBox.Show("Hi, author: " & _
                       ds.Tables(0).Rows(0)("au_lname").ToString())
End If
```

The previous code illustrates how easy it is to pass parameters to a stored procedure. You can specify values for all of the parameters by pointing to the items in the collection with either their index or their name. The code fills a DataSet with details of a specific author that are retrieved by specifying the author's identification number, and shows a message box reporting the author's last name.

Updating a Database

You've seen that each time you call the Fill() method, a fresh set of records is retrieved, and the content of the target DataSet is refreshed. In general, however, you want your DataSets to do more than that. When you've finished manipulating your in-memory representation of the data source, you need a way to write any changes you've made back to the data source, rather than just discarding them.

This discussion has two threads: understanding how to make changes to a dataset, and understanding how to have those changes reflected in the data source. To make things easier in this discussion, you're going to consider the second of those threads first: in other words, assuming that your dataset contains some changes, how do you also change the database?

Clearly, one way of adding, updating, or deleting the records in a data source to match any changes that have been made to a DataSet is to loop through the relevant tables and use command objects to execute INSERT, UPDATE, and DELETE SQL statements. In ADO.NET, however, you can use the same DataAdapter object that you used to retrieve the data to update the database with the changes made in the DataSet.

```
conn.Open()
adapter.Update(ds, "CustomerTable")
conn.Close()
```

As you'd expect, this apparent simplicity hides some complex processing that goes on underneath. Also, there are some very tight restrictions on when it's possible to use this technique. Let's show you how ADO.NET performs the trick.

Row State and Field Value Versions

ADO.NET finds out which records need to be updated by examining all of the records in the specified table in the DataSet (the fictional CustomerTable in this example). Every DataRow in a

DataTable has a RowState property that indicates the current state of the row. It can be one of the following five values, defined in the DataRowState enumeration, as shown in Table 4-1:

Table 4-1. DataRowState *Enumeration*

Value	Description
Added	The row has been added to the table.
Deleted	The row has been deleted from the table. Note that it's just been *marked* as deleted—it hasn't been physically removed. This allows ADO.NET to delete the corresponding row in the database later on, and allows you to roll back the delete operation should it become necessary to do so.
Detached	The row is not in a table. This happens when you have created a new DataRow object for a DataTable but have not yet added it to the table's Rows collection, or when you have removed the row from the table using the Remove() method.
Modified	The row has been modified. For instance, you have assigned a new value to one of the fields in the row.
Unchanged	The row has not been changed. When you first populate the DataSet using a data adapter, the state of all rows is set to Unchanged.

In addition, each field in a DataRow object may have one of the following four value versions, which come from the System.Data.DataRowVersion enumeration, as shown in Table 4-2.

Table 4-2. System.Data.DataRowVersion *Enumeration*

Version	Description
Current	The current value of the field. When the record is loaded from database, this version is identical to the original version—but it can change over the course of an application.
Original	The value that was most recently loaded from the database.
Proposed	The value to be assigned to the field as a result of the current operation.
Default	The row contains the default version for the current DataRowState. For a DataRowState value of Added, Modified, or Current, the default version is Current. For a DataRowState of Deleted, the version is Original. For a DataRowState value of Detached, the version is Proposed.

You can examine these values by specifying the version you want in an expression like one of the following:

```
row("CustomerID", DataRowVersion.Original)
row("CustomerID", DataRowVersion.Current)
row("CustomerID", DataRowVersion.Proposed)
```

This enumeration also contains a fourth value, `Default`, which represents the default version used by the field.

```
row("CustomerID", DataRowVersion.Default)
```

This returns the same result as the following familiar expression, which doesn't specify any version:

```
row("CustomerID")
```

Depending on the current state of the parent row, all of the fields in a row have at least one version, which means that you can always retrieve a value by using the default—in other words, `row("CustomerID")` is certain to return a value. However, we *can't* guarantee that a value will be returned for all of the versions listed previously, and if you try to access a version that doesn't exist, ADO.NET will throw a `System.Data.VersionNotFoundException` exception. While you may catch such an exception, it's usually better to prevent it by checking whether the version exists before you access it, using the `HasVersion()` method of the `DataRow` class.

```
If row.HasVersion(DataRowVersion.Proposed) Then
  Console.Write(row("CustomerID", DataRowVersion.Proposed).ToString())
End If
```

Whenever you fill a `DataSet` with records from a database, ADO.NET loads the field value stored in the database into both the `Original` and `Current` versions for each field. At that point, the `RowState` is set to `Unchanged` for all rows.

Modifying the Records in a DataSet

As described previously, when you create a new `DataRow` object, its `RowState` is set to `Detached`. Furthermore, each field in the row has a `Proposed` version that contains `System.Data.DBNull`; neither the `Original` version nor the `Current` version is created.

When you assign a value to each field, the `Proposed` version takes on the assigned value. When you add the row to the table's `Rows` collection, the `RowState` is changed to `Added`, `Proposed` values are moved to `Current` values, and `Proposed` values are then discarded. The following code snippet shows an example:

```
DataRow row = CustomerTable.NewRow()
row("CustomerID") = "AAAAA"
row("CompanyName") = "New Customer"
CustomerTable.Rows.Add(row)
```

The `NewRow()` method of the `DataTable` class creates a new `DataRow` object that contains fields corresponding to the table's columns. After the first three lines of code, the `RowState` property of the `DataRow` object is `Detached`, and the `Proposed` version of each field contains the new values. After the call to `Add()`, the `RowState` property of the row is `Added`, and the `Current` version of each field contains the new value.

Of course, if you wish, you can change the value of a field in an existing row with the following:

```
DataRow row = CustomerTable.Rows.Find("AAAAA")
row("CompanyName") = "VIP Customer"
```

In this example, the CompanyName field's Current value will be set to the new value, and the RowState will be set to Modified. The Original value stays unchanged, representing the value in the underlying database.

If you wish, you can call the AcceptChanges() method of a row to change the Original values of all fields to the Current value. This method also sets the RowState to Unchanged for that row. Alternatively, you can call the AcceptChanges() method on a *table* to accept changes to all rows in the table.

Equally, you can discard any changes made to a row by calling the RejectChanges() method of either the DataRow object or its parent DataTable object. Calling the row's RejectChanges() method changes its RowState back to Unchanged; if you call the RejectChanges() method of a table, changes to all rows will be lost, and the RowState of all rows will be reset to Unchanged. Calling the table's RejectChanges() method will also remove all added rows from the table.

To delete a row, you just call its Delete() method.

```
DataRow row = CustomerTable.Rows.Find("AAAAA")
row.Delete()
```

This method marks the record as deleted by changing its RowState property to Deleted, but the row itself remains in the table's Rows collection. Alternatively, you can remove a row from the Rows collection by using the latter's Remove() method. In the previous code snippet, you can replace the call to the DataRow class's Delete() method with the following call to Rows.Remove(), changing the DataRow object's RowState property to Detached.

```
CustomerTable.Rows.Remove(row)
```

Whichever of these methods you call, only the DataSet is affected—the corresponding record in the database is not deleted. However, there is a very important difference between the two. If a record is marked as Deleted, you can later attach a data adapter to the DataSet and invoke the DataAdapter's Update() method. The record will then be permanently deleted from both the database and the DataSet. On the other hand, if you're dealing with a Detached record, the corresponding row will *not* be removed from the database when you invoke the Update() method of an associated DataAdapter object. Therefore, Remove() is more useful when you only need to manipulate data in memory. If you intend to delete a record from the database, you should use DataRow.Delete().

RowState and Update Operations

You now know that rows in a table may be in different states, depending on what operations you have performed on them. When you call their Update() method, data adapters check the RowState to decide which rows should be added, updated, or deleted in the underlying database.

Each data adapter has three properties—InsertCommand, UpdateCommand, and DeleteCommand—that specify the operations the data adapter will perform when the RowState is Added, Modified, and Deleted, respectively.

■Note Out of the five possible values of RowState, only the previous three signify that the row should be updated to the database. Recall that calling AcceptChanges() on a row or its parent table sets its state to Unchanged; you should not call this method if you intend to update the row. The Update() method of data adapters will perform the required database operations and call AcceptChanges() on the table automatically.

The next question is how the data adapter knows *how* to update the records earmarked as needing to be updated. The answer can't be simpler: it doesn't know. You need SQL commands to perform these updates, insertions, and deletions—and to create those, you can choose to write your own, or you can use a CommandBuilder object. We'll discuss the second of those two options first.

Using a CommandBuilder Object

To create an application that updates the records in a database, you can use a CommandBuilder object, which analyzes the SQL SELECT statement that you provide and creates the other three statements (INSERT, UPDATE, DELETE) automatically. You have three constraints when using this object.

- You must specify a SELECT command either in the data adapter's constructor or in its SelectCommand property. In other words, the SELECT command must not use a stored procedure.

- The SELECT command must retrieve records from only one table.

- You must specify at least a primary key or a unique column as a required column within the SELECT command.

When these conditions are satisfied, you can create a CommandBuilder object, specifying the DataAdapter object in its constructor.

```
' Create the insert, delete, and update statements automatically
Dim cb As New SqlCommandBuilder(da)
```

The UPDATE statement that's created by the CommandBuilder contains a WHERE condition for identifying the correct record to update. This WHERE condition updates the record only if none of the column values has changed since the last Fill() method call. This is a useful rule in multiuser environments, where changes to the database can come from various users. It means there is no risk of overwriting a record that has been changed by another user a few moments before your updating operation.

■Note We'll return to the topic of multiuser environments later in this chapter, in the section titled "Managing Concurrency."

Figure 4-3 is from the AuthorEditor application that you'll find in the code samples for this chapter in the Downloads section of the Apress Web site (http://www.apress.com).

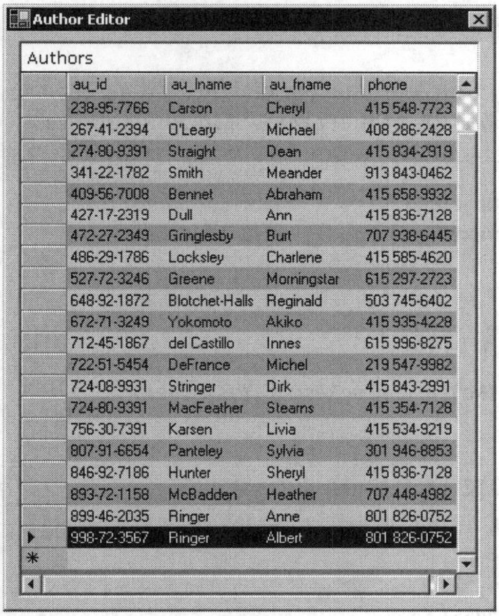

Figure 4-3. CommandBuilder *sample application*

In this sample application, a form loads and allows users to manipulate a DataSet that's retrieved from the pubs database. When the users have finished editing, they close the form. This gives them the opportunity to save their changes. Here's the form's load event handler.

```
Private da As SqlDataAdapter
Private ds As DataSet

Private Sub Form1_Load(ByVal sender As System.Object, _
        ByVal e As System.EventArgs) Handles MyBase.Load
    ' Create a Connection object
    Dim dbConn As New SqlConnection( _
        "server=(local); database=pubs; integrated security=true")
```

```
    ' Create the data adapter object pointing to the authors table
    da = New SqlDataAdapter( _
            "SELECT au_id, au_lname, au_fname, phone FROM authors", dbConn)

    ' Fill the DataSet
    ds = New DataSet("Authors")
    da.Fill(ds)

    ' Display the records in a DataGrid component
    dg.DataSource = ds.Tables(0)
End Sub
```

In the preceding code, we retrieve the records from the database and fill a DataGrid data component. Note that the SELECT statement contains the primary key (au_id), and retrieves data only from the authors table. Here's the event handler that executes when the form closes.

```
Private Sub Form1_Closing(ByVal sender As Object, _
    ByVal e As System.ComponentModel.CancelEventArgs) Handles MyBase.Closing

    ' Message box to prompt the save request
    If (MessageBox.Show("Do you want save the changes?", _
                        "Update", _
                        MessageBoxButtons.YesNo) = DialogResult.Yes) Then
        Try

            ' Create the INSERT, DELETE, and UPDATE statements automatically
            Dim cb As New SqlCommandBuilder(da)

            ' Retrieve just the changed rows
            Dim dsChanges As DataSet = ds.GetChanges()

            If Not dsChanges Is Nothing Then

                'Update the database
                da.Update(dsChanges)

                ' Accept the changes within the DataSet
                ds.AcceptChanges()
            End If
        Catch ex As Exception

            ' Error occurs, show the message
            MessageBox.Show(ex.Message)
        End Try
    End If
End Sub
```

This handler is used to prompt the user to update the database with the changes he has made to the `DataSet`. If the user clicks the Yes button, a `SqlCommandBuilder` object is created, and the `DataAdapter` object is filled with the SQL commands. Finally, the `Update()` method is called, and a new `DataSet` object containing just the changed rows is provided to it.

In this case, we've added a little complexity by using the `DataSet` object's `GetChanges()` method, which creates a new dataset containing only the records that contain changes, reducing the amount of work that the `Update()` method has to do. This is a good way to keep network traffic to a minimum, but note that when you use it, you have to call `AcceptChanges()` explicitly on the original `DataSet`. `Update()` won't do the job for you in this instance.

The advantages of using a command builder are that the approach requires only a small amount of coding, and you don't need to know the exact schema of the data source at design time. Unfortunately, it doesn't provide the best performance, you can't control the update logic, and you can't use stored procedures. An alternative is to provide your own custom update logic, which can give you improved performance and control. However, it requires high-quality SQL code for updates, and that's not always easy. You need to know more than the basics of SQL to do this successfully!

Using SQL Commands

When you have a complex query that retrieves records from several tables, or you don't want the `UPDATE` command to check for changes in the database before updating it (through the `WHERE` clause mentioned previously), you can specify your own SQL commands. To do this, assign commands to three properties of the data adapter: `InsertCommand`, `UpdateCommand`, and `DeleteCommand`.

Just like the `SelectCommand`, these three new command objects allow you to specify parameters dynamically, at run time. When you define the SQL statement, a *placeholder* is used instead of a particular value. Then, you use the `Parameters` collection of the `Command` object to define the dynamic column value. Use the @ placeholder for `SqlCommand` objects, and the ? placeholder for the other providers. The following code shows how to do this using the `OleDb` provider:

```
Dim oleDbInsert As New OleDbCommand()

oleDbInsert.CommandText = "INSERT INTO authors(" & _
            "au_id, au_fname, au_lname, phone) VALUES (?, ?, ?, ?)"
oleDbInsert.Connection = dbConn

oleDbInsert.Parameters.Add( _
            New OleDbParameter("id", OleDbType.Char, 11, "au_id"))

oleDbInsert.Parameters.Add( _
            New OleDbParameter("fname", OleDbType.Char, 20, "au_fname"))

oleDbInsert.Parameters.Add( _
            New OleDbParameter("lname", OleDbType.Char, 40, "au_lname"))
```

```
oleDbInsert.Parameters.Add( _
            New OleDbParameter("ph", OleDbType.Char, 12, "phone"))

' Define the Insert command in the data adapter
da.InsertCommand = oleDbInsert
```

And here, you use the SqlClient provider, along with a more complex object constructor that takes more arguments. In fact, you could use a constructor with the same argument list as the one used previously, but this way you get to see the full set.

```
Dim cmmInsert As New SqlCommand()

cmmInsert.CommandText = _
            "INSERT INTO authors(au_id, au_fname, au_lname, phone) " & _
            "VALUES (@au_id, @au_fname, @au_lname, @phone)"
cmmInsert.Connection = Me.dbConn

cmmInsert.Parameters.Add(New SqlParameter("@au_id", SqlType.Char, 11, _
            ParameterDirection.Input, false, CType(0, Byte), _
            CType(0, Byte), "au_id", DataRowVersion.Current, null))

cmmInsert.Parameters.Add(New SqlParameter("@au_fname", SqlType.Char, 20, _
            ParameterDirection.Input, false, CType(0, Byte), _
            CType(0, Byte), "au_fname", DataRowVersion.Current, null))
cmmInsert.Parameters.Add(New SqlParameter("@au_lname", SqlType.Char, 40, _
            ParameterDirection.Input, false, CType(0, Byte), _
            CType(0, Byte), "au_lname", DataRowVersion.Current, null))

cmmInsert.Parameters.Add(New SqlParameter("@phone", SqlType.Char, 12, _
            ParameterDirection.Input, false, CType(0, Byte), _
            CType(0, Byte), "phone", DataRowVersion.Current, null))

' Define the Insert command in the data adapter
da.InsertCommand = cmmInsert
```

The preceding code accomplishes the same task using different .NET data providers. It starts by defining the INSERT statement, where some placeholders are inserted as values of the command. Then, four parameters are added to the Parameters collection. These parameters will contain the values of the columns to be inserted in the database when the Update() method is called. To define a new parameter, you have to create a new Parameter object, to which you can give the arguments found in Table 4-3.

Table 4-3. *Parameter Arguments*

Argument Name	Description
parameterName	The parameter's name. The SQL Server .NET data provider uses this to identify which parameter you are setting. Other providers just use the order in which you define the parameters.
dbType	The parameter's data type.
size	The width of the parameter.
direction	Describes whether the parameter is an input value or an output value. If you provide the value *to* the command, use ParameterDirection.Input; if you expect a value *from* the command, use ParameterDirection.Output.
isNullable	A Boolean value indicating whether the parameter can be null (True if so; False if not).
precision	The total number of digits to the left and to the right of the decimal point (zero if the parameter is not a number).
scale	The total number of decimal places.
sourceColumn	The name that the column has in the DataTable object.
sourceVersion	The version of the DataRow to use when performing the update.
value	The parameter's default value.

■**Caution** It's very important that you specify the correct value for sourceColumn. If you don't, the data adapter will not be able to identify how the in-memory column names correspond with the database column names. If you don't specify the source column, or you make a mistake during parameter specification, an exception will be thrown.

Data Adapter Events

Data adapters expose two useful events that you can handle in order to manage the updating process. The RowUpdating and RowUpdated events are fired when the data adapter's Update() method is going to update the DataSource object and when it has updated the source, respectively. If you wish, you can define an event handler in your code to change the default behavior of the Update() method. For example, you could insert the following code (you'll find it in the DataAdapter_RowUpdating sample in the code download) to check that another user has not already updated the record that you want to update:

```
Private Sub da_RowUpdating(ByVal sender As Object, _
                    ByVal e As SqlRowUpdatingEventArgs) _
                    Handles da.RowUpdating
```

```
' Only perform processing if this is an UPDATE statement
If (e.StatementType = StatementType.Update) Then

  ' Check that the original record is not changed
  Dim strSQL As String = "SELECT au_id, au_lname, au_fname, phone " & _
                          "FROM authors WHERE "
  strSQL &= "au_id='" & e.Row("au_id", DataRowVersion.Original)
  strSQL &= "' AND "
  strSQL &= "au_lname='" & e.Row("au_lname", DataRowVersion.Original)
  strSQL &= "' AND "
  strSQL &= "au_fname='" & e.Row("au_fname", DataRowVersion.Original)
  strSql &= "' AND "
  strSQL &= "phone='" & e.Row("phone", DataRowVersion.Original) & "'"
```

Within the event handler, the code checks whether the SQL statement that's going to update the current record is the UPDATE command. Then, a SELECT command is built to check that the current record in the data source has not been changed since the last Fill() operation. As you can see, the SqlRowUpdatingEventArgs parameter, provided by the event handler, is used to retrieve the original row values that are concatenated to the SELECT command.

```
' Open the connection
dbConn.Open()

' Create a command to retrieve the number of records affected
Dim cmm As New SqlCommand(strSQL, dbConn)

' If the number of records retrieved is zero, the record has changed
If (cmm.ExecuteNonQuery() = 0) Then
```

The code goes on to retrieve the number of records affected by the query. If the value is equal to zero, then another user has already changed the row.

```
  ' Display the confirm message
  If (MessageBox.Show("The record you are attempting to modify has " & _
                      "already changed by another user. Do you " & _
                      "want to overwrite it?", "Update", _
                      MessageBoxButtons.YesNo) = DialogResult.No) Then
    ' Skip the update for the current row
    e.Status = UpdateStatus.SkipCurrentRow
  End If
End If

' Close the connection
dbConn.Close()

End If
```

In this case, a message box displays that asks the user to confirm overwriting of the record. If the user chooses to not overwrite the current row, the UpdateStatus.SkipCurrentRow value is specified in the Status property. In this way, the record will be skipped, and no updating will take place.

The SqlRowUpdatingEventArgs event handler parameter (like all such parameters in other data providers) is really useful when you use the RowUpdating event. In Table 4-4, you can see the properties exposed by the parameter.

Table 4-4. SqlRowUpdatingEventArgs *Properties*

Property	Description
Command	Get or set the command object to execute when the Update() method has been called.
Errors	Get the errors that the command object generates when the Update() method is executed.
Row	Get the row that is going to be updated.
StatementType	Get the type of the SQL statement to execute.
Status	Get the UpdateStatus value of the command object.
TableMapping	Get the DataTableMapping object used during execution of Update(). We will learn more about mapping in Chapter 9.

The SqlRowUpdatedEventArgs event handler parameter is similar in nature, having just one more property, as shown in Table 4-5.

Table 4-5. SqlRowUpdatedEventArgs *Properties*

Property	Description
RecordsAffected	Get the number of records that have been affected by execution of the Update() method.

You'll look harder at these properties, and see something of what it's possible to do with them, after you've visited our final subject for this chapter, Managing Concurrency." The real application for data adapter objects' events is the control and management of the issues surrounding concurrency, and that's where you're heading next.

Managing Concurrency

Software applications are becoming more and more complex, and even a "simple" application can be required to support a large number of users. If only one of these users updates a record, everything is simple: the application will perform whatever processing is necessary, knowing that there will be no conflicts, provided that the user follows proper business rules.

When more than one user accesses the database at the same time, however, you run into a potential minefield. A classic example of a system exposed to this danger is an airline reservation system. Assuming that there's one seat left on a flight, a single customer can book it and there's no problem. However, if two customers want that seat, things become a little more complex. The following is a possible scenario:

1. At 10:00 a.m., John uses the system to discover whether there's an empty seat. On finding that there's just one seat left, he finds a credit card and gets ready to book it.

2. At 10:02 a.m., Mary uses the system to discover whether there's an empty seat. At this point, the system still responds that there's a seat available—John hasn't booked it, yet—and Mary decides to check her accounts in order to decide which credit card she'll use to book the ticket.

3. At 10:05 a.m., John books the ticket online using his credit card. The system duly processes his request and reserves the seat for him. This reduces the number of available seats to 0.

4. At 10:08 a.m., Mary tries to book the ticket. Because the previous query indicated that there was an empty seat, the system also processes Mary's request. It has now double booked the seat.

This is an example of a system that requires you to manage data concurrency. The behavior of the airline reservation system demonstrates its lack of concurrency control. When the system processes Mary's booking request, it is in a different state (usually referred to as an inconsistent or *dirty state*) from when it processed her inquiry about the availability of tickets—the data displayed on Mary's screen is different from the data in the underlying database. The design of this hypothetical airline reservation system doesn't take into account the possibility of concurrent data access.

Types of Concurrency Control

Let's take a look at how you could improve the design of the hypothetical system to handle, or at least control, such concurrency problems. There are two common models for dealing with concurrency control.

- The pessimistic model

- The optimistic model

The main difference between these two models is whether or not the system places a "lock" on data that's being accessed. Here, we'll examine each of them in turn.

The Pessimistic Model

In the pessimistic model, you lock a record while it is being accessed. Modern relational database management systems (RDBMS) employ sophisticated locking mechanisms to provide applications with flexibility and customizability over the amount of data to be locked. In general, records are loaded into memory in blocks or pages, each of which may contain a set of records. RDBMS usually support the locking of a single record, a page, a table, or even the entire database. The size of locks, or *granularity*, and its impact on database performance are topics explained in detail in database management books. This section assumes that record-level locking is employed, but the principle of concurrency control remains the same regardless of the locking granularity.

When a record is locked, other users cannot access it until it is unlocked. The latter have to wait for the first user (or the database itself) to release the lock. If the previously mentioned airline reservation system were to use the pessimistic model, the process would be changed, as illustrated in the following steps:

1. At 10:00 a.m., John uses the system to discover whether there's an empty seat. Since there's one seat left, the system reports that the number of available seats is 1. It also places a lock on the available seat record to prevent other users from reading it. John then finds a credit card and gets ready to book it.

2. At 10:02 a.m., Mary uses the system to discover whether there's an empty seat. Since the record has been locked, the system will wait for it to be unlocked. Consequently, Mary will probably be told that the information is temporarily unavailable.

3. At 10:05 a.m., John books the ticket online using his credit card. The system duly processes his request and reserves the seat for him. It updates the database to decrement the number of seats available, and then unlocks it.

4. Shortly after 10:05 a.m., Mary's query returns a result indicating that there is no empty seat for the flight.

This solves the concurrency problem and removes the flaw that causes double booking. However, pessimistic locking has its drawbacks, the most obvious of which is that other users can't look up the availability of seats on the flight. If John goes away to get himself a cup of coffee, make a couple of phone calls, or have a chat with the neighbor before finally entering his booking, other customers will have to wait! Worse still, if John decides not to book, and to try another flight instead, the seat will be left unfilled. Other interested customers may have given up already, and the airline will lose the sale.

However, despite drawbacks like these (and other problems, such as tying up a valuable database connection), pessimistic locking can still be a valid technique. It's useful in applications such as an internal customer contact system, where you don't want your sales representatives to compete against each other. If one sales representative is looking up a customer to prepare for a presentation, you don't want others to call the same customer at the same time.

The Optimistic Model

In the optimistic model, the system doesn't lock a record while it is being accessed. Instead, it delays locking until a process *updates* the record. Immediately, you can see the concurrency problem raising its head again: when Mary decides to book the seat that was announced to her as "available," she may find that it's now gone to John. There are two techniques for handling such concurrency problems.

First In Wins

Using the "first-in-wins" strategy, the first update will be accepted, but subsequent requests to update the same data will be rejected. Each time an application tries to change a field value, the system returns to the database. If the original value matches the current value in the database, the data is clean and the update can proceed. Otherwise, the update is rejected.

In the previous example, John's booking will be processed, because its "last read" value of 1 agrees with the current value in the database. Mary's booking, on the other hand, will be rejected because the original value is 1, while the current value in the database is 0 (after John's booking has gone through).

Last Man Standing

The "last-man-standing" strategy is the opposite of "first-in-wins." Here, the most recent update request always overwrites previous updates. In the previous example, John's booking is accepted, and reduces the number of available seats to 0. When Mary's booking comes in, it will also be accepted, and the number of available seats will remain at 0.

In this particular example, "last-man-standing" is clearly a bad technique, but there are cases in which it will work well. For instance, if a customer calls to change the delivery address of an order, the operator will look up the address stored with the order and start to modify it. If the customer then realizes that the new address they just gave is actually wrong, they'll call again and (probably) talk to a different operator, who will also start to modify the address. When the second operator looks up the delivery address, they may still see the (very) old one—it could take a while for the first operator to make the change. When the second operator enters the newest address, however, it will overwrite the one that's just been entered by the first operator. At the end, the database has the newest delivery address.

Concurrency in ADO

Previous versions of ADO support both pessimistic and optimistic concurrency control. In ADO, a recordset can use a server-side cursor and maintain a connection to a database. You can choose to use either pessimistic or optimistic locking, which will then be managed by the database. This is a good solution, but maintaining a connection to the database for a long period of time is not very scalable.

ADO.NET uses a more disconnected architecture. The only time you use a server-side cursor with a live database connection is when you use a data reader to retrieve data—and because a data reader is forward-only and read-only, using it to read data doesn't require locking. ADO.NET datasets, on the other hand, are always disconnected. The optimistic model is therefore the natural choice.

In fact, as we've already mentioned, the ADO.NET data adapters have built-in support for optimistic concurrency management through the work of the command builder objects. Before you look at this more carefully, however, let's start to see how you might implement explicit, optimistic concurrency management using ADO.NET.

Controlling Concurrency Manually

Of the two optimistic concurrency strategies, "last-man-standing" is the easier of the two: you can simply use a command object to execute a SQL UPDATE query (or a stored procedure that runs the query). For example, to modify the CategoryName field of the Categories table in the sample SQL Server Northwind database, you could simply execute the following:

```
UPDATE Categories SET CategoryName = 'Category 1' WHERE CategoryID = 1
```

Because this query doesn't perform any checks on the current category *name* value in the database, the request will simply set its value to `Category 1`, overwriting any previous values. This technique is simple enough, so we can save ourselves some time by leaving it as it is.

The "first-in-wins" strategy, on the other hand, requires slightly more work. Instead of blindly setting the new value for a field, you first compare the originally read value with the current value in the database. If they're the same, you proceed with the update. If not, you back off and inform the user. Let's look at an example demonstrating the use of this technique with ADO.NET; you'll find the sample project called `Concurrency` (as shown in Figure 4-4) included in the code download (located in the Downloads section of the Apress Web site [http://www.apress.com]).

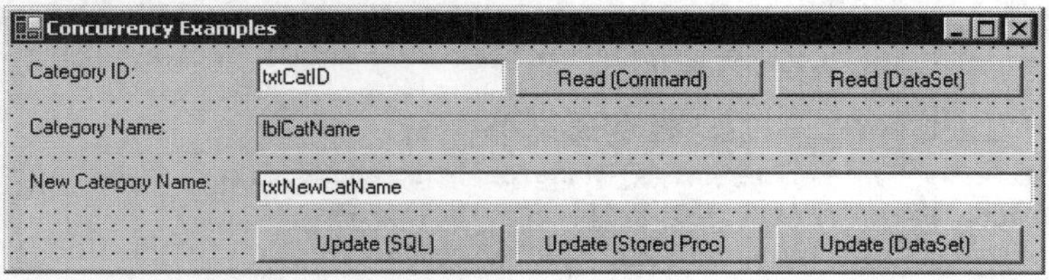

Figure 4-4. *Concurrency example*

Here, the Read (Command) button is used to read a record from the `Categories` table with the ID entered in the `txtCatID` text box. It will display the category name in `lblCatName`, which is a label control.

Once retrieved, you can enter a new name for this category in the `txtNewCatName` text box, and then click the Update (SQL) or Update (Stored Proc) button to save the change to the database using a SQL `UPDATE` statement or a SQL Server stored procedure, respectively. [The Read (DataSet) and Update (DataSet) buttons will be used in the section titled "Controlling Concurrency Using Data Adapters," where you'll look at using the concurrency control features of the `DataSet` class.]

```
Imports System.Data.SqlClient

Public Class Form1
  Inherits System.Windows.Forms.Form


  ' Connection string used by all functions
  Private Const ConnString As String = _
    "data source=(local);initial catalog=Northwind;integrated security=SSPI"


  ' Build a SQL SELECT query to read a category record from the database
  Private Function BuildSelectQuery(ByVal CatID As Int32) As String
    Return "SELECT CategoryName, CategoryID FROM Categories " & _
        "WHERE CategoryID = " & CatID
  End Function
```

```
' Given a category ID, read its name from database
Private Function ReadCatName(ByVal CatID As Int32) As String
   Dim SelectQuery As String = BuildSelectQuery(CatID)
   Dim cn As New SqlConnection(ConnString)
   Dim cmd As New SqlCommand(SelectQuery, cn)
   cn.Open()
   Dim CatName As String = cmd.ExecuteScalar()
   cn.Close()

   Return CatName
End Function
```

The Read (Command) button's click event handler just calls the ReadCatName() function and displays the category name in the lblCatName label.

```
Private Sub btnReadCmd_Click(ByVal sender As System.Object, _
                ByVal e As System.EventArgs) Handles btnReadCmd.Click
   lblCatName.Text = ReadCatName(Convert.ToInt32(txtCatID.Text))
End Sub
```

You can then enter a new category name and click the Update (SQL) button to save it to the database. The generated SQL UPDATE statement needs to look like the following:

```
UPDATE Categories SET CategoryName = 'New Category Name'
   WHERE CategoryID = 1 AND CategoryName = 'Old Category Name'
```

The key here is to compare the category name as it was last read with the name currently stored in the database. If they match, the UPDATE statement will save the new category name. Otherwise, the WHERE clause ensures that the new category name will not be saved because it can't find the record. It's a trick we've used previously, so this code should be fairly easy to understand.

```
Private Sub btnUpdateSQL_Click(ByVal sender As System.Object, _
                ByVal e As System.EventArgs) Handles btnUpdateSQL.Click
   Dim UpdateQuery As String =
      "UPDATE Categories " & _
      "SET CategoryName = '" & txtNewCatName.Text.ToString() & "'" & _
      "WHERE CategoryID = " & Convert.ToInt32(txtCatID.Text) & _
      "AND CategoryName = '" & lblCatName.Text.ToString() & "'"

   Dim cn As New SqlConnection(ConnString)
   Dim cmd As New SqlCommand(SqlQuery, cn)

   cn.Open()
   Dim RecUpdated As Int32 = cmd.ExecuteNonQuery()
   cn.Close()
```

```
  ' Check the number of records updated
  If RecUpdated = 1 Then
    MessageBox.Show("Record updated successfully")
  Else
    MessageBox.Show("Failed to update record")
  End If
End Sub
```

This handler builds a SQL UPDATE query by reading the category ID from txtCatID, the last read category name from lblCatName, and the new category name from txtNewCatName. It then connects to the database and executes the query. If the category name in the database matches the last read one, one record will be updated. Otherwise, the ExecuteNonQuery() function returns zero, indicating that the update did not succeed.

To test this out, build the project and run two instances of the executable. In each, click the Read (Command) button to read the category name for category number 1 (it should be Beverages if you haven't changed its value in Northwind), and then enter a new category name that's different from the loaded name. When you click the Update (SQL) button on the first instance, the new category name should be saved to the database. When you click the Update (SQL) button on the second instance, the update should fail because the category name value in the database has been changed to the one saved in the first instance, which will be different from its original value.

While this example uses a dynamically built SQL UPDATE statement, you can also use a stored procedure to execute the same UPDATE statement.

```
CREATE PROCEDURE spUpdateCategoryName
(@CatID int, @OriginalCatName nvarchar(15), @NewCatName nvarchar(15))
AS
UPDATE Categories
SET CategoryName = @NewCatName
WHERE CategoryID = @CatID
AND CategoryName = @OriginalCatName
```

Updating a category record using this stored procedure is very similar to the previous example that used the SQL UPDATE statement.

```
Private Sub btnUpdateSP_Click(ByVal sender As System.Object, _
                ByVal e As System.EventArgs) Handles btnUpdateSP.Click
  Dim cn As New SqlConnection(ConnString)
  Dim cmd As New SqlCommand("spUpdateCategoryName", cn)

  cmd.CommandType = CommandType.StoredProcedure
  cmd.Parameters.Add("@CatID", Convert.ToInt32(txtCatID.Text))
  cmd.Parameters.Add("@OriginalCatName", lblCatName.Text.ToString())
  cmd.Parameters.Add("@NewCatName", txtNewCatName.Text.ToString())

  cn.Open()
  Dim RecUpdated As Int32 = cmd.ExecuteNonQuery()
  cn.Close()
```

```
    ' Check the number of records updated
    If RecUpdated = 1 Then
        MessageBox.Show("Record updated successfully")
    Else
        MessageBox.Show("Failed to update record")
    End If
End Sub
```

The only difference is that it now executes the stored procedure, rather than building a dynamic SQL UPDATE statement.

Controlling Concurrency Using Data Adapters

As we've said, the UPDATE commands that are generated by command builders are very similar to the one you built in the previous section—they check the original values of the fields to be updated against the corresponding values of those fields in the database. Unlike the last example, however, a data adapter raises a DBConcurrencyException by default if it detects inconsistent data during the update process.

To see how that works, you can look at the rest of the code in the Concurrency sample application. Now, you're going to use a class-level DataSet object called CatDS—clicking the Read (DataSet) button will populate this DataSet with a category record, while clicking the Update (DataSet) button will save the new category name to the DataSet, and attempt to update the database with the new value.

```
' DataSet storing category data
Private CatDS As DataSet

Private Sub btnReadDS_Click(ByVal sender As System.Object, _
                ByVal e As System.EventArgs) Handles btnReadDS.Click
    Dim SelectQuery As String = _
                BuildSelectQuery(Convert.ToInt32(txtCatID.Text))
    Dim cn As New SqlConnection(ConnString)
    Dim cmd As New SqlCommand(SelectQuery, cn)
    Dim da As New SqlDataAdapter(cmd)

    CatDS = New DataSet()

    cn.Open()
    da.Fill(CatDS, "Categories")
    cn.Close()

    lblCatName.Text = CatDS.Tables("Categories").Rows(0)("CategoryName")
End Sub
```

The Read (DataSet) button's click event handler is fairly simple. It connects to the database, executes the SELECT query, and populates the dataset with the category record. The following update process is more interesting:

```
Private Sub btnUpdateDS_Click(ByVal sender As System.Object, _
                ByVal e As System.EventArgs) Handles btnUpdateDS.Click
    Dim CatRow As DataRow = CatDS.Tables("Categories").Rows(0)
    CatRow("CategoryName") = txtNewCatName.Text.ToString()

    Dim SelectQuery As String = BuildSelectQuery(CatRow("CategoryID"))
    Dim cn As New SqlConnection(ConnString)
    Dim da As New SqlDataAdapter(SelectQuery, cn)
    Dim cb As New SqlCommandBuilder(da)

    Try
        cn.Open()
        da.Update(CatDS, "Categories")
        MessageBox.Show("Record updated successfully")
    Catch x As DBConcurrencyException
        MessageBox.Show("Fail to update record: " & x.Message)
    Finally
        cn.Close()
    End Try
End Sub
```

First, this saves the new category name to the dataset. Second, building a SELECT query is necessary because the SqlCommandBuilder class builds the UPDATE command (as well as the INSERT and DELETE commands) for a data adapter from that query.

Because the data adapter's Update() function will raise a DBConcurrencyException if it detects inconsistent data (that is, the originally read field values don't match the corresponding field values in the database), you should catch this exception. In this example, you simply display the exception object's error message.

Resolving Concurrency Issues

Being able to catch the exception is good, but you can be more active and assert more control over the process. You have two choices. One is to set the data adapter's ContinueUpdateOnError property to True, which instructs the data adapter to ignore the problematic record and continue. This is fine as long as you don't need to know which record failed—it's equivalent to the "first-in-wins" scenario that we described earlier. If you need to take some action, however, you should use the second approach, which is to make full use of the RowUpdating event that you saw earlier—and in particular, its SqlRowUpdatingEventArgs (or OleDbRowUpdatingEventArgs, etc.) parameter.

The handler you can see following Table 4-6 gets the original category name value from the dataset, and the current value from the database, and compares them. If the name has been changed since it was loaded to the DataSet, you can decide what actions should be taken to correct the problem. You can instruct the data adapter to perform a supported action by assigning any of the following UpdateStatus enumeration values to the Status property of the SqlRowUpdatingEventArgs object.

Table 4-6. System.Data.UpdateStatus

Value	Description
Continue	Continue processing. The adapter will still try to run its UPDATE command, and consequently raise the DBConcurrencyException.
ErrorsOccurred	Abort the update and raise an exception. You can assign any exception to the SqlRowUpdatingEventArgs.Errors property.
SkipAllRemainingRows	Abort the update, but don't raise an exception.
SkipCurrentRow	Don't update the current row, but continue with the remaining records (if there are any).

For instance, you can ask the data adapter to raise an exception, which implies that the update process will be terminated.

```
    Private Sub OnRowUpdating(ByVal sender As Object, _
                             ByVal e As SqlRowUpdatingEventArgs)
                             Handles
Dim CatID As String = e.Row("CategoryID", DataRowVersion.Original)
    Dim OriginalCatName As String = _
                  e.Row("CategoryName", DataRowVersion.Original)
    Dim CatNameInDB As String = ReadCatName(CatID)

    If OriginalCatName <> CatNameInDB Then

       ' We have a concurrency violation
       e.Status = UpdateStatus.ErrorsOccurred
       e.Errors = New Exception( _
                  "Category name has changed since loaded:" & vbCrLf & _
                  "Loaded value = " & OriginalCatName & vbCrLf & _
                  "Current value = " & CatNameInDB)
    End If
End Sub
```

Here, you set SqlRowUpdatingEventArgs.Errors to a new exception containing a custom error message about the concurrency problem. You must then add code to the client function to handle this exception, as demonstrated here:

```
Private Sub btnUpdateDS_Click(ByVal sender As System.Object, _
               ByVal e As System.EventArgs) Handles btnUpdateDS.Click

   ' Code omitted for brevity
   AddHandler da.RowUpdating, AddressOf OnRowUpdating
```

```
    Try
        cn.Open()
        da.Update(CatDS, "Categories")
        MessageBox.Show("Record updated successfully")
    Catch x As DBConcurrencyException
        MessageBox.Show("Fail to update record: " & x.Message)
    Catch x As Exception
        MessageBox.Show("Fail to update record: " & x.Message)
    Finally
        cn.Close()
    End Try
End Sub
```

As you can see, while the RowUpdating event provides you with the ability to pre-process data for updating, the RowUpdated event allows you to postprocess data after the update operations have been completed. You can use them in your applications to fine-tune your data update routines.

Summary

In this chapter, you've seen how data adapters occupy a fundamental role in the ADO.NET Framework. You've looked closer at the capabilities of data adapters, focusing particularly on their ability to update, as well as to read, the data in a data store. You saw how to fill the InsertCommand, DeleteCommand, and UpdateCommand properties manually, and through the use of a CommandBuilder object. Finally, you examined the issues of concurrency that arise as soon as more than one person is using your application, and at the events exposed by DataAdapter objects that help you to deal with them.

CHAPTER 5

■ ■ ■

Typed Datasets and Dataset Schemas

So far, you've looked at how to use the `DataSet` class provided by the `System.Data` namespace. You've learned about the `Rows` collection and the `Columns` collection, and how to access individual rows and columns of data within the `DataSet`. For example, in a typical `DataSet`, you might access the first name of a customer as follows:

```
myRow = MyDataSet.Tables("Customers").Rows(0)
Console.WriteLine(myRow("FirstName"))
```

By the time you're done with this chapter, you'll be able to get access to your data in a much more programmer- (and reader-) friendly fashion.

```
Console.WriteLine(CustomerDataSet.Customers(0).FirstName)
```

As you can see, the second method is much easier to understand and write. The functionality we just described is made possible by a convention in the .NET Framework known as *strongly typed datasets*.

A typed dataset is not a built-in member of the .NET Framework. As you'll discover, it's a generated class that inherits directly from the `DataSet` class, but includes properties and methods based on an XML schema that you specify. This class also contains other classes for `DataTable` and `DataRow` objects that are enhanced in similar ways. As a result, you can create schemas and classes for data that are customized precisely for *your* data, enabling you to write data-access code more efficiently.

If you haven't come across XML schemas before, don't worry—we'll be explaining those in this chapter, too. An XML schema provides a rich definition of the data types, relationships, keys, and constraints within the data it describes. We'll be discussing how schemas and datasets fit together, and how to create strongly typed datasets, later on in this chapter. First, however, you need to have a brief overview of some of the basic elements of XSD.

Overview of XSD

Before you start double-checking the title of this chapter, we should explain why we're covering XSD here. Relational database servers like SQL Server and Oracle all have their own internal and proprietary formats for defining the structure of stored data. An Oracle table definition looks nothing like an internal SQL Server table definition. ADO.NET datasets, on the other hand, store their own internal structure in a standardized, widely used format called XSD.

The *XML Schema Definition* (*XSD*) language is an application of XML for describing data structures. It is particularly useful to you here because it allows applications to read and use schema information when handling data. A strongly typed dataset is a subclass of the (untyped) `DataSet` class, generated using an XML schema and therefore tailored to that particular XML schema.

The following overview of XSD should give you enough information to create and use strongly typed datasets. However, this is only a small part of what XSD can do. If you're already familiar with XML schemas and their use, you may want to skip directly to the "Dataset Schemas" section later in the chapter. You could at least skim the information provided in this next section as a refresher, though, so that XSD will be foremost in your mind when we start to go into more detail.

Simple Types

An XML schema is an XML document that defines the structure of other XML documents by specifying the structures and types of the elements that can be used in those documents. An XML schema also identifies the constraints on the content of those other XML documents, and describes the vocabulary (rules or grammar) that compliant XML documents must follow in order to be considered valid against the XML schema.

One of the biggest disadvantages of using *document type definitions (DTDs)* for constraining the behavior of instance documents was that the DTD syntax was not XML. So, not only did the programmer have to learn a new syntax, but validating XML parsers had to know how to parse the DTD syntax as well as XML. XML schemas are actually a dialect of XML, so any XML parser can interpret schema information.

Putting all of this another way, the XSD elements in an XML schema control how various elements and attributes can appear in a related XML document. In this section, you'll start your speedy overview of the XSD language by looking at the *simple types*—a part of XSD syntax that's used to define what types of data may appear in the content of an associated XML document.

Basic Data Types

The XSD standard defines several built-in data types, all of which are listed in Table 5-1.

Table 5-1. *Valid Data Types in an XML Schema*

Primitive XML Data Type	Description
string	Character strings.
Boolean	Represents a true or false value.
decimal	Numbers of arbitrary precision.
float	Single-precision, 32-bit floating point number.
double	Double-precision, 64-bit floating point number.
duration	Represents a length of time.
dateTime	Represents a specific point in time.
time	Represents a given time of day.

Table 5-1. *continued*

Primitive XML Data Type	Description
date	Represents a calendar date.
gYearMonth	A Gregorian month and Gregorian year.
gYear	A Gregorian year.
gMonthDay	A Gregorian month and Gregorian day. Specific date that occurs once a year.
gDay	A Gregorian day of the month.
gMonth	A Gregorian month.
hexBinary	Represents hex-encoded binary data.
base64Binary	Base64-encoded arbitrary binary data.
anyURI	Any URI (as defined by RFC 2396)—may be absolute or relative.
QName	Qualified name. Composed of a prefix and a local name, separated by a colon. The prefix must be a namespace that's been defined by a namespace declaration.
NOTATION	Represents a set of QNames.

To start making things a little clearer, the following is an example of an XSD file that (among other things) utilizes a couple of the primitive types described in Table 5-1. You might not understand all of the syntax at first, but we'll describe the remainder shortly. For now, just take a look at the attribute declarations and their associated data types.

```
<?xml version="1.0" encoding="utf-8" ?>
<xs:schema targetNamespace="http://tempuri.org/XMLSchema.xsd"
           elementFormDefault="qualified"
           xmlns="http://tempuri.org/XMLSchema.xsd"
           xmlns:xs="http://www.w3.org/2001/XMLSchema">
  <xs:element name="MyElement">
    <xs:complexType>
      <xs:attribute name="MyString" type="xs:string" />
      <xs:attribute name="MyTime" type="xs:time" />
      <xs:attribute name="MyBool" type="xs:boolean" />
      <xs:attribute name="MyDecimal" type="xs:decimal" />
    </xs:complexType>
  </xs:element>
</xs:schema>
```

This schema indicates that an element called `<MyElement>` can exist in an XML document associated with it, and that the element will have four attributes of varying data types. The following XML is part of a document that conforms to the previous schema:

```
<MyElement MyString="Hello"
           MyTime="12:00"
           MyBool="true"
           MyDecimal="3.851" />
```

You'll learn more about `<complexType>` and `<element>` elements later in this section.

Attributes

As shown in the previous example, attributes provide additional information about a given element. Attributes can only exist within the context of an element that they give additional information about—they cannot contain child elements of their own. Attributes can be defined as being any of the primitive XML data types in Table 5-1, or derived types such as positiveInteger.

The syntax for declaring an attribute in XSD is the following:

```
<attribute default = (value)
            fixed = (value)
            form = (qualified | unqualified)
            id = ID
            name = Name
            ref = (reference qualified name)
            type = (data type, qualified name)
            use = (optional | prohibited | required)
</attribute>
```

The <element> element in the previous sample schema showed how you could nest attribute declarations in order to assign them to a given element. We won't go into much more detail about the intricacies of attribute declarations here, but you can look at a few of the more important attributes of the <attribute> element in XSD.

- form: Indicates whether the attribute needs to have a valid namespace prefix in the instance document.

- type: The name of one of the primitive data types listed in Table 5-1, or a derived data type.

- use: Describes how the attribute can be used. The default value is optional, which indicates that the attribute is optional and can have any value (provided that the value doesn't contradict the type). You can also use this attribute to indicate that the attribute is prohibited in the instance document, or is required to appear.

Enumerations

Enumerations provide a way for you to restrict the values available for the XML document to those that you select. You can only provide enumerations for primitive data types, such as strings, etc. You create an enumeration by using an XSD <simpleType> element. Within the <simpleType>, you create a <restriction> with a base attribute.

The base attribute of the <restriction> tag is set with the primitive data type on which the restriction is placed. In the case of this sample, you're creating an enumeration of strings. So, at this point, your XSD fragment might look like the following:

```
<xs:simpleType name="MyEnumeration">
  <xs:restriction base="xs:string">
  </xs:restriction>
</xs:simpleType>
```

From here, you can define any number of restrictions (placed inside the `<restriction>` element) on the value that this new simple data type can accept. Keep in mind that the previous XSD snippet is defining a new data type that you're going to want to use as the data type of an attribute later on.

For your example, you're going to define an enumeration restriction that looks like this. Any attribute that's given this type will only be able to take on the values red, white, and blue.

```
<xs:enumeration value="red" />
<xs:enumeration value="white" />
<xs:enumeration value="blue" />
```

Your final schema, which indicates that your XML document can contain a `<MyElement>` element, with a MyEnum attribute and a MyString attribute, looks like the following:

```
<?xml version="1.0" encoding="utf-8" ?>
<xs:schema targetNamespace="http://tempuri.org/XMLSchema.xsd"
           elementFormDefault="qualified"
           xmlns="http://tempuri.org/XMLSchema.xsd"
           xmlns:xs="http://www.w3.org/2001/XMLSchema">
  <xs:element name="MyElement">
    <xs:complexType>
      <xs:attribute name="MyEnum" type="MyEnumeration" />
      <xs:attribute name="MyString" type="xs:string" />
  </xs:complexType>
</xs:element>
  <xs:simpleType name="MyEnumeration">
    <xs:restriction base="xs:string">
      <xs:enumeration value="red" />
      <xs:enumeration value="white" />
      <xs:enumeration value="blue" />
    </xs:restriction>
  </xs:simpleType>
</xs:schema>
```

So, if you attempted to validate the following XML against the previous schema, the validation would fail because the MyEnum attribute contains a value of "purple", which isn't allowed by the enumeration we defined:

```
<MyElement MyEnum="purple" MyString="Hello" />
```

User-Defined Types

In the context of an XML schema, a user-defined type is a restriction that's placed on the content of an element or an attribute. As you saw previously, enumerations can be used to create a kind of user-defined type, as they place a restriction on the values that primitive types can use. A user-defined simple type will always restrict the contents of the element or attribute to which it's applied, to a subset of the base type from which it's derived. In other words, when you create a user-defined simple type, you create a restriction on a primitive type.

Individual restrictions are placed on primitive types for the purpose of defining user-defined simple types through XSD elements called *facets*.

Facets

Facets are elements that are used to define a legal set of values for a simple type (which can be a user-defined simple type, or a primitive type like string or float). Constraining facets appear as child elements of a <restriction> node, which is in turn a child of a <simpleType> node. Table 5-2 is a list of the constraining facets that can be applied to a simple type (either built-in or user-defined).

Table 5-2. *Constraining Facets*

Constraining Facet	Description
enumeration	As you've already seen, this facet constrains the value of a simple type to a specified list of values.
fractionDigits	Specifies the maximum number of allowable digits in the fractional portion of the value.
length	Specifies the number of units of length. The units are determined by the base type of the simple type to which the facet is being applied. All values must be *exactly* this length.
maxExclusive	Maximum value. All values must be less than this value to qualify.
maxInclusive	Maximum value. All values must be less than *or equal to* in order to qualify.
maxLength	Maximum number of units of length. Units are determined by data type.
minExclusive	Minimum value. All values must be greater than this to qualify.
minInclusive	Minimum value. All values must be greater than *or equal to* this to qualify.
minLength	Minimum allowed length of the value. Units of length depend on the data type.
pattern	Specifies a regular expression that all values must match. A favorite!
totalDigits	Value must have a specific maximum number of total digits.
whiteSpace	Indicates whether the element should preserve, replace, or collapse whitespace.

Complex Types

As you saw in our first example, complex types in XML schemas are used to declare the attributes that can be placed on an element. They can also be used to define the names, nature, and behavior of an element's child nodes (if any). If an element in your instance document is going to be anything other than simple (meaning that it contains no child elements, no attributes, and has only a basic data type as its contents), then you must declare it as a complex type in the schema.

Let's take a look at a fairly simple XML document with just a two-level hierarchy.

```
<Book>
  <Title>Pro ADO.NET</Title>
  <Publisher>Apress Ltd</Publisher>
</Book>
```

The top-level element (the DocumentElement, if you're used to DOM programming) is the
<Book> element. It has two child elements: <Title> and <Publisher>. Based on our definition of
a complex type, the <Book> element is complex, but both the <Title> and <Publisher> elements
are simple (they are based on basic data types, and have no attributes or child elements).

Let's create a portion of a schema that represents this hierarchy. Whenever you declare a
complex type, you need to use the <complexType> XSD element.

```
<xs:element name="Book">
  <xs:complexType>
    <xs:sequence>
      <xs:element name="Title" type="xs:string" />
      <xs:element name="Publisher" type="xs:string" />
    </xs:sequence>
  </xs:complexType>
</xs:element>
```

The mixed Attribute

The <complexType> element's mixed attribute allows the content of a given element to contain
a mixture of simple character data and child nodes. This attribute is extremely helpful in mix-
ing markup tags with standard prose, such as defining reference links and information within
the context of a magazine article, a book review, or any other form of content.

You could make a slight change to your previous schema and modify the <complexType>
element to include the mixed="true" attribute, as follows:

```
<xs:element name="Book">
  <xs:complexType mixed="true">
    <xs:sequence>
      <xs:element name="Title" type="xs:string" />
      <xs:element name="Publisher" type="xs:string" />
    </xs:sequence>
  </xs:complexType>
</xs:element>
```

You could then write a valid XML document that contains mixed content, as follows:

```
<Book>
  The title of this book is <Title>Pro ADO.NET</Title> and
  the publisher of the book is <Publisher>Apress Ltd</Publisher>.
</Book>
```

Mixed content is very often seen in business-to-business (B2B) document exchanges. For example, if a media provider supplied movie reviews to dozens of online movie retailers, they could provide those reviews with mixed content, marking up the portions containing data that could be accessed or searched for, such as the rating or the title of the movie. In general, however, mixed content is best avoided if possible, due to the complexities it adds to parsing code.

Element Groups

There are only a few more things left to cover before you can get into the specifics of how schemas affect DataSet objects. One of those things is *element groups*. Any time that a set of more than one element appears as a child of another element, it is considered to be an element group. There are four main XSD elements for defining the behavior of element groups.

- The <all> element

- The <choice> element

- The <sequence> element

- The <group> element

The all Element

The <all> element indicates that all of the child elements declared beneath it can exist in the instance document, in any order. The following is how your book schema might change to accommodate such a thing:

```
<xs:element name="Book">
  <xs:complexType>
    <xs:all>
      <xs:element name="Title" type="xs:string" />
      <xs:element name="Publisher" type="xs:string" />
    </xs:all>
  </xs:complexType>
</xs:element>
```

The choice Element

The <choice> element indicates that one *and only one* of its child elements can exist in the instance document. Therefore, if you modify your book schema to use a <choice> element, you can have either a <Title> element or a <Publisher> element in your instance document, but validation will fail if you have both.

```
<xs:element name="Book">
  <xs:complexType>
    <xs:choice>
      <xs:element name="Title" type="xs:string" />
```

```
      <xs:element name="Publisher" type="xs:string" />
   </xs:choice>
  </xs:complexType>
</xs:element>
```

The sequence Element

The `<sequence>` element indicates that the order in which the child elements appear in an instance document must be the same as the order in which those elements are declared. The following is your modified book schema using the `<sequence>` element:

```
<xs:element name="Book">
  <xs:complexType>
    <xs:sequence>
      <xs:element name="Title" type="xs:string" />
      <xs:element name="Publisher" type="xs:string" />
    </xs:sequence>
  </xs:complexType>
</xs:element>
```

This means that if you try to validate the following XML document against this schema, the validation will fail, because your instance document contains the child elements in the wrong order.

```
<Book>
  <Publisher>Apress Ltd</Publisher>
  <Title>Pro ADO.NET</Title>
</Book>
```

The group Element

The `<group>` element provides a method for naming a group of elements or attributes. This becomes exceedingly useful if the same grouping will appear in more than one place. For example, if you have an instance document that contains both customers and contacts, then you might want a reusable group of elements for the name, address, and phone number. The `<group>` element can contain an `<all>` element, a `<choice>` element, or a `<sequence>` element. The following is an example portion of a schema that utilizes a `<group>`:

```
<xs:group name="ContactInfo">
  <xs:all>
    <xs:element name="Address1" type="xs:string" />
    <xs:element name="Address2" type="xs:string" />
    <xs:element name="City" type="xs:string" />
    <xs:element name="State" type="xs:string" />
  </xs:all>
</xs:group>
<xs:element name="Contact">
```

```
    <xs:complexType>
      <xs:group ref="ContactInfo" />
      <xs:element name="Company" type="xs:string" />
    </xs:complexType>
</xs:element>
<xs:element name="Customer">
    <xs:complexType>
      <xs:group ref="ContactInfo" />
      <xs:element name="Status" type="xs:string" />
    </xs:complexType>
</xs:element>
```

You can see how the ContactInfo grouping of elements was reused for two different parent elements, without having to retype the information.

Attribute Groups

This same idea of reusing groups can be applied to attributes just as easily as it can be applied to elements. If, for example, you wanted to convert your book description XML document so that the title and publisher become attributes of the <Book> element, you can group those attributes as follows, allowing them to be reused throughout the schema:

```
<xs:attributeGroup name="BookDetails">
  <xs:attribute name="Title" type="xs:string" />
  <xs:attribute name="Publisher" type="xs:string" />
</xs:attributeGroup>

<xs:element name="Book">
  <xs:attributeGroup ref="BookDetails" />
</xs:element>
```

So, your XML instance document for the new schema looks like the following:

```
<Book Title="Pro ADO.NET" Publisher="Apress Ltd" />
```

XSD Annotation

One of the biggest benefits of XML schemas is that they are written in human-readable form. Compilers and applications can interpret them for use in data manipulation scenarios, while the programmers using those schemas can read them without recourse to a translator.

Sometimes, schemas will be sent to business partners to ensure that everyone is formatting their data properly. Other times, schemas are generated by an application architect and then provided to the programmers who write the actual code. No matter what the reason, it's extremely helpful to have the ability to embed documentation and additional information into the schema itself, rather than having the programmers search for it elsewhere.

XML schemas provide two ways of annotating a schema. You can either annotate your schema with documentation that's designed to be read by a human examining the schema, or you can use annotation that's designed to provide additional detailed information to the program or process that's interpreting the schema. In fact, all annotation for an XML schema occurs within the `<annotation>` element. The two different types of annotation occur as child elements of that parent. The `<annotation>` element itself should occur as the first child of the element to which the annotation applies.

The documentation Element

The `<documentation>` element contains human-readable information that's intended for the audience of the XML schema file. The following is a quick example of a modified schema for your book document that contains some documentation:

```
<xs:element name="Book">
  <xs:annotation>
    <xs:documentation>
      This book element contains information about a single book. It
      should contain the full title and the official name of the
      publisher.
    </xs:documentation>
  </xs:annotation>

  <xs:complexType>
    <xs:sequence>
      <xs:element name="Title" type="xs:string" />
      <xs:element name="Publisher" type="xs:string" />
    </xs:sequence>
  </xs:complexType>
</xs:element>
```

The appinfo Element

The `<appinfo>` element provides a way for the schema author to supply additional information to an application interpreting the schema. This kind of information might include script code, filenames, switches, or flags of some kind indicating parameters for processing. As with the `<documentation>` element, `<appinfo>` always occurs within an `<annotation>` element.

The XmlSchema Class

The `System.Xml.XmlSchema` namespace in the .NET Framework SDK includes a class called `XmlSchema` that can be used to create and load XML schemas programmatically. We won't go into too much detail here (you can always peruse the MSDN documentation for a detailed reference), but to demonstrate the principal functionality of the `XmlSchema` class, we've cooked up a console application called SchemaGen.

Tip As with all of the code in this chapter, the sample assumes that it's using the Visual Studio .NET solution file, and the executable is in the `bin` directory beneath the main project directory. The downloadable code samples are all in this format.

This application creates the schema that we've been using for illustrative purposes so far in this chapter programmatically. The following is the source code for the SchemaGenerator.vb file:

```vb
Imports System
Imports System.Xml
Imports System.Xml.Schema
Imports System.IO

Module SchemaGenerator
  Sub Main()
    ' Create a new instance of an XML schema
    Dim Schema As XmlSchema = New XmlSchema()

    ' Produce the following XSD in the document
    ' <element name="Book">
    Dim ElementBook As New XmlSchemaElement()
    Schema.Items.Add(ElementBook)
    ElementBook.Name = "Book"

    ' <complexType>
    Dim ComplexType As New XmlSchemaComplexType()
    ElementBook.SchemaType = ComplexType

    Dim Sequence As New XmlSchemaSequence()
    ComplexType.Particle = Sequence

    ' <element name="Title" ...
    Dim ElementTitle As New XmlSchemaElement()
    ElementTitle.Name = "Title"

    ' Indicate that the data type of the Title element is not just
    ' "any" string, but the string as defined by the W3C's namespace
    ElementTitle.SchemaTypeName = New XmlQualifiedName("string", _
                              "http://www.w3.org/2001/XMLSchema")

    Dim ElementPublisher As New XmlSchemaElement()
    ElementPublisher.Name = "Publisher"
    ElementPublisher.SchemaTypeName = New XmlQualifiedName("string", _
                              "http://www.w3.org/2001/XMLSchema")
```

```
    Sequence.Items.Add(ElementTitle)
    Sequence.Items.Add(ElementPublisher)

    ' Just because we used code to create all the nodes, it doesn't mean
    ' that the schema is automatically valid. We need to compile the schema
    ' before we write it to make sure it is valid.
    Schema.Compile(New ValidationEventHandler(AddressOf ValidationHandler))
    Schema.Write(Console.Out)
  End Sub

  Sub ValidationHandler(ByVal sender As Object, _
                        ByVal args As ValidationEventArgs)
    Console.WriteLine("Schema Validation Failed.")
    Console.WriteLine(args.Message)
  End Sub
End Module
```

If all of this looks similar to building an XML document via the DOM interface, then you've been paying attention! It looks similar because the hierarchical nature of element and attribute building is inherent in *all* XML generating tools, including those that generate XSD. If your application must generate XML schemas on the fly, then the XmlSchema class will come in extremely handy. (If it must generate several similar schemas on the fly, you might want to consider deriving a class from XmlSchema, adding functionality intrinsic to your own application.)

The previous sample uses the Console class's Out stream as the destination for the new schema. This allows you either to see the schema on the screen, or, using the old DOS redirection operator (you do remember that, don't you?), to actually redirect this application's output to an .xsd file with the following command on the command line:

> **SchemaGenerator > SimpleBooks.xsd**

This generates the following XML schema file (SimpleBooks.xsd):

```xml
<?xml version="1.0" encoding="IBM850"?>
<xs:schema xmlns:xs="http://www.w3.org/2001/XMLSchema">
  <xs:element name="Book">
    <xs:complexType>
      <xs:sequence>
        <xs:element name="Title" type="xs:string" />
        <xs:element name="Publisher" type="xs:string" />
      </xs:sequence>
    </xs:complexType>
  </xs:element>
</xs:schema>
```

The class that you used to generate this schema has a default encoding format of IBM850. This could easily be changed to UTF-8 (or any other character-encoding format) by the schema generation class.

Dataset Schemas

At this point, you might be wondering when we're actually going to start talking about strongly typed datasets. However, it would have been unnecessarily confusing to rush into such a discussion without first having a thorough exploration of how DataSet objects store their internal data structures. Equally, a discussion of the internal structure of a DataSet would never be complete without having first provided an overview of XML schemas.

This next section, then, is going to cover XML schemas as they apply to DataSet objects, covering the XSD elements and structures that relate directly to various DataSet behaviors and configurations.

Schema Translation

Before you get going, it's important to bear in mind that in previous chapters, you've already manipulated and interrogated your DataSets' schemas without knowing anything at all about XSD, and you'll be doing more in the same vein later in the book. There are plenty of occasions when it's not necessary to know about the underlying XML schema in order to do useful work with ADO.NET. The schemas you're looking at here are the same as the schemas you've examined already. You're just choosing to explore and create them using XSD, rather than the ADO.NET data providers.

Here, then, we're going to talk about how XML schemas are translated into the entities that DataSets expose to their clients: tables, rows, columns, relationships, keys, and constraints. While it's theoretically possible (as you'll soon see) for you to accomplish everything you need by simply dragging a table from a database connection in Visual Studio .NET onto a new DataSet class and never looking at the underlying XSD, it may not be practical to do so. For example, there are many occasions when the structure in a database doesn't reflect the structure you want in your DataSet.

Having a thorough knowledge of which elements in XSD produce which behaviors in a DataSet can save you time, effort, redundant code, and the problem of Wizard-generated code getting *close* to your desired result, but not being exactly what you want. It's a good, defensive programming tactic to assume that a Wizard is just a starting point, and that any Wizard-generated code will have to be modified before it's ready to use. Dragging a table definition from SQL Server onto the design surface of the Visual Studio .NET DataSet designer might be sufficient to get the job done, but you can accomplish quite a bit more with some knowledge of the underlying details.

Generating Tables and Columns

In this next section, you're going to learn how to indicate tables, rows, and columns with XSD. In an XSD representation, every DataSet must have a single root element, which indicates the DataSet itself. It is beneath this root element that you can supply your definitions for the tables and columns of your DataSet.

Tables occur as complex elements beneath the root element. Columns appear as child elements of the complex elements indicating the tables (see Figure 5-1).

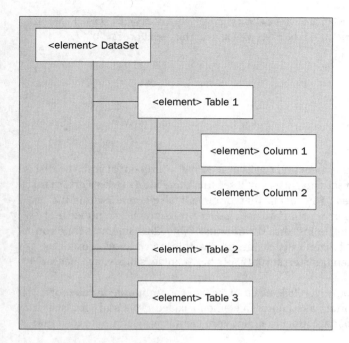

Figure 5-1. *XSD representation of a* DataSet

Let's take your simple book schema from earlier in the chapter, and make it into a DataSet schema. The first thing you need to do is define the outermost element—the DataSet itself. In your case, you'll call it <BookDataSet>. Beneath that, you'll create an element called <Books>, and lower still beneath that, you'll create two elements, <Title> and <Publisher>. Let's take a look at your XSD, modified to produce a working DataSet (BookDataSet.xsd).

```
<?xml version="1.0" encoding="utf-8" ?>
<xs:schema id="BookDataSet"
          targetNamespace="urn:apress-proadonet-chapter5-BookDataSet.xsd"
          elementFormDefault="qualified"
          xmlns="urn:apress-proadonet-chapter5-BookDataSet.xsd"
          xmlns:xs="http://www.w3.org/2001/XMLSchema"
          xmlns:msdata="urn:schemas-microsoft-com:xml-msdata">

  <xs:element name="BookDataSet" msdata:IsDataSet="true">
    <xs:complexType>
      <xs:choice maxOccurs="unbounded">
        <xs:element name="Books">
          <xs:complexType>
            <xs:sequence>
```

```
            <xs:element name="Title" type="xs:string" minOccurs="0" />
            <xs:element name="Publisher" type="xs:string" minOccurs="0" />
          </xs:sequence>
        </xs:complexType>
      </xs:element>
    </xs:choice>
  </xs:complexType>
</xs:element>
</xs:schema>
```

There are a couple of new things here that might immediately jump out at you. The first is that you've assigned an id to your schema. Also, you'll see that there is an `elementFormDefault` attribute with the value "`qualified`". This means that, by default, all elements within the schema must be qualified with their appropriate namespace prefix. You'll also notice that you've defined a target namespace, for instance documents of this XML schema. While you could get away with leaving this blank, it's a good idea to give this information in order to avoid any potential collisions when transferring `DataSets` between domains, machines, or platforms.

Looking deeper into the schema, you'll notice that we have an unlimited number of `<Books>` elements, which then contain a sequence of elements called `Title` and `Publisher`, in that order. You could create a Books.xml document for your sample application to read that looks like the following:

```xml
<BookDataSet xmlns="urn:apress-proadonet-chapter5-BookDataSet.xsd">
  <Books>
    <Title>Pro ADO.NET</Title>
    <Publisher>Apress Ltd</Publisher>
  </Books>
  <Books>
    <Title>Professional .NET Framework</Title>
    <Publisher>Apress Ltd</Publisher>
  </Books>
</BookDataSet>
```

The following list is of a small console application that creates an ordinary `DataSet`, reads the XSD file (BookDataSet.xsd), loads your Books.xml file, and then prints the information in the XML file to the console, using the relational paradigm of tables, columns, and rows. The source code for the DSSample1 example, DSSchemaSample1.vb, is listed next. The BookDataSet.xsd and Books.xml files are both in the `bin` directory beneath the project.

```vb
Imports System
Imports System.Data

Module DSSchemaSample1
  Sub Main()
    Dim BookDataSet As DataSet = New DataSet()
    BookDataSet.ReadXmlSchema("BookDataSet.xsd")
    BookDataSet.ReadXml("Books.xml")
```

```
        Console.WriteLine("Recent Books:")
        Console.WriteLine("-------------")
        Dim xRow As DataRow
        For Each xRow In BookDataSet.Tables("Books").Rows
          Console.WriteLine("{0} by {1}", xRow("Title"), xRow("Publisher"))
        Next
    End Sub
End Module
```

Constraints

As you know, constraints are rules enforced on the contents of a DataSet. It's entirely possible to use nothing but the DataSet methods to create, modify, and enforce constraints, but you should also know what constraints look like in the underlying XSD that your DataSets work with. There are several constraint types that you can enforce on the data contained within a DataSet, via its associated schema.

Key Constraints

You can use the <key> element in an XML schema to enforce key constraints on data contained within the DataSet. A key constraint must be unique throughout the schema instance, and cannot have null values.

The following addition to our BookDataSet.xsd schema creates a key on the Title column.

```
<xs:key name="KeyTitle">
  <xs:selector xpath=".//Books" />
  <xs:field xpath="Title" />
</xs:key>
```

The <selector> element contains an xpath attribute, which indicates to the DataSet the XPath query to run in order to locate the table on which the key applies. The next element, <field>, also contains an XPath query, which indicates to the DataSet how to locate the field on which the key applies (relative to the table's element).

Unique Constraints

A unique constraint is slightly more forgiving than a key constraint. A unique constraint requires only that data should be unique, *if it exists*. Individual columns can specify whether or not they allow nulls, overriding some of the default behavior of the unique constraint. You could just as easily have indicated a unique constraint on your Title column with the following XSD fragment:

```
<xs:unique name="KeyTitle">
  <xs:selector xpath=".//Books" />
  <xsd:field xpath="Title" />
</xs:unique>
```

Foreign Keys (Keyrefs) and Relationships

<keyref> elements within an XML schema provide a facility for declaring links within the document. The functionality they establish is similar in nature to that of foreign key relationships in relational databases like SQL Server. If a DataSet encounters a <keyref> element when loading a schema, the DataSet will create an appropriate foreign key constraint. It will also create a parent-child relationship (discussed shortly).

For this example, you're going to create a new table in your DataSet called BookReviews. Then, you'll use the <keyref> element to create a foreign key relationship between the BookReviews table and the Books table. To make things easier (and more realistic), you'll also add a BookID column. All of the code for this sample can be found in the DSSample2 folder of the code download for this chapter [see the Downloads section of the Apress Web site (http://www.apress.com)].

The following is the new BookDataSet.xsd file for DSSample2:

```xml
<?xml version="1.0" encoding="utf-8" ?>
<xs:schema id="BookDataSet"
           targetNamespace="urn:apress-proadonet-chapter5-BookDataSet.xsd"
           elementFormDefault="qualified"
           xmlns="urn:apress-proadonet-chapter5-BookDataSet.xsd"
           xmlns:xs="http://www.w3.org/2001/XMLSchema"
           xmlns:msdata="urn:schemas-microsoft-com:xml-msdata">

  <xs:element name="BookDataSet" msdata:IsDataSet="true">
    <xs:complexType>
      <xs:choice maxOccurs="unbounded">
        <xs:element name="Books">
          <xs:complexType>
            <xs:sequence>
              <xs:element name="BookID" type="xs:integer" minOccurs="1" />
              <xs:element name="Title" type="xs:string" minOccurs="1" />
              <xs:element name="Publisher" type="xs:string" minOccurs="1" />
            </xs:sequence>
          </xs:complexType>
        </xs:element>
```

To this point, everything should look pretty familiar. You'll notice that we've added the BookID column, an integer column that must appear any time a <Books> element appears (minOccurs="1"). Next, you create a new definition for a table. Remembering that a table in XSD is nothing more than an element that contains more elements, it's pretty easy to do.

```xml
        <xs:element name="BookReviews">
          <xs:complexType>
            <xs:sequence>
              <xs:element name="BookID" type="xs:integer" minOccurs="1" />
              <xs:element name="Rating" type="xs:integer" minOccurs="1" />
              <xs:element name="Review" type="xs:string" minOccurs="0" />
            </xs:sequence>
          </xs:complexType>
```

```
      </xs:element>
    </xs:choice>
  </xs:complexType>
```

After that, there is some more familiar-looking code. You went over the `<key>` element earlier: the xpath attribute of the `<selector>` element indicates the Books table, while the xpath attribute for the `<field>` indicates the BookID column.

```
<xs:key name="KeyTitle">
  <xs:selector xpath=".//Books" />
  <xs:field xpath="BookID" />
</xs:key>
```

Finally, you use a `<keyref>` element to indicate that you're creating a foreign key originating from the BookID column of the BookReviews table, referring to the `<key>` element named KeyTitle.

```
<xs:keyref name="KeyTitleRef" refer="KeyTitle">
  <xs:selector xpath=".//BookReviews" />
  <xs:field xpath="BookID" />
</xs:keyref>
  </xs:element>
</xs:schema>
```

With your XSD file in place, you can start the code listing for SchemaSample2.vb.

```
Imports System
Imports System.Data

Module SchemaSample2
  Sub Main()
    Dim BookDataSet As New DataSet()

    BookDataSet.ReadXmlSchema("BookDataSet.xsd")
    BookDataSet.ReadXml("Books.xml")

    Console.WriteLine("Relations Created:")
    Dim xRelation As DataRelation
    For Each xRelation In BookDataSet.Relations
       Console.WriteLine(xRelation.RelationName)
    Next

    Console.WriteLine("Apress Books")
    Console.WriteLine("----------")
    Console.WriteLine()
```

Programmers like proof. To prove that a relationship in the DataSet has been created with exactly the same name as the `<keyref>` element in the XSD file, you iterate through the Relations collection, printing out the name of the relationship. You'll see that there is indeed a relationship called KeyTitleRef in the DataSet immediately after the schema is loaded.

```
    Dim xRow As DataRow
    For Each xRow In BookDataSet.Tables("Books").Rows
      Console.WriteLine(xRow("Title"))
```

So far, this is pretty straightforward: just iterate through each of the rows in the DataSet, and print out the value in the "Title" column for each of the rows.

```
      ' Obtain child rows using the KeyTitleRef relation
      Dim zRow As DataRow
      For Each zRow In xRow.GetChildRows("KeyTitleRef")
        Console.WriteLine("  {0}", zRow("Rating"))
      Next
    Next
  End Sub
End Module
```

The GetChildRows() method obtains a list of child rows of a given row, utilizing a relationship. You can specify either the name of the relationship, or a DataRelation object. You can optionally specify a row version to further filter the results returned by querying the relation. In your source XML document, the information is stored flat, in two separate tables. With the use of GetChildRows(), you're actually forcing a hierarchical traversal of the information in the DataSet.

When you're all done, you're presented with console output like the following, showing each of the titles and the rating of each reviewer, indented to help display the hierarchy of the row relationships:

```
Relations Created:
KeyTitleRef

Apress Books
----------

Pro ADO.NET
  5
  1
Professional .NET Framework
  4
  2
```

So that you can see where the numbers are coming from, let's take a look at your updated Books.xml file that now contains information for the BookReviews table.

```
<BookDataSet xmlns="urn:apress-proadonet-chapter5-BookDataSet.xsd">
  <Books>
    <BookID>1</BookID>
    <Title>Pro ADO.NET</Title>
    <Publisher>Apress Ltd</Publisher>
  </Books>
  <Books>
```

```
    <BookID>2</BookID>
    <Title>Professional .NET Framework</Title>
    <Publisher>Apress Ltd</Publisher>
</Books>
```

The Books table information should look pretty familiar. In the following, however, we list the contents of the BookReviews table. Each row in the latter table is defined by a <BookReviews> element.

```
<BookReviews>
    <BookID>1</BookID>
    <Rating>5</Rating>
    <Review>This book was by far one of the best books on .NET ever
            written!</Review>
</BookReviews>
<BookReviews>
    <BookID>1</BookID>
    <Rating>1</Rating>
    <Review>I'm not sure this could be classified as a technical manual. It
            is worth more as a paperweight</Review>
</BookReviews>
<BookReviews>
    <BookID>2</BookID>
    <Rating>4</Rating>
    <Review>Top Notch! Excellent book! I especially liked the chapter on
            strongly typed datasets and XSD schemas!</Review>
</BookReviews>
<BookReviews>
    <BookID>2</BookID>
    <Rating>2</Rating>
    <Review>I liked the introduction. That's it.</Review>
</BookReviews>
</BookDataSet>
```

Note Even though the presence of foreign keys and relationships in a DataSet's schema can indicate a hierarchical relationship, the data does not have to appear to be nested in the instance document.

Strongly Typed Datasets

So far, you've walked through some of the more commonly used features that are available to you in XSD, and you've learned how various elements in XML schemas affect the way in which DataSets behave. You've seen how to control the data types of individual columns, and how to represent multiple tables, columns, indexes, and constraints within a DataSet.

In truth, a lot of what we've covered with regard to XSD and dataset schemas you could theoretically survive without, but knowing the internals of how your tools are working is always helpful. While most of your examples so far (and throughout this chapter) deal with using DataSets and XML data, all of this information can be applied to DataSets used in conjunction with relational databases. The essential point to remember is that whether the data came from an XML document, a relational database, or some other provider, the schemas still have the same format.

Now you'll put all of that knowledge together and get to where we promised: strongly typed datasets. You may recall that one of the first things this chapter showed was how you were going to be able to turn the following lines of code:

```
myRow = MyDataSet.Tables("Customers").Rows(0)
Console.WriteLine(myRow("FirstName"))
```

into this short, easy-to-read line of code.

```
Console.WriteLine(CustomerDataSet.Customers(0).FirstName)
```

This change is made possible by the strong support in the .NET Framework for inheritance and clear, logical object hierarchies. The essential concept behind a strongly typed dataset is that a new class is created that derives from the DataSet class. This new class implements properties and methods that are strongly typed, based on the schema that was used in order to generate it.

When this derived class is instantiated, it will provide logically named properties of integer type (if your schema called for integer columns), and further logically named properties that appear as arrays of strongly typed rows. So, rather than dealing with DataRows and DataTables, you end up dealing with task-specialized concepts, such as a CustomersRow or a CustomersTable, which may contain columns called FirstName or LastName, rather than forcing you to employ hard-to-use array indices.

In Visual Basic .NET, there are two (equally valid) approaches to creating strongly typed datasets. You can create them graphically through the tools provided within Visual Studio .NET, or you can use command-line utilities and compiler arguments. We'll cover both approaches here, and you can pick the one that best fits your skills, style, and preferences.

Building Typed Datasets in Visual Studio .NET

Visual Studio .NET provides an incredibly easy, point-and-click approach to creating strongly typed datasets. It's such a natural extension of Visual Studio .NET that if you're using Visual Studio .NET to develop your application, there's no sensible reason not to use strongly typed datasets. To start out, you'll take the concept from our "books and book reviews" example, and develop a strongly typed dataset for it in Visual Studio .NET. As usual, we're going to start out by creating a new console application, this time named TypedDS_VS1. You'll rename the module to TypedSetDemo, and the module file to TypedSetDemo.vb.

Next, right-click on the project name, choose Add ➤ Add Class, and then select the DataSet icon and type in BookDataSet.xsd as the filename. From the Toolbox, drag two elements into open areas of the design surface. From there, you can use the visual interface to add child elements (which will be columns) to each of the elements you dropped onto the surface. Create the elements according to the columns you used in DSSample2 (Books and BookReviews). Then, finish it off by creating a primary key called KeyBookID on the BookID column in the Books table, and your designer should look something like what you see in Figure 5-2.

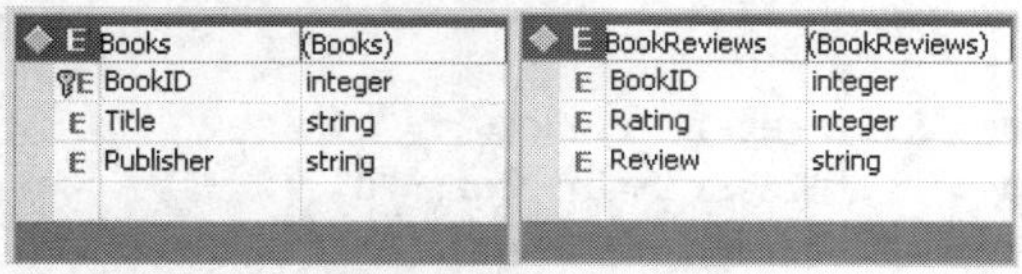

Figure 5-2. *Strongly typed dataset XSD*

At this point, what you have is two completely disjointed and unrelated tables. Now for the fun stuff: the relationship. From the Toolbox, drag a Relation onto the designer, hovering over any of the elements (or whitespace) in the BookReviews element (table). When you let go, you'll see a dialog prompting you for more information about the relation (keyref). Change the name of the keyref to KeyBookIDRef. As there's already a key in one of the tables, and there are identically named columns in each table, the dialog comes populated with all of the information you need to form the parent-child relationship. You can confirm the dialog and generate the code.

Finally, in the Properties window, change the targetNamespace property of the schema to urn:apress-proadonet-chapter5-BookDataSet.xsd, and attributeFormDefault to (Default).

Note One thing you should keep in mind is that the namespace of the data in the XML you're reading absolutely *must* be the same as the target namespace of this schema. Also, this namespace is case sensitive.

Now, take a look at the XSD for your visually designed, strongly typed dataset.

```
<?xml version="1.0" encoding="utf-8" ?>
<xs:schema id="BookDataSet"
           targetNamespace="urn:apress-proadonet-chapter5-BookDataSet.xsd"
           elementFormDefault="qualified"
           xmlns="urn:apress-proadonet-chapter5-BookDataSet.xsd"
           xmlns:mstns="urn:apress-proadonet-chapter5-BookDataSet.xsd"
           xmlns:xs="http://www.w3.org/2001/XMLSchema"
           xmlns:msdata="urn:schemas-microsoft-com:xml-msdata">
  <xs:element name="BookDataSet" msdata:IsDataSet="true">
    <xs:complexType>
      <xs:choice maxOccurs="unbounded">
        <xs:element name="Books">
          <xs:complexType>
            <xs:sequence>
              <xs:element name="BookID" type="xs:integer" minOccurs="0" />
              <xs:element name="Title" type="xs:string" minOccurs="0" />
              <xs:element name="Publisher" type="xs:string" minOccurs="0" />
            </xs:sequence>
```

```
        </xs:complexType>
      </xs:element>
      <xs:element name="BookReviews">
        <xs:complexType>
          <xs:sequence>
            <xs:element name="BookID" type="xs:integer" minOccurs="0" />
            <xs:element name="Rating" type="xs:integer" minOccurs="0" />
            <xs:element name="Review" type="xs:string" minOccurs="0" />
          </xs:sequence>
        </xs:complexType>
      </xs:element>
    </xs:choice>
  </xs:complexType>
  <xs:key name="KeyBookID">
    <xs:selector xpath=".//mstns:Books" />
    <xs:field xpath="mstns:BookID" />
  </xs:key>
  <xs:keyref name="KeyBookIDRef" refer="KeyBookID">
    <xs:selector xpath=".//mstns:BookReviews" />
    <xs:field xpath="mstns:BookID" />
  </xs:keyref>
  </xs:element>
</xs:schema>
```

It should come as no surprise that this looks remarkably similar to the document that you built manually during the schema overview. The only real difference is the use of the mstns namespace to link things together (tns is shorthand for "this namespace").

Now you'll enter some code into the main class of the console application to generate the same output as your previous example, but you'll fully utilize the features of a class that you actually did nothing to generate, other than define the schema. The following is the source listing for TypedSetDemo.vb:

```
Imports System
Imports System.Data

Module TypedSetDemo
  Sub Main()
    Dim myDS As New BookDataSet()
    myDS.ReadXml("Books.xml")

    Console.WriteLine("Relations Found:")
    Dim xRelation As DataRelation
    For Each xRelation In myDS.Relations
       Console.WriteLine(xRelation.RelationName)
    Next

    Console.WriteLine("Apress Books and Reviews")
    Console.WriteLine("----------------------")
```

Notice here that you're not instantiating a `DataSet`, but a class named `BookDataSet`. The Books.xml file you're using here is the same as the one you used in the last example, which should be copied to the `bin` directory for this project. Just like last time, you dump the relationships defined in the `DataSet` to the console. For your example, you have one called `KeyBookIDRef`.

```
Dim Book As BookDataSet.BooksRow
For Each Book In myDS.Books.Rows
```

This is where it gets almost enjoyable to write the code. Instead of iterating through the rows of some table object that you reached through an ordinal, you're indexing through each of the `BooksRow` objects in your strongly typed dataset's `Books.Rows` collection. It's much easier to read, and much easier for the programmer to write.

```
    Console.WriteLine(Book.Title)

    Dim Review As BookDataSet.BookReviewsRow
    For Each Review In Book.GetBookReviewsRows()
      Console.WriteLine("  {0}", Review.Rating)
    Next
  Next
 End Sub
End Module
```

As we said, the code generator for the strongly typed dataset will actually generate properly typed properties for each of the columns in a table. Here you can see that you're printing out the value of `Book.Title`, rather than `Tables("Books").Rows(0)("Title")`, or something similarly complex. Also, note that instead of invoking the `GetChildRows()` method, you're actually calling `GetBookReviewsRows()`, which your strongly typed dataset implemented for you. This method returns an array of `BookReviewsRow` objects.

After you've placed all the code into your solution (or you've loaded the `TypedDS_VS1` project from the code download), rebuild it, and then make sure that Show All Files is selected from the Project menu. You should see that the BookDataSet.xsd file has some child items. Expand them, and you'll see that a BookDataSet.vb file has been generated for you. This is the actual class definition that TypedSetDemo.vb uses as the strongly typed dataset.

Let's take a look at the console output generated by this sample. It should look extremely similar to your previous sample, but the key thing to remember is that this `DataSet` isn't generic—it has been derived and specialized to work *only* with Books and BookReviews, according to your schema.

```
Relations Found:
KeyBookIDRef
Apress Books and Reviews
----------------------
Pro ADO.NET
  5
  1
Professional .NET Framework
  4
  2
```

The code for BookDataSet.vb is too long to look at here in its entirety (though it is of course available in the download for this chapter), but it's certainly worth taking a look at a few key points. The first thing you'll look at is the Books property, which is a strongly typed wrapper around some inherent DataSet functionality. The following is the BookDataSet class's definition of the Books property:

```
Public ReadOnly Property Books As BooksDataTable
   Get
      Return Me.tableBooks
   End Get
End Property
```

Like so many properties, this is just a wrapper around a private member variable. The key thing to note here is the data type of the property: it's actually a nested class called BooksDataTable, which is another dynamically generated class deriving from the DataTable class.

Now let's take a look at another piece of "magic" that the strongly typed dataset is performing on your behalf: the invocation of GetChildRows() through the GetBookReviewsRows() method (a member of the BookDataSet.BooksRow class).

```
Public Function GetBookReviewsRows() As BookReviewsRow()
   Return CType(Me.GetChildRows( _
         Me.Table.ChildRelations("KeyBookIDRef")), BookReviewsRow())
End Function
```

This function locates a DataRelation object by pulling the KeyBookIDRef item out of the ChildRelations collection. It then pulls the child rows by passing the relation object to the GetChildRows() function, changing the type of the resulting array of DataRow objects to an array of BookReviewsRow objects. As with all of the items in the strongly typed dataset, this function is visible through IntelliSense in Visual Studio .NET, dramatically reducing your chances of mistyping the name of the child row's relation name.

One more useful feature of the typed dataset is its strongly typed properties. Let's take a look at the Title property of the BooksRow class.

```
Public Property Title As String
   Get
     Try
       Return CType(Me(Me.tableBooks.TitleColumn), String)
     Catch e As InvalidCastException
       Throw New StrongTypingException( _
                   "Cannot get value because it is DBNull.", e)
     End Try
   End Get
   Set
     Me(Me.tableBooks.TitleColumn) = value
   End Set
End Property
```

This property is made possible by an override for the indexer (the Item property) in the DataRow class that BooksRow inherits from. It allows an actual column object to be supplied (specifically, a `DataColumn` object, or, as in this case, an object that inherits from `DataColumn`), rather than an ordinal or a string as a field identifier, on which to set and get values.

Building Typed Datasets Manually

Now that you've looked at how to make strongly typed datasets through Visual Studio .NET, which automatically makes them available to the rest of the project, let's look at how to do it the "hard" way. Of course, that's a misnomer, because there's really nothing hard about using command-line tools to create your own strongly typed datasets.

You shouldn't confuse "manually" with the process of writing all of the code for the `DataSet` class yourself. Even without Visual Studio .NET, there's still a tool that automates generation of the class file. For your "manual" example, you'll build the same example you built under Visual Studio .NET, though all of the compilation, code editing, and `DataSet` generation will be done from the command line and Notepad. (Other text editors are available.)

The first thing you'll do is to create a new directory (we used `TypedDS_NoVS`). Into this, you'll copy the BookDataSet.xsd file that you built containing the definitions for the `Books` table, the `BookReviews` table, the keys, and the `keyref` parent-child relationship. Also, you'll copy the Books.xml file from the previous example, so that you can test that your `DataSets` are going to function identically.

With almost no changes to your TypedSetDemo.vb file (renamed to TypedSetDemo2.vb, and the `TypedSetDemo` module renamed to `TypedSetDemo2`) we went ahead and wrote a batch file to illustrate the command-line arguments to build your strongly typed dataset and associated console application. It's called BuildAll.bat.

```
xsd /d /l:VB BookDataSet.xsd
vbc /r:System.dll /r:System.xml.dll /r:System.data.dll TypedSetDemo2.vb
 BookDataSet.vb
```

The first line of the batch file invokes a utility called xsd.exe, which is used to generate schema or class files from a given source. It can take a schema and either convert it to classes, or create a typed dataset from it (the `/d` argument). Also, it can create an XSD file from an XDR file to upgrade the schema definition. The second line invokes the VB.NET compiler to compile the BookDataSet.vb file and the TypedSetDemo2.vb file with a reference to the assemblies required.

Running the BuildAll.bat file and then executing TypedSetDemo2.exe, you get screen output that's exactly the same as the output generated by the Visual Studio .NET version.

Strongly Typed Datasets and Relational Data

So far, we've spent our time describing how XSD is used to define the internal structure (schema) of a `DataSet`, and demonstrating how to use a `DataSet` created in this way to load an XML document. While it can be handy to know how to use XML-formatted data with strongly typed datasets, the reality is that most people are going to be using such datasets to store data obtained from an RDBMS such as Oracle or SQL Server.

To demonstrate the use of a strongly typed dataset in this context, you're going to create one called `CustomerOrders`. This will contain schema information for the `Customers` table and the `Orders` table in the `Northwind` sample database, as well as a relationship linking the two in a parent-child relationship.

To get started, just create a new console application called TypedDS_Northwind, renaming Module1 as NorthwindSample, and the file containing this module as NorthwindSample.vb. Right-click on the project name and choose Add ➤ Add Class, select the DataSet template, and call the new DataSet-derived class file CustomerOrders.xsd.

Once the design surface appears, you should be able to establish a connection to your Northwind database (this example uses a local instance of SQL Server 2000). With the latter visible in the Server Explorer window, click-and-drag the Customers and Orders tables onto the design surface. Then, drag a Relation item anywhere you like in the Orders table. Accept all of the defaults here and just click OK. Now you can build your solution, and if you click Show All Files, you'll see the CustomerOrders.vb file that Visual Studio .NET has generated on your behalf.

Next, enter the following code for NorthwindSample.vb, which will display all of the freight charges for the first Customer retrieved:

```
Imports System
Imports System.Data
Imports System.Data.SqlClient

Module NorthwindSample
  Sub Main()
    Dim Connection As New SqlConnection( _
       "Server=(local);Initial Catalog=Northwind;Integrated Security=SSPI;")
    Connection.Open()

    Dim CustomersDA As New SqlDataAdapter( _
                            "SELECT * FROM Customers", Connection)
    Dim OrdersDA As New SqlDataAdapter( _
                            "SELECT * FROM Orders", Connection)
    Dim CustOrders As New CustomerOrders()

    CustomersDA.Fill(CustOrders, "Customers")
    OrdersDA.Fill(CustOrders, "Orders")

    Dim FirstCustomer As CustomerOrders.CustomersRow = _
                            CustOrders.Customers(0)
    Console.WriteLine("{0}'s Freight Charges To Date:", _
                            FirstCustomer.ContactName)
    Dim Order As CustomerOrders.OrdersRow
    For Each Order In FirstCustomer.GetOrdersRows()
      Console.WriteLine("Order: Freight: {0:C}, Date: {1}", _
                   Order.Freight, Order.OrderDate.ToShortDateString())
    Next
  End Sub
End Module
```

The important thing to keep in mind about this example is foreign key relationships. When you created the Relation, you created a foreign key. This means that an Order cannot exist without a parent Customer. In other words, if you try to Fill() the Orders table before you

Fill() the Customers table, an exception will be thrown. The following is the console output of the previous program:

```
Maria Anders's Freight Charges To Date:
Order: Freight: $29.46, Date: 8/25/1997
Order: Freight: $61.02, Date: 10/3/1997
Order: Freight: $23.94, Date: 10/13/1997
Order: Freight: $69.53, Date: 1/15/1998
Order: Freight: $40.42, Date: 3/16/1998
Order: Freight: $1.21, Date: 4/9/1998
```

Filling a DataSet Object That Already Has a Schema

There's an interesting wrinkle that you need to bear in mind when you're dealing with strongly typed datasets (or indeed any DataSet object for which a schema has been preloaded). If you're filling such a DataSet with data from a source other than the one from which the schema is derived, it's possible that the schemas won't match, and the Fill() method has to take some action.

When the data adapter's Fill() method finds an existing DataSet schema, it fills those columns that are equal to the ones specified in the SELECT command. However, it could be that the data adapter retrieves more, or different, columns from the database than the ones it knows about. You can choose the action to take when a column is missing in the DataSet schema by setting the data adapter's MissingSchemaAction property. This accepts one of the MissingSchemaAction enumeration values that we tabulated in Chapter 3, when we discussed merging DataSet objects together.

Typed Dataset Performance

We've now shown you plenty of stuff demonstrating how strongly typed datasets make the jobs of creating and consuming datasets far easier. Typed datasets are easier to maintain, have strongly typed accessors, provide rigid data validation, and, because they can still be serialized, can be exposed as the return types of web service function calls.

It would be reasonable to ask, however, whether these things are any faster or slower than regular DataSets. Unfortunately, the answer is far from clear. You may already know that throwing exceptions incurs a slight overhead from the runtime, as does typecasting. All of the properties and functions in a typed dataset are wrapped in exception handling calls, and a great many are wrapped with typecasting code. This leads some people to believe that they are slightly less efficient than standard DataSets.

However, in any production application, you will be wrapping your dataset use in exception handling and typecasting code anyway, so the fact that the typed dataset does this for you should be considered an advantage, and not a performance drain.

Annotating Typed Datasets

Earlier in the chapter, during the overview of some of the commonly used features of XSD, we covered schema annotation. You saw then that annotation could take two forms: the

`<documentation>` element for human audiences, and the `<appinfo>` element. Here, you'll see another variety of (and use for) annotation that doesn't use the XSD `<annotation>` element.

As you've seen in the previous examples, when you create a strongly typed dataset using the standard techniques, the names of that DataSet class's properties, methods, relations, and constraints will be created for you. If you're going to be using a lot of typed datasets, or you plan on having them available for several other programmers or programming teams, you'll be pleased to know that you can obtain fine-grained control over the naming conventions and automated facilities of the code generator for typed dataset classes.

This is accomplished by supplying attributes from two XML namespaces provided by Microsoft: the first is the codegen namespace (defined by xmlns:codegen="urn:schemas-microsoft-com:xml-msprop") and the second is the msdata namespace (defined by xmlns:msdata="urn:schemas-microsoft-com:xml-msdata").

codegen

The codegen namespace contains a set of attributes that directly affects the code generation of a DataSet. You can apply the codegen attributes to various elements of an XSD file, providing fine-grained instructions to either xsd.exe or the VS.NET compiler on exactly how to generate the new DataSet. You'll build a sample of a Visual Studio .NET-annotated DataSet using these new attributes at the end of this section.

All of this functionality *can* be controlled by programmatically modifying the properties of the DataSet later on. However, if the functionality and control is built into the schema and the typed dataset in human-readable form, there can be no mistake about how the class creator intended it to function.

typedName

The typedName attribute indicates the name of an object, as it will appear in the new DataSet. This attribute can be applied to DataTables, DataRows, properties, and DataSet events.

typedPlural

The typedPlural attribute will indicate the name of the object when a plurality of the object is needed, as in the DataRowCollection or the DataTableCollection object.

typedParent

The typedParent attribute indicates the name of the object when it is referred to in a parent relationship. Typed datasets automatically generate accessor functions for retrieving parents and children. For example, in the previous example, the GetBookReviewsRows() function was a child accessor.

typedChildren

The typedChildren attribute indicates the name of the object when it is referred to in a child relationship. As stated previously, typed datasets generate both parent and child accessors, usually with confusing or unwieldy names. Providing the typedChildren and typedParent attributes generally makes for a much easier user experience in your typed dataset.

nullValue

The `nullValue` attribute is an incredibly useful one. It allows you to define what action will be taken in the dataset when a `DBNull` value is encountered. The following is a list of the valid values for the `nullValue` attribute:

- `"replacement"`: Rather than indicating a behavior, you can simply indicate what value your `DataSet` will store instead of `DBNull`.

- `throw`: Throws an exception any time a `DBNull` is encountered on the related element in the `DataSet`.

- `null`: Returns a null (or throws an exception if a primitive type is encountered).

- `empty`: Returns an object created from an empty constructor. For strings, it will return `String.Empty`. For any other primitive type, it will throw an exception.

msdata

The `msdata` namespace is another namespace used by Microsoft to control the behavior of a `DataSet`. It's primarily concerned with the definition, naming, and control of keys and constraints. Here are the attributes that it defines.

ConstraintName

This is the name of the constraint, as it will appear in the `DataSet`. This can apply to any kind of constraint defined in XSD, such as a `<key>` or a `<unique>` constraint.

ConstraintOnly

The default behavior of the code generator is to create a relationship whenever a foreign key constraint is found. You can override this behavior and *not* create the relationship automatically by using the `ConstraintOnly` flag. The syntax looks like the following:

```
<element msdata:ConstraintOnly="true" />
```

UpdateRule

This attribute controls the behavior of related parent-child rows when an update is made to a row. The default, if it is not supplied, is set to `Cascade`. Otherwise, it can be set to `None`, `SetDefault`, or `SetNull`, matching the settings we saw back in Chapter 3.

- `Cascade`: Cascades the update across to all related rows.

- `None`: No action will be taken on related rows.

- `SetDefault`: All of the related rows affected by the update action will be set to their default values, as indicated by their `DefaultValue` property.

- `SetNull`: All related rows will be set to `DBNull` as a result of the update action.

DeleteRule

The available values for this attribute function identically to those for the UpdateRule attribute, with the exception that they are only applied when a delete action takes place.

Relationship

Like all good rules, there's an exception to the statement we made earlier about these annotations not actually being in an <annotation> element. The <Relationship> element appears within an <appinfo> annotation element. If you wish, you can use <Relationship> to define a parent-child relationship as an alternative to using the key/keyref syntax. This is really a matter of preference, and many XSD purists prefer to use the key/keyref syntax. In any case, the syntax looks like the following:

```
<xs:annotation>
  <xs:appinfo>
    <msdata:Relationship name="KeyBookIDRef"
                         msdata:parent="Books"
                         msdata:child="BookReviews"
                         msdata:parentkey="BookID"
                         msdata:childkey="BookID" />
  </xs:appinfo>
</xs:annotation>
```

Annotated Typed Dataset Example

Now that we've covered how to annotate our DataSet in order to control how its code is generated, and to gain finer control over its behavior, constraints, and rules, let's take a look at one in action. For this example, you're going to create a Windows Forms application called TypedBindingAnnotated. Add a new class to the project and choose DataSet as the class type; name it BookDataSet.xsd. Paste the following annotated XSD into your new DataSet class XSD file:

```
<?xml version="1.0" encoding="utf-8" ?>
<xs:schema id="BookDataSet"
           targetNamespace="urn:apress-proadonet-chapter5-BookDataSet.xsd"
           elementFormDefault="qualified"
           xmlns="urn:apress-proadonet-chapter5-BookDataSet.xsd"
           xmlns:mstns="urn:apress-proadonet-chapter5-BookDataSet.xsd"
           xmlns:xs="http://www.w3.org/2001/XMLSchema"
```

The next part is new. You've already seen that Visual Studio .NET puts the msdata namespace declaration into your DataSet schemas for you, but you have to enter the following one manually in order to gain access to the codegen namespace prefix:

```
           xmlns:codegen="urn:schemas-microsoft-com:xml-msprop"
           xmlns:msdata="urn:schemas-microsoft-com:xml-msdata">
```

```
<xs:element name="BookDataSet" msdata:IsDataSet="true">
  <xs:complexType>
    <xs:choice maxOccurs="unbounded">
```

Here's a look at your first use of the codegen namespace. You're indicating that the typedName of the Books element (which matches <Books> tags in your XML instance document) is going to be called Book, and the typedPlural will be called Books.

```
      <xs:element name="Books" codegen:typedName="Book"
                              codegen:typedPlural="Books">
        <xs:complexType>
          <xs:sequence>
            <xs:element name="BookID" type="xs:integer" minOccurs="1" />
            <xs:element name="Title" type="xs:string" minOccurs="1" />
            <xs:element name="Publisher" type="xs:string" minOccurs="1" />
          </xs:sequence>
        </xs:complexType>
      </xs:element>
```

As with the <Books> tags, you're placing some logical naming conventions onto the individual items. A single row of the BookReviews table will now be considered a BookReview, rather than a "BookReviews".

```
      <xs:element name="BookReviews" codegen:typedName="BookReview"
                                   codegen:typedPlural="BookReviews">
        <xs:complexType>
          <xs:sequence>
            <xs:element name="BookID" type="xs:integer" minOccurs="0" />
            <xs:element name="Rating" type="xs:integer" minOccurs="0" />
            <xs:element name="Review" type="xs:string" minOccurs="0" />
          </xs:sequence>
        </xs:complexType>
      </xs:element>
    </xs:choice>
  </xs:complexType>

<xs:key name="KeyBookID">
  <xs:selector xpath=".//mstns:Books" />
  <xs:field xpath="mstns:BookID" />
</xs:key>
```

Finally, in the XSD file, you've got a couple of really interesting things going on. The first is that the DataGrid control you'll use shortly uses the name of the relationship to provide a visual link to the child tables. Therefore, you make sure now that this name will look good in the UI! Also, you've effectively renamed the GetBookReviewsRows() function that you saw earlier to Reviews().

```
<xs:keyref name="Reviews" refer="KeyBookID"
         codegen:typedParent="Book"
```

```
            codegen:typedChildren="Reviews">
    <xs:selector xpath=".//mstns:BookReviews" />
    <xs:field xpath="mstns:BookID" />
  </xs:keyref>
 </xs:element>
</xs:schema>
```

Next, you come to the form for the application. Rename the generated Form1 form as frmMain, and the file containing the form as frmMain.vb. Also, change the title of the form (the Text property) to Annotated Typed Dataset Binding Example. The form needs to contain two controls: a DataGrid control called dgBooks, and a button called btnSumScores with the text Sum Scores. You also need to add a private field to the form called Books, of type BookDataSet.

```
Public Class frmMain
  Inherits System.Windows.Forms.Form

  Private Books As BookDataSet
```

Now you have the constructor of the form, which you need to modify to load the XML data for the form (the Books.xml file you saw earlier, which is copied to the root directory of the application).

```
  Public Sub New()
    MyBase.New()

    ' This call is required by the Windows Form Designer.
    InitializeComponent()

    ' Add any initialization after the InitializeComponent() call
    Books = New BookDataSet()
    Books.ReadXml("../Books.xml")
    dgBooks.DataSource = Books.Books
  End Sub
```

Also, to show you how incredibly straightforward your new annotated class is, we rig up the Sum Scores button to display a message box containing the sum of all of the scores of the reviews. You could just iterate through the Reviews table, but instead you'll use the For Each syntax to demonstrate just how close the code syntax is to how you might describe the functionality out loud to another programmer.

```
  Private Sub btnSumScores_Click(ByVal sender As System.Object, _
                    ByVal e As System.EventArgs) Handles btnSumScores.Click
    Dim sum As Integer = 0
```

This is the beauty of typed datasets. Not only do you have accessors without (visibly) using array indices or collections, but also everything is named appropriately and everything is strongly typed, so if you attempt to use the wrong data type, an exception will be thrown. Iterating through a hierarchy of data has never been this easy.

```
Dim Book As BookDataSet.Book
  For Each Book In Books.Books
    Dim Review As BookDataSet.BookReview
    For Each Review In Book.Reviews()
      sum += CType(Review.Rating, Integer)
    Next
  Next

  MessageBox.Show(Me, "Score Total: " + sum.ToString())
End Sub
```

Figure 5-3 shows just how much nicer everything looks when things have been annotated and given human- (and programmer-) readable names.

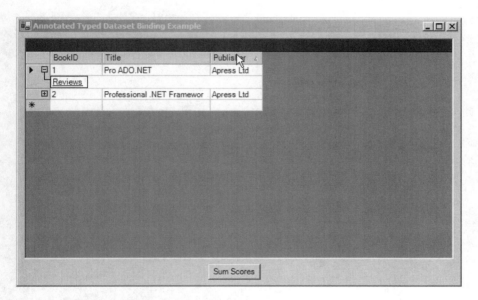

Figure 5-3. *Annotated typed dataset binding example*

Summary

In this chapter, we spent a little time giving a brief overview of the most common features of the XML Schema Definition (XSD) language. You discovered the importance of this review of XSD as you delved into the structure of the DataSet and saw how it interprets XSD to form its internal data structure of columns, tables, constraints, keys, and relations.

Once you got comfortable with how the DataSet interacts directly with XML schema information, you used such a schema to derive your own DataSet subclass that provided a strongly typed object model on top of your specific data structure.

Next, you learned how to provide additional information and instructions to the code generator, allowing us fine-grained control over the generation of the `DataSet`-derived classes. Finally, you got to bind your derived, strongly typed dataset class to a `DataGrid` control and saw how the control handled the embedded hierarchical structure of the `DataSet`.

In short, the `DataSet` is a core component of ADO.NET, and understanding its symbiotic relationship with XML schemas is essential to harnessing the true power of the `DataSet`, and creating strongly typed derivatives.

CHAPTER 6

■ ■ ■

XML and the DataSet

In one significant respect, the last chapter was not unusual: examination of many aspects of the .NET Framework reveals an inner dependence on XML or one of its related technologies. Depending on where they are, XML files can change the behavior of managed applications on the fly, override publisher policy components in the Global Assembly Cache, dictate how assemblies work, and configure ASP.NET sites. The list goes on and on.

From our point of view, the ADO.NET DataSet is particularly dependent on XML: it uses XML as its serialization format.

■**Note** Because a dataset in .NET Framework 1.1 uses XML as its default serialization format, even if you use Binaryformatter in a typical remoting setup, the impact on performance due to that is worth considering while architecting your application. For further interesting reading, please refer to Microsoft Knowledgebase article #829740.

In the previous chapter, you saw that XML schemas define the DataSet's internal data structures. As you will soon see, XML deserves as much attention when discussing .NET data access as the DataSet, or indeed any other ADO.NET component.

In this chapter, you're going to cover a range of subjects where XML and ADO.NET are complementary technologies. More specifically, you'll look at:

- How to use the XmlDocument class to create and manipulate XML documents programmatically

- How XPath expressions can be used to select parts of an XML document

- How DataSet schema inference works

- How to validate an XML document against an XML schema

- How to use the XmlDataDocument class to inspect an XML file

- The relationship between DataSets and XML documents

■Tip This chapter assumes a passing familiarity with XML and the W3C Document Object Model (DOM) specification. You might want to check out the XML specification on the W3C's Web site at `http://www.w3c.org/TR/1998/REC-xml-19980210`. Also, MSDN is full of information and samples regarding XML document manipulation.

XmlDocument (W3C DOM)

The XmlDocument class is in the System.Xml namespace of the .NET Framework class library. XmlDocument is an in-memory representation of an XML document that conforms to the W3C DOM Level 1 and Level 2 Core standards. Because of the way that DataSets hold their data, knowing how to deal with XML data in an XmlDocument can be a useful skill for an ADO.NET programmer to have.

When an XML document is loaded into an XmlDocument object, it is processed into a tree representation as a group of XmlNode objects. Each XmlNode object can have many child XmlNode objects, but only a single parent.

Before going into any more detail, you'll look at a simple example of manipulating an XML document. You will use XmlDocument and related classes to create an XML document from scratch. Then, you will save the document to disk and traverse it, displaying each of the nodes created. This will demonstrate both writing and reading with an XmlDocument object.

You'll find a console application called XmlDocumentDemo in the code download (located in the Downloads section of the Apress Web site, `http://www.apress.com`); here's the source code listing for the XmlDocumentDemo.vb file.

```
Imports System
Imports System.Xml

Module XmlDocumentDemo
  Sub Main()
    Dim FakeQuantity As Integer
    Dim Doc As New XmlDocument()
    Dim newAtt As XmlAttribute
    Dim TempNode As XmlElement

    ' Use the XmlDeclaration class to place the
    ' <?xml version="1.0"?> declaration at the top of our XML file
    Dim dec As XmlDeclaration = Doc.CreateXmlDeclaration("1.0", _
                                    Nothing, Nothing)
    Doc.AppendChild(dec)
    Dim DocRoot As XmlElement = Doc.CreateElement("Orders")
    Doc.AppendChild(DocRoot)
```

```
    ' Generate a couple of phony orders
    Dim x As Integer
    For x = 0 To 11
      Dim Order As XmlNode = Doc.CreateElement("Order")
      newAtt = Doc.CreateAttribute("Quantity")
      FakeQuantity = 10 * x + x
      newAtt.Value = FakeQuantity.ToString()
      Order.Attributes.Append(newAtt)
      DocRoot.AppendChild(Order)
    Next

    ' Saves the XML document. We can use a filename or an XmlTextWriter
    ' as the parameter.
    Doc.Save("../OutDocument.xml")
    ' This effectively wipes the document and re-loads
    ' it with the data just generated.
    Doc.Load("../OutDocument.xml")
    Console.WriteLine("Orders Loaded:")

    For x = 0 To DocRoot.ChildNodes.Count - 1
        TempNode = CType(DocRoot.ChildNodes(x), XmlElement)
        Console.WriteLine("Order Quantity: {0}", _
            TempNode.GetAttribute("Quantity"))
    Next
  End Sub
End Module
```

In the previous example, you're using XmlDocument (and some related classes) to create a new XML document and provide some feedback to users. The first thing you do after creating the actual document instance is to create an instance of an XmlDeclaration. This is the header of an XML document that defines the appropriate XML version and (optionally) some additional header information. The declaration is then appended to the existing document.

Next, you create your root node (Orders), and loop to create 12 artificial Order nodes. Once you've saved the new XML document to disk, you iterate through all of the Order nodes that you've created, displaying the values of the Quantity attribute to the console. The twin output of this application, then, is the OutDocument.xml file:

```
<?xml version="1.0"?>
<Orders>
  <Order Quantity="0" />
  <Order Quantity="11" />

  ...

  <Order Quantity="110" />
  <Order Quantity="121" />
</Orders>
```

and this in the console window:

```
Orders Loaded:
Order Quantity: 0
Order Quantity: 11


...


Order Quantity: 110
Order Quantity: 121
```

Of course, there are hundreds of different things that you can do with the various XML-related classes, and you're just scratching the surface here. In preparation for the rest of the material in this chapter, we've simply examined how to create and navigate XML documents using the W3C DOM, treating the contents of the document as nodes of a tree, and not as relational data.

XPath

Before you can move on to learn how DataSets use XML, there's one more thing that we need to cover. The *XML Path* (*XPath*) language is a non-XML language for identifying particular parts of XML documents. XPath lets you write expressions that identify particular elements in a given XML document using defined criteria (such as the relative position or the type of element). In other words, it allows you to "match and select" XML elements. For example, you could write an XPath expression that refers to the first <address> element in a document, whose content is the string "1102 Warwick Road".

■**Note** For our purposes, XPath expressions can also be called *location paths*. As you'll see, these are made up of *location steps*, which are formed by specifying an *axis*, a *node test*, and, optionally, a list of *predicates*. You form location paths by concatenating multiple location steps with forward slashes, yielding sets of nodes as a result.

XPath is used in different ways by a number of different XML technologies. XSLT uses XPath expressions to match and select particular elements for processing. XPointer uses XPath expressions to identify the particular point in (or part of) an XML document to which an XLink links, and as we saw in the last chapter, the XML Schema definition language uses XPath expressions to define uniqueness and co-occurrence constraints.

All XPath expressions have a *context*: a specific node within the document tree of the document you're searching that you can think of as a starting point. For example, if you were to ask for all of the nodes named Order from the root of a document tree, you'd get a different set of results from the one you'd get by asking for the same thing from a branch nested deep in the tree. When building your XPath expressions, you should always keep in mind the context from which the expression is being evaluated.

Table 6-1 lists some of the strings that you can place in your XPath expressions to indicate the context from which the rest of the expression should be evaluated. (You'll take a look at the structure of a full expression shortly.)

Table 6-1. *Some XPath Expressions*

String	Explanation	Example
./	A pattern that begins with ./ indicates that it should be evaluated from the current context. The current context, in this case, might be the XML node from which you are running the XPath expression.	./Order will find all child elements of the current context named <Order>.
/	A pattern that begins with a forward slash indicates that the remainder of the expression should be evaluated using the root of the document tree as the context.	/Order will find all elements named <Order> at the root of the document tree.
//	A pattern that begins with the double forward-slash indicates that the remainder of the expression should be evaluated without regard to the depth at which matching elements can be found.	//Order will find all elements named <Order> anywhere in the document tree, regardless of depth or hierarchical structure.

Forward slashes are used in forming XPath expressions in a way that's similar to how you navigate into subdirectories in UNIX or on the Web.

```
/Books/book/title
```

The forward slash in a location path indicates the *child axis*. The previous example is an XPath request for all <title> elements that are children of a <book> element that's a child of a <Books> element.

If you wish, you can mix the simple child axis steps in a location path with additional filters, as in the following example:

```
/Books/book[@Price < 21.99]/title
```

This example will return all of the <title> elements that are children of a <book> element with a Price attribute that's less than 21.99, where those <book> elements are children of a <Books> element, and that <Books> element is at the root of the document.

In fact, the two examples you've looked at so far use the abbreviated XPath syntax. More formally, the format of a location step within a location path can be represented as follows:

```
axis::node-test [predicate][predicate] ...
```

In the sections to come, you'll examine each part of this expression in detail, and then see some examples of putting the XPath expressions to use.

■**Tip** As usual, the canonical source for information on W3C standards is the W3C itself. The XPath 1.0 Recommendation is available for your perusal at http://www.w3.org/TR/xpath.

The Axis

An axis identifies a portion (sometimes called a *perspective*) of an XML document, relative to the context node. It defines a set of nodes that have a specific hierarchical relationship to the context node. The following is a list of some of the axes available to you when you're building a location step:

- `self`
- `child`
- `parent`
- `descendant[-or-self]`
- `ancestor[-or-self]`
- `attribute`
- `namespace`
- `following[-sibling]`
- `preceding[-sibling]`

Let's take a look at a couple of examples.

`child::Customer`

This indicates that the node test (`Customer`) should be performed on the `child` axis. In English, this means that the results should contain all `<Customer>` elements that are child elements of the current node.

`descendant::OrderItem`

This location step selects all descendants of the context node that match the node name `OrderItem`. Note the difference between `descendant` and `child`—the former always means an *immediate* child, but `descendant` goes deeper—a child, or a child of a child, and so on....

The Node Test

The node test can be any expression that's used to indicate the set of nodes that are to be considered valid at the current position in the location path. The node test filters the initial result subset by either name or type. You saw how you can filter by element name, so let's look now at how you can filter by type.

`child::text()`

This selects all of the child text nodes of the context node. The types available for you to filter are the types in the XPath tree model: `text`, `node`, `comment`, and `processing-instruction`.

The Predicate

To filter the results returned by a given location step still further, the use of *predicates* is required. The predicate portion of the location step is an assertion of a fact that, when evaluated within the current context node (or node set), the value is either true or false. If a node evaluates to true for all of the predicates, then it will be included in the results.

Let's look at some location steps that involve the use of predicates. The following one returns the set of child elements named <book> of the context node that has a publisher attribute equal to the value "Apress Ltd":

```
child::book[attribute::publisher = 'Apress Ltd']
```

This location step expression may look more familiar to you using the standard shorthand that most XPath processors accept, as follows:

```
book[@publisher='Apress Ltd']
```

The next expression is a bit more complicated. It uses XPath's count() function to retrieve all descendent <book> elements that have at least five chapters.

```
descendant::book[count(child::chapter) > 5]
```

This one uses the starts-with() function to retrieve all of those child <book> elements whose publisher attribute starts with "Ap".

```
child::book[starts-with(attribute::publisher, 'Ap')]
```

An Example Using XPath

XPath enables you to filter data to obtain meaningful subsets. It also provides a very fast way to access any node within an XML document. If you know a given element's XPath location, you can get at it immediately, regardless of its depth in the tree.

Here's a quick sample that illustrates how to use XPath on an XmlDocument object to obtain a relevant subset of information. This is the source code for a console application called XPDemo.

```
Imports System.Xml

Module XPathDemo
  Sub Main()
    Dim XDoc As New XmlDocument()
    XDoc.Load("../Orders.xml")

    ' The following XPath translates to: "For all those Customers whose
    ' 'Name' attribute begins with 'A', select all Order nodes beneath.
    Dim XNodes As XmlNodeList
    XNodes = XDoc.DocumentElement.SelectNodes( _
                        "//Customer[starts-with(@Name, 'A')]/Order")
```

```vbnet
' Here's the above using the XPath notation without shorthand.
' XNodes = XDoc.DocumentElement.SelectNodes( _
'             "descendant::Customer[starts-with(attribute::Name, 'A')]" & _
'                                                 "/child::Order")
Console.WriteLine("Found {0} Nodes", XNodes.Count)

Dim XNode As XmlNode
For Each XNode In XNodes
  Console.WriteLine("Customer {0} ordered {1} {2}", _
          XNode.ParentNode.Attributes.GetNamedItem("Name").Value, _
          XNode.Attributes.GetNamedItem("Quantity").Value, _
          XNode.InnerText)
Next
End Sub
End Module
```

As you can see, the listing includes both longhand and shorthand versions of the XPath expression: the // symbol indicates the descendant axis, while the @ symbol indicates the attribute axis. If you run this example against the following file (Orders.xml in the code download),

```xml
<?xml version="1.0"?>
<Orders>
  <Customer Name='Albert'>
    <Order Quantity="12">
      Roast Duck
    </Order>
    <Order Quantity="5">
      Red Wine
    </Order>
  </Customer>
  <Customer Name='John'>
    <Order Quantity="3">
      French Fries
    </Order>
    <Order Quantity="4">
      Coffee
    </Order>
  </Customer>
  <Customer Name='Stephen'>
    <Order Quantity="5">
      Milk
    </Order>
  </Customer>
  <Customer Name='Alice'>
    <Order Quantity="18">
```

```
      Frozen Pizza
    </Order>
    <Order Quantity="3">
      Potato Chips
    </Order>
  </Customer>

</Orders>
```

you get the following console output:

```
Found 4 Nodes
Customer Albert ordered 12
      Roast Duck
Customer Albert ordered 5
      Red Wine
Customer Alice ordered 18
      Frozen Pizza
Customer Alice ordered 3
      Potato Chips
```

Notice here that the whitespace surrounding the text of each of the Order nodes is completely preserved, displaying a new line and indentation—something that you won't be able to rely on later on! Essentially, however, what you've done here is to select all of the orders made by people whose names start with the letter "A". Many people feel that the hierarchical, path paradigm of XPath actually allows for more sophisticated queries than SQL does.

DataSet Schemas

Having broadened your knowledge of the .NET Framework's support for XML and related technologies, you can return to ADO.NET. In Chapter 5, you spent a good deal of time learning the relationship between XML schemas and ADO.NET DataSets. You covered everything from defining simple type restrictions on data through to foreign key relationships that established a hierarchical structure. In particular, you learned how to create strongly typed datasets using XSD files.

In this chapter, you'll see how to create data structures in a different way—you'll *infer* schemas from existing XML documents.

Schema Inference

Schema inference is a process that's performed when a DataSet object without an existing data structure attempts to load data from an XML document. The DataSet will make an initial pass through the XML document to infer the data structure, and then a second pass to load the DataSet with the information contained in the document.

There's a set of rules for inferring DataSet schemas that is always followed. Therefore, you can accurately predict what the schema inferred from a given XML document will look like.

Inference Rules

When inferring a schema from an XML document, a `DataSet` follows these rules.

- Elements with attributes become tables.

- Elements with child elements become tables.

- Repeating elements become columns in a single table.

- Attributes become columns.

- If the document (root) element has no attributes and no child elements that can be inferred to be columns, it is inferred to be a `DataSet`. Otherwise, the document element becomes a table.

- For elements inferred to be tables that have no child elements and contain text, a new column called `Tablename_Text` is created for the text of each of the elements. If an element with both child nodes and text is inferred to be a table, the text is ignored.

- For elements that are inferred to be tables nested within other elements inferred to be tables, a nested `DataRelation` is created between the two tables.

Inference Rules in Action

Let's take a look at a couple of sample XML documents and see what kind of schema the `DataSet` will infer from them. To help, you'll be using a simple program called `InferIt`, which takes two arguments: the filename of an input XML file, and the filename of an output schema.

```
> InferIt.exe Input.xml Output.xsd
```

■Tip The full source code for this utility is available in the code download for this chapter, with the XML files listed below in an XML subdirectory, and resultant schemas in an XSD directory.

`InferIt` loads the XML into a `DataSet`, which automatically infers the schema. It then uses the `DataSet` to write the schema to an XSD file. For example, consider the following XML document, Books.xml:

```
<?xml version="1.0"?>
<ApressBooks>
  <Book ISBN="1590593601" Title="Beginning C# Objects: From Concepts to Code" />
  <Book ISBN="1590591364" Title="Applied .NET Attributes" />
  <Book ISBN="1590592883" Title="Developing Application Frameworks in .NET" />
</ApressBooks>
```

If we load this into a DataSet, then the DataSet will infer that there is a single table called Book with two columns called ISBN and Title. The DataSet will set its name to ApressBooks. If we then use the DataSet to generate an XSD file using the InferIt application, we will get the following:

```
<?xml version="1.0" standalone="yes"?>
<xs:schema id="ApressBooks" xmlns=""
           xmlns:xs="http://www.w3.org/2001/XMLSchema"
           xmlns:msdata="urn:schemas-microsoft-com:xml-msdata">
  <xs:element name="ApressBooks" msdata:IsDataSet="true"
                              msdata:Locale="en-GB">
    <xs:complexType>
      <xs:choice maxOccurs="unbounded">
        <xs:element name="Book">
          <xs:complexType>
            <xs:attribute name="ISBN" type="xs:string" />
            <xs:attribute name="Title" type="xs:string" />
          </xs:complexType>
        </xs:element>
      </xs:choice>
    </xs:complexType>
  </xs:element>
</xs:schema>
```

For your second example, you're going to infer a schema from a more complex XML document. This time, you've got nesting that's three levels deep. Let's take a look at the XML file BooksComplex.xml, and see if you can figure out what the inferred structure will be before you test it with your program.

```
<?xml version="1.0"?>
<ApressBooks>
  <Book ISBN="1590593601" Title="Beginning C# Objects: From Concepts to Code" >
    <Chapter Number="1" Title="A Little Taste of C#">
      <Review Rating="5">
        One of the best introductory chapters ever written.
      </Review>
    </Chapter>
    <Chapter Number="2" Title="Abstraction and Modeling">
      <Review Rating="3">
        Good explanation of a difficult topic.
      </Review>
    </Chapter>
  </Book>
  <Book ISBN="1590591364" Title="Applied .NET Attributes">
    <Chapter Number="1" Title="Attribute Fundamentals">
      <Review Rating="3">
        I thought it was a splendid chapter.
      </Review>
```

```
  <Review Rating="5">
    Top notch intro. Two thumbs up.
  </Review>
 </Chapter>
</Book>
<Book ISBN="1590592883" Title="Application Frameworks in .NET">
 <Chapter Number="10" Title="Authorization Service">
  <Review Rating="4">
    A must read for everyone.
  </Review>
 </Chapter>
</Book>
</ApressBooks>
```

Now you've got a number of repeating elements. At the top level, you have a repeating Book element that has both attributes and child nodes. This should qualify for becoming a table. Underneath the book element, there's a Chapter element that *also* has attributes and child nodes. It, too, should qualify to become a table. Finally, beneath the Chapter elements, there is a Review element that will also become a table. With all of this nesting going on, what relationships are going to be inferred?

```
Inference Tester.
Inferred Relational Structure:
Table Book
   Book_Id
   ISBN
   Title
Table Chapter
   Chapter_Id
   Number
   Title
   Book_Id
Table Review
   Rating
   Review_Text
   Chapter_Id


Inferred Relations:
Chapter_Review
Book_Chapter
```

The inference tester indicates that it inferred three tables—Book, Chapter, and Review—just as you expected. But what's with those extra columns with underscores in their names? They weren't included in the original XML document, so where did they come from?

XSD inference is doing more work this time. As your XML file nested a couple of tables, the DataSet needed a way of relating a row from one table, to a row in another table. To do this, it created a couple of autonumbering ID columns.

From the preceding output, you can also see that two relations were created. The first, Chapter_Review, is the master-detail relationship between Chapters and Reviews. The other is the Book_Chapter relation, a master-detail relationship between Books and Chapters. Let's take a look at the XSD generated by the preceding inference.

```
<?xml version="1.0" standalone="yes"?>
<xs:schema id="ApressBooks" xmlns=""
          xmlns:xs="http://www.w3.org/2001/XMLSchema"
          xmlns:msdata="urn:schemas-microsoft-com:xml-msdata">
  <xs:element name="ApressBooks" msdata:IsDataSet="true"
                          msdata:Locale="en-GB">
    <xs:complexType>
      <xs:choice maxOccurs="unbounded">
```

After a fairly predictable beginning, the Book table's definition starts here. You'll see that the definitions in the schema are nested in the same hierarchy as the XML in the test document that we provided.

```
        <xs:element name="Book">
          <xs:complexType>
            <xs:sequence>
```

This starts the definition of the Chapter table.

```
            <xs:element name="Chapter"
                        minOccurs="0" maxOccurs="unbounded">
              <xs:complexType>
                <xs:sequence>
```

And here's the Review table.

```
                <xs:element name="Review" nillable="true"
                            minOccurs="0" maxOccurs="unbounded">
                  <xs:complexType>
                    <xs:simpleContent msdata:ColumnName="Review_Text"
                                      msdata:Ordinal="1">
                      <xs:extension base="xs:string">
                        <xs:attribute name="Rating" type="xs:string" />
                      </xs:extension>
                    </xs:simpleContent>
                  </xs:complexType>
                </xs:element>
                </xs:sequence>
```

You may have noticed that the artificially generated ID columns don't appear in this schema file.

```
                <xs:attribute name="Number" type="xs:string" />
                <xs:attribute name="Title" type="xs:string" />
              </xs:complexType>
```

```
            </xs:element>
          </xs:sequence>
          <xs:attribute name="ISBN" type="xs:string" />
          <xs:attribute name="Title" type="xs:string" />
        </xs:complexType>
      </xs:element>
    </xs:choice>
  </xs:complexType>
</xs:element>
</xs:schema>
```

Also, none of the relationships that were created appear here. This is because these relationships are created internally by the DataSet, and don't relate to the information in the XML file itself. The schema generated contains enough information for the DataSet to rebuild such relationships, and at the same time allows the schema to be used to validate the existing XML data.

Looking back at all this, you may notice that one of the limitations of schema inference is that it won't automatically detect data types for you. For instance, the Number field in the Chapter table is obviously designed to be numeric, but the inferred schema has it as type string. What this means is that unless you take action, you will gain no benefit from type checking, as every piece of data in your DataSet will be a string. If you need that facility, you'll have to modify the inferred schema in order to get it.

Supplied Schemas

Instead of allowing the DataSet to infer the schema, you can supply a schema to a DataSet object explicitly. As you saw, schema inference can only go so far before it deviates from how you'd really like the data to be organized. It can't infer data types, and it won't infer existing column relationships (instead, it will create new columns and new relationships).

In fact, there are several ways in which you can supply a schema to your DataSet objects. Obviously, you can create one yourself by creating tables and columns in a DataSet object. Alternatively, you can supply an XSD file (or an XmlSchema class) to the DataSet, or you can give the responsibility of generating the internal relational structure to a DataAdapter. Let's look at the last of those options first.

The FillSchema Method

The data adapter has a FillSchema method that executes a query on the database to fill the schema information of a table/tables into a dataset.

For an example of a situation in which this facility might be useful, imagine that you have an XML document whose data you'd eventually like to add to a SQL Server database. As a first step toward doing that, you want to load the data into an empty DataSet whose schema matches that of the database. The data in question looks like this; it's formatted for eventual insertion into the authors table of the sample pubs database that ships with SQL Server.

```
<?xml version="1.0" standalone="yes"?>
<Authors>
  <Table>
```

```
    <au_id>172-32-1176</au_id>
    <au_lname>White</au_lname>
    <au_fname>Johnson</au_fname>
    <phone>408 496-7223</phone>
  </Table>
  <Table>
    <au_id>213-46-8915</au_id>
    <au_lname>Green</au_lname>
    <au_fname>Marjorie</au_fname>
    <phone>415 986-7020</phone>
  </Table>
</Authors>
```

From here, the procedure is simply to fill a DataSet object with the schema of the authors table, and then to load the XML document with the DataSet's ReadXml() method, which you'll look at in more detail soon.

```
Imports System
Imports System.Data
Imports System.Data.SqlClient
Imports System.Xml

Module DBSchema
  Sub Main()
    ' Create the data adapter object pointing to the authors table
    Dim da As New SqlDataAdapter( _
            "SELECT au_id, au_lname, au_fname, phone FROM authors", _
            "server=localhost;database=pubs;integrated security=sspi")

    Dim ds As New DataSet("Authors")
    da.FillSchema(ds, SchemaType.Source)
    ds.ReadXml("..\SampleData.xml")

    Dim Table As DataTable = ds.Tables(0)
    Dim numCols As Integer = Table.Columns.Count

    Dim Row As DataRow
    For Each Row In Table.Rows
      Dim i As Integer
      For i = 0 To numCols - 1
        Console.WriteLine(Table.Columns(i).ColumnName & " = " & Row(i))
      Next
      Console.WriteLine()
    Next
  End Sub
End Module
```

The FillSchema() method prepares the DataSet object by adding one or more DataTables containing the columns specified in the SQL query. When the ReadXml() method is called, the DataSet looks for similar column names to fill with the data.

The ReadXmlSchema Method

As you saw briefly in the last chapter, you can supply existing schemas (typically in the form of XSD files) to a DataSet by calling its ReadXmlSchema() method. The result of this operation is that the DataSet will take on the data structure and characteristics defined by the XSD file indicated. For example, rather than inferring the data structure a second time for the samples mentioned, you could take the files that the InferIt program generated, and supply those directly to the DataSet through a call to ReadXmlSchema(). Alternatively, you could get the same XSD data by using the InferXmlSchema() method, which obtains structural information about an XML file without loading the data it contains.

Let's look at how to supply a schema from an XSD file to a DataSet, through a console application project called SuppliedSchema. This is the (fairly straightforward) code.

```
Imports System
Imports System.Data

Module SuppliedSchema
  Sub Main()
    Dim MyDS As New DataSet()
    MyDS.ReadXmlSchema("BooksComplex.xsd")

    Console.WriteLine("Supplied Relational Structure:")
    Dim Table As DataTable
    For Each Table In MyDS.Tables
      Console.WriteLine("Table {0}", Table.TableName)
      Dim Column As DataColumn
      For Each Column In Table.Columns
        Console.WriteLine("  {0}", Column.ColumnName)
      Next
    Next
  End Sub
End Module
```

Here, you load the XSD file that was generated by your second schema inference example, BooksComplex.xsd. You know enough about how the DataSet works to know that when you run this program, you'll see exactly the same relational structure as you saw when the DataSet inferred it from the XML document.

Document Validation with Schemas

In experimenting with your XML files, you may have managed to introduce enough typos to cause the DataSet to complain about improperly formed XML data. The truth is that unless the structure of an XML document meets some minimum standards that a DataSet expects, either you'll be unable to load the data into the DataSet, or the data will appear very strange.

Happily, there's a way of validating XML documents against schemas that works regardless of whether your ultimate target is a DataSet.

XmlValidatingReader

System.Xml.XmlValidatingReader is a class that provides a forward-only/read-only, fast method for traversing an XML document. In addition, it provides definitions for events to be thrown when a validation failure occurs. The XmlValidatingReader can also take a stream representing a fragment of XML to validate as an argument to its constructor, rather than requiring an entire document.

To illustrate its use, you'll create another console project: ValidatingReader. You'll also grab hold of the BooksComplex.xml and BooksComplex.xsd files from your earlier sample, and modify them so that the XML file indicates the location of its validating schema, and the XSD file properly identifies the namespace to which it applies. Here's the header of your modified XSD file.

```
<?xml version="1.0" standalone="yes"?>
<xs:schema id="ApressBooks" targetNamespace="xsdBooksComplex"
          xmlns="xsdBooksComplex"
          xmlns:xs="http://www.w3.org/2001/XMLSchema"
          xmlns:msdata="urn:schemas-microsoft-com:xml-msdata" >
```

And here's the change to the header of your XML file to point to the validating schema.

```
<?xml version="1.0"?>
<wb:ApressBooks xmlns:wb='xsdBooksComplex'
              xsi:schemaLocation='xsdBooksComplex BooksComplex.xsd'
              xmlns:xsi='http://www.w3.org/2001/XMLSchema-instance'>
```

The second of the preceding changes incorporates a couple of new pieces of information that you didn't have before. You use the xsi:schemaLocation directive to tell the XML parser the namespace of the schema, as well as the file in which the validating schema is contained. Now let's take a look at the source code for your validating reader sample (ReaderSample.vb).

```
Imports System
Imports System.IO
Imports System.Xml
Imports System.Xml.Schema

Module ReaderSample

  Sub Main()
```

After importing the namespaces you're going to be using, you open a new XmlValidating-Reader "on top of" an existing XmlTextReader.

```
    Dim xtr As New XmlTextReader("../BooksComplex.xml")
    Dim xvr As New XmlValidatingReader(xtr)

    xvr.ValidationType = ValidationType.Schema
```

Here, you've set the validating reader's ValidationType to ValidationType.Schema. The XmlValidatingReader class can handle many different types of validation, including Auto (detects validation type based on the document itself), DTD, XDR, or Schema. Next, you wire up an event handler that will be triggered if any of your element traversals encounters a validation failure.

```
AddHandler xvr.ValidationEventHandler, _
        New ValidationEventHandler(AddressOf ValidationErrorHandler)
' Traverse the entire document. If something is wrong, an event
' will be thrown and we'll display it. We don't stop traversing,
' so one error could cascade and cause dozens more after it.
While xvr.Read()
```

Here you'll display some information about the document you're traversing.

```
    If TypeOf xvr.SchemaType Is XmlSchemaComplexType Then
      Console.WriteLine("{0} - {1}", xvr.NodeType, xvr.Name)
      While xvr.MoveToNextAttribute()
        Console.WriteLine("  {0} - {1}: {2}", _
                          xvr.NodeType, xvr.Name,  xvr.Value)
      End While
    End If
  End While
End Sub


Sub ValidationErrorHandler(ByVal sender As Object, _
                          ByVal args As ValidationEventArgs)
  Console.WriteLine("XML Document Validation Failure")
  Console.WriteLine()
  Console.WriteLine("The ValidatingReader sailed with severity : {0}", _
                                              args.Severity)
  Console.WriteLine("The failure message was: {0}", args.Message)
  End Sub
End Module
```

When you first run this against your new XML file, you shouldn't encounter any problems. To see if you really *are* validating your document against the schema, you'll modify the latter so that the Number attribute of all Chapter elements must be numeric by changing the definition of the attribute to the following:

```
</xs:sequence>
<xs:attribute name="Number" type="xs:int" />
<xs:attribute name="Title" type="xs:string" />
```

Now you'll go back to your XML file and cause some damage by changing one of the chapter numbers to the string "ABC". Let's look at the final output of your program after you make that change.

```
The ValidatingReader Failed with severity : Error
The failure message was: The 'Number' attribute has an invalid value according
to its data type. An error occurred at file:///C:/Documents and Settings/Sahil
Malik/Desktop/Apress2/Malik4347/Sahil - After reviewing Chapters/Chap 06/Code/
Chapter06/ValidatingReader/BooksComplex.xml, (6, 14).
Element - Chapter
  Attribute - Number: ABC
  Attribute - Title: A Little Taste of C#
Element - Review
  Attribute - Rating: 5
```

From this, you can see the point in your traversal where the failure occurred. The message supplied with the failure is quite verbose and has lots of useful information that you can use for troubleshooting. As an exercise to work with your schema and XML skills, you might want to try doing various kinds of damage to your XML file, and see what kinds of errors you can produce in the validating reader program. The more you learn about what will violate a schema, the more you learn how to avoid violating it in the first place.

DataSets and XML Data

So far in this chapter, you've seen how to locate data within an XML document using XPath queries, and how to control the data structure of a DataSet through various means. In addition, you've seen how you can validate an XML document with an XSD file and an XmlValidatingReader object. In this next section, you'll go into more detail on how to populate a DataSet with XML data from an XML document (using the ReadXml() method that you've used once or twice already), and how to save the contents of a DataSet as XML (using the WriteXml() method).

Loading XML

There are quite a few ways in which you can populate a DataSet with XML, but the most common is probably to use one of the eight different versions of the DataSet.ReadXml() method. Here are the first four.

- ReadXml(Stream): This will load the DataSet with the XML in the stream object—that is, any object that inherits from System.IO.Stream, such as System.IO.FileStream. However, it could just as easily be a stream of data coming down from a Web site, etc.

- ReadXml(String): This will load the DataSet with the XML stored in the file whose name you provide.

- ReadXml(TextReader): This will load the DataSet with the XML processed by the given text reader—that is, any object that inherits from System.IO.TextReader.

- ReadXml(XmlReader): This will load the DataSet with the XML processed by the given XML reader. As you've seen, the XmlValidatingReader class inherits from System.Xml.XmlReader, so you can pass an XmlValidatingReader to this function.

The other four ReadXml() overloads correspond to the previous four, but with an additional parameter of type XmlReadMode. You will now look at how to use this parameter.

XmlReadMode

The System.Data.XmlReadMode enumeration is used to determine the behavior of the XML parser when loading documents from various sources. The following is a list of some members of the enumeration, and the impact they have on the DataSet and how it loads the XML:

- DiffGram: An XML representation of a "before" and "after" state for data. If you specify this argument, the DataSet will load a DiffGram and apply the changes it indicates to the DataSet.

  The input for a DiffGram operation should only come from the results of an output operation via WriteXml() on a previous DataSet state. If the schema of the source DiffGram is not the same as the schema of the target DataSet, the merge operation will fail and an exception will be thrown. We have more to say about DiffGrams later in this chapter.

- InferSchema: This option will force the DataSet to infer the schema from the XML document, ignoring any inline schema in the document, and extending any schema already in place in the DataSet.

- ReadSchema: This option will load any inline schema supplied by the DataSet and then load the data. If any schema information exists in the DataSet prior to this operation, the schema can be extended by the inline XML schema. However, if new table definitions exist in the inline schema that already exists in the DataSet, an exception will be thrown.

- Fragment: This option will read XML documents, such as those generated by FOR XML queries. In this option, the default namespace is read as the inline schema.

- Auto: This is the default. It attempts to select one of the previous options automatically. If the data being loaded is a DiffGram, then the XmlReadMode is set to DiffGram. If the DataSet has already been given a schema by some means, or the XML document has an inline schema defined, then the XmlReadMode is set to ReadSchema. If the DataSet doesn't contain a schema, there is no inline schema defined and the XML document is not a DiffGram, then the XmlReadMode is set to InferSchema.

  Depending on how much decision-making needs to take place, using the default Auto mode may perform more slowly than explicitly setting the read mode. A good rule of thumb is to supply the read mode explicitly whenever you know what it will be ahead of time.

Now that you have some information on the ReadXml() method and how to process XML when loading data, let's load some XML data into a DataSet. In the following listing, you take slightly modified Books.xsd and Books.xml files and load them both into a DataSet, thereby supplying both an XML schema and an XML document. The modifications to these files allow a new Price element.

```xml
<?xml version="1.0"?>
<ApressBooks>
 <Book ISBN="1590593601" Title="Beginning C# Objects: From Concepts to Code"
Price="33.99"/>
 <Book ISBN="1590591364" Title="Applied .NET Attributes" Price="23.79"/>
 <Book ISBN="1590592883" Title="Developing Application Frameworks in .NET"
Price="33.99"/>
</ApressBooks>
```

The schema change is as follows:

```xml
<xs:complexType>
  <xs:attribute name="ISBN" type="xs:string" />
  <xs:attribute name="Title" type="xs:string" />
  <xs:attribute name="Price" type="xs:float" />
</xs:complexType>
```

Now let's look at the code. The project is called XmlDataSet_Read, and the main module file is XmlDataReader.vb. It starts in typical fashion.

```vb
Imports System
Imports System.Data

Module XmlDataReader

  Sub Main()
```

The next section should also look familiar—you have already learned the methods used for supplying schemas to DataSets from files.

```vb
    Dim MyDS As New DataSet()
    MyDS.ReadXmlSchema("../Books.xsd")
    Console.WriteLine("Schema Loaded.")

    Dim Table As DataTable
    For Each Table In MyDS.Tables
      Console.WriteLine("Table {0}, {1} Columns", _
                        Table.TableName, Table.Columns.Count)
    Next
```

Now you load the Books.xml file into the DataSet. You use XmlReadMode.IgnoreSchema to indicate that you're using the current schema defined within the DataSet.

```vb
    MyDS.ReadXml("../Books.xml", XmlReadMode.IgnoreSchema)
    Console.WriteLine("Data Loaded.")
    Console.WriteLine()
    Dim Book As DataRow
    For Each Book In MyDS.Tables("Book").Rows
      Console.WriteLine("{0} : {1} - ${2}", _
                        Book("ISBN"), Book("Title"), Book("Price"))
```

```
      Next
   End Sub
End Module
```

Running the program will write the following to the console:

```
Schema Loaded.
Table Book, 3 Columns
Data Loaded.

1590593601 : Beginning C# Objects: From Concepts to Code - $33.99
1590591364 : Applied .NET Attributes - $23.79
1590592883 : Developing Application Frameworks in .NET - $33.99
```

Writing XML

It's just as easy to write XML from a DataSet as it is to read XML into it. Predictably, you can write XML to streams, XML writers, text writers, and files.

For this example, you're going to take the same XML and XSD files and use them to add a new row to the DataSet programmatically. You will then write an XML document containing the new DataSet. You will also write an XML document containing a DiffGram that indicates only the changes to the DataSet since you loaded it.

As usual, you create a new console project, this time called XmlDataSet_Write. We'll call the main module file DataSetWriter.vb.

```
Imports System
Imports System.Data

Module DataSetWriter
  Sub Main()
    Dim MyDS As New DataSet()
    MyDS.ReadXmlSchema("../Books.xsd")
    MyDS.ReadXml("../Books.xml")

    ' If we don't call AcceptChanges(), the DataSet thinks
    ' that _all_ data read from disk is "new". We only want
    ' the row that we add programmatically to appear as "new".
    MyDS.AcceptChanges()

    Console.WriteLine("Data loaded from disk.")
```

Here, you have loaded some information that conforms to your schema into your DataSet. Next, you'll append a new row to the Book table. Finally, you'll write the information back to disk, both as a DiffGram (XML change description) and as a complete XML document.

```
    Dim NewBook As DataRow = MyDS.Tables("Book").NewRow()
    NewBook("ISBN") = "1590594347"
```

```
    NewBook("Title") = "This ADO.NET Book"
    NewBook("Price") = 49.99
    MyDS.Tables("Book").Rows.Add(NewBook)

    ' With the new row added, the DataSet is storing
    ' "change" data. We can store this change as a DiffGram.
    MyDS.WriteXml("../Books_Changes.xml", XmlWriteMode.DiffGram)

    ' Now commit the changes and write the entire DataSet.
    MyDS.AcceptChanges()
    MyDS.WriteXml("../Books_New.xml", XmlWriteMode.IgnoreSchema)

    Console.WriteLine("Changes and entire DS have been written.")
  End Sub
End Module
```

The DiffGram resulting from the previous operation (Books_Changes.xml) looks like this.

```xml
<?xml version="1.0" standalone="yes"?>
<diffgr:diffgram xmlns:msdata="urn:schemas-microsoft-com:xml-msdata"
xmlns:diffgr="urn:schemas-microsoft-com:xml-diffgram-v1">
  <ApressBooks>
    <Book diffgr:id="Book1" msdata:rowOrder="0" ISBN="1590593601"
Title="Beginning C# Objects: From Concepts to Code" Price="33.99" />
    <Book diffgr:id="Book2" msdata:rowOrder="1" ISBN="1590591364"
Title="Applied .NET Attributes" Price="23.79" />
    <Book diffgr:id="Book3" msdata:rowOrder="2" ISBN="1590592883"
Title="Developing Application Frameworks in .NET" Price="33.99" />
    <Book diffgr:id="Book4" msdata:rowOrder="3" diffgr:hasChanges="inserted"
ISBN="1590594347" Title="This ADO.NET Book" Price="49.99" />
  </ApressBooks>
</diffgr:diffgram>
```

The final XML document, resulting from loading the three books and the programmatic addition of a fourth, looks like this.

```xml
<?xml version="1.0" standalone="yes"?>
<ApressBooks>
  <Book ISBN="1590593601" Title="Beginning C# Objects: From Concepts to Code"
Price="33.99" />
  <Book ISBN="1590591364" Title="Applied .NET Attributes" Price="23.79" />
  <Book ISBN="1590592883" Title="Developing Application Frameworks in .NET"
Price="33.99" />
  <Book ISBN="1590594347" Title="This ADO.NET Book" Price="49.99" />
</ApressBooks>
```

Fidelity Loss and DataSet Schemas

In the previous example, you read data from an XML document, and then wrote data back out again. Everything was fine and you didn't have any trouble. This will not always be the case. The DataSet is very strict about the rules it follows when reading and writing XML.

When a DataSet already has a schema—that is, it's not inferring a schema from the document—it will *only* load data defined by the schema. For example, the DataSet would ignore any XML attributes on a Book that were not defined in the DataSet's schema. Similarly, if you were to change the DataSet and then save to XML, the saved XML wouldn't contain the attributes that were not in the schema. In addition, characters, formatting, and whitespace that might be desired or meaningful in the original document will cease to exist in the DataSet-generated document.

The following example demonstrates this: You'll add a string attribute called Category to the <Book> elements in your XML document without making a change to the XSD file. You'll also throw in some additional formatting and whitespace. In a moment, you'll take a look at the XML document before and after running the following program (from the FidelityLoss project) against it, to see how it destroys the fidelity of your original:

```
Imports System
Imports System.Data

Module FidelityTester
  Sub Main()
    Dim MyDS As New DataSet()

    ' Load the schema (inferring it won't demonstrate fidelity loss)
    MyDS.ReadXmlSchema("../Books.xsd")
    ' Load the original document data
    MyDS.ReadXml("../Books.xml")

    ' We're doing nothing to the data apart from writing it out
    ' to a new XML file so that we can compare before and after
    MyDS.WriteXml("../Books_After.xml")
  End Sub
End Module
```

You're just loading an XML document and then saving it back to disk. You might expect, therefore, that the saved XML document will be no different from the original one. It doesn't work that way, though. Let's take a look at the source XML file.

```
<?xml version="1.0"?>
<ApressBooks>
 <Book ISBN="1590593601" Title="Beginning C# Objects: From Concepts to Code"
Price="33.99" Category="C#"/>
 <Book ISBN="1590591364" Title="Applied .NET Attributes" Price="23.79"
Category=".NET"/>
 <Book ISBN="1590592883" Title="Developing Application Frameworks in .NET"
Price="33.99"  Category=".NET"/>
</ApressBooks>
```

On loading this document, the DataSet removes the nonstandard whitespace, and doesn't read the Category, because the schema you supplied does not define them. Here's what the XML file looks like after being run through the DataSet.

```
<?xml version="1.0" standalone="yes"?>
<ApressBooks>
  <Book ISBN="1590593601" Title="Beginning C# Objects: From Concepts to Code"
Price="33.99" />
  <Book ISBN="1590591364" Title="Applied .NET Attributes" Price="23.79" />
  <Book ISBN="1590592883" Title="Developing Application Frameworks in .NET"
Price="33.99" />
</ApressBooks>
```

Of course, your real problem here isn't the DataSet itself. The trouble is that you're trying to enforce a relational view (the DataSet) on a hierarchical XML document. If you want to guarantee that the XML document will maintain the same structure that it had when you opened it, you need to insert a layer between the actual XML document and your view of it. As you'll see, this is accomplished using the .NET Framework's XmlDataDocument class.

The DataSet and the XmlDataDocument

What do you do if you want to have a relational view of XML data, but you don't want to destroy "extraneous" data? For example, what do you do if you have an XML document containing Orders and Customers, and you want a DataSet to manipulate only the Orders? If you used a schema detailing the Orders to load this XML document, the first change you committed to disk would completely wipe out the Customer information, because the DataSet won't read or write anything that isn't defined by its schema.

The answer to all of these questions is to use the System.Xml.XmlDataDocument class, which allows structured XML data to be stored, retrieved, and manipulated through a DataSet. More importantly, the XmlDataDocument preserves the fidelity of the XML document being used to populate the associated DataSet. The XmlDataDocument and the DataSet are synchronized so that when a change is made to one object, the other object is informed of the change.

Relational Projection of an XML Document via XSD

In this arrangement, the DataSet acts like a kind of flashlight, "illuminating" a specific part of an XmlDataDocument. The illuminated region is described by the XML schema on which the DataSet is based. To demonstrate this "projection" of relational data, you'll take as your example an XML file containing information about the students at a college. Here's the first record; you'll find the rest in Students.xml, in the code download.

```
<?xml version="1.0" encoding="utf-8" ?>
<Students>
  <Student ID="1">
    <Name>John Doe</Name>
    <Age>18</Age>
    <GPA>3.95</GPA>
    <LockerCombination>10-12-35</LockerCombination>
```

```
    <Class Title="Biology" Room="100" />
    <Class Title="English Lit" Room="101" />
  </Student>
```

...

Now, let's say that one of the intended users of this information is someone you don't think should have access to the students' locker combinations. To "hide" this information from a DataSet *without* the risk of clearing it from the source XML document, you start by creating an XML schema, StudentClasses.xsd, that doesn't include element definitions for the sensitive data, like so.

```
<?xml version="1.0" standalone="yes"?>
<xs:schema id="Students" xmlns=""
                         xmlns:xs="http://www.w3.org/2001/XMLSchema"
                         xmlns:msdata="urn:schemas-microsoft-com:xml-msdata">
  <xs:element name="Students" msdata:IsDataSet="true">
    <xs:complexType>
      <xs:choice maxOccurs="unbounded">
        <xs:element name="Student">
          <xs:complexType>
            <xs:sequence>
              <xs:element name="Name" type="xs:string"
                          minOccurs="0" msdata:Ordinal="0" />
              <xs:element name="GPA" type="xs:float"
                          minOccurs="0" msdata:Ordinal="2" />
              <xs:element name="Class"
                          minOccurs="0" maxOccurs="unbounded">
                <xs:complexType>
                  <xs:attribute name="Title" type="xs:string" />
                  <xs:attribute name="Room" type="xs:string" />
                  <xs:attribute name="StudentID" type="xs:int"
                                use="prohibited" />
                </xs:complexType>
              </xs:element>
            </xs:sequence>
            <xs:attribute name="ID" type="xs:int" />
          </xs:complexType>
        </xs:element>
      </xs:choice>
    </xs:complexType>
    <xs:unique name="StudentID" msdata:PrimaryKey="true">
      <xs:selector xpath=".//Student" />
      <xs:field xpath="@ID" />
    </xs:unique>
    <xs:keyref name="StudentClasses" refer="StudentID"
               msdata:IsNested="true">
```

```
    <xs:selector xpath=".//Class" />
    <xs:field xpath="@StudentID" />
  </xs:keyref>
 </xs:element>
</xs:schema>
```

As you can see, there's no reference to either Age or LockerCombination, effectively protecting that information from the DataSet. The following example now attempts to display that data through the use of an XmlDataDocument. The commented code tries to access an element that's not included in the schema through a DataSet; removing the comment mark will throw an exception. Here's the code, which you'll find in the XmlDataDocument1 project.

```
Imports System
Imports System.Xml
Imports System.Data

Module DataDocumentSample
  Sub Main()
    Dim DSStudentClasses As New DataSet()
    Dim tmpNode As XmlNode

    ' Load the schema into the DataSet
    DSStudentClasses.ReadXmlSchema("../StudentClasses.xsd")
    ' Load the DataSet into the data document
    Dim XDocStudents As New XmlDataDocument(DSStudentClasses)

    ' Load the data into the data document
    XDocStudents.Load("../Students.xml")

    Console.WriteLine("Students in DataSet:")
    Dim Row As DataRow
    For Each Row In DSStudentClasses.Tables("Student").Rows

      ' If we try to access the locker combination or age, we'll
      ' throw an exception!
      Console.WriteLine("{0}:{1}", Row("Name"), Row("GPA"))
      tmpNode = XDocStudents.GetElementFromRow(Row)
      Console.WriteLine( _
          "    Locker Combination (from XML, not DataSet): {0}", _
          tmpNode.SelectSingleNode("LockerCombination").InnerText)

      ' De-comment the following lines to generate an exception
      ' Console.WriteLine( _
      '       "    Locker Combination (from DataSet): {0}", _
      '       Row("LockerCombination"))
```

```
      Dim Subject As DataRow
      For Each Subject In Row.GetChildRows("StudentClasses")
        Console.WriteLine("    {0}", Subject("Title"))
      Next
    Next
  End Sub
End Module
```

The following lines, reproduced from the previous code, show how you can access data that isn't in the schema through the XmlDataDocument:

```
      tmpNode = XDocStudents.GetElementFromRow(Row)
      Console.WriteLine( _
          "    Locker Combination (from XML, not DataSet): {0}", _
          tmpNode.SelectSingleNode("LockerCombination").InnerText)
```

The first line here returns the XmlNode that corresponds to a DataRow in a table of the associated DataSet. You can use this node to access elements and attributes that are not included in the schema. Doing this has a downside, though: you need to know the exact hierarchical structure of the XML document ahead of time. A benefit of the DataSet is that you always deal with columns, rows, and tables. You don't need to know whether a given column came from an element or an attribute in the original document.

The application's output looks like this.

```
Students in DataSet:
John Doe:3.95
    Locker Combination (from XML, not DataSet): 10-12-35
    Biology
    English Lit
Albert Morris:4
    Locker Combination (from XML, not DataSet): 5-17-15
    Computer Science
    .NET Basics
    Moral Values and Ethics in Classic Cartoons
Rupert Howard:1.5
    Locker Combination (from XML, not DataSet): 35-12-20
    Biology
Esteban Colon:3.75
    Locker Combination (from XML, not DataSet): 20-14-7
    Biology
    .NET Basics
Julia Jones:2.86
    Locker Combination (from XML, not DataSet): 10-34-8
    Influence of Porky Pig on Modern Language
    An exploration of Hubris and Daffy Duck
    Biology
Kelly Norton:3.01
    Locker Combination (from XML, not DataSet): 15-13-24
```

```
   Computer Science
   .NET Basics
   Moral Values and Ethics in Classic Cartoons
Boy Genius:4.01
   Locker Combination (from XML, not DataSet): 1-2-3
   Intro to Scooby Doo Mystery Solving
```

If you de-comment the line that attempts to access the locker combination directly from the DataSet, however, you get the following rather different output:

```
Students in DataSet:
John Doe:3.95
   Locker Combination (from XML, not DataSet): 10-12-35

Unhandled Exception: System.ArgumentException: Column 'LockerCombination'
does not belong to table Student.
   at System.Data.DataRow.get_Item(String columnName)
   at XmlDataDocument1.DataDocumentSample.Main(String[] args) in
c:\apress\chapter 6\xmldatadocument1\datadocumentsample.cs:line 32
```

Relational Projection of a Typed DataSet

You've just been looking at how to use the XmlDataDocument's ability to synchronize and project XML to a standard DataSet with a supplied schema. In the previous chapter, you learned about strongly typed datasets, and as you're about to see, they can be every bit as useful now as they were then.

For your second example with XmlDataDocument, you will use the same data and the same XSD file to generate a console project that uses a *typed* DataSet called Students, generated from your StudentClasses.xsd file. Here's the source code for the DataDocumentSample.vb module file, from the project called XmlDataDocument2.

```vb
Imports System
Imports System.Xml
Imports System.Data

Module DataDocumentSample
  Sub Main()
    Dim StudentClasses As New Students()
    Dim XDocStudents As New XmlDataDocument(StudentClasses)
    XDocStudents.Load("../Students.xml")

    Console.WriteLine("Students in Typed DataSet:")
    Dim Student As Students.StudentRow
    For Each Student In StudentClasses.Student.Rows
      Console.WriteLine("{0}:{1}", Student.Name, Student.GPA)
      Dim Subject As Students._ClassRow
      For Each Subject In Student.GetClassRows()
        Console.WriteLine("   {0} in Room {1}", Subject.Title, Subject.Room)
```

```
    Next
  Next

  Console.WriteLine()
  Console.WriteLine("Students who have classes in Room 100:")
  Console.WriteLine("------------------------------------")
  Dim tmpNodes As XmlNodeList = _
          XDocStudents.SelectNodes("//Student/Class[@Room='100']")
  Dim i As Integer
  For i = 0 To tmpNodes.Count - 1
    Console.WriteLine("{0}", _
          tmpNodes(i).ParentNode.SelectSingleNode("Name").InnerText)
  Next
 End Sub
End Module
```

The following lines, reproduced from the previous code, use XPath to select specific nodes from the XmlDataDocument:

```
Dim tmpNodes As XmlNodeList = _
        XDocStudents.SelectNodes("//Student/Class[@Room='100']")
Dim i As Integer
For i = 0 To tmpNodes.Count - 1
  Console.WriteLine("{0}", _
        tmpNodes(i).ParentNode.SelectSingleNode("Name").InnerText)
Next
```

The nodes you select here are the Class nodes that are children of Student nodes, and have the Room attribute set to 100. (You are requesting all students who have classes in Room 100.) Except for displaying the two students who have classes in Room 100, the console output of this example is identical to that of the previous one.

Summary

This chapter has covered many of the things that you can do as a result of the synergy between DataSets and XML. You've seen how XML and the DataSet are interrelated, and how applications can benefit from using XML, DataSets, or both, depending on the context. It should be apparent that there are many tasks that can be simplified or automated by using these techniques, and you should now have enough information to decide if any of these techniques are right for you.

As we stated at the beginning, XML is fundamental to all aspects of the .NET Framework, and as you continue through this book you'll find XML and related technologies cropping up with some frequency. Following the work you've done in this chapter and its predecessors, though, none of it should be a problem.

■ ■ ■

CHAPTER 7

Constraints, Relations, and Views

You have seen in previous chapters that `DataSets` enable you to work with data while disconnected from the data source. You have seen the advantages of disconnected data access, particularly in multiuser and Internet systems. In this chapter, you will extend this knowledge by looking at three ADO.NET features in detail: constraints, relations, and views.

You'll start by looking at *constraints*, which force data to obey certain rules. Usually, these rules are derived from business rules. For example, you might have a rule that each account needs a unique account number. If data breaks this rule, the database will quickly cease to be very useful. You can use a constraint called a `UniqueConstraint` to ensure that this doesn't happen. You will also look at using a `ForeignKeyConstraint` to ensure that the relations between tables are not violated, and at creating your own custom constraints to ensure, for example, that string values obey certain formatting rules.

Next, you will look at *relations*. Relations represent the way tables within a `DataSet` link together. If you had a table of store information for your business, and a table of regions, the store table would have a region ID to identify the region that the store is in—a *foreign key*. The ADO.NET `DataRelation` object would make it easy to navigate between the store table and the regions table.

In the past, application developers have relied on the database server to do this kind of work. However, datasets encourage you to work with data without being connected to the database server. Using ADO.NET's features means that you can detect problems as they happen, rather than waiting until you try to update the data source.

The final object that you'll look at is designed specifically for letting users view or edit data in a controlled way. The `DataView` allows users to present a customized representation of a `DataTable`, perhaps only showing a subset of the records, for example. Users can edit a `DataView` and the changes will be made to the underlying table. `DataViews` are particularly useful because you can also control what editing operations are allowed—perhaps you can allow users to edit existing records but not add new ones, or vice versa.

Constraints

As you began to see in Chapter 3, constraints place restrictions on the data that's allowed to appear in a data column (or a set of data columns). In SQL Server, for example, a constraint might be created to ensure that a value for a column (or a set of columns) is not repeated within a table. If data is entered that does not meet this constraint, an exception is thrown. ADO.NET provides this functionality to client-side code.

Constraints in ADO.NET work primarily with `DataTables` and `DataColumns` to enforce data integrity. Of the two constraint classes in the `System.Data` namespace, `UniqueConstraint` ensures that a given column (or set of columns) contains a unique value in each row, while `ForeignKeyConstraint` constrains values in two different tables, providing for cascading updates, and deletions of related values. We'll look at each of these in more detail in the sections that follow.

ADO.NET constraints are enforced any time that data is edited or added to a data table. Specifically, the following methods initiate a check of constraints:

- `DataSet.Merge()`

- `DataTable.LoadDataRow()`

- `DataRowCollection.Add()`

- `DataRow.EndEdit()`

- `DataRow.ItemArray()`

Before we get further into the details, there are several general points to note about constraints. First, constraints are only enforced when the `EnforceConstraints` property of the `DataSet` is set to `True`. This is the default value of this property, so it should not need to be modified. However, if a method is receiving a `DataSet` as a parameter, it should ensure that the `EnforceConstraints` property is set to `True` if its code relies on constraints.

Second, if the `EnforceConstraints` property is set to `False` and changes are made to the data that would violate the constraint, and then the `EnforceConstraints` property is set to `True`, an attempt will be made to enable all of the constraints for the table. Those values that violate the constraint will cause an exception to be raised.

Third, when merging datasets, constraints are applied after *all* of the data has been merged, rather than as each item is being merged. This makes the merge process faster, as the entire set of new data can be merged without each row of data being checked.

There are two primary exception classes to be concerned with when you're working with constraints: `ConstraintException` and `InvalidConstraintException`. If a constraint is violated at the time it's checked, a `ConstraintException` will be thrown. You can catch these exceptions in order to instruct the users how they should change their input to meet the constraints. Keep in mind that exceptions should only be used for exceptional circumstances—if you think there's a good chance that a constraint will be violated, you should try to check the values first.

If the values in a data table do not meet the criteria for the constraint at the time the constraint is created, an `InvalidConstraintException` will be thrown. For example, trying to create a `UniqueConstraint` on a `DataColumn` that does not contain unique values will throw an `InvalidConstraintException`. This exception can also occur when setting the `EnforceConstraints` property to `True`. When loading data into a dataset, you don't know if the values will meet the local constraints, so it's important to catch this exception to ensure that the constraint can be applied.

Unique Constraints

As previously mentioned, the UniqueConstraint class provides a mechanism for constraining the data in a column or columns to be unique values. This can be helpful if the column in question is a key value, or if you have a requirement that this value should be unique. Keep in mind that, while any values must be unique, several rows can have null values (if you allow null values). Essentially, this constraint keeps the values, when set, from duplicating each other.

If you want to ensure that the values in your column are both unique *and* non-null, then you have two options. The first option is to set up that column as the primary key for the data table. If a primary key already exists, or if the column (or columns) to be constrained do not compose a primary key, then the second option is to apply a unique constraint and be sure to set the AllowDBNull property of the column to False.

Let's take a look at an example of a UniqueConstraint in action. The following code creates a unique constraint on the Customers table to ensure that the customer phone number is unique:

```
Dim connectionString As String = "server=(local);database=Northwind;uid=sa;pwd=;"
Dim nwindConnection As New SqlConnection(connectionString)
Dim nwindAdapter As New SqlDataAdapter("SELECT * FROM Customers;" & _
        "SELECT * FROM Orders;SELECT * FROM [order details]", nwindConnection)

Dim nwindDataSet As New DataSet()

' Fill the dataset, getting key values
nwindAdapter.MissingSchemaAction = MissingSchemaAction.AddWithKey
nwindAdapter.Fill(nwindDataSet)

' Name all of the tables appropriately
nwindDataSet.Tables(0).TableName = "Customers"
nwindDataSet.Tables(1).TableName = "Orders"
nwindDataSet.Tables(2).TableName = "OrderDetails"

' Create the unique constraint, passing in the columns to constrain
Dim constrainedColumn As DataColumn = _
                        nwindDataSet.Tables("Customers").Columns("Phone")
Dim uniqueContact = New UniqueConstraint(constrainedColumn)

' Add the constraint to the Constraints collection of the table
nwindDataSet.Tables("Customers").Constraints.Add(uniqueContact)
```

First, you load some data from the Northwind database and name the tables to match the table names in the database. You then create a new instance of the UniqueConstraint class, passing in the Phone column of the Customers table. Note that just creating the constraint is not enough—you also need to add it to the collection of constraints for the table. Only after you add it to the collection does the constraint become active.

An alternative way of adding a unique constraint to a column is simply to set its Unique property to True, as a result a UniqueConstraint is created for you automatically. This is what happens in the following listing, where you also modify the Phone column so that it will not allow nulls:

```
' Name all of the tables appropriately
nwindDataSet.Tables(0).TableName = "Customers"
nwindDataSet.Tables(1).TableName = "Orders"
nwindDataSet.Tables(2).TableName = "OrderDetails"

' Create the unique constraint by using the Unique property
nwindDataSet.Tables("Customers").Columns("Phone").Unique = True

' Do not allow null values in the phone column
nwindDataSet.Tables("Customers").Columns("Phone").AllowDBNull = False
```

Finally, you can create a unique constraint that involves more than one column. This comes in handy when you need the combination of two or more columns to be unique. For example, you might need to constrain a table of order details by having a unique combination of the product ID and the order ID. This allows the detail records to be uniquely identified for a given order and product. The only change when creating a constraint with multiple columns is that you pass an array of columns rather than a single column to the constructor.

```
Dim Columns As DataColumn()
Columns = New DataColumn(1) _
                {nwindDataSet.Tables("orderdetails").Columns("OrderID"), _
                 nwindDataSet.Tables("orderdetails").Columns("ProductID")}
Dim multiUniqueConstraint As New UniqueConstraint(Columns)
```

The unique constraint is extremely helpful in managing client-side data, and in maintaining integrity between the data on the client and the data on the server.

Foreign Key Constraints

When working with relational data, one of the ways in which data is constrained is by defining relationships between tables and creating a ForeignKeyConstraint. This constraint ensures that items in one table have a matching item in the related table. For example, if you have an Orders table that is related to a Customers table, it is important that an order does not exist without a customer. The diagram in Figure 7-1 shows what this might look like.

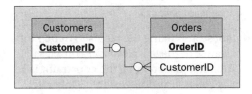

Figure 7-1. ForeignKeyConstraint—*single column*

A given order is connected to a customer by the CustomerID field. If you put a foreign key constraint on this relationship, then an order cannot be inserted or updated unless it has a valid customer ID. In this situation, the Customers table is considered to be the parent table, while the Orders table is the child. The parent table has to have a valid CustomerID for every record, so the Customers table can have CustomerID values that do not appear in the Orders table. However, a row in the parent table that is referenced from the child table cannot be deleted without the child row also being deleted. In your example, this prevents you from removing customers who have orders, which would then leave an order without customer information.

In order to use a ForeignKeyConstraint in a DataSet, you specify the column or columns from the respective DataTable objects that will be constrained. The following example loads a DataSet with data from the Northwind database's Customers and Orders tables, and creates a ForeignKeyConstraint on those tables. This constraint is then added to the Constraints collection of the child table.

```
' Name all of the tables appropriately
nwindDataSet.Tables(0).TableName = "Customers"
nwindDataSet.Tables(1).TableName = "Orders"
nwindDataSet.Tables(2).TableName = "OrderDetails"

Dim Parent As DataColumn = nwindDataSet.Tables("Customers").Columns("CustomerID")
Dim Child As DataColumn = nwindDataSet.Tables("Orders").Columns("CustomerID")
Dim customerIDConstraint As New ForeignKeyConstraint(Parent, Child)

' Add the constraint to the child table
nwindDataSet.Tables("Orders").Constraints.Add(customerIDConstraint)
```

The process of creating a ForeignKeyConstraint is rather like that for a UniqueConstraint, except that you pass in *two* DataColumn objects, the first representing the column in the parent table, and the second representing the related column in the child table. Once you have created this constraint, you add it to the *child* table's collection of constraints. It might seem odd that you add the foreign key constraint to the child and not the parent, but let's take a look at what actually happens under the covers when you do so.

First of all, when you look at a ForeignKeyConstraint, you're really trying to ensure that the child data can be related to the parent data. In the light of this alone, it begins to make more sense that the child table should contain the constraint: it is when the rows in the child table are changed that you need to be concerned about the integrity of your data. As we mentioned before, the parent table might have rows that have no corresponding data in the child table, and this is acceptable. However, it is not acceptable for the child table to have rows that do not have a companion in the parent table.

Another important aspect to consider is what happens to the parent table when the foreign key constraint is added to the child table. The parent table also gets a UniqueConstraint added to its constraint collection. This ensures that the parent table has unique values for the column that relates to the child table. If this were not the case, then there would be no way to know which row of the parent table a row in the child table was related to. This is similar to the role that the primary key plays in many relational database systems. If the column has already been identified as the primary key of the DataTable, it will already have a UniqueConstraint applied.

In addition to being able to constrain relations based on a single column in each DataTable, the ForeignKeyConstraint can be applied to a range of columns. This is useful when the key for a table is a multicolumn key. Although it's not the way things work in the Northwind database, you might have an OrderDetails table that relates to the Orders table by way of such a key. Figure 7-2 shows this relationship.

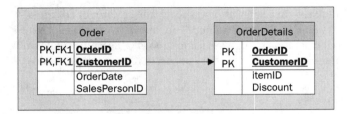

Figure 7-2. ForeignKeyConstraint—*multiple columns*

Assuming that such a relationship exists, the following example creates a ForeignKey-Constraint on the Orders and OrderDetails tables using a multicolumn key:

```
Dim Parents As DataColumn() = New DataColumn() _
                {nwindDataSet.Tables("Orders").Columns("OrderID"), _
                 nwindDataSet.Tables("Orders").Columns("CustomerID")}
Dim Children As DataColumn() = New DataColumn() _
                {nwindDataSet.Tables("OrderDetails").Columns("OrderID"), _
                 nwindDataSet.Tables("OrderDetails").Columns("CustomerID")}

Dim multiConstraint As ForeignKeyConstraint = _
                New ForeignKeyConstraint(Parents, Children)

nwindDataSet.Tables("OrderDetails").Constraints.Add(multiConstraint)
```

When you create this constraint, the OrderDetails table gets the ForeignKeyConstraint placed on the OrderID and CustomerID columns, while the Orders table gets a UniqueConstraint created on *its* OrderID and CustomerID columns. Notice, once again, that you add the constraint to the Constraints collection of the child table and not the parent. Attempting to assign the constraint to the parent table would generate an exception.

Referential Integrity

A concept that goes along with foreign key constraints is *referential integrity*, which we talked about in a couple of places previously without being specific. The kinds of thing we're talking about here are mechanisms, such as cascading deletes, which ensure that in your scenario of Customers and Orders, if a customer record is deleted, any related rows in the Orders table are also deleted automatically.

In ADO.NET, you use the AcceptRejectRule enumeration to identify the actions to be taken when the DataTable, DataSet, or DataRow objects' AcceptChanges() or RejectChanges() methods are called. Similarly, you use the Rule enumeration to identify the actions to be taken on related rows when a value in a column is updated or deleted.

Because the AcceptRejectRule is applied when the AcceptChanges() or RejectChanges() methods are called, it will *not* be put into effect during the editing process. Rather, it will only get applied when the changes made to the DataSet are either accepted or rejected, based on the values that would result from this action. There are two possible values for the AcceptRejectRule property, as defined in the AcceptRejectRule enumeration in Table 7-1.

Table 7-1. AcceptRejectRule *Enumeration*

Value	Description
Cascade	The change made in the parent table is cascaded to all related rows in the child table.
None	No action is taken on the related rows. An exception will result if there is a violation of the constraint.

Using the Cascade option, if the parent row is deleted, then the child rows are deleted as well. Also, if the column that's acting as part of the foreign key constraint in the parent table were to be updated, the change would be cascaded to the related rows in the child table, changing their key values to match the new value in the parent. When the None option is selected, none of these changes propagate to the child rows. Here's how you set things up.

```
Dim Parent As DataColumn = nwindDataSet.Tables("Customers").Columns("CustomerID")
Dim Child As DataColumn = nwindDataSet.Tables("Orders").Columns("CustomerID")
Dim customerIDConstraint As New ForeignKeyConstraint(Parent, Child)

' Indicate that on accept or reject, changes should cascade to related child rows
customerIDConstraint.AcceptRejectRule = AcceptRejectRule.Cascade

' Add the constraint to the child table
nwindDataSet.Tables("Orders").Constraints.Add(customerIDConstraint)
```

In addition to acting on changes when they're *applied* to a DataTable, you can create rules to indicate what actions should be taken on child rows when a value in the parent table is actually *changed*. It's a question of deciding whether you want to enforce the rules row-by-row, or all the rows at once. For the former, you use the UpdateRule and DeleteRule properties of the ForeignKeyConstraint to identify the action to be taken on the child rows, using an item in the Rule enumeration (an abbreviated version of Table 7-2 appeared in Chapter 3).

Table 7-2. *The* Rule *Enumeration*

Value	Description
Cascade	The change made to the parent table is cascaded to all related rows in the child table. For rows that are deleted in the parent, the related rows in the child are also deleted. For rows where the key value is updated, the related rows in the child table are updated with the new value for the key. This is the default setting for both the UpdateRule and the DeleteRule property.
SetNull	The related rows will have their key value set to DBnull. This will generate an exception if the data column does not allow null values.
SetDefault	The related rows will have their key value set to the default value for the column. If no default value has been specified, the child rows will be set to DBnull.
None	No action is taken on the related rows. An exception will result if there is a violation of the constraint and this value has been chosen for DeleteRule or UpdateRule.

The ability to indicate that child rows should have their key values set to null, or to the default value for the column, provides greater flexibility than just cascading or doing nothing. Here's an example of using DeleteRule and UpdateRule.

```
' Load data into dataset
...

Dim Parent As DataColumn = simpleForeign.Tables("Customers").Columns("CustomerID")
Dim Child As DataColumn = simpleForeign.Tables("Orders").Columns("CustomerID")
Dim customerIDConstraint As New ForeignKeyConstraint(Parent, Child)

' Indicate that when an item in the parent is deleted, the
' related child records should have their key value set to null
customerIDConstraint.DeleteRule = Rule.SetNull

' Indicate that when the parent is updated, child rows should be updated to match
customerIDConstraint.UpdateRule = Rule.Cascade

' Add the constraint to the child table
simpleForeign.Tables("Orders").Constraints.Add(customerIDConstraint)
```

Here you've expanded on your previous example to specify delete and update rules for the constraint. In this case, when a row in the parent table is deleted, the child row will have its key value set to null. When the parent has its key value updated, that change will cascade to the child rows to keep the two tables synchronized.

As mentioned previously, the DeleteRule and UpdateRule are acted upon when the constraint is enforced, which is when the value is actually changed. The AcceptRejectRule, however, is acted upon when changes to the table are accepted or rejected, using the

`AcceptChanges()` or `RejectChanges()` methods found on the `DataRow`, `DataTable`, and `DataSet` objects. If the `UpdateRule` or `DeleteRule` conflicts with the `AcceptRejectRule`, the outcome may not be as expected.

Since the update and delete rules will be acted upon first, these changes will override those defined in the `AcceptRejectRule`. For example, if the `UpdateRule` is set to `SetNull` and the `AcceptRejectRule` is set to `Cascade`, when the parent value is updated, the child rows will have their key values set to null. When the `AcceptRejectRule` is applied, the child columns will have been updated already, so no action will be taken.

Foreign key constraints are extremely useful when you're working with multiple, related tables of data in a `DataSet`. As you will see later, this functionality is enhanced when you use data relations in conjunction with the foreign key constraint. In practice, it is rather rare to create a `ForeignKeyConstraint` explicitly; creating a `DataRelation` between two `DataTable` objects within your `DataSet` creates a `ForeignKeyConstraint` in the process.

Note When working with constraints in ADO.NET, keep in mind that a `DataSet` is completely disconnected and knows nothing about the data in the data source, so constraints you define on columns and tables within your `DataSet` are valid only within that `DataSet`. The constraints are not valid on a real data source.

Custom Constraints

The `ForeignKeyConstraint` and `UniqueConstraint` both derive from the abstract `Constraint` class. This class defines much of the base functionality of the constraint classes. However, several of the abstract methods in the `Constraint` class that need to be overridden in derived classes have assembly-level protection, which means that only classes in the `System.Data` assembly can override them. Therefore, it is not possible to derive from the `Constraint` class in your own code at this time. Microsoft has indicated that this may be possible in future versions of the .NET Framework, but for now you have limited options.

While you cannot derive a class from `System.Data.Constraint` to create your own custom constraints, you *can* create a custom constraint that provides a good deal of the functionality of the included constraint classes. As an example, you'll create a custom constraint to ensure that phone numbers entered into the phone number column of a `DataTable` are in the following format: 123 456-7890.

When any constraint is created, it registers itself to receive change events from the `DataTable`, so that it can check the values of the data and throw an exception if the value does not meet the constraint. You can use this same mechanism in creating your constraint to listen for new or changed values in the column.

You start by importing the necessary namespaces, including the `System.Text.Regular-Expressions` namespace that contains the classes you'll use to validate the column value. Next, you define variables to hold the state information you'll need, including a reference to the column that should be constrained, the constraint name, and a Boolean value that will indicate if the constraint has been violated. Finally, you create a default constructor (this appears as USPhoneNumberConstraint in the examples for this chapter).

```vb
Imports System
Imports System.Data
Imports System.Text.RegularExpressions


Public Class USPhoneNumberConstraint

  ' The column we are interested in
  Private m_constrainedColumn As DataColumn

  ' The name of our constraint
  Private m_constraintName As String

  ' A test to see if the constraint is currently violated
  Private IsViolated As Boolean
  ' A static definition of the regular expression that defines
  ' the format required for a value to meet this constraint
  Private Const comparisonValue As String = "\d{3} \d{3}-\d{4}"

  ' Checks to see if the constraint and the data table are in
  ' a state in which the constraint can be successfully applied
  Private Function CanApplyConstraint() As Boolean

    ' If the column or table is null, then return False. Otherwise, check.
    If Not m_constrainedColumn Is Nothing And _
       Not m_constrainedColumn.Table Is Nothing Then

      ' Try to check the existing values.
      ' If this throws an exception, return False. Otherwise, return True.
      Try
        CheckExistingValues()
      Catch e As InvalidConstraintException
        Return False
      End Try

      Return True
    Else
      Return False
    End If
  End Function


  ' Identifies whether the constraint is currently violated
  Public Function IsConstraintViolated() As Boolean
    Return IsViolated
```

```
End Function

Public Sub New()
End Sub

'
' Other constructors and methods to follow
'

End Class
```

The other thing to notice about your initial setup is that you've created a constant representing the pattern that values must match in order to meet the constraint. The comparisonValue constant holds a regular expression that matches a phone number with the area code, separated by a space, from the rest of the string. The expression is broken down in Table 7-3.

Table 7-3. *Breakdown of the* comparisonValue *Regular Expression*

Pattern	Meaning
\d{3}	Three numeric characters
\d{3}	A space followed by three numeric characters
-\d{4}	A hyphen followed by four numeric characters

Next, you'll add some other constructors to your class to indicate the column constrained, and a constraint name. You will create a constructor that just takes the column, and one that takes the column and a name.

```
Public Sub New(ByVal constrainedColumn As DataColumn)
  Me.new("USPhoneNumberConstraint", constrainedColumn)
End Sub

Public Sub New(ByVal constraintName As String, _
               ByVal constrainedColumn As DataColumn)

  ' Make sure the column isn't null
  If constrainedColumn Is Nothing Then
    Throw New InvalidConstraintException( _
          "Constraints cannot be applied to DataColumns with Null value")
  End If

  ' Make sure our column is in a table
  If constrainedColumn.Table Is Nothing Then
    Throw New InvalidConstraintException( _
          "US Phone Number constraint can only be " & _
          "applied to columns that are in a table.")
  End If
```

```
' Set our local variable to the passed in column
m_constrainedColumn = constrainedColumn

' Set the constraint name
m_constraintName = constraintName

' Make sure the existing values meet the criteria
CheckExistingValues()

' Hook up to the DataColumn's ColumnChanged event if we have a valid column
If Not constrainedColumn Is Nothing Then
    AddHandler constrainedColumn.Table.ColumnChanged, _
            AddressOf DataColumn_OnChange
End If
End Sub
```

Your first constructor simply passes the DataColumn parameter on to the second constructor, along with a default name. In the second constructor, you do a lot of work to ensure that
you can successfully create the constraint. You check that the column is not null, and that it
belongs to a DataTable, and throw an InvalidConstraintException if either of these conditions is not met.

You then set your local variables for the constrained column and the constraint name,
and check that the values currently in the table meet the constraint. (You'll examine the
CheckExistingValues() method next.) Finally, you attach an event handler to the Column-
Changed event of the table to which your column belongs.

```
' Checks the values in the data table associated with the constrained
' column and throws an exception if they don't all meet the criteria
Private Sub CheckExistingValues()
  Dim row As DataRow
  For Each row In m_constrainedColumn.Table.Rows
    If Regex.IsMatch( _
            row(m_constrainedColumn, DataRowVersion.Current).ToString(), _
                                        comparisonValue) = False Then

        ' Nullify the column so we don't use this constraint
        m_constrainedColumn = Nothing
        Throw New InvalidConstraintException( _
            "The existing values in the data table " & _
            "do not meet the US Phone Number constraint.")
    End If
  Next
End Sub
```

The CheckExistingValues() method uses For Each to iterate through the rows in the table
and to check the current value in the constrained column against your regular expression pattern.
If you come upon any rows that do not match, you throw a new InvalidConstraintException.

You use the static `IsMatch()` method of the `RegEx` class to test the value against your pattern. This method returns a Boolean indicating whether the value matches the pattern you specify.

```
' Check any values that occur when data column we are constraining is changed
Public Sub DataColumn_OnChange(ByVal sender As Object, _
                            ByVal eArgs As DataColumnChangeEventArgs)

    ' Check to see that it is the column we are interested in,
    ' and that constraints are being enforced for the DataSet
    If eArgs.Column Is m_constrainedColumn And _
          m_constrainedColumn.Table.DataSet.EnforceConstraints = True Then

        ' If it is the constrained column, check the value
        If Regex.IsMatch( _
            eArgs.Row(m_constrainedColumn, DataRowVersion.Proposed).ToString(), _
                                    comparisonValue) = False Then

            ' If no match found, indicate violated constraint and throw exception
            IsViolated = True
            Throw New ConstraintException( _
                "The value in column " & m_constrainedColumn.ColumnName & _
                " violates the US Phone Number Constraint.")
        End If
    End If
End Sub
```

Then, as you can see, you create your event handler for the `ColumnChanged` event. In the event handler, you first need to check to see that the changing column is the one you are interested in. If it is, then you check the proposed value with the regular expression's `IsMatch()` method, as you did in the previous method. If there isn't a match, you set the `IsViolated` field to `True` and throw a `ConstraintException`, which will indicate that the constraint has been violated.

These two methods provide the bulk of the functionality for your constraint. The first ensures that the table can be constrained when you create the constraint. The second manages enforcing the constraint as the data is edited.

Next, you add some property accessors to allow a user to set the constraint name and the `DataColumn`, as well as to get the associated `DataTable`.

```
' Public accessor for the constraint name
Public Property ConstraintName() As String
    Get
        Return m_constraintName
    End Get
    Set(ByVal Value As String)
        m_constraintName = Value
    End Set
End Property
```

```
' Public read-only accessor for the data table of the constrained column
Public ReadOnly Property Table() As DataTable
  Get
    If Not m_constrainedColumn Is Nothing Then
      Return m_constrainedColumn.Table
    Else
      Return Nothing
    End If
  End Get
End Property

' Property for access to the data column to be constrained
' Allows for setting the column after the constraint has been created
Public Property Column() As DataColumn
  Get
    Return m_constrainedColumn
  End Get
  Set(ByVal Value As DataColumn)

    ' If the column is a new column then check constraint for the new column
    If Not Value Is m_constrainedColumn Then
      m_constrainedColumn = Value
      CheckExistingValues()
    End If
  End Set
End Property
```

The property accessor for the constraint name is a simple accessor for the private field. The Get for the table first checks to make sure the DataColumn is not null, and if not, returns the DataTable for the constrained column. In the property for the DataColumn, you add a check on the Set accessor, such that if the column is not the current column, you check the existing values to ensure that they can be constrained. Using these properties, calling code can set the column to be constrained and set the name of the constraint from outside the constructor.

Testing the Custom Constraint

Now that you have your constraint, you can use it in your code much as you use the predefined constraints. The following example is a simple console application (ConstraintTest.vb) that shows your constraint in action using data from the authors table of the pubs database.

You start by adding the appropriate Imports statements that includes the various namespaces you intend to use.

```
Imports System
Imports System.Data
Imports System.Data.SqlClient

Namespace ConstraintTest
```

Next, in your project, you add a reference to the USPhoneNumberConstraint.dll file. To do this, right-click on the "References" treeview in the `ConstraintTest` project under the Solution explorer. Select "Add Reference" and browse to and select the USPhoneNumberConstraint.dll file on your local filesystem.

Next, you load a `DataSet` with data from the `authors` table of the `pubs` database.

```
Class Class1
  Public Shared Sub Main()

    Dim cnn As New SqlConnection("server=(local);database=pubs;uid=sa;pwd=;")
    Dim da As New SqlDataAdapter("SELECT * FROM authors", cnn)
    Dim ds As New DataSet()
    da.Fill(ds, "Authors")
```

Now, you create your constraint, passing in the column to be constrained—in this case, the phone column of the table—and give it a name. So far, this is very like the process you used for the predefined constraints, but now it begins to differ. You do not add your constraint to the table's `Constraints` collection. (As this collection can only hold items that derive from `System.Data.Constraint`, you will get an exception if you try to do so.) However, you'll still find that trying to enter a value in this column that doesn't meet the criteria you've defined will throw an exception.

```
    Console.WriteLine("Creating Constraint")

    ' Create a new instance of our constraint, passing the phone column
    ' as the one to be constrained, and a name for our constraint
    Dim phoneConstraint As New USPhoneNumberConstraint( _
                "phoneConstraint", ds.Tables("Authors").Columns("phone"))

    Console.WriteLine("Changing number to incorrect format")
    Try
      ds.Tables("Authors").Rows(0).BeginEdit()
      ds.Tables("Authors").Rows(0)("Phone") = "(123) 222-4568"
      ds.Tables("Authors").Rows(0).EndEdit()
    Catch e As ConstraintException
      Console.WriteLine("Constraint exception encountered")
      Console.WriteLine(e.ToString())
    End Try
  End Sub
End Class
End Namespace
```

As you are not deriving from the base `Constraint` class, there are some limitations to your custom constraint. Since it's not included in the `Constraints` collection of the data table, a check of this collection could indicate that there are no constraints. One way to work around this is to use the `SetColumnError()` method of the `DataRow` object to indicate that there's a problem with the value the user has entered. This allows you to use the HasErrors property of the DataRow or DataTable objects to determine whether there are data errors.

You could see how this shortcoming manifests itself if you tried to use your constraint in a DataGrid on a Windows Form: the constraint would not prevent a user from changing the value to one that does not meet the constraint parameters. The DataGrid catches the exception you raise, but it is not able to get at the information about your constraint in order to raise a message to the user, or to stop the change from happening. If you set an error, the grid displays a red marker indicating that there is an error in the row.

To enhance your constraint, you'll add a few lines of code. You will enhance your event handler for the ColumnChanged event in such a way that you will not allow values to be entered that violate your constraint. In this way, a user of your constraint cannot catch your exception and ignore it in order to put an invalid value in your column.

```
Public Sub DataColumn_OnChange(ByVal sender As Object, _
                                ByVal eArgs As DataColumnChangeEventArgs)

    ...

    If Regex.IsMatch( _
        eArgs.Row(_constrainedColumn, DataRowVersion.Proposed).ToString(), _
                                      comparisonValue) = False Then

        ' If no match found, indicate violated constraint and throw exception
        IsViolated = True
        eArgs.Row(m_constrainedColumn) = _
                    eArgs.Row(m_constrainedColumn, DataRowVersion.Original)
        Throw New ConstraintException( _
            "The value in column " & m_constrainedColumn.ColumnName & _
            " violates the US Phone Number Constraint.")
    End If
    End If
End Sub
```

By resetting the value in the column, you ensure that the value *cannot* be changed to one that does not meet your criteria. In this way, you do not have to keep track of the column or row state after the constraint is violated. You still throw the exception, so that a program using your constraint can be notified that the constraint was violated, and take an appropriate action (such as notifying the user).

When loading your data, you're already throwing an exception if the data does not match your criteria. In that situation, you don't set the event handler for the ColumnChanged event, so you don't have to worry about a user creating your constraint when the data is already invalid.

This code sample is intended to provide a starting point for creating a custom constraint, and to give more insight into the workings of the constraint mechanism in ADO.NET. As it has some limitations, this solution is best suited for creating common constraints that can be used in many different projects, and in an environment with some guidance on how best to use them.

DataRelations

A DataRelation defines the relationship between two different DataTable objects that belong to the same DataSet. This should not be confused with the ForeignKeyConstraint, which constrains the *data* in two tables, although you'll see that DataRelation and ForeignKeyConstraint work closely together. You use DataRelations primarily for navigating between data tables. Thus, using a specific row in the parent table, you can access all of the related data rows in the related table.

We'll start this discussion by creating a simple relationship between two DataTable objects. The following example creates a new DataRelation, identifying the data columns to use for the relationship, and adds this new relation to the Relations collection of the DataSet class:

```
Dim nwindConnection As New SqlConnection(connectionString)
Dim nwindAdapter As New SqlDataAdapter("SELECT * FROM Customers;" & _
        "SELECT * FROM Orders;SELECT * FROM [order details]", nwindConnection)

Dim relationData As New DataSet()

' Fill the dataset, getting key values
nwindAdapter.MissingSchemaAction = MissingSchemaAction.AddWithKey
nwindAdapter.Fill(relationData)

' Name all of the tables appropriately
relationData.Tables(0).TableName = "Customers"
relationData.Tables(1).TableName = "Orders"
relationData.Tables(2).TableName = "OrderDetails"

' Create a new relation, giving it a name and identifying the columns to relate
Dim Parent As DataColumn = relationData.Tables("Customers").Columns("Customerid")
Dim Child As DataColumn = relationData.Tables("Orders").Columns("Customerid")

Dim customerRelation As New DataRelation("customerRelation", Parent, Child)

' Add the relation to the DataSet's Relations collection
relationData.Relations.Add(customerRelation)
```

As you can see, the creation of a data relation is very similar to that of a constraint. You create the relation, identifying the columns to use, and then add it to the collection. Creating a DataRelation will also, by default, create corresponding constraint objects, because you have not specified otherwise.

Already, you're starting to see how the DataRelation and constraints work together. By allowing the DataRelation to create constraints, you end up with a UniqueConstraint on the parent column, such that the values are required to be unique, and a ForeignKeyConstraint on the child table to ensure integrity between the two tables. You can avoid the creation of constraints by using a different version of the DataRelation constructor.

```
Public Sub New(ByVal relationName As String, _
               ByVal parentColumn As DataColumn, _
               ByVal childColumn As DataColumn, _
               ByVal createConstraints As Boolean)
```

By specifying `False` for the last parameter, you instruct the `DataRelation` not to create the constraints on the tables. This allows for the data to be related, but not constrained—in other words, you can navigate using the relationship, but you can also do things like delete rows from the parent table without receiving an exception.

As mentioned previously, the primary use for `DataRelations` is to allow for navigation between related rows in different data tables. This is accomplished by using the `GetChildRows()` and `GetParentRows()` methods of the `DataRow` object. In using these methods, you must specify the data relation to use to find the related rows. If necessary, you can set up multiple relations on a table and find only those rows that you need based on a specific relationship.

The following example shows how you might extract a set of rows from a related table using a defined `DataRelation`. `childrenData` is a `DataTable` in a `DataSet`.

```
Dim rows as DataRow() = childrenData.Rows(0).GetChildRows("customerRelation")
```

You use the `GetChildRows()` method of the `DataRow` object to get an array of `DataRow` objects. You can pass in the name of the relation, as you have here, or a reference to the relation itself. For a better understanding of how this can be applied, the following example is based on a Windows Forms application that uses this method in a master-detail situation.

Imagine that you have two data grids on a form, the first of which contains customer information. The second grid will be updated automatically to reflect the selected row in the master table. First, you load some data into the `DataSet` and create your `DataRelation` between the Customers and Orders tables.

```
' Create the relation and add it to the collection for the DataSet
Dim Parent As DataColumn = childrenData.Tables("Customers").Columns("CustomerID")
Dim Child As DataColumn = childrenData.Tables("Orders").Columns("CustomerID")

Dim customerRelation As New DataRelation("customerRelation", Parent, Child)
childrenData.Relations.Add(customerRelation)

' Set the data source of the grid to the Customers table
Grid1.DataSource = childrenData.Tables("Customers").DefaultView

' Hook up event handler so we can update the child grid when a new row is selected
AddHandler Grid1.CurrentCellChanged, AddressOf Me.CurrentCellChangedEventHandler
```

You then add an event handler for the `CurrentCellChanged` event. Here, you extract the current row from the arguments passed into the handler. You use this data, along with the `Find()` method of the `DataRowCollection` class, to identify the parent row selected. You then call `GetChildRows()` on this row, passing in the name of the relation you created.

```
Private Sub CurrentCellChangedEventHandler(ByVal sender As Object, _
                                           ByVal e As System.EventArgs)

  ' Instance values
  Dim rows As DataRow()
  Dim rowIndex As Integer
```

```
' Get the row number of the selected cell
rowIndex = CType(sender, DataGrid).CurrentCell.RowNumber

' Use the row number to get the value of the key (customerID)
Dim Key As String = CType(sender, DataGrid)(rowIndex, 0).ToString()

' Use the key to find the row we selected in the data source
Dim sourceView As DataView = _
                    CType(CType(sender, DataGrid).DataSource, DataView)
Dim row As DataRow = sourceView.Table.Rows.Find(Key)
rows = row.GetChildRows("customerRelation")
```

Next, you use this array of rows as the data source for the second grid by merging it into a new, empty DataSet and by using the default view of the table created.

```
' Merge the child rows into a new DataSet and set the source
' of the child table to the default view of the initial table
Dim tmpData As New DataSet()
tmpData.Merge(rows)
Grid2.DataSource = tmpData.Tables(0).DefaultView
End Sub
```

This is one simple example of using the GetChildRows() method to update a user interface element, but there are many other situations in which it's important to get at related child rows. Similarly, it is often useful to get the parent row for the current child row. You can access the parent row that's related to the current child row in much the same way as you access the child rows: you use the GetParentRow() or GetParentRows() methods of the DataRow class.

```
Dim rows as DataRow() = _
            childrenData.Table("Orders").Rows(0).GetParentRows("customerRelation")
```

Finally, you can further define the rows you wish to retrieve by calling an overloaded version of the GetChildRows() or GetParentRows() method to get a specific version of the DataRow in the related table. Be aware, though, that if the version requested in the GetChildRows() method is not available, an exception of type VersionNotFoundException will be thrown. In order to avoid this, you can check for the version to see if it is available with the HasVersion() method of the DataRow.

In the following example, customerRelation is the DataRelation used to query for the child rows. You first check to see that the row you are interested in has a particular version, and then query for that version.

```
Dim childRows As DataRow()
childRows = ds.Tables("Customers").Rows(0).GetChildRows(customerRelation)

If childRows(0).HasVersion(DataRowVersion.Proposed) Then
  childRows = ds.Tables("Customers").Rows(0).GetChildRows( _
                    "customerRelation", DataRowVersion.Original)
  Console.WriteLine(rows(0)(0).ToString())
End If
```

XML and DataRelations

DataSets have many built-in capabilities relating to XML. Several methods of the DataSet allow for serializing and de-serializing the data in the DataSet to and from XML. When you're creating DataRelation objects, it's possible to affect the format of the XML representation of the data by using the Nested property.

Using the GetXml() method of the DataSet, you can see that the typical XML output of a DataSet with multiple tables is structured such that each table is represented independently with its contained rows. A simple example of this is shown here; the code used to generate the XML simply loads a DataSet with data from the Customers, Orders, and Order Details tables of the Northwind database and creates relationships between them.

```
' The DataSet into which the data has been loaded is called "nested"

' Create a DataRelation using Customers and Orders
Dim parentColumns As DataColumn()
parentColumns = _
    New DataColumn() {nested.Tables("customers").Columns("customerid")}

Dim childColumns As DataColumn()
childColumns = _
    New DataColumn() {nested.Tables("orders").Columns("customerid")}

Dim customerIDrelation As New DataRelation( _
    "CustomerOrderRelation", parentColumns, childColumns)

' Create a DataRelation using Orders and Order Details
parentColumns = New DataColumn() {nested.Tables("orders").Columns("orderid")}
childColumns = New DataColumn() {nested.Tables("orderdetails").Columns("orderid")}

Dim orderDetailsRelation As New DataRelation( _
    "OrderDetailsRelation", parentColumns, childColumns)

' Add the relations to the DataSet's collection of relations
nested.Relations.Add(customerIDrelation)
nested.Relations.Add(orderDetailsRelation)

Console.WriteLine(nested.GetXml())
```

Once you've created the two relations that connect the customers' records to the orders, and the orders to the order details, you retrieve the XML with the GetXml() method of the DataSet, and see the XML output, as follows:

```
<NewDataSet>
  <Customers>
    <CustomerID>ALFKI</CustomerID>
    <CompanyName>Alfreds Futterkiste</CompanyName>
    <ContactName>Maria Anders</ContactName>
```

```xml
    <ContactTitle>Sales Representative</ContactTitle>
    <Address>Obere Str. 57</Address>
    <City>Berlin</City>
    <PostalCode>12209</PostalCode>
    <Country>Germany</Country>
    <Phone>030-0074321</Phone>
    <Fax>030-0076545</Fax>
</Customers>
<Customers>

...

<Orders>
    <OrderID>10248</OrderID>
    <CustomerID>VINET</CustomerID>
    <EmployeeID>5</EmployeeID>
    <OrderDate>1996-07-04T00:00:00.0000000-05:00</OrderDate>
    <RequiredDate>1996-08-01T00:00:00.0000000-05:00</RequiredDate>
    <ShippedDate>1996-07-16T00:00:00.0000000-05:00</ShippedDate>
    <ShipVia>3</ShipVia>
    <Freight>32.38</Freight>
    <ShipName>Vins et alcools Chevalier</ShipName>
    <ShipAddress>59 rue de l'Abbaye</ShipAddress>
    <ShipCity>Reims</ShipCity>
    <ShipPostalCode>51100</ShipPostalCode>
    <ShipCountry>France</ShipCountry>
</Orders>
<Orders>

...

<OrderDetails>
    <OrderID>10248</OrderID>
    <ProductID>11</ProductID>
    <UnitPrice>14</UnitPrice>
    <Quantity>12</Quantity>
    <Discount>0</Discount>
</OrderDetails>
<OrderDetails>
    <OrderID>10248</OrderID>
    <ProductID>42</ProductID>
    <UnitPrice>9.8</UnitPrice>
    <Quantity>10</Quantity>
    <Discount>0</Discount>
</OrderDetails>

...
```

One of the benefits of XML is that it can easily represent hierarchical data. In order to represent the data in the most logical way, you can set the Nested properties of the DataRelation objects to True. This causes the data to be output such that each element representing a row from the parent table has the child rows as nested elements. The following example shows the same data as the previous example, but with the related child rows nested within their respective parent rows. To generate this output, you simply add the following two lines of code to the last sample, just before the call to GetXml():

```
' Add the relations to the DataSet's collection of relations
nested.Relations.Add(customerIDrelation)
nested.Relations.Add(orderDetailsRelation)

' Indicate that the relations should be nested
customerIDrelation.Nested = True
orderDetailsRelation.Nested = True

Console.WriteLine(nested.GetXml())
```

Here's the output.

```
<NewDataSet>
  <Customers>
    <CustomerID>ALFKI</CustomerID>
    <CompanyName>Alfreds Futterkiste</CompanyName>
    <ContactName>Maria Anders</ContactName>
    <ContactTitle>Sales Representative</ContactTitle>
    <Address>Obere Str. 57</Address>
    <City>Berlin</City>
    <PostalCode>12209</PostalCode>
    <Country>Germany</Country>
    <Phone>030-0074321</Phone>
    <Fax>030-0076545</Fax>
    <Orders>
      <OrderID>10643</OrderID>
      <CustomerID>ALFKI</CustomerID>
      <EmployeeID>6</EmployeeID>
      <OrderDate>1997-08-25T00:00:00.0000000-05:00</OrderDate>
      <RequiredDate>1997-09-22T00:00:00.0000000-05:00</RequiredDate>
      <ShippedDate>1997-09-02T00:00:00.0000000-05:00</ShippedDate>
      <ShipVia>1</ShipVia>
      <Freight>29.46</Freight>
      <ShipName>Alfreds Futterkiste</ShipName>
      <ShipAddress>Obere Str. 57</ShipAddress>
      <ShipCity>Berlin</ShipCity>
      <ShipPostalCode>12209</ShipPostalCode>
      <ShipCountry>Germany</ShipCountry>
```

```
    <OrderDetails>
      <OrderID>10643</OrderID>
      <ProductID>28</ProductID>
      <UnitPrice>45.6</UnitPrice>
      <Quantity>15</Quantity>
      <Discount>0.25</Discount>
    </OrderDetails>
    <OrderDetails>

    ...

  </Orders>
  <Orders>

  ...
  </Customers>
</NewDataSet>
```

In the first instance, each table is represented by separate and distinct elements, and no relations are apparent. In the second, each customer element has its related orders nested beneath it—and each order, in turn, has all of the order details nested beneath it. This simple change can make the data more readable for humans and applications.

DataRelation objects are extremely helpful when working with multitable DataSet objects to manage and navigate the relationships between the tables. Soon, you'll see some more examples that demonstrate how DataRelation objects can be even more useful when used in conjunction with some of the other tools that are available to you.

DataViews

Often, data retrieved from a data source is not in exactly the form that you would like to present it. To fix this, the DataView, along with the DataTable, provides an implementation of the popular document-view design pattern. This pattern defines a model of the data, and different views that provide different representations of the data in the model. By using this design pattern, you are able to have a DataTable that contains your data, and various DataViews that provide different views of the data.

A DataView provides you with several useful mechanisms for working with data.

- Sorting: The view of the data can be sorted based on one or more columns, in ascending or descending order.

- Filtering: The data visible through the view can be filtered with expressions based on one or more columns.

- Row Version Filtering: The data visible through the view can be filtered based on the version of the rows.

These abilities provide a great deal of power when you're working with the data in a DataTable, and in this section you'll see how each of them can make working with data easier. In order to use this functionality, reasonably enough, you must first create a DataView, and there are three ways to do that.

- Retrieve the default view of a DataTable by using its DefaultView property.

- Create a new instance of a DataView that can then be associated with a DataTable.

- Use a DataViewManager to create a DataView for a DataTable.

You will examine each of these methods as you look at how to work with DataView objects.

Sorting

The DataView provides the means to sort and filter the representation of the data in a DataTable. Sorting a view orders rows based on the values in particular columns. After setting the sort criteria on a DataView, the rows will be accessed in the order specified. So if the DataView is used to present data to the user, it will appear in the sorted order.

When applying the sort criteria, you must specify the column and direction for the sort. For example, if you wanted to sort data in descending order, by a column called DateOfBirth, you would use the following:

DataView.Sort = "DateOfBirth DESC"

To sort the same column in ascending order, you would use this:

DataView.Sort = "DateOfBirth ASC"

The following example shows how to sort a view based on the Region field of the data table. It also shows one of the mechanisms for creating a data view.

```
Dim nwindConnection As New SqlConnection(connectionString)
Dim nwindAdapter As New SqlDataAdapter("SELECT * FROM Customers;" & _
        "SELECT * FROM Orders; SELECT * FROM [order details]", nwindConnection)

Dim firstSort As New DataSet()

' Fill the dataset, getting key values
nwindAdapter.MissingSchemaAction = MissingSchemaAction.AddWithKey
nwindAdapter.Fill(firstSort)

' Name all of the tables appropriately
firstSort.Tables(0).TableName = "Customers"
firstSort.Tables(1).TableName = "Orders"
firstSort.Tables(2).TableName = "OrderDetails"
```

```
' Create the DataView object and set the table to the
' Customers table by passing it in the constructor
Dim tableSort As New DataView(firstSort.Tables("Customers"))

' Set the sort criteria for the view
tableSort.Sort = "Region DESC"
```

After you've filled the DataSet, you create a new object of type DataView, and pass in a DataTable to the constructor. You then set the sort criteria for the DataView to sort the items in descending order by the Region field. Keep in mind that this does *not* change the order of the rows in the DataTable itself, only the view of the data as seen through this interface. This allows you to have multiple views of the same DataTable, with different sort criteria.

Setting DataView sorts should be familiar to you if you've worked with SQL. Just as in SQL, you can specify multiple columns to sort, providing a direction for each column. Thus, you could sort addresses in a data table by the region in descending order, followed by the city in ascending order.

```
' Create the DataView object and set the table to the
' Customers table by passing it in the constructor
Dim tableSort As New DataView(firstSort.Tables("Customers"))

' Set the sort criteria for the view
tableSort.Sort = "Region DESC, City ASC"
```

In fact, the default direction for the sort is ascending, so it's only necessary to specify the direction explicitly when you want to sort in descending order. However, explicitly identifying the sort order can make your code more readable.

It's important to remember that the sort order of a DataView is dependent on the data type of the data column. For example, a string-type column with numeric values in it will be sorted not numerically, but alphabetically.

■Note In order to ensure that the data in the view is sorted as you expect, be sure to know the data type of the column you are sorting, and the effect of sorting on that type.

Filtering

Rather than sorting the data in a DataView, you can filter records to show only those rows that meet criteria you specify. There are two ways to filter the rows in a DataView: by values in the rows, or by the version of the row data. In this section, you'll look at the first of those ways.

To filter records in the `DataView` based on their values, set the `RowFilter` property to a Boolean expression that can be evaluated against each row. Only those rows meeting the criteria will be visible in the view. Here's an example.

```
' Load the data

...

' Create a new DataView based on the Customers table
Dim tableFilter As New DataView(dataFilter.Tables("customers"))

' Set the RowFilter property of the view to filter the viewable rows
tableFilter.RowFilter = "Country='UK'"
```

Once you've set the `RowFilter` property of the view, only those rows matching the criteria will appear in the view. You can change the `RowFilter` property as needed to expose the rows you need to work with. This operation is more flexible than working directly with the data—because it's simply a *view* of the data, less information needs to be moved around, and the original data is still available to be viewed in other ways.

Notice that you put the test case (UK) in single quotation marks; this is required to specify a string value when working with the `RowFilter` property. If you're specifying a date, you surround the value with the # symbol.

Like the `Sort` property, the `RowFilter` property also allows for specifying multiple columns and expressions upon which to filter the data. However, rather than using a comma to separate the criteria, you use `AND` and `OR` to build up the criteria. Here, you filter the data based on values for both the country and the city.

```
' Create a new DataView based on the Customers table
Dim tableFilter As New DataView(dataFilter.Tables("Customers"))
' Set the RowFilter property of the view to filter the viewable rows
tableFilter.RowFilter = "Country='UK' AND City='Cowes'"
```

Operators

These operators can be used in the filter statement to combine or modify values used in the expression, as seen in Table 7-4.

Table 7-4. *Filter Statement Operators*

Operator	Meaning
AND	Logical And
OR	Logical Or
NOT	Logical Not
<	Less than
>	Greater than
<=	Less than or equal to
>=	Greater than or equal to

Table 7-4. *continued*

Operator	Meaning
<>	Not equal to
=	Equal to
IN	Values are in the specified set. Usage: IN(a, b, c)
LIKE	Tests if a given value is like the test case. Used with text values, this is similar to "="
+	Addition with numeric values or string concatenation
–	Subtraction
*	Multiplication with numeric values
/	Division
%	Modulus with numeric values or wildcard (multiple characters) for string comparisons
_	Wildcard (single character) for string comparisons

Using the comparisons with string values, you can also specify wildcard characters.

```
DataView.RowFilter = "City LIKE 'Map%'"
```

You can use the % wildcard character in any position in the string. You can also search for any set of characters in a character list, for example

```
DataView.RowFilter = "City LIKE 'm%[i]%'"
```

You can also use parentheses to indicate precedence in your expressions, as shown here.

```
DataView.RowFilter = "(City='Milan' OR City='Paris') AND Category='Fashion'"
```

Relationship Referencing

An expression can use the relationships that exist between the table behind the view and any other tables in the DataSet (see Table 7-5). In this way, the parent table can be filtered based on values in the child table, or vice versa.

Table 7-5. *Relationship Referencing*

Reference	Meaning
Child.ColumnName	References the specified column in the child table
Child(RelationshipName).ColumnName	References the specified column in the child table, as determined by the relationship specified

If there is more than one relationship in effect, the second syntax needs to be used to specify the specific relation to use. You can also reference parent columns in the same way by using Parent.ColumnName. This syntax is most often used with the aggregate functions identified in the next section—for example, you might want to filter the view to show all records where the sum of the price of the child records is greater than $50.

Aggregate Functions

Aggregate functions provide a means for operating on multiple rows of data in order to return a value (see Table 7-6). They are often used with related tables, as described previously.

Table 7-6. *Aggregate Functions*

Function	Meaning
Sum()	Sum of the column(s) specified
Avg()	Average value of the column specified
Min()	Minimum value of the column specified
Max()	Maximum value of the column specified
Count()	Count of the rows in the column specified
StDev()	Standard deviation
Var()	Statistical variance

Aggregate functions can be used on the table to which the DataView applies, or they can be computed on the data in related rows. When working with a single table, the value of this expression would be the same for all rows. For example, if you calculate the total of the price column, all rows will have the same value. This does not lend itself well to filtering the data based on the outcome. However, when working with related tables, you can choose to show only those rows in the parent table where the related rows in the child table meet your criteria. A simple example is shown here.

```
DataView.RowFilter="Sum(Child.UnitPrice) > 100"
```

This example gets those rows from the current view where the related child rows have a sum of UnitPrice that's greater than 100.

Functions

Functions provide some flexibility in creating expressions by allowing the developer to substitute or manipulate a given column value in order to test it (see Table 7-7). For example, you might want all rows where the description column starts with "Exclusive." If so, you could use the SubString() function for your test.

Table 7-7. *Various Functions*

Function	Meaning	Syntax
Convert()	Converts the given value to the specified type.	Convert(value, type)
Len()	Returns the length of the specified value.	Len(value)
IsNull()	Returns the replacement value if the expression provided evaluates to null.	IsNull(expression, replacement)
IIF()	Returns the trueResult if the expression evaluates to True, or the falseResult if the expression evaluates to False.	IIF(expression, trueResult, falseResult)
SubString()	Returns the portion of the string specified starting at startingPoint and continuing for length characters.	SubString(string, startingPoint, length)

Using the Select Method

As a brief aside, a second way to filter the content of a `DataTable` object is to use that class's `Select()` method, which returns an array of `DataRow` objects that match the criteria you specify in your query. In addition to supplying traditional filter expressions (such as `'Column = 5'` or `'Date < '01/01/2001''`), you can also supply a `DataViewRowState`, as covered in the next section.

```
' Load the data into a DataSet called ds


...


Dim SelectRows As DataRow() = ds.Tables("Customers").Select("Country = 'UK'")

Dim i As Integer
For i = 0 To SelectRows.Length - 1
  Console.WriteLine(SelectRows(i)("CompanyName"))
Next
```

As you can see, once you have the `DataRow` array, you're free to manipulate it in the usual way.

Filtering on Row State

Finally, you can filter the data in a `DataView` based on the version of the row. Using the `RowStateFilter` property, you identify the rows to be visible in the view based on the status of the data in the rows. As you saw in Chapter 4, this status changes as the data in the table is edited, which means that not all versions are always available for every row. To apply a row state filter, you set the `RowStateFilter` property to one of the `DataViewRowState` enumeration values. These values and their meanings are shown in Table 7-8.

Table 7-8. `DataViewRowState` *Constants*

Value	Meaning
Added	Includes only new rows
CurrentRows	Current rows, which includes those that have not been changed, new rows, and modified rows
Deleted	Rows that have been deleted
ModifiedCurrent	A current version of a row that has been modified
ModifiedOriginal	The original version of a modified row
None	None
OriginalRows	Original rows, which includes unchanged and deleted rows
Unchanged	A row that has not been changed

In addition to filtering the data based on a single version, you can use the Boolean `Or` operator to indicate multiple row states. For example, you can use the following code to get both the added rows and the original rows:

```
DataView.RowStateFilter = DataViewRowState.Added Or DataViewRowState.OriginalRows
```

Using these values, you can limit the rows in a DataView to a particular set, based on the edited state of the data. Using this filter, you can have different DataViews filtering on different RowStates. For example, you can have two different views: one showing the current data, and another showing the original values of those rows that have been modified. The following snippet shows this in action:

```
' Load data into a DataSet called filterVersion (code omitted)

...

' Create two new views on the Customers table
Dim currentView As New DataView(filterVersion.Tables("customers"))
Dim originalView As New DataView(filterVersion.Tables("customers"))

' Set the RowStateFilter property for each view
currentView.RowStateFilter = DataViewRowState.CurrentRows
originalView.RowStateFilter = DataViewRowState.ModifiedOriginal
```

If you used these views in a Windows Form with the DataGrid control, you would see output similar to what you see in Figure 7-3.

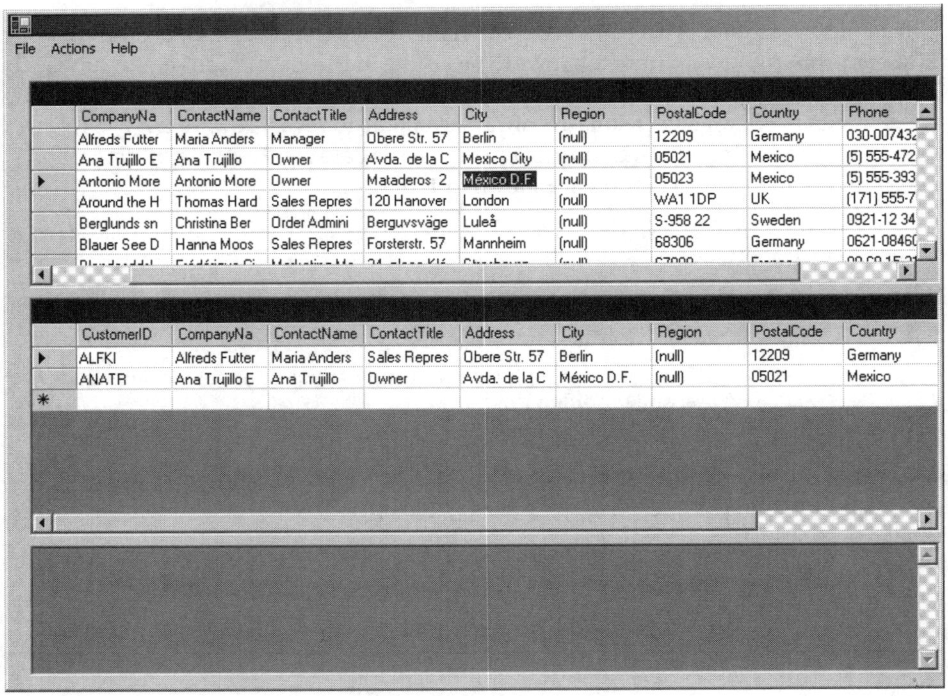

Figure 7-3. *Rollup Sample in code download*

Only those items that have been edited in the top grid show up in the bottom grid. This behavior is especially useful for working with UI elements (as shown), but it can also be useful for keeping track of the different values that a column contains during the editing process. Let's look now at how to use the DataView to help you edit data.

Editing Data in a DataView

The DataView allows for not only viewing data, but also for *editing* the data in a data table. There are three properties of the DataView that dictate its editing behavior: AllowNew, AllowEdit, and AllowDelete, which each hold a Boolean value that indicates whether the respective action can be taken. For example, if the AllowNew property is set to False, then an attempt to add a new row to the DataView using the AddNew() method will throw an exception. The default value for all of these properties is True.

An example of constraining the user's ability to edit the data is shown next. When this is applied to the DataGrid in a Windows Form, the user is not allowed to perform the action (but no error displays if he tries).

```
' Load data into a DataSet called viewEditSet

...

' Indicate that the user cannot delete items
viewEditSet.Tables("Orders").DefaultView.AllowDelete = False
' Indicate that the user cannot add new items
viewEditSet.Tables("Orders").DefaultView.AllowNew = False

' Indicate that the user can edit the current items
viewEditSet.Tables("Orders").DefaultView.AllowEdit = True
```

Using this setup, you allow the user to edit the existing data, but bar him from deleting rows or adding new rows. These properties are especially useful when building client applications that utilize the Windows Forms library. By setting these properties, a developer can control the ability of the user to edit data in a DataGrid that has a DataView as its data source. The DataGrid will automatically pick up and apply rules set in the DataView.

You can add rows to a DataView in a manner quite similar to that for the DataTable: you use the AddNew() method of the DataView to get a new DataRowView object, which can then be edited. You do not need explicitly to create and then add the row to the view, as you do when adding a row straight to a DataTable. Conversely, you delete a row by calling the Delete() method, passing in the index of the row you wish to delete, as it appears in the view. To edit data, you simply change the values of the row.

As ever, it's important to remember that the DataView is simply a view of the data contained in its associated DataTable. Therefore, when we refer to adding or editing data in the view, we are actually talking about working with the data in the table. The actions you take on the view are applied to the data in the table. Similarly, any constraints put on the data table will continue to be enforced even if you are working with the DataView. You cannot, therefore, add or edit data in such a way as to violate these constraints without an exception being raised.

The operations carried out through the DataView are a convenience to eliminate the need to manage the view and the data at the same time. All the editing actions can be taken directly on the table or the row without having to use the view. The following example shows each of the editing actions:

```
' Load DataSet

...

' Create new DataView
Dim editingView As New DataView(ds.Tables("Customers"))

' Add new row to the view
Dim newRow As DataRowView = editingView.AddNew()

' Edit the new row
newRow("CompanyName") = "Apress"

' Edit the first row in the view
editingView(0)("CompanyName") = "Apress"

' Delete the second record in the view
editingView.Delete(1)
```

Being able to edit using the DataView is extremely helpful. Considering that this is the mechanism by which you will often present the data to your users, it would be difficult to have to coordinate their actions on the data in the view, with the actual data in the data table. Being able to indicate the actions the user can take only further refines this ability.

DataViewManager

As mentioned when we began talking about DataViews, one of the ways in which a DataView can be created is by using a DataViewManager. A DataViewManager is associated with a DataSet, and is used to manage and gain access to DataView objects for each of the DataTable objects in the DataSet. The DataViewManager makes working with multitable DataSet objects much easier by providing a single object to manage the collection of DataView objects for the entire DataSet, including the relationships that have been defined between tables. The DataViewManager also allows for easy data binding, as you'll see later in this chapter.

In order to use a DataViewManager, you create and fill a DataSet, and then create a new DataViewManager and set its DataSet property to the filled DataSet. You can then use the manager's DataViewSettings property to gain access to a specific DataView. Alternatively, you can create a new DataViewManager, passing in the DataSet to the constructor. The following code provides an example of creating a DataViewManager and accessing DataView objects for specific DataTable objects in the DataSet:

```
' Load a DataSet called managerData

...
```

```
' Create a new DataViewManager based on the DataSet
Dim manager As New DataViewManager(managerData)

' Sort the data in the view for the orders table, based on the order date
manager.DataViewSettings("Orders").Sort = "OrderDate DESC"
```

Another method for accessing DataViews within the DataViewManager is to use the CreateDataView() method to create a new view based on a given table. This provides you with a direct reference to a specific view of the data. (This same method is used when accessing the DefaultView property of the DataTable.) The following example creates a DataView of the Customers table using this method:

```
' Load a DataSet called customerData


...


Dim customerTable As DataTable = customerData.Tables(0)
Dim custView As DataView = _
                customerData.DefaultViewManager.CreateDataView(customerTable)
```

When working with DataTables, it's possible to get a DataView through the DefaultView property. Similarly, you can obtain a DataViewManager using the DefaultViewManager property of the DataSet class. These default views and managers are created the first time they are accessed. For example, if you create a DataSet and then access the DefaultView property of a DataTable in that DataSet, the DataTable object will attempt to get a reference to the default DataViewManager for the DataSet, and then use it to create the DataView. If the DefaultViewManager is null, one will be created and then used to create the DataView required. Similarly, when you access a DataView for the DataSet by using the DataViewSettings property of the DataViewManager, the DataViewManager creates the DataView the first time you access it.

This "create-on-access" methodology is important to understand for performance reasons. If there is no need to create a DataView for a particular operation, then it should not be created at all, thus avoiding the creation of extra objects on the heap.

As the DataViewManager has access to DataView objects for all of the tables in a DataSet, it is most useful in situations when working with multiple tables in the DataSet. For example, when a DataSet contains multiple tables and DataRelation objects, you can use the DataViewManager to manage the many views more easily.

Data Binding

One of the main reasons for using a DataView is to bind the data represented by that view in a user interface element. The DataGrid is a common control to which DataViews are bound. The act of binding data to a UI element for display is a common practice for both Windows-based and web-based applications. When working in a Windows Forms application, the power of the DataView, Constraints, and DataRelations can be fully realized. Users interact with the data, while the DataGrid enforces properties set on the DataView and the Constraints set on the DataTable.

DataRelations also become very powerful in the Windows Forms environment. The Windows Forms DataGrid can display an entire DataSet, allowing the user to navigate the relationships between tables. When a DataRelation exists, a given row can be expanded and a specific relation selected. The related child rows then fill the grid, with the parent rows optionally appearing at the top of the grid. A user can then navigate back to the parent table using a button on the grid. Figure 7-4 shows a DataGrid with a data relation expanded. The parent row is shown in gray above the child rows.

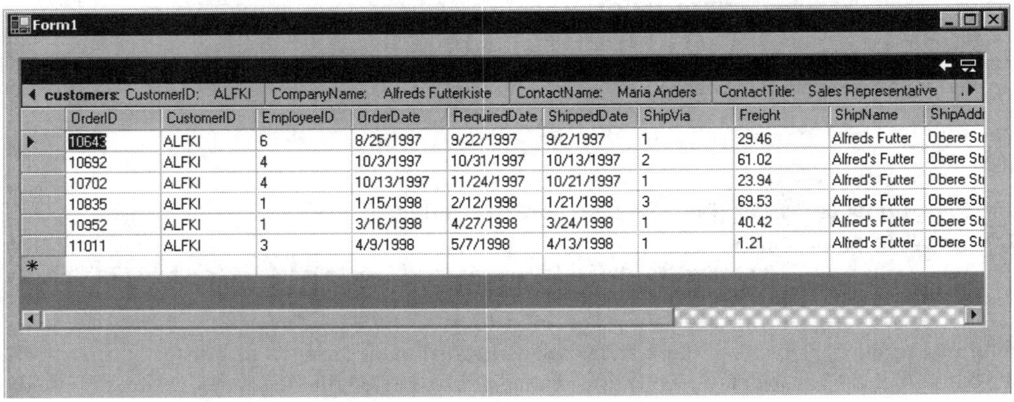

Figure 7-4. DataRelations *in a* DataGrid

There are several ways to bind data to a UI element, but each of them deals with the DataSource property of the element, and at times the DataMember property as well. The easiest way to bind data in a DataSet to a UI control is to set the DataSource property of the element to a DataView. In the following example, you bind a DataGrid to a DataView:

```
' Bind the grid to the default view of the Customers table
Grid1.DataSource = bindingData.Tables("Customers").DefaultView
```

As mentioned previously, the DataMember property often comes into play when binding data to a UI element, but its necessity will depend on the element being used, and the mechanism for identifying the source. For example, when working with a ListBox control, you have to set a display member and a value member. Alternatively, when working with a DataGrid, you might set the DataSource to a DataViewManager object, and the DataMember to the name of a table in the DataSet. The next examples show both of these binding mechanisms in action.

Here's how to bind a DataView to a ListBox—the list displays the CompanyName, but the underlying value is the selected record's CustomerID.

```
' Set the data source of the list to the default view of the Customers table
BoundCombo.DataSource = listSet.Tables("Customers").DefaultView


' Now we identify the item to be displayed
BoundCombo.DisplayMember = "CompanyName"
```

```
' And identify the item to maintain as the value of the item
BoundCombo.ValueMember = "CustomerID"
```

And here's an example of binding a DataSet to a DataGrid, and displaying the Customers table from that DataSet.

```
' Set the data source to the DataSet
Grid1.DataSource = MemberSet

' Provide the name of a data table to indicate the item to use for the data
Grid1.DataMember = "Customers"
```

You can also use this same syntax with a DataViewManager and the name of a DataTable, as shown here.

```
' Create a new DataViewManager based on the DataSet
Dim manager As New DataViewManager(ManagerData)

' Sort the data in the view for the orders table based on the order date
manager.DataViewSettings("Orders").Sort="OrderDate DESC"

' Set the grid source to be the manager, and the member to be the Orders table
Grid1.DataSource = manager
Grid1.DataMember = "Orders"
```

DataView objects provide a very flexible and powerful mechanism for working with the data in a DataTable and presenting that data to users. DataView objects can also be very helpful in a web environment by allowing the view to be cached on the server, using the new caching functionality built into ASP.NET, and reused on subsequent requests. An example of this is demonstrated in the next section.

Bringing It All Together

While each of the classes we have discussed is useful on its own, the true power of working with client-side data comes when you use them together. This section provides several quick pointers to those benefits, followed by examples of Windows Forms and Web Forms applications.

So far, we've shown how you can use a DataRelation to navigate between related DataTable objects. In addition, we gave an example showing a master-detail relationship on a Windows Form. One nice feature of the DataGrid control is that you can use a DataRelation to have the master-detail relationship managed for you automatically. Assume that you have a DataSet called CustomerData, with the following characteristics:

- Customers and Orders data tables

- A data relation between the two tables named CustomerOrderRelation

- A Windows Form with two DataGrids named Grid1 and Grid2

Given these characteristics, you can use the following code to set up your master-detail relationship:

```
Grid1.DataSource = CustomerData
Grid1.DataMember = "Customers"
Grid2.DataSource = CustomerData
Grid2.DataMember = "Customers.CustomerOrderRelation"
```

As a result of this code, the first grid is set up as described in the "Data Binding" section. However, for the second grid, you set the data source to the DataSet, and then identify the data member as a string representing the parent table concatenated, by a period, with the name of a DataRelation to use. When you use this syntax, the data grid automatically sets up event handlers to manage updating the detail grid when an item in the master row is selected.

Another helpful capability is being able to create a DataView for the child rows involved in a relationship. This allows you to start with a given row in a view of the parent table, and retrieve a view that only contains the related rows from the child table. With this view, you can further manipulate the representation of the child rows, using all of the familiar properties of the DataView class.

The following code provides an example of how to use this functionality. After loading a DataSet and creating a DataRelation between the two tables, you use the DataView of the parent table to access the related rows in the child table in a DataView that you can sort before presenting it to the user.

```
Dim cnn As New SqlConnection("server=(local);database=northwind;uid=sa;pwd=;")
Dim da As New SqlDataAdapter("SELECT * FROM Customers;" & _
                    "SELECT * FROM orders;SELECT * FROM [order details]", cnn)

Dim ds As New DataSet()
Dim rowView As DataRowView
Dim orderRowView As DataRowView

da.Fill(ds, "Customers")
ds.Tables(1).TableName = "Orders"
' Create the data relation
Dim Parent As DataColumn = ds.Tables("Customers").Columns("customerid")
Dim Child As DataColumn = ds.Tables("Orders").Columns("customerid")

Dim customerRelation New DataRelation("CustomerRelation", Parent, Child)

' Create the parent view
Dim customers As New DataView = ds.Tables("Customers").DefaultView

' Loop through the parent data view
For Each rowView In Customers

  Console.WriteLine(rowView("ContactName"))

  ' For each row, get the related child rows in a view
  Dim orders As DataView = rowView.CreateChildView(customerRelation)
```

```
' Sort the related child rows by order date
orders.Sort = "OrderDate DESC"

' Loop through the child rows and print out their value
For Each orderRowView In Orders
  Console.WriteLine(orderRowView("OrderDate") & " " & _
                    orderRowView("ShipName"))
  Next
Next
```

The following two examples show how powerful constraints, data relations, and data views can be when used in conjunction with one another. This power continues to grow as you take advantage of more and more of the features of the various classes in ADO.NET.

Examples

The two following examples pull together what you've seen in this chapter. The first is a Windows Forms application that allows the user to edit data from the pubs database; you'll find it in the code download as WinSample. It uses DataRelation objects and Constraint objects to constrain the data, and the DataView to manage the presentation of the data. (You can find the code samples for this chapter in the Downloads section of the Apress Web site [http://www.apress.com].)

WinForm Example

We start by adding two data grid controls named Grid1 and Grid2 to a file named Form1.vb. Figure 7-5 shows the form.

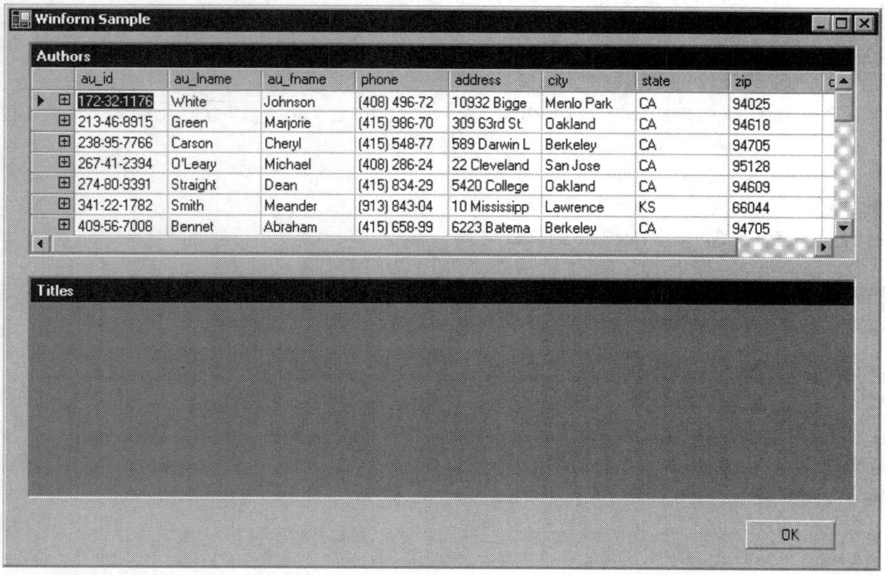

Figure 7-5. WinForm *example*

In the form's constructor, you connect to the pubs database and load a DataSet with the data from the authors, titleauthor, and titles tables.

```
Public Sub New()
  MyBase.New()

  ' Load the data into a data set
  Dim PubsConnection As New SqlConnection( _
             "server=(local);database=pubs;uid=sa;pwd=;")
  Dim PubsAdapter As New SqlDataAdapter("SELECT * FROM authors;" & _
             "SELECT * FROM titles;SELECT * FROM titleauthor", PubsConnection)
  Dim PubsDataSet As New DataSet()

  ' Identify that we want the primary key
  PubsAdapter.MissingSchemaAction = MissingSchemaAction.AddWithKey
  PubsAdapter.Fill(PubsDataSet)
```

You name the DataTables, and then create two data relations to connect the tables, which automatically creates corresponding constraints.

```
  ' Name tables
  PubsDataSet.Tables(0).TableName = "Authors"
  PubsDataSet.Tables(1).TableName = "Titles"
  PubsDataSet.Tables(2).TableName = "TitleAuthor"

  ' Create two new data relations, allowing the constraints to be created as well
  Dim AuthorTitleParent As New DataRelation("AuthorTitleParent", _
             PubsDataSet.Tables("Authors").Columns("au_id"), _
             PubsDataSet.Tables("TitleAuthor").Columns("au_id"))

  Dim AuthorTitleChild As New DataRelation("AuthorChildParent", _
             PubsDataSet.Tables("Titles").Columns("title_id"), _
             PubsDataSet.Tables("TitleAuthor").Columns("title_id"))

  ' Add the relations to the DataSet
  PubsDataSet.Relations.Add(AuthorTitleParent)
  PubsDataSet.Relations.Add(AuthorTitleChild)
```

Finally, you create a view of the data and set the appropriate properties to allow the records to be edited, but not deleted.

```
  ' Create a DataView on the data
  Dim AuthorView As New DataView(PubsDataSet.Tables("Authors"))

  ' Restrict the access to the Authors table
  AuthorView.AllowDelete = False
```

```
AuthorView.AllowEdit = True
AuthorView.AllowNew = True

' Set the grid's source to the author view
Grid1.DataSource = AuthorView

' Hook up the event handler
AddHandler Grid1.CurrentCellChanged, AddressOf Me.Grid1_CellChanging
End Sub
```

In the event handler for the CurrentCellChanged event, you make sure that this is not a new row. Next, you get the child rows of the current author. This gets you the rows in the intermediate table, TitleAuthor, but you need to get the rows in the Titles table. To do that, you iterate over the rows in the intermediate table and get the parent rows using the relationship.

```
Private Sub Grid1_CellChanging(ByVal sender As Object, ByVal eArgs As EventArgs)
  Dim grid As DataGrid = CType(sender, DataGrid)
  Dim view As DataView = CType(grid.DataSource, DataView)

  If CType(sender, DataGrid).CurrentCell.RowNumber < view.Table.Rows.Count Then

    ' Instance values
    Dim rows As DataRow()
    Dim rowIndex As Integer

    ' Get the row number of the selected cell
    rowIndex = CType(sender, DataGrid).CurrentCell.RowNumber

    ' Use the row number to get the value of the key (customerID)
    Dim Key As String = CType(sender, DataGrid)(rowIndex, 0).ToString()

    ' Use the key to find the row we selected in the data source
    rows = view.Table.Rows.Find(Key).GetChildRows("AuthorTitleParent")

    Dim tmpData As New DataSet()
    Dim row As DataRow
```

You then merge each of these sets of rows into a temporary DataSet, create a view from the initial table (if it exists), set up the editable properties of the view, sort it, and set it as the data source of the second grid.

```
    For Each row In rows
      tmpData.Merge(row.GetParentRows("AuthorChildParent"))
    Next
```

```vb
    ' If there is no data to be displayed, then don't display the
    ' data in the grid. If there is, create a view and display it.
    If (tmpData.Tables.Count > 0) Then

        Dim TitleView As New DataView(tmpData.Tables(0))
        TitleView.AllowDelete = False
        TitleView.AllowEdit = True
        TitleView.AllowNew = True
        TitleView.Sort = "Title ASC"

        Grid2.DataSource = tmpData.Tables(0).DefaultView
    Else
        Grid2.DataSource = Nothing
    End If
  End If
End Sub
```

WebSample Example

The second example is a web application that shows many of the same concepts in a web model. As usual in such an application, you have two pieces to your code, which includes the web form or ASP.NET page, and the code behind it.

In the Web Form (WebForm1.aspx) of the example called VBWebSample, you define the layout for your page. This includes two drop-down lists that will be filled with the names of the columns in the data table.

```aspx
<%@ Page language="VB" Codebehind="WebForm1.aspx.vb"
        AutoEventWireup="false" Inherits="WebSample.WebForm1" %>
<!DOCTYPE HTML PUBLIC "-//W3C//DTD HTML 4.0 Transitional//EN">
<html>
  <head>
  </head>
  <body ms_positioning="FlowLayout">
    <form id="Form1" method="post" runat="server">
      <table>
        <tr>
          <td valign="top">
            <table>
              <tr>
                <td valign="top">
                  <b>Sort &amp; Filter</b>
                  <br>
                  Sort Field
                  <br>
```

```
          <asp:dropdownlist id="SortList" runat="server" />
        </td>
      </tr>
```

You also use a radio button list to allow the user to indicate the sort direction, and a text box to specify the filter criteria.

```
      <tr>
        <td>
          Sort Direction
          <br>
          <asp:radiobuttonlist id="SortDirection" runat="server">
            <asp:ListItem value="ASC" text="Asc" selected="True" />
            <asp:ListItem value="DESC" text="Desc" />
          </asp:radiobuttonlist>
        </td>
      </tr>
      <tr>
        <td>
          Filter Field
          <br>
          <asp:dropdownlist id="FilterList" runat="server" />
        </td>
      </tr>
      <tr>
        <td>
          Filter Criteria
          <br>
          <asp:textbox id="FilterCriteria" runat="server" />
        </td>
      </tr>
```

Finally, you have a grid for displaying the results, and a button to submit the form.

```
      <tr>
        <td>
          <asp:button id="submit" runat="server" text="Update" />
        </td>
      </tr>
    </table>
  </td>
  <td valign="top">
    <asp:datagrid id="Authors" runat="server" />
  </td>
</tr>
</table>
```

```
      </form>
    </body>
</html>
```

Saving the appearance of your application for the end of this explanation, let's take a look at the code behind this page. You start with namespace and variable declarations.

```
Imports System.Data.SqlClient

Public Class WebForm1
  Inherits System.Web.UI.Page

    Protected WithEvents SortList As System.Web.UI.WebControls.DropDownList
    Protected WithEvents SortDirection As System.Web.UI.WebControls.RadioButtonList
    Protected WithEvents FilterList As System.Web.UI.WebControls.DropDownList
    Protected WithEvents FilterCriteria As System.Web.UI.WebControls.TextBox
    Protected WithEvents submit As System.Web.UI.WebControls.Button
    Protected WithEvents Authors As System.Web.UI.WebControls.DataGrid
```

Next, you put the bulk of your code in the Page_Load() event handler. You first attempt to retrieve a DataView and a DataColumnCollection object from the cache. If they are not present, you connect to the database and load a DataSet.

```
Private Sub Page_Load(ByVal sender As System.Object, _
                    ByVal e As System.EventArgs) Handles MyBase.Load

    ' If there is no view or no columns in the cache then create them
    Dim AuthorView As DataView = CType(Cache("Authors"), DataView)
    Dim Columns As DataColumnCollection = _
                                CType(Cache("Columns"), DataColumnCollection)

    ' If the data was not in the cache then we load it
    If (AuthorView Is Nothing Or Columns Is Nothing) Then

      ' Load the data into the DataSet
      Dim AuthorConnection As New SqlConnection( _
                        "server=(local);database=pubs;uid=sa;pwd=;")
      Dim AuthorAdapter As New SqlDataAdapter( _
                        "SELECT * FROM Authors", AuthorConnection)
      Dim AuthorDataSet As New DataSet()

      AuthorAdapter.Fill(AuthorDataSet)
```

You then set variables for the columns and view, and insert them into the cache so they'll be available to you next time.

```
    ' Set the view and column variables
    Columns = AuthorDataSet.Tables(0).Columns
    AuthorView = AuthorDataSet.Tables(0).DefaultView

    ' Insert the items into the cache, setting a 20 minute timeout
    Cache.Insert("Authors", AuthorView, Nothing, _
                     System.DateTime.Now.AddMinutes(20), System.TimeSpan.Zero)
    Cache.Insert("Columns", AuthorDataSet.Tables(0).Columns, Nothing, _
                     System.DateTime.Now.AddMinutes(20), System.TimeSpan.Zero)
End If
```

You then apply any filters and sorts to the view.

```
' If we are posting back, then filter and sort the view
If IsPostBack Then

    ' Sort the view
    AuthorView.Sort = SortList.SelectedItem.Text & " " & _
                     SortDirection.SelectedItem.Text

    ' Set the filter if one exists, or set it to nothing
    If (FilterCriteria.Text <> String.Empty) Then
      AuthorView.RowFilter = FilterList.SelectedItem.Text & _
                          "= '" & FilterCriteria.Text & "'"
    Else
      AuthorView.RowFilter = ""
    End If
End If
```

Then you set the drop-down lists to use the Columns collection, and the grid to use the view.

```
' Set the source of the drop-down lists to be the columns
SortList.DataSource = Columns
FilterList.DataSource = Columns

' Set the source of the DataGrid to be the view
Authors.DataSource = AuthorView

' Databind all of the controls
DataBind()
    End Sub
End Class
```

Figure 7-6 shows your results.

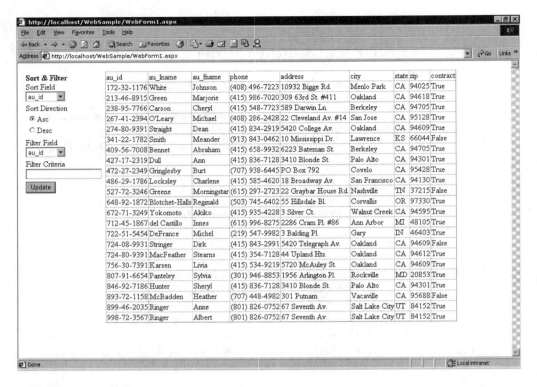

Figure 7-6. VBWebSample

Summary

In this chapter, you have examined the items in ADO.NET that allow you to have a rich client experience and maintain data integrity. You used DataRelation objects, DataView objects, and Constraint objects together to make working with data on the client side a much easier experience. More specifically, you learned how make changes cascade from parent to child tables, saw how to create custom constraints, and explained how to filter and sort the data that's eventually displayed to your users.

■ ■ ■

CHAPTER 8

Transactions

So far, you have covered ADO.NET fundamentals and various objects such as connections, commands, and DataSets. In this chapter, you are going to look at one of the important aspects of any business application—transactions. In this chapter you'll cover

- The basics of database transactions

- How ADO.NET provides transaction support

- How to write database applications that make use of ADO.NET transaction features

What Is a Transaction?

A transaction is a set of operations where either all of the operations must be successful or all of them must fail to ensure consistency and correct behavior within a system. Let's look at the traditional example of a transaction.

Suppose you need to transfer $1000 from account A to account B. This operation involves two steps:

1. $1000 should be deducted from account A.

2. $1000 should be added to account B.

Suppose that you successfully complete Step 1, but, due to some error, Step 2 fails. If you do not undo Step 1, then the entire operation will be faulty. Transactions help to avoid this. Operations in the same transaction will only make changes to the database if *all* the steps succeed. So in your example, if Step 2 fails, then the changes made by Step 1 will not be committed to the database.

Transactions usually follow certain guidelines, known as the ACID properties, which ensure that even complex transactions will be self-contained and reliable. We will look at these in the next section.

ACID Properties

Transactions are characterized by four properties popularly called ACID properties. To pass the ACID test, a transaction must be *Atomic, Consistent, Isolated*, and *Durable*. While this acronym is easy to remember, the meaning of each word is not obvious. Here is a brief explanation.

- *Atomic*: All steps in the transaction should succeed or fail together. Unless *all* the steps from a transaction complete, a transaction is not considered completed.

- *Consistent*: The transaction takes the underlying database from one stable state to another.

- *Isolated*: Every transaction is an independent entity. One transaction should not affect any other transaction running at the same time.

- *Durable*: Changes that occur during the transaction are permanently stored on some media, typically a hard disk, before the transaction is declared successful. That is, logs are maintained on a drive so that, should a failure occur, the database can be reconstructed so as to retain transactional integrity.

Note that even though these are ideal characteristics of a transaction, practically you can alter some of them to suit your requirements. In particular, you can alter the isolation behavior of a transaction, as we will discuss later. Also, constructs such as nested transactions, which we will also discuss later, allow you to control the atomicity of a transaction.

You should only change from these behaviors after careful consideration. The following sections will include discussion of when and how to change them.

Database Transactions

Transactions are frequently used in many business applications. Typically, when you develop a software system, some RDBMS is used to store the data. In order to apply the concept of transactions in such software systems, the RDBMS must support transactions. Modern databases, such as SQL Server 2000 and Oracle 9*i*, provide strong support for transactions. For instance, SQL Server 2000 provides support for Transact-SQL (T-SQL) statements such as BEGIN TRANSACTION, COMMIT TRANSACTION, and ROLLBACK TRANSACTION.

■**Tip** T-SQL is SQL Server's own dialect of structured query language.

Data access APIs, such as ODBC, OLE DB, and ADO.NET, enable developers to use transactions in their applications. Typically, RDBMSs and data access APIs provide transaction support, as long as you are working with a single database. In many large applications, more than one database is involved, and you need to use Microsoft Distributed Transaction Coordinator (MSDTC). Microsoft Transaction Server (MTS) and COM+, which are popular middleware, also use MSDTC internally to facilitate multidatabase transactions. It should be noted that .NET provides access to COM+ functionality via the System.EnterpriseServices namespace.

■Note ADO.NET transactions are not the same as MTS or COM+ transactions. ADO.NET transactions are connection-based, and span only one database at a time. COM+ transactions use MSDTC to facilitate transactions, and can span multiple databases.

Local and Distributed Transactions

Transactions can be split into the local and distributed categories.

- *Local Transaction*: Uses an aware data resource (for example, SQL Server) and has the scope of a single transaction. When a single database holds all of the data involved in a transaction, it can enforce the ACID rules discussed previously.

- *Distributed Transaction*: Spanning multiple transaction-aware data resources, distributed transactions may need to read messages from a Message Queue Server, retrieve data from a SQL Server database, and write to other databases.

  Many software packages (such as MSDTC) are available to assist with programming distributed transactions, which help ensure integrity by controlling commit and rollback behavior across all data resources, using a two-phase commit and rollback.

  MSDTC can only be used with applications that have compatible interfaces for transaction management. MSMQ, SQL Server, Oracle, Sybase, and several others are such applications, referred to as Resource Managers, which are currently available.

Manual and Automatic Transactions

A *manual transaction* model

- allows you to use explicit instructions to begin and end the transaction to control the transaction boundary.

- allows you to start a new transaction from within an active transaction (it supports nested transactions).

Unfortunately, all of the data resources need coordinating with the data boundary, and you will have to control this yourself. There is no support for distributed transactions built in, so controlling a distributed transaction manually could be difficult (i.e., controlling every resource enlistment and connection manually to maintain the ACID properties of the transaction).

A set of objects is provided by the ADO.NET data providers to help create a connection to the data source, to begin, commit, or roll back the transaction, and finally to close the connection manually.

If your transaction spans multiple transaction-aware resource managers (such as SQL Server or Microsoft Message Queue [MSMQ]), an *automatic transaction* is your best option. COM+ service will do all of the coordination work, causing an extra overhead, but the application design will be much simpler, reducing coding requirements.

COM+ uses MSDTC to manage transactions in a distributed environment, which allows a .NET application to run a transaction that combines a number of diverse activities such as the following:

- Retrieving data from a SQL Server database

- Inserting an order into an Oracle Database

- Writing a message to a MSMQ

- Sending an e-mail message

Transaction Vocabulary

There are some commands that are used frequently in the context of database transactions. They are BEGIN, COMMIT, and ROLLBACK. These are the basic building blocks used to implement transactions. Before going any further, let's take a quick look at what these commands do.

- BEGIN: Before executing any queries under a transaction, a transaction must be initiated; to do this, you use BEGIN.

- COMMIT: A transaction is said to be committed when all the changes that occurred during the transaction are written successfully to the database; to achieve this, use COMMIT.

- ROLLBACK: A rollback occurs when all changes made by the transaction are undone because some part of the transaction has failed.

Now that you know the basics of transactions, let's see how ADO.NET provides support for them.

ADO.NET Transaction Support

ADO.NET provides strong support for database transactions. Transactions covered by this support are single database transactions, and are tracked on a per-connection basis. Transaction functionality is provided with the connection object of ADO.NET. There are some differences in the implementation of transaction support in ADO.NET and in ADO.

If you have worked with ADO, you will recollect that it provides methods such as BeginTrans, CommitTrans, and RollbackTrans for the connection object itself. In the case of ADO.NET, the connection object is used simply to start a transaction. The commit or rollback of the transaction is taken care of by a dedicated object, which is an implementation of the transaction class. This enables you to associate different command objects with a single transaction object, so that those commands participate in the same transaction.

ADO.NET provides connected as well as disconnected data access, and provides support for transactions in both modes. In connected mode, the typical sequence of operations in a transaction will be as follows:

1. Open a database connection.

2. Begin a transaction.

3. Fire queries directly against the connection via the command object.

4. Commit or roll back the transaction.

5. Close the connection.

Figure 8-1 shows how transactions are handled in a connected mode.

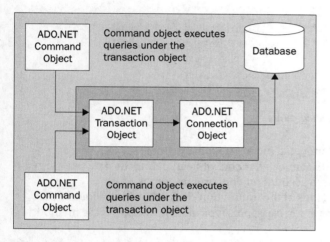

Figure 8-1. *Transactions in a connected mode*

In a disconnected mode, you generally first fetch data (usually one or more tables) into a DataSet object, manipulate it as required, and then update data back in the database. In this mode, the typical sequence of operations will be as follows:

1. Open a database connection.

2. Fetch required data in a DataSet object.

3. Close the database connection.

4. Manipulate the data in the DataSet object.

5. Again, open a connection with the database.

6. Start a transaction.

7. Update the database with changes from the DataSet.

8. Close the connection.

Figure 8-2 illustrates this sequence of events.

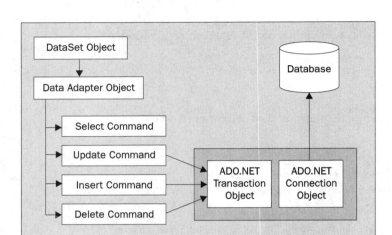

Figure 8-2. *Transactions in a disconnected mode*

Implementing transactions in connected mode is relatively simple, as you have everything happening live. However, in a disconnected mode, while updating the data back into the database, some care should be taken to account for concurrency issues.

In the following section, you will look at the transaction class. You will also look at the commonly used methods of the transaction class, plus typical ways of using these methods.

Transaction Class

There are currently four .NET Managed Providers available from Microsoft: OLEDB, SQLClient, OracleClient, and ODBC (there are other third-party alternatives available). Each of these providers has its own implementation of the transaction class: the OLEDB data provider has the OleDbTransaction class, which resides in the System.Data.OleDb namespace; the ODBC data provider has the ODBCTransaction class, which resides in the System.Data.ODBC namespace, and so on for the other providers (SQLTransaction class and OracleTransaction class).

All of these classes implement the IDbTransaction interface, from the System.Data namespace. Most of the properties and methods of these classes are identical. However, each has some specific methods of its own, as you will see later.

Methods of the Transaction Class

We mentioned commit and rollback earlier in this chapter. The transaction classes have two methods that you will use frequently.

- Commit: This method identifies a transaction as successful. Once you call this method, all the pending changes are written permanently to the underlying database.

- Rollback: This method marks a transaction as unsuccessful and pending changes are discarded. The database state remains unchanged.

Typically, both of these methods are used together. The following code snippet shows how they are used in the most common way:

```
MyConnection.Open()
MyTransaction = MyConnection.BeginTransaction()
MyCommand1.Transaction = MyTransaction
MyCommand2.Transaction = MyTransaction
Try
    MyCommand1.ExecuteNonQuery()
    MyCommand2.ExecuteNonQuery()
    MyTransaction.Commit()
Catch
    MyTransaction.Rollback()
Finally
    MyConnection.Close()
End Try
```

The command object has a `Transaction` property that you must set in order to execute your command within a transaction. The transaction classes also have other properties and methods, which you will look at later in the chapter.

Now you will move on to actually developing applications that use the transactional features of ADO.NET.

Writing Transactional Database Applications

Implementing a basic transaction using ADO.NET in an application can be fairly straightforward. The most common sequence of steps that would be performed while developing a transactional application is as follows:

1. Open a database connection using the `Open` method of the connection object.

2. Begin a transaction using the `BeginTransaction` method of the connection object. This method provides you with a transaction object that you will use later to commit or roll back the transaction. Note that changes caused by any queries executed before calling the `BeginTransaction` method will be committed to the database immediately after they execute.

3. Set the `Transaction` property of the command object to the previously mentioned transaction object.

4. Execute the SQL commands using the command object. You may use one or more command objects for this purpose, as long as the `Transaction` property of all the objects is set to a valid transaction object.

5. Commit or roll back the transaction using the `Commit` or `Rollback` method of the transaction object.

6. Close the database connection.

Note that once you have started a transaction on a certain connection, all the queries that use that particular connection must fall inside the boundary of the transaction. For example, you executed two INSERT queries and one UPDATE query inside a transaction. If you execute a SELECT query without the transaction, you will get an error indicating that a transaction is still pending. Also, one connection object can have only one pending transaction at a time. In other words, once you call the BeginTransaction method on a connection object, you cannot call BeginTransaction again, until you commit or rollback that transaction. In such situations, you will get an error message stating that parallel transactions are not supported. To overcome this error, you may use another connection to execute the query.

Let's put your knowledge about transactions into practice by developing an application that uses ADO.NET transaction features.

Implementing Transactions

In this section, you will develop a small console application that illustrates how to develop transactional applications with ADO.NET.

For your example, you will use the Northwind database that ships with SQL Server. Your application operates in the following way:

- You want to place new orders against the customer ID, "ALFKI," for product IDs 1, 2, and 3.

- You will supply quantities for product IDs.

- You will then place the order by inserting records into the Orders table and the Order Details table.

- You will then check if the requested quantity of any product is greater than the available quantity. If it is, the entire transaction is rolled back. Otherwise, the transaction is committed.

When you run the sample, the output in Figure 8-3 is produced.

Figure 8-3. *A* SimpleTransaction

Here is the complete code for the application SimpleTransaction in the code download for this chapter (located in the Downloads section of the Apress Web site [http://www.apress.com]).

```
Imports System
Imports System.Data
Imports System.Data.SqlClient

Module Module1

    Sub Main()
        'Define variables
        Dim myconnection As SqlConnection
        Dim mycommand As SqlCommand
        Dim mytransaction As SqlTransaction
        Dim ConnectionString As String
        Dim stock As Integer
        Dim qty1, qty2, qty3 As Integer

            qty1 = 2
            qty2 = 4
            qty3 = 5

        'open a database connection
        ConnectionString = "User ID=sa;Initial Catalog=Northwind;" & _
                           "Data Source=(local)"
        myconnection = New SqlConnection(ConnectionString)
        myconnection.Open()

        'start a transaction
        mytransaction = myconnection.BeginTransaction()
        'configure command object to use transaction
        mycommand = New SqlCommand()
        mycommand.Connection = myconnection
        mycommand.Transaction = mytransaction
        'execute various sql statements

        Try
            'insert into orders table
            mycommand.CommandText = "insert into orders(customerid," & _
                    "orderdate,requireddate) values('ALFKI', " & _
                    "GetDate(),DATEADD(d,15,GetDate()))"
            mycommand.ExecuteNonQuery()

            'store identity value for further queries
            mycommand.CommandText = "select @@identity from orders"
            Dim id As String = mycommand.ExecuteScalar().ToString()
```

```
'insert product details
mycommand.CommandText = "insert into [order details]" & _
            "(orderid,productid,unitprice,quantity)" & _
            " values(" & id & ",1,18," & qty1 & ")"
mycommand.ExecuteNonQuery()
mycommand.CommandText = "insert into [order details]" & _
            "(orderid,productid,unitprice,quantity)" & _
            "values(" & id & ",2,19," & qty2 & ")"
mycommand.ExecuteNonQuery()
mycommand.CommandText = "insert into [order details]" & _
            "(orderid,productid,unitprice,quantity)" & _
            "values(" & id & ",3,10," & qty3 & ")"
mycommand.ExecuteNonQuery()
'rollback if ordered quantity exceeds stock quantity
mycommand.CommandText = "select unitsinstock from products " & _
                        "where productid=1"
stock = Integer.Parse(mycommand.ExecuteScalar().ToString())
If stock < qty1 Then
    mytransaction.Rollback()
    Console.WriteLine("Quantity for Product ID 1 exceeds" & _
                      "available stock")
    Console.ReadLine()
    Return
End If
mycommand.CommandText = "select unitsinstock from products " & _
                        "where productid=2"
stock = Integer.Parse(mycommand.ExecuteScalar().ToString())
If stock < qty2 Then
    mytransaction.Rollback()
    Console.WriteLine("Quantity for Product ID 2 exceeds" & _
                      "available stock")
    Console.ReadLine()
    Return
End If
mycommand.CommandText = "select unitsinstock from products " & _
                        "where productid=3"
stock = Integer.Parse(mycommand.ExecuteScalar().ToString())
If stock < qty3 Then
    mytransaction.Rollback()
    Console.WriteLine("Quantity for Product ID 3 exceeds" & _
                      "available stock")
    Console.ReadLine()
    Return
End If
mytransaction.Commit()
Console.WriteLine("Your order has been successfully placed!")
```

```
      Console.WriteLine("Order ID :" & id)
      Console.ReadLine()
   Catch e As Exception
      Console.WriteLine(e.Message)
      Console.ReadLine()
   Finally
      myconnection.Close()
   End Try

 End Sub

End Module
```

As usual, you declare various database objects such as connection, command, and transaction. You then open a connection with the database. The following code simply opens a connection with the Northwind database:

```
ConnectionString = "User ID=sa;Initial Catalog=Northwind;Data" & _
                   "Source=(local)"
myconnection = New SqlConnection(ConnectionString)
myconnection.Open()
```

You begin the transaction by calling the BeginTransaction method of the connection object. The BeginTransaction method returns an instance of the transaction object, which you will hold in a SqlTransaction variable called mytransaction.

```
mytransaction = myconnection.BeginTransaction()
'configure command object to use transaction
mycommand = New SqlCommand()
mycommand.Connection = myconnection
```

The next step is to set the SqlCommand object's Transaction property so that all the SQL statements fired through it will participate in the transaction.

```
mycommand.Transaction = mytransaction
```

You then execute various SQL statements. You are now ready to fire your queries using the SqlCommand object.

```
   Try
      'insert into orders table
      mycommand.CommandText = "insert into orders(customerid," & _
               "orderdate,requireddate) values('ALFKI', " & _
               "GetDate(),DATEADD(d,15,GetDate()))"
      mycommand.ExecuteNonQuery()

      'store identity value for further queries
      mycommand.CommandText = "select @@identity from orders"
      Dim id As String = mycommand.ExecuteScalar().ToString()
```

```
            'insert product details
            mycommand.CommandText = "insert into [order details]" & _
                      "(orderid,productid,unitprice,quantity)" & _
                      " values(" & id & ",1,18," & qty1 & ")"
            mycommand.ExecuteNonQuery()
            mycommand.CommandText = "insert into [order details]" & _
                      "(orderid,productid,unitprice,quantity)" & _
                      "values(" & id & ",2,19," & qty2 & ")"
            mycommand.ExecuteNonQuery()
            mycommand.CommandText = "insert into [order details]" & _
                      "(orderid,productid,unitprice,quantity)" & _
                      "values(" & id & ",3,10," & qty3 & ")"
            mycommand.ExecuteNonQuery()
            'rollback if ordered quantity exceeds stock quantity
            mycommand.CommandText = "select unitsinstock from products " & _
                               "where productid=1"
```

You may change the CommandText property of the same object to fire different queries or to create new command objects. Remember that if you use new command objects, their Transaction properties need to be set. Typically, you would place the appropriate code in a Try...Catch block, so that if an error occurs, the transaction may be rolled back. You may also carry out any business validations here and decide whether to commit or roll back the transaction.

Once you are done with your operations, you must call either the Commit or Rollback method of the transaction object.

```
            stock = Integer.Parse(mycommand.ExecuteScalar().ToString())
            If stock < qty3 Then
                mytransaction.Rollback()
                Console.WriteLine("Quantity for Product ID 3 exceeds" & _
                                "available stock")
                Console.ReadLine()
                Return
            End If
            mytransaction.Commit()
            Console.WriteLine("Your order has been successfully placed!")
            Console.WriteLine("Order ID :" & id)
            Console.ReadLine()
        Catch e As Exception
            Console.WriteLine(e.Message)
            Console.ReadLine()
        Finally
            myconnection.Close()
        End Try
```

Running the Application

Try modifying the application to accept command-line arguments, and try running the application with various command-line argument values for product quantities. In order to test rollback (see Figure 8-4), supply some values that are greater than stock quantity (say 115, for Product ID 3).

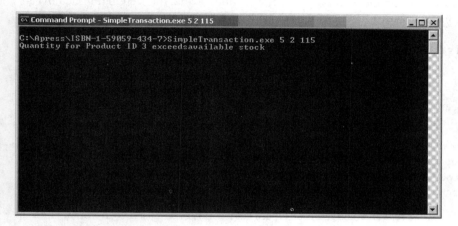

Figure 8-4. SimpleTransaction *with command-line arguments*

▪**Note** A transaction should be completed as soon as possible (started as late as possible and finished as soon as possible). An active transaction puts locks on the various resources involved, so it is always good practice to keep transactions as small as possible. If you are selecting data within a transaction, then you should only SELECT the rows you really require.

Examining the Effect of Isolation Levels

Now that you know how to implement basic transactions, let's go into some more detail. In this section, you will examine *isolation levels* and how they affect your application. In doing so, you will encounter some terms that are frequently used while discussing isolation levels. Finally, you will see how to set isolation levels in your code.

What Are Isolation Levels?

The isolation level is a measure of the extent to which changes made outside a transaction are visible inside that transaction. It determines how sensitive your transaction is to changes made by other transactions.

For example, by default, if two transactions are running independently of one another, then records inserted by one transaction are not visible to the other transaction, unless the first transaction is committed.

The isolation level concept is closely related to the locks concept, because by determining an isolation level for a given transaction you determine how long the given transaction must hold locks on resources to protect them against changes that may be made by others.

You may wish to alter the behavior of the transactions so that the second transaction can view records inserted by the first one. You can achieve this through setting isolation levels appropriately. For an ADO.NET programmer, the isolation level can be set via isolation level enumerated values. You will see shortly how these are used.

Some Related Terms

Before going any further, it is important to understand some terms that are used frequently when discussing isolation levels.

- *Dirty read*: A dirty read is a condition when a transaction reads data that has yet to be committed. Consider a case where transaction A inserts some records into the table, but is pending. Transaction B reads these records. Now, if transaction A rolls back, transaction B will refer to data that is invalid.

- *Nonrepeatable read*: Consider a case where transaction A reads a record from a table. Transaction B then alters or deletes the records, and commits the changes. Now, if transaction A tries to re-read the record, it will either be a different version, or will not be available at all. Such a condition is called a nonrepeatable read.

- *Phantom read*: Suppose that transaction A has some criteria for record selection. Initially, transaction A has, say, 100 rows matching these criteria. Now transaction B inserts some rows that match the selection criteria of transaction A. If transaction A executes the selection query again, it will receive a different set of rows than in the previous case. Rows added in this way are called phantom rows.

Possible Isolation Levels in ADO.NET

Let's now look at the different isolation level values that you can implement with ADO.NET. These values are accessible via the IsolationLevel enumeration.

- Chaos: The pending changes from more highly isolated transactions cannot be over-written. This setting is not supported by SQL Server.

- ReadCommitted: Shared locks are held while the data is being read by the transaction. This avoids dirty reads, but the data can be changed before a transaction completes. This may result in nonrepeatable reads or phantom rows. This type of isolation level is appropriate when we want to work with all the data that matches certain conditions is committed.

  Shared locks are locks that are placed when a transaction wants to read data from the database, and no exclusive lock is already held on that data item. No other transactions can modify the data while shared locks exist on a table or tables. Exclusive locks are the locks that prevent two or more transactions from modifying data simultaneously. An exclusive lock is issued when a transaction needs to update a table, or tables, and no other locks are already held on the respective tables.

- ReadUncommitted: In this case, a dirty read is possible. This means that no shared locks are placed and no exclusive locks are honored. This type of isolation level is appropriate when you want to work with all the data matching certain conditions, regardless of whether it's committed or not.

- RepeatableRead: In this case, shared locks are placed on all data that is used in a query. This prevents others from modifying the data and also prevents nonrepeatable reads. However, phantom rows are possible. This type of isolation level is appropriate when you want the records that are read to retain the same values for future reads.

- Serializable: In this case, a lock is placed on the dataset, preventing other users from updating or inserting rows into the dataset until the transaction is complete. This type of isolation level is appropriate when you want all the data you are working with to be exactly the same until you finish the processing.

- Unspecified: In this type, a different isolation level from the one specified is being used; however, the level cannot be determined.

These isolation level values can be supplied while initiating a transaction through the BeginTransaction method of the OleDbConnection or SqlConnection object. You may read the current value of isolation level using the IsolationLevel property of the transaction object.

Changing Isolation Levels

You will now develop a small application that changes the default isolation level of a SQL Server database from ReadCommitted to ReadUncommitted. The application works in the following way:

1. You will open a connection with Northwind database and begin a transaction. The isolation level for this transaction will be the default—ReadCommitted.

2. You will open another connection with the database and begin another transaction. However, you will set the isolation level to ReadUncommitted.

3. From the first transaction, you will then insert two rows into the Orders table.

4. Without committing the first transaction, you will fetch the last two order IDs in the second transaction, and output the results in the console. This will prove that, even though the first transaction is yet to be finished, the second transaction reads records inserted by it.

5. You will roll back the first transaction, and output the last two orders again from the second transaction, in order to show that they are now different.

The complete code for the application follows:

```
Imports System
Imports System.Data
Imports System.Data.SqlClient

Module Module1
    Sub Main()
        Dim myconnection1, myconnection2 As SqlConnection
        Dim mycommand1, mycommand2 As SqlCommand
        Dim mytransaction1, mytransaction2 As SqlTransaction
        Dim myreader As SqlDataReader
        Dim ConnectionString As String

        'open a database connection
        ConnectionString = "User ID=sa;Initial Catalog=Northwind; " & _
                           "Data Source=(local)"
        myconnection1 = New SqlConnection(ConnectionString)
        myconnection2 = New SqlConnection(ConnectionString)
        myconnection1.Open()
        myconnection2.Open()

        'start a transaction
        mytransaction1 = myconnection1.BeginTransaction()
        mytransaction2 = myconnection2.BeginTransaction( _
                                        IsolationLevel.ReadUncommitted)

        'configure command object to use tansaction
        mycommand1 = New SqlCommand()
        mycommand1.Connection = myconnection1
        mycommand1.Transaction = mytransaction1

        mycommand2 = New SqlCommand()
        mycommand2.Connection = myconnection2
        mycommand2.Transaction = mytransaction2

        'execute various sql statements
        Try
            mycommand1.CommandText = "insert into orders default values"
            mycommand1.ExecuteNonQuery()
            mycommand1.CommandText = "insert into orders default values"
            mycommand1.ExecuteNonQuery()

            mycommand2.CommandText = "select top 2 orderid from " & _
                                    "orders order by orderid desc"
            myreader = mycommand2.ExecuteReader()
            Console.WriteLine("Last 2 Orders - Transaction is pending")
            Console.WriteLine("=======================================")
```

```
            While myreader.Read()

                Console.WriteLine(myreader.GetInt32(0))
            End While
            myreader.Close()
            Console.ReadLine()

            mytransaction1.Rollback()
            mycommand2.CommandText = "select top 2 orderid from " & _
                                "orders order by orderid desc"
            myreader = mycommand2.ExecuteReader()

            Console.WriteLine("Last 2 Orders - Transaction rolled back")
            Console.WriteLine("=======================================")
            While myreader.Read()
                Console.WriteLine(myreader.GetInt32(0))
            End While
            Console.ReadLine()
        Catch e As Exception
            Console.WriteLine(e.Message)
            Console.ReadLine()
        Finally
            myconnection1.Close()
            myconnection2.Close()
        End Try
    End Sub
End Module
```

Here, note how you have initiated the second transaction by passing the IsolationLevel enumeration value to the BeginTransaction method.

```
mytransaction2 = myconnection2.BeginTransaction(IsolationLevel.ReadUncommitted)
```

Figure 8-5 is the result from a test run of the application.

Figure 8-5. IsolationLevel *example*

■**Note** Isolation level is the measure of the extent to which changes made outside a transaction are visible inside that transaction. The default isolation level for SQL Server is `ReadCommitted`.

Changing the default isolation level is a tricky issue that depends on the level of consistency and concurrency you want. Generally, you will find that the higher the isolation level, the higher the consistency, but the lower the concurrency.

When to Use Transactions

Even though ADO.NET provides good support for transactions, it is not necessary for you to always use transactions. In fact, every time you use a transaction you actually carry some overhead. Also, transactions involve some kind of locking of table rows. Thus, unnecessary use of transactions may cause performance penalties. So, as a rule of thumb, *use a transaction only when your operation requires one*. For example, if you are simply selecting records from a database, or firing a single query, then most of the time you will not need a transaction.

Transactional features are provided by the underlying RDBMS, ADO.NET, or COM+. The choice between these actually depends on what you are trying to accomplish. For example, suppose that you are using a stored procedure that performs a certain operation that requires a transaction. You may find that, instead of starting an ADO.NET transaction and calling the stored procedure in that transaction, it is much easier and more efficient to initialize the transaction in the stored procedure itself. On the other hand, if you are firing multiple SQL statements—inserts, for example—that require a transaction, then using ADO.NET transaction capabilities will be very easy. Also, if the commit or rollback depends on some factor external to the database, then using ADO.NET transactions would be preferable.

Almost always, there is the choice between three basic transaction techniques: RDBMS transactions, ADO.NET transactions, and COM+ transactions.

- RDBMS transactions offer the best performance, as they only need a single round trip to the database. They also provide the flexibility associated with explicitly controlling the transaction boundary. The negative sides to RDBMS transactions are that you also need code in T-SQL (which may be not so easy as using VB.NET or C#) and that your code is separated into two locations (in the .NET project and also on SQL Server).

- ADO.NET transactions are easy to code and provide the flexibility to control the transaction boundary with explicit instructions to begin and end the transaction. To achieve this ease and flexibility, a performance cost is incurred for extra round trips to the database to complete the transaction.

- COM+ transactions will be the only choice if your transaction spans multiple transaction-aware resource managers, which could include more than one SQL Server database, MSMQs, and so on. They greatly simplify the application design and reduce coding requirements. However, since COM+ service does all of the coordination work, it may have some extra overhead, plus doing COM+ programming may be not easy as ADO.NET programming.

Transactions and Performance

Always keep in mind that a lengthy transaction that performs data modification to many different tables can effectively block the work of all other users in the system. This may cause serious performance problems. While implementing a transaction, the following practices can be followed in order to achieve acceptable results:

- Keep transactions as short as possible.

- Avoid returning data with a SELECT in the middle of a transaction, unless your statements depend on the data returned.

- If you use the SELECT statement, fetch only the rows that are required so as not to lock too many resources and to keep performance as good as possible.

- Wherever appropriate, try to write transactions within stored procedures instead of always using ADO.NET transactions.

- Avoid transactions that combine multiple independent batches of work. Put such batches in individual transactions.

- Avoid large updates if at all possible.

■**Note** Transactions can generate considerable overhead and affect performance if used without thought. While developing the user interfaces of applications that deal with transactions, some care should be taken to reduce locks.

Default Behavior for Transactions

One point to also note is the default behavior of transactions. By default, if you do not explicitly commit the transaction, then the transaction is rolled back. Even though default behavior allows the rolling back of a transaction, it is always a good programming practice to explicitly call the rollback method. This will not only release any locks from data, but also make code much more readable, and less error prone.

Transactions and User Confirmation

When developing applications that deal with transactions interactively, some care must be taken in order to avoid locking issues. Consider a case where you are developing an application that transfers money from one account to another. You develop a user interface, in the form of a typical message box, which requires confirmation about the money being transferred. Now, consider that your application conforms to the following sequence of operations:

1. Open a connection.

2. Begin a transaction.

3. Execute various queries.

4. Ask user confirmation about transaction by prompting a message box.

5. On confirmation, commit the transaction.

6. In the absence of confirmation, roll back the transaction.

If, after Step 4, the user is unable to confirm the transaction (perhaps she walks out for a lunch or a meeting), the locks will still be maintained on the rows under consideration. Also, a live connection is maintained with the database. This might cause problems for other users. In such cases, you can instead perform Steps 1, 2, and 3 *after* getting confirmation from the user.

In general, you should avoid such scenarios where there is the need for user action in the middle of a transaction. If you do not know exactly how long an action within a transaction lasts, or if the length of such an action is out of your control, then it is crucial to set some kind of expiration mechanism. For example, you can give a user 30 seconds to confirm the action, otherwise it will be canceled. In such cases nothing happens and the user can start the process again.

Note that in the previous example, since you wanted to obtain user confirmation, you opted for altering the sequence. If you are simply displaying the transaction status in some user interface component, such as a status bar or a label, that does not require any user inter-action, then the previously mentioned steps can be used without any alterations. Also, you should notify the user of any changes—an account balance, for instance—just before commit-ting the changes, otherwise another transaction might alter the balance for the second time and the notification would be wrong.

Simultaneous ADO.NET and RDBMS Transactions

Although rare, you might encounter cases where you use ADO.NET transactions as well as RDBMS transactions. Suppose that you have one stored procedure that uses transactions internally, and you call this stored procedure as a part of your own ADO.NET transaction. In such cases, both the transactions work as if they are nested. The ADO.NET commit or rollback decides the outcome of the entire process. However, there are chances of getting into errors if you roll back from the stored procedure or place improper nesting levels (see "Nested Trans-actions" later in this chapter).

Advanced Techniques

Up to now, you have seen how to implement transactions using ADO.NET. You also saw how to change a transaction's isolation level. Now it's time to move on to some advanced topics. These topics include savepoints, nested transactions, and using transactions with disconnected data access techniques.

Savepoints

Whenever you roll back a transaction, it nullifies the effects of every statement from that transaction. In some cases, you may not want to roll back each and every statement, so you need a mechanism to roll back only part of a transaction. You can implement this through the use of *savepoints*.

Savepoints are markers that act like bookmarks: you may mark a certain point in the flow of transaction and then roll back up to that point, rather than completely rolling back the transaction. To accomplish this, use the Save method of the transaction object. Note that the Save method is available only for the SqlTransaction class and not for the OleDbTransaction class.

You will now develop a simple example that illustrates the use of the Save method. Here is the complete code for the example.

```vb
Imports System
Imports System.Data
Imports System.Data.SqlClient

Module Module1
    Sub Main()
        Dim myconnection As SqlConnection
        Dim mycommand As SqlCommand
        Dim mytransaction As SqlTransaction
        Dim myreader As SqlDataReader

        'open a database connection
        myconnection = New SqlConnection("User ID=sa; " & _
                    "Initial Catalog=Northwind;Data Source=(local)")
        myconnection.Open()

        'start a transaction
        mytransaction = myconnection.BeginTransaction()
        'configure command object to use transaction
        mycommand = New SqlCommand()
        mycommand.Connection = myconnection
        mycommand.Transaction = mytransaction

        'execute various sql statements
        Try
            'insert into orders table
            mycommand.CommandText = "insert into orders default values"
            mycommand.ExecuteNonQuery()
            mytransaction.Save("firstorder")
            mycommand.CommandText = "insert into orders default values"
            mycommand.ExecuteNonQuery()
            mycommand.CommandText = "insert into orders default values"
            mycommand.ExecuteNonQuery()
            mytransaction.Rollback("firstorder")

            mycommand.CommandText = "insert into orders default values"
            mycommand.ExecuteNonQuery()
            mycommand.CommandText = "insert into orders default values"
```

```
            mycommand.ExecuteNonQuery()
            mytransaction.Commit()

            mycommand.CommandText = "select top 3 orderid from " & _
                                    "orders order by orderid desc"
            myreader = mycommand.ExecuteReader()
            Console.WriteLine("Last 3 Orders")
            While myreader.Read()
                Console.WriteLine(myreader.GetInt32(0))
            End While
        Catch e As Exception
            Console.WriteLine(e.Message)
            Console.ReadLine()
        Finally
            myconnection.Close()
        End Try
    End Sub
End Module
```

Here, you have executed a total of five queries that insert orders. After inserting the first order, you have inserted a savepoint by using the following statement:

```
mytransaction.Save("firstorder")
```

You then insert two more rows and roll back up to the savepoint called firstorder. Note how the same Rollback method is used with the savepoint name as a parameter (to roll back the whole transaction you don't use the parameter). You then insert another two rows and, finally, commit the transaction. You then display the last three order IDs to confirm that the effect of the first insert is indeed committed to the database.

Figure 8-6 shows a sample run of this application.

Figure 8-6. SavePoints *example*

Note that the missing order IDs are due to the fact you rolled back some inserts.

There are a couple of things that can make savepoints messy. One of the common mistakes novice programmers make while working with savepoints is forgetting to call either Commit or Rollback after rolling back to a certain savepoint. Savepoints can be thought of as bookmarks, but you still need to explicitly call Commit or Rollback. Another point to be noted is that once you roll back to a savepoint, all the savepoints defined after that savepoint are lost. You must set them again if they are needed.

Nested Transactions

As you saw in the previous section, savepoints allow a transaction to be arranged as a sequence of actions that can be rolled back individually. Nesting, on the other hand, allows a transaction to be arranged as a hierarchy of such actions. In cases of nested transactions, one transaction can contain one or more other transactions. To initiate such nested transactions, the Begin method of the transaction object is used. This method is available only for the OleDbTransaction class and not for the SqlTransaction or the OracleClientTransaction class. The following code snippet illustrates the usage of the Begin method:

```
Mytransaction = myconnection.BeginTransaction()
myanothertransaction = mytransaction.Begin()
```

Tip With MS SQL Server 2000, nested transactions are perfectly valid in T-SQL, but it is important to bear in mind that nested T-SQL transactions aren't really nested. You just see their blocks nested in the source code. Inner transactions do not increment @@TRANCOUNT. In other words, ROLLBACK on any level of a nested transaction rolls back a whole transaction, and COMMIT TRAN commits a transaction only if it is part of the outermost transaction block. COMMIT TRAN in nested level simply does nothing. This behavior gives you the illusion of nesting and it is acceptable and predictable.

The Begin method returns an instance of another transaction object, which you can use just like the original transaction object. However, rolling back this transaction simply rolls back the current transaction, and not the entire transaction.

Note Savepoints and nested transactions provide a means of dividing a transaction into multiple "subtransactions." The SqlClient data provider and ODP.NET support savepoints with the Save method of the transaction object, whereas the OleDb data provider supports nested transactions with the Begin method of the transaction object.

Using Transactions with a DataSet and DataAdapter

In the previous examples, you used the command object directly to fire queries against the database. However, you can also use the DataSet and DataAdapter objects. You might want to do this, for instance, if you had bound data in a DataSet to control and you wanted to implement batch updates.

You would first fetch all the records needed, place them in the DataSet, and then manipulate them as required. Finally, you might send new values back to the database. Since the DataAdapter uses command objects, internally, to update changes back to the database, you would, essentially, be using the same techniques as discussed previously. The following example illustrates how you can use transactions with the DataSet and DataAdapter objects.

In this example, you want to fetch order details for an order ID into a DataSet. We then change the order quantity for various products and update the data source from the DataSet, via the DataAdapter.

```
Imports System
Imports System.Data
Imports System.Data.SqlClient

Module Module1
    Sub Main()
        Dim ConnectionString As String
        Dim myconnection As SqlConnection
        Dim mytransaction As SqlTransaction
        Dim mycommand1 As SqlCommand
        Dim myparam As SqlParameter
        Dim da As SqlDataAdapter
        Dim ds As New DataSet()
        Dim args() As String = Environment.GetCommandLineArgs

        ConnectionString = "User ID=sa;Initial Catalog=Northwind;" & _
                        "Data Source=(local)"
        myconnection = New SqlConnection(ConnectionString)
        myconnection.Open()

        da = New SqlDataAdapter("select * from [order details] where" & _
                        "orderid=10635", myconnection)
        da.Fill(ds, "orderdetails")
        myconnection.Close()

        ds.Tables(0).Rows(0)("Quantity") = 2

        mycommand1 = New SqlCommand("update [order details] set " & _
                    "quantity=@qty " & "where " & _
                    "orderid=@ordid and productid=@prdid", myconnection)
        myparam = New SqlParameter("@qty", SqlDbType.SmallInt)
        myparam.SourceColumn = "Quantity"
        myparam.SourceVersion = DataRowVersion.Current
```

```
        mycommand1.Parameters.Add(myparam)

        myparam = New SqlParameter("@ordid", SqlDbType.Int)
        myparam.SourceColumn = "OrderID"
        myparam.SourceVersion = DataRowVersion.Current
        mycommand1.Parameters.Add(myparam)

        myparam = New SqlParameter("@prdid", SqlDbType.Int)
        myparam.SourceColumn = "ProductID"
        myparam.SourceVersion = DataRowVersion.Current
        mycommand1.Parameters.Add(myparam)

        myconnection.Open()
        mytransaction = myconnection.BeginTransaction()
        mycommand1.Transaction = mytransaction
        da.UpdateCommand = mycommand1
        Try
            da.Update(ds, "orderdetails")
            mytransaction.Commit()
            Console.WriteLine("Order modified successfully !")
            Console.ReadLine()
        Catch e As Exception
            mytransaction.Rollback()
            Console.WriteLine(e.Message)
            Console.ReadLine()
        Finally
            myconnection.Close()
        End Try
    End Sub
End Module
```

The program works as follows:

- You first establish a connection with the database and fetch order details for Order ID 11116 into a DataSet. Note that you may have to change this Order ID to suit data from your database.

- The connection with the database is closed.

- You then modify the order quantities in the DataSet.

- You, again, open a connection with the database and begin a transaction.

- You, then, set the UpdateCommand property of the SqlDataAdapter to run within this transaction.

- You finally call the Update method of the DataAdapter. Since the update command is running within a transaction, you must call the Commit method of the transaction object to save the changes.

Figure 8-7 shows a sample run of the previous application.

Figure 8-7. *TransactionDataSet.exe sample*

Summary

In this chapter, we started with a general discussion about transactions and how ADO.NET supports them. You looked at the details of implementing transactions: using Commit, Rollback, and Savepoint. You also saw how to initialize a transaction using the BeginTransaction method, and how to use the transaction object that is returned. In order to commit a transaction, you would call the Commit method of a transaction object, whereas in order to roll back a transaction, you would call the Rollback method of a transaction object. You then looked at isolation levels and how they affect the data read within a transaction.

CHAPTER 9

■ ■ ■

Mapping

Frequently, object names in a database are inappropriate for a particular application. For example, you might want to provide a web service for English-speaking Americans using a database with Spanish table and column names. In this chapter you will learn how to *map* different names to one another—so that your code can refer to objects by the name you choose, regardless of the names the objects have in the database.

SQL has a built-in feature for mapping column names—the AS keyword. Many of you will be familiar with this method, and in some cases it can be the simplest solution. We will discuss how to use this in your ADO.NET applications and how to identify its shortcomings.

You will then examine using the DataTableMapping and DataColumnMapping objects, which provide a far more comprehensive solution.

Finally, you will apply your knowledge to building an XML web service. You will use mapping objects so that the table and column names provided by our service will be clearer and more consistent than the names in the underlying database.

Using the SQL AS Keyword

Before you examine the mapping facilities provided by ADO.NET, let's have a look at the traditional mapping methods provided by the SQL language.

In the following code, you load a DataSet with data from an imaginary database with very terse column names. You use the SQL AS keyword to map these short names to longer, more meaningful names for use in your application. You then write the rows to the console, using the following mapped names:

```
Imports System.Data.OleDb
Module Module1

    Sub Main()
        Try
```

Initially, you define a connection object.

```
        ' Define a connection object
        Dim dbConn As New _
OleDbConnection("Provider=Microsoft.Jet.OLEDB.4.0;" & _
    "Password=;User ID=Admin;Data Source=db.mdb")
```

You then create a `DataAdapter` to retrieve records from the database.

```
' Create a data adapter to retrieve records from db
Dim strSELECT As String = "SELECT ID AS UserID, " & _
"fn AS FirstName, ln AS LastName, " & _
"cty AS City, st AS State FROM tabUsers"
Dim daUsers As New OleDbDataAdapter(strSELECT, dbConn)
Dim dsUsers As New DataSet("Users")
```

You then fill the dataset.

```
' Fill the dataset
daUsers.Fill(dsUsers)

' Go through the records and print them using the mapped names
Dim r As DataRow
For Each r In dsUsers.Tables(0).Rows
    Console.WriteLine("ID: {0}, FirstName: {1}, " & _
"LastName: {2}, City: {3}, State: {4}", _
r("UserID"), r("FirstName"), r("LastName"), _
r("City"), r("State"))
Next
Catch ex As Exception
' An error occurred. Show the error message
Console.WriteLine(ex.Message)
End Try
End Sub

End Module
```

This method has succeeded in giving you new column names, which in many cases will be enough. However, it does not automatically map table names. You can do that yourself using the `DataTable TableName` property.

The `Fill()` method provided by the `DataAdapter` object doesn't create mapping classes when it encounters the aliased column names. In fact, the database software, not .NET, handles the mapping.

The ADO.NET Mapping Mechanism

Now, let's take a look at the new mapping mechanisms provided by ADO.NET. You will introduce the objects by using mappings when filling a `DataSet`. Then you will move on to using mappings when making updates to the data source.

There is a big difference between the SQL method and the ADO.NET method. The ADO.NET mapping objects allow developers to manage `DataSet` data and schemas that have been created using XML documents and XML schemas. With the SQL AS keyword, you can use the aliased column names only when you deal with the database and records.

Using Mapping When Retrieving Data

When you fill a DataSet, the DataAdapter looks at its own TableMappings property to see if the developer has defined mapping rules. By default, the TableMappings property is empty, so the same column names used in the database are used in the DataSet table.

Let's take a look at how you would use the ADO.NET mapping mechanism to rename very terse column names in a DataSet to more meaningful alternatives. You will use the same Microsoft Access database that you used in the previous example.

To use ADO.NET mappings, you create a DataTableMapping object. This object enables you to map between two names for the same table, and it also contains the ColumnMappings property—a collection of DataColumnMapping objects that map between names of the column in the table. Once you have created this object and added all of the required column mappings, you add it to the DataAdapter object's TableMappings property.

Let's look at an example that puts this into practice.

The following is just a class outline. To keep the new code clear, you will use a separate method to handle the mapping—DoDataMappings. Notice that we introduce the System.Data.Common namespace, which you need to use the mapping classes.

```
Imports System
Imports System.Data
Imports System.Data.OleDb
Imports System.Data.Common


Module Module1
    Sub Main()
        ' implemented later
    End Sub
    Sub DoDataMappings(Dim da As OleDbDataAdapter)
        ' implemented later
    End Sub
End Module
```

The Main() method looks like this.

```
Sub Main()
    Try
        ' Define a connection object
        Dim dbConn As New _
    OleDbConnection("Provider=Microsoft.Jet.OLEDB.4.0;" & _
        "Password=;User ID=Admin;Data Source=db.mdb")

        ' Create a data adapter to retrieve records from DB
        Dim daUsers As New OleDbDataAdapter("SELECT ID,fn,ln,cty,st" & _
            "FROM tabUsers", dbConn)
        Dim dsUsers As New DataSet("User")

    DoDataMapping(da)
```

```
' Fill the dataset
daUsers.Fill(dsUsers)

' Go through the records and print them using the mapped names
Dim r As DataRow
For Each r In dsUsers.Tables("tabUsers").Rows
    Console.WriteLine("ID: {0}, FirstName: {1}, " & _
"LastName: {2}, City: {3}, State: {4}", _
r("UserID"), r("FirstName"), r("LastName"), _
r("City"), r("State"))
Next
        Catch ex As Exception
            ' An error occurred. Show the error message
            Console.WriteLine(ex.Message)
        End Try
    End Sub
```

Notice the call to DoDataMappings, which comes before calling the DataAdapter Fill() method. This method means that although you have retrieved columns from the database with names like ln and cty, you can refer to them as LastName and City. Let's take a look at the DoDataMappings method now.

You start by declaring DataColumnMapping objects. You create a new DataColumnMapping object for each database column that you want to map to a DataSet column.

```
Sub DoDataMappings(Dim da As OleDbDataAdapter)
    Try
        ' Define each column to map
        Dim dcmUserID As New DataColumnMapping("ID", "UserID")
        Dim dcmFirstName As New DataColumnMapping("fn", "FirstName")
        Dim dcmLastName As New DataColumnMapping("ln", "LastName")
        Dim dcmCity As New DataColumnMapping("cty", "City")
        Dim dcmState As New DataColumnMapping("st", "State")
```

The DataColumnMapping object contains the relation between the column within the database and the column inside the DataSet. You construct it by providing two strings. The first string specifies the column name in the data source; the second string defines the column name that will appear in the DataSet.

Once you have created these DataColumnMapping objects, you create a DataTableMapping object and add the DataColumnMapping objects to it.

```
' Define the table containing the mapped columns
Dim dtmUsers As New DataTableMapping("Table", "tabUsers")
dtmUsers.ColumnMappings.Add(dcmUserID)
dtmUsers.ColumnMappings.Add(dcmFirstName)
dtmUsers.ColumnMappings.Add(dcmLastName)
dtmUsers.ColumnMappings.Add(dcmCity)
dtmUsers.ColumnMappings.Add(dcmState)
```

The DataTableMapping object has a constructor that takes two strings. The first string specifies the name of the source table, and is case sensitive. This name must correspond to the table name used during the filling or updating process accomplished by the DataAdapter object. If you do not specify a source table name you must use the default name assigned by the DataAdapter object: Table.

The second parameter is the DataTable object's DataSet. The DataTableMapping object exposes the ColumnMappings collection property that must contain every column you want to map from the database to the DataSet.

Finally, you add the DataTableMapping object to the TableMappings property of the DataAdapter. Now when you fill the DataSet, the DataAdapter will find the DataTableMapping in its TableMappings collection, and use it.

```
        ' Activate the mapping mechanism
        daUsers.TableMappings.Add(dtmUsers)
    Catch ex As Exception
        // An error occurred. Show the error message
        Console.WriteLine(ex.Message);
    End Try
End Sub
```

This has taken quite a bit more code than just using the SQL AS keyword. The good news is that there is a shorter way to use the data mapping objects—you've just looked at the longer version to get a better idea of what is happening. The bad news is that it is still not quite as short as using the AS keyword. Let's look at a shortened version of the DoDataMappings method.

```
    Sub DoDataMappings(Dim da As OleDbDataAdapter)
        Try
            ' Define an array of columns to map
            Dim dcmMappedColumns() As DataColumnMapping = { _
                    New DataColumnMapping("ID", "UserID"), _
                    New DataColumnMapping("fn", "FirstName"), _
                    New DataColumnMapping("ln", "LastName"), _
                    New DataColumnMapping("cty", "City"), _
                    New DataColumnMapping("st", "State")}

            ' Define the table containing the mapped columns
            Dim dtmUsers As New DataTableMapping("Table", "tabUsers", _
            dcmMappedColumns)
            ' Activate the mapping mechanism
            daUsers.TableMappings.Add(dtmUsers)
        Catch ex As Exception
            // An error occurred. Show the error message
            Console.WriteLine(ex.Message);
        End Try
    End Sub
```

This time you create an array of DataColumnMapping objects, instead of declaring them all separately. You then use another DataTableMapping constructor that accepts an array of DataColumnMapping objects in the constructor, rather than adding each DataColumnMapping separately.

There are no substantial differences between using one method over the other. The first case requires more code, but it is slightly more readable than the second one. However, with a few clear comments, the shorter version is perfectly understandable.

MissingMappingAction and MissingSchemaAction

We have seen that when the DataAdapter fills a DataSet, it checks to see what table mappings have been specified. If none have been specified, then it uses the original names. However, this is only the default. You can choose how you want the DataAdapter to react if it meets columns that you have no specified mappings for. The MissingMappingAction property of the DataAdapter has three settings.

- Passthrough (the default): If a mapping is not specified, the DataAdapter will assume the name is the same in the data source and the DataSet.

- Error: If a mapping is not specified, the DataAdapter will raise a SystemException exception.

- Ignore: If a mapping is not specified, the DataAdapter will ignore that column.

Moreover, when you use the Fill() and the Update() methods, you can choose what the DataAdapter should do when a DataSet schema does not meet expectations. The MissingSchemaAction property of the DataAdapter can accept four values.

- Add (default option): When the schema is missing for the current column, the DataAdapter will create it and add it to the DataSet object without creating information on primary keys or unique columns.

- AddWithKey: The same as the Add option, but with the difference that primary keys and unique columns will be created. Remember that the identity column will be created without identity seed and identity increment values. You should add them after the Fill() or the Update() calls.

- Ignore: When the schema is missing for the current column, the DataAdapter will ignore it and continue analyzing the other columns.

- Error: When the schema is missing for the current column, the DataAdapter will raise a SystemException exception.

These settings also apply when using the DataAdapter to update a data source, which you will look at now.

Inserting Records Using Mapped Names

Until now, you have focused your attention on retrieving records. But mapping means that even the database's other operations, such as inserting a new record or updating an existing one, are easier to write and manage. After mapping column names, you can use them throughout your code to accomplish every kind of database task. Let's see an example of adding a new record inside the Microsoft Access DB.MDB database.

```
Imports System.Data.OleDb
Imports System.Data.Common

Module Module1
    Sub Main()
        Dim dsUsers As New DataSet("Users")

        Try
            ' Define a connection object
            Dim dbConn As New _
        OleDbConnection("Provider=Microsoft.Jet.OLEDB.4.0;" & _
        "Password=;User ID=Admin;Data Source=db.mdb")

            ' Create a data adapter to retrieve records from DB
            Dim daUsers As New OleDbDataAdapter("SELECT ID,fn,ln,cty,st" & _
                " FROM tabUsers", dbConn)

            ' Define each column to map
            Dim dcmUserID As New DataColumnMapping("ID", "UserID")
            Dim dcmFirstName As New DataColumnMapping("fn", "FirstName")
            Dim dcmLastName As New DataColumnMapping("ln", "LastName")
            Dim dcmCity As New DataColumnMapping("cty", "City")
            Dim dcmState As New DataColumnMapping("st", "State")

            ' Define the table containing the mapped columns
            Dim dtmUsers As New DataTableMapping("Table", "User")
            dtmUsers.ColumnMappings.Add(dcmUserID)
            dtmUsers.ColumnMappings.Add(dcmFirstName)
            dtmUsers.ColumnMappings.Add(dcmLastName)
            dtmUsers.ColumnMappings.Add(dcmCity)
            dtmUsers.ColumnMappings.Add(dcmState)

            ' Activate the mapping mechanism
            daUsers.TableMappings.Add(dtmUsers)

            ' Fill the dataset
            daUsers.Fill(dsUsers)
```

```vbnet
                    ' Declare a command builder to create SQL instructions
                    ' to create and update records.
                    Dim cb As New OleDbCommandBuilder(daUsers)

                    ' Insert a new record in the DataSet
                    Dim r As DataRow = dsUsers.Tables(0).NewRow()
                    r("FirstName") = "Eddie"
                    r("LastName") = "Robinson"
                    r("City") = "Houston"
                    r("State") = "Texas"
                    dsUsers.Tables(0).Rows.Add(r)

                    ' Insert the record in the database
                    daUsers.Update(dsUsers.GetChanges())

                    ' Align in-memory data with the data source ones
                    dsUsers.AcceptChanges()

                    ' Print successfully message
                    Console.WriteLine("A new record has been" & _
                        " added to the database.")
            Catch ex As Exception
                    ' Reject DataSet changes
                    dsUsers.RejectChanges()

                    ' An error occurred. Show the error message
                    Console.WriteLine(ex.Message)
            End Try
        End Sub
End Module
```

In the previous highlighted snippet of code, a new row has been created and filled using the mapped column names. In the following code, you update a column using the mapping mechanism:

```vbnet
Imports System.Data.Common
Imports System.Data.OleDb

Module Module1
    Sub Main()
        Dim dsUsers As New DataSet("Users")

        Try
            ' Define a connection object
            Dim dbConn As New _
        OleDbConnection("Provider=Microsoft.Jet.OLEDB.4.0;" & _
        "Password=;User ID=Admin;Data Source=db.mdb")
```

```vb
' Create a data adapter to retrieve records from db
Dim daUsers As New OleDbDataAdapter("SELECT ID,fn,ln,cty,st" & _
    " FROM tabUsers", dbConn)

' Define each column to map
Dim dcmUserID As New DataColumnMapping("ID", "UserID")
Dim dcmFirstName As New DataColumnMapping("fn", "FirstName")
Dim dcmLastName As New DataColumnMapping("ln", "LastName")
Dim dcmCity As New DataColumnMapping("cty", "City")
Dim dcmState As New DataColumnMapping("st", "State")
' Define the table containing the mapped columns
Dim dtmUsers As New DataTableMapping("Table", "User")
dtmUsers.ColumnMappings.Add(dcmUserID)
dtmUsers.ColumnMappings.Add(dcmFirstName)
dtmUsers.ColumnMappings.Add(dcmLastName)
dtmUsers.ColumnMappings.Add(dcmCity)
dtmUsers.ColumnMappings.Add(dcmState)

' Activate the mapping mechanism
daUsers.TableMappings.Add(dtmUsers)

' Fill the dataset
daUsers.Fill(dsUsers)

' Set the primary key in order to use the Find() method
' below.
Dim dcaKey() As DataColumn = _
{dsUsers.Tables(0).Columns("UserID")}
 dsUsers.Tables(0).PrimaryKey = dcaKey

' Declare a command builder to create SQL instructions
' to create and update records.
Dim cb = New OleDbCommandBuilder(daUsers)

' Update an existing record in the DataSet
Dim r As DataRow = dsUsers.Tables(0).Rows.Find(3)

If Not r Is Nothing Then
    r("FirstName") = "Venus"
    r("LastName") = "Williams"
    r("City") = "Houston"
    r("State") = "Texas"

    ' Update the record in the database
    daUsers.Update(dsUsers.GetChanges())
```

```
            ' Align in-memory data with the data source ones
            dsUsers.AcceptChanges()

            ' Print success message
            Console.WriteLine("The record has been updated " & _
                "successfully.")
        Else
            Console.WriteLine("No record found...")
        End If
    Catch ex As Exception
        ' Reject DataSet changes
        dsUsers.RejectChanges()

        ' An error occurred. Show the error message
        Console.WriteLine(ex.Message)
    End Try
End Sub
End Module
```

In the previous code, you can see how the Find() method retrieves the DataRow object reference that is used in the updating process. The code has to define a primary key within the DataSet in order to use the Find() method, which needs a valid primary key value as a parameter to retrieve the correct record.

Web Services with Mapping

You have seen how mapping classes can help you create more easily readable code by allowing you to use your preferred column names throughout your code. However, mapping classes are even more useful when you need to deal with XML documents and XML schemas. Imagine you receive an XML document containing different elements from those in your database, or from the necessary names used by the parser to analyze the document. You can use the ADO.NET mapping mechanisms to solve this problem.

In this section of the chapter, you will analyze a typical scenario that will be common in the next few years: exchanging documents between different companies.

Imagine a big company that, over the years, has spent a lot of money on implementing electronic systems and software applications to automate its own bureaucracy. Now, try telling that company that it has to change some of its systems because other big companies use different systems! If this were the case, faxes and couriers would remain the preferred method of intercompany communication.

Fortunately, the .NET Framework offers a better solution based on XML document exchange, using TCP/IP protocols such as HTTP, FTP, and SMTP. In this scenario, the big company has only to develop a new system to produce a text file that contains XML elements describing its own document, and then use the preferred TCP/IP protocol to send its data. With .NET, you don't even need to worry about the XML or the transmission protocol. Using web services, you can transmit objects such as DataSets over the Web with almost no effort, as the following example shows.

Our "big company," called Pet Lovers, supplies pet materials to affiliated pet shops. The pet shops order the supplies from Pet Lovers by phone. Pet Lovers communicates with its supplier using a web service. This web service has a method that will return a list of items along with the available quantity. Moreover, the supplier will provide a web method that accepts incoming orders from its customers. Figure 9-1 clarifies this sequence of events.

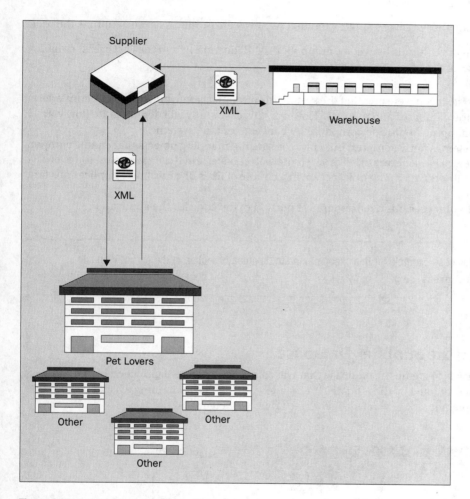

Figure 9-1. PetLovers *sample setup*

The supplier provides a method that returns a complete list of products within an XML document. The Pet Lovers Company, as with as every affiliated company, retrieves the document and sends back a new one having the same XML elements describing the required goods. Another scenario could be where XML documents are exchanged between the supplier and its warehouse to retrieve the quantities of the available items.

You will focus your attention on the document exchange between supplier and customer. Let's see the steps you are going to undertake.

1. Create the supplier's database containing the products, the orders, and the customers.

2. Create the web service providing two methods: one for retrieving the list of products and one for storing the order.

3. Create the PetLovers application that retrieves the products list and submits the order.

4. Map the columns between the supplier's XML document and the PetLovers' database to store the order's information.

Of course, if you were creating the system from scratch, you would try to use consistent names for the databases and the XML. However, this case study will demonstrate how you could use mapping to provide compatibility between existing systems.

The system is fairly complex, but at its core are the mapping objects that enable compatibility between a DataSet, returned by a remote web service, and the database on the client. This shows how the mapping objects can, in a couple of lines of code, make applications far more useful.

This chapter presents a representative portion of the code for the application.

■**Tip** The full code example for this chapter is in the Downloads section of the Apress Web site (http://www.apress.com).

Creating the Supplier Database

The first task is to create the database that will contain the products provided by the supplier, the orders completed by the affiliated companies, and a table containing a list of customers. In your implementation, you will have three tables (see Figure 9-2).

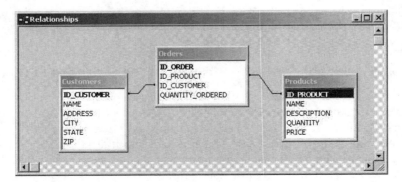

Figure 9-2. *Pets.mdb relationship diagram*

Figure 9-3 shows the Customers table design. It has an auto-number primary key containing the identification for each customer and other fields containing generic information, such as the customer's name and the customer's address.

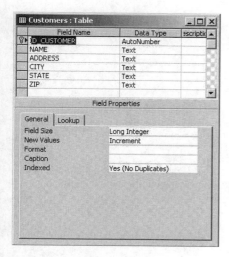

Figure 9-3. *Pets.mdb—*Customers *table*

Figure 9-4 shows the Products table structure. It has an auto-increment primary key to identify each product in the table, plus text fields that describe it.

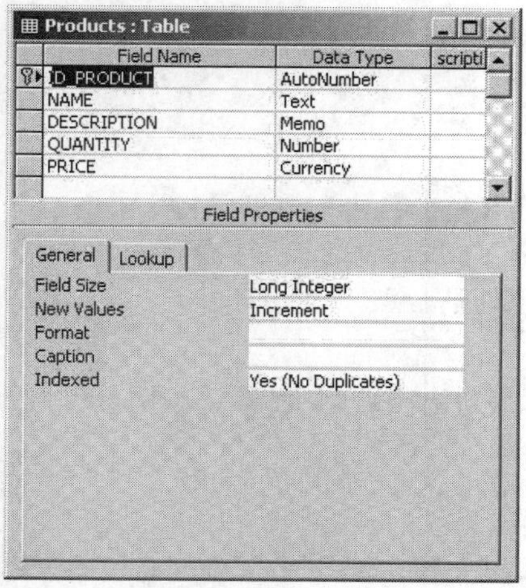

Figure 9-4. *Pets.mdb—*Products *table*

Orders is the last table, illustrated in Figure 9-5. It contains each order submitted by the customers. It has an auto-number primary key that identifies the order and the primary keys from the other tables to identify the product and the customer. Finally, it has a field to store the quantity ordered by the customer.

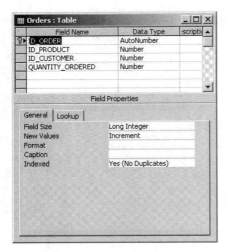

Figure 9-5. *Pets.mdb—*Orders *table*

Creating the Supplier Web Service

The supplier will provide a web service containing a method used to retrieve an up-to-date list of products available, along with their related stock level. Creating a web service in Visual Studio .NET is easy: just choose the Visual Basic .NET Projects ➤ ASP.NET Web Service option from the New Project dialog (see Figure 9-6).

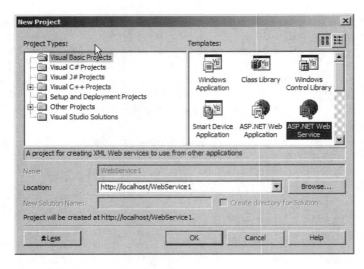

Figure 9-6. *New web service dialog*

After choosing a valid name and selecting the OK button, Visual Studio .NET generates all the necessary code to implement the web service. You just add your web method, which retrieves the product list from the respective table in the database.

```
<WebMethod()> Public Function RetrieveList() As DataSet
    ' Create a dataset that will contain products list
    Dim ds As New DataSet("Products")

    Try
        ' Create the connection object
        Dim dbConn As New _
    OleDbConnection("Provider=Microsoft.Jet.OLEDB.4.0;" & _
    "Password=;User ID=Admin;Data Source=C:\pets.mdb")

        ' Create the data adapter specifying the SQL
        ' statement used to fill the dataset
        Dim da As New OleDbDataAdapter("SELECT ID_PRODUCT, NAME, " & _
    "DESCRIPTION, QUANTITY, PRICE FROM Products", dbConn)

        da.Fill(ds)
    Catch
        ds = Nothing
    End Try

    ' return the dataset
    Return ds

End Function
```

Eventually, the web service will contain a second method called Order, which you will see later.

Creating the PetLovers Application

You will now look at the construction of the code for the PetLovers application. Initially, you'll look at the section that is concerned with ordering materials from the supplier.

■Note The full application can be found in the associated code for the book.

In Figure 9-7, you can see the application running.

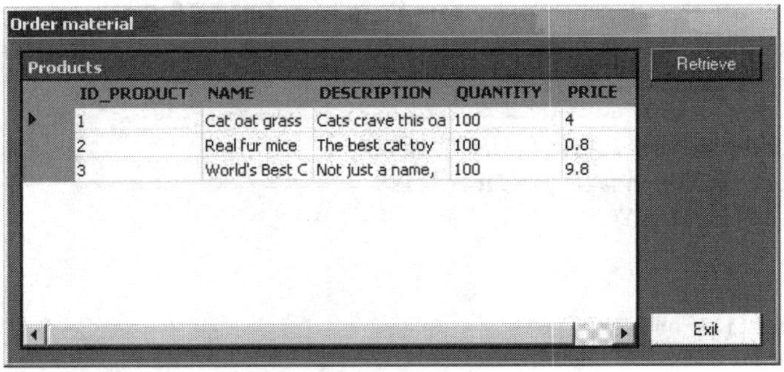

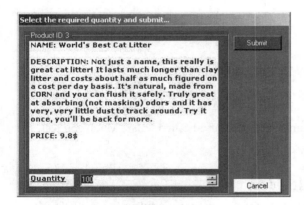

Figure 9-7. `PetLovers` *application—frmOrders.vb*

The application is composed of a `DataGrid` data component that shows the products, quantities, and prices retrieved directly from the supplier web service and two buttons, one to exit from the application and one to retrieve the available products from the supplier. By pressing the Retrieve button, the application calls the web method and fills the list using the retrieved `DataSet` object. Double-clicking on the selected record within the list causes the product details to be shown on screen (see Figure 9-8).

Figure 9-8. `PetLovers` *application—frmSubmit.vb*

After you select the quantity to order and press the Submit button, the `Order` web method is called and a `DataSet` object containing the product and quantity ordered is passed to the supplier. (You will see how the `Order` method works later.) The `Order` method will return a `DataSet` containing the order information as the quantity and the product identifier. This information will be stored in the local `PetLovers` database, which contains a similar `Orders` table, only with different column names. The application will use the mapping mechanism to update the table.

Let's see some code for the `PetLovers` Windows application. The following code illustrates how the Retrieve button click event is managed by the application. First, the mouse pointer changes to the wait cursor and then an object pointing to the web service is created. The `RetrieveList()` web method returns the `DataSet` object reference that is used as the data source for the `DataGrid` component. Finally, the mouse pointer returns to the default cursor.

```
Private Sub btnRetrieve_Click(ByVal sender As System.Object,_
    ByVal e As System.EventArgs) Handles btnRetrieve.Click
      ' Change mouse pointer to wait cursor
      Me.Cursor = Cursors.WaitCursor

      ' create an object from the web service
      Dim service As New localhost.PetGoodsDistribution()

      ' Retrieve the products' list
      ds = service.RetrieveList()

      ' Restore the original cursor
      Me.Cursor = Cursors.Default

      If Not ds Is Nothing Then
          ' Fill the data grid with the dataset content
          dgProducts.DataSource = ds.Tables(0)
      Else
          MessageBox.Show("Unable to retrieve the list")
      End If
End Sub
```

The next snippet shows what happens when the user double-clicks the selected item within the `DataGrid` component. The first operation retrieves the index of the selected row. The `DataGrid` will return the –1 value when the user has made a wrong selection. The code checks this value and continues only when the user selects a valid row. You then load `frmSubmit` and set member variables in that form to the `DataSet` and the selected row. The following is the method:

```
Private Sub dgProducts_DoubleClick(ByVal sender As Object, _
ByVal e As System.EventArgs) Handles dgProducts.DoubleClick
      ' Retrieve the current row index selected
      Dim iIndex As Integer = CType(sender, DataGrid).CurrentRowIndex

      ' If the row is valid
      If iIndex <> -1 Then
          ' Create an object from the Submit form
          Dim dialog As New frmSubmit()
          ' Pass to submit form some parameters
          dialog.iIndex = iIndex
          dialog.dsSubmit = ds
          ' Show the modal submit form
          dialog.ShowDialog()
```

```
        ' Refresh the product list
        btnRetrieve_Click(sender, e)
    End If
End Sub
```

When you call the ShowDialog() method, before the Submit form is shown, the Load() event is called and you can see the code within its body, as follows. After retrieving the content of the record from the DataSet using the index of the DataGrid selected row, the code fills a label with the name, description, and price of the selected product. Moreover, a NumericUpDown control is filled with the product's quantity and the maximum quantity purchasable.

```
Private Sub frmSubmit_Load(ByVal sender As System.Object, _
    ByVal e As System.EventArgs) Handles MyBase.Load
    Dim drSubmit As DataRow
    drSubmit = dsSubmit.Tables(0).Rows(iIndex)
    groupBox.Text = groupBox.Text & drSubmit("ID_PRODUCT")
    Dim txt As String = "NAME: " & drSubmit("NAME") & _
      vbCrLf & vbCrLf & "DESCRIPTION: " & _
              drSubmit("DESCRIPTION") & _
      vbCrLf & vbCrLf & "PRICE: " & _
      drSubmit("PRICE") & "$"
    lbText.Text = txt
    txtQuantity.Maximum = CInt(drSubmit("QUANTITY"))
    txtQuantity.Value = CInt(drSubmit("QUANTITY"))
End Sub
```

The following code represents the code executed when the user presses the Submit button. At the beginning, a new object is created to manage the supplier service. Then, the quantity value contained in the DataSet object is updated with the required product quantity. The modified DataSet object is passed back to the web service, which will use it to update the database.

```
Private Sub btnSubmit_Click(ByVal sender As System.Object, _
  ByVal e As System.EventArgs) Handles btnSubmit.Click
    Dim service As New localhost.PetGoodsDistribution()
    dsSubmit.Tables(0).Rows(iIndex)("QUANTITY") = txtQuantity.Value

  ' 1 is the Customer ID assigned by the supplier
    Dim ds As DataSet = _
service.Order(dsSubmit.GetChanges(DataRowState.Modified), 1)

    If Not ds Is Nothing Then
        InsertOrder(ds)
        Me.Close()
    Else
        MessageBox.Show("Error occurred during order processing.")
    End If
End Sub
```

The Order() web method will return a new DataSet containing order information. You will use the InsertOrder() method to update the local database with this DataSet. Let's see what the Order() web method contains. A new DataSet object has been created to contain the orders stored in the Orders table. Naturally, this is an example, but when you work in real situations you rarely retrieve all the records contained in the table. You should filter the SELECT statement with an ad hoc WHERE condition. The following is the code:

```
<WebMethod()> Public Function Order(ByVal d As DataSet, _
        ByVal iCustomerID As Integer) As DataSet
    ' Create a dataset that will contain products list
    Dim ds As New DataSet("Orders")

    Try
        ' Create the connection object
        Dim dbConn As New _
    OleDbConnection("Provider=Microsoft.Jet.OLEDB.4.0;" & _
    "Password=;User ID=Admin;Data Source=C:\pets.mdb")

        ' Create the data adapter specifying the SQL
        ' statement used to fill the dataset
        Dim da As New OleDbDataAdapter("SELECT ID_ORDER, " & _
        "ID_PRODUCT, ID_CUSTOMER, QUANTITY_ORDERED" & _
        " FROM Orders", dbConn)

        da.Fill(ds)
```

In the following loop, every new row contained in the source DataSet object is used to create a new row in the Orders table of the Supplier database:

```
        ' Go through each row that has to be inserted
        Dim r As DataRow
        For Each r In d.Tables(0).Rows
            Dim newRow As DataRow = ds.Tables(0).NewRow()
            newRow("ID_PRODUCT") = r("ID_PRODUCT")
            newRow("QUANTITY_ORDERED") = r("QUANTITY")
            newRow("ID_CUSTOMER") = iCustomerID
            ds.Tables(0).Rows.Add(newRow)
        Next
```

Finally, the code creates a CommandBuilder object that automatically generates every SQL statement to insert, update, and delete records in the table. Then the DataAdapter object is used to update the database with the DataSet changes that will be returned to the calling application if no errors occur. Before that, the private UpdateQuantity() method is used to update the quantity of the product, subtracting the required quantity to obtain the available one.

```
        ' Update the database with new records
        Dim cm As New OleDbCommandBuilder(da)
        da.Update(ds.GetChanges())
```

```
        ' Update the available quantity
        UpdateQuantity(d)
        ' Return
        Return ds.GetChanges()
    Catch
        Return Nothing
    End Try
End Function
```

You now arrive at the main code where the mapping mechanism is used to map DataSet columns to the Orders table contained in the PetLovers database. As you can see from Figure 9-9, the field names of the Orders table are different from the ones contained in the DataSet returned from the web service. This is a typical case where the mapping mechanism is useful to store the information without changing the table structure.

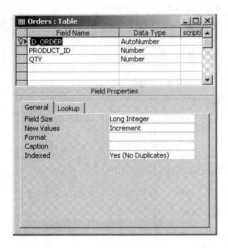

Figure 9-9. *Pets.mdb—*Orders *table*

The code starts by creating a connection object pointing to the local database and to a DataAdapter object that will be used to update the database. Here, you use the SELECT statement to inform the DataAdapter about the DataSet structure, but not to fill it.

```
Private Sub InsertOrder(ByVal d As DataSet)
    Dim dbConn As New _
OleDbConnection("Provider=Microsoft.Jet.OLEDB.4.0;" & _
Password=;User ID=Admin;Data Source=PetLovers.mdb")
    Dim da As New OleDbDataAdapter("SELECT ID_ORDER,PRODUCT_ID," & _
            "QTY FROM Orders", dbConn)
```

The code goes on to create the mapped columns that will be used by the Update() method during the database updating process. The first parameter of the DataColumnMapping object's constructor is equal to the physical table's column in the local database. The second parameter is equal to the column of the DataSet retrieved from the web service. The DataTableMapping object is then created, using the constructor that accepts an array of mapped columns.

```
Dim dcm() As DataColumnMapping = _
    {New DataColumnMapping("PRODUCT_ID", "ID_PRODUCT"), _
            New DataColumnMapping("QTY", "QUANTITY_ORDERED")}
    Dim dtm As New DataTableMapping("Table", "Table", dcm)
```

The DataAdapter class contains two properties, MissingMappingAction and Missing-SchemaAction, that are useful to inform the code about the action to take when there is either a mapping column or an element in the XML schema that cannot be found in the DataSet object. In the following code, every column not declared as a mapped column will be ignored.

```
' Inform the application about the action to undertake
' whether a missing mapped column or a missing schema
' is found in the dataset
da.MissingMappingAction = MissingMappingAction.Ignore
da.MissingSchemaAction = MissingSchemaAction.Ignore
```

Finally, the code starts the mapping mechanism before calling the Update() method, which will insert the new record in the local database.

```
' Start the mapping mechanism
da.TableMappings.Add(dtm)

' Update the database
Dim cm As New OleDbCommandBuilder(da)
da.Update(d)
End Sub
```

Summary

In this chapter, you have seen how to use mapping to make code easier to read and modify, and how to map column and table names so that data can be passed easily between different data sources.

You started by reviewing how to use the AS keyword in SQL, which is a simple but inflexible way to achieve column mappings.

You then moved on to looking at the ADO.NET mapping objects, with the DataAdapter object's ColumnMappings property, and the DataColumnMapping and DataTableMapping classes.

Finally, you built a client-server application using a web service and Windows Forms application to demonstrate mapping in action.

CHAPTER 10

■ ■ ■

Making a Data Services Component

Here we are again, another chapter on making a Data Services component, sometimes called a Data Application Layer (DAL) component. If you are reading this book you are probably all too familiar with what a DAL component is and have probably contributed to or developed an entire one by yourself.

If you are not familiar with them, here's a summary: it is one layer within an *n*-tier (multitier) application that encapsulates data access. We will not be going into great detail on what the Data Layer is or on *n*-tier architecture, but we will be showing you how to create a DAL component for .NET applications.

The coming of .NET has made the development, organization, and distribution of DAL components a very simple process because of features like the Common Language Runtime (CLR), base class libraries (BCL), and the "all-in-one" development environment, Visual Studio .NET!

In this chapter you will learn how to develop, compile, deploy, and use a DAL component using .NET—specifically we will be covering the following topics:

- What is a DAL and why use one?

- How to build a DAL component

- How to deploy a DAL component

- How to use the DAL in a web form and a web service

- Performance and optimization tips through object pooling and database transactions

By the end of this chapter you will have a firm grasp on how to develop data service components in a .NET development environment. The following list contains everything you will need and what you will need to do to complete this chapter. You'll notice that you should have Microsoft SQL Server, Microsoft Access, Oracle 8.1.7 or above, and a System DSN. You'll be using all four of these so that you will see how to connect to a data store using the SQL Server, OLE DB, OracleClient, and ODBC .NET data providers.

Things you will need for this chapter are the following:

- Microsoft SQL Server with the Northwind sample database installed, for the SqlClient examples

- Microsoft Access Northwind database, for the OleDb examples

- A System DSN setup going to the SQL Server Northwind database, for ODBC examples

- ODBC .NET data provider (System.Data.ODBC)

- OracleClient provider (System.Data.OracleClient)

- ASP.NET installed and configured on a .NET-compatible operating system

What Is a Data Service Component and Why Use It?

Many "new generation" developers have not been developing for many years and can't develop in assembly code. This fact comes with many problems, but also many benefits. A big benefit is that systems designers develop solutions that solve the problem in a logical way, rather than tying the solution tightly to the system architecture. object orientation and *n*-tier development are ways of solving problems in a solution-centered way. In this section, we will introduce a high-level look at what *n*-tier architecture is, where DAL components fit into the picture, and some of the benefits of using DAL components.

There are a few things that have been introduced over the years that have been really exciting: *n*-tier software architecture getting more robust, plus newer and better Windows operating systems to run programs on, XML, and now .NET (the logical next step). In this chapter we are going to be using each one of these…how convenient!

It is often assumed that most developers know what a "Data Services" or "Data Layer" component is. However, *not* everyone knows what one is and some might have heard of it, but don't really have a firm grasp of the concept—to this end, here is a short section to give you an overview of what a DAL component is and some of its many benefits. By no means will this section tell you everything you should know, but it will get you going in the right direction.

What Is the Data Services Component?

A data services component is an *n*-tier object encapsulating data access for any application that needs to access data from a data store. What does this mean? As Figure 10-1 illustrates, you will have one or more DAL components that one or more applications use for all data access, resulting in absolute control over how data is accessed. The diagram consists of three levels or tiers. The first is the "Presentation Layer," which would be the user interfaces—for example, a console application, GUI, or a web application's web page. The second layer is the "Business Layer," which contains business rules that would consist of routines that do things like data validation or formatting. Then comes the "Data Services Layer," which consists of routines to manipulate data from backend data stores such as a Microsoft SQL Server database. Business objects are designed to be data-source independent and therefore do not interact with the data stores. Instead, they access data by invoking appropriate methods provided by data service components. An important thing to note is that this model can be on a single machine (known as logical layers) or multiple machines (known as physical layers).

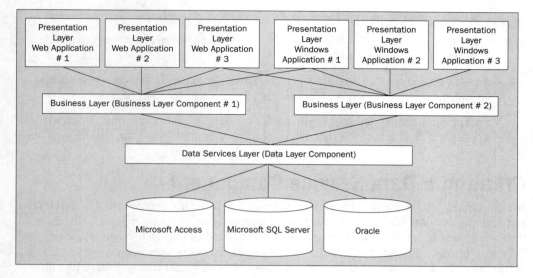

Figure 10-1. *A typical* n-*tier application layout*

As Figure 10-1 illustrates, the Data Services Layer is completely separated from both the Business Layer and Presentation Layer. What this means to you as a developer and designer is that you can have one DAL component that is used by multiple business layer objects and in turn can be used by many different applications.

While this example demonstrates a classic 3-tier architecture, the data access components can be used in other architectures that support componentized application development. For instance, you can use the design pattern to further encapsulate the business logic and provide a more robust interface to the Business Layer. An example of this architecture is the Microsoft Duwamish 7 sample application at `http://msdn.microsoft.com/library/en-us/dnbda/html/bdasampduwam7.asp`.

What Are the Benefits?

DAL components are located in a centralized location and one or more applications use them. This is of great benefit, because there is now a centralized place for application updates. For instance, say that your company decides to switch the backend database from Oracle to Microsoft SQL Server 2000 to take advantage of its vast XML support. As all of your data access is done in one place, you will only have to change, edit, or add features in the DAL component, rather than in every application that connects to this database as long as the DAL component's interface doesn't change.

Another benefit is your ability to control all database activity. Instead of 15 applications all connecting to your database from different locations and in different ways, you can create one component that connects to your database and control what type of data can be returned to clients. For instance, in this chapter you are going to make a component that will only return a DataSet, DataReaders, or an XmlDataDocument, and nothing else. Some benefits of using a DAL component are

- *Centralized code*: If you need to make a code change, you only make it in one place.

- *Security*: You control how connections are made to a database and what type of data can be returned from the data store.

- *Performance*: One way it improves performance is by ensuring that components use specific technologies such as object pooling and connection pooling.

- *Ease of maintenance*: Subsequent features need to be added in only one place and the application data access behavior can be controlled centrally from the data access layer.

Creating a Data Service Component

In this section, you are going to jump right into building your DAL component, but first let's see a description of the component. Your DAL component encapsulates all classes used for data access into one place. The component is universal and can be used to connect to any database supported by .NET: SQL, OLE DB, ODBC (still in beta so database support is limited at this time). There are two classes in this example and two enumerations—Figure 10-2 illustrates the basic structure of the DataLayer namespace.

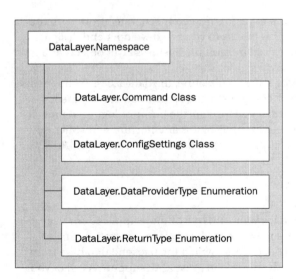

Figure 10-2. *Your* DataLayer *structure*

- Commands: This class is used to execute commands against the database.

- ConfigSettings: This class is used to set up configuration data used by the Commands class to execute database commands. For example, a connection string for database access.

- `DataProviderType` enumeration: This is used to set what type of data provider to use.

- `ReturnType` enumeration: This is used to set what type of data object to return from queries.

It might be worth mentioning that the DAL component you are designing is rather simplistic. It does not use `DataAdapters`, while a true enterprise level data layer would make use of both `DataReaders` and `DataAdapters`. Also, issues like concurrency etc. have to be dealt with in a manner specific to the database, but in concept all of those can be abstracted to your data layer. A good starting point would be the data access application block that can be downloaded from Microsoft's Web site.

Before you jump into making your DAL component, let's go over its features. Many enterprise-level applications these days need access to many types of data stores (for example, databases). For this reason, your DAL component will have features that enable it to connect not only to SQL Server using the SQL Server .NET data provider, but also to any database supported by the OLEDB.NET data provider, ODBC .NET data provider, and Oracle database using the OracleClient data provider. As you will see in the code example, this is easily accomplished by taking advantage of the `IDbConnection`, `IDbCommand`, and `IDataAdapter` interfaces.

The second feature you need is the ability for the client (any object that uses the DAL component) to execute not only stored procedures, but also straight SQL commands. To accommodate this, you will take advantage of function overloading—creating multiple versions of a function with different arguments (parameters).

The third feature you need is the ability for the DAL component to return multiple types of data. For instance, in one situation the client may need a `DataSet` and in another a `DataReader` object (`SqlDataReader`).

So now that you have an overview of the component, let's take a look at the code for the component. First, run Visual Studio .NET to create a Visual Basic .NET Class Library project and name it `DataLayer`. Next, add a reference to the `System.Data.OracleClient`. The following are your enumerations for the component—we are going over these first because they are used in the other two classes.

The DataLayer Namespace—Public Enumerators

You will define two enumerations that enable the user to set what type of data they want to return from a database query and to indicate what type of data store they want to connect to. Tables 10-1 and 10-2 list all the enumeration values and their descriptions.

Table 10-1. `ReturnType` *Enumeration*

Enumeration Value	Type Returned	Description
`DataReaderType`	`DataReader`	A `SqlDataReader`, `OleDbDataReader`, or `OdbcDataReader` will be returned.
`XmlDocumentType`	`XmlDataDocument`	An `XmlDataDocument` will be returned.
`DataSetType`	`DataSet`	A `DataSet` will be returned.

Table 10-2. DataProviderType *Enumeration*

Enumeration Value	Provider Used	Description
Sql	SQL Data Provider	The SQL data provider will be used.
OleDb	OLE DB Data Provider	The OLE DB data provider will be used.
Odbc	ODBC Data Provider	The ODBC data provider will be used.
Oracle	Oracle Data Provider	The OracleClient data provider will be used.

To define the two enumerations in your project, rename the automatically generated Class1.vb as DataLayerEnums.vb. You will then delete the automatically generated class skeleton code and add the following code to the file:

```
Public Enum ReturnType
    DataSetType
    DataReaderType
    XmlDocumentType
End Enum

Public Enum DataProviderType
    Sql
    OleDb
    Odbc
    Oracle
End Enum
```

The Pair Class

Stored procedures can define a set of parameters. In ADO.NET, parameters in the stored procedures and parameterized queries are specified using the Parameter class defined in .NET data providers. While a parameter has many attributes such as name, type, size, and value, in this chapter you will only use the parameter name and value.

Client objects can request to run a stored procedure and pass in an array of parameter name-value pairs. One of many possible ways to support the passing of parameters is to wrap their name-value pairs in a Pair class. .NET Framework defines a Pair class in the System.Web.UI namespace in System.Web.dll, but it's not very effective to reference this assembly only to get access to the Pair class. It's actually pretty simple to define such a class yourself. Just add a new class to the project and name it Pair. The following code listing shows a simple implementation:

```
Public Class Pair
    Public Sub New(ByVal First As Object, ByVal Second As Object)
        mFirst = First
        mSecond = Second
    End Sub

    Public Property First() As Object
        Get
```

```
            Return mFirst
        End Get
        Set(ByVal Value As Object)
            mFirst = Value
        End Set
    End Property

    Public Property Second() As Object
        Get
            Return mSecond
        End Get
        Set(ByVal Value As Object)
            mSecond = Value
        End Set
    End Property

    Private mFirst As Object
    Private mSecond As Object
End Class
```

It's pretty self-explanatory, so we won't waste your time going over it in detail.

The ConfigSettings Class

Next, add a new class to the project and name it ConfigSettings. This class is used to configure the DAL components settings and must be initialized before any methods are called in this component, because it is used by the other classes' methods to create database connections and execute commands. The client uses this class to specify the .NET data provider to use and the connection strings for the backend database. The following is the code for this class:

```
Imports System.Data.SqlClient
Imports System.Data.OleDb
Imports System.Data.Odbc
Imports System.Data.OracleClient

Public Class ConfigSettings
    '
    ' Constructor
    '
    Public Sub New(ByVal Provider As DataProviderType, ByVal ConnString As String)
        mProvider = Provider
        mConnString = ConnString
    End Sub

    '
    ' Properties accessing the class members
    '
```

```
' Data provider
Public Property Provider() As DataProviderType
    Get
        Return mProvider
    End Get
    Set(ByVal Value As DataProviderType)
        mProvider = Value
    End Set
End Property
' Connection string to the backend database
Public Property ConnectionString() As String
    Get
        Return mConnString
    End Get
    Set(ByVal Value As String)
        mConnString = Value
    End Set
End Property


    '
    ' Internal class members
    '
    ' Data provider
    Private mProvider As DataProviderType

    ' Connection string to the backend database
    Private mConnString As String
End Class
```

There are two properties in this class.

- Provider: Indicates what type of database to connect to. The value for Provider will be one of the DataProviderType enumeration values that you saw previously.

- ConnectionString: Set or retrieve the connection string that should be used to connect to a database—its value should be a string.

The constructor simply initializes the properties.

The Command Class

The Commands class is where all database activity happens and is completely dependent on the ConfigSettings class for execution. Remember that the ConfigSettings class contains the connection string that should be used to connect to the database, and what type of database to connect to. The Commands class will use those settings to access the database. You should add a new class to the project and name it Commands.

The Commands class has two private class variables, an IDbConnection object and an IDbCommand object. They are all defined as interfaces so that you can use them to connect and access different types of databases.

```
Imports System.Data.OracleClient
Imports System.Data.SqlClient
Imports System.Data.OleDb
Imports System.Data.Odbc
Imports System.Xml

Public Class Commands

    ' Generic connection
    ' - must be instantiated to a data provider specific connection
    Private mConnection As IDbConnection
    ' Command object to access the backend database
    Private mCommand As IDbCommand

End Class
```

The next task is to define internal functions that support the communications to different types of data providers. An obvious operation is to establish a connection to a database using a specific data provider.

The Connect Method

IDbConnection is an interface that all concrete connection classes must implement. However, you must instantiate a concrete connection class such as SqlConnection in order to connect to a database. The following code is a possible implementation of a generic connection function:

```
' Create and open a provider specific connection
Private Sub Connect(ByVal Config As ConfigSettings)
    Select Case Config.Provider
        Case DataProviderType.Odbc
            mConnection = New OdbcConnection(Config.ConnectionString)
        Case DataProviderType.OleDb
            mConnection = New OleDbConnection(Config.ConnectionString)
        Case DataProviderType.Oracle
            mConnection = New OracleConnection(Config.ConnectionString)
        Case DataProviderType.Sql
            mConnection = New SqlConnection(Config.ConnectionString)
    End Select

    mConnection.Open()
End Sub
```

The Connection function is used to create an active connection for all other methods to use to execute commands against the database. It accepts a ConfigSettings object and uses its Provider value to create a connection object based on the database type. Then the connection object's Open method is invoked and the routine is finished.

The CreateCommand Function

The next internal function is to create a concrete command object to execute either a dynamic SQL statement or a stored procedure with parameters.

```
' Create a provider specific command object with a SQL Statement
Private Sub CreateCommand(ByVal Config As ConfigSettings, _
                    ByVal CommandText As String, _
                    ByVal CommandType As System.Data.CommandType, _
                    ByVal ParamArray Params() As Pair)
    Dim Param As Pair

    Select Case Config.Provider
        Case DataProviderType.Odbc
            mCommand = New OdbcCommand(CommandText)
            Dim OdbcParam As OdbcParameter
            For Each Param In Params
                OdbcParam = _
                    New OdbcParameter(Param.First.ToString(), Param.Second)
                mCommand.Parameters.Add(OdbcParam)
            Next

        Case DataProviderType.OleDb
            mCommand = New OleDbCommand(CommandText)

            Dim OleDbParam As OleDbParameter
            For Each Param In Params
                OleDbParam = _
                    New OleDbParameter(Param.First.ToString(), Param.Second)
                mCommand.Parameters.Add(OleDbParam)
            Next

        Case DataProviderType.Sql
            mCommand = New SqlCommand(CommandText)

            Dim SqlParam As SqlParameter
            For Each Param In Params
                SqlParam = _
                    New SqlParameter(Param.First.ToString(), Param.Second)
                mCommand.Parameters.Add(SqlParam)
            Next
```

```
        Case DataProviderType.Oracle
            mCommand = New OracleCommand(CommandText)

            Dim OracleParam As OracleParameter
            For Each Param In Params
                OracleParam = _
                    New OracleParameter(Param.First.ToString(), Param.Second)
                mCommand.Parameters.Add(OracleParam)
    End Select

    mCommand.CommandType = CommandType
End Sub
```

The first parameter of this function is a ConfigSettings object, which specifies the data provider and connection string. The second is either a dynamic SQL statement or a stored procedure in a format supported by the data provider. The third is the type of the command. The last is an array of parameter name-value pairs.

The code to actually create a concrete command object is straightforward—it simply instantiates a data-provider-specific command object, sets its command text and type, and adds parameters if necessary. The only thing that is worth pointing out is that this function creates concrete parameter objects using a constructor accepting the parameter name and value, which are retrieved from the passed-in parameter array. If you are designing a more flexible data access utility, you might want to expand it to support more parameter attributes.

The CreateAdapter Function

You will also need to create data adapters if you are to populate a DataSet containing the retrieved records. Again the IDataAdapter interface allows you to write generic code, but you still need to instantiate concrete data adapters.

```
' Create a provider specific data adapter object
Private Function CreateAdapter(ByVal Config As ConfigSettings) As IDataAdapter
    Select Case Config.Provider
        Case DataProviderType.Odbc
            Return New OdbcDataAdapter(mCommand)
        Case DataProviderType.OleDb
            Return New OleDbDataAdapter(mCommand)
        Case DataProviderType.Sql
            Return New SqlDataAdapter(mCommand)
        Case DataProviderType.Oracle
            Return New OracleDataAdapter(mCommand)
    End Select
End Function
```

Please note that this function assumes that the mCommand object is initialized and ready to use. Some checking may be necessary to verify this, but we omit such checking code to simplify the code.

The ExecuteQuery Functions

Assuming that you have already initialized the mCommand object properly, executing its SelectCommand to get a result set can be done as shown in the following code:

```
' This function is the one that performs the real work
Private Function ExecuteQuery(ByVal Config As ConfigSettings, _
                              ByVal ResultType As ReturnType) As Object
    Connect(Config)
    mCommand.Connection = mConnection

    If ResultType = ReturnType.DataReaderType Then
        Return mCommand.ExecuteReader(CommandBehavior.CloseConnection)
    End If

    Dim Adapter As IDataAdapter = CreateAdapter(Config)
    Dim ds As DataSet = New DataSet()
    Adapter.Fill(ds)
    mConnection.Close()

    If ResultType = ReturnType.DataSetType Then
        Return ds
    Else
        Return New XmlDataDocument(ds)
    End If
End Function
```

The first parameter is a ConfigSettings object that will be used by other internal functions, while the second parameter specifies the type of object to be returned. This function connects to the database using the Connect function defined earlier. The mCommand object is then attached to an established connection. If the client object expects a data reader, this function simply invokes the ExecuteReader function and returns the created data reader.

■**Tip** Note that the ExecuteReader function specifies the command behavior to close the connection when the reader is returned. The client object is always responsible for closing the reader, which also closes the connection.

If the expected return type is either a DataSet or an XML document, this function creates a data adapter and uses it to fill a DataSet object. Depending on the actual return type, the DataSet is either returned or converted into an XML document, which is then returned.

Obviously, you should not expect the client objects to create the command object for you. After all, the whole purpose of creating a data access layer like this is to shield the client objects from performing low-level data-access operations. In other words, you should not let client objects call this version of ExecuteQuery directly. Therefore, it's declared as Private.

If a client object wants to run a dynamic SQL statement, it should be able to simply pass the statement and expect the correct result to be returned. Therefore, you should overload the ExecuteQuery function to accept a SQL statement.

```
' Accepts a dynamic SQL statement
Public Function ExecuteQuery(ByVal Config As ConfigSettings, _
                            ByVal ResultType As ReturnType, _
                            ByVal CommandText As String) As Object
    CreateCommand(Config, CommandText, CommandType.Text)
    Return ExecuteQuery(Config, ResultType)
End Function
```

The first two parameters are identical to the private ExecuteQuery function discussed previously. The third parameter will store the SQL statement. This function simply uses the internal CreateCommand function to create a command object. As there is no parameter, the ParamArray parameter of the CreateCommand function will be empty.

If a client object needs to execute a stored procedure, possibly with parameters, it should be able to pass the stored procedure name and its parameter list. You create another overloaded ExecuteQuery function to facilitate this.

```
' Accepts a stored procedure with parameter name-value pairs
Public Function ExecuteQuery(ByVal config As ConfigSettings, _
                            ByVal ResultType As ReturnType, _
                            ByVal CommandText As String, _
                            ByVal CommandType As CommandType, _
                            ByVal ParamArray Params() As Pair) As Object
    CreateCommand(config, CommandText, CommandType, Params)
    Return ExecuteQuery(config, ResultType)
End Function
```

The first three parameters are the same as the previous overloaded version of ExecuteQuery. The fourth parameter specifies the type of command and the last parameter is an array of parameter name-value pairs. Again, this function passes all parameters to the CreateCommand function to create a command object. Finally, it calls the private ExecuteQuery function and returns the expected object to the calling object.

You might think that the CommandType parameter is rather redundant, as you know this version of ExecuteQuery is designed to run stored procedures. The reason it's here is that you can, in fact, use this version to execute parameterized queries as well. For instance, you can assign CommandText the following SQL query:

```
SELECT ProductID, ProductName FROM Products
 WHERE CategoryID = @CategoryID
```

It's not a stored procedure, but it requires a parameter, which can be passed in the Param-Array. In such cases, the command type will be Text rather than StoredProcedure.

That's it! Can it get much easier? You can add any number of data return types; for instance, if you use a custom XML schema, you can dynamically create XML documents here, or you can return the data as an array. The possibilities are (almost) endless.

The ExecuteNonQuery Functions

The ExecuteNonQuery functions follow the same pattern as the ExecuteQuery functions. There are three overloaded versions: two public and one private. The following code snippet demonstrates an implementation:

```
'
' Execute a SQL statement that will not return a result
' This function has several overloaded versions
'
' Accepts a dynamic SQL statement
Public Sub ExecuteNonQuery(ByVal config As ConfigSettings, _
                           ByVal CommandText As String)
    CreateCommand(config, CommandText, CommandType.Text)
    ExecuteNonQuery(config)
End Sub

' Accepts a stored procedure with parameter name-value pairs
Public Sub ExecuteNonQuery(ByVal config As ConfigSettings, _
                           ByVal CommandText As String, _
                              ByVal CommandType As CommandType, _
                              ByVal ParamArray Params() As Pair)
    CreateCommand(config, CommandText, CommandType, Params)
    ExecuteNonQuery(config)
End Sub

' This function is the one that performs the real work
Private Sub ExecuteNonQuery(ByVal config As ConfigSettings)
    Connect(config)
    mCommand.Connection = mConnection
    mCommand.ExecuteNonQuery()
    mConnection.Close()
End Sub
```

Again, the two public versions differ in whether or not they accept an explicit command type and parameter name-value pairs. They first create a command object by calling the CreateCommand function and then invoke the private version to do the real work. The latter is slightly simpler than its ExecuteQuery counterpart. As you are by now quite familiar with ADO.NET, the private ExecuteNonQuery function should be pretty clear to you.

Deploying a Data Service Component

Deploying a solution developed by utilizing the .NET Framework is a very easy task, due to the very nature of .NET—the use of self-describing components and a CLR. You aren't going to go into every aspect of packaging and deploying a .NET application because all you are concerned with is deploying your DAL component.

There are two categories of assemblies with regards to distribution: private and shared. A private assembly will be located within an application's directory structure: the /bin directory.

However, what is the use of this if multiple applications need to use the object, as with your component? This is where the Global Assembly Cache (GAC) and shared assemblies come into play.

The Global Assembly Cache

The GAC is an assembly cache that is accessible machine-wide. What this means is that it is accessible from an ASP.NET application, a Windows Form application, a web service, or any other .NET application running on the machine. There are several advantages to installing assemblies in the GAC.

- Components are located in a centralized location.

- Components are secure—you must be an administrator on the machine to install or manipulate any assemblies in the GAC.

- Side-by-side versioning—you can have multiple versions of the same assembly running side by side.

Before you can install a component into the GAC, there are some things you must do and attributes that your component must possess. Your assembly must be a strong-named assembly. A *strong name* is essentially your assembly's identity—that is, what distinguishes it from all other assemblies. No two assemblies can have the same name. A strong name can include information about your assembly's name, version, public key, and digital signature.

A public and private key pair is used to create an assembly's strong name and this key-pair file is used during the component's compilation to create its strong name. Microsoft has included a utility with the .NET SDK that you can use to generate a key-pair file that will be used to sign an assembly. This tool is called the Strong Name utility, sn.exe.

Strong Name Utility—sn.exe

You use the Strong Name tool to create a file containing a cryptographic key pair. You should be able to use sn.exe directly from the command line. It will usually be in the `C:\Program Files\Microsoft.NET\FrameworkSDK\Bin` folder.

Table 10-3 contains some of the more widely used features of this tool. For a complete list of features, please see the .NET SDK Help files section on "Strong Name Tool (sn.exe)" or type **sn.exe /?** at the command prompt.

Table 10-3. *sn.exe Switch Descriptions*

Switch	Description
- k OutFile	Generates a new key pair and writes it to the specified file
- v Assembly	Verifies the strong name for an assembly
- e Assembly OutFile	Extracts the public key from an assembly and stores it in the specified file
- ?	Displays all command syntax for sn.exe

The following code snippet will automatically generate the .snk file you will be using in your example. .snk is a Microsoft recommended extension-naming convention for these files:

```
sn.exe -k D:\ProAdo.Net\DataLayer\OurKeyPair.snk
```

Tip Remember to replace the directory name with your project directory.

Now that you have your .snk file, you have to add an attribute to your assembly to use the specified file. To do this, use the `AssemblyKeyFileAttribute` class, as illustrated in the following code:

```
<Assembly: AssemblyKeyFile("D:\ProAdo.Net\DataLayer\OurKeyPair.snk")>
```

Put this code in the AssemblyInfo.vb file and rebuild the assembly. Now, you are ready to install the assembly in the GAC.

Global Assembly Cache Utility—gacutil.exe

The Global Assembly Cache utility (gacutil.exe) is used to manipulate the contents of the GAC—to install, uninstall, and list assemblies.

Note The GAC is usually located at `C:\WINNT\assembly`. Be careful with this directory, because once it is lost, the only way to get it back is to reinstall the framework.

Table 10-4 contains some of the more often used commands.

Table 10-4. *gacutil.exe Switch Descriptions*

Switch	Description
/i Assembly	Installs an assembly into the GAC
/u Assembly	Uninstalls an assembly from the GAC
/l	Lists the contents of the GAC
/cdl	Deletes the contents of the download cache
/?	Displays all commands

Now let's install your `DataLayer` component into the GAC. Use the following code in the command prompt window or in a .bat file to install it:

```
gacutil.exe -I D:\ProAdo.Net\DataLayer\bin\DataLayer.dll
```

As you can see in Figure 10-3, the assembly was added to the GAC.

Global Assembly Name △	Type	Version	Culture	Public Key Token
CustomMarshalers		1.0.3300.0		b03f5f7f11d50a3a
DataLayer		1.0.952.19733		df6d6c9edb69f08e
EnvDTE		7.0.3300.0		b03f5f7f11d50a3a
Extensibility		7.0.3300.0		b03f5f7f11d50a3a
IEExecRemote		1.0.3300.0		b03f5f7f11d50a3a
IEHost		1.0.3300.0		b03f5f7f11d50a3a
IIEHost		1.0.3300.0		b03f5f7f11d50a3a

Figure 10-3. *GAC with your data layer in it*

Using the Data Service Component

Using this new DAL component is the same from one type of .NET application to another. In this section of the chapter, we will demonstrate this by using the DAL component from a couple of different places. There is code illustrating how to use the DAL component in a web form and a web service. Within the web form code, you will use the DAL component to do the following tasks:

- Execute SQL INSERT, UPDATE, SELECT, and DELETE commands with SQL statements using the SqlClient, OleDb, OracleClient, and ODBC .NET data providers

- Execute SQL stored procedures

- Return different types of data objects: DataSet, DataReader, and XmlDataDocument

Using the DAL Component in an ASP.NET Web Form

The first example illustrates how to use the DAL component from a web form environment. This first example illustrates how to execute SELECT, UPDATE, DELETE, and INSERT statements using the DAL component. You must have all the requirements for the chapter, as explained in the introduction, for this example to work properly.

Executing SQL Text

First, create a new Visual Basic ASP.NET web application project with any name you like, for instance, DALWebApp, and rename the automatically created web form class Client_SQL. Before you start working on this form, make sure that you add a reference to the data layer assembly, DataLayer.dll. Because all data access operations are performed by DataLayer.dll, this web form doesn't access the database directly. Therefore, there is no need to reference System.Data.OracleClient.

This web form contains the following five server controls:

- A DropDownList named ddlDataSource that is used to pick a data store: SQL Server, Access, Oracle, or ODBC. You need to manually create three strings into this control's Items collection.

- A DropDownList named ddlSqlType that is used to pick what type of function to execute: SELECT, DELETE, UPDATE, or INSERT. Again, you need to manually add strings representing those operations into this control's Items collection.

- A Button that is used to POST the page back to the server. Each time a user clicks this button, the form is posted to the server. The default name of this button is RUN, as we won't explicitly work with this button.

- A Label named lblMessage that is used to display messages to users.

- A DataGrid named grdProducts that is used to display the contents of the Product table—the table you are manipulating.

Figure 10-4 illustrates the form.

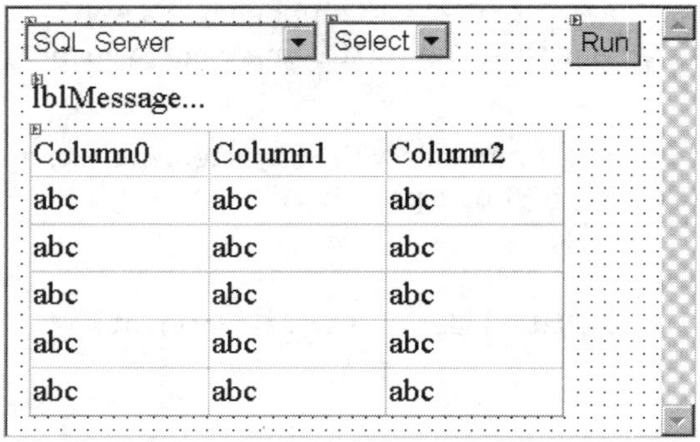

Figure 10-4. *Client_SQL.aspx*

In this sample web form, you will perform data access using any of the three supported .NET data providers—SQL Server, OLE DB, and ODBC. The data layer, however, will work just as well for Oracle, but since we do not have a Northwind database for Oracle, you will skip that for now. You will display all product records in the relevant databases. You will also insert, update, and delete an arbitrary new product record using each of the data providers.

```
Public Class Client_SQL
    Inherits System.Web.UI.Page

    ' SQL Statements for testing
    Private Const mcTestProductOldName As String = "Macks Fried Chicken"
    Private Const mcTestProductNewName As String = "Macks Spicy Fried Chicken"
    Private Const mcSqlSelect As String = "SELECT * FROM Products"
```

```
    Private Const mcSqlInsert As String = _
      "INSERT INTO Products (ProductName) VALUES ('" & mcTestProductOldName & "')"
    Private Const mcSqlUpdate As String = _
        "UPDATE Products SET ProductName = '" & mcTestProductNewName & _
        "' WHERE ProductName = '" & mcTestProductOldName & "'"
    Private Const mcSqlDelete As String = _
        "DELETE FROM Products WHERE ProductName = '" & mcTestProductNewName & "'"


    ' Connection strings
    Private Const mcSqlConnString As String = _
        "Data Source=(local);User ID=sa;Password=;Initial Catalog=Northwind"
    Private Const mcOdbcConnString As String = "DSN=NorthWind;UID=sa"
    Private Const mcOleDbConnString As String = _
        "Provider=Microsoft.Jet.OLEDB.4.0;Data Source=D:\Northwind.Mdb"
    Private Const mcOracleConnString As String = _
        "Data Source=Oracle8i;Integrated Security=SSPI"
    ' Data Layer configuration settings object
    Private mDalConfig As DataLayer.ConfigSettings
    Private mDalCommands As DataLayer.Commands
End Class
```

You will define a set of class-level constants to store SQL statements for the four operations, select, insert, update, and delete. mcTestProductOldName stores the initial product name of the new record to be inserted, while mcTestProductNewName stores the new product name entered by the SQL UPDATE statement. This name is then used to delete this record. When you play with this example web form, please note that you must perform the INSERT, UPDATE, and DELETE operations in sequence because the SQL UPDATE and DELETE statements use the hard-coded product names to find the record.

The next set of constants, mcSqlConnString, mcOdbcConnString, mcOracleConnString, and mcOleDbConnString, stores the connection strings for the three data providers to connect to corresponding databases. In this example, you connect to the local sample Northwind database shipped with SQL Server using both SQL Server and ODBC .NET data providers. The data access layer will, however, work in a similar fashion for Oracle. You need to change the connection string for the SQL Server .NET data provider if you use a remote SQL Server. You should also create an ODBC data source named Northwind to point to your SQL Server Northwind database in order for the ODBC .NET data provider to connect to it.

This example also connects to an Access database, Northwind, that is shipped with Access using the OLE DB data provider. The OLE DB connection string assumes that the database is in the root directory of the D drive; you will need to adjust its path to point to its location on your machine.

Finally, you define a reference for an instance of each of the data layer classes. When an ASP.NET page is loaded or posted back, the Page.Load event fires and triggers its event handler, Page_Load.

```
Private Sub Page_Load(ByVal sender As System.Object, _
        ByVal e As System.EventArgs) Handles MyBase.Load
    CreateDalObjects()
```

```
    Select Case UCase(ddlFunction.SelectedItem.Value)
        Case "SELECT"
            ShowProducts()

        Case "INSERT"
            InsertProduct()

        Case "EDIT"
            UpdateProduct()

        Case "DELETE"
            DeleteProduct()

        Case Else
            ShowProducts()
    End Select
End Sub
```

The code in this event handler is simple, as it should be. It just calls methods that actually do the dirty work. The first, CreateDalObjects, instantiates the two data layer classes for other functions to use. Page_Load will then extract the type of data access operations from the ddl-Function drop-down list and call the corresponding functions to perform the selected operation.

Here's the complete code of the CreateDalObjects method.

```
Private Sub CreateDalObjects()
    Select Case UCase(ddlDataSource.SelectedItem.Value)
        Case "ODBC"
            mDalConfig = New DataLayer.ConfigSettings( _
                DataLayer.DataProviderType.Odbc, mcOdbcConnString)
        Case "OLEDB"
            mDalConfig = New DataLayer.ConfigSettings( _
                DataLayer.DataProviderType.OleDb, mcOleDbConnString)
        Case "SQL"
            mDalConfig = New DataLayer.ConfigSettings( _
                DataLayer.DataProviderType.Sql, mcSqlConnString)
            Case "ORACLE"
                mDalConfig = New DataLayer.ConfigSettings( _
                    DataLayer.DataProviderType.Oracle, mcOracleConnString)
        Case Else
            mDalConfig = New DataLayer.ConfigSettings( _
                DataLayer.DataProviderType.Sql, mcSqlConnString)
    End Select

    mDalCommands = New DataLayer.Commands()
End Sub
```

This method creates a new ConfigSettings object and passes in the selected data provider in the ddlDataSource drop-down list. It also passes in the corresponding connection string for the selected data provider. The Commands object is then created.

Once the data layer objects have been created, actually performing the data access operations is a simple matter of calling the Commands object's ExecuteQuery or ExecuteNonQuery functions. Let's start by looking at the ShowProducts method.

```
Private Sub ShowProducts()
  Dim ds As DataSet = mDalCommands.ExecuteQuery( _
        mDalConfig, DataLayer.ReturnType.DataSetType, mcSqlSelect)
  grdProducts.DataSource = ds
  grdProducts.DataBind()
  lblMessage.Text = ""
End Sub
```

Since the Commands class doesn't know anything about the data provider to be used. It's the client object's responsibility to provide a ConfigSettings object specifying the desired data provider and connection string. In this function, you also specify the return type, an ADO.NET DataSet, and the SQL statement to be executed. You then bind the DataGrid, grdProducts, to the returned DataSet so that all product records are displayed in the page returned to the browser. The label, lblMessage, is left empty in this case.

The InsertProduct method is just as simple. The following is its code:

```
Private Sub InsertProduct()
  mDalCommands.ExecuteNonQuery(mDalConfig, mcSqlInsert)
  ShowProducts()
  lblMessage.Text = "Record inserted"
End Sub
```

Since a SQL INSERT statement doesn't return a result set, it invokes the Commands object's ExecuteNonQuery function. As usual, it passes in a ConfigSettings object containing the selected data provider and corresponding connection string, and the actual SQL INSERT statement to be executed. Once the new record is added, this function calls the ShowProducts function to display all product records. This time, it also notifies the user about the outcome by displaying a message, Record inserted, in the lblMessage label.

As you can imagine, the UpdateProduct and DeleteProduct methods will be very similar to the InsertProduct method. Therefore, we will not repeat the explanations but rather just present the code listing as follows:

```
' Edit the test product record created in InsertProduct
Private Sub UpdateProduct()
  mDalCommands.ExecuteNonQuery(mDalConfig, mcSqlUpdate)
  ShowProducts()
  lblMessage.Text = "Record updated"
End Sub
' Delete the modified test product record
Private Sub DeleteProduct()
  mDalCommands.ExecuteNonQuery(mDalConfig, mcSqlDelete)
```

```
        ShowProducts()
        lblMessage.Text = "Record deleted"
    End Sub
```

Figure 10-5 illustrates the form after the new product record is inserted.

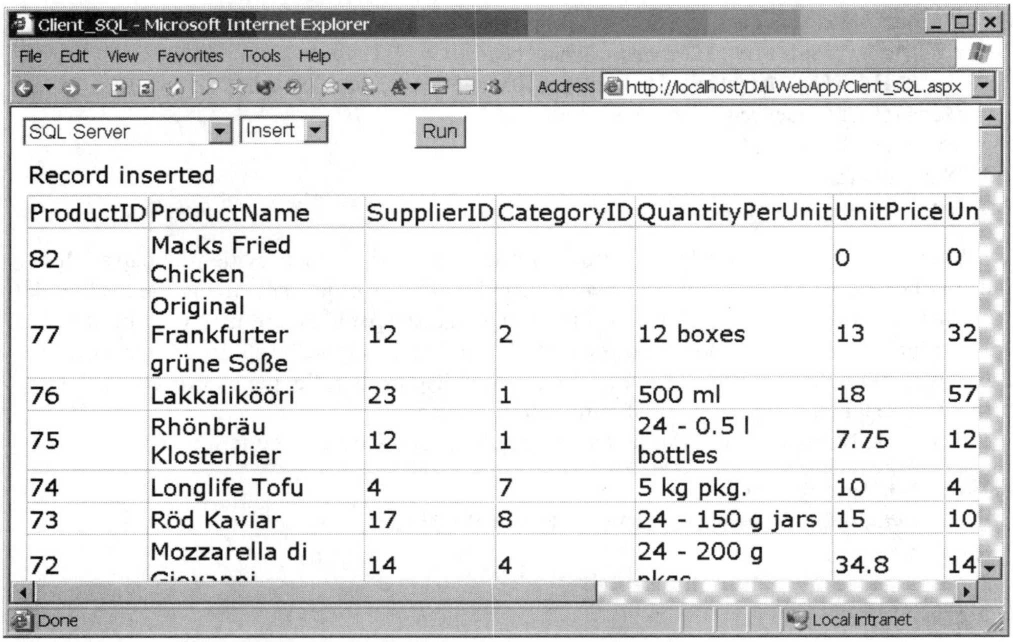

Figure 10-5. *Client_SQL.aspx after a record is inserted*

As you can see, the hard work you have done on the data layer component pays off handsomely for the client applications. A client application doesn't have to know how to use different data providers to access databases. All it has to do is specify the data provider, its connection string, and a SQL statement and let the data layer component do the hard work for it.

If you have worked with more than one database such as SQL Server, Oracle, or Access, you will know the reality about performing data access on heterogeneous databases. While most databases claim to support standard SQL, their implementations often differ slightly. For instance, SQL Server denotes a wildcard character with the % symbol while Access uses the * symbol. You must construct SQL statements with such subtle differences in mind.

Executing Stored Procedures

Unlike plain SQL statements, stored procedures are not standardized at all. Different databases implement stored procedures using different syntax, and some, such as Access, don't support stored procedures at all. In the case of Access, you can still use queries to simulate the stored procedures. Different data providers also use different stored procedure syntax. While the data layer component presented in this chapter supports the use of stored procedures and provides features to simplify their usage, it doesn't offer a unified stored procedure invocation capability for different data providers and databases. Providing the latter functionality would require an in-depth understanding about the implementation of stored procedures in every database and data provider it supports, and therefore is far beyond what this chapter, and this book, can reasonably cover.

In this second example, you will see what a client application needs to do to deal with such implementation discrepancies. You will find, however, that the data layer will greatly reduce the programming efforts required for the rest of your data access tasks.

Just add a new web form into the ASP.NET web application project you created earlier and name it Client_StoredProc.

In this web form there are three server controls.

- A DropDownList named ddlDataSource that is used to pick a data store—SQL Server, Access, or ODBC. You need to manually create three strings into this control's Items collection.

- A Button that is used to POST the page back to the server. Each time a user clicks this button, the form is posted to the server. The default name of this button is Run, as you won't explicitly work with this button.

- A DataGrid named grdProducts that is used to display the contents of the Product table—the table you are manipulating.

Figure 10-6 illustrates the form.

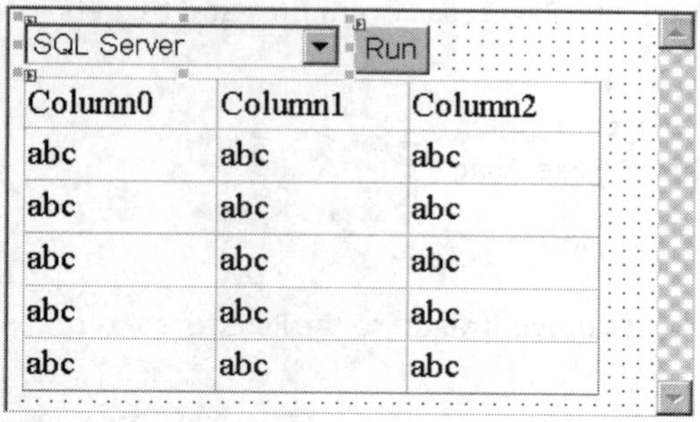

Figure 10-6. *Client_StoredProc.aspx*

In this sample web form, you will execute the stored procedure Sales by Year in SQL Server using SQL Server and ODBC .NET data providers. You will also run its counterpart, the Sales by Year query, in Access using the OLE DB .NET data provider. You will display sales by year figures returned by the SQL Server stored procedure and Access query.

```
Public Class Client_StoredProc
    Inherits System.Web.UI.Page
```

```
    ' Stored procedure name and parameter values
    Private Const mcStoredProc As String = "[Sales by Year]"
    Private Const mcStartDateParamName As String = "@Beginning_Date"
    Private mStartDateParamValue As DateTime = New DateTime(1996, 7, 1)
    Private Const mcEndDateParamName As String = "@Ending_Date"
    Private mEndDateParamValue As DateTime = New DateTime(1996, 8, 1)

    ' Connection strings
    Private Const mcOdbcConnString As String = "DSN=NorthWind;UID=sa"
    Private Const mcOleDbConnString As String = _
        "Provider=Microsoft.Jet.OLEDB.4.0;Data Source=D:\Northwind.Mdb"
    Private Const mcSqlConnString As String = _
        "Data Source=(local);User ID=sa;Password=;Initial Catalog=Northwind"
    Private Const mcOracleConnString As String = _
        "Data Source=Oracle8i;Integrated Security=SSPI"
    ' Data Layer configuration settings object
    Private mDalConfig As DataLayer.ConfigSettings
    Private mDalCommands As DataLayer.Commands
End Class
```

Again, you will define a set of class-level constants to store the stored procedures and their parameter names, mcStartDataParamValue and mcEndDataParamValue store arbitrary starting and ending time, respectively, for the query.

The next set of constants, mcSqlConnString, mcOdbcConnString, mcOracleConnString, and mcOleDbConnString, are the same as in the last example. They store the connection strings for the three data providers to connect to corresponding databases. You also define a reference for an instance of each of the data layer classes.

When an ASP.NET page is loaded or posted back, the Page.Load event fires and triggers its event handler, Page_Load.

```
Private Sub Page_Load(ByVal sender As System.Object, _
        ByVal e As System.EventArgs) Handles MyBase.Load
    RunStoredProc()
End Sub
```

This is even simpler than in the last example. Let's move straight to the RunStoredProc method.

```
Private Sub RunStoredProc()
    Dim StoredProcName As String = mcStoredProc

    Select Case UCase(ddlDataSource.SelectedItem.Value)
    Case "ODBC"
        mDalConfig = New DataLayer.ConfigSettings( _
            DataLayer.DataProviderType.Odbc, mcOdbcConnString)
        StoredProcName = "{call [Sales by Year](?, ?)}"

    Case "OLEDB"
        mDalConfig = New DataLayer.ConfigSettings( _
            DataLayer.DataProviderType.OleDb, mcOleDbConnString)
```

```
   Case "SQL"
       mDalConfig = New DataLayer.ConfigSettings( _
           DataLayer.DataProviderType.Sql, mcSqlConnString)


           Case "ORACLE"
               mDalConfig = New DataLayer.ConfigSettings( _
                   DataLayer.DataProviderType.Oracle, mcOracleConnString)
   Case Else
       mDalConfig = New DataLayer.ConfigSettings( _
           DataLayer.DataProviderType.Sql, mcSqlConnString)
   End Select

   mDalCommands = New DataLayer.Commands()
   Dim ds As DataSet = mDalCommands.ExecuteQuery( _
       mDalConfig, DataLayer.ReturnType.DataSetType, _
       StoredProcName, CommandType.StoredProcedure, _
       New DataLayer.Pair(mcStartDateParamName, mStartDateParamValue), _
       New DataLayer.Pair(mcEndDateParamName, mEndDateParamValue))

   grdProducts.DataSource = ds
   grdProducts.DataBind()
End Sub
```

As in the previous example, you instantiate a ConfigSettings class to store the preferred data provider and connection string in the Select block. When you run a stored procedure on a SQL Server using SQL Server and OLE DB .NET data providers, you can simply specify the name of the stored procedure and its parameters and execute it. This example only tests the SQL Server .NET data provider, but you can easily test the OLE DB .NET data provider by replacing the corresponding connection, mcOleDbConnString. In fact, the OLE DB .NET data provider simply passes the stored procedure command to the correct OLE DB provider to execute. For instance, if you assign the Provider property in the OLE DB connection string with "SQLOLEDB", the stored procedure command will be passed to the OLE DB provider for SQL Server. Similarly, you could build suitable functionality for the OracleClient for the appropriate stored procedure or package within Oracle.

In this example, you use the OLE DB .NET data provider to connect to an Access database. Therefore, you assign OLE DB .NET data provider's Provider property with "Microsoft.Jet.OLEDB.4.0", which specifies that it should use Microsoft OLE DB provider for Jet to perform data access operations. This OLE DB provider supports the execution of Access queries using a Command object of StoredProcedure type. As you can see from the previous function, you can take advantage of this feature by simply specifying the name of the query as the stored procedure name and passing in the parameter name-value pairs.

Similarly, the ODBC .NET data provider also uses the underlying database-specific ODBC driver to connect to ODBC data sources. In this example, the ODBC .NET data provider reads from the given DSN to work out that the ODBC data source connects to a SQL Server database. Therefore, it uses the ODBC driver for SQL Server to execute the stored procedure. Being an older technology, the ODBC driver for SQL Server uses a different stored procedure invocation syntax that requires you to specify the full calling code including place holders for the parameters, as you can see in the Case block for ODBC.

```
StoredProcName = "{call [Sales by Year](?, ?)}"
```

In this example, each question mark (?) denotes a parameter for the stored procedure. You must also include the T-SQL stored procedure invocation keyword (call).

Once it works out the preferred data provider, connection string, and stored procedure name in correct format, this function calls the Commands object's ExecuteQuery function to execute the stored procedure. This time, it calls the overloaded version that accepts an array of stored procedure parameters.

```
Public Function ExecuteQuery(ByVal config As ConfigSettings, _
                             ByVal ResultType As ReturnType, _
                             ByVal CommandText As String, _
                             ByVal CommandType As CommandType, _
                             ByVal ParamArray Params() As Pair) As Object
```

Once the SQL Server stored procedure or Access query is executed, the results are returned in a DataSet. You can bind the DataGrid, grdProducts, to the returned DataSet to display the sales figures. Figure 10-7 shows a sample result.

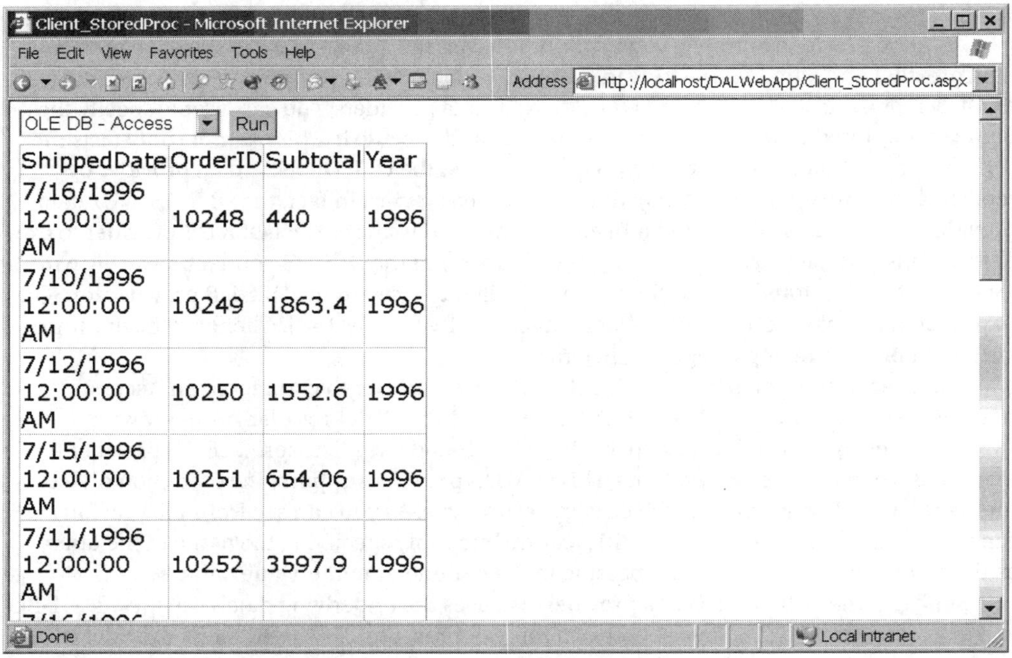

Figure 10-7. *Client_StoredProc.aspx sample results*

This example demonstrates that while different databases implement stored procedures differently, a .NET data provider can work with the database-specific OLE DB provider to offer a unified programming interface through ADO.NET. As you have seen, the code to execute a SQL Server stored procedure and an Access query is identical. You have also seen that different .NET data providers may require different stored procedure invocation syntax, as in the case of accessing the same Sales by Year SQL Server stored procedure using SQL Server and ODBC .NET data providers.

Using the DAL Component in a Web Service

As previously mentioned, now that you have registered the DAL component in the GAC, it can be used from anywhere without the need to put the .dll file in the /bin directory of the application. In this section, we'll illustrate this through a simple web service example.

First, create a new Visual Basic ASP.NET web service project and name it DALWebService. Next, add a reference to DataLayer.dll and change its Copy Local property value to False. This change prevents the DLL from being copied to the /bin directory of DALWebService. To be precise, the DLL is copied when the reference is added and changing the Copy Local property to False just deletes it from the \bin directory. You can then delete the automatically generated Service1.asmx and add a new web service named Client_WebService.

Switch to the code view of Client_WebService and enter the code as show here.

```
<WebService(Namespace := "http://tempuri.org/")> _
Public Class Client_WebService
    Inherits System.Web.Services.WebService

    <WebMethod()> _
    Public Function GetProducts(ByVal CustomerID As String) As DataSet
        ' Connection string
        Const cSqlConnString As String = _
            "Data Source=(local);User ID=sa;Password=;Initial Catalog=Northwind"

        ' Data Layer objects
        Dim DalConfig As DataLayer.ConfigSettings = _
            New DataLayer.ConfigSettings(DataLayer.DataProviderType.Sql, _
                                    cSqlConnString)
        Dim DalCommands As DataLayer.Commands = New DataLayer.Commands()

        Return DalCommands.ExecuteQuery( _
                    DalConfig, DataLayer.ReturnType.DataSetType, _
                    "CustOrderHist", CommandType.StoredProcedure, _
                    New DataLayer.Pair("@CustomerID", CustomerID))
    End Function
End Class
```

By now, the code in the GetProducts function should be pretty familiar to you. This function invokes the Commands object's ExecuteQuery function to retrieve in a DataSet all order history data for a given customer. It then simply returns the DataSet to the client object.

You can test this web service function by setting Client_WebService.asmx as the start page and running the project. Figure 10-8 illustrates the result from the execution of this web method.

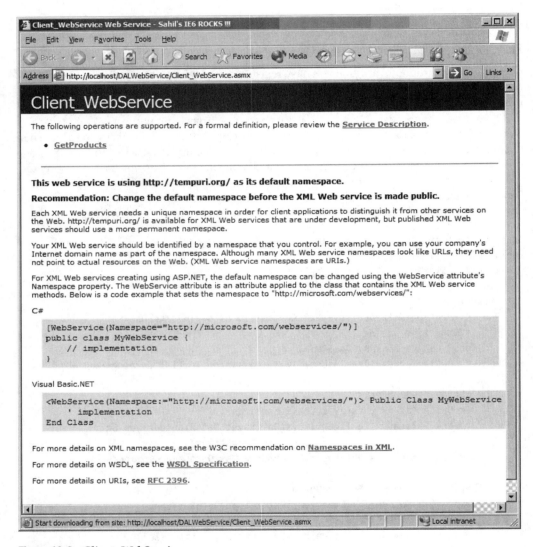

Figure 10-8. *Client_WebService.asmx*

Also, you can click the "Service Description" link to view the associated WSDL, as shown in Figure 10-9.

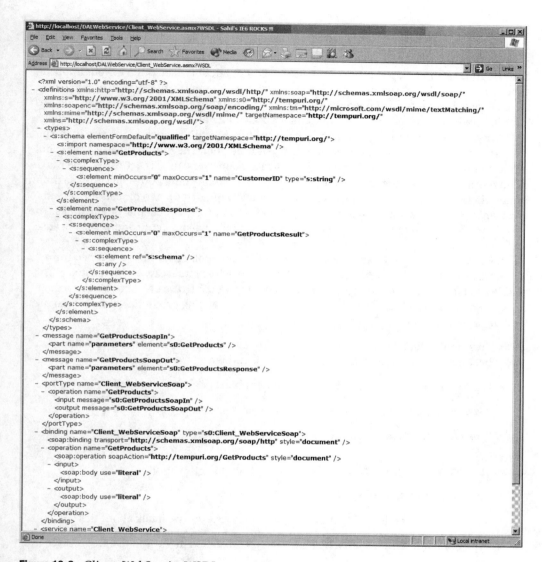

Figure 10-9. *Client_WebService WSDL*

Performance and Optimization Tips

In this last section, we will go over a few optimization and performance tips with regards to creating business and data service components. In addition, we will cover object pooling and transactions.

Object Pooling

Before .NET arrived on the scene, object pooling in COM+ was only available to the Visual C++ developer so programmers who used Visual Basic or FoxPro were out of luck. Object pooling in .NET is still utilized as a COM+ service. For those who aren't familiar with object pooling, it is technology that enables you to create one or more objects and put them in a pool. Once these objects are in the pool, clients can use them without having to create them from scratch. For example, say there is a component named CheckOut and it is used often in your applications. You can enable object pooling for the CheckOut component and when an application needs to use the object it simply requests the object from the pool, uses it, and then releases it back into the pool so it can be used by another application later.

When you enable object pooling, you have control over things such as the size of the pool. You can set both a minimum and maximum size for the pool. The minimum size of the pool is how many objects are created and ready for use as soon as the pool is activated. The maximum number is the maximum number of objects that can be in the pool. Once the maximum is met, clients' requests for the objects are automatically queued up and objects are served to the clients as they become available—you can also set a timeout for clients' queue times. The best thing about object pooling is the performance gain that client applications see because they rarely need to create an object from scratch.

If you want a component to take advantage of object pooling, it must be derived from the ServicedComponent class—a member of the System.EnterpriseServices namespace. This enables you to use ObjectPoolingAttribute to enable and configure object pooling for the component. The ObjectPoolingAttribute contains the following properties that you can use to configure object pooling for components:

- CreationTimeout: Sets the length of time, in milliseconds, to wait for an object to become available after which an exception is thrown

- Enabled: A Boolean value indicating whether object pooling is enabled

- MaxPoolSize: The maximum number of objects that can be in the pool

- MinPoolSize: The minimum number of objects that can be in the pool

Additionally your component must possess the following attributes:

- Must be strong named (sn.exe)

- Must be registered in the Windows registry (regsvcs.exe—we'll talk about this soon)

- Type library definitions must be registered and installed in the application (regsvcs.exe)

The following example will illustrate how to develop and deploy a pooled object. This object is used as a "Hit Tracker." It contains only two methods; the first is used to update a database with unique Web site hits and the second is used to update every Web site hit. The reason we chose this example is because it isn't economical to put an object in the pool if it isn't used that often. If your Web site is anything like ours, http://www.dotnetjunkies.com/, it gets hit quite often so pooling the tracking component just makes sense. The pooled object in this example is used by the global.asax file because there are events that you can handle within this file that are fired for both unique requests and every request for the documents in a web application.

Building a Hit Tracker Component

There will be three aspects to this example: the database, which you will create in SQL Server; the code for the pooled component; and the global.asax file.

Creating a Database

The first thing you need to do is create a new database to use with the example. This example uses SQL Server, but the code can be adapted to use any other database. The following script (HitTracker.sql) can be used to generate the needed database:

```
CREATE TABLE [dbo].[PageViews] (
  [HitDate] [datetime] NULL ,
  [TotalHits] [float] NULL
) ON [PRIMARY]
GO


CREATE TABLE [dbo].[Unique] (
  [HitDate] [datetime] NOT NULL ,
  [TotalHits] [float] NOT NULL
) ON [PRIMARY]
GO


SET QUOTED_IDENTIFIER OFF
GO
SET ANSI_NULLS ON
GO


CREATE PROCEDURE [dbo].[HitsTotal]
@todaysdate datetime
AS
DECLARE @TOTAL int
SET @TOTAL = (SELECT COUNT(*) FROM [PageViews] WHERE HitDate = @todaysdate)

IF @TOTAL > 0
  BEGIN
    UPDATE PageViews
      SET TotalHits =
            ((SELECT TotalHits FROM PageViews WHERE HitDate = @todaysdate) + 1)
      WHERE HitDate = @todaysdate
  END
ELSE
  BEGIN
    INSERT INTO PageViews
      (
        HitDate,
        TotalHits
      )
```

```
      VALUES
      (
        @todaysdate,
        1
      )
  END
GO
SET QUOTED_IDENTIFIER OFF
GO
SET ANSI_NULLS ON
GO

SET QUOTED_IDENTIFIER OFF
GO
SET ANSI_NULLS ON
GO

CREATE PROCEDURE [dbo].[HitsUnique]
@todaysdate datetimeAS
DECLARE @TOTAL int

SET @TOTAL = (SELECT COUNT(*) FROM [Unique] WHERE HitDate = @todaysdate)

IF   @TOTAL > 0
  BEGIN
    UPDATE [Unique]
      SET
      TotalHits =
          ((SELECT TotalHits FROM [Unique] WHERE HitDate = @todaysDate ) +1)
      WHERE HitDate = @todaysdate
  END
ELSE
  BEGIN
    INSERT INTO [Unique]
      (
        HitDate,
        TotalHits
      )
      VALUES
      (
        @todaysdate,
        1
      )
  END
GO
SET QUOTED_IDENTIFIER OFF
```

```
GO
SET ANSI_NULLS ON
GO
```

Creating the Component

Next, you will create your Hit Tracker serviced component. In Visual Studio.NET, create a new Visual Basic Class Library project and name it `ObjectPoolingServer`. Since Visual Studio .NET doesn't automatically reference the `System.EnterpriseServices` component, you will have to manually add a reference to it.

When developing serviced components, you need to specify several attributes for the assembly. The best place to put them is in the automatically generated AssemblyInfo.vb class.

```
Imports System.Reflection
Imports System.Runtime.InteropServices
Imports System.EnterpriseServices

' Enterprise Services Application Attributes
<Assembly: ApplicationName("Object Pooling Sample")>
<Assembly: ApplicationActivation(ActivationOption.Server)>
<Assembly: AssemblyKeyFile("D:\ObjectPoolingServer\OPSKey.snk")>
<Assembly: AssemblyVersion("1.0.0.1")>
```

An attribute you may not have seen before is included here—the `ApplicationActivation` attribute. The `ApplicationActivation` attribute is used to specify whether the component should run in the creator's process or in a system process. The constructor expects one parameter, a value from the `ActivationOption` enumeration. If you want a component to run in COM+ as a server, you must use `ActivationOption.Server`. The other possible value is `ActivationOption.Library`, which causes the component to run as a library. That is, it will run in the client assembly's process. Remember to replace the path to the strong key file with your own directory, and with your own filename if you name it differently.

The workhorse of this serviced component is the `HitTracker` class. You should rename the automatically generated Class1.vb to HitTracker.vb and change the class name to `HitTracker`. You also need to decorate this class to tell the CLR that it will be managed by the .NET enterprise services.

```
Imports System.Data.SqlClient
Imports System.EnterpriseServices
Imports System.Runtime.InteropServices

<ObjectPooling(MinPoolSize:=1, MaxPoolSize:=5, CreationTimeout:=90000), _
 JustInTimeActivation(True), ClassInterface(ClassInterfaceType.AutoDual)> _
Public Class HitTracker
    Inherits ServicedComponent

End Class
```

The class you are creating is named HitTracker and it is derived from ServicedComponent. Three additional attributes are used to describe this class: ObjectPooling controls the object pooling attributes for the component; JustInTimeActivation, also a member of the System.EnterpriseServices namespace, enables or disables Just-in-Time activation (JIT); and ClassInterface identifies what type of interface should be generated for the class. The value for this constructor must be a member of the ClassInterfaceType enumeration. The available values are as follows:

- AutoDispatch: Only an IDispatch interface is generated for the class.

- AutoDual: A dual interface is generated for the class.

- None: No interface is generated for this class.

The rest of the code is exactly the same as any other class you may create with one exception: the AutoCompleteAttribute found before each method. The AutoCompleteAttribute indicates that the object should automatically return to the pool after the object is finished with.

```
Private Const mcSqlConnString As String = _
    "Data Source=(local);User ID=sa;Password=;Initial Catalog=LocalHits"
Private mConnection As SqlConnection = New SqlConnection(mcSqlConnString)
Private mCommand As SqlCommand
Private mHitDateTime As DateTime = DateTime.Today

Protected Overrides Function CanBePooled() As Boolean
    Return True
End Function

<AutoComplete()> _
Public Sub AddUnique()
    mCommand = New SqlCommand("HitsUnique", mConnection)
    mCommand.CommandType = CommandType.StoredProcedure
    mCommand.Parameters.Add("@TodaysDate", mHitDateTime)

    mConnection.Open()
    mCommand.ExecuteNonQuery()
    mConnection.Close()
End Sub

<AutoComplete()> _
Public Sub AddPageView()
    mCommand = New SqlCommand("HitsTotal", mConnection)
    mCommand.CommandType = CommandType.StoredProcedure
    mCommand.Parameters.Add("@TodaysDate", mHitDateTime)

    mConnection.Open()
    mCommand.ExecuteNonQuery()
    mConnection.Close()
End Sub
```

There are three methods in the class: AddUnique, AddPageView, and CanBePooled. The AddUnique method is used to execute the HitsUnique stored procedure and the AddPageView method is used to execute the HitsTotal method. The last method is CanBePooled, which is a member of the base class ServicedComponent, and is used to specify whether or not the object can be pooled.

Once you have compiled the project, you can use the following commands to register it in COM+ and add it to the GAC so it can be used machine-wide:

regsvcs.exe bin\ObjectPoolingServer.DLL
gacutil.exe /i bin\ObjectPoolingServer.DLL

Now let's take a look at how to use the component. Create a new Visual Basic ASP.NET web application and name it anything you like, for instance OPSClient. Next, add two references to it, ObjectPoolingServer and System.EnterpriseServices. The latter is necessary for all client assemblies that use a serviced component. In this example, you only need to add hit counting code to Global.asax.

```
Public Class Global
    Inherits System.Web.HttpApplication

Private mHitTracker As ObjectPoolingServer.HitTracker = _
    New ObjectPoolingServer.HitTracker()

    Sub Session_Start(ByVal sender As Object, ByVal e As EventArgs)
        ' Fires when the session is started
        mHitTracker.AddUnique()
    End Sub

    Sub Application_BeginRequest(ByVal sender As Object, ByVal e As EventArgs)
        ' Fires at the beginning of each request
        mHitTracker.AddPageView()
    End Sub
End Class
```

After you have built the project, execute any page within the web application. For instance, you can simply load the automatically created WebForm1.aspx.

- If you run the application for the first time, for instance when you click the Run button from Visual Studio .NET, the HitsTotal in both Unique and PageViews tables should increment.

- If you request a page after the application has started, for instance when you refresh the WebForm1.aspx page, only the HitsTotal in the PageViews table should increment.

You can also keep an eye on the serviced component in the COM+ Component Services console.

1. Go to Start ➤ Settings ➤ Control Panel ➤ Administration Tools ➤ Component Services.

2. Open Component Services.

3. Open Computers.

4. Open and select the COM+ Applications folder.

5. Notice in the right pane that Object Pooling Sample is there with the spinning ball. This is your component.

6. Now open Object Pooling Sample on the left pane.

7. Open Components, right-click, and go to Properties on `ObjectPoolingServer.Hit-Tracker`.

8. Click on the Activation tab—notice the minimum and maximum pool sizes are there along with the creation timeout.

That's it, your object is now pooled and ready for use. Figure 10-10 shows your object spinning happily in COM+.

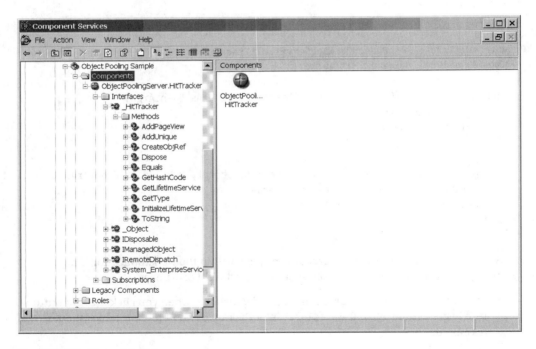

Figure 10-10. *Your object*

Uninstalling the Components

To uninstall the `ObjectPoolingServer` component, you can use regsvcs.exe with the /u switch.

```
regsvcs.exe /u bin\ObjectPoolingServer.dll
```

You can also remove it from the GAC using gacutil.exe, again using the /u switch.

gacutil.exe /u ObjectPoolingServer

■Tip You can also remove the DataLayer assembly from the GAC following the same process.

Summary

In this chapter you learned how easy it is to make and distribute a Data Application Layer (DAL) component using .NET. You saw how to make a component that supports three different data providers, how to execute different types of SQL statements using both Text and Command objects (such as SqlCommand), and how to return different types of data object. Next, you saw how to create a strong-named assembly that can be installed in the Global Assembly Cache (GAC). Finally, you learned how to use the DAL component from a web form and from a web service.

In the second part of the chapter, you looked at some performance and optimization tips, including how you can use object pooling to reduce costly object creation by keeping ready-made objects in an object pool within COM+.

In this chapter you were introduced to quite a few different aspects of development and deployment using .NET and ADO.NET. Some were covered in more detail than others. The following list summarizes these, and provides a quick reference for topics you might like to look at later in more detail:

- *n*-tier architecture concepts
- IDbConnection interface
- IDbDataAdapter interface
- SqlCommand, OleDbCommand, OdbcCommand, and IDbCommand interfaces
- ODBC .NET provider
- Strong Naming tool (sn.exe)
- Global Assembly Cache tool (gacutil.exe)
- Assembly information files
- SqlTransaction class
- ServicedComponent class
- .NET Services Installation tool (regsvcs.exe)

CHAPTER 11

■ ■ ■

ADO.NET and Web Services

In this day and age it is nearly inconceivable to think of building a new Enterprise application that does not include the Internet in its architectural diagram. Whether the Internet is used to transfer data from clients to a central processing application or to link multiple servers in separate geographic locations, the Internet has become an integral part of application architecture, and it is only becoming more critical.

Enter the web service.

A web service is a piece of application logic that is publicly exposed and available to any number of potentially disparate systems through the use of common Internet standards, such as HTTP, XML, and SOAP. Essentially, a web service is code that you expose in an application that can be accessed locally, over an intranet, or over the Internet. You have the option of allowing any number of possible clients to access your web service, or restricting the access to authenticated clients only.

Web services rely heavily on the acceptance of XML in the public arena. Web services use XML as the means for serializing data to receive from, or return to, the client. Any client that can parse XML can use the data returned, regardless of whether the client and the web service host are using the same operating system, or the applications are written in the same language. In the same manner, if the web service expects complex data to be passed into it, the client can pass that data as an XML document in a SOAP message.

Web services provide a high level of abstraction between the application logic, or the provider, and the client that uses, or consumes, the web service. The only thing the provider and the consumer need to know about each other is what input the consumer needs to provide, and what output the provider will return. The simplicity of this "contract" frees the consumer from any need to be concerned with the application logic itself. As long as the web service interface—the input and output definition—doesn't change, the provider can make code changes to the web service, and the consumer never needs to know about it, and never needs to be given any code to implement the updated service.

As you will discover in this chapter, web services are opening the door to a newer and simpler distributed application-programming model and, dare we say, a paradigm shift in distributed programming. The following documentation that is provided with the .NET Framework SDK says it best:

> *"As the next revolutionary advancement of the Internet, Web services will become the fundamental structure that links together all computing devices."*

—Web services Overview, Microsoft .NET Framework SDK documentation

In this chapter you will learn the following:

- What a web service is

- How to build a web service

- How to build a web service consumer in Visual Studio .NET

- How to build a web service consumer using a proxy client

- How to work with datasets in web services

- How to work with custom objects in web services

- How to secure a web service

Setting Up the Code Samples

In this chapter you will build three projects: two ASP.NET web applications named VBProvider and VBConsumer, and one Windows Forms project named VBWinFormsConsumer. The sample code has all three projects as Visual Studio .NET projects. (You can find the code samples for this chapter in the Downloads section of the Apress Web site [http://www.apress.com].)

The following is only a general direction toward setting up the code for this chapter on your system. Expect to do some fine tweaking as you go by. To set up the projects on your system, follow these steps:

■**Note** Skip Steps 5–8 if you will be building all of the examples. Steps 5–8 add the sample code to the project so you do not have to build it yourself. In this chapter, we will assume you are building the project and give explicit instruction on what file types and filenames to add.

---

1. Create a new directory named c:\Inetpub\wwwroot\ProADONET\.

2. Launch Visual Studio .NET and create a new Blank Solution.

3. In the New Project dialog window, create a new Visual Basic ASP.NET web application in the http://localhost/ProADONET location, named VBProvider.

4. Next, create a New Project in the Solution named VBConsumer (be sure to select Visual Basic ASP.NET web application and check the Add to Solution radio button).

5. Copy the contents of the VBProvider folder into the C:\Inetpub\wwwroot\ProADONET\ VBProvider folder that was created by Visual Studio .NET (choose "Yes to All" in the Confirm File Replace dialog box).

6. In Visual Studio .NET, you will be prompted with a dialog indicating that the project/solution was changed outside of Visual Studio .NET. Choose the Reload button to discard your changes, and update the project with the files you copied into the directory.

7. Copy the contents of the VBConsumer folder into the C:\Inetpub\wwwroot\ProADONET\ VBConsumer folder that was created by Visual Studio .NET (choose "Yes to All" in the Confirm File Replace dialog box).

8. In Visual Studio .NET, you will be prompted with a dialog indicating that the project/solution was changed outside of Visual Studio .NET. Choose the Reload button to discard your changes, and update the project with the files you copied into the directory.

9. Finally, create a new Visual Basic .NET Windows Application project in the solution, named VBWinFormsConsumer.

10. *Do not* copy the files into this project directory as you did with the others. You will be building this project later in this chapter.

You should now have three projects in the Solution Explorer, VBProvider, VBConsumer, and VBWinFormsConsumer, looking something like what you see in Figure 11-1.

Figure 11-1. *Solution Explorer for this chapter's code*

> **Note** In this chapter, we refer to some command-line utilities included with the .NET Framework. If you have installed only the .NET Framework SDK, these should work fine. If you have installed Visual Studio .NET, you must execute these from the Visual Studio .NET Command Prompt. To open this, click Start ➤ Programs ➤ Visual Studio .Net ➤ Visual Studio .Net Tools ➤ Visual Studio .Net Command Prompt.

Web Services—The New DCOM

Creating applications that enable multiple servers to communicate and exchange information is not new; the advent of web services didn't bring this on. As a developer, it is likely that you have had some involvement in building an application that required two systems to exchange data, whether via Microsoft's Distributed Component Object Model (DCOM) or Sun's Remote Method Invocation (RMI). The difference between using DCOM, or RMI, and .NET web services is how much time you get to enjoy your social life! You see, web services make the process of enabling data exchange between disparate systems easier, enabling you to get the job done more quickly.

Are web services the new DCOM? The answer lies in how web services work—in how web services enable data exchange between disparate systems. A web service exposes an interface for invoking a method on one system from another. A call to this method can be made using one of three Internet protocols: HTTP GET, HTTP POST, or SOAP. Once the web service method is invoked, any data that needs to be returned is serialized as XML and returned, either as raw XML, or as XML in the body of a SOAP message. This data exchange model allows for any object that can be serialized as XML—strings, integers, arrays, ADO.NET `DataSets`, or even custom objects—to be exchanged between the provider and the consumer. While web services may not work the same way DCOM does, they are certainly likely candidates to replace DCOM in the near future.

Common Standards

There was nearly nothing worse than trying to get a Java-based system to exchange data with a COM-based system in the pre-web services era. Data type marshaling and the incompatibilities of the two systems made this type of functionality less than desirable to implement. Since web services rely on a set of common standards, such as HTTP, XML and SOAP, this task becomes child's play—almost.

The use of common standards ensures that any number of disparate systems can exchange data easily and flawlessly, enabling true multiplatform, distributed applications. Following is a short description of the five technologies that web services make use of: XML, SOAP, WSDL, DISCO, and UDDI.

- *XML (eXtensible Markup Language)*: XML has become an accepted Internet standard for data description and exchange, much as HTML became a standard for information display many years ago. Behind the scenes, web services use XML as the data transmission format. When a web service method is invoked, the data returned (whether it is a string, an integer, a `DataSet`, or a custom object) is serialized as XML and sent back to the consumer.

- *SOAP (originally Simple Object Access Protocol)*: SOAP is an XML-based message protocol. Web services can use SOAP as the carrier for the XML data that is being exchanged between the web service provider and the web service consumer. If a web service method expects a complex object, such as a custom object that defines a product with properties that describe it, as part of its input, a SOAP message is required to carry that object, serialized as XML in the SOAP message body.

- *WSDL (web service Description Language)*: WSDL is an XML-based description of a web service. For all intents and purposes, the WSDL is the contract that a provider and a consumer agree on. The WSDL describes the interfaces of a web service and how the messages are to be formatted when using HTTP GET, HTTP POST, or SOAP protocols.

- *DISCO (web service Discovery)*: DISCO is the process of locating (discovering) the WSDL file associated to a web service. The discovery process identifies a web service and its location. The discovery process is primarily used by tools, such as Visual Studio .NET, to locate a WSDL file and build proxy clients that can remotely invoke the web service methods (proxy clients are covered later in this chapter).

- *UDDI (Universal Description, Discovery, and Integration)*: UDDI is an industry effort to enable businesses to quickly, easily, and dynamically find web services and interact with one another. UDDI is a distributed directory, or registry of businesses and web services. UDDI enables a business to describe itself and its services, discover other businesses offering desired services, and integrate with them. The UDDI community includes Microsoft, IBM, Sun Microsystems, Ariba, and many others, and is lead by a committee of these industry leaders.

Supply and Demand—Web Service Providers and Consumers

Web services work by exchanging data between two primary entities: the web service provider and the web service consumer. The web service provider is an application that exposes a piece of functionality, which other applications—web service consumers—will access. The provider application exposes the WSDL that the consumer must comply with to use the web service.

The consumer discovers the web service, either by finding it in the UDDI registry or some other means of discovery. Once the consumer understands the web service, via the WSDL document, a method can be invoked using any of the three acceptable protocols, HTTP GET, HTTP POST, or SOAP. When the web service method is invoked, the provider returns the data to the consumer in the form of an XML document, either as a web response, or embedded in a SOAP message. The data exchange can be protected either with SSL or by encrypting the XML payload.

In the following sections, you will build a few different web services and make use of the different protocols, varied data types, and security options. For simplicity purposes, you will not be doing very much database access, since what is really important here is that you understand how web services can be used to exchange any data, not just how to exchange data from a database. You will work with data, however: data from an XML file and objects serialized to XML. The concepts demonstrated here can easily be implemented with data from a database as well.

Building a Basic Web Service

Building a web service is not drastically different to building any public class and method. A web service takes a typical method and exposes it via Internet protocols. You can build a web service by adding a few lines of code to any public method in a public class, provided that if there is data returned it is an XSD-compliant data type.

The steps to build a web service are shown here, and you will explore each of them in this section:

1. Build a public class that inherits from System.Web.Services.WebService.

2. Create a public method.

3. Apply the WebMethod() attribute to the method.

4. Create a web service file using the .asmx extension (MyWebService.asmx).

5. Add the @ WebService attribute to the .asmx file and inherit from the class defined in Step 1.

The following code shows a basic class that exposes one method, the RandomNumber-Generator() method:

```
Imports System
Imports System.Web

Namespace VBProvider
  Public Class TrivialFunTools
    Public Function RandomNumberGenerator(ByVal LowNumber As Int32, _
      ByVal HighNumber As Int32) As Int32
      Dim RandNumber As New Random()
      Return RandNumber.Next(LowNumber, HighNumber)
    End Function
  End Class
End Namespace
```

The RandomNumberGenerator method uses the System.Random class to create a random number between the two values passed into the method. A new instance of the Random class is constructed and a value between the LowNumber and the HighNumber is returned. To convert the RandomNumberGenerator method to a web service requires only a few lines of code.

Create a new web service file in the VBProvider project named TrivialFunTools.asmx. Open the TrivialFunTools.asmx.vb code-behind file by clicking the Click Here to Switch to Code View link.

■**Note** Visual Studio .NET inserts additional code in the class file that the Integrated Design Environment (IDE) needs. In the code samples in for this chapter, we have excluded most of it as it is not pertinent to building a web service. We will note anywhere that it is important.

The Imports statement for the System.Web.Services namespace is automatically added by Visual Studio .NET so that you don't have to use fully qualified names when referencing a class in this namespace.

```
Imports System.Web.Services
```

The optional <WebService()> attribute can be used in the class declaration to add a description, namespace, etc. to the web service. This attribute is optional, but by using it you can provide greater value to your web service by including a brief description, a unique name-space, and more. The .NET Framework SDK documentation provides a full list of options for the WebService() attribute class. The .NET Framework will automatically generate an informa-tion and test page for the web service, and the information passed into the <WebService()> attribute will be used on this page.

```
<WebService(Description:="This is a collection of silly web services " & _
    "that demonstrate various web service capabilities.", _
    Namespace:="http://www.dotnetjunkies.com"))> _
Public Class TrivialFunTools
    Inherits System.Web.Services.WebService
```

The class itself inherits from the System.Web.Services.WebService class, so your class will have all of the same capabilities as the WebService class, plus whatever properties, methods or events you create.

```
<WebService(Description:="This is a collection of silly web services " & _
    "that demonstrate various web service capabilities.", _
    Namespace:="http://www.dotnetjunkies.com"))> _
Public Class TrivialFunTools
    Inherits System.Web.Services.WebService
```

The <WebMethod()> attribute is used preceding any public method that you want to expose as a web service method. Like the <WebService()> attribute, the <WebMethod()> attribute enables you to add a description of the web service method for display in the automatically generated information and test page. The <WebMethod()> attribute enables your public method as a web service method, giving it the ability to be invoked over the Internet using HTTP GET, HTTP POST, or SOAP.

Not all methods in a web service need to be web service methods—you can create meth-ods in the web service that will not be exposed via the Internet. Any method, public, private, or protected, will not be accessible via the Internet unless it has the <WebMethod()> attribute applied to it; only public methods may have the <WebMethod()> attribute.

Add the following method to the TrivialFunTools class:

```
<WebMethod(Description:="Generate a random number between " & _
    "two values.<br>This web service demonstrates how a " & _
    "basic web service works.")> _
    Public Function RandomNumberGenerator( _
  ByVal LowNumber As Int32, _
      ByVal HighNumber As Int32) As Int32
      Dim RandNumber As New Random()
      Return RandNumber.Next(LowNumber, HighNumber)
    End Function
```

Methods that you are exposing as web service methods (using the `<WebMethod()>` attribute) must be declared publicly and must be in a public class.

You can build the project by clicking the Build option in the Build menu. If you are building this project with a text editor, you can use the VBC.exe (Visual Basic .NET Compiler) command-line compiler with the following statement:

```
> vbc.exe /t:library TrivialFunTools.asmx.vb /r:System.dll,System.Web.dll
```

If you open the TrivialFunTools.asmx file in a text editor other than Visual Studio .NET (you cannot view this type of file in Visual Studio .NET, only the code-behind class file), you will see the following code:

```
<%@ WebService Language="vb" Codebehind="TrivialFunTools.asmx.vb"
  Class="VBProvider.TrivialFunTools" %>
```

The @ `WebService` directive identifies the class that implements the web service. When the TrivialFunTools.asmx page is browsed to, the .NET Framework will create the information and test page. To do this, right-click on the TrivialFunTools.asmx file in the Solution Explorer, and choose Set as Start Page. Now run the project.

The application will be compiled and a browser will open with the page as seen in Figure 11-2.

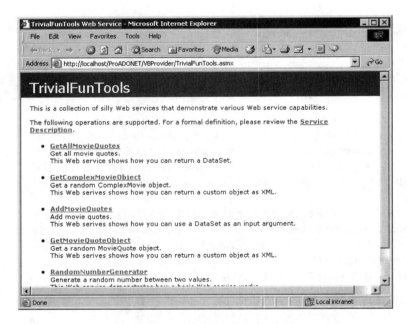

Figure 11-2. *TrivialFunTools.asmx as viewed through a web browser*

The information and test page provides a link to the Service Description (WSDL), and a link to test any web service methods in the web service. Clicking the link to the Service Description will show you the actual XML-based WSDL document, as shown in Figure 11-3.

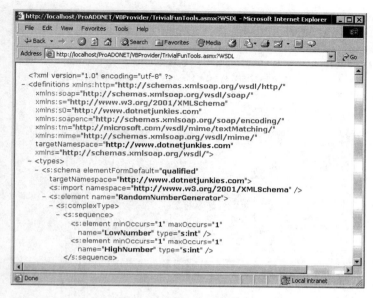

Figure 11-3. TrivialFunTools *web service WSDL*

Clicking the web service method link on the web service information page will bring you to a test interface for the web service method, as shown in Figure 11-4.

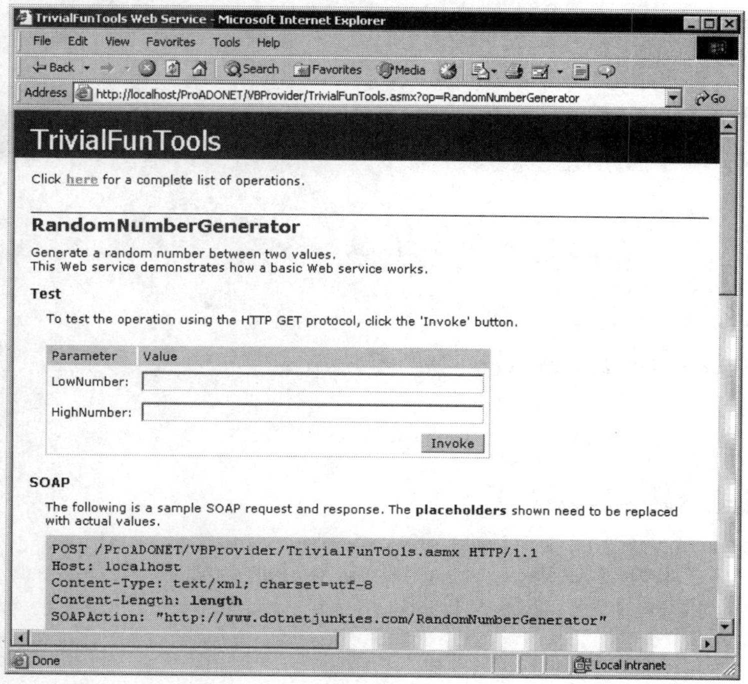

Figure 11-4. TrivialFunTools *web-based test interface to invoke individual methods*

The test interface provides a text box for each input argument and a button to invoke the web service method. Below the test interface is a list of the acceptable protocols for this web service method, and sample requests and responses for the web method.

To test this web service method, enter values into the text boxes and click Invoke. The web service method is invoked, and the return data is displayed in a new window, formatted as XML data, as shown in Figure 11-5.

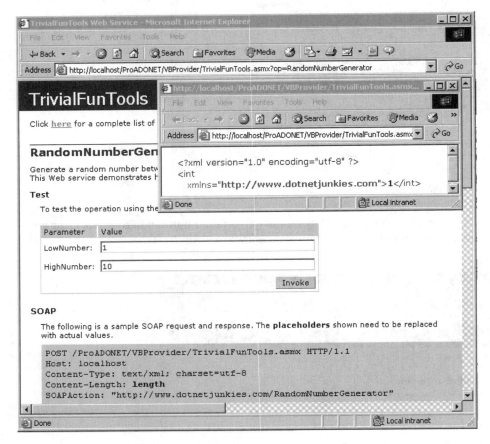

Figure 11-5. *TrivialFunTools.asmx web-based test interface return value*

Building a Basic Consumer

A consumer application can access the web service in, as we have mentioned, any of three protocols, HTTP GET, HTTP POST, or SOAP. Each protocol has advantages and disadvantages, some of which are listed in Table 11-1.

Table 11-1. *Various Web Service Protocol Access Comparisons*

Protocol	Advantages	Disadvantages
HTTP GET	Easy to implement	Any input values are passed in the query string. Cannot exchange complex data types.
HTTP POST	Easy to implement	Cannot exchange complex data types.
SOAP	Can exchange complex data types	Uses more bandwidth.

Web services enable the consumer application to have any type of user interface necessary, including a web or a desktop (Windows) application interface. The web service will be accessed in code, and the return data can then be formatted and displayed as is appropriate. You can build a consumer using a text editor, and if necessary, a command-line compiler, or a tool such as Visual Studio .NET.

Building an HTTP Consumer

You can build a consumer that accesses the web service using HTTP GET or HTTP POST by simply adding a <FORM> tag to an HTML web page, using GET or POST as the METHOD and the web service URL as the ACTION.

```
<FORM METHOD="GET" ACTION="http://webserver/webservice.asmx/WebMethod">
```

or

```
<FORM METHOD="POST" ACTION="http://webserver/webservice.asmx/WebMethod">
```

The FORM tag instructs the web server how to handle the form when a user submits it. The METHOD attribute indicates which protocol should be used, HTTP GET or HTTP POST. The ACTION attribute indicates where the web server should redirect the action. In the first example, the form will be redirected to the URL in the ACTION attribute as an HTTP GET, with any submitted values as query string parameters. The second example will redirect to the specific URL with any submitted values in the HTTP POST request header.

Add the following page to the VBConsumer project as an HTML page named HttpGet-Consumer.htm.

```
<!DOCTYPE HTML PUBLIC "-//W3C//DTD HTML 4.0 Transitional//EN" >
<HTML>
 <HEAD>
  <META NAME="GENERATOR" Content="Microsoft Visual Studio 7.0">
  <TITLE></TITLE>
 </HEAD>
 <BODY>
  <FORM METHOD="GET"
ACTION="http://localhost/ProADONET/VBProvider/TrivialFunTools.asmx/↵
RandomNumberGenerator" ID="Form1">
   <H3>
   Random Number Consumer
   </H3>
```

```
<P>
 To get a random number, enter your number range and click Go.
</P>
<B>Low Number:</B>
<BR>
<INPUT TYPE="text" NAME="LowNumber" ID="Text1">
<BR>
<B>High Number:</B>
<BR>
<INPUT TYPE="text" NAME="HighNumber" ID="Text2">
<BR>
<BR>
<INPUT TYPE="submit" VALUE="Go" ID="Submit1" NAME="Submit1">
 </FORM>
</BODY>
</HTML>
```

When the preceding HTML page is filled out and the Go button is clicked, the Web site visitor sees the raw XML returned from the web service. To test this, right-click in the IDE and choose View In Browser (see Figure 11-6).

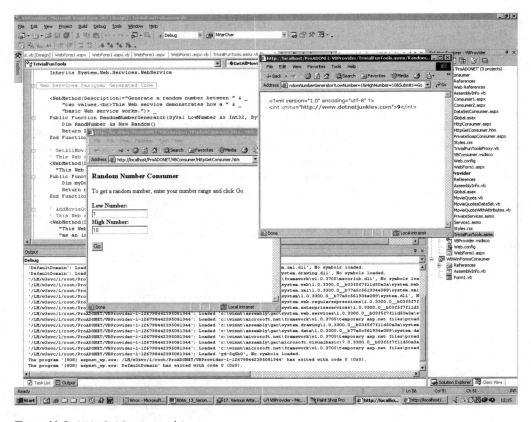

Figure 11-6. HttpGetConsumer.htm

In the preceding example, the browser is simply redirected to the web service, and the result of the web service method is shown in the browser as an XML document. What would be better (and what web services are intended for) is if you invoked the web service in code and captured the returned value to display to the visitor.

To invoke a web service method using HTTP GET and capture the return value, first build a web form that will be the consumer's interface to the web service. Create a new web form in the VBConsumer project named HttpConsumer.aspx, and model its layout after the screenshot in Figure 11-7.

Don't forget you can download this from the Downloads section of the Apress Web site at http://www.apress.com.

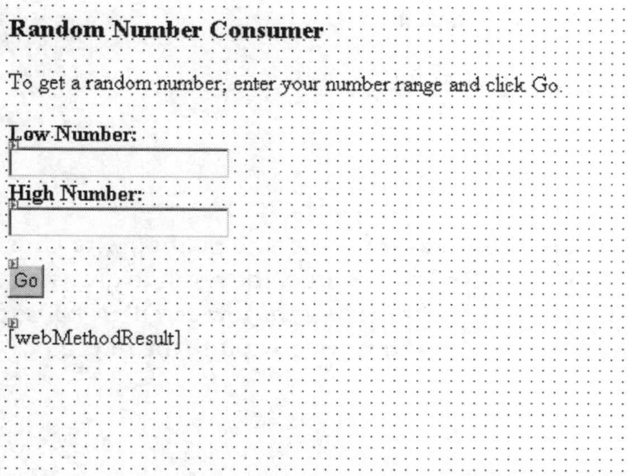

Figure 11-7. *HttpConsumer.aspx—design view*

Following is the code for the web form shown in Figure 11-7:

```
<%@ Page language="vb" Codebehind="HttpConsumer.aspx.vb"
  AutoEventWireup="false" Inherits="VBConsumer.HttpConsumer" %>
<!DOCTYPE HTML PUBLIC "-//W3C//DTD HTML 4.0 Transitional//EN" >
<HTML>
  <HEAD>
    <meta name="GENERATOR" Content="Microsoft Visual Studio.NET 7.0">
    <meta name="CODE_LANGUAGE" Content="Visual Basic 7.0">
    <meta name="vs_defaultClientScript" content="JavaScript">
    <meta name="vs_targetSchema"
      content="http://schemas.microsoft.com/intellisense/ie5">
  </HEAD>
  <body MS_POSITIONING="GridLayout">
    <form id="Form1" method="post" runat="server">
      <h3>
        Random Number Consumer
      </h3>
      <p>
```

```
        To get a random number, enter your number
        range and click Go.
    </p>
    <b>Low Number:</b>
    <br>
    <asp:TextBox Runat="server" ID="lowNumber" />
    <br>
    <b>High Number:</b>
    <br>
    <asp:TextBox Runat="server" ID="highNumber" />
    <br>
    <p>
      <asp:Button Runat="server" Text="Go" id="Button1" />
    </p>
    <asp:Label Runat="server" ID="webMethodResult" />
  </form>
 </body>
</HTML>
```

What you want to do is invoke the RandomNumberGenerator web service method when the
Go button is clicked—in the Button.Click event handler—and capture the result to display in
the webMethodResult Label control. This will enable the user to enter the low and high values,
and post the form. Behind the scenes, you will invoke the web service, capture the return
value, and display it for the user.

Capturing the Data in an XmlDocument

You can capture the returned XML with an XmlDocument object and pull the value out of the
appropriate child node of the object. The XmlDocument class represents an XML document in
code as an object. The XmlDocument class exposes several methods and properties for traversing
the XML node tree and extracting the inner and outer XML values, specifically the ChildNodes
property, which is a collection of XmlNode objects in the form of an XmlNodeList object. Using
the XmlDocument class will enable you to capture the data returned from the web service (which
is returned as an XML document), and render only the data in the consumer application rather
than the entire XML document.

Following is the Button1_Click() event handler for the previous web form. While in the
design view of the HttpConsumer.aspx web form, you can double-click the button control and
Visual Studio .NET will inject the framework for the Button1_Click() event handler into the
code-behind class, and display it in the IDE. Add the following code:

```
Private Sub Button1_Click(ByVal sender As System.Object, _
   ByVal e As System.EventArgs) Handles Button1.Click
        'Add the TextBox values into the HTTP GET query string
        Dim httpGetUrl As String = _
          "http://localhost/ProADONET/VBProvider/" & _
          "TrivialFunTools.asmx/RandomNumberGenerator?LowNumber=" & _
          lowNumber.Text.Trim() & _
```

```
            "&HighNumber=" & _
            highNumber.Text.Trim()

        'Use an XmlDocument to load the XML returned
        Dim xmlDoc As New System.Xml.XmlDocument()
        xmlDoc.Load(httpGetUrl)

        'Pull the value out of the second node
        '   1st Node: <?xml version="1.0" encoding="utf-8" ?>
        '   2nd Node: <int xmlns="http://www.dotnetjunkies.com">7</int>
        webMethodResult.Text = "<hr><b>Your number is: </b>" & _
            xmlDoc.ChildNodes.Item(1).InnerText()
    End Sub
```

After the web form has been built and the Button1_Click() event handler is in place, you
can run the project to test the code. First, set the VBConsumer project as the start-up project by
right-clicking on the VBConsumer item in the Solution Explorer, and selecting Set As StartUp
Project. Next, set the HttpConsumer.aspx web form as the start form, as you did previously,
and click the Start button (see Figure 11-8).

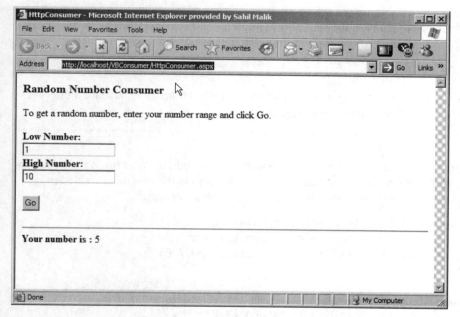

Figure 11-8. *HttpConsumer.aspx—running through a browser*

When the Go button is clicked, the Button1_Click() event handler is invoked. In the event
handler, you create a string that is the web service method URL with the input arguments as
query string values. Using the XmlDocument class, you create an object that is a representation

of the XML file returned by the RandomNumberGenerator web service method. The first node of the XML file is

```
<?xml version="1.0" encoding="utf-8" ?>
<int xmlns="http://www.dotnetjunkies.com">5</int>
```

In the second element, int refers to the XML data type of the element—an integer in this case—and xmlns refers to the XML namespace—defined in the <WebService()> attribute in the TrivialFunTools web service.

The return value of the web service method is the InnerText of the <int> tag (the text between the opening and closing <int> tags). Since the XmlDocument.ChildNodes property is a zero-based collection, the ordinal "1" references the second node (xmlDoc.Child-Nodes.Item(1).InnerText refers to the value returned by the web service method), the integer "5" in this example.

Building a SOAP Consumer in Visual Studio .NET

While you can consume a web service using HTTP GET and HTTP POST, either by setting the <FORM> action and method or by invoking the web service method in code and capturing the return value, you also can consume a web service using SOAP. One of the easiest ways to implement a SOAP consumer is by using a tool, such as Visual Studio .NET. Tools such as this may provide wizards or utilities, which abstract the process of building a SOAP consumer away from the developer, making it very easy to implement. The consumer can be any application that can access the Internet (or an intranet in the case of private web services).

■**Note** Later in this chapter, you will use some of the command-line utilities provided by the .NET Framework to create a consumer without using Visual Studio .NET.

Before writing the code for consuming the web service, build the user interface—you can copy the HTML between the opening and closing <FORM> tags in the web form created previously, HttpConsumer.aspx, to a new web form named Consumer1.aspx.

```
<%@ Page language="vb" Codebehind="Consumer1.aspx.vb"
  AutoEventWireup="false" Inherits="VBConsumer.Consumer1" %>
<!DOCTYPE HTML PUBLIC "-//W3C//DTD HTML 4.0 Transitional//EN" >
<HTML>
  <HEAD>
    <meta name="GENERATOR" Content="Microsoft Visual Studio.NET 7.0">
    <meta name="CODE_LANGUAGE" Content="Visual Basic 7.0">
    <meta name="vs_defaultClientScript" content="JavaScript">
    <meta name="vs_targetSchema"
      content="http://schemas.microsoft.com/intellisense/ie5">
```

```
</HEAD>
<body MS_POSITIONING="GridLayout">
  <form id="Form1" method="post" runat="server">
    <h3>
      Random Number Consumer
    </h3>
    <p>
      To get a random number, enter your number
      range and click Go.
    </p>
    <b>Low Number:</b>
    <br>
    <asp:TextBox Runat="server" ID="lowNumber" />
    <br>
    <b>High Number:</b>
    <br>
    <asp:TextBox Runat="server" ID="highNumber" />
    <br>
    <p>
      <asp:Button Runat="server" Text="Go" id="Button1" />
    </p>
    <asp:Label Runat="server" ID="webMethodResult" />
  </form>
</body>
</HTML>
```

With the web interface constructed, you can begin building the code-behind class that will connect to the web service and invoke the RandomNumberGenerator method. In the previous examples, we have assumed you knew exactly where the web service was located—you knew the URL to the TrivialFunTools.asmx page. For this example, you will use some discovery tools to find the web service.

Discovering Web Services

As a consumer, you would know the web service URL by either getting it directly from the provider company or discovering it in the UDDI registry (http://www.uddi.org or http://uddi.microsoft.com). In the UDDI registry, you can search for web services that are publicly available in many ways, including by business name, location, or classification (see Figure 11-9).

Additionally, if you know the location of the .disco or .vsdisco discovery files, you can discover available web services with either the Add Web Reference functionality in Visual Studio .NET or with a discovery tool, such as disco.exe.

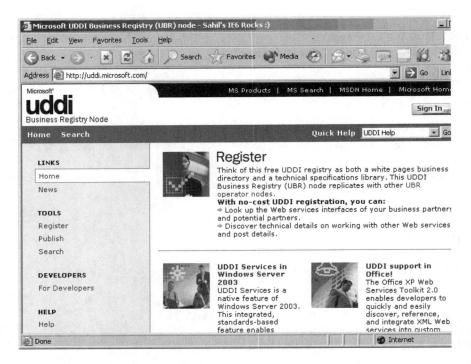

Figure 11-9. `http://uddi.microsoft.com`

Using disco.exe to Discover Web Services

If you know the URL for the discovery file (.disco, .vsdisco, or .discomap) or the WSDL file (.wsdl or .xsd), you can use the disco.exe utility to discover what web services are available.

The disco.exe utility allows the following optional arguments:

- `/nologo`: Suppress the banner (the text that displays in the command window before the results are displayed).

- `/nosave`: Does not save the discovered documents or results (.wsdl, .xsd, .disco, and .discomap files) to disk. The default is to save these documents.

- `/out` (shorthand is `/o:`): Specifies the output directory in which to save the discovered documents. The default is the current directory.

- `/username` (shorthand is `/u:`): Specifies the username to use when connecting to a proxy server that requires authentication.

- `/password` (shorthand is `/p:`): Specifies the password to use when connecting to a proxy server that requires authentication.

- `/domain` (shorthand is `/d:`): Specifies the domain name to use when connecting to a proxy server that requires authentication.

- /proxy: Specifies the URL of the proxy server to use for HTTP requests. The default is to use the system proxy setting.

- /proxyusername (shorthand is /pu:): Specifies the username to use when connecting to a proxy server that requires authentication.

- /proxypassword (shorthand is /pp:): Specifies the password to use when connecting to a proxy server that requires authentication.

- /proxydomain (shorthand is /pd:): Specifies the domain to use when connecting to a proxy server that requires authentication.

- /?: Displays command syntax and options for the tool.

In a command window, execute the following command:

```
disco.exe /nosave http://localhost/ProADONET/VBProvider/TrivialFunTools.asmx
```

The result should look similar to the screenshot in Figure 11-10.

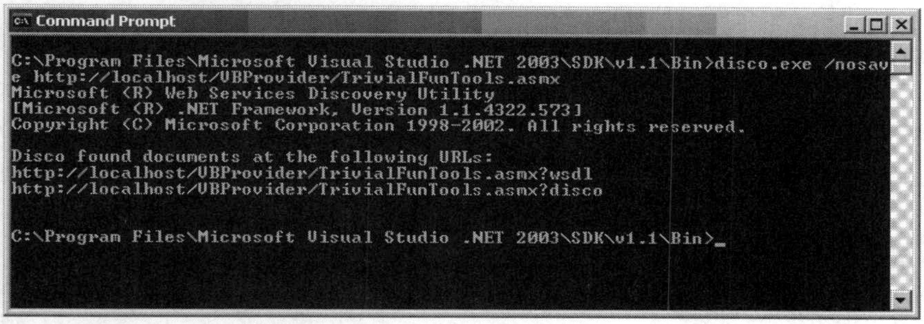

Figure 11-10. *disco.exe results for your web service*

When this command is executed, the disco.exe utility discovers the DISCO and WSDL documents related to the web service. Visual Studio .NET automatically generates a .vsdisco file for every web application or web service project. The .vsdisco file is a dynamic discovery file, which checks the root directory and all subdirectories of the web application for web services.

Adding a Web Reference in Visual Studio .NET

When you make a web reference in Visual Studio .NET, a lot more is done than just discovery of the web service. When you complete the steps to add a web reference, a proxy client class is automatically generated for you. The proxy client is created based on the WSDL provided by the web service. The proxy client exposes the web service interfaces to the consumer application as if the web service was a local class in the consumer application. The proxy client class will be used to invoke the methods of the web service.

■Note Proxy client classes are explored in detail later in this chapter.

To create a web reference in Visual Studio .NET, select Project ➤ Add Web Reference. Then, in the Add Web Reference dialog window (see Figure 11-11), you can enter either the web service URL or the discovery file URL into the Address text box, or click on one of the UDDI links to search the Microsoft UDDI registry.

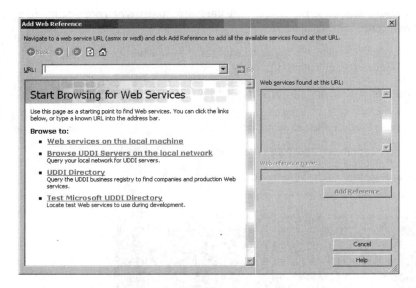

Figure 11-11. *Visual Studio 2003 Add Web Reference dialog*

If you type in the URL to the .disco file, you will see an XML document that lists all of the available web services from this web application (see Figure 11-12).

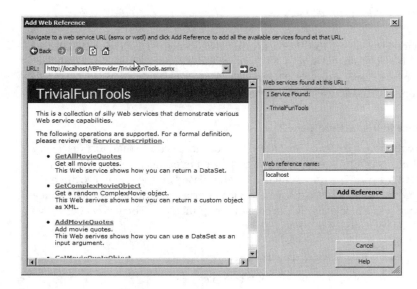

Figure 11-12. `TrivialFunTools` *web service*

Once you've decided on the web service that you want, you simply click the Add Reference button at the bottom of the window.

When a web reference is added, behind the scenes Visual Studio .NET uses the web service's WSDL to create a proxy client class, which includes the URL of the web service, and interfaces for invoking the web service methods, both synchronously and asynchronously. *Synchronous execution* is the typical "invoke and wait for a response" type of method execution. *Asynchronous execution* is similar to fire-and-forget; the method is invoked, but the caller does not wait for a response. The proxy client is automatically created with methods for both types of execution.

If you build the project (click on Build ➤ Build), you can view the project assembly in the Microsoft Intermediate Language Disassembler (ILDASM.exe). From the command line, type the following:

```
> ildasm.exe
```

When the utility launches, drag the project DLL `C:\Inetpub\wwwroot\ProADONET\VBConsumer\bin\VBConsumer.dll` into the ILDASM window (see Figure 11-13).

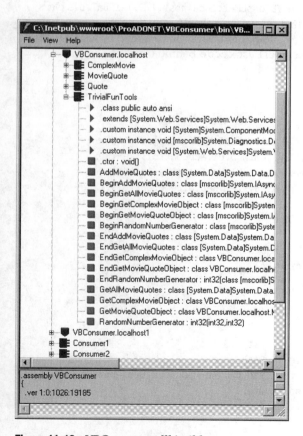

Figure 11-13. *VBConsumer.dll in ildasm.exe*

As you can see in the Figure 11-13, a new namespace was added to your project, the VBConsumer.localhost namespace, which has one class, TrivialFunTools. The class has public methods, for each of the web services that can be invoked. An object instance of the proxy client class can be constructed and the proxy methods can be invoked, causing the web service methods to be invoked.

■Note The namespace created for the proxy client class is based on the URL that was used to create the web reference. For example, creating a web reference to http://www.dotnetjunkies.com/services/TrivialFunTools.asmx creates a proxy client class with VBConsumer.com.dotnetjunkies.www as the namespace.

Building the Consumer Code-Behind Class

In the code-behind class, you instantiate the VBConsumer.localhost.TrivialFunTools class, and invoke the RandomNumberGenerator() method on a postback—any time the page is posted from a button click. Most of the code in the code-behind class will be added by Visual Studio .NET. Add the highlighted code to the Consumer1.aspx code-behind class.

```
Imports VBConsumer.localhost

Public Class Consumer1
    Inherits System.Web.UI.Page
    Protected WithEvents lowNumber As System.Web.UI.WebControls.TextBox
    Protected WithEvents highNumber As System.Web.UI.WebControls.TextBox
    Protected WithEvents Button1 As System.Web.UI.WebControls.Button
    Protected WithEvents webMethodResult As System.Web.UI.WebControls.Label

#Region " Web Form Designer Generated Code "

    'This call is required by the Web Form Designer.
    <System.Diagnostics.DebuggerStepThrough()> _
    Private Sub InitializeComponent()

    End Sub

    Private Sub Page_Init(ByVal sender As System.Object, _
    ByVal e As System.EventArgs) Handles MyBase.Init
        'CODEGEN: This method call is required by the Web Form Designer
        'Do not modify it using the code editor.
        InitializeComponent()
    End Sub
```

```
#End Region

    Private Sub Page_Load(ByVal sender As System.Object, _
    ByVal e As System.EventArgs) Handles MyBase.Load
        If Page.IsPostBack Then
            'Create two integer objects to hold
            'the low and high values
            Dim low As Int32 = Int32.Parse(lowNumber.Text.Trim())
            Dim high As Int32 = Int32.Parse(highNumber.Text.Trim())

            'Create an instance of the
            'TrivialFunTools proxy client class
            Dim tft As New TrivialFunTools()

            'Invoke the web service method and catch
            'the return value
            Dim result As Int32 = tft.RandomNumberGenerator(low, high)
            'Set the return value to the Label.Text property
            webMethodResult.Text = _
             "<hr><b>Your number is: </b>" & _
             result.ToString()
        End If
    End Sub

End Class
```

In the Consumer1.aspx code-behind class, you add an `Imports` statement to include the proxy client's namespace, `VBConsumer.localhost`, so that you do not have to use fully qualified class names. Visual Studio .NET added variable instances that map to the server controls on the web form that you need programmatic access to—the `lowNumber` and `highNumber` text boxes, and the `webMethodResult` label.

In the `Page_Load` event handler, you evaluate for a page postback. If the current request is the result of a page postback (the Go button was clicked), you invoke the web service method. This is done by creating an instance of the `VBConsumer.localhost.TrivialFunTools` class and invoking the `RandomNumberGenerator` method.

When the `RandomNumberGenerator` proxy client method is invoked, a SOAP message is created, and it is sent to the web service URL that was used when creating the web reference. The method in the web service executes on the provider server, and the return data is sent back to the consumer as a SOAP message, where the proxy client returns the data to the calling component as if the method executed locally (see Figure 11-14).

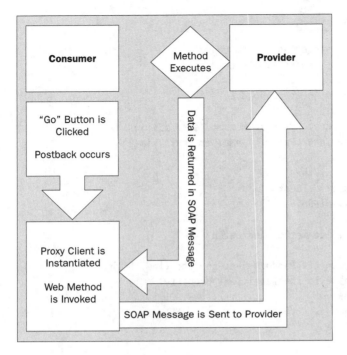

Figure 11-14. *Message flow in your projects*

The SOAP message structure that is sent to the provider is shown here.

```xml
<?xml version="1.0" encoding="utf-8"?>
<soap:Envelope xmlns:xsi="http://www.w3.org/2001/XMLSchema-instance"
 xmlns:xsd="http://www.w3.org/2001/XMLSchema"
 xmlns:soap="http://schemas.xmlsoap.org/soap/envelope/">
  <soap:Body>
   <RandomNumberGenerator xmlns="http://www.dotnetjunkies.com">
    <LowNumber>1</LowNumber>
    <HighNumber>10</HighNumber>
   </RandomNumberGenerator>
  </soap:Body>
</soap:Envelope>
```

The web service receives the SOAP message and extracts the `<LowNumber>` and `<HighNumber>` values from the SOAP message body. The `RandomNumberGenerator` method in the web service is invoked, using the `<LowNumber>` and `<HighNumber>` values, and a random number is returned in a SOAP message to the consumer.

```xml
<?xml version="1.0" encoding="utf-8"?>
<soap:Envelope xmlns:xsi="http://www.w3.org/2001/XMLSchema-instance"
 xmlns:xsd="http://www.w3.org/2001/XMLSchema"
```

```
xmlns:soap="http://schemas.xmlsoap.org/soap/envelope/">
 <soap:Body>
  <RandomNumberGeneratorResponse xmlns="http://www.dotnetjunkies.com">
   <RandomNumberGeneratorResult>5</RandomNumberGeneratorResult>
  </RandomNumberGeneratorResponse>
 </soap:Body>
</soap:Envelope>
```

The SOAP message is received and de-serialized into a .NET object—an integer in this example. The object then has all the functionality provided by its class definition.

■**Note** All error handling for the web service execution is the responsibility of the consumer application. The provider has clearly defined, in the WSDL, what is expected and returned by this web service—the interfaces. Since this has been clearly defined by the provider, it is expected that the consumer will abide by it. Any incorrect values entered, for instance, will cause the web service to return an exception that must be handled by the consumer.

When the web form interface is invoked, you see the web form in Figure 11-15.

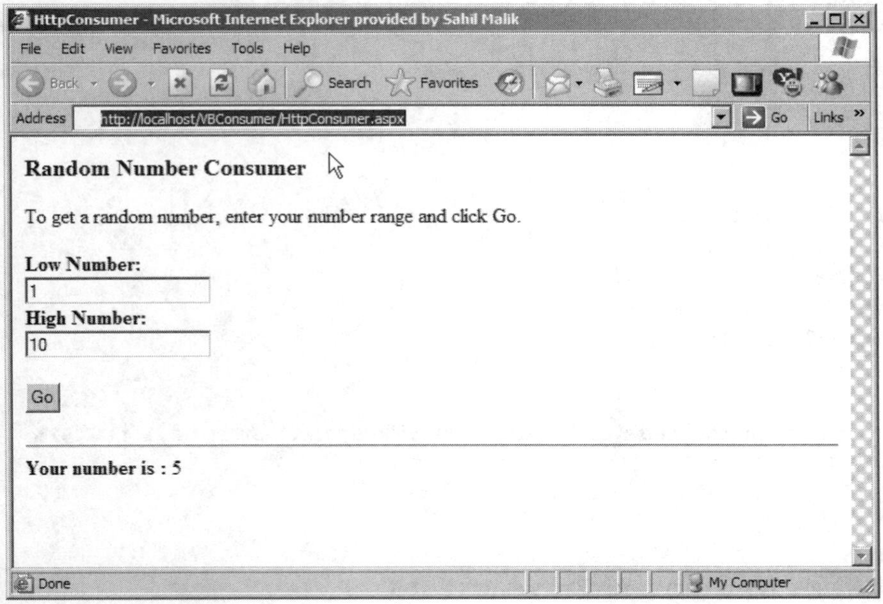

Figure 11-15. *HttpConsumer.aspx*

What Is a Proxy Client?

In the previous example, you used Visual Studio .NET to create a web service proxy client class by adding a web reference to your project. A proxy client class can also be created using a command-line utility that ships with the .NET Framework—the wsdl.exe utility. Before you investigate the WSDL.exe utility, let's look at what a proxy client class is.

A proxy client is a local object that simulates the functionality of a remote object. For instance, in the previous example, a proxy client class is created for you by Visual Studio .NET. This proxy client class is a local representation of the remote class. The proxy client class contains all of the method declarations that the remote class has, but the proxy does not include the functionality. Instead, the proxy client is a surrogate class for you to use when implementing the remote object.

Let's take a look at the proxy client class that was created by Visual Studio .NET when you made a web reference. This class file can be found at C:\Inetpub\wwwroot\ProADONET\ VBConsumer\Web References\localhost\Reference.vb.

```
'-----------------------------------------------------------------------
' <autogenerated>
'     This code was generated by a tool.
'     Runtime Version: 1.1.4322.573
'
'     Changes to this file may cause incorrect behavior and will be lost if⤶
'     the code is regenerated.
' </autogenerated>
'-----------------------------------------------------------------------

Option Strict Off
Option Explicit On

Imports System
Imports System.ComponentModel
Imports System.Diagnostics
Imports System.Web.Services
Imports System.Web.Services.Protocols
Imports System.Xml.Serialization

'
'This source code was auto-generated by Microsoft.VSDesigner, Version 1.1.4322.573.
'
Namespace localhost

    '<remarks/>
    <System.Diagnostics.DebuggerStepThroughAttribute(), _
     System.ComponentModel.DesignerCategoryAttribute("code"), _
     System.Web.Services.WebServiceBindingAttribute(Name:="TrivialFunToolsSoap", _
    [Namespace]:="http://www.dotnetjunkies.com")> _
    Public Class TrivialFunTools
        Inherits System.Web.Services.Protocols.SoapHttpClientProtocol
```

The proxy class includes a specification of what URL was used when creating the proxy. This is the URL that will be used each time a web service method is invoked. In this example the URL property specifies http://localhost as the domain where this web service is. That is because making a web reference to a web service on the local machine created the proxy client. The URL property will have whatever URL was used to create the proxy class.

For example, http://www.dotnetjunkies.com/services/TrivialFunTools.asmx:

```
'<remarks/>
Public Sub New()
    MyBase.New
    Me.Url = _
"http://localhost/ProADONET/VBProvider/TrivialFunTools.asmx"
    End Sub
```

Note If you create a proxy client using the WSDL for a web service on a development server whose URL will change on a production server, you can create a proxy client that gets the URL from a configuration file <appSetting>. See "The wsdl.exe Utility" later in this chapter for information on creating proxy client classes.

The RandomNumberGenerator method is included, using the SoapDocumentMethodAttribute attribute. This attribute specifies how the SOAP message should be formatted.

```
'<remarks/>
 <System.Web.Services.Protocols.SoapDocumentMethodAttribute( _
 "http://www.dotnetjunkies.com/RandomNumberGenerator", _
 RequestNamespace:="http://www.dotnetjunkies.com", _
 ResponseNamespace:="http://www.dotnetjunkies.com", _
 Use:=System.Web.Services.Description.SoapBindingUse.Literal, _
 ParameterStyle:= _
 System.Web.Services.Protocols.SoapParameterStyle.Wrapped)> _
    Public Function RandomNumberGenerator(ByVal LowNumber As Integer, _
ByVal HighNumber As Integer) As Integer
        Dim results() As Object = _
 Me.Invoke("RandomNumberGenerator", _
    New Object() {LowNumber, HighNumber})
        Return CType(results(0),Integer)
    End Function
```

Also included in the proxy client class are methods for invoking the web service method asynchronously. These methods are added by the proxy generator (wsdl.exe or Visual Studio .NET) to enable asynchronous calls to the web service.

```
'<remarks/>
 Public Function BeginRandomNumberGenerator( _
ByVal LowNumber As Integer, _
```

```
        ByVal HighNumber As Integer, _
        ByVal callback As System.AsyncCallback, _
        ByVal asyncState As Object) As System.IAsyncResult
              Return Me.BeginInvoke("RandomNumberGenerator", _
          New Object() {LowNumber, HighNumber}, _
          callback, asyncState)
             End Function


           '<remarks/>
           Public Function EndRandomNumberGenerator( _
        ByVal asyncResult As System.IAsyncResult) As Integer
              Dim results() As Object = Me.EndInvoke(asyncResult)
              Return CType(results(0),Integer)
             End Function
        End Class
End Namespace
```

While the proxy client class provides an interface for invoking the web service methods, the code for the web service method's functionality remains on the provider server. The proxy client class enables the constructing of an object in your code that represents the remote object.

The wsdl.exe Utility

You can use the wsdl.exe utility that is shipped with the .NET Framework to create a proxy client class without Visual Studio .NET. You may want to do this in situations where you will be reading the web service URL from the configuration file, or if you are not using Visual Studio .NET to build your application. The wsdl.exe utility includes a number of optional arguments that can be used to customize the proxy client class when it is generated. As you go through the rest of this chapter, you will discover and use many of the optional arguments. For an entire list of wsdl.exe arguments, open a command window and execute the following command:

`wsdl.exe /?`

To create a proxy client class for the TrivialFunTools web service using the wsdl.exe utility, open a command window, and execute the following command:

`wsdl.exe http://localhost/ProADONET/VBProvider/TrivialFunTools.asmx?WSDL`

The previous command indicates that a proxy client class should be created using the WSDL document at the specified URL. By default, proxy classes generated by the wsdl.exe utility *are in C#*. You can use the /l: argument to specify the language you would like the proxy client to be created with—possible values are CS (C#), VB (Visual Basic .NET), JS (JScript .NET), or you can also specify the fully qualified name of a class that implements the System.Code-Dom.Compiler.CodeDomProvider class (see the .NET Framework SDK documentation for more information on the CodeDomProvider class).

Executing the previous command creates a file named TrivialFunTools.vb; the file is named after the web service class name. You can create a file using any name you specify by adding the /out: argument to the wsdl.exe command.

```
wsdl.exe http://localhost/ProADONET/VBProvider/TrivialFunTools.asmx?WSDL↵
/out:TrivialFunToolsProxy.vb /l:vb
```

The proxy client class, by default, is generated without a specified .NET namespace. You can create the class in a specified namespace by adding the /n: argument (shorthand for /namespace:).

```
wsdl.exe http://localhost/ProADONET/VBProvider/TrivialFunTools.asmx?WSDL↵
/out:TrivialFunToolsProxy.vb /l:vb /n:VBConsumer.Proxies
```

The resulting proxy client class is nearly identical to the proxy client class created previously by Visual Studio .NET. The only difference is the namespace (VBConsumer.localhost vs. VBConsumer.Proxies).

This proxy class can be compiled into your application assembly by including the assembly in your Visual Studio .NET project and rebuilding it.

1. Copy the TrivialFunTools.vb file into the VBConsumer directory.

2. Click the Show All Files button in the Solution Explorer.

3. Right-click on the TrivialFunTools.vb file and choose Include In Project.

4. Build the project.

The web service methods of the new namespace can be invoked in the same way as the previous example.

Following is the code for the Page_Load event handler of the Consumer1.aspx web form's code-behind class using the proxy you just built:

```
Private Sub Page_Load(ByVal sender As System.Object, _
        ByVal e As System.EventArgs) Handles MyBase.Load
    If Page.IsPostBack Then
        'Create two integer objects to hold
        'the low and high values
        Dim low As Int32 = Int32.Parse(lowNumber.Text.Trim())
        Dim high As Int32 = Int32.Parse(highNumber.Text.Trim())

        'Create an instance of the
        'TrivialFunTools proxy client class
        Dim tft As New VBConsumer.Proxies.TrivialFunTools()

        'Invoke the web service method and catch
        'the return value
        Dim result As Int32 = tft.RandomNumberGenerator(low, high)
        'Set the return value to the Label.Text property
        webMethodResult.Text = _
          "<hr><b>Your number is: </b>" & _
          result.ToString()
    End If
End Sub
```

There is no functional difference between the proxy client class you created with Visual Studio .NET using a web reference and the proxy client class you created using the wsdl.exe utility.

Storing a Web Service URL in a Configuration File

The wsdl.exe utility enables creating a proxy client class that will check the application configuration file for the URL. This is useful when you will have different URLs for the web service while your consumer application is in development vs. in production. When creating the proxy client class, you can provide the /appsettingurlkey: argument, which identifies the key name of an <appSettings> key-value pair in the configuration file.

```
wsdl.exe http://localhost/ProADONET/VBProvider/TrivialFunTools.asmx?WSDL ⏎
/out:TrivialFunToolsProxy.vb /l:vb /n:VBConsumer.Proxies ⏎
 /appsettingurlkey:TrivialFunToolsUrl
```

The preceding command will create a proxy client class, like you created in the previous example; however, the constructor for the class will have an evaluator to check the <appSettings> section of the configuration file for the specified key-value pair. If a pair is found with the specified key name, the value will be used as the URL to connect to when invoking the web service; if no pair is found with the specified key name, the URL that was used when creating the proxy client will be used.

```
Public Sub New()
            MyBase.New
            Dim urlSetting As String = _
        System.Configuration.ConfigurationSettings.AppSettings( _
        "TrivialFunToolsUrl")
            If (Not (urlSetting) Is Nothing) Then
                Me.Url = urlSetting
            Else
                Me.Url = _
        "http://localhost/ProADONET/VBProvider/TrivialFunTools.asmx"
            End If
        End Sub
```

The format for including an <appSetting> key-value pair is shown here.

```
<?xml version="1.0" encoding="utf-8" ?>
<configuration>
 <appSettings>
  <add key="TrivialFunToolsURL"
   value="http://www.dotnetjunkies.com/services/TrivialFunTools.asmx"
  />
 </appSettings>
</configuration>
```

Using an <appSetting> key-value pair for the web service URL enables you to use one URL while in development, and another while in production, without having to recompile the proxy client class.

Exchanging Data in Web Services

In the previous example, you built and consumed a web service that took two integer objects as input arguments, and returned a third integer object. Web services are capable of working with several data types, both simple types—like string and integer—and complex types—like DataSets and serialized custom classes. A web service can have the following data types as input arguments, or returned results (see Table 11-2).

Table 11-2. *XML Schema Definition and CLR Data Type Mapping*

XML Schema Definition	CLR Data Type
boolean	Boolean
byte	SByte
double	Double
datetime	DateTime
decimal	Decimal
enumeration	Enum
float	Single
int	Int32
long	Int64
Qname	XmlQualifiedName
short	Int16
string	String
timeInstant	DateTime
unsignedByte	Byte
unsignedInt	UInt32
unsignedLong	UInt64
unsignedShort	UInt16

■**Note** The protocol being used to invoke a web service is directly related to the data types that the web service is using. HTTP GET and HTTP POST both use key-value string pairs, which limit the data types that can be passed into a web service to simple data types, such as strings. If complex data types, such as DataSets or custom classes, are being passed into the web service, SOAP must be used, as the objects can be serialized to XML and transmitted in the body of a SOAP message.

Working with DataSets

The DataSet is a terrific container for exchanging data in web services. Using DataSets, you can exchange tremendous amounts of data in a structured, relational data format. .NET consumers can work with the DataSet in its ADO.NET format, while non-.NET consumers can use the DataSet in its XML format, or de-serialize it to a proprietary format.

■**Note** A .NET 1.1 Framework dataset sent over the Internet (serialized even using BinaryFormatter) will still be XML serialized, which can place tremendous demands on bandwidth. There are, however, ways around this. Look for *datasetsurrogate* in Microsoft Knowledgebase, or you can write your own formatter as explained in the Apress book *Advanced .NET Remoting* (Rammer 2002).

Building a Pre-populated DataSet-Derived Class

To demonstrate how to make a web service that returns a DataSet, you'll add a new web service method to the TrivialFunTools web service. This web service method, GetAllMovie-Quotes(), will return a DataSet that is an instance of a custom class, MovieQuotesDataSet. The custom class derives from the DataSet class, but it is populated from an XML file in the constructor. You are creating this custom class because other web service methods you will be creating are going to be using the same data (see Figure 11-16).

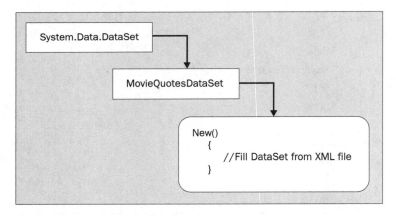

Figure 11-16. *The* MovieQuotesDataSet

First you create the MovieQuotesDataSet class. This class derives from the DataSet class and uses the FileStream and StreamReader classes in its constructor to populate the DataSet from an XML file (MovieQuotes.xml).

Create a new class file in the VBProvider project, named MovieQuotesDataSet.vb, and add the highlighted code as follows:

```
Imports System.IO

Public Class MovieQuotesDataSet
    Inherits System.Data.DataSet

    Public Sub New()
        'Open a FileStream to stream in the XML file
        Dim fs As New FileStream( _
```

```
      HttpContext.Current.Server.MapPath( _
      "MovieQuotes.xml"), _
      FileMode.Open, FileAccess.Read)
    Dim xmlStream As New StreamReader(fs)
    'Use the ReadXml() method to create a
    'DataTable that represents the XML data
    MyBase.ReadXml(xmlStream)

  End Sub

End Class
```

In the preceding code you create a custom class, MovieQuotesDataSet, which derives from the System.Data.DataSet class. In the constructor for the custom class, you create a new System.IO.FileStream object, passing in the path to the MovieQuotes.xml file, and the enumeration arguments to open and grant read access to the file. Using a System.IO.StreamReader you create an object to read the characters from the FileStream. The DataSet.ReadXml method uses the StreamReader object to read the XML data into the DataSet, creating a new DataTable to hold the data. As a result, anytime you create an instance of the MovieQuotesDataSet, the object is automatically populated with the data from the MovieQuotes.xml file.

The MovieQuotes.xml file is formatted as follows:

```
<?xml version="1.0" ?>
<MovieQuotes>
  <MovieQuote>
    <Quote>Honestly, this isn't really a brains kind of operation.</Quote>
    <Movie>The Way of the Gun</Movie>
    <ActorOrCharacter>Benicio del Toro</ActorOrCharacter>
  </MovieQuote>

  <MovieQuote>
    <Quote>I've got to return some video tapes.</Quote>
    <Movie>American Psycho</Movie>
    <ActorOrCharacter>Patrick Bateman (Christian Bale)</ActorOrCharacter>
  </MovieQuote>
<MovieQuotes>
```

■**Note** The entire MovieQuotes.xml file can be downloaded from the Downloads section of the Apress Web site (http://www.apress.com).

Building the Web Service Method

The GetAllMovies web service method creates and returns an instance of the MovieQuotesDataSet. This is a simple method, since all you need to do is create a new instance of the class, which is populated when it is constructed, and return it to the consumer.

Add this web service method to the TrivialFunTools.asmx.vb file (the code-behind file for the TrivialFunTools web service).

```
' GetAllMovieQuotes-Get all movie quotes.
' This Web serives shows how you can return a DataSet.
<WebMethod(Description:="Get all movie quotes.<br>" & _
    "This web service shows how you can return a DataSet.")> _
Public Function GetAllMovieQuotes() As DataSet
    Dim myDataSet As New MovieQuotesDataSet()
    Return myDataSet
End Function
```

In the GetAllMovieQuotes web service method, you simply create an instance of the MovieQuotesDataSet class and return it to the consumer. You can test this web service method using the automatically generated test page that is created when you run the project. First, set the VBProvider project as the start-up project and the TrivialFunTools.asmx file as the Start Page; then click the Start button.

In the web service information page, click the GetAllMovieQuotes link, and click the Invoke button (as seen in Figure 11-17):

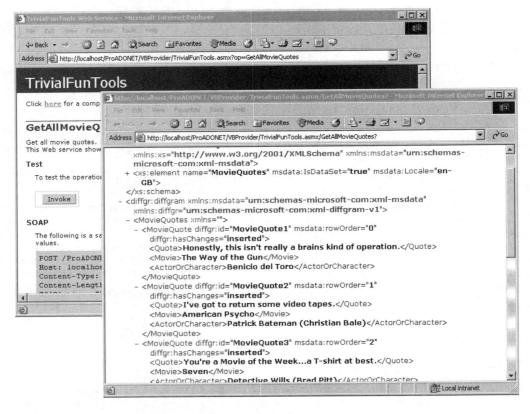

Figure 11-17. *Testing the* GetAllMovieQuotes *method*

Building a Windows Form Consumer with Visual Studio .NET

A Windows Forms application can consume a web service just as an ASP.NET application can—provided the application will always have access to the web service URL. As far as the web service is concerned, there is no difference between an ASP.NET consumer and a Windows Forms consumer. Both consumers invoke the web service method by making a call using one of the three protocols, so the platform, architecture, and language used are irrelevant. As long as the consumer can use one of the protocols, and understand the data returned to it, the web service can be used—Windows, Linux, Solaris, Macintosh, and so on.

To build the Windows Form consumer, follow these steps:

1. In the `VBWinFormsConsumer` project, add a web reference to the `TrivialFunTools` WSDL file.

2. By default, Visual Studio .NET creates a Windows Form named `Form1`. In the Properties Explorer, change the File Name value to GetAllMovieQuotesConsumer.vb.

3. Change the `Text` property of the form to Get All Movie Quotes.

4. Add `GroupBox`, `DataGrid`, and `Button` controls to the Windows Form.

5. Change the `Text` property of the `Button` control to &Get Movie Quotes.

6. Change the `Text` property of the `GroupBox` to Movie Quotes.

The Windows Form should look like the form shown in Figure 11-18.

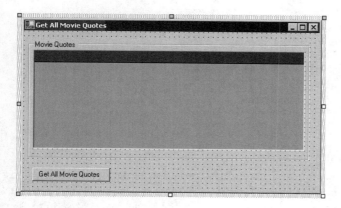

Figure 11-18. *GetAllMovieQuotesConsumer.vb designer view*

7. Double-click the `Button` in the Windows Form designer view. This will open up the code view where you can add the following code:

```
Private Sub Button1_Click(ByVal sender As System.Object, _
ByVal e As System.EventArgs) Handles Button1.Click
    Dim tft As New VBWinFormsConsumer.localhost.TrivialFunTools()
    Dim ds As DataSet = tft.GetAllMovieQuotes()
    DataGrid1.DataSource = ds.Tables(0)
End Sub
```

In this code, you create an instance of the proxy client class for the web service and invoke the GetAllMovieQuotes() method. The returned data is instantiated as an instance of the System.Data.DataSet class (since our MovieQuotesDataSet class is really just a pre-populated DataSet). The dataGrid1.DataSource is set to the first (and only) DataTable in the DataSet.

Running the Windows Form Project

Build the project and run it by setting the VBWinFormsConsumer project as the start-up project and by clicking the Start button.

When you run the application, the Windows Form will launch. When you click the Get Movie Quotes button on the Windows Form, the button1_Click event handler will fire. When the TrivialFunTools object is created and the GetAllMovieQuotes() method is invoked, a SOAP message is created and sent to the provider, the GetAllMovieQuotes() web service method is invoked, and a DataSet is returned to the consumer in a SOAP message. The first DataTable in the DataSet is set as the dataGrid1.DataSource property, and the movie quotes are displayed in the DataGrid, as seen in Figure 11-19.

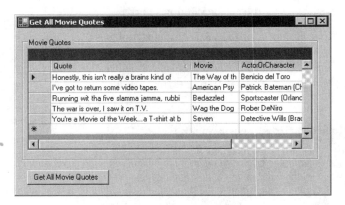

Figure 11-19. VBWinFormsConsumer *in action*

DataSets as Input Arguments

DataSets can also be used as input arguments for a web service method, much as you used integers as input arguments in the RandomNumberGenerator web service method previously. In the following example, you create a new web service method, AddMovieQuotes, in the Trivial-FunTools web service, which takes a DataSet as an input argument, merges it with the existing MovieQuotesDataSet object, and returns the merged DataSet.

In the TrivialFunTools code-behind class, add the following web service method:

```
' AddMovieQuotes-Adds a DataSet of MovieQuotes to the existing DataSet.
' This Web serives shows how you can use a DataSet as an input argument.
<WebMethod(Description:="Add movie quotes.<br>" & _
    "This Web serives shows how you can use a DataSet " & _
    "as an input argument.")> _
Public Function AddMovieQuotes(ByVal MovieQuotes As DataSet) As DataSet
    Dim myDataSet As New MovieQuotesDataSet()
```

```
    myDataSet.Merge(MovieQuotes, False, MissingSchemaAction.Add)
    Return myDataSet
End Function
```

When you declare the method, the input argument is defined with its data type. In the preceding sample code, you define a DataSet (MovieQuotes) as an input argument, and use the DataSet.Merge() method to merge the input DataSet into the existing DataSet (Movie-QuotesDataSet).

Note For more information on the DataSet and the Merge method, see Chapter 3.

Web service methods that accept complex data types, such as DataSets and bytes, as input arguments cannot be invoked in the same way as web service methods that use simple data types, like strings and integers. Web service methods that require complex data types as input arguments cannot be invoked using HTTP GET or HTTP POST, since the complex data types cannot be passed in the query string (HTTP GET) or in the request body (HTTP POST). SOAP is the only protocol that can be used when invoking a web service method that requires complex data type input arguments. As a result, the information and test page generated by the .NET Framework does not include test mechanisms for HTTP GET and HTTP POST (see Figure 11-20).

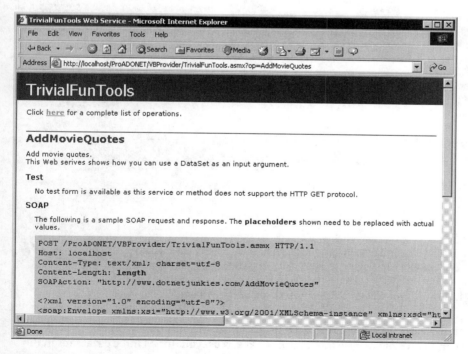

Figure 11-20. TrivialFunTools.AddMovieQuotes

Building a Web Form Consumer

Now you've seen web forms consuming web services returning simple data, and Windows Forms retrieving `DataSets` from web services, let's complete the roundup by creating a web form that manipulates a `DataSet` returned by a web service.

For this example, you will build an ASP.NET Web Form consumer. The web form, named DataSetConsumer.aspx, will invoke the `GetAllMovieQuotes` web method to populate a Data-Grid server control and load another XML file (MovieQuotes2.xml) to populate a `DataSet` and another `DataGrid`. When the `AddMovieQuotes` web service method is invoked, the `DataSet` created from MovieQuotes2.xml will be passed as the input argument, and the merged `DataSet` will be used to populate a third `DataGrid`.

Before creating the web form, right-click on Local Host, under the web references directory in the Solution Explorer. Choose Update Web Reference. This will rebuild the proxy client class with the newly added web service methods.

The web form for this example should look like what you see in Figure 11-21.

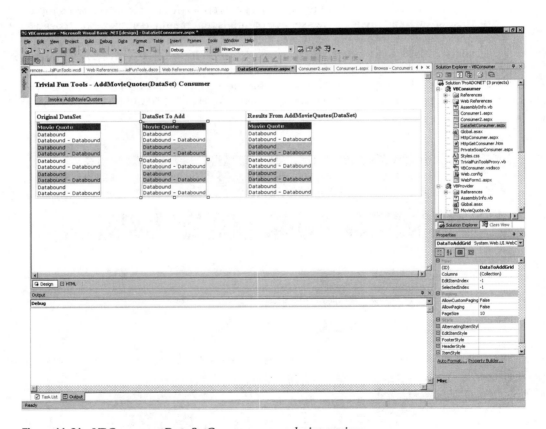

Figure 11-21. *VBConsumer.DataSetConsumer.aspx designer view*

The `DataGrids` all use a `TemplateColumn` to customize the output. All three `DataGrids` should have the same layout. Use the following `DataGrid` layout for all three `DataGrids` in the web form:

```
<asp:DataGrid id="OriginalDataGrid" runat="server" AutoGenerateColumns="False"
  Font-Names="Verdana, Arial, sans-serif" Font-Size="x-small"
  HeaderStyle-BackColor="Maroon" HeaderStyle-ForeColor="White"
  HeaderStyle-Font-Bold="True" AlternatingItemStyle-BackColor="Tan">
  <Columns>
    <asp:TemplateColumn HeaderText="Movie Quote">
      <ItemTemplate>
        <%# DataBinder.Eval(Container.DataItem, "Quote") %>
        <br>
        <%# DataBinder.Eval(Container.DataItem, "ActorOrCharacter") %>
        -
        <%# DataBinder.Eval(Container.DataItem, "Movie") %>
      </ItemTemplate>
    </asp:TemplateColumn>
  </Columns>
</asp:DataGrid>
```

In the code-behind file for the web form, you will populate the first DataGrid by invoking the GetAllMovieQuotes web service method, and populate the second DataGrid by loading a new DataSet with data from the MovieQuotes2.xml file. Let's build a GetData() method to encapsulate this functionality.

Open the code-behind class in Visual Studio .NET and add an Imports statement for the System.IO namespace, and declare a class-level DataSet object to work with.

```
Imports System.IO

Public Class DataSetConsumer
    Inherits System.Web.UI.Page
    Protected WithEvents OriginalDataGrid As _
    System.Web.UI.WebControls.DataGrid
    Protected WithEvents DataToAddGrid As System.Web.UI.WebControls.DataGrid
    Protected WithEvents ResultGrid As System.Web.UI.WebControls.DataGrid
    Protected WithEvents Button1 As System.Web.UI.WebControls.Button
    Private WithEvents myDataSet As DataSet
```

Now build the GetData method. In the method, construct a new instance of myDataSet, and populate it with the MovieQuotes2.xml file. Then construct an instance of the Trivial-FunTools proxy client class and set the OriginalDataGrid.DataSource property to the DataSet returned by the GetAllMovies web service method.

```
#Region " Web Form Designer Generated Code "

    'This call is required by the Web Form Designer.
    <System.Diagnostics.DebuggerStepThrough()> _
    Private Sub InitializeComponent()

    End Sub
```

```
    Private Sub Page_Init(ByVal sender As System.Object, _
    ByVal e As System.EventArgs) Handles MyBase.Init
        'CODEGEN: This method call is required by the Web Form Designer
        'Do not modify it using the code editor.
        InitializeComponent()
    End Sub

#End Region
    Private Sub GetData()
        myDataSet = New DataSet()

        'Open a FileStream to stream in the XML file
        Dim fs As New FileStream( _
        HttpContext.Current.Server.MapPath( _
        "MovieQuotes2.xml"), _
        FileMode.Open, FileAccess.Read)

        Dim xmlStream As New StreamReader(fs)
        'Use the ReadXml() method to create a
        'DataTable that represents the XML data
        myDataSet.ReadXml(xmlStream)
        xmlStream.Close()

        Dim tft As New localhost.TrivialFunTools()

        OriginalDataGrid.DataSource = tft.GetAllMovieQuotes()
        DataToAddGrid.DataSource = myDataSet
    End Sub
```

In the Page_Load() event handler, invoke the GetData() method, then use the Page.Data-Bind() method to databind all of the server controls in the Page.Controls collection only on the first request (not on a postback).

```
    Private Sub Page_Load(ByVal sender As System.Object, _
    ByVal e As System.EventArgs) Handles MyBase.Load
        If Not Page.IsPostBack Then
            GetData()
            Page.DataBind()
        End If
    End Sub
```

At this point, when the page is first requested, the Page_Load() event handler will be invoked and the first two DataGrids will be populated (as seen in Figure 11-22).

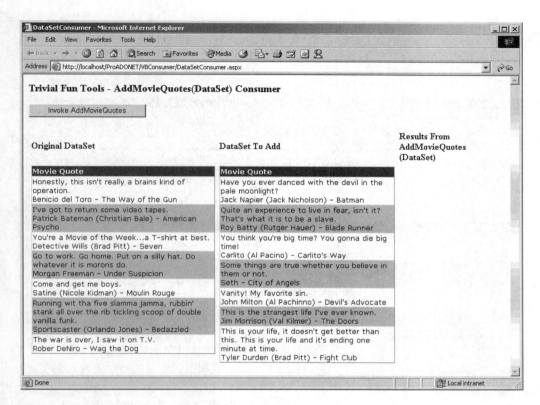

Figure 11-22. *VBConsumer.DataSetConsumer.aspx in action*

In the Button1_Click event handler, you want to invoke the AddMovieQuotes() web service method. Since the page is reloaded when the postback occurs, you first call GetData to create the myDataSet object, then declare a new DataSet, myMergedDataSet, and instantiate it by invoking the AddMovieQuotes() web service method with myDataSet as the input argument.

```
Private Sub Button1_Click(ByVal sender As System.Object, _
ByVal e As System.EventArgs) Handles Button1.Click
    'Populate myDataSet
    GetData()
    'Create the TrivialFunTools object
    Dim tft As New localhost.TrivialFunTools()
    'Invoke the AddMovieQuotes() method, passing in myDataSet
    'Put the returned DataSet into the myMergedDataSet object
    Dim myMergedDataSet As DataSet = tft.AddMovieQuotes(myDataSet)
    'Set the DataSource of the third DataGrid
    ResultGrid.DataSource = myMergedDataSet
    'Bind all of the controls
    Page.DataBind()
End Sub
```

When the button is clicked, and the `Button1_Click` event handler is invoked, the `AddMovieQuotes()` web service method is invoked, and a merged `DataSet` is returned and bound to the third `DataGrid` (as seen in Figure 11-23).

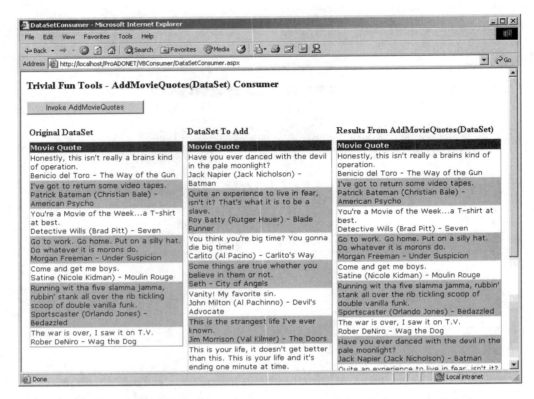

Figure 11-23. *VBConsumer.DataSetConsumer.aspx in action after the button is clicked*

Using XML with Web Services

As we previously discussed, web services use XML as their transmission format. In the previous web service examples, `RandomNumberGenerator` and `GetAllMovieQuotes`, you saw how the return values of the web service methods were serialized as XML before being returned to the consumer. The .NET Framework also enables serializing custom classes that can be returned from a web service method. You can create a custom class in the web service and set the return type of a web service method as that custom class as follows:

```
<WebMethod()> _
Public Function MyMethod() As MyClass
  Dim obj As New MyClass()
  Return obj
End Function
```

Working with Custom Classes as XML

You can create a custom class that your web service can use. The proxy client that you create, either with a web reference in Visual Studio .NET or using the wsdl.exe utility, can have proxy classes for your custom class as well as for the web service class. This enables consumers to create an instance of the custom class in their application and use it as if it were a resident class.

The provider application can define a class. By including this class as either a return data type or an input data type, this class' interfaces will be included in the web service proxy class that is created by the consumer. This enables the consumer to instantiate this class and use the object as if it were resident, when in fact it is a remote object (see Figure 11-24).

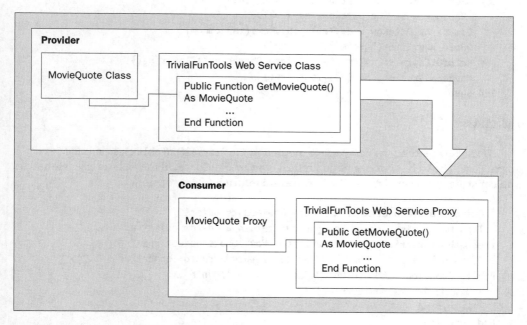

Figure 11-24. VBProvider *and* VBConsumer *interaction*

Exposing a Custom Class with a Web Service

To demonstrate this, let's start by building a custom MovieQuote class in the VBProvider project. This class will be used to represent a random <MovieQuote> element from the MovieQuotes.xml file—it will expose Quote, ActorOrCharacter, and Movie properties.

Create a new class file in the VBProvider project, named MovieQuote.vb, as follows:

```
Public Class MovieQuote

    Public Quote As String
    Public ActorOrCharacter As String
```

```
Public Movie As String

Public Sub New()
    Dim ds As New MovieQuotesDataSet()
    'Create a random number to select one of the quotes
    Dim randNumber As New Random()
    'The random number should be between 0 and
    'the number of rows in the table
    Dim randomRow As Int32 = _
        randNumber.Next(0, ds.Tables(0).Rows.Count)
    'Set the MovieQuote properties using the
    'RandomRow as the DataRow index value
    Dim dr As DataRow = ds.Tables(0).Rows(randomRow)
    Quote = dr.Item("Quote").ToString()
    ActorOrCharacter = dr.Item("ActorOrCharacter").ToString()
    Movie = dr.Item("Movie").ToString()
End Sub

End Class
```

Next, you create a new web service method in the TrivialFunTools class, named Get-MovieQuote. The web service method's return type is MovieQuote. In the web service method, you construct a new instance of MovieQuote and return it to the consumer.

```
' GetMovieQuoteObject-Get a random MovieQuote object.
' This Web serives shows how you can return a custom object as XML.
<WebMethod(Description:="Get a random MovieQuote object.<br>" & _
    "This Web serives shows how you can return a custom object as XML.")> _
Public Function GetMovieQuoteObject() As MovieQuote
    Dim mq As New MovieQuote()
    Return mq
End Function
```

Make VBProvider the start-up project and TrivialFunTools.asmx the Start Page. Click the Start button to run the applications and test the web service method from the test page (see Figure 11-25).

When the web service method is invoked, the custom object is automatically serialized as XML. Each of the properties becomes an element in the XML node tree. At the consumer application you can construct an instance of the MovieQuote custom class, using the proxy client, and have full access to its properties.

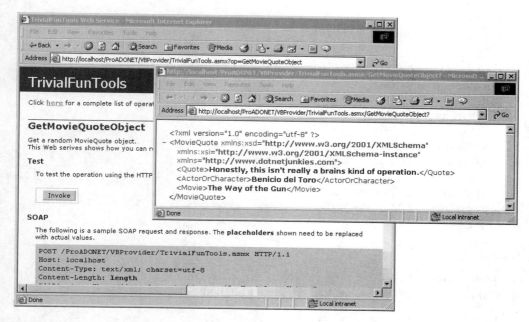

Figure 11-25. `TrivialFunTools.GetMovieQuoteObject`

Consuming a Custom Class from a Web Service

In the `VBConsumer` project, you can consume the `TrivialFunTools` web service, and use a proxy `MovieQuote` object in your application.

You start by updating the web reference again. Right-click on it in the Solution Explorer and choose Update Web Reference. Next, you create the consumer web form, Consumer2.aspx, in the `VBConsumer` project.

```vb
<%@ Page Language="vb" AutoEventWireup="false"
  Codebehind="Consumer2.aspx.vb" Inherits="VBConsumer.Consumer2"%>
<!DOCTYPE HTML PUBLIC "-//W3C//DTD HTML 4.0 Transitional//EN">
<HTML>
  <HEAD>
    <title>Consumer2</title>
    <meta name="GENERATOR"
      content="Microsoft Visual Studio.NET 7.0">
    <meta name="CODE_LANGUAGE" content="Visual Basic 7.0">
    <meta name="vs_defaultClientScript" content="JavaScript">
    <meta name="vs_targetSchema"
      content="http://schemas.microsoft.com/intellisense/ie5">
  </HEAD>
```

```
<body MS_POSITIONING="GridLayout">
  <form id="Form1" method="post" runat="server">
    <h3>
      TrivialFunTools - GetMovieQuoteObject() Consumer
    </h3>
    <b>Movie:</b>
    <asp:Label id="Movie" runat="server" />
    <br>
    <b>Quote:</b>
    <asp:Label id="Quote" runat="server" />
    <br>
    <b>Actor or Character:</b>
    <asp:Label id="ActorOrCharacter" runat="server" />
  </form>
</body>
</HTML>
```

In the code-behind class for the web form, you can instantiate the MovieQuote custom class and invoke the GetMovieObject() web service method.

```
Private Sub Page_Load(ByVal sender As System.Object, _
ByVal e As System.EventArgs) Handles MyBase.Load
    Dim tft As New localhost.TrivialFunTools()
    Dim myMovieQuote As New localhost.MovieQuote()
    myMovieQuote = tft.GetMovieQuoteObject()
    Movie.Text = myMovieQuote.Movie
    Quote.Text = myMovieQuote.Quote
    ActorOrCharacter.Text = myMovieQuote.ActorOrCharacter
End Sub
```

The resulting consumer web form is shown in Figure 11-26.

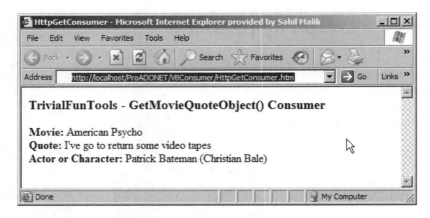

Figure 11-26. VBConsumer/HttpGetConsumer.htm

Working with XML Attributes

The System.Xml.Serialization namespace includes a collection of classes that can be used to control how an object is serialized or de-serialized. Controlling how an object is serialized or de-serialized can be very beneficial particularly in B2B applications, where a specific XML schema is required. For instance, you may build an application that exchanges customer information with a vendor, and for business reasons it is required to have the ID value as an attribute of the root element and the address as a child element, with the address detail as child elements of the address element.

```
<?xml version="1.0" encoding="utf-8" ?>
<Customer
  xmlns:xsi="http://www.w3.org/2001/XMLSchema-instance"
  xmlns:xsd="http://www.w3.org/2001/XMLSchema"
  ID="DNJCOM"   xmlns=http://www.dotnetjunkies.com>
  <Address>
    <Street>123 Main</Street>
    <City>Seattle</City>
    <State>WA</State>
  </Address>
</Customer>
```

The first of the "attribute" classes that you will look at is the XmlAttribute class. This attribute specifies that the class member that it is applied to should be serialized as an XML attribute.

■**Note** To use the attribute classes that you are going to be working with in the following examples, you must add a using statement to the classes to eliminate the need to use fully qualified class names: Imports System.Xml.Serialization.

You can create another custom class, MovieQuoteWithAttributes, in the VBProvider project, which represents one random movie quote, with the Quote, ActorOrCharacter, and Movie values as XML attributes of the <MovieQuote> element.

Create a new class file named MovieQuoteWithAttributes.cs and add the following highlighted code:

```
Imports System.Xml.Serialization

Public Class MovieQuoteWithAttributes
    <XmlAttribute ()> Public Quote As String
    <XmlAttribute()> Public ActorOrCharacter As String
    <XmlAttribute()> Public Movie As String

    Public Sub New()
        Dim mq As New MovieQuote()
        Quote = mq.Quote
```

```
        ActorOrCharacter = mq.ActorOrCharacter
        Movie = mq.Movie
    End Sub

End Class
```

If you build a web service method to return this custom object, the XML document that is generated looks like the following:

```xml
<?xml version="1.0" encoding="utf-8" ?>
<MovieQuoteWithAttributes
  xmlns:xsi="http://www.w3.org/2001/XMLSchema-instance"
  xmlns:xsd="http://www.w3.org/2001/XMLSchema"
  Quote="Come and get me boys."
  ActorOrCharacter="Satine (Nicole Kidman)"
  Movie="Moulin Rouge"
  xmlns="http://www.dotnetjunkies.com" />
```

The properties of the object are still exposed as properties in the proxy client class. The only thing you have done here is change how the XML representation of this object appears.

Working with XML Elements and Attributes

Another of the XML attribute classes is the XmlTextAttribute. This attribute specifies that the class member that it is applied to should be serialized as XML text.

```vb
' Movie
' An object that has elements and attributes.
Public Class Movie
    <XmlTextAttribute()> Public Title As String
    <XmlAttribute()> Public Quote As String
    <XmlAttribute()> Public ActorOrCharacter As String

    Public Sub New()
        Dim mq As New MovieQuote()
        Quote = mq.Quote
        ActorOrCharacter = mq.ActorOrCharacter
        Title = mq.Movie
    End Sub
End Class
```

The Title property has the XmlTextAttribute class applied to it, specifying that this property should be serialized as the XML text value of the <Movie> element, while the Quote and ActorOrCharacter properties are to be serialized as attributes of the <Movie> element.

```xml
<?xml version="1.0" encoding="utf-8" ?>
<Movie xmlns:xsi="http://www.w3.org/2001/XMLSchema-instance"
  xmlns:xsd="http://www.w3.org/2001/XMLSchema"
```

```
Quote="You're a Movie of the Week...a T-shirt at best."
ActorOrCharacter="Detective Wills (Brad Pitt)"
xmlns="http://www.dotnetjunkies.com">Seven</Movie>
```

Working with Multiple Custom Classes as XML

You can also build a custom class that has another custom class as one of its properties. Both classes can have XML attribute classes applied to them to specify how they should be serialized. In the following code, you create a custom Quote class that has a property, MovieQuote, with the XmlTextAttribute class applied to it, and a property, ActorOrCharacter, with the XmlAttribute class applied to it:

```
' Quote
' Only the quote element of a Movie object.
Public Class Quote
    <XmlTextAttribute()> Public MovieQuote As String
    <XmlAttribute()> Public ActorOrCharacter As String
End Class
```

By itself, this class would be serialized like this:

```
<?xml version="1.0" encoding="utf-8" ?>
<Quote ActorOrCharacter="Robert DeNiro">The war is over, I saw it on T.V.</Quote>
```

Of course, you want to know what great movie this fabulous quote came from, so you create another class, to act as a parent class, which will have a property whose type is Quote. For this, you build another custom class, Movie. The Movie class has a MovieQuote property and a Movie property.

```
' ComplexMovie
' An object with an attribute, and an element that also has an attribute.
Public Class ComplexMovie
    <XmlElementAttribute(ElementName:="Quote")> _
    Public MovieQuote As Quote
    <XmlAttribute()> _
    Public Movie As String
    Public Sub New()
        Dim mq As New MovieQuote()
        Dim q As New Quote()
        q.MovieQuote = mq.Quote
        q.ActorOrCharacter = mq.ActorOrCharacter
        MovieQuote = q
        Movie = mq.Movie
    End Sub
End Class
```

The MovieQuote property has the XmlElementAttribute class applied to it, specifying that this property should be serialized as an XML element—a child element of the `<ComplexMovie>`

element. You use the `ElementName` property to specify that in the XML document this element should be named `<Quote>` even though the property's name is `MovieQuote`. Effectively, you are overriding the property name and applying a name that is more appropriate for what you are doing.

The XML document created by this class is shown in the following code:

```
<?xml version="1.0" encoding="utf-8" ?>
<ComplexMovie xmlns:xsi="http://www.w3.org/2001/XMLSchema-instance"
  xmlns:xsd="http://www.w3.org/2001/XMLSchema"
  Movie="Wag the Dog" xmlns="http://www.dotnetjunkies.com">
  <Quote ActorOrCharacter="Robert DeNiro">The war is over, I saw it on
    T.V.</Quote>
</ComplexMovie>
```

Through the use of the attribute classes in the `System.Xml.Serialization` namespace, you can completely customize the XML output generated by a web service. This enables, for example, two businesses to agree on a standard format for data exchange, such as customer information or a product order, and automate a business process using web services. Changing the XML serialization does not affect the use of a proxy client at all. The properties exposed by a class are still exposed in the proxy class; the only thing that has changed is the XML format of the object while it is in transit between the provider and the consumer.

Web Service Security

In many cases you may want to create a web service that you want to expose for your business partners to consume, but you don't want everyone to have access to it. In much the same way that you may secure a web application so that only a predefined set of users are granted access to some or all of the resources, you can secure web services using a couple of different security schemas.

The two most likely candidates for securing a web service are Windows Authentication and SOAP-based Authentication.

- *Windows Authentication* uses Windows account credentials to grant access to resources. You can secure your application, or a part of your application, to allow only users with valid accounts on your Windows domain access to the resources. This, of course, requires that every user you want to grant access to be given a user account on your domain. This type of authentication is mainly intended for intranets and extranets, where the users are likely to have accounts in your network.

- With *SOAP-based Authentication*, you can secure your web services at a very granular level: securing each web service method individually. Additionally, you can enable access based on usernames, passwords, customer ID number, or any combination of any data you want. The required authentication data is sent in the SOAP message header when the web service method is invoked. The credentials can be validated at the method level allowing anonymous access to some methods, such as those you are allowing anyone access to, and restricting access to others.

Using Windows Authentication

ASP.NET applications can implement Windows Authentication to prevent unauthenticated users from accessing resources. In an application that implements Windows Authentication, the user's Windows login credentials are evaluated to determine if the user should be granted access to the resource. The same type of authentication can be implemented in a web service.

To implement Windows Authentication in an ASP.NET application, set the <authentication> configuration setting in the root web.config file.

```
<authentication mode="Windows">
```

You can then restrict access to your web service in one of two ways:

1. Use a <location> element in the root web.config file that includes a <deny> element. This is useful when you only want to restrict access to a single resource. This will restrict access to only the specified file.

```
<location path="Private/SuperPrivateServices.asmx">
  <system.web>
    <authorization>
      <deny users="?" />
    </authorization>
  </system.web>
</location>
```

2. Put the web service file in a sub-directory with a web.config file that includes a <deny> element. This is useful when you have multiple resources you are restricting access to. This will restrict access to all .NET managed files in the sub-directory.

```
<?xml version="1.0" encoding="utf-8" ?>
<configuration>
  <system.web>
    <authorization>
      <deny users="?" />
    </authorization>
  </system.web>
</configuration>
```

The <deny> element specifies what type of users or roles to deny access to. Setting the users attributes to ? indicates that all unauthenticated users should be denied access.

Adding Credentials to a Consumer

In order for a consumer application to be granted access to a web service that is restricted using Windows Authentication, the consumer application must supply the appropriate Windows credentials. Normally, as a user accessing a restricted resource, you would be prompted with a login window, where you could supply your username, password, and possibly the domain name that your Windows account belongs to. Since you want the consumer application to access the resource without any user intervention, you can supply appropriate credentials to the proxy client when you attempt to invoke the web service method.

The proxy client class that you create to access the web service derives from the SoapHttpClientProtocol. This class exposes a Credentials property (inherited from the Web-ClientProtocol class) that takes an instance of a class that implements the ICredentials interface, such as NetworkCredential or CredentialCache.

The NetworkCredential class is used to provide credentials for password-based authentication schemes such as basic, digest, NTLM, and Kerberos authentication, while CredentialCache provides a storage mechanism for multiple credentials.

You can use the NetworkCredential class to supply Windows credentials to your proxy object before invoking the web service method.

```
Dim sps As New VBConsumer.SuperPrivate.SuperPrivateServices()
sps.Credentials =
  New System.Net.NetworkCredential("myUserName", "myPassword")
Dim Result As String = sps.GetMySuperSecret()
```

In the preceding code, an instance of the SuperPrivateServices proxy class is constructed, and the Credentials property is set to an instance of the NetworkCredential class. In the constructor for the NetworkCredential class, you pass in the username and password for your Windows account.

Note The NetworkCredential class has an overloaded constructor that takes a domain name as a third argument, if it is necessary in your application: sps.Credentials = New System.Net.Network-Credential("myUserName", "myPassword", "myDomain").

When the web service method is invoked, the credentials are passed to the provider in the SOAP message. If the credentials are valid, the web service method is invoked and the appropriate data is returned; if the credentials are invalid, a System.Net.WebException is raised:

- System.Net.WebException: The request failed with HTTP status 401: Access Denied.

You can add error-handling code in the consumer to catch and handle this error—the key here is that this error is up to the consumer to handle. If the consumer does not provide valid credentials, then the consumer is never granted access to the web service. The provider never has the option of handling the exception—the exception happens in the consumer application (in the proxy client object) and the provider has no knowledge of it.

Using SOAP-based Authentication

Another means of securing a web service is by implementing restrictions via custom headers in a SOAP message. You can use a class attribute, SoapHeaderAttribute, to specify a SOAP message header that you are expecting in the incoming request to invoke the web service method. For example, you can create a web service method that requires a SOAP header containing a username and password. You can use the data passed in the SOAP header to authenticate the request.

This type of authentication opens up a broad range of authentication possibilities, including authenticating users from a database or XML document.

To implement this type of authentication, you create a custom class that derives from the System.Web.Services.Protocols.SoapHeader class. This class represents the data that will be passed in the SOAP header—the username and password. The values passed in the SOAP header are clear text. The values can be encrypted before being put in the SOAP headers, and decrypted when pulled out. Encryption is out of the scope of this chapter, but we will demonstrate how the authentication works.

■**Tip** You can read a little more about encryption in Chapter 13.

Building a Private Web Service

Create a new web service file in the VBProvider project, named PrivateServices.asmx. Add the following highlighted code to the web service code-behind class:

```
Imports System.Web.Services
Imports System.Web.Services.Protocols

<WebService(Description:="This is a web service that demonstrates " & _
  "SOAP Authentication.", _
  Namespace:="http://www.dotnetjunkies.com")> _
Public Class PrivateServices
    Inherits System.Web.Services.WebService

#Region " web services Designer Generated Code "

    Public Sub New()
        MyBase.New()

        'This call is required by the web services Designer.
        InitializeComponent()

        'Add your own initialization code after the InitializeComponent() call

    End Sub

    'Required by the web services Designer
    Private components As System.ComponentModel.IContainer
    'NOTE: The following procedure is required by the web services Designer
    'It can be modified using the web services Designer.
    'Do not modify it using the code editor.
    <System.Diagnostics.DebuggerStepThrough()> Private Sub InitializeComponent()
        components = New System.ComponentModel.Container()
    End Sub
```

```
    Protected Overloads Overrides Sub Dispose(ByVal disposing As Boolean)
        'CODEGEN: This procedure is required by the web services Designer
        'Do not modify it using the code editor.
        If disposing Then
            If Not (components Is Nothing) Then
                components.Dispose()
            End If
        End If
        MyBase.Dispose(disposing)
    End Sub

#End Region

    'Create a property of the web service that is
    'the SOAP Header class
    Public Header As mySoapHeader

    <WebMethod(Description:="Get a secret that no " & _
        "one else can get."), _
        SoapHeader("Header")> _
    Public Function GetMySecret() As String
        If Header.ValidUser() Then
            Return "This is my secret."
        Else
            Return "The username or password was incorrect."
        End If
    End Function

End Class

Public Class mySoapHeader
    Inherits SoapHeader

    Public Username As String
    Public Password As String

    Public Function ValidUser() As Boolean
        If Username = "WillyWonka" AndAlso Password = "GoldenTicket" Then
            Return True
        Else
            Return False
        End If
    End Function

End Class
```

In the preceding code you create two things, a web service method, GetMySecret(), and a class that derives from the SoapHeader class, mySoapHeader.

In the mySoapHeader class you declare two properties, Username and Password. Additionally, you create a method for validating the user. While in the example you validate the user against a hard-coded username-password pair, you could add logic in the ValidUser() method to validate the credentials against a data store.

In the web service, you declare a property, Header, whose data type is that of the derived SoapHeader class you just created.

In the web service method declaration you apply the SoapHeaderAttribute, providing the name of the web service member that represents the SOAP header contents (the Header property). The SoapHeaderAttribute class has three properties you can set to specify how the SOAP header should be used.

- *Direction*: Gets or sets whether the SOAP header is intended for the web service, the web service client, or both. SoapHeaderDirection.In is the default—InOut and Out are the other possible enumerations.

- *MemberName*: Gets or sets the member of the web service class representing the SOAP header contents. There is no default value.

- *Required*: Gets or sets a value indicating whether the SOAP header must be understood and processed by the recipient web service or web service client. The default value is true.

In the web service method, you can evaluate the SOAP header contents—in this example you can invoke the mySoapHeader.ValidUser method to see if the credentials are valid—if they are, you execute the code and return the appropriate data to the consumer. If the credentials are invalid, you can return a message, a null value, or exit the method without returning a value.

■Note By applying the SoapHeaderAttribute to the web service method, you eliminate support for HTTP GET or HTTP POST protocols—SOAP is the only allowed protocol for accessing web service methods that use the SoapHeaderAttribute.

Building the Consumer

The consumer application is responsible for adding the username and password credentials to the SOAP header before invoking the web service method. Since the mySoapHeader class is part of the web service, the proxy client has a mySoapHeader class.

Build the VBProvider project. You need to add a new web reference for the PrivateServices WSDL file.

Create a new web form in the VBConsumer project, named PrivateSoapConsumer.aspx. Add the following highlighted code in the web form:

```
<%@ Page Language="vb" AutoEventWireup="false"
  Codebehind="PrivateSoapConsumer.aspx.vb"
  Inherits="VBConsumer.PrivateSoapConsumer"%>
```

```
<!DOCTYPE HTML PUBLIC "-//W3C//DTD HTML 4.0 Transitional//EN">
<HTML>
  <HEAD>
    <title>PrivateSoapConsumer</title>
    <meta name="GENERATOR"
      content="Microsoft Visual Studio.NET 7.0">
    <meta name="CODE_LANGUAGE" content="Visual Basic 7.0">
    <meta name="vs_defaultClientScript" content="JavaScript">
    <meta name="vs_targetSchema"
      content="http://schemas.microsoft.com/intellisense/ie5">
  </HEAD>
  <body MS_POSITIONING="GridLayout">
    <form id="Form1" method="post" runat="server">
      <h3>
        PrivateServices - GetMySecret() SOAP Authentication
      </h3>
      <P>
        User Name:
        <BR>
        <asp:TextBox id="Username" runat="server" />
      </P>
      <P>
        Password:
        <BR>
        <asp:TextBox id="Password" runat="server" />
      </P>
      <P>
        <asp:Button id="Button1" runat="server"
          Text="Get Secret!" />
      </P>
      <P>
        <asp:Label id="Result" runat="server" />
      </P>
    </form>
  </body>
</HTML>
```

With the web form in design view, double-click on the Button control to add a Button1_Click event handler. In the code-behind class, add the following highlighted code:

```
Public Class PrivateSoapConsumer
    Inherits System.Web.UI.Page
    Protected WithEvents Username As System.Web.UI.WebControls.TextBox
    Protected WithEvents Password As System.Web.UI.WebControls.TextBox
    Protected WithEvents Button1 As System.Web.UI.WebControls.Button
    Protected WithEvents Result As System.Web.UI.WebControls.Label
```

```
#Region " Web Form Designer Generated Code "

    'This call is required by the Web Form Designer.
    <System.Diagnostics.DebuggerStepThrough()> _
    Private Sub InitializeComponent()
    End Sub

    Private Sub Page_Init(ByVal sender As System.Object, _
    ByVal e As System.EventArgs) Handles MyBase.Init
        'CODEGEN: This method call is required by the Web Form Designer
        'Do not modify it using the code editor.
        InitializeComponent()
    End Sub

#End Region

    Private Sub Page_Load(ByVal sender As System.Object, _
    ByVal e As System.EventArgs) Handles MyBase.Load
        'Put user code to initialize the page here
    End Sub

    Private Sub Button1_Click(ByVal sender As System.Object, _
    ByVal e As System.EventArgs) Handles Button1.Click
        Dim header As New localhost1.mySoapHeader()
        header.Username = Username.Text.Trim()
        header.Password = Password.Text.Trim()
        Dim ps As New localhost1.PrivateServices()
        ps.mySoapHeaderValue = header

        Result.Text = ps.GetMySecret()
    End Sub
End Class
```

The mySoapHeader class exposes two public properties: Username and Password. These properties are accessible in the proxy client. For this example, you are setting the Username and Password properties of the mySoapHeader proxy object to the values input by the user in the web form.

Once the mySoapHeader object is constructed and the properties are set, you construct the web service proxy class—PrivateServices—and set the mySoapHeader object as its mySoap-HeaderValue property.

The SOAP message is constructed with the mySoapHeader object serialized in the <soap:Header> element.

```
<?xml version="1.0" encoding="utf-8"?>
<soap:Envelope xmlns:xsi=http://www.w3.org/2001/XMLSchema-instance
  xmlns:xsd=http://www.w3.org/2001/XMLSchema
  xmlns:soap="http://schemas.xmlsoap.org/soap/envelope/">
```

```
<soap:Header>
  <mySoapHeader xmlns="http://www.dotnetjunkies.com">
    <Username>WillyWonka</Username>
    <Password>GoldenTicket</Password>
  </mySoapHeader>
</soap:Header>
<soap:Body>
  <GetMySecret xmlns="http://www.dotnetjunkies.com" />
</soap:Body>
</soap:Envelope>
```

As we mentioned previously, the username and password values are passed in the SOAP header as clear text. Encryption can be used before setting the values, and when the SOAP message is received they can be decrypted. Another security option is to have the web service method call go across SSL for encryption of the entire SOAP message.

Summary

In this chapter, you learned about web services and how you can use them to exchange data in a variety of formats. Web services are entities of application programming logic that are exposed to remote consumers via standard Internet protocols, such as HTTP, XML, SOAP, and WSDL.

You can use web services with three protocols:

- HTTP GET

- HTTP POST

- SOAP

With web services, you can exchange simple data types, like strings and integers, as well as more complex data types, like ADO.NET DataSets, images, and custom-defined classes. The data objects are serialized to XML and transmitted from the provider to the consumer. This enables disparate systems to exchange data regardless of platform or programming language.

You saw several ways of customizing the XML output from a web service, and finally, you saw two different schemas for providing security to your web services—Windows Authentication and SOAP-based Authentication.

CHAPTER 12

■ ■ ■

SQL Server Native XML Support

The introduction of SQL Server 2000 heralded a suite of new XML-related features that can be readily exploited by an ADO.NET application. In this chapter, you'll investigate two of the key SQL Server 2000 XML features.

- FOR XML: The FOR XML clause of a SQL SELECT statement allows a rowset to be returned as an XML document. The XML document generated by a FOR XML clause is highly customizable with respect to the document hierarchy generated, per-column data transforms, representation of binary data, the XML schema generated, and a variety of other XML nuances.

- OPENXML: The OPENXML extension to Transact-SQL (T-SQL) allows a stored procedure call to manipulate an XML document as a rowset. Subsequently, this rowset can be used to perform a variety of tasks including SELECT, INSERT, DELETE, and UPDATE.

To take an example, SELECT queries containing FOR XML clauses could be used to generate an XML document using tables such as Doctors, Pharmacies, and Medications. The results of such a query (an XML document) could correspond with a properly formed medical prescription, and could be used by both an insurance company and the pharmacy that will ultimately dispense the prescription. In such a case, the XML document is immediately generated in the appropriate format using FOR XML, and therefore doesn't require the kind of programmatic massaging that's supported by the classes in System.Xml.

As suggested previously, where FOR XML generates XML, OPENXML is utilized in the consumption of XML. Imagine a pharmacy that receives prescriptions in the form of XML documents. These prescriptions could be used to update an underlying SQL Server database, in conjunction with SQL INSERT, UPDATE, and DELETE commands. There is no need to parse the XML document and generate the appropriate SQL command from that process. Instead, the XML document is included as part of the SQL command.

What's elegant about the XML-specific features of SQL Server is that no intricate steps are required by ADO.NET in order to exploit them. Queries containing a FOR XML clause, for example, require no extra ADO.NET coding in order to execute them. However, you do need to be aware that a query contains a FOR XML clause when it's executed because you have to execute it using the ExecuteXmlReader() method of the SqlCommand class.

In this chapter, you'll investigate the construction of two console applications that demonstrate these SQL Server XML features being exploited using ADO.NET.

- ForXmlDemo demonstrates each of the three styles of FOR XML query (RAW, AUTO, and EXPLICIT).

- OpenXMLDemo demonstrates using OPENXML to INSERT, DELETE, and UPDATE in a table using data provided in an XML document.

You're also going to look at a variety of ways to construct SQL script files that demonstrate FOR XML and OPENXML. In some instances, these scripts must be run before sample applications can be run.

FOR XML

The T-SQL extension to the SELECT statement, FOR XML, is defined in the following way:

FOR XML mode [, XMLDATA][, ELEMENTS][, BINARY BASE64]

The permissible FOR XML modes are RAW, AUTO, and EXPLICIT, listed in order from the least sophisticated to the most sophisticated. These modes generate SQL as follows:

- RAW generates a two-dimensional XML grid, where each row returned by the query is contained in an element named <row>. The values of the column returned by the query are represented by attributes in the <row> elements.

- AUTO generates a potentially hierarchal XML document, where the value returned for every column is contained in an element or an attribute.

- EXPLICIT allows you to specify the precise form used to contain the value of each column returned by the query. The values of columns can be returned as attributes or elements, and this distinction can be specified on a per-column basis. The exact data type used to represent a column can also be specified, as can the precise XML document hierarchy generated by the query.

■Tip The optional components of a FOR XML query (XMLDATA, ELEMENTS, and BINARY BASE64) will be discussed in conjunction with the detailed overview of each mode.

A FOR XML RAW query is the most basic form of FOR XML query. As stated previously, the XML document generated contains one type of element, named <row>. Each <row> element corresponds to a row returned by the query. This simplicity can lead to a great deal of replicated data, since there is no hierarchy within the generated XML document.

An example of a FOR XML RAW query, to be executed against SQL Server's Northwind database, is as follows:

```
SELECT Region.RegionID, Territories.TerritoryID
FROM Region
INNER JOIN Territories ON Region.RegionID = Territories.RegionID
ORDER BY Territories.TerritoryID
FOR XML RAW
```

The XML document generated by this query contains *dozens* of elements named `<row>`—one per row of data returned. True to form, the FOR XML RAW query generates duplicate data, since every element shown contains the attribute RegionID, but the value of the RegionID attribute is the same for many different `<row>` elements.

```
XML_F52E2B61-18A1-11d1-B105-00805F49916B
---------------------------------------------------------------------
<row RegionID="1" TerritoryID="01581"/>
<row RegionID="1" TerritoryID="01730"/>
<row RegionID="1" TerritoryID="01833"/>
<row RegionID="1" TerritoryID="02116"/>
<row RegionID="1" TerritoryID="02139"/>
...
```

The results of a FOR XML query are returned in a rowset containing a single row and a single column. The column, in this case, is arbitrarily named XML_F52E2B61-18A1-11d1-B105-00805F49916B, and the value stored in this single column/row is the XML document. In fact, this column name is identical for *every* FOR XML query, so it provides no additional information with regard to the query or how it will be used.

A FOR XML query of type AUTO exploits the hierarchal nature of certain SQL queries. Each table associated with a FOR XML AUTO query is represented as an XML element (for example, the Region table corresponds to the XML `<Region>` element). The values of each column within the query are contained within each table-specific element (for example, the columns of the Region table retrieved by the query are contained in attributes of the XML `<Region>` element). The per-table elements are nested within the XML hierarchy in the order in which they appear in the query. For example, the Territories table would be a subelement of the `<Region>` element if the FROM clause of the FOR XML AUTO query were to be the following:

```
FROM Region, Territories
```

The values of each of the columns of each table are represented as attributes (by default) or elements (if ELEMENTS is specified as an option to the FOR XML AUTO clause). The ELEMENTS option applies to *all* column attributes returned by the query and cannot be applied to only a few selected ones. Swapping the FOR XML RAW for a FOR XML AUTO in the initial query results in the following:

```
SELECT Region.RegionID, TerritoryID
FROM Region, Territories
WHERE Region.RegionID = Territories.RegionID
ORDER BY TerritoryID
FOR XML AUTO
```

The data generated by this query is as follows:

```
<Region RegionID="1">
  <Territories TerritoryID="01581"/>
  <Territories TerritoryID="01730"/>
  <Territories TerritoryID="01833"/>

  ...

</Region>
<Region RegionID="3">
  <Territories TerritoryID="03049"/>

  ...

</Region>
```

FOR XML EXPLICIT is the most complicated and customizable form of the FOR XML query. Using this form, a specific position within the XML data hierarchy can be specified for each table-column pairing. FOR XML EXPLICT queries use per-column *directives* to control the form of the XML data generated, so that one column from a table may generate an XML element, while another column may generate an attribute. The following snippet from a FOR XML EXPLICIT query's SELECT clause demonstrates how the RegionID from Northwind's Region table could be specified as both an attribute and an element within the same XML document:

```
SELECT 1 AS Tag,
       0 AS Parent,
       RegionID AS [Region!1!RegionIDAsAttribute],
       RegionID AS [Region!1!RegionIDAsElement!element]
FROM Region
FOR XML EXPLICIT
```

Ignoring the Tag and Parent parts of this query for now, the alias following the first instance of RegionID contains no directive, so it's treated as an attribute (the default). However, the element directive in the alias following the second RegionID causes that column to be represented as an element. We'll go into more detail later on, but a portion of the XML generated by the previous SQL is as follows:

```
<Region RegionIDAsAttribute="1">
  <RegionIDAsElement>1</RegionIDAsElement>
</Region>
<Region RegionIDAsAttribute="2">
  <RegionIDAsElement>2</RegionIDAsElement>
</Region>
...
```

FOR XML's Optional Arguments

The following optional arguments can be used in conjunction with a FOR XML query:

- ELEMENTS is only applicable to a FOR XML AUTO query, and specifies that the value of each column returned will be represented as an element within the XML document, rather than as an attribute (the default).

- BINARY BASE64 causes any binary data within the XML document to be represented in base-64 encoding. Such data is found in columns of type BINARY, VARBINARY, or IMAGE. The BINARY BASE64 option must be specified in order for FOR XML RAW and FOR XML EXPLICIT queries to retrieve binary data.

  By default, a FOR XML AUTO query handles binary data by creating a reference within the XML document to the location of the binary data. The disadvantage of doing this, however, is that it limits an XML document's portability. When BINARY BASE64 is specified for a FOR XML AUTO query, the generated XML document will contain the binary data.

- XMLDATA generates a schema for the XML document generated by the FOR XML query. This schema is placed at the start of the XML document.

The following SQL is identical to one of your earlier examples, save that it contains the optional XMLDATA argument:

```
SELECT Region.RegionID, TerritoryID
FROM Region, Territories
WHERE Region.RegionID = Territories.RegionID
ORDER BY TerritoryID
FOR XML AUTO, XMLDATA
```

A portion of the XML document generated by this query (including the schema) is as follows:

```
<Schema name="Schema1" xmlns="urn:schemas-microsoft-com:xml-data"
                        xmlns:dt="urn:schemas-microsoft-com:datatypes">
  <ElementType name="Region" content="eltOnly" model="closed" order="many">
    <element type="Territories" maxOccurs="*" />
    <AttributeType name="RegionID" dt:type="i4" />
    <attribute type="RegionID" />
  </ElementType>
  <ElementType name="Territories" content="empty" model="closed">
    <AttributeType name="TerritoryID" dt:type="string" />
    <attribute type="TerritoryID" />
  </ElementType>
</Schema>
<Region xmlns="x-schema:#Schema1" RegionID="1">
  <Territories TerritoryID="01581" />
  <Territories TerritoryID="01730" />
...
```

■Note Note that the schema is neither a document type definition (DTD) nor a W3C schema of the kind that you saw at in Chapter 5—it's an XML-Data schema.

Microsoft proposed and implemented XML-Data schemas in January 1998, three years before the W3C adopted the XML Schema specification. Such schemas are used to validate XML documents in homogeneous Microsoft environments.

Since Microsoft is now committed to supporting the W3C's XML Schema specification, it seems likely that FOR XML's XMLDATA option will be altered or superseded in a future version of SQL Server.

FOR XML RAW

Let's now start looking more closely at SQL Server's FOR XML queries. Another example of a FOR XML RAW query is the following:

```
SELECT FirstName, LastName, Photo
FROM Employees
ORDER BY LastName, FirstName
FOR XML RAW, BINARY BASE64
```

The presence of the BINARY BASE 64 argument here causes the binary data (the Photo column of type IMAGE) to be encoded and placed within the XML generated document. In fact, although BINARY BASE64 is classified as an "optional" argument, it's *required* for queries of type RAW and EXPLICIT when the query contains a column of binary type. A portion of the output generated by this query is as follows:

```
<row FirstName="Steven" LastName="Buchanan" Photo="FRwv ... atBf4=" />
<row FirstName="Laura" LastName="Callahan" Photo="FRwvA ... +tBf4=" />
<row FirstName="Nancy" LastName="Davolio" Photo="FRwvAA ... StBf4=" />
<row FirstName="Anne" LastName="Dodsworth" Photo="FRwv   ... 6tBf4=" />
...
```

Had we not specified BINARY BASE64 here, the previous query would have produced a very clear error message, as seen in Figure 12-1.

```
Server: Msg 6829, Level 16, State 1, Line 1
FOR XML EXPLICIT and RAW modes currently do not support addressing binary data
as URLs in column 'Photo'. Remove the column, or use the BINARY BASE64 mode,
or create the URL directly using the 'dbobject/TABLE[@PK1="V1"]/@COLUMN' syntax.
```

Figure 12-1. *Error message upon trying to retrieve a binary column without the Binary argument*

Using FOR XML RAW with ADO.NET

To test the use of FOR XML RAW with ADO.NET, you'll use a query that's nearly the same as the one you used previously.

```
SELECT FirstName, LastName
FROM Employees
ORDER BY LastName, FirstName
FOR XML RAW, XMLDATA
```

We've excluded the Photo column because it generates too much data, meaning that the BINARY BASE64 option is not required as part of this query. Instead, we've used the XMLDATA option in order to generate a schema for the XML document. The rationale for generating such a schema will be introduced later in this example.

To execute this query, a System.Data.SqlClient.SqlCommand instance is created and associated with an instance of SQL Server containing a Northwind database. At the same time, the query is specified as a parameter to the SqlCommand object's constructor. This is demonstrated in the following excerpt from the VB.NET source file ForXMLDemo.vb:

```
Dim strQuery As String = _
                "SELECT FirstName, LastName FROM Employees " & _
                "ORDER BY LastName, FirstName FOR XML RAW, XMLDATA"
Dim strConnection As String = _
                "Data Source=(local);Integrated Security=SSPI;" & _
                "Initial Catalog=Northwind"

Dim sqlConnection As New SqlConnection(strConnection)
Dim forXMLCommand As New SqlCommand(strQuery, sqlConnection)

Try
  sqlConnection.Open()
```

Once the SqlCommand instance has been created and the connection opened, the SqlCommand object's ExecuteXmlReader() method can be called. The prototype for this method is as follows:

```
Public Function ExecuteXmlReader() As XmlReader
```

ExecuteXmlReader() executes a query containing a FOR XML clause and returns an instance of type System.Xml.XmlReader. The DataSet class exposes the ReadXml() method that can consume an instance of XmlReader and the WriteXml() method that can persist an XML dataset to a file. A DataSet instance can therefore be used to persist the XML document as follows:

```
Dim ds As New DataSet()
ds.ReadXml(forXMLCommand.ExecuteXmlReader(), XmlReadMode.Fragment)
ds.WriteXml("DemoOutRaw.xml")
Catch ex As Exception
  Console.Error.WriteLine(ex)
Finally
  sqlConnection.Close()
End Try
```

When `XmlReadMode.Fragment` is specified to the `ReadXml()` method, the latter assumes that the data to be read into the `DataSet` is an XML document that includes an inline XDR (XML-Data Reduced) schema. The `XMLDATA` option was specified in the query's `FOR XML RAW` clause in order to ensure that this was the case. If you take a look at DemoOutRaw.xml, you should see something like the following:

```
<?xml version="1.0" standalone="yes"?>
<Schema1>
  <row FirstName="Steven" LastName="Buchanan" />
  <row FirstName="Laura" LastName="Callahan" />

...

  <row FirstName="Michael" LastName="Suyama" />
  <row FirstName="Jane" LastName="Zerdeni" />
</Schema1>
```

FOR XML AUTO

`FOR XML`'s `AUTO` mode supports the use of `BINARY BASE64`, but doesn't require it. When the `BINARY BASE64` option *isn't* specified, *references* to any binary data will be included in the generated XML document. In order to demonstrate such references, consider the following SQL query:

```
SELECT EmployeeID, FirstName, LastName, Photo
FROM Employees
ORDER BY LastName, FirstName
FOR XML AUTO
```

Here, we've deliberately requested the `EmployeeID` column of the `Employees` table—it's the primary key, and it will be used to generate an XPath reference to the employee's `Photo`. The following is the kind of thing you get:

```
<Employees EmployeeID="5" FirstName="Steven" LastName="Buchanan"
          Photo="dbobject/Employees[@EmployeeID='5']/@Photo" />
<Employees EmployeeID="8" FirstName="Laura" LastName="Callahan"
          Photo="dbobject/Employees[@EmployeeID='8']/@Photo" />
<Employees EmployeeID="1" FirstName="Nancy" LastName="Davolio"
          Photo="dbobject/Employees[@EmployeeID='1']/@Photo" />
...
```

Referencing XML data is clearly more readable than including binary data; the trouble is that doing so is only supported in conjunction with SQL Server and Internet Information Server. Since the binary data itself is not contained in the XML document, copying the document to another location results in references that can no longer be resolved—references to binary data are not portable. Microsoft-specific references to binary data should be avoided unless the deployment environment is Microsoft-homogeneous.

Moving on, the `Region` table of the `Northwind` database contains a primary key called `RegionID`, which is also the name of a foreign key in the `Territories` table (there can be multiple territories per region). An example of a `FOR XML AUTO` mode that accesses the `Region` and Territories can be found here, in the creation statement for a stored procedure called RegionTerritory (see ForXmlAutoStoredProc.sql in the Downloads section of the Apress Web site [http://www.apress.com]).

```
CREATE PROCEDURE RegionTerritory AS
SELECT R.RegionID, RTRIM(R.RegionDescription) AS RegionDesc,
       T.TerritoryID, RTRIM(T.TerritoryDescription) AS TerritoryDesc
FROM Region AS R, Territories AS T
WHERE R.RegionID = T.RegionID
ORDER BY R.RegionID, T.TerritoryID
FOR XML AUTO, XMLDATA
```

A portion of the output generated by this stored procedure without the prefixed schema (courtesy of the XMLDATA option) is as follows:

```
<R RegionID="1" RegionDesc="Eastern">
  <T TerritoryID="01581" TerritoryDesc="Westboro" />
  <T TerritoryID="01730" TerritoryDesc="Bedford" />
  ...

  <T TerritoryID="27511" TerritoryDesc="Cary" />
  <T TerritoryID="40222" TerritoryDesc="Louisville" />
</R>
<R RegionID="2" RegionDesc="Western">
  <T TerritoryID="60179" TerritoryDesc="Hoffman Estates" />
  <T TerritoryID="60601" TerritoryDesc="Chicago" />
  ...
```

This document exploits the relationship between Region and Territories—there is no repeated data for each region. Each Region (element <R>) contains subelements corresponding to that region's Territories (element <T>). The columns of the Region table are represented by the RegionID and RegionDesc attributes, while the columns of the Territories table are represented by the TerritoryID and TerritoryDesc attributes.

If you wish, you can use the ELEMENTS option with this FOR XML AUTO mode, as follows:

```
FOR XML AUTO, ELEMENTS, XMLDATA
```

As a consequence of doing this, the attributes used to contain per-column data in the generated document would be replaced by elements, like so:

```
<R>
  <RegionID>1</RegionID>
  <RegionDesc>Eastern</RegionDesc>
  <T>
    <TerritoryID>01581</TerritoryID>
    <TerritoryDesc>Westboro</TerritoryDesc>
  </T>
  <T>
    <TerritoryID>01730</TerritoryID>
    ...
```

This ability to choose between elements and attributes is useful, but there's no way to indicate that *some* columns should have their data contained in attributes, while *other* columns should have their data contained in elements. What's lacking is the ability for each column to declare its own representation within the XML document (attribute or element, the level of the hierarchy at which it is to be placed, etc.). The FOR XML EXPLICIT mode, which we'll present shortly, will address that shortcoming.

Using FOR XML AUTO with ADO.NET

Earlier, we demonstrated that a FOR XML RAW query could be executed using ADO.NET. In that example, the query was in the form of a SQL statement placed directly into the source code. With respect to FOR XML AUTO, a stored procedure called RegionTerritory has already been presented that can be used in conjunction with ADO.NET to retrieve an XML document. This stored procedure is executed in the ShowOffForXMLAuto() function in the VB.NET source file named ForXMLDemo.vb by first establishing a connection to a SQL Server database.

```
Dim strConnection As String = _
                "Data Source=(local);Integrated Security=SSPI;" & _
                "Initial Catalog=Northwind"
Dim sqlConnection As New SqlConnection(strConnection)
Try
  sqlConnection.Open()
```

Once a connection has been set up, the SqlCommand instance, forXMLCommand, can be created. This SQL command is associated with the RegionTerritory stored procedure, so CommandType is set to StoredProcedure.

```
Dim forXMLCommand As New SqlCommand("RegionTerritory")
forXMLCommand.CommandType = CommandType.StoredProcedure
forXMLCommand.Connection = sqlConnection
```

Once the stored procedure has been set up, it can be executed using the SqlCommand object's ExecuteXmlReader() method. The XmlReader returned by this method is, again, associated with a DataSet instance, and the DataSet's WriteXml() method is used to write the generated XML to a file called DemoOutAuto.xml.

```
Dim ds As New DataSet()
ds.ReadXml(forXMLCommand.ExecuteXmlReader(), XmlReadMode.Fragment)
ds.WriteXml("DemoOutAuto.xml", XmlWriteMode.IgnoreSchema)
Catch ex As Exception
  Console.Error.WriteLine(ex)
Finally
  sqlConnection.Close()
End Try
```

The contents of the file produced by the execution of this code are identical to the output we showed when first describing the previous stored procedure.

FOR XML EXPLICIT

The EXPLICIT mode of FOR XML provides a tremendous amount of flexibility when it comes to the generation of XML documents, but the tradeoff is a fair amount of complexity with respect to the writing of such queries. To understand this fully, you'll experiment with a FOR XML EXPLICIT query that will be executed against the following set of tables (see Figure 12-2) that can be created on your RDBMS using the SQL script called ForXMLExplicit.sql:

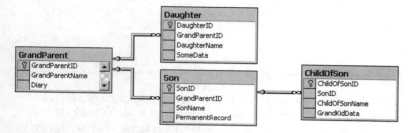

Figure 12-2. *Schema for the* FamilyDB *database*

These tables are not meant to be realistic. Rather, they're intended to demonstrate how to represent a relational hierarchy as an XML hierarchy. In subsequent code examples, we've assumed that these tables have been created in a database called FamilyDB. However, you can create them in any database you like, so long as you make the appropriate changes to the code. The tables are related as follows:

- GrandParent contains a primary key called GrandParentID.

- Daughter contains a primary key called DaughterID and a foreign key called Grand-ParentID that refers to an entry in the GrandParent table.

- Son contains a primary key called SonID and a foreign key called GrandParentID that refers to an entry in the GrandParent table.

- ChildOfSon contains a primary key called ChildOfSonID and a foreign key called SonID that refers to an entry in the Son table.

Using FOR XML EXPLICIT and this hierarchy of relational database tables, you would like to generate an XML document with the following format:

- A root element named <GParent>, which will contain each row of the GrandParent table and all of the grandparent's children and grandchildren. This root element will contain the data retrieved from the GrandParent table by the FOR XML EXPLICIT query.

- Directly below the <GParent> element will exist elements named <Daughter> and <Son>. Each of these elements will contain the data retrieved from their respective tables, Daughter and Son.

- At the level below the <Son> element will exist the <ChildOfSon> element. This will contain the data retrieved from the ChildOfSon table.

The mechanism that FOR XML EXPLICIT uses to support the generation of a specific hierarchy is to assign a tag to each element within the XML hierarchy. Every element declares a tag value, and the value of its parent (see Table 12-1). For your proposed hierarchy, this is as follows:

Table 12-1. Hierarchy Description for Your Query

Level	Tag	Parent
GParent	1	0
Son	2	1
Daughter	3	1
ChildOfSon	4	2

The GParent has a tag value of 1, and a parent value of 0. (When the parent of a level in the XML hierarchy is set to zero, this indicates that the element is at the root of the XML document.) Notice that both Son (tag 2) and Daughter (tag 3) have a parent value of 1 (the GParent level of the XML hierarchy). Daughter is at the second, rather than the third, level of the hierarchy because its parent's value is 1. The ChildOfSon is assigned a tag value of 4, and is associated with a parent whose tag value is 2 (a Son).

Each column of a FOR XML EXPLICIT query specifies a per-column encoding that includes a tag value. The form that this per-column encoding takes is as follows:

columnName AS [ContainedElementName!Tag!AttributeOrElementName!Directive]

The subcomponents that make up the explicit declaration of a column are the following:

- ContainedElementName: The name of the element in which this column returned by the query will be contained. For example, each column of the GrandParent table will be contained in the <GParent> element, whether as an element or an attribute.

- Tag: The tag value associated with a column. For example, each column of the Son table is associated with a tag value of 2, while each column of the Daughter table is associated with a tag value of 3.

- AttributeOrElementName: The name of the element or attribute that will contain this returned column's data.

  - If no Directive is specified, then this is the name of the attribute (for example, [Son!2!SonID] where the attribute containing the data is named SonID).

  - If the Directive specified is xml, element, or CDATA, then AttributeOrElementName specifies the name of the element that will contain this column's data (for example, [GrandKid!4!GrandKidData!xml], where the element containing the data is named GrandKidData).

  - If a Directive is specified, then AttributeOrElementName is optional.

  - If no AttributeOrElementName is specified, then the column's data is included as child content of the element specified by ContainedElementName.

- Directive: The directive is used to specify the format that data should take (hide, element, xml, xmltext, or CDATA), and to specify references between columns. Supplying a directive for a column is optional. You will review the directives in full a little later on.

FOR XML EXPLICIT: Two-Level Example

Before things get out of hand, we'll demonstrate a query that works with only two levels of the three-level database that you just created. This query is designed to demonstrate how a FOR XML EXPLICIT hierarchy can be created, by using UNION ALL to combine the results of multiple queries.

```
-- SubQuery1 -- This sub-query retrieves columns from the GrandParent table
SELECT 1 As Tag,
       0 As Parent,
       GrandParentID AS [GrandParent!1!GrandParentID],
       0 AS [Son!2!SonID]
FROM GrandParent
UNION ALL

-- SubQuery2 -- This sub-query retrieves columns from the Son table
SELECT 2, -- The tag
       1, -- Identifying GrandParent as the parent element
       0,
       SonID
FROM GrandParent G, Son S
WHERE G.GrandParentID = S.GrandParentID

FOR XML EXPLICIT
```

Here you can see two subqueries: SubQuery1 and SubQuery2. The first of these retrieves columns from the GrandParent table—on this occasion, just GrandParentID. Specifying a Tag of 1 and a Parent of 0 means that the data retrieved will be at the root of the XML document. The children of this <GrandParent> element will use the tag value in order to indicate it as their parent in the XML hierarchy.

SubQuery2 retrieves the SonID column from the Son table and, by specifying a Tag value of 2 and a Parent value of 1, dictates that the elements of this subquery are to be stored in a subelement of a <GrandParent> element.

The subqueries of your FOR XML EXPLICIT query are combined using UNION ALL. Using a SQL union means that every subquery must retrieve the same columns as every other sub-query. Notice that SubQuery1 returns a value for the Son table's SonID.

```
0 AS [Son!2!SonID]
```

The value for SonID in each row returned by SubQuery1 is 0, but the value isn't displayed because its Tag value is specified as 2. In other words, the data associated with this column only appears at Tag level 2. Similarly, the Son's subquery, SubQuery2, contains a 0 representing the GrandParentID column. This value is never displayed either, because the data displayed for the Son table is at Tag level 2, and the GrandParentID is at Tag level 1.

The XML document generated by the previously mentioned query is as follows:

```
<GrandParent GrandParentID="1">
  <Son SonID="3" />
</GrandParent>
<GrandParent GrandParentID="2">
  <Son SonID="1" />
  <Son SonID="2" />
</GrandParent>
<GrandParent GrandParentID="3" />
```

Since both GrandParentID and SonID are represented as attributes here, this document could have been generated using FOR XML AUTO. However, it would have been possible to specify that the data in the GrandParentID column should be contained in an attribute, and the data in the SonID column should be contained in an element, by means of the element directive. Directives are optional, and since the query didn't contain any, you got attributes.

Entity Encoding

Before delving further into the tantalizing world of FOR XML EXPLICIT directives, we need to introduce an equally important concept: *entity encoding*. Entity encoding is the means by which XML special characters can be included in data. What do we mean by special characters? The less-than character (<) is special, because it's used to start each element within an XML document. How would an XML parser handle data of the following form?

<CompareThis> MassOfEarth < MassOfJupiter </CompareThis>

This is not actually well-formed XML, because the "< m" character inside the element's data leads to a parsing ambiguity. In this XML-like snippet, the less-than character indicates the start of each tag, and is also part of the data associated with the element: MassOfEarth < MassOfJupiter. The previous snippet could be made well-formed by using entity encoding to change how the less-than character is represented.

<CompareThis> MassOfEarth < MassOfJupiter </CompareThis>

< is the entity-encoded form of the less-than character, so there is no ambiguity for XML parsers here. The characters deemed as special by XML include &, ', >, <, and ". When you need them, they should by written within an XML document using the alternative representations shown in Table 12-2.

Table 12-2. *Various Entity Encoding Representations*

Character Name	Character Literal	Entity Encoding Representation
Ampersand	&	&amp;
Apostrophe	'	&apos;
Greater-than	>	&gt;
Less-than	<	&lt;
Quotation mark	"	&quot;

The concept of entity encoding is pertinent to the next section's discussion of the FOR XML EXPLICIT directive, xml.

Directives

The short SQL query we just demonstrated was really only an aside, designed to show how FOR XML EXPLICIT can be used to generate a specific hierarchy. Our true goals are loftier, and will be presented using a query that's designed to exercise the majority of directives. The FOR XML EXPLICIT directives presented in this section are shown in Table 12-3.

Table 12-3. FOR XML EXPLICIT *Directives*

Directive	Description
element	Causes a particular column in the query to be represented by an element rather than an attribute.
hide	Causes a column in the SELECT clause of the query not to generate XML, and therefore not to be included in the XML document generated.
xml	Causes the data associated with a column to be included in the XML document, but not to be entity encoded.
xmltext	Causes the data associated with a column to be included in the XML document as XML. A column can contain XML, and this will be placed in the generated XML document.
CDATA	Causes the data associated with a column to be included in the generated XML document as data type CDATA.
ID	Causes the data associated with a column to be included in the generated XML document as data type ID.
IDREF	Causes the data associated with a column to be included in the generated XML document as data type IDREF.
IDREFS	Causes the data associated with a column to be included in the generated XML document as data type IDREFS.

Just before you get to your main example, let's take a closer look at a few of these directives. For a start, the data associated with a column specified using the element directive is contained within an XML element in the generated document. An example of this is as follows:

```
[GrandKid!4!ChildOfSonName!element]
```

The data associated with a column that's been configured like this will be contained in an element called <ChildOfSonName>, like this:

```
<GrandKid>
  <ChildOfSonName>Kyle</ChildOfSonName>

  ...

</GrandKid>
```

Next, the xml directive causes the data in the column to which it applies not to be entity encoded when placed in the XML document. This means, for example, that any < characters are not converted to <. An example of such a specification is

```
[GrandKid!4!GrandKidData!xml]
```

The XML generated by this directive is as follows, where quote and question-mark characters are not entity encoded, even though they are classified as special characters within XML:

```
<GrandKid>
  <GrandKidData>"/?%#</GrandKidData>
  ...

</GrandKid>
```

Moving on, when the xmltext directive is specified for a column, the data associated with this column is assumed to be well-formed XML, and is included in the document at the beginning of the child content of the element containing it. An example of using the xmltext directive is

```
Diary AS [GParent!1!!xmltext]
```

The output generated by this part of a SQL query is completely dependent on the data contained in the Diary column. For the case of the GrandParent named Olivia, the Diary column contains XML corresponding to the chapters of a diary. The <Chapter> elements in the following XML snippet are not generated by SQL Server, but rather extracted as data from the Diary column of the GrandParent table, courtesy of the xmltext directive:

```
<GParent GParentName="Olivia">
  <Chapter>ChapNum="1" Body="It was the best of times"</Chapter>
  <Chapter>ChapNum="2" Body="It is a far, far"</Chapter>
```

Finally, for now, when the hide directive is specified for a column, the column is not included in the generated XML document. Such hidden columns can be used to affect the overall architecture without having their data appearing in the XML document. These columns will ultimately be included in an ORDER BY clause, because they are typically used to order data.

An example of specifying a hidden column is

```
[GParent!1!OrderByGrandParentName!hide]
```

Each subquery of the large FOR XML EXPLICIT query that you'll look at next contains a column corresponding to GrandParentName, aliased to OrderByGrandParentName. This column is not displayed because of the hide directive. In fact, the ORDER BY clause of your sample query looks like the following; a total of four hidden columns are used to specify the order of the data generated:

```
ORDER BY [GParent!1!OrderByGrandParentName!hide],
         [Son!2!OrderBySonName!hide],
         [Daughter!3!OrderByDaughterName!hide],
         [GrandKid!4!OrderByChildOfSonName!hide]
```

It's worth bearing in mind that the directives are not the only controllers of per-column encoding. To understand this, consider the following portion of a query:

```
GrandParentID AS [GParent!1!],
GrandParentName AS [GParent!1!OrderByGrandParentName!hide],
RTRIM(GrandParentName) AS [GParent!1!GParentName],
Diary AS [GParent!1!!xmltext],
```

Here, the values retrieved from the GrandParent table will all be contained in the XML element, <GParent>. The data associated with the GrandParentName column is contained in the attribute GParentName (third line). For the GrandParentID column, however, there is no attribute name specified, and therefore there is no attribute to contain this column's data. Under these circumstances, the data associated with the GrandParentID column is contained directly in the <GParent> element. A sample of the XML generated by this portion of your query is as follows:

```
<GParent GParentName="Jeb">
  <Chapter> ChapNum="1" Body="They call me Ishmael"</Chapter>
  <Chapter> ChapNum="2" Body="Whale sinks"</Chapter>
  1
</GParent>
```

The <Chapter> elements and their corresponding attributes are again retrieved from the Diary column, but notice that in this snippet of XML, the "1" is not associated with an attribute. This "1" is the value of the GrandParentID column.

FOR XML EXPLICIT: Three-Level Example

So far, each directive has been presented in piecemeal fashion, but all of the pieces you've seen so far have actually been part of a larger query—a query that generates a three-level XML hierarchy in the following form:

```
<GParent> contains Son and Daughter elements
  <Son> contains GrandKid elements
    <GrandKid> </GrandKid>
  </Son>
  <Daughter> </Daughter>
</GParent>
```

The query in question is a union of four separate queries combined using UNION ALL. These subqueries perform the following tasks in generating the XML document:

- Retrieve the grandparent data at level 1 of the hierarchy
- Retrieve the son data at level 2 of the hierarchy
- Retrieve the daughter data at level 2 of the hierarchy
- Retrieve the grandchild (child of son) data at level 3 of the hierarchy

The query itself looks like the following (you'll find it in ForXmlExplicitStoredProcFull.sql, which is available in the code download for this book):

```
-- Generate the Grandparent level of the hierarchy
SELECT 1 AS Tag,
       0 AS Parent,
       GrandParentID AS [GParent!1!],
       GrandParentName AS [GParent!1!OrderByGrandParentName!hide],
       RTRIM(GrandParentName) AS [GParent!1!GParentName],
       Diary AS [GParent!1!!xmltext],
       0 AS [Son!2!SonID],
       '' AS [Son!2!OrderBySonName!hide],
       '' AS [Son!2!SonName],
       '' AS [Son!2!!CDATA], -- PermanentRecord
       0 AS [Daughter!3!DaughterID!element],
       '' AS [Daughter!3!OrderByDaughterName!hide],
       '' AS [Daughter!3!DaughterName!element],
       '' AS [Daughter!3!SomeData!element],
       0 AS [GrandKid!4!ChildOfSonID!element],
       '' AS [GrandKid!4!OrderByChildOfSonName!hide],
       '' AS [GrandKid!4!ChildOfSonName!element],
       '' AS [GrandKid!4!GrandKidData!xml]


FROM GrandParent

UNION ALL

-- Generated the Son level of the hierarchy
SELECT 2 AS Tag,
       1 AS Parent,
       0, -- GrandParent.GrandParentID
       G.GrandParentName AS [GParent!1!OrderByGrandParentName!hide],
       '', -- GrandParent.Name
       '', -- GrandParent.Diary
       SonID,
       RTRIM(SonName),
       RTRIM(SonName),
       PermanentRecord,
       0, -- Daughter.DaughterID
       '', -- Daughter.OrderByDaughterName
       '', -- Daughter.DaughterName
       '', -- Daughter.SomeData,
       0, -- ChildOfSon.ChildOfOnID,
       '', -- ChildOfSon.OrderByChildOfSonName
       '', -- ChildOfSon.ChildOfSonName
       '' -- ChildOfSon.GrandKidData
```

```
FROM GrandParent AS G, Son AS S
WHERE G.GrandParentID = S.GrandParentID

UNION ALL

-- Generate the Daughter level of the hierarchy
-- that is in the same level as the Son's data
SELECT 3 AS Tag,
       1 AS Parent,
       0, -- GrandParent.GrandParentID
       G.GrandParentName AS [GParent!1!OrderByGrandParentName!hide],
       '', -- GrandParent.Name
       '', -- GrandParent.Diary
       0, -- Son.SonID
       '', -- Son.SonName (hidden)
       '', -- Son.SonName
       '', -- Son.PermentRecord
       DaughterID,
       RTRIM(DaughterName),
       RTRIM(DaughterName),
       SomeData,
       0, -- ChildOfSon.ChildOfOnID,
       '', -- ChildOfSon.OrderByChildOfSonName
       '', -- ChildOfSon.ChildOfSonName
       '' -- ChildOfSon.GrandKidData

FROM GrandParent AS G, Daughter AS D
WHERE G.GrandParentID = D.GrandParentID

UNION ALL

-- Execute grandchild (child of son) level of the query
SELECT 4 AS Tag,
       2 AS Parent,
       0, -- GrandParent.GrandParentID
       G.GrandParentName AS [GParent!1!OrderByGrandParentName!hide],
       '', -- GrandParent.Name
       '', -- GrandParent.Diary
       0, -- Son.SonID
       RTRIM(S.SonName),
       '', -- Son.SonName
       '', -- Son.PermentRecord
       0, -- Daughter.DaughterID
       '', -- Daughter.OrderByDaughterName
       '', -- Daughter.DaughterName
       '', -- Daughter.SomeData,
```

```
        CS.ChildOfSonID,
        RTRIM(CS.ChildOfSonName),
        RTRIM(CS.ChildOfSonName),
        CS.GrandKidData

FROM GrandParent AS G, Son AS S, ChildOfSon AS CS
WHERE G.GrandParentID = S.GrandParentID AND S.SonID = CS.SonID

ORDER BY [GParent!1!OrderByGrandParentName!hide],
         [Son!2!OrderBySonName!hide],
         [Daughter!3!OrderByDaughterName!hide],
         [GrandKid!4!OrderByChildOfSonName!hide]

FOR XML EXPLICIT
```

A portion of the output generated by this sizable query is as follows:

```
<GParent GParentName="Jeb">
  <Chapter> ChapNum="1" Body="They call me Ishmael"</Chapter>
  <Chapter> ChapNum="2" Body="Whale sinks"</Chapter>
  1
  <Daughter>
    <DaughterID>1</DaughterID>
    <DaughterName>Sade</DaughterName>
    <SomeData>abcd&lt;&gt;&apos;</SomeData>
  </Daughter>
  <Son SonID="3" SonName="Han">
    <![CDATA[<Book><Chapter> ChapNum="1" Body="Bye, Bye Yoda"</Chapter>
                  <Chapter> ChapNum="2" Body="Yet another Death Star,
                            boom boom"</Chapter></Book>]]>
    <GrandKid>
      <ChildOfSonID>3</ChildOfSonID>
      <ChildOfSonName>Kyle</ChildOfSonName>
      <GrandKidData>?????"""???</GrandKidData>
    </GrandKid>
  </Son>
</GParent>
```

Using FOR XML EXPLICIT with ADO.NET

As you might expect, your example query could just as well be executed using ADO.NET, in similar fashion to the way you dealt with FOR XML RAW and FOR XML AUTO—there's nothing special about the EXPLICIT option in that respect. Given the size that such queries can reach, though, it's worth bearing in mind that using stored procedures gets you better performance than storing SQL queries in your code, making the former technique the preferred way of dealing with FOR XML EXPLICIT. You'll find demonstrations of both styles in the code download.

Conclusion

FOR XML EXPLICIT is powerful and can produce highly customized XML documents. Your extremely complicated FOR XML EXPLICT query could be used to generate exactly the data needed for consumption by a third-party application with explicit needs.

Using FOR XML EXPLICIT to generate XML data makes sense in a development environment that is SQL Server savvy. Development shops that primarily use high-level languages such as VB.NET, on the other hand, should consider using a simpler type of query in conjunction with the XML-shaping functionality exposed by the System.Xml and System.Xml.Xsl namespaces.

OPENXML

The OPENXML function of SQL Server's T-SQL allows an XML document to be viewed as a rowset without the need for any involvement of .NET code. Once opened, this rowset can immediately be manipulated using SQL statements such as SELECT, INSERT, UPDATE, and DELETE.

This tying of SQL Server to an XML document results in certain complexities. For example, what happens if the XML document inserted into a SQL Server table contains extra elements or attributes that weren't taken into account by the OPENXML command? We refer to this as *overflow*, and it results in the elements and tags in question being *unconsumed*. As you'll see, the OPENXML mechanism has the ability to handle unconsumed XML by placing it in a designated column.

The OPENXML function of T-SQL is defined as follows, where parameters surrounded by square brackets ([flags byte[in]]) and clauses surrounded by square brackets ([WITH (Schema-Declaration | TableName)]) are optional:

```
OPENXML(idoc int [in], rowpattern nvarchar [in], [flags byte [in]])
    [WITH (SchemaDeclaration | TableName)]
```

The parameters to OPENXML are defined as follows:

- idoc (input parameter of type int): A document handle referring to the parsed XML document. This document handle is created by calling the sp_xml_preparedocument stored procedure.

- rowpattern (input parameter of type nvarchar): An XPath pattern specifying the node of the XML document to be processed as a rowset. For example, the following pattern indicates that the Region node is the level of the XML document to be interpreted: N'/Top/Region'.

- flags (input parameter of type byte): A flag that indicates how the XML node is to be interpreted. 1 indicates that attributes in the document become columns in the rowset, while 2 indicates that elements in the document become columns. This flag can also be used to specify that data not consumed by the rowset should be placed in an overflow column.

Two forms of WITH clause can be specified with OPENXML.

- WITH SchemaDeclaration allows an XML-Data schema to be specified.

- WITH TableName indicates that the schema associated with a specified table should be used to interpret the XML document specified. This is the simpler of the two variants.

In this section, we'll demonstrate how to use OPENXML in an example that requires you to add a stored procedure called RegionInsert to the Northwind database. This stored procedure contains an INSERT statement that uses OPENXML. The steps involved in the creation of the RegionInsert stored procedure are as follows:

1. Call the system-provided stored procedure, sp_xml_preparedocument, passing the XML document to be processed (@xmldoc). This stored procedure parses the XML document and returns a handle (an integer, @docIndex) that's used by OPENXML to process the parsed document.

```
CREATE PROCEDURE RegionInsert @xmlDoc NVARCHAR(4000) AS
DECLARE @docIndex INT
EXECUTE sp_xml_preparedocument @docIndex OUTPUT, @xmlDoc
```

2. Call OPENXML to create a rowset from the XML document. This rowset can then be processed by any applicable SQL command. The following INSERT statement demonstrates OPENXML creating a rowset using the schema associated with the Region table (WITH Region), and then inserting the data into that table.

```
-- 1 is ATTRIBUTE-centric mapping
INSERT Region
SELECT RegionID, RegionDescription
FROM OPENXML(@docIndex, N'/Top/Region', 1) WITH Region
```

3. Call the system-provided stored procedure, sp_xml_removedocument, in order to clean up the handle to the XML document.

```
EXECUTE sp_xml_removedocument @docIndex
```

You can add this stored procedure to the Northwind database by executing the OpenXMLSP.sql SQL script from the code download. Once that's in place, an example of SQL code (including the XML document with data to insert) that executes the RegionInsert stored procedure is as follows (OpenXMLDemo.sql):

```
DECLARE @newRegions NVARCHAR(2048)

SET @newRegions = N'
<Top>
  <Region RegionID="11" RegionDescription="Uptown" />
  <Region RegionID="22" RegionDescription="Downtown" />
</Top>'

EXEC RegionInsert @newRegions
```

This calls RegionInsert to add two rows to the Region table (one with RegionID 11, and one with RegionID 22). Remember that XML is case sensitive, but SQL Server's SQL is not. When OPENXML was specified (OPENXML(@docIndex, N'/Top/Region', 1)) in the RegionInsert stored procedure, the row pattern was /Top/Region. The XML document's elements must match these exactly (<Top> and <Region>). If <TOP> or <top> had been specified as the root element name, then the insertion would have failed, as there would have been a case mismatch.

OPENXML Stored Procedures: Deletion and Updates

Another of the SQL scripts in OpenXMLSP.sql demonstrates OPENXML being used in conjunction with a SQL DELETE operation (in a stored procedure called RegionDelete).

```
CREATE PROCEDURE RegionDelete @xmlDoc NVARCHAR(4000) AS
DECLARE @docIndex INT
EXECUTE sp_xml_preparedocument @docIndex OUTPUT, @xmlDoc

DELETE Region
FROM OPENXML(@docIndex, N'/Top/Region', 1) WITH Region AS XMLRegion
WHERE Region.RegionID = XMLRegion.RegionID

EXECUTE sp_xml_removedocument @docIndex
```

Here, the FROM clause of the DELETE statement uses the OPENXML function to generate a rowset named XMLRegion.

```
OPENXML(@docIndex, N'/Top/Region', 1) WITH Region AS XMLRegion
```

OpenXMLSP.sql also includes a stored procedure called RegionUpdate, which uses an XML document to provide the data used to *update* the Region table.

```
CREATE PROCEDURE RegionUpdate @xmlDoc NVARCHAR(4000) AS
DECLARE @docIndex INT
EXECUTE sp_xml_preparedocument @docIndex OUTPUT, @xmlDoc

UPDATE Region
SET Region.RegionDescription = XMLRegion.RegionDescription
FROM OPENXML(@docIndex, N'/Top/Region',1) WITH Region AS XMLRegion
WHERE Region.RegionID = XMLRegion.RegionID

EXECUTE sp_xml_removedocument @docIndex
```

The RegionUpdate stored procedure's UPDATE statement contains a FROM clause that uses OPENXML. The OPENXML function uses an XML document to generate a rowset containing the entries in the Region table to be updated. The values in the Region table are matched to the values specified in the OPENXML-generated rowset, XmlRegion, using the UPDATE statement's WHERE clause.

Using OPENXML with ADO.NET

So far, you've created three stored procedures that use OPENXML: RegionInsert, RegionUpdate, and RegionDelete. The OpenXMLDemo console application uses ADO.NET to demonstrate each of these stored procedure calls being executed.

The implementation of OpenXMLDemo contains a method called DemoOpenXML(). In it, you begin by creating a SqlCommand instance that's wired to the first stored procedure you want to execute, RegionInsert.

```
Const strConnection As String = _
    "Data Source=(local);Integrated Security=SSPI;Initial Catalog=Northwind"
```

```
Const strXMLDoc As String = _
    "<Top>" & _
      "<Region RegionID=""11"" RegionDescription=""Uptown""/>" & _
      "<Region RegionID=""22"" RegionDescription=""Downtown""/>" & _
    "</Top>"

Dim sqlConnection As New SqlConnection(strConnection)
Dim openXMLCommand As New SqlCommand("RegionInsert", sqlConnection)
openXMLCommand.CommandType = CommandType.StoredProcedure
```

Next, you create a parameter for this command's Parameters collection, setting its value to the XML document (strXMLDoc) that will be inserted using the RegionInsert stored procedure.

```
Dim xmlDocParm As SqlParameter = _
    openXMLCommand.Parameters.Add("@xmlDoc", SqlDbType.NVarChar, 4000)
xmlDocParm.Value = strXMLDoc
```

The ExecuteNonQuery() method of the openXMLCommand instance can now be called to insert the data. (ExecuteNonQuery() is a good choice here because RegionInsert only inserts data and does not return the results of a query.)

```
sqlConnection.Open()
openXMLCommand.ExecuteNonQuery()
```

The next stored procedure to demonstrate is RegionUpdate. To facilitate this, the data associated with the parameter (the XML document) is tweaked by changing each instance of the word "town" to "state" (so "Uptown" becomes "Upstate" and "Downtown" becomes "Downstate"), courtesy of the String class's Replace() method. Once the data is tweaked, the command's text is set to RegionUpdate and the command is executed using ExecuteNon-Query().

```
xmlDocParm.Value = strXMLDoc.Replace("town", "state")
openXMLCommand.CommandText = "RegionUpdate"
openXMLCommand.ExecuteNonQuery()
```

The remainder of DemoOpenXML() sets the command's text to the stored procedure that handles deletion, RegionDelete. Once this is set, ExecuteNonQuery() can work its magic again.

```
openXMLCommand.CommandText = "RegionDelete"
openXMLCommand.ExecuteNonQuery()

SqlConnection.Close()
```

The elegance of this technique is that VB.NET is blissfully unaware of how the XML document it passes to the stored procedure is eventually written to SQL Server. Ultimately, the stored procedure calls OPENXML, but ADO.NET neither knows nor cares what's going on under the covers.

SQLXML Managed Classes

As you've seen in the first part of this chapter, working with ADO.NET presents you with some powerful XML features that can be used when working with databases. However, the ability to use XML to access database information from SQL Server has been around for some time, in the form of the SQLXML COM library.

SQLXML, which is available at `http://msdn.microsoft.com/library/default.asp?url=/library/en-us/dnanchor/html/anch_SQLXML.asp`, is a set of components that were created to enable developers to work with XML rather than ADO.NET when querying SQL Server. You can create queries to select and update data in the database using pure XML, FOR XML, SQLXML templates, XPath, UpdateGrams and DiffGrams, and XSLT transformations, all of which we'll discuss in the following sections.

The SQLXML 3.0 managed classes actually use COM interoperability (a fully managed version is expected with the next release of SQL Server) to provide access to the unmanaged SQLXMLOLEDB provider, which is a COM DLL. You will get some performance hit when working with these classes, compared to the unmanaged classes (which do not have an interop layer to cross) or ADO.NET classes (which are fully managed).

SQLXML and ADO.Net?

Having said that, what reasons could you have for using SQLXML from .NET code—especially when ADO.NET has so many XML features? Most of the time, ADO.NET is the way to go, but you'll want to consider using SQLXML managed classes in the following conditions:

- You're migrating to the .NET Framework from a previous version that used SQLXML in unmanaged code. In this case, it will be easier simply to migrate the SQLXML code to .NET code, rather than rewrite everything in ADO.NET.

- You want to do client-side XML formatting, which is currently not available in ADO.NET.

- You want to represent multidimensional table relations, as this cannot be done in ADO.NET.

Let's now look at the architecture of SQLXML and the managed classes, and begin to see how you might use them.

Architecture of SQLXML Managed Classes

The SQL Server .NET data provider is recommended when connecting to SQL Server databases from ADO.NET applications. When you're working with the SQLXML managed classes, however, the SQLOLEDB provider plays a major role. When XML queries get involved, this OLE DB provider also relies on Sqlxml3.dll, which performs the translation of XML to T-SQL statements. Furthermore, an extra provider called SQLXMLOLEDB implements features such as client-side formatting, but again uses the SQLOLEDB provider to actually interact with SQL Server.

The SQLXMLOLEDB provider actually pre-parses the submitted XML on the client and converts it to pure T-SQL, so that only SQL code is ever submitted to SQL Server. The rowset that's returned from SQL Server is formatted back into XML on the client by the same provider.

Obviously, this makes it essential that the SQL client machine should have the SQL client libraries installed, and that the SQLXMLOLEDB provider (and underlying SQLOLEDB provider) is available.

Figure 12-3 shows how SQLXML is used in managed classes with these providers. Each step is numbered and discussed here.

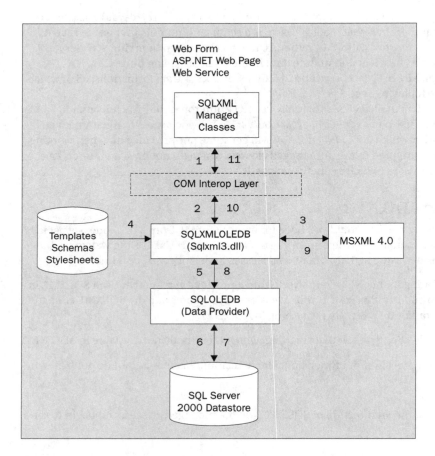

Figure 12-3. *How SQLXML fits into the picture*

1. One of the SQLXML managed classes is used in a .NET application, and a method is invoked. The call must cross an interop boundary from the .NET Framework to a COM environment.

2. The SQLXMLOLEDB provider (SqlXml3.dll) interprets the SQLXML query.

3. The XML of the query is interpreted, and the MSXML 4.0 is used to convert the XML to a T-SQL query.

4. Any templates or schemas that may be required are loaded and used during the conversion process.

5. The resultant T-SQL query is sent to the SQLOLEDB provider, which actually performs the job of interfacing with SQL Server.

6. The T-SQL query is sent to SQL Server 2000 data store.

7. The resultant rowset or XML from the query (there may be server-side XML conversion) is returned to the SQLOLEDB provider.

8. The rowset or XML is returned to the SQLXMLOLEDB layer.

9. The rowset may require conversion to XML and/or an XSL transformation. The MSXML 4.0 is used in this process.

10. The result of the conversion is sent back to the client.

11. The result goes back into the managed environment and is interpreted by the SQLXML managed classes on the client.

The SQLXML Object Model

Now that you understand a little about the architecture, it's time to look at how to use these managed classes. To access them at all, you need to install SQLXML 3.0 SP1 from the URL provided at the start of this section: http://msdn.microsoft.com/library/default.asp?url=/library/en-us/dnanchor/html/anch_SQLXML.asp.

The SQLXML managed classes themselves are implemented in the Microsoft.Data.SqlXml.dll assembly (typically located in the C:\Program Files\SQLXML 3.0\ bin folder). If you're using Visual Studio .NET, you'll need to add a reference to this assembly before you can use the following four classes it contains:

- SqlXmlCommand

- SqlXmlParameter

- SqlXmlAdapter

- SqlXmlException

The SqlXmlCommand Object

A SqlXmlCommand object is similar to an ADO.NET SqlCommand object, but it's used for working with SQLXML in SQL Server. As you'll see, however, the SqlXmlCommand class is slightly more useful in certain scenarios.

The first is that it can be used to make the SQL client do more work, rather than pushing the load onto the SQL Server. When you perform a FOR XML query using the SqlCommand class, the work of transforming the selected rowset into XML format is done in the SQL Server process on the database. When you use a SqlXmlCommand object and FOR XML, you have the option of saying that you want this process to occur on the middle tier, and hence reduce the load on your database.

Furthermore, the SqlXmlCommand class allows you to write the result to a new or existing stream instance (a class derived from the System.IO.Stream class), an option that's not available in ADO.NET. Table 12-4 displays the properties of the SqlXmlCommand.

Table 12-4. SqlXmlCommand *Properties*

Property	Description
BasePath	Contains a directory path or base URL that relative filenames can be resolved from. So if you specify the XSLPath to be a.xsl, and the BasePath to be http://localhost/, then the fully resolved path will be http://localhost/a.xsl.
ClientSideXml	When set to True, this indicates that the rowset returned from SQL Server should be converted to XML in the client process. By default, the conversion is done on the SQL Server.
CommandStream	Contains a stream (such as a file) that contains a query to be executed.
CommandText	Allows you to set the XML query to be executed.
CommandType	One of the SqlXmlCommandType enumeration values, which can be Sql, XPath, Template, TemplateFile, UpdateGram, or DiffGram.
Namespaces	Allows qualified XPath queries to be made. This is needed when the XML document contains namespaces, and you want to select a node from one of them.
OutputEncoding	Allows you to specify the encoding of the XML that is output and sets the encoding attribute on the XML declaration (such as encoding="UTF-8").
RootTag	Allows you to specify a root XML element that will wrap the XML returned from the query. This is especially important where the XML that is returned doesn't have a root element (a list of "row" elements, for example).
SchemaPath	Similar to the XslPath property, but used for XML schema files.
XslPath	Specifies the absolute or relative path to an XSL file. If a relative path is used, the BasePath is used to get the full path to the file.

Table 12-5 displays the various methods of SqlXmlCommand.

Table 12-5. SqlXmlCommand *Methods*

Method	Description
ClearParameters()	Clears all parameters that have been bound to the command—useful when you want to reuse the command instance with new parameters.
CreateParameter()	Returns an instance of a new parameter object that can have its name and value set, and will be passed to the command.
ExecuteNonQuery()	Simply executes the query and returns nothing—useful for update and delete queries.
ExecuteStream()	Executes the query and returns the resulting XML as an instance of a stream object.
ExecuteToStream(Stream)	Similar to ExecuteStream(), except that it will output the resulting XML to the existing stream instance that's passed as an argument.
ExecuteXmlReader()	Executes the query and returns the result in an XMLReader instance.

Now that you know what methods and properties are available, let's look at how they can be used. First, you create a new instance of the SqlXmlCommand object by passing the SQLOLEDB connection string to construct the object as follows (using the SQL Server Northwind database):

```
Dim strConnection As String = _
                "Provider=SQLOLEDB;Data Source=(local);" & _
                "Integrated Security=SSPI;Initial Catalog=Northwind"
Dim sqlxmlcommand As New SqlXmlCommand(strConnection)
```

You can specify the SQLXML query to execute in two ways. The first is to set the CommandText property to the query string.

```
sqlxmlcommand.CommandText = "SELECT * FROM Customers FOR XML AUTO"
```

Alternatively, you may use the CommandStream property to set a stream instance where the query to be executed is stored. In the following case, you use the file employees.xml to get the query, which must be a Template, an UpdateGram, or a DiffGram (you'll see how these work shortly):

```
Dim employeesFile As New FileStream("employees.xml", FileMode.Open)
sqlxmlcommand.CommandStream = employeesFile
```

The final parameter that should be set is CommandType, which takes one of the enumeration values discussed previously and determines the type of query to be made. In the current case, you're executing a pure SQL-based query, so you set this as follows:

```
sqlxmlcommand.CommandType = SqlCommandType.Sql
```

When this is run from the SQLXML example in the code download, the following XML will be returned (edited for clarity):

```
<products ProductID="1" ProductName="Chai" SupplierID="1"
          CategoryID="1" QuantityPerUnit="10 boxes x 20 bags" UnitPrice="18"
          UnitsInStock="39" UnitsOnOrder="0" ReorderLevel="10"
          Discontinued="0" />
<products ProductID="2" ProductName="Chang" SupplierID="1"
          CategoryID="1" QuantityPerUnit="24 - 12 oz bottles" UnitPrice="19"
          UnitsInStock="17" UnitsOnOrder="40" ReorderLevel="25"
          Discontinued="0" />
...
```

Example of Client-side XML Processing

In this example, you'll see how the conversion from rowset to XML can be moved from the database to the client process. The code is shown as follows:

```
Dim cmd As New SqlXmlCommand( _
                "Provider=SQLOLEDB;Data Source=(local);" & _
                "Integrated Security=SSPI;Initial Catalog=Northwind")
cmd.CommandText = "SELECT * FROM Customers FOR XML NESTED"
cmd.ClientSideXml = True
```

```
cmd.RootTag = "CustomerData"
cmd.OutputEncoding = "utf-16"

Dim rdr As XmlTextReader = cmd.ExecuteXmlReader()
rdr.MoveToContent()

While rdr.ReadState <> ReadState.EndOfFile
  TextBox1.Text = rdr.ReadOuterXml()
End While

rdr.Close()
```

Here you use a nested XML format and set the `ClientSideXml` property to `True`, so that you can customize the XML output from the query. Then, you wrap the XML in a `<CustomerData>` root element by setting the `RootTag` property. After that, you encode the output in UTF-16 by setting the `OutputEncoding` property appropriately.

Now when the `ExecuteXmlReader()` method of the command class is executed, an `XmlText-Reader` instance is returned. You use its `MoveToContent()` method to move to the root element of the returned XML document, and then employ the `ReadState` property to read through the results. You output the XML content of the document by writing it to a text box, and then close the text reader. When this code is executed, the following is output:

```
<CustomerData>
  <Customers CustomerID="ALFKI"
             CompanyName="Alfreds Futterkiste"
             ContactName="Maria Anders" ContactTitle="Sales Representative"
             Address="Obere Str. 57"
             City="Berlin" PostalCode="12209"
             Country="Germany" Phone="030-0074321" Fax="030-0076545" />
  <Customers CustomerID="ANATR"
             CompanyName="Ana Trujillo Emparedados y helados"
             ContactName="Ana Trujillo" ContactTitle="Owner"
             Address="Avda. de la Constitución 2222"
             City="México D.F." PostalCode="05021"
             Country="Mexico" Phone="(5) 555-4729" Fax="(5) 555-3745" />
  ...

</CustomerData>
```

Working with XSL Transforms

Next, you'll look at how you can transform the results of a SQL Server query to HTML format using an XSL transform. The following code will add this functionality to the example you were working with previously:

```vb
Dim cmd As New SqlXmlCommand( _
                "Provider=SQLOLEDB;Data Source=(local);" & _
                "Integrated Security=SSPI;Initial Catalog=Northwind")
cmd.CommandText = "SELECT * from Customers FOR XML NESTED"
cmd.ClientSideXml = True
cmd.RootTag = "CustomerData"

cmd.CommandType = SqlXmlCommandType.Sql
cmd.XslPath = "trans.xsl"
cmd.BasePath = "http://localhost/"

' Create stream for result XML
Dim ms As MemoryStream = cmd.ExecuteStream()

' Read the data from that stream and insert into text box
Dim sr As New StreamReader(ms)
TextBox1.Text = sr.ReadToEnd()
' Create HTML file to store the result of the transform
Dim fileStream As New FileStream( _
                "CustomerData.htm", FileMode.OpenOrCreate, FileAccess.Write)

' Write the data from the stream to the file
ms.WriteTo(fileStream)

' Close the streams
fileStream.Close()
sr.Close()
ms.Close()
```

Before you see the results, let's look through the code so that you understand what's happening. Once again, you create a command object and configure its CommandText, ClientSideXml, and RootTag properties. The next two lines then allow you to apply the transform to the XML that's returned from the query.

The XslPath property defines a path relative to the value in BasePath, where the XSL to be used to transform the XML can be found. In your case, the stylesheet trans.xsl should be placed in the root directory of the local web server, so you set the XslPath and BasePath properties as shown here.

```vb
cmd.XslPath = "trans.xsl"
cmd.BasePath = "http://localhost/"
```

Following this, you want to do two things. First, you'll write the result of the transformation to a text box, so that you can see the HTML that was output. Second, you're going to create an HTML file and write the result to that, so you can view it in a browser. You start by executing the SQLXML query and sending the result to a MemoryStream instance.

```vb
Dim ms As MemoryStream = cmd.ExecuteStream()
```

Next, a `StreamReader` instance is used to read the data from the stream in memory, and the result is written to a text box.

```
Dim sr As StreamReader = New StreamReader(ms)
TextBox1.Text = sr.ReadToEnd()
```

Last, you create an HTML file called CustomerData.htm using a `FileStream` instance, using the `MemoryStream`'s `WriteTo()` method.

```
Dim fileStream As New FileStream( _
              "CustomerData.htm", FileMode.OpenOrCreate, FileAccess.Write)
ms.WriteTo(fileStream)
```

After this step, the various stream instances that you created in the course of your processing are all closed. The XSL document that converts the XML output to HTML, trans.xsl, is shown here.

```xml
<?xml version="1.0" encoding="UTF-8"?>
<xs:stylesheet version="1.0"
                xmlns:xs="http://www.w3.org/1999/XSL/Transform">

  <xs:template match="/">
    <html>
      <head><title>Customer Data</title></head>
      <body bgcolor="lightblue">
        <xs:apply-templates select="CustomerData" />
      </body>
    </html>
  </xs:template>

  <xs:template match="CustomerData">
    <table>
      <tr align="left">
        <th>Company Name</th>
        <th>Contact Name</th>
        <th>Country</th>
      </tr>
      <xs:apply-templates select="Customers">
        <xs:sort select="@Country" />
        <xs:sort select="@CompanyName" />
      </xs:apply-templates>
    </table>
  </xs:template>

  <xs:template match="Customers">
    <tr>
      <td>
```

```
        <xs:value-of select="@CompanyName" />
      </td>
      <td>
        <xs:value-of select="@ContactName" />
      </td>
      <td>
        <xs:value-of select="@Country" />
      </td>
    </tr>
  </xs:template>
</xs:stylesheet>
```

The first section of the stylesheet will match the document root, so you create the outline of the HTML document and then use the `<apply-templates>` element to tell the processor to find any elements called `<CustomerData>` and process the matching template for this element.

```
<xs:template match="/">
  <html>
    <head><title>Customer Data</title></head>
    <body bgcolor="lightblue">
      <xs:apply-templates select="CustomerData" />
    </body>
  </html>
</xs:template>
```

The template that matches `<CustomerData>` elements creates a table element with three headings for the columns you want to display.

```
<xs:template match="CustomerData">
  <table>
    <tr align="left">
      <th>Company Name</th>
      <th>Contact Name</th>
      <th>Country</th>
    </tr>
```

Before you close the table, you apply a template that finds any `<Customers>` elements and uses the XSL `<sort>` element to sort by the Country and then the CompanyName attributes.

```
    <xs:apply-templates select="Customers">
      <xs:sort select="@Country" />
      <xs:sort select="@CompanyName" />
    </xs:apply-templates>
  </table>
</xs:template>
```

Finally, there's a template for `<Customers>` elements that creates a new table row for each such element, and writes the values of the relevant attributes to the appropriate column in the row.

```
<xsl:template match="Customers">
  <tr>
    <td>
      <xs:value-of select="@CompanyName" />
    </td>
    <td>
      <xs:value-of select="@ContactName" />
    </td>
    <td>
      <xs:value-of select="@Country" />
    </td>
  </tr>
</xs:template>
```

When you run this code, you will get the following output:

```
<html>
<head>
<META http-equiv="Content-Type" content="text/html; charset=utf-8">
<title>Customer Data</title></head>
<body bgcolor="lightblue">
<table>
<tr align="left">
<th>Company Name</th>
<th>Contact Name</th>
<th>Country</th>
</tr>
<tr>
<td>Cactus Comidas para llevar</td>
<td>Patricio Simpson</td>
<td>Argentina</td>
</tr>
<tr>
<td>Océano Atlántico Ltda.</td>
<td>Yvonne Moncada</td>
<td>Argentina</td>

...

</table>
</body>
</html>
```

If you open the CustomerData.htm file in Internet Explorer, you should see the screen represented in Figure 12-4.

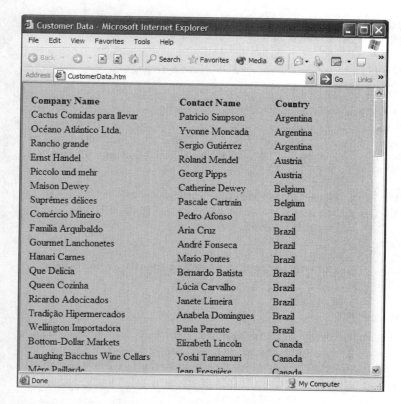

Figure 12-4. *CustomerData.htm in Internet Explorer*

The SqlXmlParameter Object

Beyond the simple queries you've looked at so far, commonly you will want to pass one or more parameters, so let's look at how the SQLXML managed classes allow this. Objects of the SqlXmlParameter class have two properties.

- Name is used to specify the name of the parameter, as it appears in the query.

- Value is the value to associate with this parameter.

So if you wished to extend your earlier example to return only those products that start with the letter Z, you could do so as follows:

```
Dim strConnection As String = _
                "Provider=SQLOLEDB;Data Source=(local);" & _
                "Integrated Security=SSPI;Initial Catalog=Northwind"
Dim sqlxmlcommand As New SqlXmlCommand(strConnection)

sqlxmlcommand.CommandText = _
        "SELECT * FROM Products WHERE ProductName LIKE ? FOR XML AUTO"
```

```
Dim sqlxmlparam As SqlXmlParameter = sqlxmlcommand.CreateParameter()
sqlxmlparam.Value = "Z%"

Dim employeesFile As New FileStream("employees.xml", FileMode.Open)
sqlxmlcommand.CommandStream = employeesFile
```

The query you've set in the CommandText property allows for a single parameter, and then a new SqlXmlParameter is created using the CreateParameter() method of the SqlXmlCommand instance. The Value property of the SqlXmlParameter is set to Z%, matching products where the value in the ProductName column starts with a Z. When this is run, the following XML will be returned:

```
<products ProductID="47" ProductName="Zaanse koeken" SupplierID="22"
          CategoryID="3" QuantityPerUnit="10 - 4 oz boxes" UnitPrice="9.5"
          UnitsInStock="36" UnitsOnOrder="0" ReorderLevel="0"
          Discontinued="0" />
```

Let's look at an example of how you can use templates and parameters to improve the flexibility of your SQLXML queries.

Using Templates and Parameters

The SQL queries you've used so far have been defined inline with the code, and although parameters give you a bit more flexibility in the query that's sent to SQL Server, it would be better if you could separate entirely the SQL from the code, and host that in a separate file. This would provide for a more flexible architecture, promote reuse of XML query formats (which also improves deployment time), and perhaps even improve performance.

SQLXML provides this functionality through the use of *templates*, which allow you to create an XML document containing the details of the query that can then be passed to the command object and processed normally.

The following template allows you to define a query that selects products with a ProductName similar to the string that's passed in as a parameter:

```
<ROOT xmlns:sql='urn:schemas-microsoft-com:xml-sql'>
  <sql:header>
    <sql:param name="ProductName" />
  </sql:header>
  <sql:query>
    SELECT * FROM Products WHERE ProductName LIKE @ProductName FOR XML AUTO
  </sql:query>
</ROOT>
```

The parameters must be defined in the <header> section (this is optional if you have no parameters), with a <param> element *with a suitable name* representing each one. (In your case, ProductName is the name of the parameter.) The query to be executed is defined in the <query> element; it's a normal SQL query with the name of each parameter included in the form @ParamName.

How does this change your code? The new version is shown here.

```
Dim strConnection As String = _
                  "Provider=SQLOLEDB;Data Source=(local);" & _
                  "Integrated Security=SSPI;Initial Catalog=Northwind"

Dim xmlquery As New FileStream("../FindProducts.xml", FileMode.Open)

Dim sqlxmlcommand As New SqlXmlCommand(strConnection)

sqlxmlcommand.CommandStream = xmlquery
sqlxmlcommand.CommandType = SqlXmlCommandType.Template

Dim sqlxmlparam As SqlXmlParameter = sqlxmlcommand.CreateParameter()
sqlxmlparam.Name = "@ProductName"
sqlxmlparam.Value = "Z%"

Dim sr As New StreamReader(sqlxmlcommand.ExecuteStream())
TextBox1.Text = sr.ReadToEnd()
sr.Close ()
```

Now, you have to load the XML template file from the filesystem; you use the `FileStream` class to do this. After that, you set this stream as the input to the command using the `CommandStream` property, and set the `CommandType` property to `Template` rather than `Sql`.

Next, you have to arrange to pass the parameter to the query, but unless you give it a name, it won't work. You called the parameter `ProductName` in the template XML file, so that's what you use here. Again, you set the `Value` property, execute the query, and write the result to the text box. The result when this is run is shown in the following code:

```
<ROOT xmlns:sql="urn:schemas-microsoft-com:xml-sql">
  <products ProductID="47" ProductName="Zaanse koeken" SupplierID="22"
            CategoryID="3" QuantityPerUnit="10 - 4 oz boxes" UnitPrice="9.5"
            UnitsInStock="36" UnitsOnOrder="0" ReorderLevel="0"
            Discontinued="0" />
</ROOT>
```

This is almost the same result as the last query, but this time it's wrapped in a `<ROOT>` element that's added automatically when you're working with templates. If you wanted to get back the XML without this element, you'd do better to load the result into an `XmlReader` instance. This would require you to modify the last three lines of the previous code and replace them with the following:

```
Dim rdr As XmlTextReader
rdr = sqlxmlcommand.ExecuteXmlReader()
rdr.MoveToContent()
TextBox1.Text = rdr.ReadInnerXml()
rdr.Close()
```

If you make these changes and run the code, the following will once again be output:

```
<products ProductID="47" ProductName="Zaanse koeken" SupplierID="22"
          CategoryID="3" QuantityPerUnit="10 - 4 oz boxes" UnitPrice="9.5"
          UnitsInStock="36" UnitsOnOrder="0" ReorderLevel="0"
          Discontinued="0" />
```

Updating with an UpdateGram

At some stage, you're going to want to update data that's been modified on the client. In SQLXML, this is typically performed using an UpdateGram when you create the update XML document yourself, but the way the SqlXmlAdapter object has been implemented means it will use the DiffGram format, as featured in ADO.NET.

An UpdateGram is very useful for operating in distributed systems and applications that can't use ADO.NET (or even the managed classes—Java applications, perhaps), because you can use HTTP and a web server to make updates to the database. An UpdateGram can be created as an XML message and sent to a .NET application that can then use the SQLXML managed classes to update SQL Server.

The following XML file is an example of an UpdateGram that could be used to update a product with an ID of 2:

```
<ROOT xmlns:updg='urn:schemas-microsoft-com:xml-updategram'>
  <updg:sync>
    <updg:before>
      <Products ProductID='2' ProductName='Chang' />
    </updg:before>
    <updg:after>
      <Products ProductName='My New Name' />
    </updg:after>
  </updg:sync>
</ROOT>
```

The UpdateGram namespace must be specified in the root of the document, and in this case it's associated with the updg prefix. The root element is the <sync> element that says you want a synchronization to take place with "before" and "after" data definitions, and contains the specific details of the modifications you want to make.

On this occasion, you want to update the data in the column where the ProductID is 2 and the ProductName is "Chang", so you place that information in the <before> element. The containing element for this information has the same name as the table you want to select from (Products), and the attributes you specify effectively form an AND clause in the SQL statement. If any of them cause the query to return no rows, a SqlXmlException is thrown. In this case, if the ProductName were "Chong", you'd get an exception.

The new value of the row(s) that you select should be specified in the <after> element, and again you use a child element with the same name as the table you want to update, and use attributes to indicate the new values. You want to change the ProductName column, so you specify that as an attribute.

The code to perform the update that uses this UpdateGram is shown here.

```
Dim strConnection As String = _
                    "Provider=SQLOLEDB;Data Source=(local);" & _
                    "Integrated Security=SSPI;Initial Catalog=Northwind"

Dim xmlquery As New FileStream("../UpdateGram.xml", FileMode.Open)

Dim sqlxmlcommand As New SqlXmlCommand(strConnection)

sqlxmlcommand.CommandStream = xmlquery
sqlxmlcommand.CommandType = SqlXmlCommandType.UpdateGram

sqlxmlcommand.ExecuteNonQuery()
xmlquery.Close()
```

The `UpdateGram` that's stored in an XML file called UpdateGram.xml is loaded into a `FileStream` instance, and this is set as the value of the `CommandStream` property. The `CommandType` property then has to be set to `UpdateGram`, and finally the `ExecuteNonQuery()` method of the `SqlXmlCommand` object is called. When complete, the `FileStream` is closed.

If you check the `Products` table of the `Northwind` database before executing this code, you'll see the product you want to update in the second row of Figure 12-5.

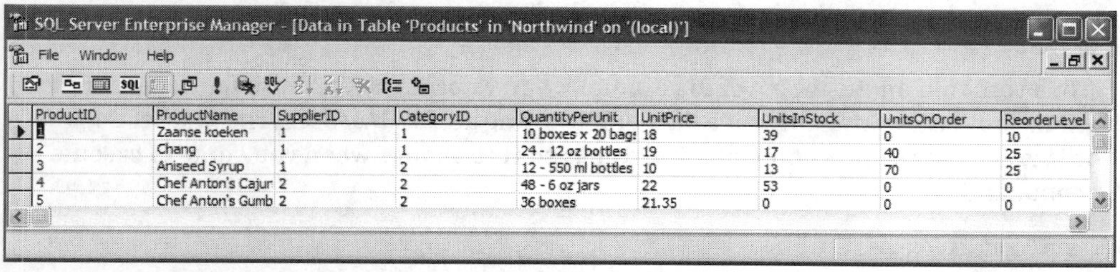

ProductID	ProductName	SupplierID	CategoryID	QuantityPerUnit	UnitPrice	UnitsInStock	UnitsOnOrder	ReorderLevel
1	Zaanse koeken	1	1	10 boxes x 20 bag	18	39	0	10
2	Chang	1	1	24 - 12 oz bottles	19	17	40	25
3	Aniseed Syrup	1	2	12 - 550 ml bottles	10	13	70	25
4	Chef Anton's Cajur	2	2	48 - 6 oz jars	22	53	0	0
5	Chef Anton's Gumb	2	2	36 boxes	21.35	0	0	0

Figure 12-5. `Products` *table before your update*

If you now run this code and refresh the SQL view, you should see that the update has been successful, as seen in Figure 12-6.

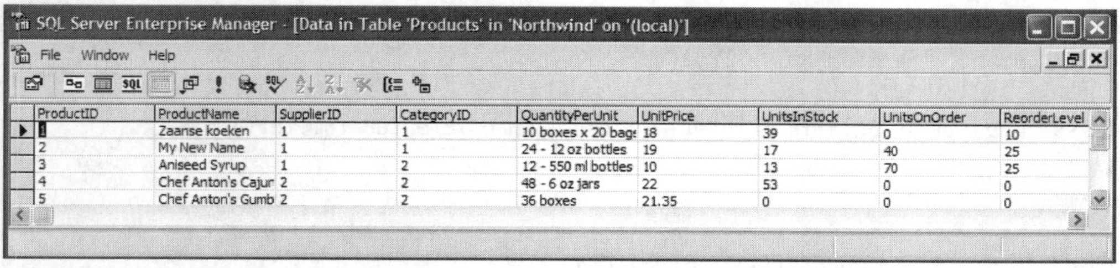

ProductID	ProductName	SupplierID	CategoryID	QuantityPerUnit	UnitPrice	UnitsInStock	UnitsOnOrder	ReorderLevel
1	Zaanse koeken	1	1	10 boxes x 20 bag	18	39	0	10
2	My New Name	1	1	24 - 12 oz bottles	19	17	40	25
3	Aniseed Syrup	1	2	12 - 550 ml bottles	10	13	70	25
4	Chef Anton's Cajur	2	2	48 - 6 oz jars	22	53	0	0
5	Chef Anton's Gumb	2	2	36 boxes	21.35	0	0	0

Figure 12-6. `Products` *table after your update*

The SqlXmlAdapter Object

The SqlXmlAdapter object is similar to ADO.NET's data adapter classes. It can be used to fill a DataSet with the results from a query, or to post back changes to the database when the DataSet is updated. There are three constructors that are used to initialize an instance of this object. The first takes a SqlXmlCommand instance as an argument, as follows:

SqlXmlAdapter(SqlXmlCommand)

The second constructor takes a string containing the query, the type of command specified in the first argument, and finally a connection string to connect to the data source.

SqlXmlAdapter(String, SqlXmlCommandType, String)

The final constructor uses a *stream* containing the command, rather than the *string* used in the previous code example.

SqlXmlAdapter(Stream, SqlXmlCommandType, String)

There are no properties and only two methods associated with this class, as follows:

- Fill(DataSet) allows you to fill the DataSet passed as an argument with the XML results retrieved from the query.

- Update(DataSet) is the inverse of the Fill(DataSet) method, and allows you to update the database with the data specified in the DataSet.

In a variation on the theme of the examples you've been looking at so far, you can put the XML you retrieve straight into a data grid by using a SqlXmlAdapter. The first section of code is exactly the same as previous, but things start to change when you come to execute the command.

```
Dim strConnection As String = _
                "Provider=SQLOLEDB;Data Source=(local);" & _
                "Integrated Security=SSPI;Initial Catalog=Northwind"

Dim xmlquery As New FileStream("../FindProducts.xml", FileMode.Open)

Dim sqlxmlcommand As New SqlXmlCommand(strConnection)
sqlxmlcommand.CommandStream = xmlquery
sqlxmlcommand.CommandType = SqlXmlCommandType.Template
sqlxmlcommand.ClientSideXml = True

Dim sqlxmlparam As SqlXmlParameter = sqlxmlcommand.CreateParameter()
sqlxmlparam.Name = "@ProductName"
sqlxmlparam.Value = "Z%"

Dim da As New SqlXmlAdapter(sqlxmlcommand)
Dim dsProducts As New DataSet()
da.Fill(dsProducts)
DataGrid1.DataSource = dsProducts.Tables("Products")
```

Rather than executing the command explicitly, a new SqlXmlAdapter is created, and the SqlXmlCommand object is passed as an argument to the constructor of this class. Following this, a DataSet is created, and the Fill() method of the SqlXmlAdapter class is used to execute the command and fill the DataSet with the results (see Figure 12-7). On the final line, you set the DataSource property of a data grid and fill it with the data from the Products table in the returned XML.

	ProductID	ProductName	SupplierID	CategoryID	QuantityPerU	UnitPrice	UnitsInStocl
▶	47	Zaanse koek	22	3	10 - 4 oz box	9.5	36
*							

Figure 12-7. *Sample results of* SqlXmlAdapter

Updating with XPath and a Schema

To make updates using the SqlXmlAdapter class, you must use XPath and a schema. In the schema, you map elements in the XML document that are returned from your query to equivalent tables and columns in a SQL Server database. This allows XPath to work on the XML data as elements and attributes, and the SQL Server client to map back to equivalent tables and columns in the SQL query that's passed to that database.

What does an XML schema look like for your tables? The schema that we've created for this sample is shown here—it's called Products.xsd, and it can be found in the SQLXML project in the code download.

```
<xs:schema xmlns:xs="http://www.w3.org/2001/XMLSchema"
           xmlns:sql="urn:schemas-microsoft-com:mapping-schema">

<!-- XML output we want to map
<products ProductID="47" ProductName="Zaanse koeken" SupplierID="22"
          CategoryID="3" QuantityPerUnit="10 - 4 oz boxes" UnitPrice="9.5"
          UnitsInStock="36" UnitsOnOrder="0" ReorderLevel="0"
          Discontinued="0" />
-->

  <xs:element name="products" sql:relation="Products">
    <xs:complexType>
      <xs:attribute name="ProductID"
                    sql:field="ProductID" type="xs:int" />
      <xs:attribute name="ProductName"
                    sql:field="ProductName" type="xs:string" />
      <xs:attribute name="SupplierID"
                    sql:field="SupplierID" type="xs:int" />
```

```
        <xs:attribute name="CategoryID"
                      sql:field="CategoryID" type="xs:int" />
        <xs:attribute name="QuantityPerUnit"
                      sql:field="QuantityPerUnit" type="xs:string" />
        <xs:attribute name="UnitPrice"
                      sql:field="UnitPrice" type="xs:decimal" />
        <xs:attribute name="UnitsInStock"
                      sql:field="UnitsInStock" type="xs:int" />
        <xs:attribute name="UnitsOnOrder"
                      sql:field="UnitsOnOrder" type="xs:int" />
        <xs:attribute name="ReorderLevel"
                      sql:field="ReorderLevel" type="xs:int" />
        <xs:attribute name="Discontinued"
                      sql:field="Discontinued" type="xs:int" />
      </xs:complexType>
    </xs:element>
</xs:schema>
```

You've seen plenty of schemas before, but because we've annotated this one with information specific to SQL Server, an additional namespace is defined on the root element: the namespace urn:schemas-microsoft-com:mapping-schema is mapped to the prefix sql.

```
<xs:schema xmlns:xs="http://www.w3.org/2001/XMLSchema"
           xmlns:sql="urn:schemas-microsoft-com:mapping-schema">
```

Next, the element that will represent the elements returned from your queries has been called <products> and the <sql:relation> attribute maps this to the Products table.

```
    <xs:element name="products" sql:relation="Products">
```

Now, you want to define the columns that are part of this table, and in this case you represent them as attributes on the <products> element. The relationship between the attribute name and the column name is made by using the name attribute and the sql:field attribute. With this schema in place, you can adapt your code to make use of it.

```
Dim strConnection As String = _
                   "Provider=SQLOLEDB;Data Source=(local);" & _
                   "Integrated Security=SSPI;Initial Catalog=Northwind"

Dim sqlxmlcommand As New SqlXmlCommand(strConnection)

sqlxmlcommand.CommandText = "products"
sqlxmlcommand.CommandType = SqlXmlCommandType.XPath
sqlxmlcommand.SchemaPath = "../Products.xsd"
sqlxmlcommand.ClientSideXml = True
sqlxmlcommand.RootTag = "ProductData"
Dim da As SqlXmlAdapter = New SqlXmlAdapter(sqlxmlcommand)
```

```
Dim dsProducts As New DataSet()
da.Fill(dsProducts)
DataGrid1.DataSource = dsProducts.Tables("products")
```

dsProducts.Tables("products").Rows(0).Item("ProductName")="Zaanse koeken 3"
da.Update(dsProducts)

The CommandText that's being set here is actually an XPath query against an XML document that conforms to the XML schema we defined previously. In your case, you select the <products> elements by setting the CommandText property to the string "products".

After setting the CommandType to XPath, you must then define a schema, which you do in the next line.

```
sqlxmlcommand.CommandType = SqlXmlCommandType.XPath
sqlxmlcommand.SchemaPath = "../Products.xsd"
```

The ClientSideXml property is set to True so that the work is done in the client process, and the RootTag property is set to "ProductData" to encapsulate the XML elements that are returned from the query.

After using a data adapter to fill a DataSet in the same way as you did it last time, you can prove that everything's working as it should by running the code without the last two lines of the previous listing (see Figure 12-8).

	CategoryID	Discontinued	ProductName	UnitPrice	ProductID	SupplierID	Quan ▲
▶	1	0	Zaanse koeken	18	1	1	10 bo:
	1	0	Chang	19	2	1	24 - 1
	2	0	Aniseed Syrup	10	3	1	12 - 5 ▼

Figure 12-8. *SQLXML solution, Adapter button in action*

The first of the two remaining lines updates the ProductName column of the first row of data in the data grid. Admittedly, the name you're changing to is not inspirational, but it illustrates the point:

```
dsProducts.Tables("products").Rows(0).Item("ProductName")="Zaanse koeken 2"
```

Finally, to persist these changes, you call the Update() method of the SqlXmlAdapter instance, passing in the updated DataSet.

```
da.Update(dsProducts)
```

In response to this instruction, the DataSet generates a DiffGram containing the data that has changed in the data grid. When the Update() method is called, the changes specified in the DiffGram are applied to the Products table. Figure 12-9 illustrates what's happening.

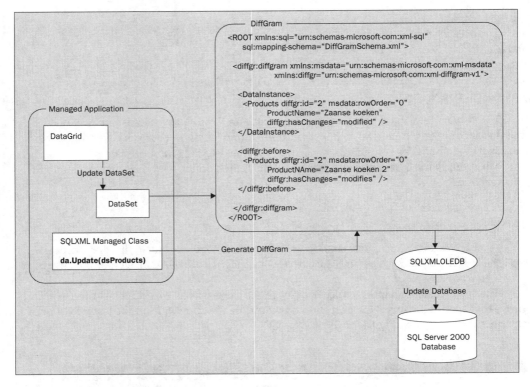

Figure 12-9. *SQLXML solution, Adapter button behind the scenes*

Executing this code will give the output shown in Figure 12-10.

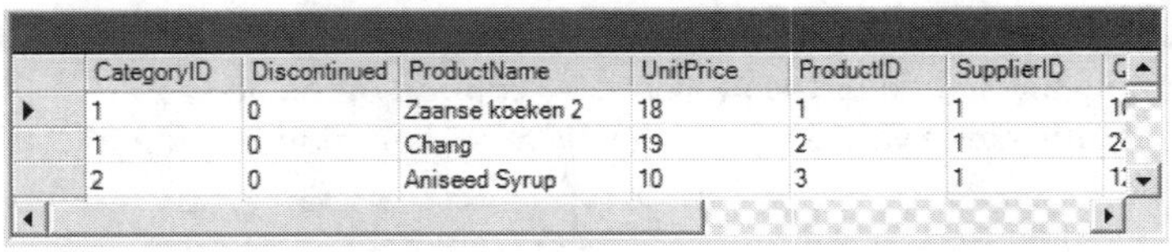

	CategoryID	Discontinued	ProductName	UnitPrice	ProductID	SupplierID	C
▶	1	0	Zaanse koeken 2	18	1	1	1
	1	0	Chang	19	2	1	2
	2	0	Aniseed Syrup	10	3	1	1

Figure 12-10. *SQLXML solution, Adapter button in action*

You can confirm that the update has actually taken place by checking the Products table of the Northwind database. Sure enough, the update was successful (see Figure 12-11).

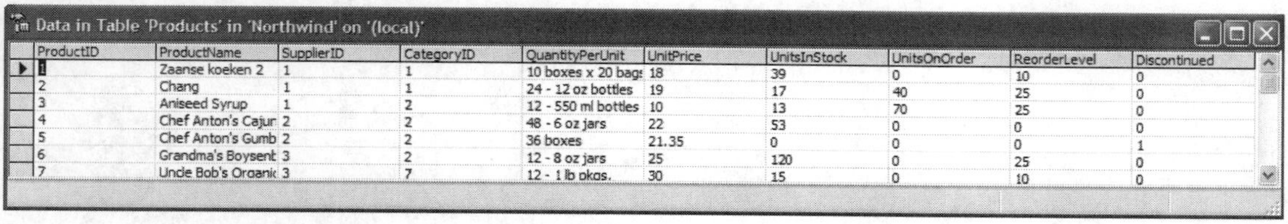

ProductID	ProductName	SupplierID	CategoryID	QuantityPerUnit	UnitPrice	UnitsInStock	UnitsOnOrder	ReorderLevel	Discontinued
1	Zaanse koeken 2	1	1	10 boxes x 20 bag:	18	39	0	10	0
2	Chang	1	1	24 - 12 oz bottles	19	17	40	25	0
3	Aniseed Syrup	1	2	12 - 550 ml bottles	10	13	70	25	0
4	Chef Anton's Cajur	2	2	48 - 6 oz jars	22	53	0	0	0
5	Chef Anton's Gumb	2	2	36 boxes	21.35	0	0	0	1
6	Grandma's Boysent	3	2	12 - 8 oz jars	25	120	0	25	0
7	Uncle Bob's Organic	3	7	12 - 1 lb pkgs.	30	15	0	10	0

Figure 12-11. *Confirming the update through Enterprise Manager*

Summary

Before the advent of SQL Server's `FOR XML` and `OPENXML`, a large amount of time was spent translating the results of queries to XML documents (the service provided by `FOR XML`) and translating XML documents to SQL statements (the services provided by `OPENXML`). In the first part of this chapter, you saw how the `FOR XML` and `OPENXML` features of SQL Server can be remarkable timesavers in the development process. They may seem to be a bit of SQL voodoo, but with practice you'll find that they'll give you more time to spend on the golf course!

In the second part of the chapter, you looked at the popular SQLXML technology, which was created as a COM library to allow people using COM and SQL Server to work with XML to perform queries and updates. The managed classes that provide a bridge from the managed .NET environment to the unmanaged COM implementation were covered in detail, and you looked at the `SqlXmlCommand`, `SqlXmlParameter`, `SqlXmlAdapter`, and `SqlXmlException` classes. You worked through numerous examples demonstrating how the SQLXML classes can be used, and learned when they're the best option even under .NET.

CHAPTER 13

■ ■ ■

Performance and Security

Once you've become accustomed to the basics of working with ADO.NET—using the `DataSet`, `DataAdapters`, SQL Client, and OLE DB data providers, and so on—you can focus more on some of the details generally left out of most overview texts on the subject. Among such details are performance and security issues.

In this chapter, you'll learn about the issues surrounding the creation of high-performance applications and components for use with ADO.NET in the .NET Framework, as well as issues concerning code and data security. Performance is a problem that plagues even the most well-designed and well-programmed solutions. In this chapter, you'll see how to take ADO.NET solutions and make them faster and more secure by using some optimization techniques, asynchronous execution, connection pooling, and various security technologies. By the time this chapter is complete, you should have a thorough understanding of the following topics:

- Various methods to optimize data access

- Connection pooling

- Message queuing

- Security issues and tradeoffs concerning data access

Optimizing Data Access

We all want our applications to run fast. That much should be a given for any programmer, on any project. Not too many of us have ever sat in on a design meeting in which people said, "Our application is fine the way it is, there's really nothing to be gained by making it faster." However, the unfortunate fact of life is that many of us have been in meetings where it was decided that it was too expensive in terms of time or money to improve an application's performance.

Traditionally, optimizing applications for the highest performance possible has often been a black art left to programmers who disappear into the basement for weeks at a time. However, this is changing with some of the features of ADO.NET and the .NET Framework. In the past, optimizing ADO for performance has been difficult, because so many of its components were multifaceted; using a component for one purpose often incurred performance overhead from another purpose, not currently being used. This is most obvious when looking at the classic ADO `Recordset`, which performs so many tasks that you often incur performance overhead from completely unrelated code just by using it.

This next section should give you an insight on some techniques and tips you can incorporate into your applications that will help speed them up, and keep code easy to read and maintain.

DataReader or DataSet?

The choice of whether to use a DataSet should be a fairly straightforward decision, provided you know enough about the type of data you need to access, and the ways in which you intend to process it. Unlike many multifaceted ADO components, both of these components have well-defined roles. As long as you know which roles each of these is designed for, you can choose the most effective solution for your needs. There are a number of major differences between these two components.

An important thing to keep in mind is that, regardless of which solution is *faster*, it doesn't necessarily mean that either component is *better*. Each is suited for a particular task, and each will excel at that task. Conversely, each will perform poorly (if at all) when used to perform a task it isn't suited for.

Memory Consumption

One of the main differences between the DataReader and the DataSet is that the DataReader consumes less memory than a DataSet. Depending on the amount of data and the memory resources available, the performance advantages associated with using less memory can be enormous. You will look at how best to handle large result sets later in the chapter.

A DataReader is an object that contains information on only *a single row of data* at a given time. What this means is that, regardless of the size of a result set, traversing this result set with a DataReader will only ever have a single record loaded in memory at a given time.

A DataSet, on the other hand, is designed specifically to be an in-memory cache of large amounts of data. In this regard, the DataSet will consume more memory than the DataReader.

To summarize, if you are tight on memory, then you should consider using a DataReader rather than a DataSet. However, if memory concerns are not at the top of your list of priorities, the increased functionality of an entirely disconnected in-memory data cache may suit your needs better.

Traversal Direction

Whenever you plan on traversing data for a particular task, you need to consider the direction of the traversal. Just as with ADO, you can reap enormous performance benefits if you know in advance exactly how you will need to access data.

If you plan on accessing data to do something simple, such as display all of the records in a result set in HTML form through an ASP.NET page, for instance, then the choice is simple. The DataReader is a read-only/forward-only component designed specifically for the task of reading and traversing data rapidly in a single direction. So, when looking at what an application is going to need to do with the data, if you don't need to be able to write changes to an in-memory cache, or if you won't need to have indexed access to any row at any given time, then the DataReader will definitely provide you with some performance benefits.

Note If you don't need to modify data, or access rows in random order, then you can probably gain a considerable performance advantage by using a `DataReader`.

Multiple Result Sets

Both the `DataReader` and the `DataSet` support the notion of multiple result sets. The `DataSet` supports this through using `Tables`. The `DataReader` enables you to access additional result sets by providing the `NextResult` method. Just as with row access with the `DataReader`, accessing additional result sets in the `DataReader` is a forward-only/read-only operation.

It is important to reiterate here that the `DataReader` will actually only hold one row of information at any given time. This means that even though ten different result sets may be available, only one row of any given result set will be available at any given time. Once a row has been passed in a `DataReader` traversal, that row is disposed of, and there is no way to retrieve it again without resetting the reader and starting over from the beginning.

For those of you who like using the `SHAPE` statement in your SQL statements to create hierarchical record sets, you can rest assure that you can still use this with the `DataReader`. Whereas in ADO you would set a `Recordset` object to the individual field object of a row, instead, you now set a `DataReader` object to the value of a column in the `DataReader` of the parent row.

There is plenty of information on the details of working with the `DataReader` component in Chapter 2, and information on using the `DataSet` object in Chapter 3.

Roundtrips

Any time you create an application designed for data access of any kind, one of the first things you learn is to keep roundtrips to the data source to an absolute minimum. Actually, hitting the database server for information should be considered a slow and expensive operation, which should be done sparingly. The reason for this is that while operating under minimum load, you may not notice anything, but when connection resources are in use for long periods of time in a heavily burdened application, you will encounter all sorts of problems, such as resource locks, resource contention, race conditions, and the dreaded command timeout.

Note Always strive to achieve the highest possible ratio of tasks to database roundtrips. The optimal situation is where more than one task is accomplished by a single database roundtrip.

Stored Procedures

Discussing stored procedures can be tricky. Many programmers will tell you that they don't buy you all that much. Others, especially database administrators, will tell you that stored procedures are the answer to all of your problems.

A programmer with an open mind and a stopwatch can probably tell you that the real answer is somewhere in between. Marathons are not won by runners with a great sprint speed, and 100-meter dashes are not won by endurance runners. The key to optimal performance when working with stored procedures is making sure that the task is given to the appropriate process.

One of the things mentioned about reducing roundtrips is to keep the ratio of tasks to database requests high. One way in which you can accomplish this is to use stored procedures. For example, consider an application that has to create a new order item in response to a customer purchase request. Once an item has been ordered, a table must be updated that reduces the available stock of that item by one. If the component created the order item, and then issued a SQL statement to reduce that item's stock quantity, that would result in two full roundtrips. However, if a stored procedure was invoked to purchase the item, the stored procedure could then automatically decrease its stock quantity without incurring the overhead and performance hit of performing another roundtrip between the component's process space and the database server. This roundtrip becomes painfully slow when the database server is not on the same physical machine as the component issuing the requests, and, of course, the more roundtrips incurred, the higher the network traffic, which can impact the perceived speed of your application.

One of the other benefits of stored procedures is that, in general, they are less prone to failure due to simple mistakes. For example, let's take the following simple example code snippet of how you might insert a record into the database manually with a standard SQL statement:

```
Dim strSQL As String = "INSERT INTO Books(UPC, Title, Price) " _
    & "VALUES('" & _UPC & "', '" & _Title & "', " & _Price & ")"
Connection.Execute(strSQL, RecordsAffected)
```

First of all, you're looking at an extremely ugly string concatenation. Not only is it extremely cumbersome to try to place the apostrophes in the right places, but because floating point values also support the ToString method, you won't get any type mismatch errors when you try to place a floating point value into a string field or vice versa. The other problem is that if the book's title happens to have an apostrophe in it somewhere, it will crash the statement execution. Therefore, you have to modify the previous SQL statement to replace all occurrences of apostrophes with two apostrophes to make sure they don't interfere with the statement parser. If you've ever done this kind of SQL work from ADO, you know that it gets very ugly, very quickly and becomes nightmarish to debug and maintain for large queries.

Alternatively, let's take a look at what performing the same task looks like when done with a stored procedure (this can also be performed using inline SQL and parameters, but we'll just show the stored procedure here).

```
Dim myCommand As SqlCommand = New SqlCommand("sp_InsertBook", myConnection)
myCommand.CommandType = CommandType.StoredProcedure
myCommand.Parameters.Add(New SqlParameter("@UPC", SqlDbType.VarChar, 30))
myCommand.Parameters.Add(new SqlParameter("@Title", SqlDbType.VarChar, 45))
myCommand.Parameters.Add(New SqlParameter("@Price", SqlDbType.Float))
myCommand.Parameters(0).Value = _UPC
myCommand.Parameters(1).Value = _Title
myCommand.Parameters(2).Value = _Price
RowsAffected = myCommand.ExecuteNonQuery()
```

This might actually take up more lines of code, but believe us it runs faster. Even if it didn't run faster, most programmers consider code that is easy to read and maintain far more useful than fast code. Just from looking at the code without a single comment in it, you know the data types of each of your arguments, you know that you're executing a stored procedure, and you know that you've deliberately told SQL to skip the overhead of attempting to return parameters. The other major gain, here, is that instead of potentially corrupting data with type mismatches for the previous SQL statement, you can be assured that a type mismatch in the stored procedure will throw an exception before data is committed to the database, and, if a transaction is active, it will be rolled back.

■**Note** In general, stored procedures are faster, more reliable, less error-prone, and more scalable than building SQL statement strings manually within your components.

A final concern is that building SQL queries from template text with variable content being inserted where appropriate (as per the previous simple example) is vulnerable to SQL insertion attack. If the variable content is taken directly from data entered by a user, it can be difficult to see exactly what the effects will be.

For example, instead of setting a `String` variable called `CustomerName` to a sensible string such as `"Richard Attenborough"`, it could be set to a string that effectively terminated the query you think you are running and executed a potentially dangerous stored procedure. Depending on the privileges granted to the current login, malicious users could cause considerable damage to data. Using parameterized queries, including stored procedures, can prevent this from happening since the parameters will be verified before being used.

Compiled Query Caching

One of the features of most RDBMSs available today that many people take for granted is the ability to compile and cache stored procedures and their results based on certain parameters. As an example, let's say that your application has several different pages that all retrieve customer order history. It is possible that instead of having your component (or ASP.NET page, or Windows Forms application) issue the SQL statement to retrieve the history directly, you could simply have the component issue a request for a stored procedure and retrieve the results faster.

This performance benefit comes from the fact that SQL Server can compile the stored procedure and actually cache various results for it in memory. This means that repeated calls to the same stored procedure for the same customer could actually retrieve cached results from memory. However, you should also keep in mind that the standard query processor that processes SQL strings sent from ADO and ADO.NET components can also compile and cache queries. The ultimate test will be wiring a test harness for both modes of operation (with or without stored procedures) to see which performs best in the conditions of your application.

Configuring DataAdapter Commands

As you've seen throughout this book, the DataAdapter is the plug that can transfer information from a data store to a DataSet, as well as transfer changes from the DataSet into the data store. In most examples of a DataAdapter, you'd probably see something like the following:

```
Dim MyDA As SqlDataAdapter = _
    New SqlDataAdapter("SELECT * FROM Table", MyConn)
```

What you don't see behind the scenes is this code populating one of the properties of the DataAdapter, the SelectCommand property. Each DataAdapter has four main objects that it holds to use for the four main operations that can be performed on data.

- InsertCommand

- SelectCommand

- UpdateCommand

- DeleteCommand

When an adapter is associated with a DataSet, and the DataSet invokes the Update method, the adapter is then asked to propagate any changes made (be they creates, deletes, updates, or inserts) across to the data source.

The problem is that it is all too easy to have another object do your work for you and create these commands on the fly. There are countless examples floating around in various books that recommend that you use the CommandBuilder objects (SqlCommandBuilder or OleDbCommand-Builder) to generate automatically the commands to perform the data update operations. While this may reduce the amount of code you have to write, chances are this won't help you in the long run, because there are many problems with using CommandBuilder related to performance and reliability.

The bottom line is that, in order to make sure that changes are carried across to the data source as fast as possible, you should be building your own commands for your adapters. Not only that, but in many cases the commands that are automatically built by the CommandBuilder might actually cause exceptions to be thrown, because the SQL generated is faulty.

Let's take a look at some code that takes a DataAdapter and links the CommandBuilder object to it. The way the CommandBuilder object works is by building the appropriate command object as needed. So, if you have a DataAdapter that has a SelectCommand, when the DataSet invokes the Update method, the CommandBuilder object will generate commands that it deems appropriate for the intended operations. The conflict arises when the command the builder deems appropriate is either inefficient or nonfunctional.

Here is the source listing for your code that links a CommandBuilder to a DataAdapter and then prints out what the CommandBuilder thinks is an appropriate UpdateCommand.

The project containing this code is called DACommands, and this module is found in the file CommandBuilderSample.vb. (You can find the code samples for this chapter in the Downloads section of the Apress Web site [http://www.apress.com].)

```
Imports System
Imports System.Data
```

```
Imports System.Data.SqlClient

Module CommandBuilderSample

    Sub Main()
        Dim MyDS As DataSet = New DataSet()
        Dim Connection As SqlConnection = New SqlConnection( _
            "Data Source=(local); Initial Catalog=Northwind; " _
            & "Integrated Security=SSPI;")
        Connection.Open()

        Dim MyDA As SqlDataAdapter = New SqlDataAdapter( _
                "SELECT * FROM [Order Details] OD", Connection)
```

Here is the code that creates a new CommandBuilder based on the instance of our DataAdapter. It works by inferring what it thinks should be reasonable commands based on whatever information is available to it already.

```
        Dim myBuilder As SqlCommandBuilder = New SqlCommandBuilder(MyDA)

        Console.WriteLine(myBuilder.GetUpdateCommand().CommandText)
    End Sub

End Module
```

Much to our chagrin, Figure 13-1 shows the SQL Update command produced by the "automatic" CommandBuilder.

Figure 13-1. DACommands, *output of the* CommandBuilderSample

What's the first thing you notice about this query? Well, one of the most obvious things about the query is that its WHERE clause is needlessly large. Essentially, what is happening is that the CommandBuilder is assuming that the DataSet will provide the DataAdapter two *states* of data—an original state and a new state. So, parameters 1 through 5 indicate the *new* state and are the arguments to the SET clause. Parameters 6 through 13 indicate the *original* state of the row and are used to locate the row in the database on which to perform the update. This is the way the CommandBuilder will always function, because it cannot make any assumptions about the underlying data source.

What kind of performance would you be looking at if none of the other fields were indexed, some of the fields were memos (SQL Text data type), and the table consisted of a few thousand rows? The situation would be grim to the say the least. You know that the OrderID column and ProductID column combine to form the unique row indicator for that table. Therefore, you could build your own UpdateCommand that only required the *original state* OrderID and ProductID and it would be far more efficient than the automatically generated version.

The other problem with this automatically generated command is that it contains update columns for the OrderID and ProductID columns. Together, these two columns form the primary key for this table. We're sure you know by now that you cannot use an UPDATE command to modify the values of autoincrement columns. If you execute your UpdateCommand generated by the CommandBuilder against the Northwind database, an exception will be thrown, indicating that you cannot modify the values of a primary key column.

One other reason for manually building your own commands instead of using the Command-Builder is that you can indicate to the DataAdapter that it should use a stored procedure for an operation instead of an inline SQL command.

To show an example of building your own command object for a DataAdapter for a stored procedure, you'll create a console application called DACommands2, with a module file called CommandSample.vb as follows:

```
Imports System
Imports System.Data
Imports System.Data.SqlClient

Module CommandSample

    Sub Main()
        Dim MyDS As DataSet = New DataSet()
        Dim Connection As SqlConnection = New SqlConnection( _
            "Data Source=(local); Initial Catalog=Northwind; " _
            & "Integrated Security=SSPI;")
        Connection.Open()
```

Rather than providing a simple SQL SELECT statement in the constructor to the DataAdapter object, you'll instead create a new command entirely, setting its type to Command-Type.StoredProcedure. Once you have that, you can define parameters just as you normally would. In your case, we're providing the arguments ourselves to indicate the 1996 annual sales for the "Sales by Year" stored procedure that comes with the Northwind database (we're using the copy that comes with SQL Server 2000).

```
        Dim MyDA As SqlDataAdapter = New SqlDataAdapter()
        MyDA.SelectCommand = New SqlCommand("Sales by Year", Connection)
        MyDA.SelectCommand.CommandType = CommandType.StoredProcedure
        MyDA.SelectCommand.Parameters.Add(New SqlParameter("@Beginning_Date", _
            SqlDbType.DateTime))
```

```
MyDA.SelectCommand.Parameters("@Beginning_Date").Value = _
    DateTime.Parse("01/01/1996")

MyDA.SelectCommand.Parameters.Add(New SqlParameter("@Ending_Date", _
    SqlDbType.DateTime))
MyDA.SelectCommand.Parameters("@Ending_Date").Value = _
    DateTime.Parse("01/01/1997")
```

Here, you might be looking for some kind of "execute" method to be called on the stored procedure command we created. This is actually done behind the scenes for you when the Fill method is called on the DataAdapter.

```
MyDA.Fill(MyDS, "SalesByYear")
```

Here, you're iterating through each of the columns programmatically and displaying them to further illustrate the point that even though you used a stored procedure to obtain your records in the DataAdapter, the DataSet has been populated with a full schema.

```
Dim _Column As DataColumn
Dim tabChar = Chr(9)
For Each _Column In MyDS.Tables("SalesByYear").Columns
    Console.Write("{0}" & tabChar, _Column.ColumnName)
Next
Console.WriteLine()
Console.WriteLine( _
    "-------------------------------------------------------")

Dim _Row As DataRow
For Each _Row In MyDS.Tables("SalesByYear").Rows
    For Each _Column In MyDS.Tables("SalesByYear").Columns
        Console.Write("{0}" & tabChar, _Row(_Column))
    Next
    Console.WriteLine()
Next
End Sub

End Module
```

Figure 13-2 is a screenshot of the console output generated by this program. The output on its own isn't entirely impressive; however, if you compile the sample and run it, and then run it again over and over again (Up arrow/Enter is good for this), you'll notice that, beyond the initial execution, it runs *really* fast. This is because (if configured properly) SQL has cached the compiled stored procedure, *and* the results it returns for the arguments we supplied. This allows SQL to service the request for the result set without requerying the database for the information.

```
C:\WINDOWS\System32\cmd.exe                                    _□×
11/8/1996 12:00:00 AM      10340    2436.1800       1996
11/5/1996 12:00:00 AM      10341    352.6000        1996
11/4/1996 12:00:00 AM      10342    1840.6400       1996
11/6/1996 12:00:00 AM      10343    1584.0000       1996
11/5/1996 12:00:00 AM      10344    2296.0000       1996
11/11/1996 12:00:00 AM     10345    2924.8000       1996
11/8/1996 12:00:00 AM      10346    1618.8800       1996
11/8/1996 12:00:00 AM      10347    814.4200        1996
11/15/1996 12:00:00 AM     10348    363.6000        1996
11/15/1996 12:00:00 AM     10349    141.6000        1996
12/3/1996 12:00:00 AM      10350    642.0600        1996
11/20/1996 12:00:00 AM     10351    5398.7200       1996
11/18/1996 12:00:00 AM     10352    136.3000        1996
11/25/1996 12:00:00 AM     10353    8593.2800       1996
11/20/1996 12:00:00 AM     10354    568.8000        1996
11/20/1996 12:00:00 AM     10355    480.0000        1996
11/27/1996 12:00:00 AM     10356    1106.4000       1996
12/2/1996 12:00:00 AM      10357    1167.6800       1996
11/27/1996 12:00:00 AM     10358    429.4000        1996
11/26/1996 12:00:00 AM     10359    3471.6800       1996
12/2/1996 12:00:00 AM      10360    7390.2000       1996
12/3/1996 12:00:00 AM      10361    2046.2400       1996
11/28/1996 12:00:00 AM     10362    1549.6000       1996
12/4/1996 12:00:00 AM      10363    447.2000        1996
12/4/1996 12:00:00 AM      10364    950.0000        1996
12/2/1996 12:00:00 AM      10365    403.2000        1996
12/30/1996 12:00:00 AM     10366    136.0000        1996
12/2/1996 12:00:00 AM      10367    834.2000        1996
12/2/1996 12:00:00 AM      10368    1689.7800       1996
12/9/1996 12:00:00 AM      10369    2390.4000       1996
12/27/1996 12:00:00 AM     10370    1117.6000       1996
12/24/1996 12:00:00 AM     10371    72.9600 1996
12/9/1996 12:00:00 AM      10372    9210.9000       1996
12/11/1996 12:00:00 AM     10373    1366.4000       1996
12/9/1996 12:00:00 AM      10374    459.0000        1996
12/9/1996 12:00:00 AM      10375    338.0000        1996
12/13/1996 12:00:00 AM     10376    399.0000        1996
12/13/1996 12:00:00 AM     10377    863.6000        1996
12/19/1996 12:00:00 AM     10378    103.2000        1996
12/13/1996 12:00:00 AM     10379    863.2800        1996
12/13/1996 12:00:00 AM     10381    112.0000        1996
12/16/1996 12:00:00 AM     10382    2900.0000       1996
12/18/1996 12:00:00 AM     10383    899.0000        1996
12/20/1996 12:00:00 AM     10384    2222.4000       1996
12/23/1996 12:00:00 AM     10385    691.2000        1996
12/25/1996 12:00:00 AM     10386    166.0000        1996
12/20/1996 12:00:00 AM     10387    1058.4000       1996
12/20/1996 12:00:00 AM     10388    1228.8000       1996
12/24/1996 12:00:00 AM     10389    1832.8000       1996
12/26/1996 12:00:00 AM     10390    2090.8800       1996
12/31/1996 12:00:00 AM     10391    86.4000 1996
1/1/1997 12:00:00 AM       10392    1440.0000       1997
C:\Apress\ISBN-1-59059-434-7>
```

Figure 13-2. DACommands2, *CommandSample.vb using a stored procedure*

Taken on its own, this little bit of information about building your own commands might not seem all that impressive. However, when you take into account that the DataAdapter is used to populate DataSets, which can then be visually bound to controls either on Windows Forms applications or on ASP.NET Forms, the power becomes clear. By supplying your own commands, you not only get fine-grained control over how the DataAdapter transfers data, but you can also optimize it to transfer data in the fastest way possible using stored procedures, etc.

■**Note** The CommandBuilders are excellent at enabling you to update data when you don't know the schema of the data you're working with ahead of time. However, in most other cases, you should try to avoid using the CommandBuilders.

High-Volume Data Processing

When working with small applications, you can often ignore performance issues. However, when working with large amounts of data, large numbers of users, or both, these seemingly small issues can magnify and cause an application to grind to a halt. Here, we've listed a couple of things you can do to try to prepare yourself for some of the pitfalls that occur in high-volume and high-activity applications.

Latency

One of the most important things you can remember about large applications is that latency is your enemy. Latency, in our context, is the delay and lock of resources incurred while obtaining and opening a connection. You want to perform this activity as *infrequently* as possible throughout an application. If you keep this in mind, performance tuning an application may be easier than expected.

In small applications or desktop applications, when accessing local data stores such as an Access database or an Excel spreadsheet, the overhead of opening and closing connections may not be noticeable. However, when the component opening and closing the connection is on a different machine in a network (or worse, across the Internet) from the actual database server, the cost of opening a connection is very high.

For example, let's suppose a user of an application clicks a button to retrieve a list of orders. This opens a connection, obtains the orders, and closes the connection, because we've all been taught that leaving a connection open too long is also bad practice. Then, the user double-clicks on an order item and obtains a list of order details. This also opens the connection, obtains the result set, and then closes the connection again. Assuming the user continues with this browsing behavior for ten minutes, the user could be consuming an enormous amount of time and resources needlessly opening and closing connections.

One way to prevent situations like this is to anticipate the intended use of data. You should weigh the memory cost of obtaining the information on the initial database connection against the cost of waiting until the information is needed.

DataSets are designed to be in-memory data caches. They are also designed to hold on to more than one table of information. They are an ideal candidate for storing large amounts of data in anticipation of disconnected browsing behavior.

■Note Retrieving a large volume of data within the context of a single connection will always be faster than retrieving small portions and opening and closing the connection each time. This is because large-block retrieval causes less network roundtrips and incurs less latency.

Cached Data

Many applications suffering from undiagnosed performance problems are often plagued by the same problem. This problem is often the fact that the application is needlessly performing multiple redundant queries for the same data.

If an application is consistently hitting the database for the same data, then it can probably benefit from caching. Many performance benchmarks have been done using ASP.NET object caching and have shown remarkable speed improvements over noncached ASP.NET applications and classic ASP.

Let's suppose that you're building an e-commerce Web site. All of your products are arranged in a hierarchy of categories and subcategories. Through some usage testing, you've found that one of the most frequently performed activities on the Web site is the browsing of items within a category.

Add to the example the fact that the site gets over 100,000 hits per day. If only 40 percent of customers browse products within categories, that is still 40,000 requests per day for information that probably isn't going to change except on a weekly or monthly basis.

What many companies do is retrieve the information once only at some predetermined time. Until the next time the data needs to be changed, all of the code on the entire Web site can hit the cached information instead of the actual database information. This may not seem like all that big a deal, but when you are dealing with high volumes of traffic, every single database request you can avoid is one worth avoiding. Relieving the database server of the drudgery of fetching the same item browse list information 40,000 times a day frees it up to handle more taxing things like retrieving order histories, storing new orders, and performing complex product searches.

There are several methods available for caching data. You can find information about caching ADO.NET datasets in ASP.NET in Chapter 3 of this book. In addition, you can use the COM+ (or Microsoft Transaction Server [MTS]) package itself to cache information for you. COM+ provides a facility known as Property Groups that allows you to cache information in the package's own memory space. This way, your COM+ application that is driving your Web site (you *are* using COM+ to drive your data components, aren't you?) can avoid actually hitting the database if the information has been cached. Before continuing on with your example here, I highly recommend doing some reading on COM+ if you have not done so already, or if you are not familiar with the service.

Let's look at the Northwind database for an example. The category listing in the database (Categories table) contains binary columns that store images for the categories. If Northwind were running a high-volume Web site, every single user browsing through the system would hit the database needlessly for the same, nearly static binary data, over and over again. Obviously, that's not the situation you want.

The solution is to create a component (COM+) that fetches the category listing. First, it will check to see whether the category listing has been cached. If not, it will fetch it from the database, add it to the cache, and then return that result. The beauty of this solution is that anytime a Web site administrator adds a new category, all they need to do is right-click the COM+ application, choose Shut Down, and then hit the Web site again and the cache will be populated with the new information. If the category is added programmatically by a component, then the component can also automatically trigger a refresh of the cache. The act of shutting down the package removes the cache. As you'll see, the cache is actually tied directly to the process in which the component is running.

Here's the source code for your COM+ component, created in a new VB.NET Class Library project called PropGroupAssembly. The project needs a reference to System.EnterpriseServices, and the component needs to derive from the ServicedComponent class. The following is the listing for the class, PropGroupClass:

```
Imports System
Imports System.Data
Imports System.EnterpriseServices
Imports System.Data.SqlClient

Public Class PropGroupClass
  Inherits ServicedComponent

    Public Function FetchCategoryList(ByRef FromCache As Boolean) As String
      Dim fExist As Boolean
      fExist = True
```

You're going to use the COM+ Shared Property Group Manager to do some work for you. You'll create an instance of a group and be told whether that group already exists. Then, you'll create an instance of a property and be told whether that property existed. If, by the time you have the instance of your property, the fExist variable is True, then you know that you're working from a cache. Otherwise, you need to hit the database for your categories. Take special note of the ReleaseMode we've chosen. This indicates that the property will not be cleared until the process in which it is being hosted has been terminated. This is of vital importance when deciding between library activation packages (applications) and server-activation applications.

```
      Dim oLock As PropertyLockMode = PropertyLockMode.SetGet
      Dim oRel As PropertyReleaseMode = PropertyReleaseMode.Process
      Dim grpMan As SharedPropertyGroupManager = _
        New SharedPropertyGroupManager()
      Dim grpCache As SharedPropertyGroup = _
        grpMan.CreatePropertyGroup("CategoryCacheGroup", oLock, oRel, _
                            fExist)
      Dim propCache As SharedProperty = _
        grpCache.CreateProperty("CategoryCache", fExist)
      If fExist Then
        FromCache = True
        Return CType(propCache.Value, String)
      Else
        FromCache = False
```

You didn't get your information from the in-memory, process-specific cache, so now you'll get it from the database. Remember that opening and closing the connection is a task that is your enemy, so you only want to do this when the data hasn't already been cached.

```
      Dim Connection As SqlConnection = New SqlConnection( _
          "Data Source=(local); Initial Catalog=Northwind; " _
          & "Integrated Security=SSPI;")
      Dim MyDA As SqlDataAdapter = New SqlDataAdapter( _
          "SELECT CategoryID, CategoryName, Description, Picture FROM " _
          & "Categories", Connection)
      Dim MyDS As DataSet = New DataSet()
      MyDA.Fill(MyDS, "Categories")
```

You're storing the string representation of the `DataSet`'s internal XML data. This allows for maximum flexibility of consumers of the cache. It allows consumers of the cache that have access to the `DataSet` component to utilize it, but it also allows traditional COM/COM+ components invoking this component to access the data via traditional DOM or SAX components and traversals.

```
        propCache.Value = MyDS.GetXml()
        Connection.Close()
        MyDA.Dispose()
        Return CType(propCache.Value, String)
    End If
End Function
```

```
End Class
```

The AssemblyInfo.vb file for this project (called `PropGroupAssembly`) contains the following custom attribute (defined by the `System.EnterpriseServices` namespace, which you need to add to an `Imports` statement at the top of this file):

```
[assembly:ApplicationName("Property Group Test")]
```

This tells the Common Language Runtime (CLR) that the first time this assembly has a class invoked in it, all of the classes within it will be registered in COM+, belonging to a new, library-activation application called "Property Group Test." This is where it is important to remember the difference between activation models in a COM+ application. A library-activation application will activate the components *within the context of the calling process*. A server-activation application will activate the components within its own separate process. So, if your client (or consumer) component expects the cache to persist, even though the client process has terminated, you *must* reconfigure your COM+ application to activate server-side. We'll come back to this in a little while.

In order for this component to work as a COM+ component, you also need to give the generated assembly a strong name. Here, the first step is to generate a key pair to use to sign the assembly, which can be achieved from the command line as follows:

```
sn -k PGAKey.snk
```

■**Tip** You'll see more about .snk files later in the chapter, when you examine security issues.

The generated key-pair file, PGAKey.snk, should be placed in the project directory of `PropGroupAssembly`. Next, you need to link this file with the assembly, which you do using the following attribute in AssemblyInfo.vb:

```
<Assembly: AssemblyKeyFileAttribute("..\..\PGAKey.snk")>
```

One more thing before you look at the code to test this caching component: always remember to place your .NET COM+ assemblies in the Global Assembly Cache (GAC); otherwise, .NET components attempting to use them will be unable to locate them, even if they are in the same directory.

To add your newly generated assembly to the GAC, you need to run the following from the command line:

```
gacutil -i PropGroupAssembly.dll
```

Next, you have your testing harness, PropGroupTester, a console application. This application needs a reference to your COM+ assembly, PropGroupAssembly. To add this, browse to the PropGroupAssembly entry in the GAC (found in C:\Windows\assembly\) and add the reference. The code for the main module of this project, TestPropGroupClass.vb, starts as follows:

```
Imports System
Imports PropGroupAssembly

Module TestPropGroupClass

    Sub Main()
        Dim oClass As PropGroupClass = New PropGroupClass()
        Dim strXML As String
        Dim fExist As Boolean
```

Your testing harness is storing the XML, but isn't actually doing anything with it. Quite easily, you could have a DataSet load the XML for use in a databound grid or some ASP.NET server-side control.

```
        Console.WriteLine("First Execution")
        strXML = oClass.FetchCategoryList(fExist)
        Console.WriteLine("From Cache: {0}", fExist)

        Console.WriteLine("Second Execution")
        strXML = oClass.FetchCategoryList(fExist)
        Console.WriteLine("From Cache: {0}", fExist)
    End Sub

End Module
```

The first time this application is run a COM+ application is automatically created for you. As mentioned previously, this will be a library application. This means that the PropGroupClass instance will be created in the same process as the console application, and will be destroyed afterward. The result of this is shown in Figure 13-3.

Figure 13-3. PropGroupTester—*cache demonstration*

The data from the database is being cached, but only as long as the console application runs. You can see this as the first execution in each case doesn't get data from the cache, but the second execution does.

To convert the COM+ application to a server application, you need to modify it via the Component Services tool found in the Administrative Tools section of Control Panel. Navigate through the tree structure, as shown in Figure 13-4, to find the new application.

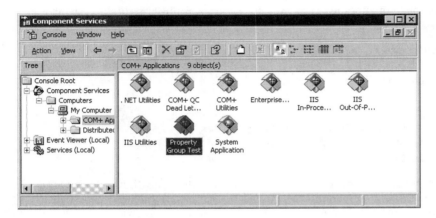

Figure 13-4. *Your COM+ application under Component Services*

From the Properties of this application, change the Activation Type to Server Application as shown in Figure 13-5 (ignore the warnings that appear when you do this).

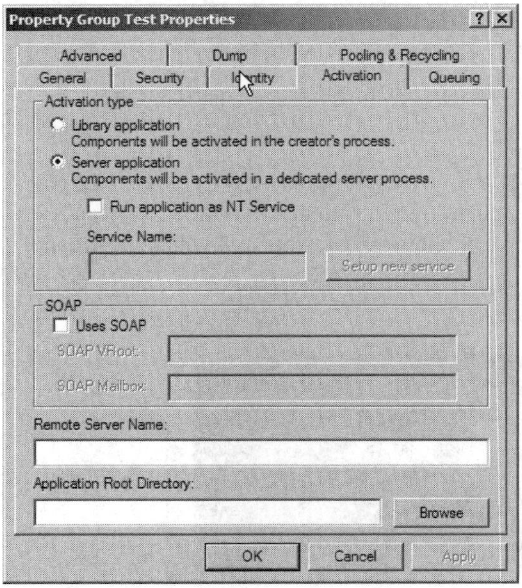

Figure 13-5. *Changing your application to Server Application*

Also tab over to the Security tab, and uncheck the "Enforce access checks for this application" as shown in Figure 13-6.

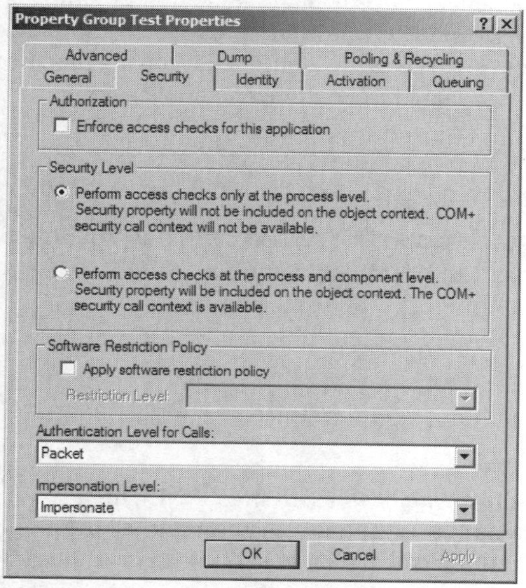

Figure 13-6. *Changing the security of your application*

What can you expect from the output of the example now? Well, if your COM+ component is running in a server-activated application, then the first time you run this you should get a False and then a True. The first execution will have needed to query the database for the information. On the second execution, the information should be in the cache and you should see a True. To further prove that the cache is being maintained separately from your client process (it is a server-activated COM+ application), you run the application again, and you should expect a True value for both the first and second execution. Let's test this out (see Figure 13-7).

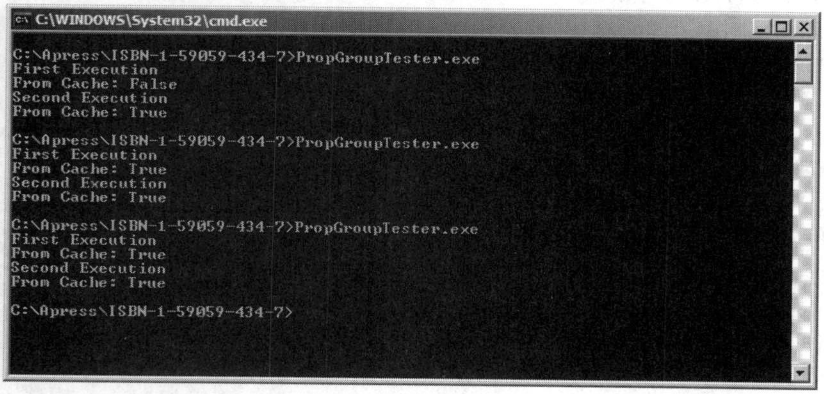

Figure 13-7. *Executing your application as a server*

You can see from this screenshot of your console that the first time you ran the application, the first execution shows that the information was *not* cached. You then see that every time you ran the program after that, the information you retrieved was from the cache. As an experiment, right-click the application in Component Services (which should now be spinning to indicate that it is active) and choose Shut Down. Then rerun the application and you should see that the results are the same as Figure 13-7. The cache is emptied when the process hosting the cache is terminated. This process is terminated when the server application is shut down.

■Note Examine the data needs of the consumers of your application and consider caching any data that is accessed far more frequently than it changes. Two popular methods of caching are using ASP.NET's caching or COM+ Shared Property Groups.

ASP.NET Object Caching

If you are lucky enough to be writing your data-driven application within ASP.NET, then you actually have a considerably large toolbox available at your disposal. For example, all of the work you did previously to allow you to cache arbitrary data within the COM+ server application process is completely unnecessary when you're working in ASP.NET.

ASP.NET provides a feature called *object caching* that automates the work you did earlier. It also provides methods for caching page and partial-page output, but those topics are better left for an ASP.NET book.

The caching mechanism is provided by an object named Cache, which exposes a dictionary-like interface, allowing you to store arbitrary objects indexed by a string key, much like the classic ASP Session object. The difference is that you can not only decide how long that information should stay cached, but you can also determine if that information should automatically become uncached (dirty) if a change occurs in a file on disk or a database table, etc.

To quickly demonstrate caching, you'll cache a string that contains the date and time at the time of caching. You'll create an ASP page that displays the cached date/time and the current date/time so that you can see the cached time remain the same as you refresh the page.

To do this, let's create a page called CacheSample.aspx, with a code-behind class of CacheSample.aspx.vb. You'll drop two labels onto the design surface, one called CacheLabel and the other called LiveLabel, making the ASP.NET code as follows:

```
<form id="Form1" method="post" runat="server">
  <asp:Label Runat="server" id="CacheLabel" />
  <br>
  <asp:Label Runat="server" ID="LiveLabel" />
</form>
```

The code behind simply needs some additions to Page_Load. In the following code, you test to see if there is anything stored in the named cache variable CachedValue. If there isn't, then you populate it with the current time and set the expiration date of the cached value to one minute from now.

```
Private Sub Page_Load(ByVal sender As System.Object, _
                    ByVal e As System.EventArgs) Handles MyBase.Load
    'Put user code to initialize the page here
    If Cache("CachedValue") = Nothing Then
        Cache.Insert("CachedValue", _
                    "Cached At : " + DateTime.Now.ToString(), _
                    nothing, DateTime.Now.AddMinutes(1), _
                    System.Web.Caching.Cache.NoSlidingExpiration)
    End If
```

In keeping with the standard dictionary model, you simply obtain an object from the cache by name, and cast it to the appropriate type in order to use it.

```
    CacheLabel.Text = CType(Cache("CachedValue"), String)
    LiveLabel.Text = DateTime.Now.ToString()
End Sub
```

The first time you run this in a browser, both of the labels have the same time displayed. After waiting a few seconds, you hit Refresh and get the display as shown in Figure 13-8.

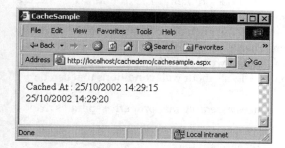

Figure 13-8. Cachedemo *sample before the cache value has expired*

You then wait a minute and hit Refresh again to see if the cached value expired, causing your code to place a new string into the cache (see Figure 13-9).

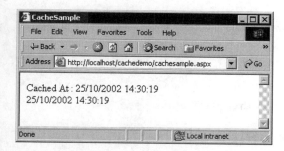

Figure 13-9. Cachedemo *sample after the cache value has expired*

So, in conclusion, if you are writing a web application and you want to store frequently accessed information in order to increase performance, then the Cache object is your new best friend. However, if you are working on a distributed or server-side application that is using some of the performance benefits of COM+ (object pooling, etc.), you can take advantage of COM+/MTS property groups to utilize their in-memory data caching features. As you've seen, it is far easier to cache data within ASP.NET than it is within COM+, but at least you know that there are options regardless of your architecture.

Birds of a Feather (Functionality Grouping)

With a small application that performs very few data operations, you probably wouldn't need to be concerned with functionality grouping. However, if you're concerned about performance; you're probably not working with a small application to begin with.

Most texts on performance tuning in the Windows DNA world include rules about making sure that you never house transactional processing in the same component as you house nontransactional processing, as this incurs the overhead of transactional processing for read-only operations that don't need it.

The same holds true for .NET, only with slightly looser restrictions. Due to the way assemblies are built, you can actually include a transactional and a nontransactional class in the same assembly without worrying about the performance problems. The trouble arises when you use the same class to perform write operations and read operations.

In a slow-paced, single-user world, this wouldn't be much of a consideration. However, in high-volume applications, you want your components to start and finish their operations as quickly as possible. If a class instance is busy making a write operation when 30 other users want to use it for a simple read operation, you needlessly incur wait conditions that can be avoided.

Here you'll look at the skeleton of a data services assembly that properly separates read and write operations.

```
' The following is an illustration only and is not intended
' to be compiled. It is intended as a guideline and starting
' point for creating a data services component that provides
' proper separation of functionality for optimum performance


Imports System
Imports System.EnterpriseServices
Imports System.Data
Imports System.Data.SqlClient
Imports System.Data.SqlTypes
Imports MyApplication.Common


Namespace MyApplication.DAL
    ' Define read-only data service class for this particular
    ' entity.
    <Transaction(TransactionOption.NotSupported)> _
    Public Class MyObject
        Inherits DALObject
```

In most cases, the nontransactional component will have at least one method that allows for the loading of data corresponding to an individual item. Some components may have more, including loading lists or searching, but a single-item load is the most common read operation.

Tip Note that you could easily use a `DataReader` here instead of the `DataSet` for more performance if you didn't intend to modify any of the information.

```
    Public Function Load(ByVal ID As Integer) As DataSet
        ' Load a single item from the database
    End Function
End Class
```

Next, you have the transactional portion of the code, as follows:

```
Namespace Transactional
    ' define write-access service class for this particular
    ' entity.
    <Transaction(TransactionOption.Supported)> _
    Public Class MyObject
        Inherits DALObject
```

The transactional portion of the data access component should more than likely provide the remainder of the CRUD (Create/Retrieve/Update/Delete) functionality, providing methods for creating a new item, updating an existing item, and deleting an existing item.

```
    Public Function Create(...) As Integer
        ' use supplied arguments to create a new item in the DB.
    End Function

    Public Function Update(int ID, ...) As Integer
        ' use supplied arguments to update an item in the DB.
    End Function

    Public Function Delete(int ID, ...) As Integer
        ' use supplied arguments to delete an item in the DB.
    End Function
    End Class
    End Namespace
End Namespace
```

Note Data service classes should provide either a read-access layer or a write-access layer surrounding the data store. They should *never* provide both within the same class.

Marshaling Considerations

Unless an application is a single, standalone executable, or something similar, then more than likely you will encounter data marshaling at some point. Whether it is COM InterOp marshaling of data between the various wrappers, or marshaling data between two .NET processes, you will still need to be aware of how data is being marshaled in your application.

Marshaling is an expensive operation that involves moving data from one process to another without any data loss. This is a simple operation for some types, such as integers, strings, and decimals. However, for complex types, such as custom classes and user-defined types, the operation is considerably more expensive.

Object serialization, however, is a much faster process. The reason it is faster is that, rather than going through the expensive process of determining how to convert the complex data into a form that is suitable for transmission, the CLR can simply identify a class that supports serialization, and ask that class to serialize itself. Serialization essentially reduces the entire class to a single stream that is already in a form that is easy to transmit. This stream can then be used to reconstitute an exact duplicate of the class instance on the other side of the function call.

■**Note** When deciding on data formats to send between tiers or processes, try to use classes that support serialization to avoid costly reference-marshaling overhead.

The following is a brief list of classes that you might be using on a regular basis that already support automatic serialization:

- DataSet: The DataSet will serialize everything, including its own schema.

- DBNull: A constant representing a NULL database value.

- Exception: The base class for all exceptions in the system.

- Hashtable: A collection of name-value pairs much like a Scripting Dictionary.

- SoapFault: This contains error information wrapped in a SOAP envelope. When web services throw exceptions, they are carried back to the client in a SoapFault.

DataSet Serialization

The DataSet can actually be serialized in several ways: into binary format, into a SOAP envelope, or into an XML document. Each of the various serialization formats has its advantages. For example, the binary format is highly optimized for quick parsing and deserialization. The SOAP format is used to transfer data to and from web services, and the XML format is used widely throughout the CLR, including passing data between processes or application domains.

If you want to use a specific format for data serialization, then instead of passing or returning the actual object (forcing the CLR to serialize the object for us), you can pass a stream onto which you have already serialized an object.

Let's take a look at a quick example that illustrates serializing a DataSet into various different formats. To create this example, we created a new console application called SerializeDS
that references System.Runtime.Serialization.Formatters.Soap in addition to the defaults.
The code for the main module file, SerializeSample.vb, is as follows:

```
Imports System
Imports System.Data
Imports System.Data.SqlClient
Imports System.IO
Imports System.Runtime.Serialization.Formatters
Imports System.Runtime.Serialization.Formatters.Soap
Imports System.Runtime.Serialization.Formatters.Binary
Imports System.Xml.Serialization

Module SerializeSample
  Sub Main()
```

Your first task is going to be to populate an initial DataSet with some data from the
Northwind database in your SQL Server 2000. You'll be selecting all of the customers in the
system.

```
    Dim Connection As SqlConnection = New SqlConnection( _
      "Server=(local); Initial Catalog=Northwind; " _
      & "Integrated Security=SSPI;")
    Dim MyDA As SqlDataAdapter = New SqlDataAdapter( _
      "SELECT * FROM Customers", Connection)
    Dim MyDS As DataSet = New DataSet()
    Dim MyDS2 As DataSet = New DataSet()
    MyDA.Fill(MyDS, "Customers")
```

The first serialization you're going to do is into a SOAP envelope, the format used to communicate with web services. To do this, all you have to do is create a new SoapFormatter. Then
to serialize, all you do is invoke the Serialize function, indicating the stream onto which the
object will be serialized, and the object whose graph is to be serialized.

```
    Dim s As Stream = File.Open("MyDS.soap", _
      FileMode.Create, FileAccess.ReadWrite)
    Dim sf As SoapFormatter = New SoapFormatter()
    sf.Serialize(s, MyDS)
    s.Close()
```

To reconstitute a DataSet from the SOAP envelope we stored on disk, you basically reverse
the process. You need a SOAPFormatter (a class that specializes in serializing and deserializing
object graphs using SOAP) and an input stream, and then you simply call DeSerialize on it.

```
    Console.WriteLine("Serialization Complete.")
    Console.WriteLine("De-Serializing Graph from SOAP Envelope...")
    Dim r As Stream = File.Open("MyDS.soap", _
      FileMode.Open, FileAccess.Read)
    Dim sf2 As SoapFormatter = New SoapFormatter()
```

```
    MyDS2 = CType(sf2.Deserialize(r), DataSet)
    r.Close()

    Console.WriteLine( _
        "After Deserialization, MyDS2 contains {0} Customers", _
        MyDS2.Tables("Customers").Rows.Count)
```

Just because you can, and to continue demonstrating the various serialization formats, you're going to serialize your recently populated DataSet into an XML file. Again, the procedure is very similar. You create a stream, which will be the destination of the serialization process, and then you use the appropriate formatter to perform the serialization.

```
    Console.WriteLine("Serializing DataSet into an XML DOM...")
    Dim xStream As Stream = File.Open("MyDS2.xml", _
        FileMode.Create, FileAccess.ReadWrite)
    Dim xs As XmlSerializer = New XmlSerializer(GetType(DataSet))
    xs.Serialize(xStream, MyDS2)
    xStream.Close()
```

Finally, for the smallest of the serialization formats, you'll output your DataSet in serialized binary. Again, you create a stream, a binary formatter, and then have the formatter invoke the Serialize method. Much like the SOAPFormatter and an XML Formatter, the BinaryFormatter is a class that specializes in serializing and deserializing object graphs in a binary format.

```
    Console.WriteLine("Now Serializing to Binary Format...")
    Dim bs As Stream = File.Open("MyDS2.bin", _
        FileMode.Create, FileAccess.ReadWrite)
    Dim bf As BinaryFormatter = New BinaryFormatter()
    bf.Serialize(bs, MyDS2)
    bs.Close()
    End Sub

End Module
```

XML over HTTP

It would be difficult to discuss performance and security within ADO.NET without mentioning the use of XML over HTTP. It is also worth mentioning that XML over HTTP is *not* the same thing as SOAP. SOAP began as the **S**imple **O**bject **A**ccess **P**rotocol, and is an industry standard that allows methods and properties to be exposed and utilized over the Internet. It is a wire protocol that, as of version 1.1, makes no requirement about the *transport* used.

The System.Net namespace contains two classes called HttpWebRequest and HttpWebResponse. These two classes allow code to communicate directly with any server exposing a port to the HTTP protocol. An additional benefit of these classes is that they expose streams to enable you to send large amounts of data to a web server, or receive large amounts of data from a web server. This provides a facility for all kinds of enhanced communications and back-end functionality that previously all had to be coded by hand.

You could take the code from the previous DataSet serialization example and convert it into two portions: a client and a server. The server would be an ASP.NET page that deserializes a

DataSet directly off the request stream. The client would be a console application that populates a DataSet and then serializes it directly onto a stream obtained by calling the GetRequestStream method.

Using the previous DataSet serialization code as an example for working with streams, you should be able to take the knowledge that both the Request and Response in an HTTP conversation can be treated as streams and build this exercise fairly easily.

Connection Pooling

Opening and closing database connections is a very expensive operation. The concept of *connection pooling* involves preparing connection instances ahead of time in a pool. This has the upshot that multiple requests for the same connection can be served by a pool of available connections, thereby reducing the overhead of obtaining a new connection instance. Connection pooling is handled differently by each data provider: we'll cover how the SQL Client and OLE DB .NET data providers handle connection pooling. You can find more information on the OracleClient.

SqlConnection

The SqlConnection object is implicitly a pooled object. It relies solely on Windows 2000 Component Services (COM+) to provide pooled connections. Each pool of available connections is based on a single, unique connection string. Each time a request for a connection is made with a distinct connection string, a new pool will be created. The pools will be filled with connections up to a maximum defined number. Requests for connections from a full pool will be queued until a connection can be re-allocated to the queued request. If the queued request times out, an exception will be thrown.

There are some arguments that can be passed in the connection string to manually configure the pooling behavior of the connection.

■**Tip** Note that these arguments count towards the uniqueness of the string, and two otherwise identical strings with differing pool settings will create two different pools.

The following is a list of SQL connection string parameters that affect pooling:

- *Connection Lifetime* (0): This is a value that indicates (in seconds) that a connection will remain live after having been created and placed in the pool. The default value of 0 indicates that the connection will never time out.

- *Connection Reset* (True): This Boolean value indicates whether or not the connection will be reset when removed from the pool. A value of False avoids hitting the database again when obtaining the connection, but may cause unexpected results as the connection state will not be reset. The default value for this option is True, and it should be set to False only when you can be certain that *not* resetting the connection state when obtaining the connection will not have any adverse effects on code.

- *Enlist* (True): This Boolean value indicates whether or not the connection should auto-matically enlist the connection in the current transaction of the creation thread (if one exists). The default value for this is True.

- *Max Pool Size* (100): Maximum number of connections that can reside in the pool at any given time.

- *Min Pool Size* (0): The minimum number of connections maintained in the pool. Set-ting this to at least 1 will guarantee that, after the initial startup of your application, there will always be at least one connection available in the pool.

- *Pooling* (True): This is the Boolean value that indicates whether or not the connection should be pooled at all. The default is True.

The best thing about SQL connection pooling is that, besides optionally tuning pooling configuration in the connection string, you don't have to do any additional programming to support it.

■Note SQL connection pooling can drastically reduce the cost of obtaining a new connection in your code, as long as the connection string of each connection is exactly the same.

OleDbConnection

The OLE DB .NET data provider provides connection pooling automatically through the use of OLE DB session pooling. Again, there is no special code that you need to write to take advan-tage of the OLE DB session pooling; it is simply there for you. You can configure or disable the OLE DB session pooling by using the OLE DB Services connection string argument. For exam-ple, if the connection string contains the following parameter, it will disable session pooling and automatic transaction enlistment:

```
Provider=SQLOLEDB; OLE DB Services=-4; Data Source=(local); Integrated⌂
  Security=SSPI;
```

For more information on what values for this parameter affect the OLE DB connection and in what way, consult the OLE DB Programmer's Reference that is available at http://msdn.microsoft.com/library.

Message Queuing

Message queuing is, quite simply, placing messages in a queue to be processed at a later time by another application or component. Users will frequently be sitting in front of either a web or Windows application and have to wait an extended period of time for some processing to complete. In many cases, this is both tolerated and expected. However, when hundreds of users are waiting for processing to complete and their tasks are all burdening the same server, the wait may be unacceptable, assuming that none of the clients experience timeout failures.

Messaging is used to create the perception of increased performance by taking the user's request for a task to be performed and placing it in a queue. Some other service or process then reads the requests out of the queue and processes those tasks in an offline fashion, relieving the load on the main server.

In addition to being able to send and receive messages containing arbitrary objects from within your code, you can also make the components you write queued components. This allows method calls on your components to be serialized into a queue and then serviced at a later time by another process, not only allowing you to asynchronously send messages, but also asynchronously send and respond to method calls. We'll just discuss simple Microsoft Message Queuing (MSMQ) in this chapter. Microsoft has plenty of documentation on how to create queued components that will be fairly easy to read and understand once you have a grasp of the basics of using Microsoft Message Queues.

To Queue or Not to Queue?

You might wonder, if messaging is such a handy tool for offloading burdensome tasks, then why it is not used all the time for everything? Just like all specialized technologies, messaging is very good at solving certain problems, but is far from ideal for solving other issues. For example, any time the user needs direct feedback as to the success or failure of their task, messaging is probably not a good idea. The reason being that the task might well not even have begun to be processed: the only feedback the user can receive is that their message has been placed in a queue.

The other reason why you might avoid using messaging concerns user feedback. Suppose a user's request is submitted to a queue, but then the service that was processing the information in the queue unexpectedly dies. If adequate precautions are not taken, thousands of messages carrying critical information could be stranded in a queue with no place to go.

Messaging is a perfectly viable tool for reducing the load on your back-end systems, as well as communicating with other loosely connected systems throughout a network or the world. Just be sure to prepare for some of the pitfalls of loosely connected messaging before you deploy your messaging solution.

■**Note** In order for the examples in this section to work, you must have installed the Message Queuing component on your computer, which you can do via your Windows 2000 or Windows XP installation disks.

Sending Messages

You're going to create an example that places a string containing the highly overused phrase "Hello World" into a queue. When you create a message, you wrap an object in some header information, which includes a label for that message. The body (object) of the message can contain any object, including a DataSet. This can be an extremely valuable tool to take data from one data source, place it in a queue in the form of a DataSet, and then pick up the message to be stored in another data store.

To create your sample, you create a console application called QueueSender. Make sure that the project has a reference to the System.Messaging namespace. Type in the following code into the main module file (MessageSample.vb) to create a simple message-sending application:

```
Imports System
Imports System.Messaging

Module MessageSample

    Sub Main()
```

It's all pretty straightforward. You use a private queue here just to make things simpler. MSMQ has three main kinds of queues: outgoing, private, and system. The outgoing queues can participate in complex publishing policies that allow the contents of the queue to be sent to other MSMQ servers in a domain. System queues are, obviously, used by the operating system for internal asynchronous messaging.

```
        Dim Greeting As String = "Hello World!"
        Dim mQ As MessageQueue
        If MessageQueue.Exists(".\Private$\HelloWorld") Then
            mQ = New MessageQueue(".\Private$\HelloWorld")
        Else
            mQ = MessageQueue.Create(".\Private$\HelloWorld")
        End If

        mQ.Send(Greeting, "HelloWorld")
        Console.WriteLine("Greeting Message Sent to Private Queue.")
    End Sub

End Module
```

What you've done in this code is test for the existence of a queue by using the shared method Exists in the MessageQueue class. If it doesn't exist, then you create it. Once you know you have a valid reference to your message queue, you simply send your string to the queue. The messaging system is going to wrap up your object in a message. By default, MSMQ will use an XML serialization scheme to store objects; however, you can choose to use a binary storage system that is more efficient for transmitting things like pictures.

When you run the previous example, you get the simple message that the greeting message has been sent to the queue. To see the impact of what you've just done, you'll open the Computer Management console on Windows 2000 (or XP) and open up the Message Queuing item. From there, you can open the Private Queues folder and find your newly created queue. This is illustrated in a Figure 13-10.

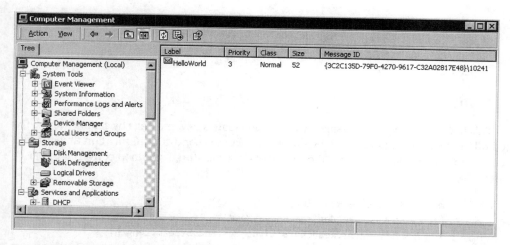

Figure 13-10. *A message in your private queue*

As you can see from the screenshot, you have a 52-byte message sitting in a queue called helloworld with the label of HelloWorld. You can also see that the message has been given a priority and a GUID for unique identification. Even though this screenshot was taken on Windows XP Professional, this example works just fine on Windows 2000 Professional.

Receiving Messages

Now that you've seen how you can place messages into a queue, let's take a look at pulling them out. True to their name, the queues work in FIFO order (First In, First Out). Messages are plucked out of the queue in the order in which they were placed into it. Create another console application and call it QueueReceiver. Again, you must make sure that the application has a reference to the System.Messaging assembly. The main module file, ReceiverSample.vb, is as follows:

```vb
Imports System
Imports System.Messaging
Imports System.IO

Module ReceiverSample

    Sub Main()
        Dim mQ As MessageQueue
        Dim mes As Message
        Dim X As String
        Dim br As BinaryReader

        If MessageQueue.Exists(".\Private$\HelloWorld") Then
            mQ = New MessageQueue(".\Private$\HelloWorld")
```

```
Else
    Console.WriteLine("Queue doesn't exist.")
    Return
End If

Try
```

This is the meat of your message receiver. You create a new message by calling the Receive method in the message queue, also by supplying a three second communication timeout. You then use a BinaryReader to pull out the stream of data you stored and then convert it into a string.

```
    mes = mQ.Receive(New TimeSpan(0, 0, 3))
    br = New BinaryReader(mes.BodyStream)
    X = New String(br.ReadChars(CType(mes.BodyStream.Length, _
                                    Integer)))
    Console.WriteLine("Received Message: {0}", X)
Catch
    Console.WriteLine("No Message to Receive.")
End Try

End Sub

End Module
```

When you execute this code after placing a message in the private queue, your console contains the following output:

```
Received Message: <?xml version="1.0"?>
<string>Hello World!</string>
```

Now, not only do you know that your original text has been preserved, but also that it has been wrapped in the XML document created when a string is serialized.

■**Tip** Note, also, that if you run this application again no message will be received, since messages are removed from queues as they are processed.

■**Note** Message Queues are an excellent tool for relieving the burden of critical back-end systems by providing a mechanism for offline processing and loosely coupled message-based interapplication communication.

Security Concerns

Now that you've spent some time covering some of the ways in which you might be able to increase or maintain the performance of an application, let's talk about security. The .NET Framework provides several ways in which you can not only secure data, but also an application (or component). The most common ways to secure an application involve either using the Code Access Security (CAS) system or using an encryption scheme or SSL (Secure Sockets Layer) encryption for Web sites.

Code Access Security

Every single .NET application interacts with the CLR's security system. This security system is a fully configurable set of policies and permission sets that allows administrators to dictate policy at the enterprise, machine, or user level.

What it means to you, as programmers, is that it is now possible for an administrator on a machine running an application to dictate security policy. This could have the effect of preventing your application from executing. Even more interesting is that the same administrator can dictate an enterprise-wide policy that prevents *any code published by a particular company* from executing.

A very common misconception is that the CAS system works in a similar fashion to the NTFS security permissions that can be assigned to individual files, directories, and resources on NT/2000/XP machines. While NTFS is a system of locking down access to files and filesystem resources, CAS is a system of restricting the resources available to certain .NET Assemblies. The CAS administration has a very similar structure and feel to editing security policy files for locking down workstations. Windows 95/98 had *policy files* that dictated which users had access to which resources, etc. Anyone familiar with the POLEDIT.EXE utility will feel comfortable navigating the .NET Framework CAS administration.

So, what does CAS have to do with ADO.NET? Well, if you're using ADO.NET, then you are undoubtedly accessing resources of some kind. These resources include a SQL Server, an OLE DB Data Source, an ODBC Data Source, an Access database file, a text file, or an XML file. All of these resources are security controlled, and you should be aware of how your code functions in a secure environment.

Administration

Using the Microsoft .NET Framework Configuration utility from the Control Panel, you can administer the runtime security policy on three different scope levels: enterprise, machine, and user. When policy is evaluated, it is evaluated separately for each scope level and then intersected. The result of this is that code is granted the minimum set of permissions available from each scope.

Code Groups

The way the security policy works is that an administrator (or Microsoft, in the case of the system defaults) defines a set of *code groups*. These code groups are simply *statements of membership*. Any time an assembly is invoked, its evidence (public key, zone, version, application directory, name, etc.) is compared against the applicable code groups defined within the system. If the assembly's evidence matches a code group, that assembly is granted the applicable permission sets. You'll see a real-world example of how to apply all of this information shortly.

The code groups that ship with the framework are:

- *LocalIntranet_Zone:* Identifies all assemblies whose zone is "Intranet."

- *Internet_Zone:* Identifies all assemblies whose zone is "Internet."

- *Restricted_Zone:* Identifies all assemblies from the "Untrusted" zone.

- *Trusted_Zone:* Identifies all assemblies from the "Trusted" zone.

- *Microsoft_Strong_Name:* Identifies all assemblies built with the Microsoft public key.

- *ECMA_Strong_Name:* Identifies all assemblies built with the ECMA public key. ECMA is a standards body that stands for the *European Computer Manufacturer's Association*.

- *My_Computer_Zone:* Identifies all assemblies residing on your computer.

Permission Sets

Permission sets are named groups of code access permissions. Each code group is assigned to a given permission set. This essentially provides for the ability to grant a named set of permissions to all code matching a given criterion (or *policy*). The following is a list of the default permission sets that ship with the Framework:

- *FullTrust:* Gives complete and unrestricted access to all protected resources.

- *SkipVerification:* Grants the matching code the right to bypass security verification.

- *Execution:* Allows the code to execute.

- *Nothing:* Denies the code all rights, including the right to execute.

- *LocalIntranet:* The default set of permissions granted to code on your local intranet.

- *Internet:* The default set of permissions given to Internet applications.

- *Everything:* Allows complete unrestricted access to all resources that are governed by the built-in permissions. This differs from `FullTrust` in that `FullTrust` allows unrestricted access to everything, even if those resources are not governed by built-in permissions.

Permissions

Permissions are the individual access points that protect specific system resources. Code must have been granted (either directly or indirectly through assertions, etc.) the appropriate permission before it can access the given resource. If code attempts to access a resource to which it has not been granted the appropriate permission, the CLR will throw an exception. We'll show how to grant or revoke these permissions to assemblies in the next section.

- *DirectoryServicesPermission*: Allows access to `System.DirectoryServices` classes.

- *DnsPermission*: Allows the code to access the Domain Name System (DNS).

- *EnvironmentPermission*: Governs access to reading and/or writing environment variables.

- *EventLogPermission*: Allows read and write access to the event logging services.

- *FileDialogPermission*: Allows access to files chosen by a user from an Open File dialog box.

- *FileIOPermission*: Allows the code to read, append, or write files or directories.

- *IsolatedStorageFilePermission*: Allows access to private virtual filesystems.

- *IsolatedStoragePermission*: Allows access to isolated storage, which is a system of storage associated with a given user and some portion of the code's identity (Web site, publisher, or signature). Isolated storage allows downloaded code to maintain an offline data store without encroaching on the user's otherwise protected filesystem/hard disk. The data will be stored in a directory structure on the system depending on the operating system and whether user profiles have been enabled. For example, on a Windows 2000 machine, the files will be in `<SYSTEM>\Profiles\<user>\Application Data`, or `<SYSTEM>\Profiles\<user>\Local Settings\Application Data` for a nonroaming profile.

- *MessageQueuePermission*: Allows access to Message Queues via MSMQ.

- *OleDbPermission*: Allows access to resources exposed by the OLE DB data provider.

- *PerformanceCounterPermission*: Allows the specified code to access performance counters.

- *PrintingPermission*: Allows access to the printing system.

- *ReflectionPermission*: Allows access to the reflection system to discover type information at runtime. The lack of this permission can be potentially crippling to a lot of code that the programmer or administrator might not expect to be affected. In other words, if your application depends on the use of reflection in order to function properly, an administrator could cripple it by revoking this permission.

- *RegistryPermission*: Allows the specified code to read, write, create, or delete keys and values in the system registry.

- *SecurityPermission*: Actually, kind of a multifaceted permission. Allows execution, asserting permissions, calls into unmanaged code (InterOp), verification skip, and other things.

- *ServiceControllerPermission*: Allows code to access system services.

- *SocketPermission*: Allows the code access low-level sockets.

- *SqlClientPermission*: Allows the code to access resources exposed by the SQL data provider.

- *StrongNameIdentityPermission*: Allows one piece of code to restrict calling access to only code that matches certain identity characteristics. Often used to distribute assemblies callable only by the publisher.

- *UIPermission*: Allows access to the user interface.

- *WebPermission*: Allows access to make or accept connections on web addresses.

CAS in Action

Now that you've seen a bit of what functionality CAS provides for programmers and adminis-trators, let's take a look at CAS in action. There are two examples you're going to go through: the first is an illustration of how to create an assembly that can be callable only by other assemblies built with the same public key—in other words, the secured assembly can only be invoked by other assemblies built with the same strong-name key file (typically a .snk file generated with the SN.EXE tool or Visual Studio .NET); the second will be an example of locking down some code and seeing the results of attempting to execute code with insufficient permission.

For your first example, create a class library project called SecureLibrary. Then, hit the command prompt and type the following in the new project directory:

```
> sn -k Secure.snk
```

This generates your RSA signature file used for establishing a unique publisher ID for the component. You need the RSA signature file to guarantee you a public key that will uniquely identify you as a distinct publisher. All assemblies built upon this RSA file will have the same public key, and hence the same publisher. *RSA* is an algorithm for obtaining digital signa-tures and public-key cryptosystems. It was named after its three inventors: R.L. **R**ivest, A. **S**hamir, and L.M. **A**delman.

To give your assembly a strong name using this file, you need to add the attribute you saw earlier in this chapter to AssemblyInfo.vb:

```
<Assembly: AssemblyKeyFile("../../Secure.snk")>
```

Now, you'll type the following into the main class file for your library (SecureClass.cs):

```
Imports System
Imports System.Security
Imports System.Security.Permissions

Public Class SecureClass

    Public Function GetSecureString() As String
        Return "Secret Phrase: Confucious say, Penny Saved a Day is " _
        & "Seven Cents a Week."
    End Function
End Class
```

Compile the project then enter the following at the command prompt in the bin directory:

```
> secutil -hex -strongname SecureLibrary.dll
```

This will display the public key portion of the key used to sign the assembly. Copy this key into the clipboard and add it to the code for SecureClass.vb as follows, removing the 0x prefix:

```
Public Class SecureClass

    <StrongNameIdentityPermissionAttribute(SecurityAction.LinkDemand, _
        PublicKey:="0024000004800000940000000602000000240000525341 3" _
        & "100040000010001 0067106E89E1 8E7CA82EA95CE79D2D6CCF6C22B30F1" _
        & "70B094F20F2DB4480C4E9FC13B79CABC808879C93498FEB20C2003F748" _
        & "D469B44A5176D15FB788C10E85E6456337BE54ACEF7348A6AD4CC4294F" _
        & "2367C39597F7344A6E83B0846DCA3A63262F867EA8ABCC09FB7F7F8319" _
        & "DFF17DDA38A9FDC3885397459715D11B57C66BD98")> _
    Public Function GetSecureString() As String
        Return "Secret Phrase: A Penny Saved a Day is Seven Cents a Week."
    End Function

End Class
```

Effectively, what you're doing is telling the CLR that any code attempting to access the Get-SecureString function must have a strong name identity that contains the public key listed.

There, now you have an assembly that you're pretty sure will be completely useless to anyone who compiles an assembly against a different .snk file from yours. This kind of code is extremely handy in applications that have a business rule tier in that it can prevent tricky, programming-savvy customers from writing code to bypass the business rules, because they will not have access to your .snk file.

■**Note** If you ever plan to distribute assemblies outside your own company, *never* allow your .snk file to fall into the wrong hands. Not only can it allow customers to tamper with your application, but it can also allow them to create new assemblies that appear to come from your organization.

Let's test your new assembly. First, you'll create a console application using your Secure.snk file as the AssemblyKeyFile, called SecureClient. Make sure the following attribute is in the AssemblyInfo.vb file:

```
<Assembly: AssemblyKeyFile("../../../SecureLibrary/Secure.snk")>
```

Next, add a reference to the SecureLibrary.dll assembly created in the previous example. Here is the source code for the main module in your application, SecureClientSample.vb:

```
Imports System

Module SecureClientSample

    Sub Main()
        Dim oClass As SecureLibrary.SecureClass = _
            New SecureLibrary.SecureClass()
        Console.WriteLine(oClass.GetSecureString())
    End Sub

End Module
```

It's pretty simple. It should generate the secure string as a result. When you run this application, you get the following console output:

`Secret Phrase: A Penny Saved a Day is Seven Cents a Week.`

Well, that's all well and good: everything works just fine. Now, let's actually prove that the code will fail against a client compiled without the right public key (or, for that matter, with no strong name at all). To do this, you'll create another console application, called `UnsecureClient`. You won't bother setting any key file attributes for this one. As previous, add a reference to SecureLibrary.dll, and add code to the module file UnsecureClientSample.vb.

The following is the short source code for your unauthorized client application:

```vb
Imports System

Module UnsecureClientSample

    Sub Main()
        Dim oClass As SecureLibrary.SecureClass = _
            New SecureLibrary.SecureClass()
        Console.WriteLine(oClass.GetSecureString())
    End Sub

End Module
```

The code should look pretty familiar. In fact, it is the same. The only difference is that your second client application has no strong name, so it should fail the identity test. Well, let's run it and take a look at the console output (see Figure 13-11).

Figure 13-11. *Running the example without a strong name*

It's certainly ugly, but it's also what was expected. The CLR has thrown an exception indicating that the permission request on the part of the calling assembly (your client) failed. The CLR is even nice enough to not only tell us that you failed an identity check, but also what identity the CLR was looking for. Don't worry; the only way to generate this public key for your DLL is to have the accompanying private key in your .snk file (which is why it is a very good idea to keep the .snk file locked up somewhere safe if you're distributing any assemblies commercially).

Now, let's see what happens when you try to revoke some permissions from existing code. To do this, you're going to go into the DACommands2 project (a sample from earlier in this chapter) and use the Secure.snk key file built previously to create a strongly named assembly with a public key you can use. To do this, you just need to add the same attribute you saw earlier.

```
<Assembly: AssemblyKeyFile("../../../SecureLibrary/Secure.snk")>
```

Once it is compiled, open the Microsoft .NET Framework Configuration tool from the Administrative Tools section of the Control Panel. In order to apply some security policy to your specific assembly, it needs to be a member of a specific code group. To do this, you're going to go into the machine scope and create a new custom code group beneath the My_Computer code group. You're presented with a wizard that allows you to supply a name (DACommands2) and description for your code group.

You then choose the membership condition. In your case, the membership condition will be Strong Name, with a public key. Again, the wizard is nice enough to allow you to browse to a specific assembly and import that public key. You can also check the Name and Version boxes to limit the rule to the assembly loaded. The last step is to choose which permission set should be applied to group members. Let's be really extreme and set that to Nothing (which means that no permissions will be granted to code matching your policy).

You also need to make sure that you check the boxes that indicate that the group members will be granted only this permission set, which we do from the properties of the code group once it is created. This prevents members from inheriting other permissions from different scopes when you've explicitly denied them. When you're all done creating some tyrannical security policy for this assembly, you have an admin tool that looks like what you see in Figure 13-12.

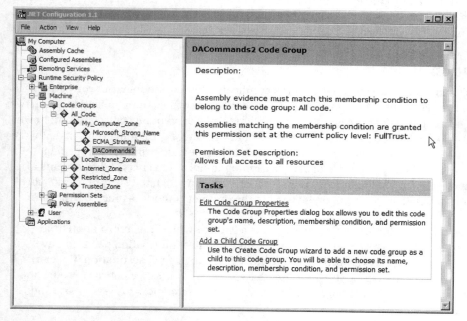

Figure 13-12. *Microsoft .NET Framework 1.1 configuration*

This should be suitably restrictive. Now, let's try to run the DACommands2 executable, which you know worked earlier in the chapter. The following is your console output:

Unhandled Exception: System.Security.Policy.PolicyException: Execution permission cannot be acquired.

You just modified some XML files sitting in the system somewhere with a graphic tool, and now this application cannot execute. If you were to go to the Enterprise scope and use the same public key to establish a code group, but left off the name and version, you could effectively prevent all code built against your Secure.snk from executing anywhere in your enterprise.

The bottom line is that you need to be aware of the fact that, no matter what, your code will be interacting with CAS somehow. Whether it is simply to verify that no security checks are being enforced or to perform detailed security checks, code will still interact with CAS on some level. What this means is that any time you need access to a resource, your code should make sure that it has sufficient permission to do so, and if not, it should gracefully trap that failure and explain the issue to the user.

SSL

In addition to securing your code through permissions or identity checks, we can also secure your data. SSL (Secure Sockets Layer) is a protocol that allows encrypted, secure communications across the Internet. It works by requiring the IIS server to maintain an authentication certificate that is used in the encryption of the data. Traditionally, SSL has been used on Web sites to encrypt transmissions of confidential information, such as credit card numbers during e-commerce sessions.

With the advent of web services, however, SSL is being used to guarantee that transmission of all kinds of data to and from web services is kept completely secure and private. Users can rest assure that any conversation they have with a web service, be it through a browser or a Windows Forms client, is completely private and no one else will be able to access that information.

Encryption

If you don't happen to have an authentication certificate (they cost money, but you can get them from companies like VeriSign at http://www.verisign.com) or your application doesn't have a permanent Internet presence, you might want to take encryption control into your own hands and deal with your data privacy issues on your own. One way in which you can do this is to use some of the Cryptographic APIs that are available in the framework to encrypt data.

You'll take a look at an example of using a Cryptographic API to encrypt the contents of a DataSet, and then decrypt that into another DataSet. This can be a handy way of transferring private information between components across the Internet without as much overhead as using SSL.

The basic plan of your example is to populate a DataSet with some information from the Northwind database. Then, you're going to assume that this information needs to travel securely across a nonsecure network, such as the Internet, to its final destination. You can do this by creating a cryptographic stream. To set this sample up yourself, create a console application and call it Encryption. Then, make sure that you have references to System.Data and

System.Security (Visual Studio should give you System.Data and System.XML by default), and type in the following code for the main module, EncryptionSample.vb:

```
Imports System
Imports System.Data
Imports System.Data.SqlClient
Imports System.Security
Imports System.Security.Cryptography
Imports System.IO
Imports System.Xml


Module EncryptionSample

    Sub Main()
```

The first thing you're going to do is create a file stream that will create a new file called DSencrypted.dat. This file will hold the encrypted contents of your DataSet. The only reason you're using a permanent storage for the encrypted data is so that, when you download the sample, you can examine this file and verify that it truly is impossible to glean any useful information from its encrypted form.

```
        Dim fs As FileStream = New FileStream("DSencrypted.dat", _
            FileMode.Create, FileAccess.Write)
```

Next, you'll populate a DataSet with some source data. In your case, you're going to select all of the columns from the Customers table in the Northwind database.

```
        Dim MyDS As DataSet = New DataSet()
        Dim MyDS2 As DataSet = New DataSet()
        Dim Connection As SqlConnection = New SqlConnection( _
            "Initial Catalog=Northwind;Integrated Security=SSPI;" _
            & "Server=(local);")
        Connection.Open()
        Dim MyDA As SqlDataAdapter = New SqlDataAdapter( _
            "SELECT * FROM Customers", Connection)
        MyDA.Fill(MyDS, "Customers")
```

Now you'll start doing some actual encryption work. The first thing to do in any encryption scheme is obtain a reference to the *Cryptographic Service Provider* (*CSP*) that you are looking for. In your case, you're using the *Data Encryption Standard* (*DES*). One reason for this is you don't have to seed it with any information in order for it to be able to encrypt your data.

```
        Dim DES As DESCryptoServiceProvider = _
            New DESCryptoServiceProvider()

        Dim DESencrypter As ICryptoTransform = _
            DES.CreateEncryptor()
        Dim cryptStream As CryptoStream = _
            New CryptoStream(fs, DESencrypter, CryptoStreamMode.Write)
```

This next line is actually doing an incredible amount of work behind the scenes that you just don't have to worry about. You've created this object, cryptStream, that is a stream-based on a DESencrypter transformation object. This means that anything placed on this stream is automatically encrypted according to the DES algorithm. Conveniently enough, the DataSet has an overload of the WriteXml method that will take a simple stream abstract as an argument. Notice, here, that not only are you writing the entire contents of the DataSet to the encryption stream, but also you are writing the schema. This means that when the DataSet is decrypted, all of its internal data types can be preserved.

```
MyDS.WriteXml(cryptStream, XmlWriteMode.WriteSchema)
cryptStream.Close()
```

Now you'll actually begin the task of loading your second DataSet with the decrypted information. To do this, you'll grab a read-access file stream, and create a DES decryption stream based on that. Then, you'll create an XmlTextReader based on that stream and use that as the source for your DataSet. Once that has been done, you'll display some basic information about the data in the DataSet to prove that it loaded successfully.

```
Dim fsRead As FileStream = New FileStream("DSencrypted.dat", _
    FileMode.Open, FileAccess.Read)
Dim DESdecrypter As ICryptoTransform = DES.CreateDecryptor()
Dim decryptStream As CryptoStream = New CryptoStream(fsRead, _
    DESdecrypter, CryptoStreamMode.Read)
Dim plainStreamR As XmlTextReader = New XmlTextReader(decryptStream)
MyDS2.ReadXml(plainStreamR, XmlReadMode.ReadSchema)

Console.WriteLine("Customers Table Successfully" _
    & " Encrypted and Decrypted.")
Console.WriteLine("First Customer:")
Dim _Column As DataColumn
For Each _Column In MyDS2.Tables("Customers").Columns
    Console.Write("{0}, ", _
        MyDS2.Tables("Customers").Rows(0)(_Column))
Next
Console.WriteLine()
End Sub


End Module
```

You can adapt the previous example so that a component in a class library returns an encrypted stream based on some data, and then the consuming application or component decrypts the data and loads it into its own DataSet. The resulting output should look like what you see in Figure 13-13.

Figure 13-13. Encryption *demo*

If you really want to get fancy, you can hook up a packet sniffer and watch the encrypted data travel across your network. If you've been paying attention, you may have noticed that there is no key exchange happening, so there's no key required to decrypt the stream. This means that anyone else using the same decryption scheme could watch all of your data if they were clever and patient enough. To really secure your data you'll want to use a keyed security system.

■**Note** If keeping your data private is a concern, and SSL is unavailable, you can still manually encrypt DataSets for securely traveling across nonsecure networks.

Summary

In this chapter, you've gained some insight on how you might be able to increase the performance of an application. In addition, you have looked at some of the ways in which you might be able to protect data from prying eyes. It is worth bearing in mind that what might be an acceptable level of performance for one programmer or one application might be considered too slow and unacceptable for another application. Also, what might be considered an adequate level of protection and security by one application might be considered a nonsecure situation for another application.

CHAPTER 14

■ ■ ■

Integration and Migration

While ADO.NET may be an incredibly useful and powerful tool, many people learning ADO.NET might well have been programming with various technologies already. One of those technologies is ADO. Many programmers and software companies have invested considerable amounts of time, money, and resources making applications that use ADO for their data access.

In a perfect world, with any new technology, all code written in the old technology would magically transform itself to be a part of the next "Big Thing." However, this isn't usually the case. The chances are you will be forced to make the decision between reusing your existing code from your .NET-managed assemblies or rewriting your existing data access code in ADO.NET.

In this chapter, you will look at how to perform the following tasks in order to reuse as much of your existing code as possible:

- Invoking COM objects from managed (.NET) code

- Invoking functions in existing DLLs from managed code

- Migrating your existing ADO code to ADO.NET

- Deciding when to upgrade and when to reuse

- Reusing classic code that returns ADO Recordsets from .NET

All of the examples in this chapter were run against the SQL Server 2000 version of the Northwind database.

InterOp

The Common Language Runtime (CLR) provides automatic facilities for code interoperability. It allows existing COM components to make use of .NET components, and .NET components to make use of COM components. Within the .NET Framework, you can also invoke functions in standard DLLs such as those composing the Win32 API.

The RCW and COM InterOp

COM interoperability is implemented through an object called the *Runtime Callable Wrapper* (*RCW*). In order for code to use classic COM objects, a .NET Assembly is created that contains a wrapper for that COM object's functionality. This assembly is referred to as an *InterOp Assembly*.

When you use Visual Studio .NET to create a reference to a COM component, if the publisher has not specified an official InterOp Assembly—called the Primary InterOp Assembly—then one is created automatically.

Each method that the COM object exposes is also a method available on the RCW object created to communicate with that COM object. The method arguments and return value are then *marshaled* to and from the COM object.

In this chapter, you'll focus on using COM InterOp with ADO components from within .NET managed code.

Accessing ADO from .NET

There are a couple of things to keep in mind when accessing the ADO COM objects from within .NET. The first and foremost is that whenever you invoke a method on an ADO object, you are using the RCW, which incurs a slight per-call performance overhead. If you are making lots of function calls in a row, the performance overhead may become noticeable. The second thing to keep in mind is that data-bindable controls cannot be bound to ADO Recordsets.

Whether to Access ADO from .NET

The most important decision you should make when creating your new .NET applications is whether you want to use ADO or ADO.NET. ADO.NET is designed to run very quickly from within managed code, and is definitely the faster choice. You should only use ADO from .NET if you absolutely have to. If there is some data source that ADO.NET cannot connect to that ADO can (though with the release of the ODBC data provider for .NET, these occurrences are quite rare), then you will be forced to use ADO.

Despite Microsoft urging people to use ADO only when technically necessary, there are typically other concerns. Companies might have a considerable amount of time and effort invested in existing code, and invoking this code from .NET and avoiding the rewrite might be the only practical solution available.

Another case when ADO may be required is in the case where your managed code needs to access files that were used to persist ADO Recordsets. While an ADO.NET DataSet can load an ADO 2.7 XML-persisted DataSet, the results are not pretty, and the DataSet cannot load the Advanced Data Tablegram (ADTG) binary Recordset persistence format at all.

■Note Use classic ADO only when the situation requires it, not as a preferred method of data access for managed code.

Accessing ADO from .NET

Thankfully, Microsoft has done most of the work for you to allow .NET components to interact with existing COM components. To demonstrate this, create a Windows application in Visual Studio .NET, called ADOInterOp, and add a reference to the ADO 2.7 COM type library (Microsoft ActiveX Data Objects 2.7 Library) from the COM tab in the Add Reference dialog. Rename Form1 as frmMain with a title of "ADO InterOp Example," add a label to the top of the form with the text "Northwind Customers:", and a listbox called lbCustomers below it (see Figure 14-1).

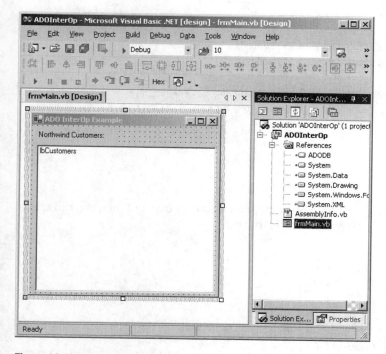

Figure 14-1. ADOInterOp *at design time*

What you're going to do for this example is create an ADO connection, then use that Connection to populate an ADO Recordset. From there, you'll iterate through the Recordset to populate a simple control on your form. All the code to do this can be added to a new frmMain_Load event handler in the frmMain.vb file.

Because you've got a reference to the ADO type library, you can create ADODB and ADOMD [ActiveX Data Objects Multi-Dimensional, used for Online Analytical Processing (OLAP) features] objects just as if they were standard .NET components. The RCW automatically wraps up the managed calls for you and forwards them on to the actual COM components.

```
Private Sub frmMain_Load(ByVal sender As System.Object, _
            ByVal e As System.EventArgs) Handles MyBase.Load
   Dim Connection As ADODB.Connection = New ADODB.Connection()
   Connection.Open("DRIVER={SQL Server};SERVER=Localhost;" _
            & "DATABASE=Northwind;", "sa", "", 0)
```

This code should all look pretty familiar to ADO programmers. You simply create a new Recordset, and then open it by supplying a SQL SELECT statement, a cursor type, and a lock type. Then you can iterate through the Recordset using the same methods and functions as you used to when invoking ADO from classic VB or C++ code.

```
    Dim RS As ADODB.Recordset = New ADODB.Recordset()
    RS.Open("SELECT * FROM Customers", _
            Connection, _
            ADODB.CursorTypeEnum.adOpenDynamic, _
            ADODB.LockTypeEnum.adLockReadOnly, 0)
    While Not RS.EOF
       lbCustomers.Items.Add(RS.Fields("ContactName").Value _
                  & " From " & RS.Fields("CompanyName").Value)
       RS.MoveNext()
    End While
    RS.Close()
    Connection.Close()
End Sub
```

The rest of the Windows Form code isn't reproduced here for brevity. When you run this program, you get the form display shown in Figure 14-2.

Figure 14-2. ADOInterOp *in action*

There is something else you can do in order to access your ADO data. In the previous example, you had to manually add each and every customer to the ListBox because the List-Box is incapable of binding directly to an ADO Recordset. However, you can use the OLEDB data provider to take the contents of an ADO Recordset and use it to fill an ADO.NET DataSet. Since the ADO.NET DataSet *can* participate in binding, you can bind the control to your DataSet. Even more useful is the fact that once the data is in the DataSet, you can do all of the things to it that a DataSet can do to it, such as obtain its XML representation, generate an XML schema for it, or even hook up another DataAdapter to it to transfer data to another data store.

Let's take a look at an example that accomplishes the same as the earlier example, but this time you'll use the OleDbDataAdapter to fill your DataSet using the ADO Recordset as the source. To do this, create a new Windows application project called ADOInterOp2, with the same two controls on the form (frmMain) as stated previously and the same reference to the ADO 2.7 type library. Then enter the following code for the frmMain_Load event handler in frmMain.vb (along with an Imports statement for System.Data.OleDb):

```
Private Sub frmMain_Load(ByVal sender As System.Object, _
             ByVal e As System.EventArgs) Handles MyBase.Load
  Dim Connection As ADODB.Connection = New ADODB.Connection()
  Connection.Open("DRIVER={SQL Server};SERVER=LOCALHOST;" _
            & "DATABASE=Northwind;", "sa", "", 0)
  Dim RS As ADODB.Recordset = New ADODB.Recordset()
  RS.Open("SELECT Customers.*, ContactName + ' from ' + " _
          & "CompanyName AS FullName FROM Customers", _
          Connection, _
          ADODB.CursorTypeEnum.adOpenDynamic, _
          ADODB.LockTypeEnum.adLockReadOnly, 0)
```

This is where you can really start to get the most out of code used to write to the ADO components. The OleDbDataAdapter has an overloaded version of the Fill method that allows it to Fill a DataSet from an ADODB Recordset object, instead of a SELECT string or a Select-Command.

```
  Dim DA As OleDbDataAdapter = New OleDbDataAdapter()
  Dim DS As DataSet = New DataSet()

  DA.Fill(DS, RS, "Customers")
  lbCustomers.DataSource = DS.Tables("Customers")
  lbCustomers.DisplayMember = "FullName"

  Connection.Close()
End Sub
```

The immediate value of this might not seem all that obvious—after all, if you're selecting out of a database, why not select straight into an adapter rather than an ADODB Recordset? That's an extremely good point. The only reason we used the procedure we did was to demonstrate loading an ADO Recordset into a DataSet. The real power of this technique comes from when you have existing COM components that return ADO Recordsets. Using this technique, you can leverage and reuse those existing components, and still gain access to all of the advanced features found in the DataSet and Windows/Web Forms control binding.

■Note You can populate ADO.NET DataSets with ADO Recordsets returned from your existing COM objects through the COM InterOp layer without having to rewrite your existing components.

Platform Invocation Services (PInvoke)

Need to access data that isn't exposed via a COM interface? Don't worry, because the .NET Framework has another built-in facility supporting code interoperability that might come in handy. If you need to access a classic API exposed in the form of a standard DLL (such as the Win32 API or older database APIs like Btrieve), then you can use something called *Platform Invocation Services (PInvoke)*.

Not only can you declare an external function stored in a DLL, but also you can configure how information is marshaled to and from that external function. This is quite an obscure technology, so we will not cover it in detail here.

We will give a brief sample of how you might use PInvoke Services to gain access to functions in existing DLLs. To do this, create a console application called PInvokeTest, then enter the following code for the main file PInvokeSample.vb:

```
Imports System
Imports System.Runtime.InteropServices

Class PInvokeTest

    <DllImport("winmm.dll")> _
    Public Shared Function sndPlaySound(ByVal lpszSound As String, _
                                        ByVal flags As UInt32) As Boolean
    End Function

    Public Shared Sub Main()
        sndPlaySound("Windows XP Startup", New UInt32())
    End Sub

End Class
```

This example is pretty simple. We used the Windows API Text Viewer that comes with Visual Studio 6.0 to get the definition for the sndPlaySound function. We found out from this that it is defined in the winmm.dll library and that it takes two arguments—a string and an unsigned integer. We use the DllImport attribute to indicate that the following Public Shared function is defined in the indicated DLL. Once declared, you can use the function as if it were a standard, native Framework function. When you run the application (on Windows XP) the default startup noise is played. To change this to work with any other WAV file in the \Windows\ Media (or \Winnt\media) directory, just supply the filename of the WAV file without the .WAV extension.

The point here isn't to show how to play a sound in Windows (although that is a nice bonus). The point is to demonstrate that even though you might be planning to write new code for the .NET Framework, your old code is not lost. You don't have to rewrite all of your old DLLs, nor do you have to rewrite all of your old COM components. Both types of functions can be accessed via code InterOp provided automatically in the .NET Framework.

Migration

Migration is an extremely important topic when talking about moving to ADO.NET. Many people learning how to use ADO.NET are also thinking about how their old data-access code written in classic ADO can be translated. While there may be some wizards available to perform language upgrades from Visual Basic 6.0 to Visual Basic .NET, these wizards are not smart enough to interpret classic ADO access and migrate it to ADO.NET.

The biggest reason for this is that the object model and data access strategy have an entirely different focus in ADO.NET from that of their predecessors. ADO's object model seems to treat offline, disconnected data access, and manipulation as an afterthought, whereas this is at the core of ADO.NET's design. This next section will give you an object-by-object instruction on how to convert your existing code to work in the .NET world. In most of the previous chapters in this book, you have focused on how to do things the new way: using ADO.NET. This next section will provide a handy side-by-side comparison of old and new.

The old-style ADO samples are written in Visual Basic 6.0 for clarity, while the new-style ADO.NET samples are provided in VB.NET.

ADO Data Types

When using ADO, all of the various data types were represented by constants that began with the ad prefix. In certain languages, especially Visual Basic, it was occasionally difficult to figure out what intrinsic (language-supplied) data type to use for each of the ADO constants when supplying values for stored procedures, for instance. With ADO.NET, all of the data types are part of the Common Type System (CTS), so no matter what language you access ADO.NET from, the data types will always remain the same.

Table 14-1 gives you a handy reference for migrating your ADO data types to .NET data types. This list is not complete, and only covers some of the more commonly used data types.

Table 14-1. *ADO Data Types and Their Equivalent .NET Data Types*

ADO 2.7 Data Type	.NET Framework Data Type
adEmpty	Null
adBoolean	Boolean
adTinyInt	Byte
adSmallInt	Int16
adInteger	Int32
adBigInt	Int64
adUnsignedTinyInt	Byte
adUnsignedSmallInt	UInt16
adUnsignedInt	UInt32
asUnsignedBigInt	UInt64
adSingle	Single
adDouble	Double

continues

Table 14-1. *continued*

ADO 2.7 Data Type	.NET Framework Data Type
adCurrency	Decimal
adDecimal	Decimal
adNumeric	Decimal
adDate	DateTime
adDBDate	DateTime
adDBTime	DateTime
adDBTimeStamp	DateTime
adFileTime	DateTime
adError	ExternalException
adVariant	Object
adBinary	Byte[]
adChar	String
adWChar	String
adBSTR	String
adUserDefined	(not supported)

Migrating Connections

The connection is the lifeline of RDBMS-based data access. All data comes through a connection, and all changes to data return through a connection. ADO connections followed the black-box model, allowing a connection to any data source supported by OLEDB or ODBC Drivers. But ADO.NET uses different connection classes to provide connections that are optimized to work as fast as possible with their particular connection type.

Syntactically, the ADO connection object and ADO.NET connection object are probably the closest in terms of duties performed and object models. The following code should look pretty familiar to ADO programmers, especially those who used Visual Basic:

```
Private Sub Command1_Click()
    Dim myConn As ADODB.Connection

    Set myConn = New ADODB.Connection
    myConn.Open "DRIVER={SQL Server};DATABASE=Northwind;" & _
                "SERVER=Localhost;UID=sa;PWD=;"
    MsgBox "Connection Object Version: " & myConn.Version
    myConn.Close
End Sub
```

The previous code displays the connection version (2.7 on our test machine) in a message box after opening it.

The following is the VB.NET source code for opening and closing a SQL connection:

```
Imports System.Data
Imports System.Data.SqlClient
```

You need to make sure that the appropriate namespaces are imported so that when you reference SqlConnection, the compiler knows that it is the System.Data.SqlClient.Sql-Connection class.

```
Public Class Form1
    Inherits System.Windows.Forms.Form
```

To keep things clear and easy-to-read, the code generated by the Forms Designer is not included.

```
Private Sub Button1_Click(ByVal sender As System.Object, _
                          ByVal e As System.EventArgs) Handles Button1.Click
    Dim myConnection As SqlConnection
    myConnection = New SqlConnection( _
        "Server=(local); Integrated Security=SSPI; " _
        & "Initial Catalog=Northwind;")
    myConnection.Open()
    MessageBox.Show("SQL Server Version: " + myConnection.ServerVersion)
    myConnection.Close()
End Sub
End Class
```

One thing that sticks out is the difference in connection strings. Because, when using ADO.NET, you get to choose whether you're using OLEDB, ODBC, or SQL, the connection strings can be specialized rather than generic. This connection string tells SQL that you want the Northwind database on the local server, and to use NT integrated security. Also, because this connection is a SQL-specific connection, you can ask it for SQL Server's version, which is far more useful than asking it for the version of ADO used to connect to the database. In our case, this application executes and displays the SQL version 8.00.0193 (SQL 2000) in a modal dialog box (see Figure 14-3).

Figure 14-3. *Retrieving SQL Server version in VB.NET*

For more details on using ADO.NET connections with non-SQL data sources, consult the introductory chapters in this book that detail making database connections.

Migrating the Recordset

The connection object seemed pretty simple. Unfortunately, the same is not true for the Recordset. As with so many other ADO components, the Recordset encapsulates an incredible amount of functionality.

ADO.NET, on the other hand, takes an entirely different approach. For read-only/result-set traversal, ADO.NET uses a DataReader object, while ADO still must use the Recordset. For storing an in-memory cache of rows, ADO uses a disconnected Recordset while ADO.NET uses a DataSet, which provides a wealth of functionality that simply doesn't exist anywhere in classic ADO. For publishing data back to the database, ADO uses either a connected Recordset or SQL statements or stored procedures. ADO.NET can accomplish this using DataAdapters hooked to a DataSet and a connection or stored procedures or simple SQL statements.

Table 14-2 is a quick reference to help you determine which classes in ADO.NET you need to use based on the purpose for which you were using the classic ADO Recordset.

Table 14-2. *ADO* Recordset *to ADO.NET*

ADO Recordset Task	ADO.NET Classes Involved
Forward-only iteration for display	DataReader, connection, command
Connected random (indexed) row access	DataSet, DataAdapter, connection
Publishing Recordset changes to DB	DataSet, DataAdapter, connection, command
Reading/writing persisted data (XML or binary)	DataSet
GetString or GetRows	DataSet (the purpose of GetString and GetRows is removed by the DataSet object's disconnected, random-access nature)

The first one you'll look at is one of the most common data-related tasks: forward-only iteration. This is usually done when obtaining lists of read-only information to be displayed to users such as category lists, order history, or any other kind of "view" information. In ADO.NET, this operation is highly optimized by the DataReader, while ADO still uses a Recordset.

Forward-Only Data Access

You'll start by looking at a VB6 example that populates a ListBox control with the customers list from the Northwind database (much like the COM InterOp sample you went through earlier).

The following is VB6 source code for forward-only Recordset iteration:

```
Private Sub Form_Load()
    Dim myRS As New ADODB.Recordset
    Dim myConnection As New ADODB.Connection

    myConnection.ConnectionString = _
        "Driver={SQL Server}; Server=localhost; Database=Northwind;" _
        & " Uid=sa;Pwd=;"
    myConnection.Open
```

```
    myRS.Open "SELECT * FROM Customers", myConnection, adOpenForwardOnly, _
            adLockReadOnly
    Do While Not myRS.EOF
        List1.AddItem (myRS("ContactName") & " FROM " & myRS("CompanyName"))
        myRS.MoveNext
    Loop
    myRS.Close
    myConnection.Close

    Set myConnection = Nothing
    Set myRS = Nothing
End Sub
```

It's all pretty straightforward. You use an ADO connection and an ADO Recordset to iterate through the customers, adding each one individually to the ListBox control on your VB6 form. Let's take a look at how you accomplish this the fast way in VB.NET using a data reader.

The following is a VB.NET forward-only data access example:

```
Imports System.Data
Imports System.Data.SqlClient

Public Class Form1
    Inherits System.Windows.Forms.Form

    Private Sub Form1_Load(ByVal sender As System.Object, _
                            ByVal e As System.EventArgs) Handles MyBase.Load
        Dim myConnection As SqlConnection
        Dim myReader As SqlDataReader
        Dim myCommand As SqlCommand

        myConnection = _
            New SqlConnection("Server=localhost; Initial Catalog=Northwind;" _
                            & " Integrated Security=SSPI;")
        myConnection.Open()
        myCommand = New SqlCommand("SELECT * FROM Customers", myConnection)
        myReader = myCommand.ExecuteReader()

        While myReader.Read
            ListBox1.Items.Add(myReader.GetString( _
                myReader.GetOrdinal("ContactName")) & " from " _
                & myReader.GetString(myReader.GetOrdinal("CompanyName")))
        End While
    End Sub
End Class
```

Both of the previous examples generate output that looks similar to what you see in Figure 14-4.

Figure 14-4. *VB.NET forward-only data access using a* DataReader

Publishing Recordset Changes

One of the other common things to do with a Recordset is to leave it connected, make the
appropriate changes, and then post the changes back to the database. To illustrate this example in classic ADO, you're going to use VB6 to open a connected Recordset and insert a new
customer, carrying that change across to the connected database. Then, to contrast, you'll
accomplish the same goal using different techniques in VB.NET.

The VB6 source code to update a database using a Recordset could look something like
the following:

```
Private Sub Command1_Click()
  Dim myConnection As ADODB.Connection
  Dim myRS As ADODB.Recordset

  Set myConnection = New ADODB.Connection
  myConnection.ConnectionString = _
    "DRIVER={SQL Server};DATABASE=Northwind;UID=sa;PWD=;SERVER=localhost;"
  myConnection.Open
```

You are going to open the Recordset in Dynamic mode with an optimistic lock to give you
sufficient access to allow the Recordset to modify the underlying table directly.

```
  Set myRS = New ADODB.Recordset
  myRS.Open "SELECT * FROM Customers", myConnection, adOpenDynamic, _
    adLockOptimistic

  myRS.AddNew
  myRS("CustomerID").Value = "SDOO"
  myRS("CompanyName").Value = "Scooby Doo Detective Agency"
  myRS("ContactName").Value = "Scooby Doo"
  myRS("ContactTitle").Value = "Canine Detective"
  myRS("Address").Value = "1 Doo Lane"
```

```
myRS("City").Value = "Springfield"
myRS("PostalCode").Value = "111111"
myRS("Country").Value = "USA"
myRS("Phone").Value = "111-111-1111"
myRS.Update

myRS.Close
myConnection.Close
Set myConnection = Nothing
Set myRS = Nothing

    MsgBox "New Customer Added"
End Sub
```

This is probably pretty familiar. ADO Recordsets use the AddNew method to create a new row and move the current row pointer to that new row. Then, they use the Update method to post those changes back to the database.

As you have seen in previous chapters, ADO.NET has no connected equivalent for enabling this kind of functionality. Not in a single class, anyway. ADO.NET uses a DataSet to store an in-memory, disconnected cache of data. A DataAdapter is then used to pump information to and from the database, in and out of the DataSet. Next we'll take a look at the source code for a VB.NET application that uses a DataSet and a DataAdapter to load a DataSet with the Customers table, and then update the database with a customer added to the DataSet. This combination of classes is far more powerful than the single ADO Recordset, in that it allows us not only to configure what information is updated in the database, but also how it is updated. The ADO.NET design of focusing the entire system around the offline data cache facilitates all kinds of features previously unavailable to classic ADO, such as the ability to work with the offline data cache from within portable devices such as PocketPCs.

Now, let's take a look at how the VB.NET comparison stands up. What you're doing is using a DataAdapter to load the DataSet, and then allowing the SqlCommandBuilder to automatically generate the necessary InsertCommand for you.

```
Imports System.Data
Imports System.Data.SqlClient

Public Class Form1
    Inherits System.Windows.Forms.Form


    Private Sub Button1_Click(ByVal sender As System.Object, _
                    ByVal e As System.EventArgs) Handles Button1.Click

        Dim myConnection As SqlConnection
        Dim myDS As DataSet
        Dim myDA As SqlDataAdapter
        Dim NewRow As DataRow
        Dim SqlCB As SqlCommandBuilder
```

```
myConnection = New SqlConnection( _
    "Server=localhost; Initial Catalog=Northwind; " _
    & "Integrated Security=SSPI;")
myConnection.Open()
myDS = New DataSet()
myDA = New SqlDataAdapter("SELECT * FROM Customers", myConnection)
```

Here you're instantiating a new SqlCommandBuilder. This object will automatically create the appropriate UPDATE, INSERT, and DELETE SQL statements based on the SELECT statement that you provide to the DataAdapter. This is different from classic ADO in that the ADO Recordset would automatically generate these commands for you without you requesting it, often incurring a performance overhead each time a classic ADO Recordset was created. You're going to use this to automatically generate your insert command so that it most closely resembles the VB6 version (which is also creating an insert statement behind the scenes in the Recordset object).

```
SqlCB = New SqlCommandBuilder(myDA)
myDA.Fill(myDS, "Customers")
```

The NewRow method creates a new row object. Unlike the Recordset AddNew method, however, this new row is not automatically part of the originating table. It is simply a new, disconnected DataRow object that has the same columns and column data types as the originating table.

```
NewRow = myDS.Tables("Customers").NewRow()
NewRow("CustomerID") = "SDOO"
NewRow("CompanyName") = "Scooby Doo Detective Agency"
NewRow("ContactName") = "Scooby Doo"
NewRow("ContactTitle") = "Canine Detective"
NewRow("Address") = "1 Doo Lane"
NewRow("City") = "Springfield"
NewRow("PostalCode") = "11111"
NewRow("Country") = "USA"
NewRow("Phone") = "111-111-1111"
```

In order to make sure that your new row is actually placed back into the DataSet, you'll add the new DataRow to the Rows collection in your DataTable object (Customers table).

```
myDS.Tables("Customers").Rows.Add(NewRow)
```

Calling the Update method on your Customers table in the DataSet actually performs quite a bit of work in the background. First, it finds all *new* rows, and then uses the appropriate object, returned by the InsertCommand method, to place those new rows in the database. In addition, it finds all *modified* rows and uses the appropriate UpdateCommand to make those changes in the database. All *deleted* rows in the DataSet are then removed from the database using the adapter's DeleteCommand. These commands can either be standard SQL statements or they can be stored procedures in the server. As you can see, there is quite a bit of versatility and power in the DataSet/DataAdapter combination that simply didn't exist in previous ADO incarnations.

```
        myDA.Update(myDS.Tables("Customers"))
        MsgBox("New Customer Added")
    End Sub
End Class
```

As you learned in the performance chapter, the preferred way of accomplishing things is to build your own commands instead of using the command builder, but this works fine for this comparison.

Migrating Commands and Stored Procedures

So far you have seen a side-by-side comparison of ADO `Recordsets` and `Connections`, detailing what the ADO.NET code looks like to accomplish the same task as the classic ADO code. This next section will cover using stored procedures. You have seen some of the places where ADO.NET commands can be used, such as with the `DataAdapter`, but now you'll cover using a stored procedure rather than SQL strings. To do this, you'll enter the following stored procedure into your local SQL Server's `Northwind` database:

```
CREATE PROCEDURE sp_InsertCustomer
@CustomerID nchar(5),
@CompanyName nvarchar(40),
@ContactName nvarchar(30),
@ContactTitle nvarchar(30),
@Address nvarchar(60),
@City nvarchar(15),
@Region nvarchar(15) = null,
@PostalCode nvarchar(10),
@Country nvarchar(15),
@Phone nvarchar(24),
@Fax nvarchar(24) = null
AS
    INSERT INTO Customers(CustomerID, CompanyName, ContactName, ContactTitle,
    Address, City, Region, PostalCode, Country, Phone, Fax)
    VALUES(@CustomerID, @CompanyName, @ContactName, @ContactTitle, @Address,
    @City, @Region, @PostalCode, @Country, @Phone, @Fax)
```

The SQL statement should look pretty familiar. It is very similar to the SQL statements supplied to the `InsertCommand` property of the `SqlDataAdapter` in the previous example. The only difference between the two is that this procedure will be compiled ahead of time and saved on the server, while the procedure in the previous example will be compiled and cached only when first executed, and the caching rules will be different. In other words, the server-side stored procedure is a faster solution.

Let's take a quick look at the VB6, classic ADO source code for creating a new customer in the `Northwind` database using this stored procedure.

```
Private Sub Command1_Click()
    Dim myConnection As ADODB.Connection
    Dim myCommand As ADODB.Command
```

```
    Set myConnection = New ADODB.Connection
    myConnection.ConnectionString =
        "DRIVER={SQL Server};DATABASE=Northwind;SERVER=localhost;UID=sa;PWD=;"
    myConnection.Open

    Set myCommand = New ADODB.Command

    myCommand.CommandText = "sp_InsertCustomer"
    myCommand.CommandType = adCmdStoredProc
    Set myCommand.ActiveConnection = myConnection

    myCommand.Parameters.Append myCommand.CreateParameter("CustomerID", _
        adChar, adParamInput, 5, "SDOO")
    myCommand.Parameters.Append myCommand.CreateParameter("CompanyName", _
        adVarChar, adParamInput, 40, "Scooby Doo Detective Agency")
    myCommand.Parameters.Append myCommand.CreateParameter("ContactName", _
        adVarChar, adParamInput, 30, "Scooby Doo")
    myCommand.Parameters.Append myCommand.CreateParameter("ContactTitle", _
        adVarChar, adParamInput, 30, "Canine Detective")
    myCommand.Parameters.Append myCommand.CreateParameter("Address", _
        adVarChar, adParamInput, 60, "1 Doo Lane")
    myCommand.Parameters.Append myCommand.CreateParameter("City", _
        adVarChar, adParamInput, 15, "Springfield")
    myCommand.Parameters.Append myCommand.CreateParameter("Region", _
        adVarChar, adParamInput, 15)
    myCommand.Parameters.Append myCommand.CreateParameter("PostalCode", _
        adVarChar, adParamInput, 10, "11111")
    myCommand.Parameters.Append myCommand.CreateParameter("Country", _
        adVarChar, adParamInput, 15, "USA")
    myCommand.Parameters.Append myCommand.CreateParameter("Phone", _
        adVarChar, adParamInput, 24, "111-111-1111")
    myCommand.Parameters.Append myCommand.CreateParameter("Fax", _
        adVarChar, adParamInput, 24)

    myCommand.Execute
    MsgBox "New Customer Added"
    myConnection.Close
    Set myCommand = Nothing
    Set myConnection = Nothing
End Sub
```

This is the standard setup for invoking a stored procedure using ADO: you instantiate a connection, then instantiate a Command object. This command object then gets parameters populated with values, and finally you execute the command. It is a pretty straightforward operation.

In your VB.NET example, you're going to bind your ListBox control to a DataSet, and you'll have a button that will add a new customer to the DataSet. However, this time you're going to custom build an InsertCommand that uses your new stored procedure rather than plain SQL text.

The following is the VB.NET source code for using a stored procedure in the InsertCommand property:

```
Imports System.Data
Imports System.Data.SqlClient

Public Class Form1
    Inherits System.Windows.Forms.Form

    Private myConnection As SqlConnection
    Private myCommand As SqlCommand
    Private myDS As DataSet
    Private myDA As SqlDataAdapter
```

This is the event handler for the button-click event on your form. In response to the button, you create a new DataRow object, populate the values appropriately, and then add the new row to the Rows collection on your Customers DataTable. Once you do that, you call the Update method, which then invokes your stored procedure. If you had added two rows, your stored procedure would be invoked twice, once for each row.

```
    Private Sub Button1_Click(ByVal sender As System.Object, _
                            ByVal e As System.EventArgs) Handles Button1.Click
        Dim NewRow As DataRow

        NewRow = myDS.Tables("Customers").NewRow()
        NewRow("CustomerID") = "SDOO"
        NewRow("CompanyName") = "Scooby Doo Detective Agency"
        NewRow("ContactName") = "Scooby Doo"
        NewRow("ContactTitle") = "Canine Detective"
        NewRow("Address") = "1 Doo Lane"
        NewRow("City") = "Springfield"
        NewRow("PostalCode") = "11111"
        NewRow("Country") = "USA"
        NewRow("Phone") = "111-111-1111"
        NewRow("FullName") = NewRow("ContactName") &" from " _
                & NewRow("CompanyName")
        myDS.Tables("Customers").Rows.Add(NewRow)
        ListBox1.SelectedIndex = ListBox1.Items.Count - 1
        myDA.Update(myDS, "Customers")
    End Sub

    Private Sub Form1_Load(ByVal sender As System.Object, _
                            ByVal e As System.EventArgs) Handles MyBase.Load
        myConnection = _
            New SqlConnection("Server=localhost; Initial Catalog=Northwind;" _
                            & " Integrated Security=SSPI;")
```

```
myCommand = New SqlCommand()
myDS = New DataSet()
myDA = _
    New SqlDataAdapter("SELECT Customers.*, ContactName & ' from ' _
            & " CompanyName as FullName FROM Customers", myConnection)
myDA.Fill(myDS, "Customers")
```

As usual, the databinding operation is incredibly simple and straightforward. It doesn't get much easier than this.

```
ListBox1.DataSource = myDS.Tables("Customers")
ListBox1.DisplayMember = "FullName"
```

Now you actually attend to the business of building your InsertCommand. You've initialized a private member variable called myCommand to be of type SqlCommand. You indicate that you want this command to be a stored procedure and set the CommandText property to be the actual name of the stored procedure. The rest of the parameter population should look nearly identical to what you did in the previous example.

```
myCommand.CommandType = CommandType.StoredProcedure
myCommand.Connection = myConnection
myCommand.CommandText = "sp_InsertCustomer"
myCommand.Parameters.Add(New SqlParameter
    ("@CustomerID", SqlDbType.NChar, 5, "CustomerID"))
myCommand.Parameters.Add(New SqlParameter
    ("@CompanyName", SqlDbType.NVarChar, 40, "CompanyName"))
myCommand.Parameters.Add(New SqlParameter
    ("@ContactName", SqlDbType.NVarChar, 30, "ContactName"))
myCommand.Parameters.Add(New SqlParameter
    ("@ContactTitle", SqlDbType.NVarChar, 30, "ContactTitle"))
myCommand.Parameters.Add(New SqlParameter
    ("@Address", SqlDbType.NVarChar, 60, "Address"))
myCommand.Parameters.Add(New SqlParameter
    ("@City", SqlDbType.NVarChar, 15, "City"))
myCommand.Parameters.Add(New SqlParameter
    ("@Region", SqlDbType.NVarChar, 15, "Region"))
myCommand.Parameters.Add(New SqlParameter
    ("@PostalCode", SqlDbType.NVarChar, 10, "PostalCode"))
myCommand.Parameters.Add(New SqlParameter
    ("@Country", SqlDbType.NVarChar, 15, "Country"))
myCommand.Parameters.Add(New SqlParameter
    ("@Phone", SqlDbType.NVarChar, 24, "Phone"))
myCommand.Parameters.Add(New SqlParameter
    ("@Fax", SqlDbType.NVarChar, 24, "Fax"))

myDA.InsertCommand = myCommand
  End Sub
End Class
```

■Note The ADO.NET `Command` objects have quite a bit of power, and can be used in a variety of ways, such as being attached to `DataAdapters` to facilitate data communication between `DataSets` and databases or executing stored procedures or a combination of both.

Changes in XML Persistence

As ADO progressed and advanced, so too did its support of XML as a persistence format. Attempting to load a `Recordset` persisted to XML via ADO 2.1 into a `Recordset` under ADO 2.6 often lead to compatibility problems. But otherwise, ADO's XML persistence support was good.

However, there have been some changes to the way data is persisted in ADO.NET.

In ADO, the `Recordset` was the only construct that could persist itself to XML. .NET allows virtually any class to persist itself to a vast array of different formats, including binary, XML, and SOAP formats.

ADO XML-persisted `Recordsets` all stored an XDR (XML-Data Reduced) Schema at the top of the file or stream that indicated the structure of the `Recordset`. ADO.NET supports either leaving off the schema entirely or storing the data with an inline XML Schema Definition (XSD). XSD is the W3C (World Wide Web Consortium) standard for XML Schemas. Microsoft created XDR because it needed something with regard to XML Schemas to work with, and XSD wasn't finished at the time. Now XSD is the official standard and the .NET Framework is fully compliant with it; there is no reason to use XDR.

First, let's take a look at a snippet of what the `Customers` table looks like when persisted via Visual Basic 6.0 and ADO 2.7.

```
<xml xmlns:s='uuid:BDC6E3F0-6DA3-11d1-A2A3-00AA00C14882'
  xmlns:dt='uuid:C2F41010-65B3-11d1-A29F-00AA00C14882'
  xmlns:rs='urn:schemas-microsoft-com:rowset'
  xmlns:z='#RowsetSchema'>
<s:Schema id='RowsetSchema'>
  <s:ElementType name='row' content='eltOnly' rs:CommandTimeout='30'>
    <s:AttributeType name='CustomerID' rs:number='1' rs:writeunknown='true'>
      <s:datatype dt:type='string' dt:maxLength='5' rs:fixedlength='true'
              rs:maybenull='false'/>
    </s:AttributeType>
    <s:AttributeType name='CompanyName' rs:number='2'
                rs:writeunknown='true'>
      <s:datatype dt:type='string' dt:maxLength='40' rs:maybenull='false'/>
    </s:AttributeType>
```

The schema at the top of this persisted `Recordset` is a `RowSetSchema`. According to the schema, the actual data portion of the document will consist of row elements. Each of those row elements will have attributes that indicate the columns in the `Recordset`, such as `CustomerID` and `CompanyName`.

If you skip down through the file a bit (it is quite large and not all that pretty) to the actual data portion, you'll see that the data for each row is, indeed, contained within the attributes of a row element.

```
<z:row CustomerID='REGGC' CompanyName='Reggiani Caseifici'
  ContactName='Maurizio Moroni' ContactTitle='Sales Associate'
  Address='StradaProvinciale 124' City='Reggio Emilia' PostalCode='42100'
  Country='Italy' Phone='0522-556721' Fax='0522-556722'/>
<z:row CustomerID='RICAR' CompanyName='Ricardo Adocicados'
  ContactName='Janete Limeira' ContactTitle='Assistant Sales Agent'
  Address='Av. Copacabana, 267' City='Rio de Janeiro' Region='RJ'
  PostalCode='02389-890' Country='Brazil' Phone='(21) 555-3412'/>
```

Looking at this file, you notice some of its limitations. The main limitation is that the only type of element you'll ever get is a row element; you'll never be able to call it anything else. Additionally, even though it is XML, it is not easy to read, and you have no choice as to whether the columns are attributes or nested child elements. ADO.NET allows for all of these flexibilities and quite a bit more. However, if all you are using is purely the WriteXml method of the DataSet object, your output is going to look remarkably similar. The following is a snippet of the Customers table persisted to XML. We've decided to write the schema into the file as well so it is easier to compare side-by-side the two different implementations of XML persistence.

The following is a snippet of the schema header of the persisted XML file:

```
<?xml version="1.0" standalone="yes"?>
<xml>
  <xsd:schema id="xml" xmlns="" xmlns:xsd="http://www.w3.org/2001/XMLSchema"
            xmlns:msdata="urn:schemas-microsoft-com:xml-msdata"
            xmlns:app1="#RowsetSchema"
            xmlns:app2="urn:schemas-microsoft-com:rowset">
    <xsd:import namespace="#RowsetSchema" schemaLocation="app1_NS.xsd" />
    <xsd:import namespace="urn:schemas-microsoft-com:rowset"
              schemaLocation="app2_NS.xsd" />
    <xsd:element name="xml" msdata:IsDataSet="true">
      <xsd:complexType>
        <xsd:choice maxOccurs="unbounded">
          <xsd:element name="Customers">
            <xsd:complexType>
              <xsd:sequence>
                <xsd:element name="CustomerID" type="xsd:string"
                           minOccurs="0" />
                <xsd:element name="CompanyName" type="xsd:string"
                           minOccurs="0" />
                <xsd:element name="ContactName" type="xsd:string"
                           minOccurs="0" />
```

It looks fairly similar, though it is a bit easier to read. The main difference is that the previous schema is in XSD format while the previous schema was an XDR Schema. ADO.NET DataSets *can* load data described by XDR Schemas. And following you have some of the data generated by ADO.NET listed:

```
<rs:data xmlns:rs="urn:schemas-microsoft-com:rowset">
  <z:row CustomerID="ALFKI" CompanyName="Alfreds Futterkiste"
         ContactName="Maria Anders"
         ContactTitle="Sales Representative"
         Address="Obere Str. 57" City="Berlin"
         PostalCode="12209" Country="Germany"
         Phone="030-0074321" Fax="030-0076545" xmlns:z="#RowsetSchema" />
  <z:row CustomerID="ANATR" CompanyName="Ana Trujillo Emparedados y helados"
         ContactName="Ana Trujillo"
         ContactTitle="Owner"
         Address="Avda. de la Constitución 2222" City="México D.F." ...
```

The difference is pretty limited. The main difference between the two XML persistence formats is which standard they conform to. The first (ADO) conforms to the XDR Schema standard while the ADO.NET persistence format conforms to the XSD standard. The two standards are very similar, and in general the DataSet should be able to interpret most flat ADO XML-persisted Recordsets. Another main difference is that ADO.NET supports multiple tables and relationships and constraints. Once these are placed into an XML file, the compatibility ends completely. By default, whenever an ADO Recordset is persisted, and an ADO.NET DataSet attempts to load it, it will think the main table name is a table called "row".

The following is a quick code listing that demonstrates loading ADO persisted Recordset data into an ADO.NET DataSet:

```
Imports System
Imports System.Data
Imports System.Data.SqlClient

Module XMLPersistSample

  Sub Main()
    Dim myDS As DataSet = New DataSet()
    myDS.ReadXml("..\..\Customers_ADO.XML")

    Console.WriteLine("Customers Table, Persisted from ADO 2.7")
    Dim Row As DataRow
    For Each Row In myDS.Tables("row").Rows
      Console.WriteLine("{0} from {1}", Row("ContactName"), _
                        Row("CompanyName"))
    Next
    myDS.Dispose()
  End Sub

End Module
```

This example loads a DataSet with the Customers table and then displays each row to the console. Figure 14-5 is a screenshot of the console output of this program.

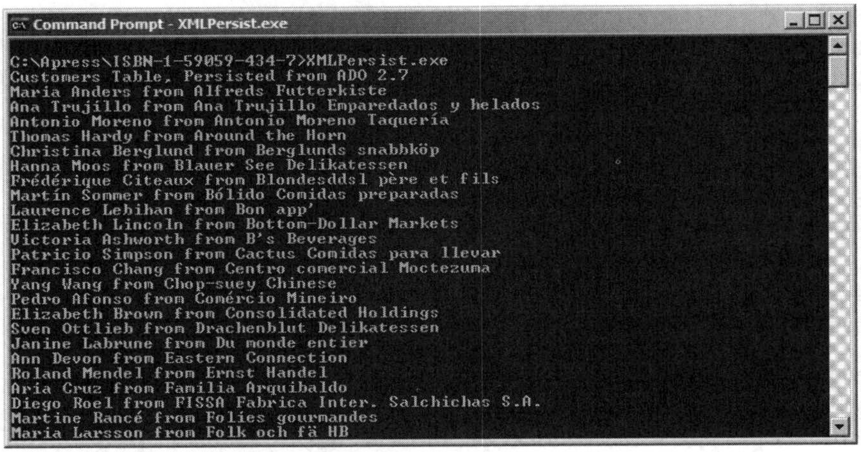

Figure 14-5. XMLPersist

XML persistence has changed between ADO and ADO.NET even though an ADO.NET DataSet can load a simple ADO 2.7 XML-persisted Recordset. In simple cases, where a Recordset is made up of just a few tables, this may work, but in complex real-world scenarios, with many related tables, such an approach is unusable.

■**Note** If you can avoid using the old ADO format in favor of the ADO.NET persistence format, do so. There is no guarantee that a newer version of ADO.NET will still be able to load ADO 2.7 XML Recordsets.

Handling Exceptions and Errors

Catching exceptions in .NET data-access applications is much more of a language and CLR function than it is of ADO.NET itself. ADO.NET provides its own class of exception called the DataException. All exceptions thrown by ADO.NET derive from the DataException class. In addition, certain ADO.NET objects, such as the DataSet, support properties that contain additional error information. The DataSet has a property called HasErrors, which indicates whether there is something wrong with the DataSet.

The biggest benefit in error handling from using ADO.NET actually extends beyond just ADO.NET. In VB6, the only real way to trap errors was to use the On Error construct. This was moderately effective, but hardly what most people would consider robust error handling.

.NET languages support Try/Catch/Finally exception trapping blocks. These are far more versatile and powerful in trapping error conditions than the On Error construct. First, you'll look at a classic VB6 example in which you are going to forget the trailing "s" on the Customers table and blindly report that something happened.

The following is the source code to the VB6 error-handling example:

```
Private Sub Command1_Click()
    On Error GoTo FuncFailed
    Dim myConnection As ADODB.Connection
    Dim myRS As ADODB.Recordset

    Set myConnection = New ADODB.Connection
    myConnection.ConnectionString = _
        "DRIVER={SQL Server};SERVER=localhost;UID=sa;PWD=;DATABASE=Northwind;"
    myConnection.Open

    Set myRS = New ADODB.Recordset
    myRS.Open "SELECT * FROM Customer", myConnection, adOpenForwardOnly
    MsgBox "Opened Customers"
    myRS.Close
    myConnection.Close
    Set myConnection = Nothing
    Set myRS = Nothing
    Exit Sub
FuncFailed:
    MsgBox "Operation Failed: " + Err.Source & vbCrLf & vbCrLf _
        & Err.Description, vbCritical, "Data Operation Failure"
End Sub
```

Figure 14-6 is a screenshot of the VB6 application trapping an error.

Figure 14-6. *Error handling, or lack thereof, in VB6*

Even though you're only looking specifically for when a data failure occurs, you will actually trap other kinds of runtime errors that you might not be expecting (such as COM failures, if ADO 2.7 isn't installed). The following code block illustrates more advanced exception handling:

```
Imports System.Data
Imports System.Data.SqlClient

Module ErrorSample

    Sub Main()
        Dim myConnection As SqlConnection
        Dim myDS As DataSet
```

```
        Dim myDA As SqlDataAdapter

        myConnection = New SqlConnection( _
           "Server=(local);Initial Catalog=Northwind; " _
           & "Integrated Security=SSPI;")
        myConnection.Open()
```

Here is your slightly more robust error-handling system. You have two lines of code that you're going to wrap in your handler. If either of those two lines of codes generates an exception that derives from (can be cast to) a `SqlException`, then it will trigger the code in the `SqlException Catch` code block. If that code block does not catch it (that is, if there was an exception, but it wasn't a `SqlException`), then the fallback handler will be called.

Microsoft's documentation indicates that the `DataException` class is used whenever ADO.NET components throw exceptions. However, the `SqlException` class does *not* inherit from the `DataException` class. When using the `SqlClient` classes, `SqlExceptions` are thrown. Therefore, if your code is handling the generic `DataException` class without a fallback handler, it is quite possible that SQL errors will slip right through the cracks.

```
        Try
           myDA = New SqlDataAdapter("SELECT * FROM Customer", myConnection)
           myDA.Fill(myDS, "Customers")
        Catch E As SqlException
           Console.WriteLine("A Data Exception Occurred.")
           Console.WriteLine("Source: {0}", E.Source)
           Console.WriteLine("Message: {0}", E.Message)
           If Not E.InnerException Is Nothing Then
              Console.WriteLine("Inner: {0}", E.InnerException.Message)
           End If
           End
        Catch RE As Exception
           Console.WriteLine("An unexpected Exception has occurred.")
           Console.WriteLine(RE.Message)
           End
        End Try
        Console.WriteLine("Filled DataSet")
        myDS.Dispose()
        myDA.Dispose()
        myConnection.Close()

    End Sub

End Module
```

Let's run the application and see what results.

```
An unexpected Exception has occurred.
Value cannot be null.
Parameter name: dataset
```

It looks like we forgot to instantiate a new DataSet. All we did was declare it. You will fix that error by adding the instantiation line up at the top of the Sub.

```
Dim myConnection As SqlConnection
Dim myDS As DataSet = New DataSet()
Dim myDA As SqlDataAdapter
```

It's a good thing we had a fallback error handler. Now you can rerun the application after making the change and see what results.

```
A SQL Exception Occurred.
Source: SQL Server Managed Provider
Message: Invalid object name 'Customer'.
```

This is actually the exception we were expecting. You *cannot* trap this exception using the DataException class. You knew that we deliberately misspelled the Customers table, so you knew you were going to cause a failure in the SQL Managed Provider.

One of the enormous advantages to exception handling in the .NET Framework is that you can create your own classes that derive from standard exceptions. This allows you to create Exception classes that automatically log themselves in the Event Log, or even automatically send e-mail or pager notifications to system administrators.

Streams

The Stream object was introduced to ADO with the release of version 2.5. The main benefit to this was that it enabled a Recordset to be persisted to a Stream object, rather than to a single flat file. This allowed persisted Recordsets to be placed in streams, converted into strings, and transferred between tiers in enterprise applications, as well as having a host of other uses.

Streams are used throughout the entire framework. There are Reader and Writer objects that perform operations on Streams, and there are custom implementations of streams such as the NetworkStream and the MemoryStream object. Basic file input and output all takes place through the use of streams. When objects are serialized by the CLR they are serialized into Streams. There are, in fact, too many types of streams in the .NET Framework to list here.

To keep the focus on migration, you'll look at a VB6 example that uses a Stream in a way that was common in ADO 2.5, 2.6, and 2.7. Then you'll take a look at how things like that are accomplished using ADO.NET components. The key concept to remember is that streams are an integral part of nearly all I/O operations throughout the framework, and not an optional set of additional features as they were in classic ADO.

The following is the VB6 code to populate a text box with the XML contents of an ADO Recordset:

```
Private Sub Command1_Click()
    Dim x As ADODB.Stream
    Dim myConnection As ADODB.Connection
    Dim myRS As ADODB.Recordset
    Dim strXML As String

    Set myConnection = New ADODB.Connection
```

```
myConnection.ConnectionString = _
    "Driver={SQL Server};Database=Northwind;UID=sa;PWD=;Server=localhost;"
myConnection.Open

Set myRS = New ADODB.Recordset
myRS.Open "SELECT * FROM Customers", myConnection, adOpenForwardOnly, _
        adLockReadOnly

Set x = New ADODB.Stream
x.Open
```

Being able to save a Recordset to an object (any object that implements IStream) rather than simply a filename was a welcome addition that arrived with ADO version 2.5. Here we save the Recordset to the stream and then read all of the text in the stream into a simple string variable.

```
myRS.Save x, adPersistXML
myRS.Close
myConnection.Close
Set myRS = Nothing
Set myConnection = Nothing
x.Position = 0
strXML = x.ReadText
Text1.Text = strXML
End Sub
```

The DataSet object, on the other hand, natively gives you the ability to retrieve the XML representation of the data with the GetXml method. You have already seen how to use a stream to encrypt the contents of a DataSet in the "Encryption" section of the previous chapter. In your next console application, you see that you don't even need a Stream object to obtain the XML stored within a DataSet.

```
Imports System
Imports System.Data
Imports System.Data.SqlClient
Imports System.Xml
Imports System.IO

Module StreamSample

    Sub Main()
        Dim myConnection As SqlConnection = New SqlConnection( _
                "Server=(local); Initial Catalog=Northwind; " _
                & "Integrated Security=SSPI;")
        myConnection.Open()
        Dim myDA As SqlDataAdapter = New SqlDataAdapter( _
                "SELECT * FROM Customers", myConnection)
        Dim myDS As DataSet = New DataSet()
```

```
        myDA.Fill(myDS, "Customers")

        Console.WriteLine(myDS.GetXml())
        myConnection.Close()
        myDS.Dispose()
    End Sub

End Module
```

The XML generated from the previous code is a well-formed XML document that doesn't include any concept of rows or columns—it is simply an XML document. The following is a portion of that document:

```
<Customers>
  <CustomerID>WOLZA</CustomerID>
  <CompanyName>Wolski  Zajazd</CompanyName>
  <ContactName>Zbyszek Piestrzeniewicz</ContactName>
  <ContactTitle>Owner</ContactTitle>
  <Address>ul. Filtrowa 68</Address>
  <City>Warszawa</City>
  <PostalCode>01-012</PostalCode>
  <Country>Poland</Country>
  <Phone>(26) 642-7012</Phone>
  <Fax>(26) 642-7012</Fax>
</Customers>
```

Even though we don't use streams here, streams are used in many places throughout the framework and are an invaluable tool.

Summary

In this chapter, you have investigated writing ADO.NET code from the perspective of the current ADO 2.7 programmer. You covered some of the procedures and decisions involved in either migrating or reusing existing ADO code. ADO.NET is an incredibly powerful tool, but there may be times when you need to keep the existing ADO code. If not, then you should now have a good understanding of how to perform some of the most common ADO tasks using ADO.NET classes. At this point, you should feel comfortable with the following tasks:

- Invoking COM objects from managed (.NET) code

- Invoking functions in existing DLLs from managed code

- Upgrading your existing ADO code to ADO.NET

- Deciding when to upgrade and when to reuse classic ADO code

- Reusing existing code that returns ADO Recordsets from within .NET

CHAPTER 15

■■■

Creating a Custom .NET Data Provider

A .NET data provider is an object-oriented abstraction around a particular form of data access. The providers that come with the framework, such as the SQL Server .NET data provider and the OLE DB .NET data provider, expose an object hierarchy that allows access to those data sources in a standard, uniform, and often highly optimized manner.

Some vendors might choose to create their own .NET data providers to provide a more specialized or native method for accessing their particular data source. For example, it's possible to access a Paradox table using the ODBC Driver for Paradox and the ODBC .NET data provider, but doing so involves several levels of abstraction and overhead. If someone were to provide their own Paradox-specific .NET data provider, it could be highly optimized for performing Paradox tasks, and not incur the overheads of COM interoperability, bridging across ODBC Drivers, etc.

Other reasons that someone might choose to create their own data provider are if the data source to which they want access is a nontraditional data source (that is, not a relational database), or there is no available ODBC or OLE DB Driver. This might include things like the Active Directory, complex filesystems, proprietary (vendor-specific) binary file formats, or (as we'll demonstrate in this chapter) the Microsoft Message Queuing (MSMQ) subsystem.

This chapter will give you step-by-step directions on how to create your own .NET data provider in tutorial fashion, by creating a .NET data provider specialized for the MSMQ technology that's available on Windows operating systems such as Windows NT, Windows 2000, and Windows XP Professional. In particular, it will provide you with the information you'll need to achieve the following goals:

- Designing a .NET data provider

- Using the data provider interfaces as a guideline for creating your own data provider

- Creating a custom connection class

- Creating a custom command class

- Creating a custom data reader class

- Creating a custom data exception class

- Creating a custom class that can be serialized to and from MSMQ messages

- Using the custom data provider for reading, writing, displaying, and data binding

- Putting all of the technology and information together to create a distributed order-entry system

A Data Provider Library

Historically, programmers have been at the mercy of the data access APIs that they've been more-or-less forced to use, simply because there weren't too many alternatives. To access SQL Server from Visual Basic, for example, the chances are that you used ADO.

With the .NET Framework and ADO.NET, Microsoft has changed all that. Now, anyone who wants to can implement their own data provider library: a single assembly containing all of the classes, enumerations, types, constants, etc. that are required in order for that data provider to operate. Unlike the black art of creating OLE DB providers, Microsoft has made the creation of data provider assemblies relatively simple. All you have to do is follow the guidelines defined by the appropriate interfaces, and you can create your own.

Application Requirements

This chapter is going to illustrate the creation of a custom .NET data provider by applying a tutorial-style approach to a fictitious application need. For the purposes of our examples, a large merchant company has decided that it wants to be able to allow for an enterprise-wide, distributed order entry system. This system will allow orders for stock to be taken from a traditional "bricks-and-mortar" retail store, as well as from an e-commerce Web site, and from a telephone service linked to a phone-order catalog.

The Retail Store

The retail store application must be able to take orders from customers who walk into the store and pay at a cash register. The cashier operating the application should be able to transmit the list of orders taken during a certain period of time into the MSMQ system by simply pressing a button. There's no urgency to this operation, however, as the orders have already been fulfilled, and the need to transmit from the retail store is only for bookkeeping and central accounting purposes. The backend order processing system (fulfillment) would have a complete order history for the retail store, and be able to issue restock requests automatically on its behalf.

e-Commerce Site

The needs of the e-commerce site are a bit different. This site needs to be able to allow customers to browse the electronic catalog, select products and quantities, and finally check out through some form of shopping cart process. The results of this checkout should then be immediately sent into the queued backend system for processing as quickly as possible. It should also be possible for customers to specify an alternative shipping address and name from the one that's tied to their customer record in the case of gifts, office deliveries, and so on.

Telephone Sales

The telephone sales application will function in a similar way to that of the e-commerce site—the main difference lies in the type of audience for the application, rather than any technical matter. The salespeople sitting at desks at our fictitious company should be able to answer a call and create an order for a given customer. As soon as the salesperson has created the order, it should then be transmitted into the queue for fulfillment as soon as possible. (Fulfillment is the process by which the product ordered is actually shipped and billed to the customer.)

Architecture and Design

Figure 15-1 illustrates the type of architecture that our fictitious company is trying to accomplish. There are two retail stores shown in the diagram, both of which are connected to the corporate intranet by some means. In addition, there are two call centers also attached to the corporate intranet. The primary responsibility of both the stores and the call centers is to take orders for customers and stuff them into the amorphous "cloud" that represents the corporate intranet/backbone. We know at this point that the "cloud" will be some form of linked and propagated network of MSMQs.

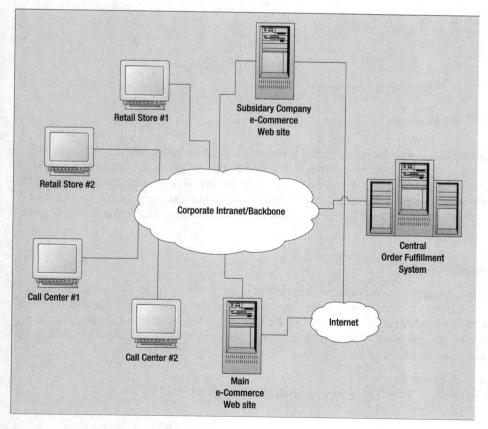

Figure 15-1. *Our fictitious application design*

The last two order-entry systems are two different Web sites. The first could be the main corporate Web site, and the second could be a Web site of an owned subsidiary (maybe our fictitious company bought out its competition?). All of these input systems need to be able to place orders into a queue that will eventually be read and serviced by the central order fulfillment system.

Before we discuss the mechanics of messaging and queues and so forth, we need to tackle a more basic issue: interchange format. We need to settle on some standard form that will represent a single "order" entity. As all of the programmers at this fictitious company are hard-line OOP designers, they decide to come up with a class whose instances can be serialized into an XML format, allowing for both portable transmission and a simple object model for access (see Figure 15-2).

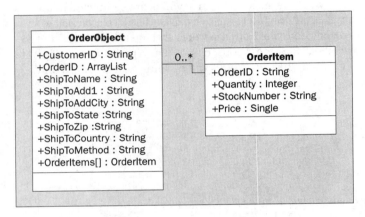

Figure 15-2. *Order format*

This design evolved from an original proposal in which an order, and an item from an order, were completely separate entities that would be reconciled by the fulfillment system. This sounded like a good idea, but it could have run into problems if something happened to (say) the message containing an order item, but the original order message remained intact. In the final scheme, a single class encapsulates the entire concept of an "order," including the individual order items.

A Sample Order

We're going to use the XmlSerializer class (found in the System.Xml.Serialization namespace) to convert an instance of an OrderObject into a portable XML format suitable for being placed into the body of an MSMQ message. We'll go into more detail about the intricacies of MSMQ later; for now, the following is a sample of what our OrderObject class looks like after being serialized into XML format:

```
<?xml version="1.0"?>
<Order xmlns:xsi="http://www.w3.org/2001/XMLSchema-instance"
```

```
        xmlns:xsd="http://www.w3.org/2001/XMLSchema"
        OrderID="ORDER1"
        ShipToName="John Doe"
        ShipToAddr1="1 Anonymous Blvd"
        ShipToAddr2=""
        ShipToCity="Somewhere"
        ShipToState="MS"
        ShipToZip="111111"
        ShipToCountry="USA"
        ShipMethod="USPS Priority">
  <OrderItem xsi:type="OrderItem" OrderID="ORDER1" Quantity="12"
          StockNumber="ITEM1" Price="14.99" />
  <OrderItem xsi:type="OrderItem" OrderID="ORDER1" Quantity="15"
          StockNumber="ITEM2" Price="12.25" />
</Order>
```

Even though this may be similar to what the rows in a `DataSet` might look like, it's important here not to confuse the two. The previous is a *serialized XML* format, and should not be compared with the storage format that's used to represent the same data in a `DataSet`.

While it's certainly possible to have a `DataSet` configured to load this information, keep in mind that we'll be creating a custom class that's designed to serialize and deserialize itself using the previous format. We'll talk more about the actual `OrderObject` and `OrderItem` classes in the next section.

Implementing the Data Provider Assembly

The `System.Data` namespace is the root from which all of Microsoft's .NET data providers begin. For example, the SQL Server .NET data provider exists entirely within the `System.Data.SqlClient` namespace, while the OLE DB .NET data provider is contained in the `System.Data.OleDb` namespace. Microsoft has provided some guidelines in the MSDN library (under the heading *Implementing a .NET Data Provider*) to help you create your own data provider. In addition, of course, there are the interfaces that define the contracts to which your components must comply in order to be considered valid portions of a data provider.

Microsoft's first guideline is that all of the components of your data provider must reside in a unique namespace. In this case, a unique namespace is one that has a reasonable guarantee that there are no other namespaces with the same name in the world. In general, the recommendation for creating unique namespaces is to create an outer namespace for your company, then one within for the project, and so on. For our example, we're going to create an assembly that will eventually be called OQProvider.DLL, containing all of the entities in the namespace `Apress.ProADONET.OQProvider`.

The OQProvider Namespace

Figure 15-3 illustrates the layout of our `Apress.ProADONET.OQProvider` data provider namespace.

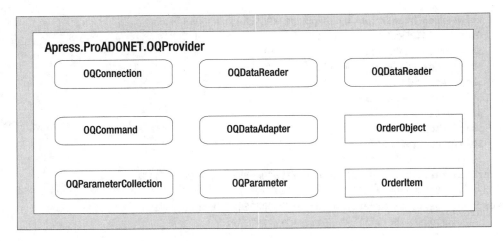

Figure 15-3. *Components of our provider namespace*

Microsoft has a detailed list of the interfaces that a data provider must support in its classes in order to be considered a valid data provider. Therefore, our custom provider assembly must contain classes (represented by the rounded rectangles in Figure 15-3) that implement the interfaces shown in Table 15-1.

Table 15-1. *Required Interfaces*

Interface	Description
IDbConnection	Represents a "live" connection to a data source.
IDbCommand	Represents a statement that is executed against a data source. For traditional providers, this can be a stored procedure or a SQL statement.
IDataAdapter	Data adapters are "plugs" that transfer information to and from DataSets.
IDataReader	Represents a means of accessing one or more forward-only/read-only streams of data obtained by a class implementing the IDbCommand interface.
IDataParameterCollection	In order to supply parameters to a command, they must be in the form of a class that implements the IDataParameterCollection interface.
IDataParameter	Classes that implement the IDataParameterCollection interface maintain collections of classes implementing the IDataParameter interface.

An assembly containing classes that provide implementations of all of the interfaces in Table 15-1 can be considered to be a data provider. It's possible to create a "limited" provider that only provides an implementation of IDataAdapter, but such a provider has no concept of a connection, and can only transfer data to and from DataSets. Keep in mind that we don't need to implement our own `DataSet`, as those objects are completely indifferent to the source or the final destination of the data they contain.

The OrderObject

Before we get into the detail of implementing the interfaces, we're going to create our `Order-Object` class. This class is entirely implementation-specific, and has no relationship with data providers—it's just the container we're going to use to house our proprietary order data.

Instances of the `OrderObject` class will represent a single "order" entity, and the class will be designed so that it can be serialized onto a stream automatically by the CLR, through the use of code attributes. (Serialization is the process by which an object instance can be converted into a stream of data.) This will allow the object to be serialized into the body of an MSMQ message. Such functionality is allowed through the use of the XML serialization attributes available in the `System.Xml.Serialization` namespace, such as `XmlAttribute`, `XmlRoot`, `XmlElement`, and `XmlInclude`.

The `OrderObject` class is contained in the `OQProvider` class library project in the code download, but if you want to enter the code into Visual Studio .NET yourself, create a new class library project using this name, and set the root namespace to `Apress.ProADONET.OQ-Provider`. Then, just add a class file called OrderObject.vb. (You can find the code samples for this chapter in the Downloads section of the Apress Web site [http://www.apress.com].)

There's nothing particularly fancy about the `OrderObject` class—it's really nothing more than a container for some private member variables and an `ArrayList` that represents the internal list of `OrderItem` classes. Before starting on the code, add the `System.Xml.Serialization` namespace to the Project Imports list in the project's property page.

Next, the `XmlRoot` attribute tells the serializer in the CLR that the class should be serialized with a root element named `<Order>`, while the `XmlInclude` attribute tells the serialization to include a schema reference to a type called `OrderItem`. Without that directive, we couldn't serialize an `ArrayList` of `OrderItem` instances.

Tip For more information on code attributes, see *Applied .NET Attributes* by Tom Barnaby and Jason Bock (Apress, 2003).

```
<XmlRoot(ElementName:="Order"), XmlInclude(GetType(OrderItem))> _
Public Class OrderObject
```

Here we declare all of the private member variables that the class instance will use to maintain the information it needs to store an order. This includes an `ArrayList` of `OrderItem` instances.

```
Private _OrderItems As ArrayList
Private _CustomerID As String
Private _OrderID As String
```

```
Private _ShipToName As String
Private _ShipToAddr1 As String
Private _ShipToAddr2 As String
Private _ShipToCity As String
Private _ShipToState As String
Private _ShipToZip As String
Private _ShipToCountry As String
Private _ShipMethod As String
Public Sub New()
  _OrderItems = New ArrayList()
End Sub
```

In the next section, we've created an overloaded constructor so that we can build the entire class instance (except for the OrderItems) in a single constructor. Keep in mind that a class cannot be serialized unless it provides a default constructor, and that any private variables that don't have public property accessors won't be able to be reconstructed properly by the serializer. Therefore, for every private member variable that our class contains, we provide both Set and Get accessors.

```
Public Sub New(ByVal CustomerID As String,    ByVal OrderID As String, _
               ByVal ShipToName As String,    ByVal ShipToAddr1 As String, _
               ByVal ShipToAddr2 As String,   ByVal ShipToCity As String, _
               ByVal ShipToState As String,   ByVal ShipToZip As String, _
               ByVal ShipToCountry As String, ByVal ShipMethod As String)
  _OrderItems = New ArrayList()
  _CustomerID = CustomerID
  _OrderID = OrderID
  _ShipToName = ShipToName
  _ShipToAddr1 = ShipToAddr1
  _ShipToAddr2 = ShipToAddr2
  _ShipToCity = ShipToCity
  _ShipToState = ShipToState
  _ShipToZip = ShipToZip
  _ShipToCountry = ShipToCountry
  _ShipMethod = ShipMethod
End Sub
```

Next, we have a method that the client application supplying the order would call in order to add OrderItem instances to an instance of an OrderObject. Note that we don't need to supply the OrderID parameter in the parameter list, because it is already a private member of the containing instance. When the method is called, we create a new instance of an OrderItem class, and then add a reference to it to the private ArrayList we maintain.

```
Public Sub AddItem(ByVal StockNumber As String, _
                   ByVal Quantity As Integer, ByVal Price As Single)
  Dim newItem As New OrderItem(StockNumber, Quantity, Price, _OrderID)
  _OrderItems.Add(newItem)
End Sub
```

```
Public Sub ClearItems()
   _OrderItems.Clear()
End Sub
```

The XmlAttributeAttribute code attribute we use next tells the Common Language Runtime (CLR) serialization routine that the following property should be serialized (and deserialized) as an XML attribute, rather than as an element. If you look back at the example we gave of a serialized order, you'll see that all of the main properties of the order are stored as XML attributes of the main Order XML element.

```
<XmlAttributeAttribute()> _
Public Property CustomerID() As String
   Get
      Return _CustomerID
   End Get
   Set(ByVal Value As String)
      _CustomerID = Value
   End Set
End Property
<XmlAttributeAttribute()> _
Public Property OrderID() As String
   Get
      Return _OrderID
   End Get
   Set(ByVal Value As String)
      _OrderID = Value
   End Set
End Property
```

In an effort to avoid boring you to tears, we've left out the rest of the property definitions. They all follow the same pattern, and all of them sport the XmlAttributeAttribute code attribute. If you want to, you can see all of the property definitions in the code download for this chapter.

Finally, we use the XmlElementAttribute code attribute to indicate that the following property is to be serialized in the form of an element called OrderItem. As it's an ArrayList, this property will be serialized once for each item in the list, creating a sequence of <OrderItem> XML elements.

```
' Other properties omitted for brevity

<XmlElementAttribute()> _
Public ReadOnly Property OrderItems() As ArrayList
   Get
      Return _OrderItems
   End Get
End Property
End Class
```

The OrderItem

Now that we've covered our portable, XML-serializable OrderObject class, let's take a look at the class we're using to represent an OrderItem. This is even simpler than OrderObject, containing only a few member variables and no ArrayList properties. Let's take a look at the source code.

As we did with the OrderObject class, we'll use a code attribute to define the name of the root element to be used to serialize this class. This time, we're calling the class's root element OrderItem. We're also using the Serializable attribute to reiterate to the CLR (and to any coder examining the source) that this class can, indeed, be serialized.

```
<XmlRoot(ElementName:="OrderItem"), Serializable()> _
Public Class OrderItem
```

There are only a handful of private member variables to keep track of: the Quantity, the StockNumber, the Price, and the OrderID of the order to which it belongs. The OrderID property is there to reinforce the link between OrderObject and OrderItem, and is especially handy for creating DataRelation objects when placing data into a DataSet.

```
Private _Quantity As Integer
Private _StockNumber As String
Private _Price As Single
Private _OrderID As String

Public Sub New()
  _Quantity = 0
  _Price = 0
  _StockNumber = "--"
  _OrderID = ""
End Sub
```

Again, as we did with the OrderObject class, we've created an overloaded constructor that allows OrderObject objects to instantiate items quickly and easily. In the following listing, we've cut out most of the property definitions for brevity; all of the properties are defined with the XmlAttributeAttribute code attribute:

```
Public Sub New(ByVal StockNumber As String, ByVal Quantity As Integer, _
               ByVal Price As Single, ByVal OrderID As String)
  _Quantity = Quantity
  _Price = Price
  _StockNumber = StockNumber
  _OrderID = OrderID
End Sub

<XmlAttributeAttribute()> _
Public Property Quantity() As Integer
  Get
    Return _Quantity
  End Get
  Set(ByVal Value As Integer)
```

```
      _Quantity = Value
    End Set
  End Property

' Other properties omitted for brevity

End Class
```

We've defined a class that represents an individual order, and a class that represents an individual item in a given order. We've also shown how we can dictate the serialization properties of these classes by using the various code attributes provided for us. Now we have a completely portable, serializable class that can be passed around through various client applications, and placed in the body of an MSMQ message. Before we jump into implementing all of the various interfaces that we're required to implement, let's go through a very brief review of the MSMQ technology we're going to be using.

An MSMQ Review

Microsoft Message Queuing (MSMQ) is a service provided by Windows that allows asynchronous, loosely coupled messaging between applications. We looked at it briefly in Chapter 13 as a way of deferring computationally expensive tasks until such time as the user is unaware of the cost or delay. We can also use message queues to send informational messages to other applications that may or may not be connected live on a network. By placing a message in a queue, another application can receive that message whenever it gets a chance, be it an hour or a week from the time it was sent.

This is exactly the architecture that our application wants to take advantage of. By allowing disparate, disconnected, loosely coupled data entry systems to place orders into a queue (or a system of queues) that can then be processed asynchronously by a fulfillment system, we solve an enormous logistical problem and save countless hours and dollars in manpower trying to force disparate systems to communicate and translate in real time.

Sending Messages

You saw how to send a simple text message in Chapter 13; what we'll cover here is the technology used to serialize one of our OrderObject objects into a MessageQueue object. (You'll need to understand how this works in order to understand the logistics of building an entire data provider assembly around this technology.) The following is a modified version of the Queue-Sender sample from Chapter 13, tailored to work with an OrderObject object. You'll find it in the code download for this chapter under the same name.

```
Imports System
Imports System.Messaging
Imports Apress.ProADONET.OQProvider

Module MessageSample

  Sub Main()
```

```
' Create an Order and populate it with some data.
Dim myOrder As New OrderObject("HOFF", "ORDER1", "Kevin Hoffman", _
                               "101 Queue Lane", "", "ADOville", _
                               "MS", "000000", "USA", "FEDEX")

' Create a MessageQueue object and point it at OrderQueue
Dim mQ As MessageQueue
If MessageQueue.Exists(".\Private$\OrderQueue") Then
  mQ = New MessageQueue(".\Private$\OrderQueue")
Else
  mQ = MessageQueue.Create(".\Private$\OrderQueue")
End If
mQ.Formatter = New XmlMessageFormatter()

' Send an OrderObject to the Queue, automatically invoking XML serialization
mQ.Send(myOrder, myOrder.OrderID)

Console.WriteLine("Order Sent to OrderQueue.")
End Sub

End Module
```

The code obtains a reference to an existing `MessageQueue` object, and then makes sure that all messages placed into that queue are formatted using the `XmlMessageFormatter` (which uses XML serialization). When the code is run, you can open up the message it created by running the Computer Management console (Start ➤ Programs ➤ Administrative Tools on Windows 2000) and examine the XML-serialized `OrderObject` that resides in the message's body (see Figure 15-4).

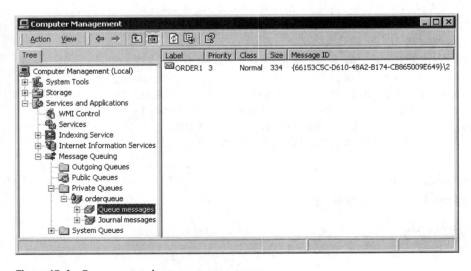

Figure 15-4. *Our message in our message queue*

By double-clicking the ORDER1 message in the right-hand view and then selecting the Body tab, we can actually verify that our OrderObject has been serialized and stored in XML in the body of our message (see Figure 15-5).

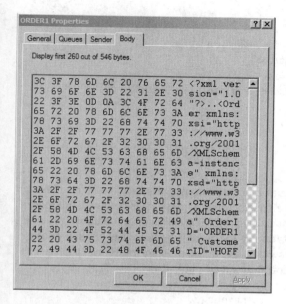

Figure 15-5. *Details of our message*

Receiving Messages

To receive an order that has already been placed in a message queue, we simply reverse the process we used to store the message to begin with. Some steps, such as deserialization, are not completely automatic, so it takes a line or two more code, but it's still fairly straightforward. The following is a modified version of the QueueReceiver application from Chapter 13:

```
Imports System
Imports System.Messaging
Imports System.Xml.Serialization
Imports System.IO
Imports Apress.ProADONET.OQProvider

Module ReceiverSample

  Sub Main()

    ' Get queue reference
    Dim mQ As MessageQueue
    If MessageQueue.Exists(".\Private$\OrderQueue") Then
      mQ = New MessageQueue(".\Private$\OrderQueue")
```

```
      Else
        Console.WriteLine("Queue doesn't exist.")
        Return
      End If

      ' Get message and extract order
      Dim msg As Message = mQ.Receive(New TimeSpan(0, 0, 3))
      Dim sr As New StreamReader(msg.BodyStream)
      Dim xs As New XmlSerializer(GetType(OrderObject))
      Dim myOrder As OrderObject = CType(xs.Deserialize(sr), OrderObject)

      ' Do something with received order...
    End Sub

End Module
```

This code instantiates a new MessageQueue object, and then attempts to receive a message from that queue. If more than three seconds elapse before the message is received, the messaging system will throw an exception. The body of an MSMQ message can be treated as a stream, which is especially handy for serialization of XML and large amounts of binary data. We create a StreamReader object to pull the raw data out of the message body, and then use the XmlSerializer class to deserialize the information it contains into a new OrderObject instance. As the Deserialize() method returns an Object, and there is no implicit typecast between object and an OrderObject, we have to cast explicitly.

Note Sending and receiving OrderObject objects through MSMQ forms the core functionality of our data provider.

The OQConnection

An ADO.NET connection object represents a connection to a data source or some other resource. Traditionally, it represents the physical link to a SQL Server or Oracle database, or even to a Microsoft Access database file (.mdb). In our particular example, the OQConnection class represents a connection to a message queue.

Microsoft's IDbConnection interface requires that the following properties and methods be implemented in order to implement a custom connection class (see Table 15-2). A key point to remember, though, is that when you're building your own data provider, you may be required to provide certain implementations, but you're not required to make those implementations meaningful. This allows you, for example, to not bother with database transactions if you choose, giving you the option of throwing a NotSupportedException exception when transaction-related functions are called on your provider.

Table 15-2. IDBConnection *Interface Requirements*

Name	Type	Description
ConnectionString	Property	String used to open the resource.
ConnectionTimeout	Property	Time to wait for a connection to be established before throwing an exception.
Database	Property	Name of the current database, or the database to be used once the connection is opened.
State	Property	Indicates the current state of the connection. This property is of type ConnectionState.
BeginTransaction()	Method	Begins a database transaction.
ChangeDatabase()	Method	Changes the current database for an open connection.
Close()	Method	Closes the current connection.
CreateCommand()	Method	Creates a command object, automatically setting its connection property.
Open()	Method	Opens the current connection.

Now that we've seen what's required of us in terms of implementing the interface, let's take a look at the code we use to create our OQConnection class (you'll need to import the System.Messaging namespace and add a reference to the System.Messaging.dll assembly to get access to the messaging functionality required by the class).

```
Public Class OQConnection
  Implements IDbConnection
```

In order to maintain some of the information that the IDbConnection interface requires us to maintain, we'll need to create some private member variables for the connection state, the connection string, and the timeout period. In addition, the Boolean private member, called AutoCreateQueue, indicates whether the connection should create the queue upon opening (the queue to be created is indicated by the connection string). While the interface may define what properties we are to expose, it's still up to us to maintain the private variables that support them.

```
Private _cState As ConnectionState
Private _ConnStr As String
Private _TimeOutPeriod As Integer
Private _AutoCreateQueue As Boolean

Private _Queue As MessageQueue

Public Sub New()
  _TimeOutPeriod = 3
  _cState = ConnectionState.Closed
  _AutoCreateQueue = True
End Sub
```

Other classes within our assembly, such as the OQDataReader, will need to be able to modify the connection state. In order to avoid allowing the end user (that is, the application programmer) to modify the connection state manually, we use the Friend keyword, which allows us to indicate that only classes contained within this particular assembly are allowed to access this method.

```
Friend Sub SetState(ByVal newState As ConnectionState)
  _cState = newState
End Sub

Public Property AutoCreateQueue() As Boolean
  Get
    Return _AutoCreateQueue
  End Get
  Set(ByVal Value As Boolean)
    _AutoCreateQueue = Value
  End Set
End Property
```

Furthermore, classes such as OQCommand will need to be able to access the message queue directly in order to send and receive data in a fashion that appears as though the information is simply passing through the connection. We facilitate this by allowing all classes within our data provider assembly to access the MessageQueue object itself, via the connection. No other client component or application can directly access this queue.

```
Friend ReadOnly Property MQ() As MessageQueue
  Get
    Return _Queue
  End Get
End Property

Public Property ConnectionString() As String _
  Implements IDbConnection.ConnectionString

  Get
    Return _ConnStr
  End Get
  Set(ByVal Value As String)
    If (_cState <> ConnectionState.Closed) Then
      Throw New InvalidOperationException( _
          "Cannot set the Connection String unless the Connection is Closed.")
    Else
      _ConnStr = Value
    End If
  End Set
End Property
```

```
    Public ReadOnly Property ConnectionTimeout() As Integer _
      Implements IDbConnection.ConnectionTimeout

      Get
        Return _TimeOutPeriod
      End Get
    End Property


    ' Database property will return ""; this provider does not work with databases
    Public ReadOnly Property Database() As String _
      Implements IDbConnection.Database

      Get
        Return ""
      End Get
    End Property
```

There is no ability to set the ConnectionState property manually; it can only be set by other classes contained within the assembly, through the SetState() method we defined earlier.

```
    Public ReadOnly Property State() As ConnectionState _
      Implements IDbConnection.State

      Get
        Return _cState
      End Get
    End Property
```

Our data provider does not support transactions. The goal of this chapter is to give you a practical example of why and how to build a data provider, and while adding transactions might be a useful exercise for you to do once you have a full grasp of how data providers work (MSMQ has full support for transactions), it's not a priority right now.

```
    Public Function BeginTransaction() As IDbTransaction _
      Implements IDbConnection.BeginTransaction

      Throw New NotSupportedException("Transactions not supported by this provider")
    End Function


    Public Function BeginTransaction(ByVal iLevel As IsolationLevel) _
      As IDbTransaction _
      Implements IDbConnection.BeginTransaction
      Throw New NotSupportedException("Transactions not supported by this provider")
    End Function
    Public Sub ChangeDatabase(ByVal databaseName As String) _
      Implements IDbConnection.ChangeDatabase

      Throw New NotSupportedException("Changing DB not supported by this provider")
    End Sub
```

The CreateCommand() method provides a shortcut for not only instantiating a new OQCommand object, but also associating the newly created command object with the current instance of the connection class, saving the programmer a few lines of code and a few potential mistakes. By always using the CreateCommand() method, rather than creating commands on their own, client programs can be written to be completely provider-independent.

```
Public Function CreateCommand() As IDbCommand _
  Implements IDbConnection.CreateCommand

  Dim nCommand As New OQCommand()
  nCommand.Connection = Me
  Return nCommand
End Function
```

Typically, when a connection is opened, resources are allocated to provide for the physical connection to the data source. When the connection is closed, those resources are then disposed of. Our case is no different. When we open the connection, depending on whether the connection is configured to create the queue automatically, it will either obtain a reference to an existing queue, or create a new one.

```
Public Sub Open() _
  Implements IDbConnection.Open

  If (Not MessageQueue.Exists(_ConnStr)) Then
    If (Not _AutoCreateQueue) Then
      Throw New InvalidOperationException( _
                "Cannot Open Queue: Queue Does not Exist")
    Else
      _Queue = MessageQueue.Create(_ConnStr)
    End If
  Else
    _Queue = New MessageQueue(_ConnStr)
  End If

  _Queue.Formatter = New XmlMessageFormatter()
  _cState = ConnectionState.Open
End Sub

Public Sub Close() _
  Implements IDbConnection.Close

  _Queue.Dispose()
  _cState = ConnectionState.Closed
End Sub
Public Sub Dispose() _
  Implements IDisposable.Dispose
```

```
    _Queue.Dispose()
  End Sub
End Class
```

The following few lines of code might be seen in a client application that uses the previous OQConnection class to open and close a connection to a queue:

```
Dim Conn As New OQConnection()
Conn.ConnectionString = ".\Private$\OQTester"
Conn.Open()

Conn.Close()
```

The OQCommand

Classes that implement the IDbCommand interface are responsible for generating requests and passing them on to the data source. In a typical relational database situation, there are four types of commands: select, update, delete, and insert. These have a one-to-one mapping to the four different kinds of SQL statements available. In our case, there are only two things that we can do to messages in a queue: we can send them, and we can receive them. Table 15-3 is the list of items that we're required to deal with in an implementation of the IDbCommand interface.

Table 15-3. IDBCommand *Interface Requirements*

Name	Type	Description
CommandText	Property	String representing the text command to run against the command's associated connection.
CommandTimeout	Property	Timeout period for a command to complete before an exception will be thrown.
CommandType	Property	Indicates how the CommandText property will be interpreted.
Connection	Property	Object reference indicating the associated connection for this command object.
Parameters	Property	Retrieves the object that implements IDbParameterCollection.
Transaction	Property	Gets or sets the transaction context in which the IDbCommand instance is to execute.
UpdatedRowSource	Property	Gets or sets how the results of command execution are to be applied to the DataRow when used by the Update() method of a data adapter.
Cancel()	Method	Cancels execution of an IDbCommand instance.
CreateParameter()	Method	Creates a new instance of an IDBDataParameter object.
ExecuteNonQuery()	Method	Executes the CommandText with any parameters, returning only the number of rows affected.

continues

Table 15-3. *continued*

Name	Type	Description
ExecuteReader()	Method	Executes the command, returning the results in an appropriately initialized IDataReader object.
ExecuteScalar()	Method	Executes the command, returning the first column in the result set. All additional columns are ignored.
Prepare()	Method	Creates a prepared (pre-processed or compiled) version of the command on the data source (if applicable).

Let's take a look at the code we wrote to implement the previous methods for our specific need of allowing commands to execute against a connection that houses an active message queue.

```
Public Class OQCommand
  Implements IDbCommand
```

Again, we're maintaining some private member information. This time, we're holding information for the CommandTimeOut property, the Connection property, the CommandText property, and some others, including the Parameters property.

```
Private _TimeOutPeriod As Integer
Private _Connection As OQConnection
Private _CmdText As String
Private _UpdatedRowSource As UpdateRowSource = UpdateRowSource.None
Private _Parameters As New OQParameterCollection()

Public Sub New()
End Sub
```

Next, we add a little bit of specialization code. As there's nothing all that complex about the operation we're performing against the OQConnection, we only support two different words in the CommandText property. Where the SQL Server .NET data provider supports fully featured SQL queries and even temporary stored procedures, our commands can only be "send" or "receive" operations. If any client code attempts to configure the command to do anything else, an exception is thrown.

```
Public Property CommandText() As String _
  Implements IDbCommand.CommandText

  Get
    Return _CmdText
  End Get
  Set(ByVal Value As String)
    If ((Value <> "Send") And (Value <> "Receive")) Then
      Throw New NotSupportedException( _
              "CommandText must be either Send or Receive")
```

```
      Else
         _CmdText = Value
      End If
   End Set
End Property


Public Property CommandTimeout() As Integer _
   Implements IDbCommand.CommandTimeout

   Get
      Return _TimeOutPeriod
   End Get
   Set(ByVal Value As Integer)
      _TimeOutPeriod = Value
   End Set
End Property
```

Time for some more specialization. We have to implement the CommandType property, but we don't have to allow all possible values of that property. Instead, we throw an exception if any client code attempts to supply any value other than CommandType.Text: we don't support any command types beyond simple words. The reason we don't simply force CommandType to be read-only and initialized to CommandType.Text is because the IDbCommand interface requires a Set accessor for the CommandType property.

```
Public Property CommandType() As CommandType _
   Implements IDbCommand.CommandType

   Get
      Return CommandType.Text
   End Get
   Set(ByVal Value As CommandType)
      If (Value <> CommandType.Text) Then
         Throw New NotSupportedException("Only supported CommandType is Text")
      End If
   End Set
End Property


Public Property Connection() As IDbConnection _
   Implements IDbCommand.Connection

   Get
      Return _Connection
   End Get
   Set(ByVal Value As IDbConnection)
      _Connection = CType(Value, OQConnection)
   End Set
End Property
```

```
Public ReadOnly Property Parameters() As IDataParameterCollection _
  Implements IDbCommand.Parameters
  Get
    Return _Parameters
  End Get
End Property

Public Property Transaction() As IDbTransaction _
  Implements IDbCommand.Transaction

  Get
    Return Nothing
  End Get
  Set(ByVal Value As IDbTransaction)
    Throw New NotSupportedException()
  End Set
End Property

Public Property UpdatedRowSource() As UpdateRowSource _
  Implements IDbCommand.UpdatedRowSource

  Get
    Return _UpdatedRowSource
  End Get
  Set(ByVal Value As UpdateRowSource)
    _UpdatedRowSource = Value
  End Set
End Property

Public Sub Cancel() _
  Implements IDbCommand.Cancel

  Throw New NotSupportedException()
End Sub

Public Function CreateParameter() As IDbDataParameter _
  Implements IDbCommand.CreateParameter

  Return New OQParameter()
End Function
```

Up next is the first section of code that does anything beyond meeting the requirements of the interface specification. Here, we are supplying code for the ExecuteNonQuery() method.

The method assumes that it's performing a "send" operation. As we'll see shortly, as a business rule in our provider, the OQCommand only accepts a single parameter called Order in the case of a "send" command, and accepts no parameters in the case of a "receive" command. The reason for this is that we're only going to send a single OrderObject at a time, and when we receive OrderObjects, we don't need to provide any additional information that the connection doesn't already have. The code pulls the OrderObject reference out of the Order parameter, and then uses code similar to what we saw earlier in order to transmit the OrderObject into the queue.

```
Public Function ExecuteNonQuery() As Integer _
  Implements IDbCommand.ExecuteNonQuery
  _Connection.SetState(ConnectionState.Executing)
  If (_Parameters.Contains("Order")) Then
    Dim tmpParam As OQParameter = CType(_Parameters("Order"), OQParameter)
    Dim tmpOrder As OrderObject = CType(tmpParam.Value, OrderObject)
    _Connection.MQ.Send(tmpOrder, tmpOrder.OrderID)
    _Connection.SetState(ConnectionState.Open)
    Return 1
  Else
    Throw New IndexOutOfRangeException("Order parameter does not exist.")
  End If
End Function
```

The ExecuteReader() method simply returns a new copy of the data reader object. You can't see it from here—you'll see it when we get to the code for the OQDataReader class—but the constructor we're invoking is a Friend. This means that the only way to obtain an OQDataReader is to invoke the ExecuteReader() method on an OQCommand object. (This is the way things work in the other data providers as well.) Due to the nature of the data reader in our implementation, no work is actually done, nor is any reading accomplished, until the Read() method of the retrieved reader is invoked.

```
Public Function ExecuteReader() As IDataReader _
  Implements IDbCommand.ExecuteReader

  Return New OQDataReader(_Connection)
End Function
```

To keep things simple, we don't support any change in functionality based on supplying different values to a CommandBehavior parameter. However, because the IDbCommand interface dictates that we have a method that supports this argument, we simply ignore it and create a new OQDataReader, just as we did in the previous method.

```
Public Function ExecuteReader(ByVal behavior As CommandBehavior) _
  As IDataReader Implements IDbCommand.ExecuteReader

  Return New OQDataReader(_Connection)
End Function
```

As you know, ExecuteScalar() is supposed to return the first column in a result set. We didn't feel this method would get much use when dealing with messaged order objects, so we didn't provide an implementation.

```
Public Function ExecuteScalar() As Object Implements IDbCommand.ExecuteScalar
  Return Nothing
End Function
```

```
Public Sub Prepare() Implements IDbCommand.Prepare

    ' Do nothing
End Sub
Public Sub Dispose() Implements IDisposable.Dispose
    _Connection.Dispose()
End Sub
End Class
```

The OQParameterCollection and OQParameter

The OQParameterCollection class that we're going to create implements the IDataParameter-Collection interface. Even though we really have no need for the ability to store multiple parameters for our particular implementation, the IDbCommand interface dictates that the Parameters property be an object reference to a class that implements the IDataParameter-Collection interface. This interface has the requirements shown in Table 15-4.

Table 15-4. IDataParameterCollection *Interface Requirements*

Name	Type	Description
Item	Property	The parameter at the specified index
Contains()	Method	Indicates whether or not the ParameterCollection contains a given parameter name
IndexOf()	Method	Returns the index of a given parameter name
RemoveAt()	Method	Removes the parameter from the collection

We get around the fact that the IDataParameterCollection interface also requires that the basic Collection interface should be implemented by inheriting our class from the CollectionBase class as well as implementing the IDataParameterCollection interface. This provides our class with basic collection functionality without us having to code all of that detail by hand. The following is the source listing for the OQParameterCollection class:

```
Public Class OQParameterCollection
    Inherits System.Collections.CollectionBase
    Implements IDataParameterCollection

    Private _Param As OQParameter

    Public Sub New()
    End Sub
```

Our particular implementation only supports the notion of a single parameter called Order. Therefore, rather than maintaining an internal collection, we're actually only maintaining a single Parameter. Any attempt to obtain *any* parameter will always give you the Order parameter.

```
Default Public Overloads Property Item(ByVal parameterName As String) _
    As Object Implements IDataParameterCollection.Item

    Get
        Return _Param
    End Get
    Set(ByVal Value As Object)
        _Param = CType(Value, OQParameter)
    End Set
End Property
```

The basic interface requirements dictate that we provide a Contains() method. Ours is a pretty simple string check. If the parameterName supplied is Order, and we've already had the Order parameter created, then we return True. Otherwise, we return a False indicator.

```
Public Function Contains(ByVal parameterName As String) As Boolean _
    Implements IDataParameterCollection.Contains

    If ((parameterName = "Order") And (Not _Param Is Nothing)) Then
        Return True
    Else
        Return False
    End If
End Function

Public Function IndexOf(ByVal parameterName As String) As Integer _
    Implements IDataParameterCollection.IndexOf

    Return 0
End Function

Public Overloads Sub RemoveAt(ByVal parameterName As String) _
    Implements IDataParameterCollection.RemoveAt

    _Param = Nothing
End Sub
End Class
```

The OQParameter class has a smaller footprint than OQParameterCollection, as it only has to implement details concerning itself—it doesn't have to conform to any interfaces requiring the maintenance of list information. Table 15-5 is the list of requirements for the IDataParameter interface.

Table 15-5. IDataParameter *Interface Requirements*

Name	Type	Description
DbType	Property	Property indicating the DbType of the parameter
Direction	Property	Indicates the direction (in, out, return value, etc.) of the parameter
IsNullable	Property	Indicates whether this parameter accepts Null values
ParameterName	Property	String/textual name of the parameter
SourceColumn	Property	Name of the source column that's mapped to the DataSet and is used for reading/writing the value
SourceVersion	Property	Indicates the DataRowVersion when loading a value
Value	Property	Gets/sets the value of the parameter itself

Let's take a look at the source code for the OQParameter class.

```
Public Class OQParameter
  Implements IDataParameter

  Private _Order As OrderObject

  Public Sub New()
  End Sub
```

Our own overload of the constructor takes a single object, an OrderObject, as an argument. This allows for quick access to the private member variable storing the parameter's internal OrderObject reference.

```
  Public Sub New(ByVal Order As OrderObject)
    _Order = Order
  End Sub

  Public Property DbType() As DbType _
    Implements IDataParameter.DbType

    Get
      Return DbType.Object
    End Get
    Set(ByVal Value As DbType)

      ' Do nothing
    End Set
  End Property

  Public Property Direction() As ParameterDirection _
    Implements IDataParameter.Direction

    Get
```

```
      Return ParameterDirection.Input
   End Get
   Set(ByVal Value As ParameterDirection)

      ' Do nothing
   End Set
End Property


Public ReadOnly Property IsNullable() As Boolean _
   Implements IDataParameter.IsNullable

   Get
      Return False
   End Get
End Property
Public Property ParameterName() As String _
   Implements IDataParameter.ParameterName

   Get
      Return "Order"
   End Get
   Set(ByVal Value As String)

      ' Do nothing
   End Set
End Property
```

An `OrderObject` parameter actually contains information for multiple columns and multiple rows within a `DataSet`, so using the `SourceColumn` property in our case is quite useless.

```
Public Property SourceColumn() As String _
   Implements IDataParameter.SourceColumn

   Get
      Return ""
   End Get
   Set(ByVal Value As String)

      ' Do nothing
   End Set
End Property


Public Property SourceVersion() As DataRowVersion _
   Implements IDataParameter.SourceVersion

   Get
      Return DataRowVersion.Original
   End Get
```

```
      Set(ByVal Value As DataRowVersion)

        ' Do nothing
      End Set
    End Property
```

Rather than retrieving and storing the information in a completely generic manner, we are instead storing an actual OrderObject reference as the parameter's value.

```
    Public Property Value() As Object _
      Implements IDataParameter.Value

      Get
        Return _Order
      End Get
      Set(ByVal Value As Object)
        _Order = CType(Value, OrderObject)
      End Set
    End Property
End Class
```

The OQDataReader

The data reader is an object that provides forward-only/read-only access to the result set returned by a command of some kind. In our case, the OQDataReader will provide forward-only/read-only access to the list of messages in the queue that's indicated by the OQConnection and returned by executing an ExecuteReader() method against a command object.

Table 15-6 is the list of the requirements specified by the IDataReader interface.

Table 15-6. IDataReader *Interface Requirements*

Name	Type	Description
Depth	Property	Indicates the depth of the current nesting for the current row. It is possible for nesting to be quite high when hierarchical result sets are returned from some data sources.
IsClosed	Property	Indicates whether or not the reader is closed.
RecordsAffected	Property	Indicates the number of rows changed, inserted, or deleted by execution of the associated command.
Close()	Method	Closes the current reader.
GetSchemaTable()	Method	Returns a DataTable that describes the column definitions of the IDataReader.
NextResult()	Method	Advances to the next result set in the list of result sets obtained by the reader.
Read()	Method	The core function of the data reader. It advances the IDataReader to the next record.

There are some other functions (such as GetInt16(), GetInt32(), etc.) that must be present in order to complete the definition of an IDataReader class, and those are specified by the IDataRecord interface. We won't go into the list of requirements here, though, as we'll see them in our following code. (This code requires System.Xml and System.IO to be added to the project's import list.)

```
Public Class OQDataReader
  Implements IDataReader

  Private _Connection As OQConnection
  Private _Message As Message
  Private _Order As OrderObject
  Private _ReadCount As Integer
```

Take note of the Friend keyword here; it means that an OQDataReader cannot be instantiated by client objects defined outside the assembly.

```
Friend Sub New()
  _Order = New OrderObject()
  _ReadCount = 0
End Sub
```

Here's another Friend constructor, this one taking the associated connection as an argument. A DataReader cannot function without a connection, and it can't read from a Connection that isn't open.

```
Friend Sub New(ByVal Connection As OQConnection)
  _Connection = Connection
  _Order = New OrderObject()
  _ReadCount = 0
End Sub
```

In place of all of the many GetXXX functions, such as GetInt32(), GetInt64(), GetString(), etc., we supply our own method. This retrieves an OrderObject instance from the current message. We use a private counter so that we can detect whether an attempt to obtain an OrderObject reference occurs before the first call to the Read() method.

```
Public Function GetOrder() As OrderObject
  If (_ReadCount = 0) Then
    Throw New IndexOutOfRangeException( _
              "Must first call Read method to load current data.")
  End If
  Return _Order
End Function
```

We don't support any kind of nesting, so our Depth is always going to be 0 (top-level).

```
Public ReadOnly Property Depth() As Integer _
  Implements IDataReader.Depth
```

```
      Get
         Return 0
      End Get
   End Property
```

Also, we don't support opening and closing a data reader. The data reader is only instantiated to pull live information from a live connection to an MSMQ. There is no reason to close
or reopen a data reader while the connection remains live. Other data providers written for
other purposes may contain logic to support the opening and closing of the data reader class.

```
   Public ReadOnly Property IsClosed() As Boolean _
      Implements IDataReader.IsClosed

      Get
         Return False
      End Get
   End Property

   Public ReadOnly Property RecordsAffected() As Integer _
      Implements IDataReader.RecordsAffected

      Get
         Return 0
      End Get
   End Property

   Public ReadOnly Property FieldCount() As Integer _
      Implements IDataReader.FieldCount

      Get
         Return 1
      End Get
   End Property

   Default Public ReadOnly Property Item(ByVal name As String) _
      Implements IDataReader.Item

      Get
         If (_ReadCount = 0) Then
            Throw New IndexOutOfRangeException( _
                        "Must first call Read method to load current data.")
         End If
         If (name <> "Order") Then
            Throw New IndexOutOfRangeException("No Such Column")
         End If
         Return _Order
      End Get
   End Property
```

The interface allows for named and numeric indexing into the data reader itself for access to individual columns. Due to the fact that we only have a single column (called Order), at least in terms of the data reader, we can return the OrderObject reference so long as the column index is 0.

```
Default Public ReadOnly Property Item(ByVal i As Integer) _
   Implements IDataReader.Item

   Get
     If (_ReadCount = 0) Then
       Throw New IndexOutOfRangeException( _
                  "Must first call Read method to load current data.")
     End If
     If (i > 0) Then
       Throw New IndexOutOfRangeException("No Such Column")
     End If
     Return _Order
   End Get
End Property
```

The IDataRecord interface specifies a GetXXX method for every single data type supported by the CLR. In order to spare your eyes the strain and avoid putting you to sleep rapidly, we've snipped out those definitions from the code listed in the book (though of course they exist in the downloads). The essential idea is that we throw a NotSupportedException for each of the inappropriate data types.

```
' Retrieval of the unsupported types removed for clarity

Public Function GetFieldType(ByVal i As Integer) As Type _
   Implements IDataReader.GetFieldType

   If (_ReadCount = 0) Then
     Throw New IndexOutOfRangeException( _
                 "Must first call Read method to load current data.")
   End If
   If (i > 0) Then
     Throw New ArgumentOutOfRangeException("Only Possible Column Index is 0")
   End If
   Return GetType(OrderObject)
End Function

Public Function GetValue(ByVal i As Integer) As Object _
   Implements IDataReader.GetValue

   If (_ReadCount = 0) Then
     Throw New IndexOutOfRangeException( _
                 "Must first call Read method to load current data.")
   End If
```

```vb
    If (i > 0) Then
        Throw New ArgumentOutOfRangeException("Only Possible Column Index is 0")
    End If
    Return _Order
End Function

Public Function GetValues(ByVal values As Object()) As Integer _
    Implements IDataReader.GetValues

    If (_ReadCount = 0) Then
        Throw New IndexOutOfRangeException( _
                    "Must first call Read method to load current data.")
    End If
    values(0) = _Order
    Return 0
End Function

Public Function GetOrdinal(ByVal name As String) As Integer _
    Implements IDataReader.GetOrdinal

    If (_ReadCount = 0) Then
        Throw New IndexOutOfRangeException( _
                    "Must first call Read method to load current data.")
    End If
    If (name <> "Order") Then
        Throw New IndexOutOfRangeException("No such Column")
    End If
    Return 0
End Function
Public Sub Close() _
    Implements IDataReader.Close

End Sub

Public Function GetSchemaTable() As DataTable _
    Implements IDataReader.GetSchemaTable

    Throw New NotSupportedException()
End Function

Public Function NextResult() As Boolean _
    Implements IDataReader.NextResult

    Return False
End Function
```

The following code is the core of our IDataReader implementation. The Read() method uses the associated connection to "advance" to the next record by pulling another message out of the queue. This message is then converted into an OrderObject reference, which is then used internally by other GetXXX functions.

```
Public Function Read() As Boolean _
   Implements IDataReader.Read

   If (_Connection Is Nothing) Then
     Throw New OQException("Invalid Connection Object")
   End If
   If (_Connection.State <> ConnectionState.Open) Then
     Throw New OQException("Connection must be open before Reading")
   End If
   If (_Connection.MQ Is Nothing) Then
     Throw New OQException("Connection's Internal Queue is invalid.")
   End If
```

Some of the next code should look familiar—it's very similar to the simple message-receiving code snippet we went through earlier in the chapter. The message is obtained by reading from the message queue with a TimeSpan class indicating the timeout period, as defined by the connection object. Then, the XmlSerializer is used to deserialize the object directly into memory in the form of an OrderObject.

```
   Try
       _Connection.SetState(ConnectionState.Fetching)
       _Message = _Connection.MQ.Receive( _
                    New TimeSpan(0, 0, _Connection.ConnectionTimeout))

       Dim reader As New StreamReader(_Message.BodyStream)
       Dim xs As New XmlSerializer(GetType(OrderObject))
       _Order = CType(xs.Deserialize(reader), OrderObject)
       xs = Nothing
       reader = Nothing
       _ReadCount += 1
       Return True
   Catch e As MessageQueueException
       Return False
   Catch e As InvalidOperationException
       Return False
   Finally
       _Connection.SetState(ConnectionState.Open)
   End Try
End Function


Public Sub Dispose() _
   Implements IDisposable.Dispose
```

```
      _Connection.Dispose()
      _Message.Dispose()
   End Sub
End Class
```

The OQDataAdapter

As we said earlier, the data adapter is essentially a "plug" that connects the data source and the DataSet via the connection (in our case, a connection to a queue). It is responsible for carrying changes from a DataSet across to the connection, and for carrying information from the connection to the DataSet. Table 15-7 is the list of requirements for a class implementing the IDataAdapter interface.

Table 15-7. IDataAdapter *Interface Requirements*

Name	Type	Description
MissingMappingAction	Property	Action to take when DataSet mappings for the affected columns are not found
MissingSchemaAction	Property	Indicates whether missing source tables, columns, and relationships are added to the DataSet schema, ignored, or generates an exception
TableMappings	Property	Indicates how a source table is to be mapped to a DataSet table
Fill()	Method	Adds or refreshes rows in the DataSet to match those in the data source
FillSchema()	Method	Adds schema definition information for a table called "Table"
Update()	Method	Takes all appropriately affected rows and uses appropriate commands to populate the data source

Now let's look at the code for our custom OQDataAdapter class.

```
Public Class OQDataAdapter
   Implements IDataAdapter

   Private _SendCommand As OQCommand
   Private _ReceiveCommand As OQCommand

   Public Sub New()
   End Sub
```

In our implementation, we always do the same thing whether or not mappings are supplied, so here we just supply a simple property to satisfy the requirements of the interface. We never actually use the information contained in this property internally.

```
   Public Property MissingMappingAction() As MissingMappingAction _
      Implements IDataAdapter.MissingMappingAction
```

```
  Get
    Return MissingMappingAction.Passthrough
  End Get
  Set(ByVal Value As MissingMappingAction)

    ' Do nothing
  End Set
End Property
```

We have a similar situation with the `MissingSchemaAction` property, although here we're indicating that the value will *always* be `MissingSchemaAction.Add`.

```
Public Property MissingSchemaAction() As MissingSchemaAction _
  Implements IDataAdapter.MissingSchemaAction

  Get
    Return MissingSchemaAction.Add
  End Get
  Set(ByVal Value As MissingSchemaAction)

    ' Do nothing
  End Set
End Property
```

The `TableMappings` property isn't supported, so we simply return `Nothing`.

```
Public ReadOnly Property TableMappings() As ITableMappingCollection _
  Implements IDataAdapter.TableMappings

  Get
    Return Nothing
  End Get
End Property
```

The `Fill()`, `FillSchema()`, and `Update()` methods of the `IDataAdapter` interface compose the core functionality of the data adapter. In our case, when `Fill()` is called, we validate whether our `ReceiveCommand` is functioning properly. Once we've cleared that hurdle, we ensure that the supplied `DataSet`'s `Orders` table will be removed. Then, we call our `FillSchema()` method to define a `DataSet` schema that will re-create the tables. From there, an `OQDataReader` is used to populate the `Orders` items in the table.

```
Public Function Fill(ByVal dataSet As DataSet) As Integer _
  Implements IDataAdapter.Fill

  If (_ReceiveCommand Is Nothing) Then
    Throw New OQException("Cannot Fill without a valid ReceiveCommand.")
  End If
  If (dataSet.Tables.Contains("Orders")) Then
    dataSet.Tables.Remove("Orders")
  End If
```

In the first line of the following code, we supply the parameter SchemaType.Mapped only because the interface requires us to supply something, even though our FillSchema() implementation ignores that parameter.

```
FillSchema(dataSet, SchemaType.Mapped)
Dim Orders As DataTable = dataSet.Tables("Orders")
Dim OrderItems As DataTable = dataSet.Tables("OrderItems")

Dim myReader As OQDataReader = _
                CType(_ReceiveCommand.ExecuteReader(), OQDataReader)
Dim myOrder As OrderObject

While (myReader.Read())
  myOrder = myReader.GetOrder()
  Dim newOrder As DataRow = Orders.NewRow()
  newOrder("CustomerID") = myOrder.CustomerID
  newOrder("OrderID") = myOrder.OrderID
  newOrder("ShipToName") = myOrder.ShipToName
  newOrder("ShipToAddr1") = myOrder.ShipToAddr1
  newOrder("ShipToAddr2") = myOrder.ShipToAddr2
  newOrder("ShipToCity") = myOrder.ShipToCity
  newOrder("ShipToState") = myOrder.ShipToState
  newOrder("ShipToCountry") = myOrder.ShipToCountry
  newOrder("ShipMethod") = myOrder.ShipMethod
  newOrder("ShipToZip") = myOrder.ShipToZip
  Orders.Rows.Add(newOrder)

  Dim itm As OrderItem
  For Each itm In myOrder.OrderItems
    Dim newItem As DataRow = OrderItems.NewRow()
    newItem("Quantity") = itm.Quantity
    newItem("StockNumber") = itm.StockNumber
    newItem("Price") = itm.Price
    newItem("OrderID") = myOrder.OrderID
    OrderItems.Rows.Add(newItem)
  Next
End While

' This will make everything we just put into the DataSet appear as
' unchanged. This allows us to distinguish between items that came
' from the queue and items that came from the DataSet.
dataSet.AcceptChanges()
Return 0
End Function
```

The FillSchema() method creates all of the appropriate metadata in the DataSet by defining the appropriate tables (Orders and OrderItems), their columns, and the DataRelations between the two tables. It is called each time the Fill() method is called, to make sure that the DataSet is never corrupted, and that it *always* has the metadata/schema structure appropriate for the OrderObject and OrderItem classes.

```
Public Function FillSchema(ByVal dataSet As DataSet, _
                            ByVal schemaType As SchemaType) As DataTable() _
    Implements IDataAdapter.FillSchema

    Dim x(2) As DataTable
    Dim OID_Parent As DataColumn
    Dim OID_Child As DataColumn
    Dim ParentKeys(1) As DataColumn
    Dim ChildKeys(2) As DataColumn

    x(0) = New DataTable("Orders")
    x(1) = New DataTable("OrderItems")

    x(0).Columns.Add("CustomerID", GetType(String))
    x(0).Columns.Add("OrderID", GetType(String))
    x(0).Columns.Add("ShipToName", GetType(String))
    x(0).Columns.Add("ShipToAddr1", GetType(String))
    x(0).Columns.Add("ShipToAddr2", GetType(String))
    x(0).Columns.Add("ShipToCity", GetType(String))
    x(0).Columns.Add("ShipToState", GetType(String))
    x(0).Columns.Add("ShipToZip", GetType(String))
    x(0).Columns.Add("ShipToCountry", GetType(String))
    x(0).Columns.Add("ShipMethod", GetType(String))
    OID_Parent = x(0).Columns("OrderID")
    ParentKeys(0) = OID_Parent
    x(0).PrimaryKey = ParentKeys

    x(1).Columns.Add("Quantity", GetType(Integer))
    x(1).Columns.Add("StockNumber", GetType(String))
    x(1).Columns.Add("Price", GetType(Single))
    x(1).Columns.Add("OrderID", GetType(String))
    OID_Child = x(1).Columns("OrderID")
    ChildKeys(0) = OID_Child
    ChildKeys(1) = x(1).Columns("StockNumber")
    If (dataSet.Tables.Contains("Orders")) Then
      dataSet.Tables.Remove("Orders")
    End If
    If (dataSet.Tables.Contains("OrderItems")) Then
      dataSet.Tables.Remove("OrderItems")
    End If

    dataSet.Tables.Add(x(0))
    dataSet.Tables.Add(x(1))
    dataSet.Relations.Add("OrderItems", OID_Parent, OID_Child, True)
```

```
    Return x
End Function

Public Function GetFillParameters() As IDataParameter() _
    Implements IDataAdapter.GetFillParameters

    Return Nothing
End Function
```

Aside from Fill(), Update() is the most important method on a data adapter. This method (defined later) will use the DataTable class's Select() method to obtain all of the "added" rows in the DataSet. We're ignoring anything other than "added" rows, because we're maintaining the queue model in which data can only be sent in or pulled out, and never modified while already there.

Then, for each of those added rows, a "send" command is executed, which, as we know, converts the row into an OrderObject (complete with items), and then serializes that object into the MSMQ message's body.

```
Public Function Update(ByVal dataSet As DataSet) As Integer _
    Implements IDataAdapter.Update

    Dim rowCount As Integer = 0
    If (_SendCommand Is Nothing) Then
      Throw New OQException( _
                "Cannot Update Queued DataSet without a valid SendCommand")
    End If

    Dim UpdatedOrders As DataRow() = _
                dataSet.Tables("Orders").Select("", "", DataViewRowState.Added)

    Dim _Order As DataRow
    For Each _Order In UpdatedOrders
      Dim Items As DataRow() = _Order.GetChildRows("OrderItems")
      Dim myOrder As New OrderObject()
      myOrder.CustomerID = _Order("CustomerID").ToString()
      myOrder.OrderID = _Order("OrderID").ToString()
      myOrder.ShipToName = _Order("ShipToName").ToString()
      myOrder.ShipToAddr1 = _Order("ShipToAddr1").ToString()
      myOrder.ShipToAddr2 = _Order("ShipToAddr2").ToString()
      myOrder.ShipToCity = _Order("ShipToCity").ToString()
      myOrder.ShipToState = _Order("ShipToState").ToString()
      myOrder.ShipToZip = _Order("ShipToZip").ToString()
      myOrder.ShipToCountry = _Order("ShipToCountry").ToString()
      myOrder.ShipMethod = _Order("ShipMethod").ToString()
      Dim _Item As DataRow
      For Each _Item In Items
        myOrder.AddItem(_Item("StockNumber").ToString(), _
```

```
                    CType(_Item("Quantity"), Integer), _
                    CType(_Item("Price"), Single))
        Next

        _SendCommand.Parameters("Order") = New OQParameter(myOrder)
        _SendCommand.ExecuteNonQuery()
        rowCount += 1
    Next

    dataSet.Tables("OrderItems").Clear()
    dataSet.Tables("Orders").Clear()
    Return rowCount
  End Function
```

The SendCommand and ReceiveCommand are both stored completely independent of each other. This allows each of the respective commands to maintain its own connection, which in turn allows information to be read from one queue, displayed through a DataSet, and then pumped into another queue. This provides for some extremely sophisticated distributed processing.

```
  Public Property SendCommand() As OQCommand
    Get
        Return _SendCommand
    End Get
    Set(ByVal Value As OQCommand)
        _SendCommand = Value
    End Set
  End Property

  Public Property ReceiveCommand() As OQCommand
    Get
        Return _ReceiveCommand
    End Get
    Set(ByVal Value As OQCommand)
        _ReceiveCommand = Value
    End Set
  End Property
End Class
```

The OQException

The last class that we're going to implement in our custom .NET data provider for our distributed, queued order-entry system is a derivation of the DataException class. The reason for this is that there might be some times when the client application is trapping specifically for one of the exceptions that we throw deliberately. This is why we throw an OQException rather than a standard one.

Doing this also provides us with the opportunity to upgrade the OQException class at a later date to allow it to use the Event Logging system and other complex features. (For more information, see *Professional .NET Framework*, ISBN 1-86100-556-3).

The following is the brief source code for our derived OQException class:

```
Public Class OQException
  Inherits DataException

  Public Sub New()
  End Sub

  Public Sub New(ByVal message As String)
    MyBase.New(message)
  End Sub

  Public Sub New(ByVal message As String, ByVal inner As Exception)
    MyBase.new(message, inner)
  End Sub
End Class
```

As you can see, all we're doing is creating a new exception class that can be thrown and caught via Try...Catch facilities. At some later date, we could go back into this class and add event-logging features, or more robust error tracking.

The last thing we need to do to this project in Visual Studio .NET is to ensure that it's strongly named, as we will want the generated assembly to go in the Global Assembly Cache (GAC). To do this, we need the following command line call to create a key pair, OQueue.snk:

```
> sn -k OQueue.snk
```

and we also need to specify that this pair is to be used, in AssemblyInfo.vb:

```
<Assembly: AssemblyKeyFile("..\..\OQueue.snk")>
```

Using the Custom Data Provider

Utilizing the custom data provider that we've just built should appear quite familiar—in fact, that's rather the point! By complying with all of the appropriate interfaces set out by the System.Data namespace, we've created a standard and uniform way to access our data source. Even though we don't provide full support for all the methods, they're all there, and the data-access paradigm is similar enough that we'll be reusing our knowledge of the SQL Server .NET and OLE DB .NET data providers when we use our custom provider.

At the very beginning of the chapter, we discussed that our fictitious company that was creating this queued backend infrastructure was planning on three main consumer types: a retail store, an e-commerce Web site, and a telephone sales call center. We'll now go through each of these and create a small sample application that demonstrates how each of them might be created for our custom data provider.

A Retail Store Interface

According to the design that our fictitious company came up with, the retail store interface simply needs to be able to provide the ability for a clerk behind the cash register to enter orders. To do this, we'll use a DataGrid bound to a DataSet. This way, they can simply enter the information they need free-form, and then hit a button to post the orders to the queue. Obviously, in the real world, this application would be much more robust, with a full suite of business rules, lookups, and error checking.

To create this example, we can use Visual Studio .NET to start a new Visual Basic .NET Windows application called RetailStore (see Figure 15-6). The next step after that is to add a reference to the DLL we generated by compiling our data provider assembly (OQProvider.dll), which is in the OQprovider\bin directory in the download. Before compiling our retail store interface, we need to make sure that our OQProvider assembly is in the GAC (either by using the gacutil utility, or by opening the \Winnt\Assembly folder and using the GAC shell extension). If we don't, the system will throw a FileNotFound exception when our application attempts to start.

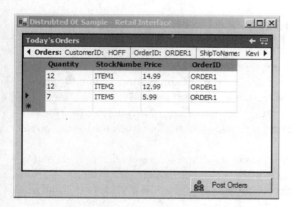

Figure 15-6. RetailStore *application—Windows application*

Rather than go into detail about the UI for this application, which you can examine at your leisure from the code download (the project's called RetailStore), we'll concentrate here on the code that makes it work. When the application's form first loads, we save ourselves some time by using the OQDataAdapter's FillSchema() method to prestructure our DataSet before we even have any data in it. This way, we don't have to write code that populates the schema over and over again, and we don't have to worry about accidentally getting the schema wrong.

```
Private Sub Form1_Load(ByVal sender As System.Object, _
                        ByVal e As System.EventArgs) Handles MyBase.Load
    myDS = New DataSet()
    Dim oqDA As New OQDataAdapter()
    oqDA.FillSchema(myDS, SchemaType.Mapped)
    oqDA = Nothing
    dgOrders.DataSource = myDS.Tables("Orders")
End Sub
```

The rest of the action takes place in the handler for the Post Orders button, listed here:

```
Private Sub button1_Click(ByVal sender As System.Object, _
                        ByVal e As System.EventArgs) Handles button1.Click
    Dim myConnection As New OQConnection()
    myConnection.ConnectionString = ".\Private$\OQTester"
    myConnection.Open()

    Dim oqDA As New OQDataAdapter()
    Dim SendCmd As New OQCommand()
    SendCmd.CommandText = "Send"
    SendCmd.Connection = myConnection
    oqDA.SendCommand = SendCmd
```

The `myDS` variable in the following line of code is a private member of type `DataSet` that's initialized when the form starts up.

```
    oqDA.Update(myDS)
    myConnection.Close()
    MessageBox.Show(Me, "Orders Transmitted.")
End Sub
```

Just like normal ADO.NET data access, everything starts with the connection. Once we've created and opened our connection, we then create our data adapter. Then, we create a new `SendCommand` object, which is just an `OQCommand` instance with the `CommandText` set to `"Send"`. With that done, all we have to do is call the `Update()` method on the data adapter, passing our `DataSet` as an argument. As a result, the changes are all automatically transferred to the queue for us.

Recalling the `Update()` code from the previous code listings, we iterate through each of the newly added rows in the `DataSet`, and create an `OrderObject` instance for each row (including its child item rows). Then, the `OrderObject` is transferred to the queue via a `Send()` call on the message queue, which is stored in the connection object.

Of course, our retail store example is lacking in a couple of areas—it's not as fully featured as it might be, and it doesn't contain as much error handling as it should. Another problem is that when you've entered data into the `DataGrid`, but you haven't moved the cursor off the current line, the `DataSet` doesn't know about it. This can cause difficulties when the user hits the Post Orders button.

One of the application requirements mentioned at the beginning of this chapter was that some distinction should be made between "fulfilled" orders and "unfulfilled" orders. To accomplish this, you could add a `Status` field to the `OrderObject` class, and allow it to be a value of an enumerated type that would include such values as `Open`, `Fulfilled`, `Pending`, etc. That way, the distributed order entry system could incorporate a workflow or pipeline-like process, where the `Order` travels from place to place affecting various company operations, until it is finally closed weeks later after the customer receives their product.

An e-Commerce Web Site Interface

Our e-commerce Web site example is going to be fairly small. Rather than go through the effort of simulating the process of going through a product catalog, logging a valid customer into the system, and all the other details that make a large Web site function, we'll just simulate the checkout page of an e-commerce site. The "checkout" button is going to place the customer's order into the queue by way of our custom data provider, and inform the customer that their order is on its way to the warehouse.

Let's take a look at a sample of the user interface for this simulated checkout page (see Figure 15-7), and then we'll look at the ASP.NET code that drives it.

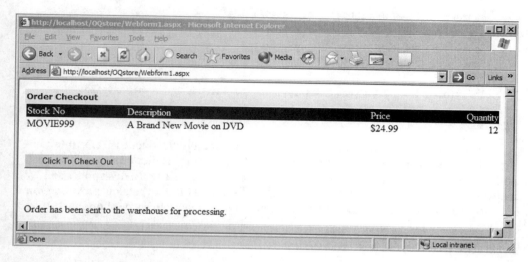

Figure 15-7. *Web site interface—*OQStore

What you're looking at is a *very* bare-bones mock-up of a Web site's checkout page. When the user activates the Click To Check Out button, they're informed that the order has been sent to the warehouse for processing. Here's the code in the code-behind page for the Page_Load() event handler (we could just as easily have wired the event to the button click itself):

```
Private Sub Page_Load(ByVal sender As System.Object, _
                      ByVal e As System.EventArgs) Handles MyBase.Load
   If (Page.IsPostBack) Then

      ' They hit the checkout button.
      Dim myConnection As New OQConnection()
      myConnection.ConnectionString = ".\Private$\OQTester"
      myConnection.Open()

      Dim SendCmd As New OQCommand()
      SendCmd.Connection = myConnection
      SendCmd.CommandText = "Send"

      Dim myOrder As New OrderObject("HOFF", _
                                     "ORDER99", _
                                     "Kevin", _
                                     "101 Nowhere", _
```

```
                                    "", _
                                    "Somewhere", _
                                    "OR", _
                                    "97201", _
                                    "USA", _
                                    "FedEx")

        myOrder.AddItem("MOVIE999", 12, 24.99F)
        Dim myParam As New OQParameter(myOrder)
        SendCmd.Parameters("Order") = myParam
        SendCmd.ExecuteNonQuery()

        lblInfo.Text = "Order has been sent to the warehouse for processing."
    End If
End Sub
```

As you can see, the process of actually getting an order into the queue isn't terribly complex. (Or rather, it isn't complex for the user of the data provider, as they don't see all of the work that went into facilitating that action!) To hone your ASP.NET skills, this application could be improved by hooking it up to an XML or SQL-based product catalog, providing some forms-based authentication, and having the shopping cart maintain a true shopping list.

The Telephone Sales Interface

The telephone sales interface works very much like the Web site interface. The differences are that it will be Windows-based, and it will work on only one order at a time—the telephone salespeople are going to be working a single call at a time, and when they're done, they should be finished. The order should already have been transmitted to the queue, with the salesperson being none the wiser.

Figure 15-8 shows a screenshot of our telephone sales interface in action (for the detail, look at the TelephoneSales project in the code download).

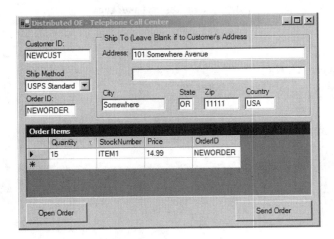

Figure 15-8. TelephoneSales

So, the telephone salesperson gets a phone call and hits the Open Order button, which wipes the data from the previous order and gives him or her a clean slate to work with. (Again, this is just a sample, and you'll find out quickly that it has a few holes, but those can be corrected with a little effort.) Let's take a look at the code that's executed in response to the Send Order button.

```
myDA.Update(myDS)
ClearOrder()
button1.Enabled = False
MessageBox.Show(Me, "Order Transmitted.")
```

We've done the work of instantiating and configuring new OQConnection and OQDataAdapter objects (the myDA variable) in the form's initialization code. All we have to do here is simply call the Update() method in the data adapter, and everything else is handled for us!

In that case, we'd better take a look at the initialization code, which goes through the motions of binding the DataGrid to the OrderItems table in our DataSet, and binding the standard controls to various columns in our Orders table. Before that, it creates and configures the core connection, and creates a SendCommand object that the data adapter will use to publish DataSet changes.

```
Private Sub Form1_Load(ByVal sender As System.Object, _
                       ByVal e As System.EventArgs) Handles MyBase.Load
  myConnection.ConnectionString = ".\Private$\OQTester"
  myConnection.Open()
  SendCmd.Connection = myConnection
  SendCmd.CommandText = "Send"
  myDA.SendCommand = SendCmd
```

We preconfigure the DataSet with the appropriate structure so that we can bind to controls even when there's no data in the DataSet.

```
myDA.FillSchema(myDS, SchemaType.Mapped)
dgItems.DataSource = myDS.Tables("OrderItems")
```

We can then bind the text boxes to the individual columns of our Orders table by creating new Binding objects and adding them to the controls' Bindings collections.

```
txtCustomerID.DataBindings.Add( _
                New Binding("Text", myDS.Tables("Orders"), "CustomerID"))
txtOrderID.DataBindings.Add( _
                New Binding("Text", myDS.Tables("Orders"), "OrderID"))
txtShipToAddr1.DataBindings.Add( _
                New Binding("Text", myDS.Tables("Orders"), "ShipToAddr1"))
txtShipToAddr2.DataBindings.Add( _
                New Binding("Text", myDS.Tables("Orders"), "ShipToAddr2"))
txtShipToCity.DataBindings.Add( _
                New Binding("Text", myDS.Tables("Orders"), "ShipToCity"))
txtShipToState.DataBindings.Add( _
                New Binding("Text", myDS.Tables("Orders"), "ShipToState"))
txtShipToCountry.DataBindings.Add( _
                New Binding("Text", myDS.Tables("Orders"), "ShipToCountry"))
```

```
   cboShipMethod.DataBindings.Add( _
                  New Binding("Text", myDS.Tables("Orders"), "ShipMethod"))
   button1.Enabled = False
End Sub
```

Finally, let's take a look at the ClearOrder() method, which wipes the current order and sets up the application user with a fresh new order. Note that we don't have to do anything to the controls, as they will be updated automatically whenever the DataSet changes.

```
Private Sub ClearOrder()
  Dim Order As DataRow = myDS.Tables("Orders").NewRow()

  Order("CustomerID") = "NEWCUST"
  Order("OrderID") = "NEWORDER"
  Order("ShipToAddr1") = ""
  Order("ShipToAddr2") = ""
  Order("ShipToCity") = ""
  Order("ShipToState") = ""
  Order("ShipToZip") = ""
  Order("ShipToCountry") = ""
  Order("ShipMethod") = ""
  myDS.Tables("Orders").Rows.Clear()
  myDS.Tables("Orders").Rows.Add(Order)
  myDS.Tables("OrderItems").Rows.Clear()

  button1.Enabled = True
End Sub
```

As you can see, we're obtaining a new row, populating it with empty strings (since our schema does not allow nulls), and then adding this new row to the Orders table. The visual controls bound to the columns of the Orders table will automatically update and clear to reflect that the original data is no longer there.

As another exercise to polish your skills at working with the custom data provider, you could write a fourth application that represents the backend administration system that continuously pulls orders out of the queue and simulates some processing on them, or even places them in a database using the SQL Server .NET data provider or OLE DB .NET data provider. The possibilities are limitless, not only for this particular data provider, but also for any custom provider you choose to write.

Summary

This chapter has provided thorough, in-depth coverage of the tasks involved in creating your own .NET data provider. You've covered the reasons why you might do this, as well as the steps involved in doing it. In addition, we've developed a fairly complex tutorial data provider that provides an infrastructure backbone for a distributed order entry system.

APPENDIX A

■ ■ ■

Visual Studio .NET and ADO.NET

Throughout the book you may use Visual Studio .NET to write code, to compile, and to debug. Visual Studio .NET offers more features to manage ADO.NET classes. Thanks to the data components, you can write ADO.NET applications without writing any code by using various wizards. By the end of this appendix, you'll be able to use every data component offered by Visual Studio .NET to create applications that use ADO.NET classes.

In this appendix, you'll look at the following:

- Using `SqlConnection` and `OleDbConnection` to specify connection parameters

- Using `SqlCommand` and `OleDbCommand` to specify SQL commands

- Using `SqlDataAdapter` and `OleDbDataAdapter` to retrieve records from the database and to fill `DataSet` and `DataTable` objects

- Using the `DataSet` to manage in-memory database structures and data

- Using the `DataView` component to filter and sort data in a dataset

- Using the `DataGrid` to display and edit data on a web page or Windows Form

You'll also look at the code that Visual Studio .NET generates automatically, so you can customize it to your specific needs.

Connection Classes

As you have seen, the .NET Framework includes two data providers—one for OLE DB data sources, and one especially for SQL Server 7.0 and above. You use both of these providers in a very similar way, but the components have different names to differentiate them. `OleDb-Connection` provides connections to OLE DB data sources, and `SqlConnection` provides connections to SQL Server 7.0 and above.

SqlConnection and OleDbConnection Data Components

ADO.NET connection objects establish a connection to a specified database. Visual Studio .NET offers two data components to help you manage your connection objects, as follows:

- The OleDbConnection data component to connect to a database using the OLE DB .NET data provider

- The SqlConnection data component to connect to a Microsoft SQL Server database using the SQL .NET data provider

Figure A-1 shows the Visual Studio .NET toolbox, where these components are located (if the toolbox is not showing in Visual Studio .NET, press Ctrl+Alt+X).

Figure A-1. *The Visual Studio .NET toolbox*

To use them, just drag either one *onto* the Web or Window Form and observe the new object inserted automatically *below* the form, in an area called the *tray* (see Figure A-2).

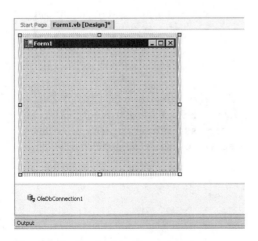

Figure A-2. *Control in the system tray*

This drag operation generates code automatically. The first snippet declares the object.

```
Me.OleDbConnection1 = New System.Data.OleDb.OleDbConnection()
```

The second snippet is generated inside the `InitializeComponent` method, which the Visual Studio .NET designer generates to initialize every object contained in the form (if you can't see this snippet of code in your application's script, you have to click the "+" next to the Windows Form Designer generated code to expand the code).

```
#Region " Windows Form Designer generated code "

    Public Sub New()
        MyBase.New()

        'This call is required by the Windows Form Designer.
        InitializeComponent()

        'Add any initialization after the InitializeComponent() call

    End Sub

    ...


#End Region
```

This snippet of code shows the connection object creation inside a #Region/#End Region code zone generated by the Designer, which delimits private code.

Note Visual Studio .NET does allow you to change the code inside the private region, but it would be better to think of this code as "untouchable," because these directives are used to make the code more maintainable, so changing anything here could cause untold damage elsewhere.

Adding the Connection String

The connection string contains the information used by the object to connect to the database. Usually, a connection string contains the database server name, the database name, and the username and password to use. Sometimes a connection string also contains specific data provider information, such as the security model or data encryption method.

You can add a connection string to the data component in two ways.

1. Using the `ConnectionString` property from the Properties window

2. Using the Data Link Properties dialog box

A connection string looks something like the following:

```
Provider=Microsoft.Jet.OLEDB.4.0;Data Source=C:\PRO.ADO.NET\example1\example1.mdb
```

Using the first method, you write the connection string directly into the `ConnectionString` property in the Properties window, as illustrated in Figure A-3.

Figure A-3. *Properties for the* `OleDbConnection` *in Visual Studio .NET*

Setting the `ConnectionString` property in the Properties window will add the following line of code within the Designer region:

```
Me.oleDbConnection1.ConnectionString="Provider=Microsoft.Jet.OLEDB.4.0;" & _
     "Data Source=C:\PRO.ADO.NET\example1\example1.mdb"
```

To use the second method, you create a new data connection item by selecting <New Connection…> from the drop-down list for the `ConnectionString` property in the Properties window. This will generate a connection string by letting you select settings in a dialog box. If the connection is successful, the generated connection string will be assigned to the `Connection` object, and added to the Data Connections listed in the Server Explorer window (which you can display by selecting Server Explorer from the View menu).

You can also add a connection to the Server Explorer by right-clicking on the Data Connections item and selecting Add Connection. It will then appear as an option in the drop-down list in the `ConnectionString` property of `Connection` components. If you can't see the Server Explorer window, you can use the Ctrl+Shift+S keys combination in order to display it, as well as the View menu.

You will now take a look at the dialog box that this method of generating a connection string uses. Although the same dialog box appears for both OLE DB and SQL connections, you use it in a slightly different way for the different connections.

For an OLE DB connection, the first step is to choose an OLE DB data provider from the Provider tab in the Data Link Properties dialog box (see Figure A-4).

For `SqlConnection` objects, you do not specify a provider. The default choice of provider, Microsoft OLE DB provider for SQL Server, will provide you with the choice of connection settings that you need.

After selecting the correct provider, click Next to move to the Connection tab. There are various parameters that need to be set—the exact parameters are dictated by the choice of provider. Figure A-5 shows the connection settings for the Microsoft Jet 4.0 OLE DB Provider.

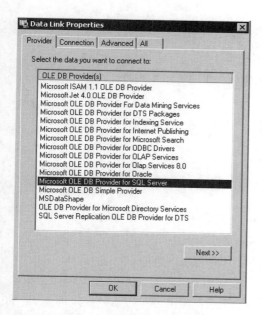

Figure A-4. *Setting up your* OleDbConnection—*choosing a provider*

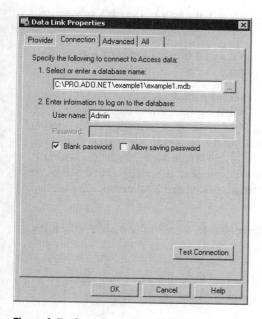

Figure A-5. *Setting up your* OleDbConnection—*specifying connection properties*

For this particular provider you need to specify the database filename, and optionally a username and password. You can check the settings using the Test Connection button.

Just for completeness, Figure A-6 shows the parameters for SqlConnection, or an OLE DB connection to SQL Server.

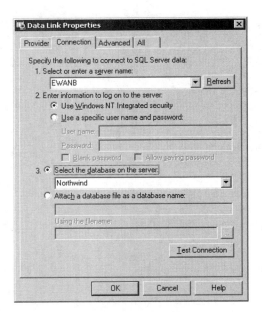

Figure A-6. *Setting up your* OleDbConnection—*for SQL Server*

As you can see, there are more parameters for this type of connection. Here is a summary of how to use them:

- **Server name**: The server that contains the database. If the database will run on the same machine as the application, use Localhost.

- **Log on information**: You need to choose the security model to use to connect to the database. The Use Windows NT Integrated Security option allows users who are logged into NT to connect to the database without SQL Server-specific accounts. To implement this kind of security model, you have to set the Microsoft SQL Server database to use the Windows NT Authentication Mode or the Mixed Mode. Using the second option, Use a Specific Username and Password, you need to specify a valid SQL Server account that gives appropriate permission for accessing the database. For the Northwind database, you can use **sa**.

- **Database**: Select the database that you wish to access, in one of two ways—the logon credentials must be valid for that database.

Going back to your Microsoft Jet connection, clicking OK will create a new data connection item and display it in the Data Connections tree within the Server Explorer window (see Figure A-7).

If you use the <New Connection...> option in the ConnectionString pull-down, the new connection string will be assigned automatically. If you use Add Connection in the Server Explorer, you can assign the connection string to the Connection component by selecting it from the ConnectionString pull-down on the Connection's Property window. Of course, this means that the same connection string can be used for several Connection objects, by selecting an existing string from the pull-down.

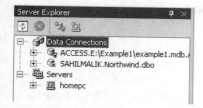

Figure A-7. *The new data connection in Server Explorer*

Choosing a connection string will add some new code in the region used by the Designer, as follows:

```
#Region " Windows Form Designer generated code "
    <System.Diagnostics.DebuggerStepThrough()> _
            Private Sub InitializeComponent()
  Me.oleDbConnection1 = New System.Data.OleDb.OleDbConnection()
  '
  ' oleDbConnection1
  '
Me.oleDbConnection1.ConnectionString = _
"Provider=Microsoft.Jet.OLEDB.4.0;Password="""";User ID=Admin;" & _
"Data Source=C:\ProADONET\Example1\example1.mdb;Mode=Share Deny None;" & _
"Extended Properties="";Jet OLEDB:System database="";" & _
"Jet OLEDB:Registry Path="";" & _
"Jet OLEDB:Database Password="";Jet OLEDB:Engine Type=5;" & _
"Jet OLEDB:Database Locking Mode=1;Jet OLEDB:Global Partial Bulk Ops=2;" & _
"Jet OLEDB:Global Bulk Transactions=1;Jet OLEDB:New Database Password="""";" & _
"Jet OLEDB:Create System Database=False;Jet OLEDB:Encrypt Database=False;" & _
"Jet OLEDB:Don't Copy Locale on Compact=False;" & _
"Jet OLEDB:Compact Without Replica Repair=False;Jet OLEDB:SFP=False"
  '
  ' dbConn
  '
dbConn.ConnectionString = _
"Provider=Microsoft.Jet.OLEDB.4.0;Password="""";User ID=Admin;" & _
"Data Source=C:\ProADONET\Example1\example1.mdb;Mode=Share Deny None;" & _
"Extended Properties="""";Jet OLEDB:System database="""";" & _
"Jet OLEDB:Registry Path="""";Jet OLEDB:Database Password="""";" & _
"Jet OLEDB:Engine Type=5;Jet OLEDB:Database Locking Mode=1;" & _
"Jet OLEDB:Global Partial Bulk Ops=2;Jet OLEDB:Global Bulk Transactions=1;" & _
"Jet OLEDB:New Database Password="""";Jet OLEDB:Create System Database=False;" & _
"Jet OLEDB:Encrypt Database=False;Jet OLEDB:Don't Copy Locale on Compact=False;" & _
"Jet OLEDB:Compact Without Replica Repair=False;Jet OLEDB:SFP=False"
. . .
```

The previous code snippet shows two different connections to two different Microsoft Access databases using the Microsoft Jet provider. Every giant connection string has been added to the code automatically after the connection string was specified in the Properties window. If you were coding the connection string manually, you would be able to leave out many of these settings so the string would be much shorter.

Adding an Event

Managing an event from the Visual Studio .NET application is a piece of cake. From the code editor, by selecting the object name from the first combo box, the second will be populated with all the supported events (see Figure A-8).

Figure A-8. *Events for an* OleDbConnection *object*

A new empty event handler managing method will be inserted at the end of the code, as follows:

```
Private Sub OleDbConnection1_StateChange(ByVal sender As Object, _
    ByVal e As System.Data.StateChangeEventArgs) _
    Handles OleDbConnection1.StateChange
End Sub
```

The StateChange event is fired each time the connection state changes (see Figure A-9). For example, you can use this event to inform the user of the database connection state by displaying a message in the status bar of the application (you can find this example in the Example1 folder of the code samples for this Appendix in the Downloads section of the Apress Web site [http://www.apress.com]).

Figure A-9. StateChange *event demonstration*

The code behind the "big" button retrieves the data using an OleDbDataAdapter together with a DataSet object, while the StateChange event handler writes every connection change inside the status bar.

```
Private Sub button1_Click(ByVal sender As Object, _
        ByVal e As System.EventArgs) Handles button1.Click
        Dim da As New OleDbDataAdapter("SELECT ID FROM tabUsers", _
                OleDbConnection1)
        Dim ds As New DataSet("ds")
        da.Fill(ds)
End Sub


Private Sub OleDbConnection1_StateChange(ByVal sender As Object, _
        ByVal e As System.Data.StateChangeEventArgs) _
        Handles OleDbConnection1.StateChange
        Dim strMessage As String
        strMessage = "Connection state changed from " & _
            e.OriginalState.ToString() & " to " & _
            e.CurrentState.ToString()
        sb.Text = strMessage
End Sub
```

Command Data Components

The Connection object alone is not sufficient to retrieve data or to modify a record from the database, because it indicates only which are the parameters to use to connect to the database, and establishes a connection based on these parameters. ADO.NET offers two classes that use the Connection object: either a DataAdapter object to fill a DataTable or a DataSet, or the Execute method series provided by the Command class itself. You can use an object created from one of these classes—DataAdapter or Command—to retrieve data, to update some records, to add a new record, and to delete records.

You use the Command object that corresponds to the connection you are using—OleDbCommand for an OleDbConnection, and SqlCommand for a SqlConnection.

SqlCommand and OleDbCommand Data Components

Visual Studio .NET offers two data components to execute commands against a database connection.

- The SqlCommand data component manages SQL commands specific for a Microsoft SQL Server database, accessed using a SqlConnection object.

- The OleDbCommand data component manages SQL commands for data sources accessed through an OLE data provider.

They can be accessed from the toolbox, as before. To use the command components, first you need a corresponding connection component. After that, simply drag the command data component onto the form in Visual Studio .NET (see Figure A-10).

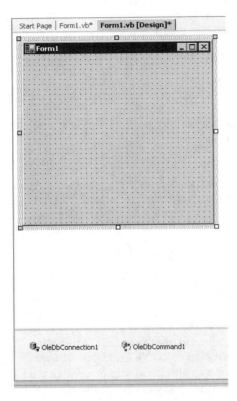

Figure A-10. `OleDbCommand` *object in the tray*

The drag operation inserts two new lines of code automatically in your source code. The first is added within the main class, in order to declare an `OleDbCommand` variable.

```
Private oleDbCommand1 As System.Data.OleDb.OleDbCommand
```

▮Note The `Private` data-hiding descriptor can be modified either manually or better from the `Modifiers` property inside the Properties window.

The second line is added within the Designer and creates a new object from the `OleDb-Command` class, assigning it to the `oleDbCommand1` variable.

```
#Region " Windows Form Designer generated code "
    <System.Diagnostics.DebuggerStepThrough()> _
            Private Sub InitializeComponent()
  Me.oleDbConnection1 = New System.Data.OleDb.OleDbConnection()
  Me.oleDbCommand1 = New System.Data.OleDb.OleDbCommand()


  . . .
#End Region
```

Note If you want to change the default auto-assigned object name, you can write a new name within the (Name) property inside the Properties window. Visual Studio .NET will change every command reference to the new name, automatically.

Before executing the SQL command, you need to specify the database connection that the command data component will use. From the Properties window, selecting the `Connection` property means that you can select from the combo box the name of the connection object previously inserted in the project. The Visual Studio .NET IDE (Integrated Design Environment) gives you the opportunity to create a new connection object directly from the combo box by selecting the New item (see Figure A-11).

Figure A-11. *Specifying the connection for an* `OleDbCommand` *object*

In Figure A-11, you can select the connection component that you already added to the form.

Executing a Stored Procedure

A stored procedure is a SQL function that is compiled and stored in the Microsoft SQL Server database. You can call it from your .NET applications, and these procedures can take parameters and return values—like procedures in other programming languages. As it is compiled into the database, it will be a lot faster than writing complex SQL commands into your .NET application, where they will need to be re-interpreted by the database every time the query is run. Let's look at a simple stored procedure, called InsertNewAuthor, that inserts a new record into the tab-Authors table in the ApressDB database (scripts for this are available in the code download).

```
CREATE PROCEDURE InsertNewAuthor
@FirstName varchar(50),
@LastName varchar(50)
AS
INSERT INTO tabAuthors (Author_FirstName,Author_LastName)
VALUES (@FirstName,@LastName)
return @@IDENTITY
```

The table you are looking at requires three columns.

- An identity column identifier called AuthorID as primary key, which is autonumbered

- A varchar column data type called Author_FirstName

- A varchar column data type called Author_LastName

This procedure creates a new row, assigning the Author_FirstName and Author_LastName values. Finally, @@IDENTITY is a parameter that will contain the AuthorID column value just created (as @@IDENTITY is a special way of returning the primary key of a table).

To use the previous stored procedure, you provide two parameters, the FirstName and the LastName, which you can see defined as input parameters in the previous code (@FirstName and @LastName). For example, the next snippet of code adds a new record using the EXEC SQL command within the database to execute the stored procedure.

```
EXEC InsertNewAuthor 'Fabio Claudio','Ferracchiati'
```

Executing a stored procedure in a .NET application is really simple using Visual Studio .NET. The following are the required steps (you can see this in Example2):

1. Set the CommandType property to StoredProcedure using the drop-down menu in the Properties window, as shown in Figure A-12.

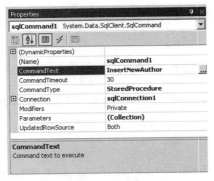

Figure A-12. SqlCommand *properties in Visual Studio .NET—specifying* CommandType

2. Specify the name of the stored procedure to use in the CommandText property of the Properties window.

3. Select Yes on the Regenerate Parameters dialog box that appears after Step 2 (see Figure A-13).

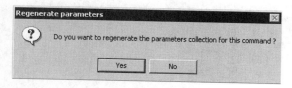

Figure A-13. *Regenerate Parameters dialog box*

After these steps, Visual Studio .NET will insert several lines of code to prepare the command object to execute the correct stored procedure.

```
'
'sqlCommand1
'
Me.sqlCommand1.CommandText = "InsertNewAuthor"
Me.sqlCommand1.CommandType = System.Data.CommandType.StoredProcedure
Me.sqlCommand1.Connection = Me.sqlConnection1
Me.sqlCommand1.Parameters.Add(New _
        System.Data.SqlClient.SqlParameter("@RETURN_VALUE", _
        System.Data.SqlDbType.Int, 4, _
        System.Data.ParameterDirection.ReturnValue, True, _
        CType(10, Byte), CType(0, Byte), "", _
        System.Data.DataRowVersion.Current, Nothing))
Me.sqlCommand1.Parameters.Add(New _
        System.Data.SqlClient.SqlParameter("@FirstName", _
        System.Data.SqlDbType.Char, 50, _
        System.Data.ParameterDirection.Input, True, _
        CType(0, Byte), CType(0 , Byte), "", _
        System.Data.DataRowVersion.Current, Nothing))
Me.sqlCommand1.Parameters.Add(New _
        System.Data.SqlClient.SqlParameter("@LastName", _
        System.Data.SqlDbType.Char, 50, _
        System.Data.ParameterDirection.Input, True, _
        CType(0, Byte), CType(0, Byte), "", _
        System.Data.DataRowVersion.Current, Nothing))
```

Visual Studio .NET has retrieved the stored procedure's parameters automatically, and it has obtained properties like the parameter data type, size, name, and so on.

You can change the parameters collection by calling the SqlParameter Collection Editor (see Figure A-14), which you do by selecting the "..." button for the Parameters property in the Properties window.

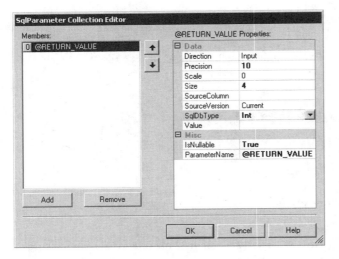

Figure A-14. SqlParameter *collection modification dialog box in Visual Studio .NET*

The left panel of the dialog box, Members, lists all the parameters that the stored procedure exposes. In the right panel, you have to define the parameter's characteristics. Let's review every option in detail.

- Direction: Indicates whether the member is just an input parameter, just an output parameter, or both. You have to use the input parameter when you want to provide a value to the stored procedure. You have to specify an output parameter when you expect a returning value from the stored procedure. Finally, you can select the input/output parameter type when you first want to provide a value to the stored procedure, and then you expect a returning value filled by the stored procedure within the same parameter.

- Precision: This property is valid just for the number data types and indicates the number of digits in a number.

- Scale: This property is valid just for the number data types and indicates the number of digits after the decimal point.

- Size: This property is valid just for the alphanumeric data types and indicates the parameter size. It has to be exactly the same size as was declared for the stored procedure parameter.

- SourceColumn: Use this field to associate the parameter to the source column in the database. It is very useful in update processes, but not useful for a stored procedure retrieving records.

- SourceVersion: Use this field to specify the version of the data within the data source. This is very useful for update operations, but not useful in a stored procedure that retrieves records.

- SqlDbType: Indicates the parameter data type.

- Value: In this property, you can set a value for the parameter. Not really useful in the case of a stored procedure.

- IsNullable: Indicates whether the parameter can be a null value (true) or not (false).

- ParameterName: Indicates the name of the parameter. For Microsoft SQL Server stored procedures, the name must start with an @ character.

After the stored procedure's parameter declaration, you have to follow these steps in order to execute the stored procedure from your code.

1. Open the database connection.

2. Set each value to supply to the stored procedure.

3. Call the ExecuteNonQuery method.

4. Close the database connection.

Imagine that you want to insert a new record, with details supplied by the user. The form would have text boxes to supply the record details. The code behind an "insert" button could be like the following:

```
Private Sub btnInsert_Click(ByVal sender As System.Object, _
    ByVal e As System.EventArgs) Handles btnInsert.Click
    Try
        If ((txtFirstName.TextLength > 0) And _
           (txtLastName.TextLength > 0)) Then
            ' Open the connection to the database
            sqlConnection1.Open()

            ' Fill the stored procedure parameters
            ' with text fields values
            sqlCommand1.Parameters(1).Value = txtFirstName.Text
            sqlCommand1.Parameters(2).Value = txtLastName.Text

            ' Execute the stored procedure
            sqlCommand1.ExecuteNonQuery()

            ' Close the connection
            sqlConnection1.Close()

            ' Print to video the final result
            MessageBox.Show("The new author has been added with " & _
        "the following identifier: " & _
        sqlCommand1.Parameters(0).Value)

            ' Clear text fields
            txtFirstName.Clear()
            txtLastName.Clear()
        End If
    Catch excpt As Exception
```

```
                    ' If the connection has been opened, close it
                    If (sqlConnection1.State = ConnectionState.Open) Then
                        sqlConnection1.Close()
                    End If

                    ' Show error message
                    MessageBox.Show(excpt.Message)
            End Try
    End Sub
```

Data Adapter Components

The DataAdapter transfers data from a data source to a DataSet, and back again—a key ability of ADO.NET. DataSets allow us to work with data without remaining connected to the data source. Also, the same DataSet class can handle data retrieved from many different sources—SQL Server connections, OLE DB connections, XML, or the user interface. The DataAdapter enables the DataSet to update a database using SQL commands stored within the Insert-Command, UpdateCommand, and DeleteCommand properties.

Once again, you have a separate class for OLE DB connections, and direct connections to SQL Server 7 or above databases: OleDbDataAdapter and SqlDataAdapter. DataAdapters will probably start to appear for all kinds of data sources, and it is possible to write your own—see Chapter 15 on creating .NET data providers.

Visual Studio .NET offers a wizard for developers to create a working DataAdapter object for their data source by selecting a few options.

The wizard offers similar features for SQL and OLE DB connections. However, some OLE databases do not support stored procedures, Microsoft Access for example. In these cases, the wizard will disable these options.

Dragging a DataAdapter component onto the form will display the wizard. After the welcome step, which summarizes all the operations available using the tool, the wizard gives you a choice between available database connections, and the option to create a new one (see Figure A-15).

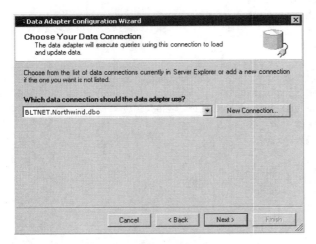

Figure A-15. *Data Adapter Configuration Wizard—choose your connection*

Choosing a New Connection will display Data Link Properties, and you can create a connection in the way you saw earlier in the appendix. Once the connection has been chosen, you move on to select the method that the data adapter will use to access the database (see Figure A-16).

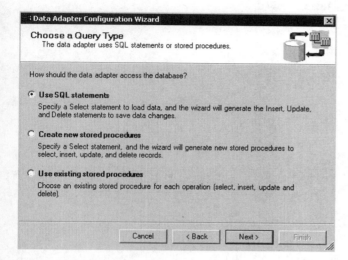

Figure A-16. *Data Adapter Configuration Wizard—choose your query type*

Each of these is worth considering. The following is an overview of your choices:

- Use SQL statements: Allows developers either to specify a SQL statement to retrieve data from the database or to build a new query using the Query Builder visual tool. The wizard will automatically generate update, delete, and insert commands based on the select statement.

- Create new stored procedures: Creates stored procedures instead of SQL statements in the application's code. The wizard will automatically generate update, delete, and insert commands based on the select statement. **This option is disabled for databases that do not implement stored procedures.**

- Use existing stored procedures: Allows developers to choose existing stored procedures to select, update, insert, and delete records.

Note The wizard allows a developer to generate SQL statements automatically only when the query does not contain more than one table. So, you will have to manually add your insert, update, and delete statements if you have tables joined together in your query.

The Use SQL Statements Option

In this case, the wizard will ask you to specify a new Select statement (see Figure A-17), which it will use to fill the dataset and to generate the three update commands.

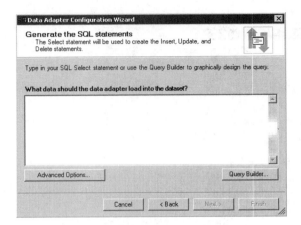

Figure A-17. *Data Adapter Configuration Wizard—use SQL statements*

In Figure A-17, you have the following two possibilities:

- Insert the SQL query instruction manually in the text field

- Use the Query Builder visual tool

If you prefer writing the SQL straight out, just write it in the box. Otherwise, use the Query Builder button, which builds a Select statement using the Query Builder visual tool.

At this stage, you can click Advanced Options and set some additional details, as shown in Figure A-18.

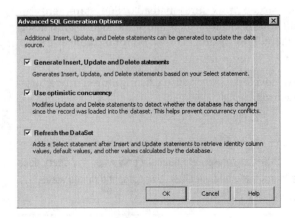

Figure A-18. *Data Adapter Configuration Wizard—Advanced SQL Generation Options*

Let's review each option in detail.

- Generate Insert, Update, and Delete statements: Generates three statements based on the SELECT query instruction. The other two options are related to this one, so if you clear this option you will clear the other two automatically.

- Use optimistic concurrency: Adds a WHERE condition to the INSERT, UPDATE, and DELETE statements generated automatically by the wizard in order to guarantee users that they are not going to change records that have been modified by other users, otherwise the command will fail.

- Refresh the DataSet: Appends a SELECT statement after the Insert and Update statements in order to retrieve the newly added or modified record. This is necessary when you want to always have a fresh set of records after every access to the database.

Clicking the Next button moves onto a final summary, and then clicking Finish will close the wizard and add the data adapter and its associated code (see Figure A-19).

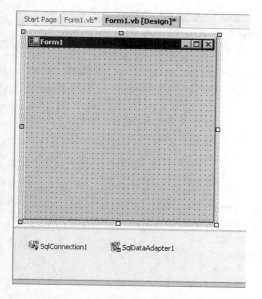

Figure A-19. *The* DataAdapter *added to your form*

Note The wizard can be rerun at any time by right-clicking the DataAdapter component in the form's tray and selecting Configure Data Adapter....

It's worth taking a look at the code that the wizard generates. Let's see how different code is generated depending on the Advanced Options that you select.

If you clear every Advanced Option, so that the wizard does not generate any update commands, you get the following code. Three variables are declared.

```
Friend WithEvents sqlSelectEmployees As System.Data.SqlClient.SqlCommand
Friend WithEvents dbConn As System.Data.SqlClient.SqlConnection
Friend WithEvents daEmployee As System.Data.SqlClient.SqlDataAdapter
```

In the body of the `InitializeComponent` function, the three objects are constructed and initialized, as follows:

```
Me.sqlSelectEmployees = New System.Data.SqlClient.SqlCommand()
Me.dbConn = New System.Data.SqlClient.SqlConnection()
Me.daEmployee = New System.Data.SqlClient.SqlDataAdapter()

...

'
'sqlSelectEmployees
'
Me.sqlSelectEmployees.CommandText = "SELECT Title, FirstName, LastName," & _
          " HomePhone, EmployeeID FROM Employees"
Me.sqlSelectEmployees.Connection = Me.dbConn
```

The `Command` object, `sqlSelectCommand1`, contains the `Select` statement specified in the related wizard step, and the `Command` property of the `DataAdapter` object is set to the `sqlSelect-Command1` object.

With only the Generate Insert, Update and Delete Statements option selected, the wizard will analyze your query to create the following three statements:

```
'
'daEmployee
'
Me.daEmployee.DeleteCommand = Me.sqlDeleteEmployee
Me.daEmployee.InsertCommand = Me.sqlInsertEmployee
Me.daEmployee.SelectCommand = Me.sqlSelectEmployees
Me.daEmployee.UpdateCommand = Me.sqlUpdateEmployee
'
'sqlInsertEmployee
'
Me.sqlInsertEmployee.CommandText = _
      "INSERT INTO Employees(Title, FirstName, LastName, HomePhone) " & _
      "VALUES (@Title, @FirstName," & _
      " @LastName, @HomePhone); SELECT Title, FirstName, LastName, " & _
      "HomePhone, EmployeeID FROM Employees WHERE (EmployeeID = @@IDENTITY)"

Me.sqlInsertEmployee.Connection = Me.dbConn
Me.sqlInsertEmployee.Parameters.Add( _
      New System.Data.SqlClient.SqlParameter("@Title", _
```

```vb
            System.Data.SqlDbType.NVarChar, _
                30, System.Data.ParameterDirection.Input, _
            True, CType(0, Byte), CType(0, Byte), _
            "Title", System.Data.DataRowVersion.Current, _
        Nothing))

...


...


'
'sqlUpdateEmployee
'
Me.sqlUpdateEmployee.CommandText = _
        "UPDATE Employees SET Title = @Title, " & _
        "FirstName = @FirstName, LastName = @LastName" & _
        ", HomePhone = @HomePhone WHERE " & _
        "(EmployeeID = @Original_EmployeeID) AND (FirstNam" & _
        "e = @Original_FirstName) AND (HomePhone " & _
        "= @Original_HomePhone OR @Original_HomeP" & _
        "hone1 IS NULL AND HomePhone IS NULL) AND " & _
        "(LastName = @Original_LastName) AND (Ti" & _
        "tle = @Original_Title OR @Original_Title1 " & _
        "IS NULL AND Title IS NULL); SELECT Tit" & _
        "le, FirstName, LastName, HomePhone, EmployeeID " & _
        "FROM Employees WHERE (EmployeeID " & _
        "= @Select_EmployeeID)"

Me.sqlUpdateEmployee.Connection = Me.dbConn

Me.sqlUpdateEmployee.Parameters.Add( _
        New System.Data.SqlClient.SqlParameter("@Title", _
            System.Data.SqlDbType.NVarChar, _
                30, System.Data.ParameterDirection.Input, _
            True, CType(0, Byte), CType(0, Byte), _
                "Title", System.Data.DataRowVersion.Current, _
        Nothing))

...


...


'
'sqlDeleteEmployee
'
Me.sqlDeleteEmployee.CommandText = _
```

```
        "DELETE FROM Employees WHERE (EmployeeID = @EmployeeID) AND " & _
        "(FirstName = @FirstName) AND (HomePhone = @HomePhone OR " & _
        "@HomePhone1 IS NULL AND HomePhone IS NULL) AND" & _
        " (LastName = @LastName) AND (Title = @Title OR " & _
        "@Title1 IS NULL AND Title IS NULL)"

Me.sqlDeleteEmployee.Connection = Me.dbConn

Me.sqlDeleteEmployee.Parameters.Add( _
        New System.Data.SqlClient.SqlParameter("@EmployeeID",   _
        System.Data.SqlDbType.Int, 4, System.Data.ParameterDirection.Input,   _
        False, CType(0, Byte), CType(0, Byte), "EmployeeID",   _
        System.Data.DataRowVersion.Original, Nothing))
```

As you can see from the previous code, the Insert, Update, and Delete commands have been created automatically. The wizard has recognized the primary key column, even if it was not present in the query, adding a WHERE condition inside both the Update and Delete statements.

In an application it could happen that you are attempting to update a record that has been removed by another user; using the previous code, an exception would be raised and the program would fail the operation. To obtain major control over these kinds of exceptions, you can select the Use Optimistic Concurrency option, which will create extra code, as follows:

```
'
'sqlUpdateEmployee
'
Me.sqlUpdateEmployee.CommandText = _
        "UPDATE Employees SET Title = @Title, " & _
        "FirstName = @FirstName, LastName = @LastName" & _
        ", HomePhone = @HomePhone WHERE " & _
        "(EmployeeID = @Original_EmployeeID) AND (FirstName" & _
        " = @Original_FirstName) AND " & _
        "(HomePhone = @Original_HomePhone OR " & _
        "@Original_HomePhone1 IS NULL AND HomePhone IS NULL) " & _
        "AND (LastName = @Original_LastName) " & _
        " AND (Title = @Original_Title OR @Original_Title1 " & _
        "IS NULL AND Title IS NULL); SELECT " & _
        "Title, FirstName, LastName, HomePhone, " & _
        "EmployeeID FROM Employees WHERE (EmployeeID " & _
        "= @Select_EmployeeID)"
```

In the previous snippet, the Update statement has changed and the record will be updated only if the original column values have not been changed. The Delete statement also changes, so that a row will only be deleted if it has not been modified in the data source since the dataset was filled.

Finally, to ensure that you always have a set of fresh records inside your DataSet object, you can select the Refresh the DataSet advanced option in order to retrieve the records each time a new database operation is performed.

```
'
'sqlInsertEmployee
'
Me.sqlInsertEmployee.CommandText = _
"INSERT INTO Employees(Title, FirstName, LastName, HomePhone) " & _
        "VALUES (@Title, @FirstName, @LastName, @HomePhone); " & _
"SELECT Title, FirstName, LastName, HomePhone " & _
",EmployeeID FROM Employees WHERE (EmployeeID = @@IDENTITY)"
```

In the previous statement, a SELECT instruction has been appended to the INSERT command in order to retrieve the last record inserted. However, if you have many records to insert or to update, it is better not to use this option and refresh the DataSet at the end of your database operations. Using the Refresh the DataSet option will execute two commands for each database operation, slowing down general performance.

The Create New Stored Procedures Option

This option allows you to create four stored procedures to select, update, insert, and delete records, instead of using SQL statements in your application. The first two wizard steps are identical to those for if you were using SQL statements—you choose the database connection parameters and the Select string. The third step is different because it asks you to choose four stored procedure names that will be created in the database automatically (based on the Select string you have provided), as shown in Figure A-20.

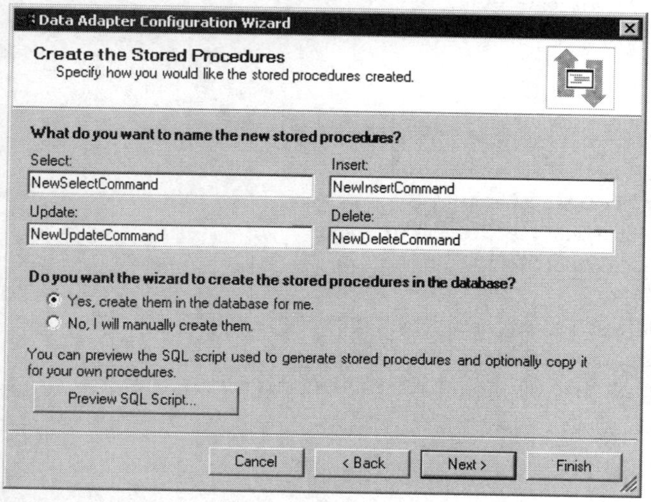

Figure A-20. *Data Adapter Configuration Wizard—create the Stored Procedures option*

You can change the default names for the stored procedures and choose whether to let the wizard create the stored procedures in the database automatically. The Preview SQL Script button shows the script that the wizard will run against the database, but does not provide the ability to modify the instructions (see Figure A-21).

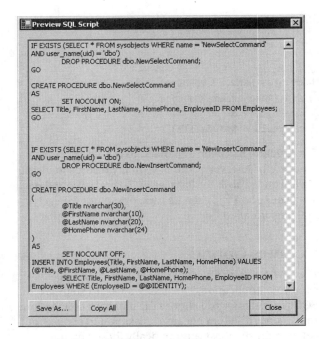

```
IF EXISTS (SELECT * FROM sysobjects WHERE name = 'NewSelectCommand'
AND user_name(uid) = 'dbo')
          DROP PROCEDURE dbo.NewSelectCommand;
GO

CREATE PROCEDURE dbo.NewSelectCommand
AS
          SET NOCOUNT ON;
SELECT Title, FirstName, LastName, HomePhone, EmployeeID FROM Employees;
GO


IF EXISTS (SELECT * FROM sysobjects WHERE name = 'NewInsertCommand'
AND user_name(uid) = 'dbo')
          DROP PROCEDURE dbo.NewInsertCommand;
GO

CREATE PROCEDURE dbo.NewInsertCommand
(
          @Title nvarchar(30),
          @FirstName nvarchar(10),
          @LastName nvarchar(20),
          @HomePhone nvarchar(24)
)
AS
          SET NOCOUNT OFF;
INSERT INTO Employees(Title, FirstName, LastName, HomePhone) VALUES
(@Title, @FirstName, @LastName, @HomePhone);
          SELECT Title, FirstName, LastName, HomePhone, EmployeeID FROM
Employees WHERE (EmployeeID = @@IDENTITY);
```

Save As...   Copy All   Close

Figure A-21. *New stored procedure, preview before save*

After this step, the wizard will display a summary of every operation it is going to do. Clicking the Finish button will create the stored procedures, and add the following code to the project:

```
'
' sqlSelectCommand1
'
sqlSelectCommand1.CommandText = "NewSelectCommand"
sqlSelectCommand1.CommandType = CommandType.StoredProcedure
sqlSelectCommand1.Connection = sqlConnection1

sqlSelectCommand1.Parameters.Add(New SqlParameter("@RETURN_VALUE", _
  SqlDbType.Int, 4, ParameterDirection.ReturnValue, False, _
    ((System.Byte)(0)), ((System.Byte)(0)), "", DataRowVersion.Current, _
    Nothing))


'
' sqlInsertCommand1
'
sqlInsertCommand1.CommandText = "NewInsertCommand"
sqlInsertCommand1.CommandType = CommandType.StoredProcedure
sqlInsertCommand1.Connection = sqlConnection1
```

```vbnet
sqlInsertCommand1.Parameters.Add(New SqlClient.SqlParameter("@RETURN_VALUE", _
  SqlDbType.Int, 4, ParameterDirection.ReturnValue, False, _
    CType(0, Byte), CType(0, Byte), "", DataRowVersion.Current, _
    Nothing))

sqlInsertCommand1.Parameters.Add(New SqlClient.SqlParameter("@Title", _
  SqlDbType.NVarChar, 30, ParameterDirection.Input, True, _
    CType(0, Byte), CType(0, Byte), "Title", DataRowVersion.Current, _
    Nothing))

. . .

'
' sqlUpdateCommand1
'
sqlUpdateCommand1.CommandText = "NewUpdateCommand"
sqlUpdateCommand1.CommandType = CommandType.StoredProcedure
sqlUpdateCommand1.Connection = sqlConnection1
sqlUpdateCommand1.Parameters.Add(new SqlClient.SqlParameter("@RETURN_VALUE", _
  SqlDbType.Int, 4, ParameterDirection.ReturnValue, False, _
    CType(0, Byte), CType(0, Byte), "", DataRowVersion.Current, _
    Nothing))

sqlUpdateCommand1.Parameters.Add(New _
  System.Data.SqlClient.SqlParameter("@Title", _
    System.Data.SqlDbType.NVarChar, 30, _
    System.Data.ParameterDirection.Input, True, CType(0, Byte), _
    CType(0, Byte), "Title", System.Data.DataRowVersion.Current, Nothing))

sqlUpdateCommand1.Parameters.Add(New SqlClient.SqlParameter("@FirstName", _
  SqlDbType.NVarChar, 10, ParameterDirection.Input, False, _
    CType(0, Byte), CType(0, Byte), "FirstName", _
    DataRowVersion.Current, Nothing))

. . .

'
' sqlDeleteCommand1
'
sqlDeleteCommand1.CommandText = "NewDeleteCommand"
sqlDeleteCommand1.CommandType = CommandType.StoredProcedure
sqlDeleteCommand1.Connection = sqlConnection1

sqlDeleteCommand1.Parameters.Add(New SqlClient.SqlParameter("@RETURN_VALUE", _
  SqlDbType.Int, 4, ParameterDirection.ReturnValue, False, _
    CType(0, Byte), CType(0, Byte), "", DataRowVersion.Current, _
    Nothing))
```

```
sqlDeleteCommand1.Parameters.Add(New SqlClient.SqlParameter("@EmployeeID", _
   SqlDbType.Int, 4, ParameterDirection.Input, False, CType(0, Byte), _
      CType(0, Byte), "EmployeeID", DataRowVersion.Original, Nothing))
```

. . .

In this fragment of code, you can see how the wizard has inserted the stored procedures in the code.

The Use Existing Stored Procedures Option

You can use the last wizard option when you want to use existing stored procedures to select, insert, update, and delete records in the database (see Figure A-22). The wizard will analyze every parameter that you have to provide to the stored procedures, creating all the code necessary to execute them.

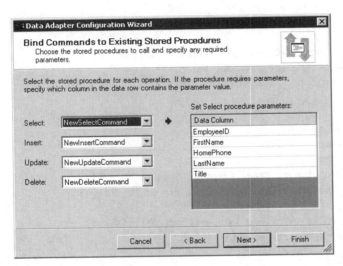

Figure A-22. *Data Adapter Configuration Wizard—using existing stored procedures*

Figure A-22 shows four combo boxes where you can select every stored procedure that you want to use in your code. The Select stored procedure is mandatory, while you can omit the other three (Insert, Update, and Delete).

Note If you remove a parameter from a stored procedure and then use the wizard to update your code, you will continue to see the same parameters, even the deleted one. The same behavior is encountered when you add a new parameter to the stored procedure or when you change its name, dimension, data type, and so on. Actually, the only thing you can do in order to retrieve the correct stored procedure structure is close Visual Studio .NET and then restart it.

The code generated by the wizard will contain calls to the stored procedures specified during these steps.

Table Mappings

The ADO.NET class library offers a way to map column names from the database to the DataSet using the DataTableMapping and DataColumnMapping objects. Usually, mapping classes are really useful when you have to manage tables that have unclear or short column names. In fact, you can define new names for the columns used by the DataSet object in order to improve the code readability. For more information on Mapping, see Chapter 9. Visual Studio .NET offers a visual tool that allows developers to map the column names generating the code automatically. You can display the Table Mappings visual tool by clicking on the "..." button in the DataAdapter object's TableMappings property contained in the Properties window. The resulting window is shown in Figure A-23.

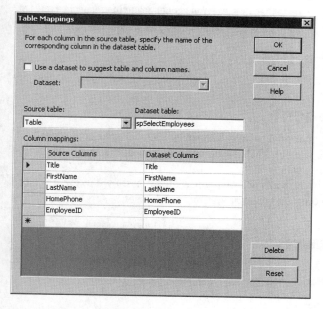

Figure A-23. *Modifying* TableMappings *and* ColumnMappings *for the* DataAdapter

In Figure A-23, you can decide how columns map from the database to the dataset by relating names from the Source Columns and the Dataset Columns in the grid. You can check Use a Dataset to Suggest Table and Column Names if your project contains one or more dataset files whose schema will be used to suggest the table and column names to map to.

A typical scenario where you can use the Table Mappings dialog box would be receiving a DataSet object from a web service and wanting to insert its data into a database. Often, the database table and column names will be different from the names in the dataset, so you must map the database names to the dataset names.

Finally, you can remove a mapping row by selecting it and pressing the Delete button, or you can roll back all the changes you have made by using the Reset button.

Let's see the code generated by the wizard.

```
sqlDataAdapter1.TableMappings.AddRange(New Common.DataTableMapping() { _
    New Common.DataTableMapping("Table", "spSelectEmployees", New _
    Common.DataColumnMapping() {New Common.DataColumnMapping("Title", _
    "Title"), _
New Common.DataColumnMapping("FirstName", "FirstName"), New _
    Common.DataColumnMapping("LastName", "LastName"), New _
    Common.DataColumnMapping("HomePhone", "HomePhone"), New _
    Common.DataColumnMapping("EmployeeID", "EmployeeID")})})
```

The code creates a new `DataTableMapping` object, with related `DataColumnMapping` objects.

■**Note** Even if you don't want to create a mapping mechanism, because the source column names are the same as in the dataset, Visual Studio .NET will create them anyway. You cannot delete the respective rows of code because they have been written in the private code region, and changing its content would render the tool useless.

DataSet Data Component

The `DataSet` implements a disconnected mechanism to improve database connection performance, and to manage data exchange using XML. Visual Studio .NET offers many visual tools to help developers manipulate datasets.

Dragging the data component onto the form will raise the dialog box shown in Figure A-24, where you select whether you want to create a typed or an untyped dataset.

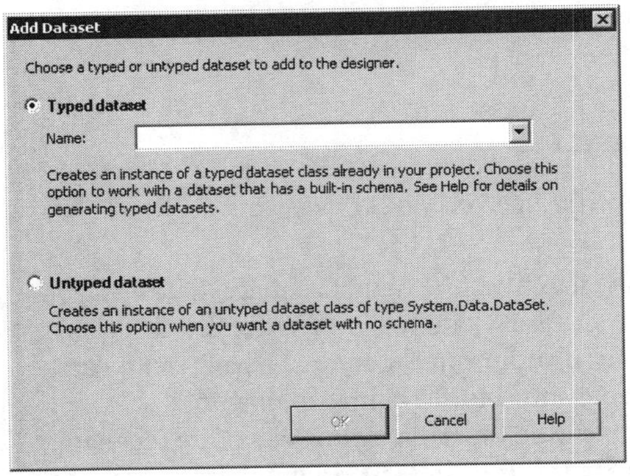

Figure A-24. *Adding a dataset to your project*

This dialog box allows developers to choose between two options.

- Typed dataset: Create an object based on an existing subclass of the DataSet class that incorporates schema information into the class definition.

- Untyped dataset: Create an instance of the DataSet class, which incorporates no schema information. This option allows you to create an empty dataset with no initial schema.

Visual Studio .NET offers a complete set of tools to manage typed datasets, so in the following section of the chapter you will focus your attention on this aspect. Adding an untyped dataset is more or less the same as declaring a DataSet object with coding instructions—you have the ability to set a few properties at design time, such as the namespace and the prefix. The really interesting Visual Studio .NET features are offered by typed datasets.

The Typed Dataset

A typed dataset is a subclass of the DataSet class that implements properties and methods specific to the data structure that it will be used to manipulate; it also includes column type information. These properties and methods provide easy ways to access tables, columns, relations, and so on. They also ensure that the dataset is only used to store data of the appropriate type for its columns, helping to avoid errors when the dataset is written back to the data source.

Imagine you want to manage a myTable that has a myID column. With the typed dataset it will be as simple as calling the following instruction:

```
myDataSet.myTable.myID
```

Creating a typed dataset manually can be complicated, but Visual Studio .NET offers the tools to accomplish this easily.

Adding a Typed Dataset to the Project

Adding a DataSet object inside the Visual Studio .NET project is really easy. From the Project menu, select Add New Item, and choose Data Set from the dialog box, as shown in Figure A-25.

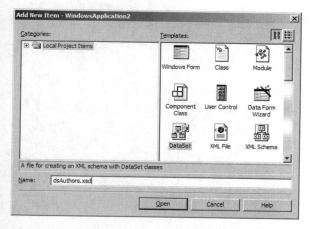

Figure A-25. *Adding a new typed dataset to the project*

After choosing a valid filename and pressing the Open button, a new `DataSet` class will be generated automatically. The class does not contain database information, but it has overridden all the necessary methods to serialize the data and the constructor to initialize internal variables to the default values.

Note In order to display the code generated by the Visual Studio .NET tool, you have to select the Show All Files button within the Solution Explorer window, as shown in Figure A-26.

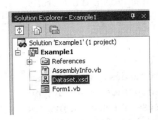

Figure A-26. *The typed dataset in Solution Explorer*

There are two ways to create the dataset schema: you can drag tables from a database connection in the Server Explorer onto the dataset, or you can drag the XML schema components in the Toolbox window onto the Dataset Designer (this option allows for creating the dataset manually). Usually, the first method is used to retrieve information from a database, and the second method is used when the data will be retrieved from an XML document. However, you can use whichever one you like, even if retrieving a schema automatically is faster than if you had made it manually.

Figure A-27 shows the complete list of XML schema components that you can use for your dataset schema definition (the best way to get more information on these components is to use the Help files that come with Visual Studio .NET).

Figure A-27. *XML schema items in the XML Schema Toolbox*

Although you need a sound understanding of XML to manually create an XML schema, you can, if you do not have such a solid basis, always choose either to infer the XML schema using the `DataSet`'s `InferXmlSchema` method, or load an existing one using an untyped dataset object.

When you work with database information, you can drag the desired tables directly onto the Dataset Designer from the Server Explorer—Visual Studio .NET will create the related schema automatically. It will analyze every column contained in the selected tables and create element keys and other elements with the correct data types. Moreover, if the tables are joined by relationships, then Visual Studio .NET will automatically create relations inside the XML schema.

Figure A-28 shows what it would look like if you dragged a table onto it from the Server Explorer.

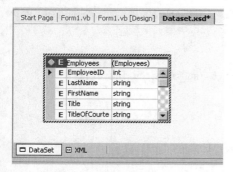

Figure A-28. *The typed dataset opened in Visual Studio .NET*

You can see the XML tags that define the typed dataset by clicking on the XML tab underneath the Dataset Designer. You can remove XML elements (whole tables or individual columns) graphically by right-clicking them and choosing Delete from the Context menu, or by selecting them and pressing the Delete key.

As you define the dataset's schema, Visual Studio .NET will generate a class that inherits from the `DataSet` and implements the schema.

Let's see what has been added.

- The main class derived from the `DataSet` parent class will contain a new `DataTable`-derived class wrapped around the table specified in the designer. Naturally, for each table inserted in the `DataSet`, the tool will create a related `DataTable`-derived class.

- A new `DataRow`-derived class is added to the main class, which wraps the table's row information.

- A new `EventArgs`-derived class will be added in the main class to implement the row change event.

- The `DataSet`-derived class will offer a new property for each table inserted into the dataset; the properties will be named after the table that they point to.

- Every new class will contain an ad hoc method to add a row to the data table contained in the dataset, a read-only property for each column present in the table, a method to find a row providing the primary key, and, finally, four event handlers specific for the rows contained in the table.

These features make it easy to manage the data, and code that uses a typed dataset is clearer than code that uses an untyped dataset. To show the difference, let's see a snippet of code that uses your generated dataset to add a row to the authors table.

```
Dim ds As New dsAuthors()
ds.authors.AddauthorsRow("222-22-2222", "Ferracchiati", "Fabio Claudio", _
                        True)
```

This snippet of code uses a typed dataset wrapped around four columns of the authors table. As you can see, it's really a piece of cake using the new AddauthorsRow method to add a row to the dataset. Using an untyped dataset means that things became contorted, as shown in the following code:

```
Dim dbConn As new SqlConnection("data source=BLTNET;initial" & _
    "catalog=pubs;integrated security=SSPI;persist security " & _
    "info=True;workstation id=BLTNET;packet size=4096")

Dim daAuthors As New SqlClient.SqlDataAdapter("SELECT au_lname,au_fname" & _
            ",contract, au_id FROM authors", dbConn)

Dim ds As New DataSet("dsAuthors")

daAuthors.Fill(ds)
```

Retrieving data from the typed dataset is easier. With a typed dataset, you can use the read-only properties added by the tool, as follows:

```
ds.authors.au_lname
```

However, when using an untyped dataset, you must use the following:

```
ds.Tables("authors").Rows(0)(" au_lname")
```

Relating Two or More Tables

Relating two or more tables in the DataSet object is as important as relating them in the database. You can assign constraints between tables that cascade updates and deletes, or check for integrity rules.

The Dataset Designer makes it easy to create relationships between tables. You have to drag the tables onto the designer and drag the column that composes the relation over to the other column in the other table. If two or more columns compose the relation, you can select all of them and drag them directly onto the other table.

■**Note** Visual Studio .NET offers a different dragging mechanism from Microsoft Access and Microsoft SQL Server: when you have two tables side by side in the diagram and you want to relate the column from the left table to one in the right table, you must drag the source column from the left-hand side of the parent table. Also, it doesn't matter what column you drag to—the Dataset Designer will select one for you, and give you the option to change it if you wish.

After dragging a column onto a related table, the Dataset Designer prompts you to define the relationship's details, as shown in Figure A-29.

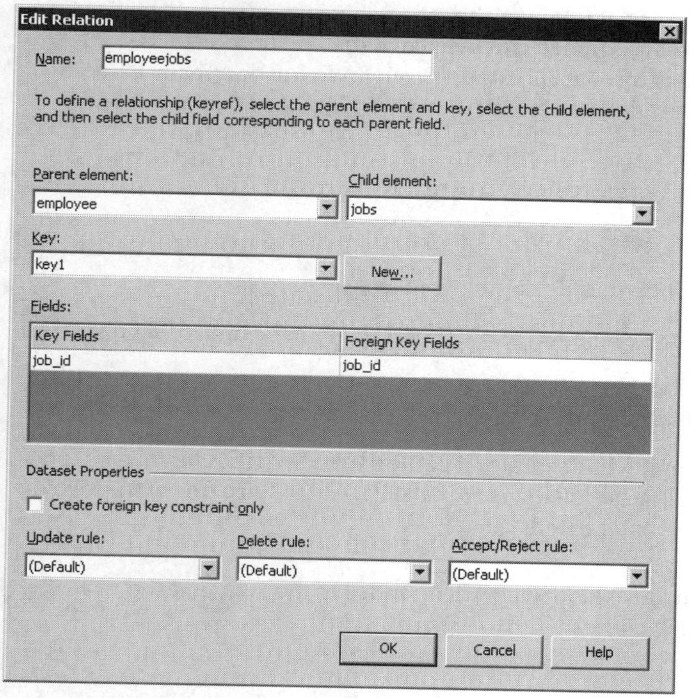

Figure A-29. *Specifying relation details in Visual Studio .NET*

Let's see what you can do with this dialog box.

- The Name text field allows you to specify the name that will be assigned to this relationship in the DataSet object.

- The Parent Element combo box enables you to select a different parent table for the relationship.

- The Child Element combo box enables you to select a different child table for the relationship.

- The Key combo box enables you to select a parent key. This could be a single column or a set of columns. If you have created the relationship by dragging, you don't need to change this. The New button enables you to specify a column or set of columns to act as the key in the parent table.

- The Fields list view allows you to set columns in the child table that correspond with the key columns you have selected for the parent table. Visual Studio .NET will attempt to choose these automatically, but sometimes it is necessary to change them.

- The Create Foreign Key Constraint Only option specifies that a dataset should only enforce constraints between the tables, and not to retrieve data from both the tables. The resulting dataset will be more efficient, but will contain fewer methods.

- Update Rule and Delete Rule enable you to choose how the dataset should behave when a row in the parent table is updated or deleted. If the Create Foreign Key Constraint Only check box has been enabled, the constraint rule will be applied to these operations, guaranteeing the data's referential integrity. They can assume one of the following values:

  - (Default): Set to whatever the default is set to.

  - None: No action will be taken on related rows.

  - Cascade: Cascades the update/delete across to all related rows.

  - SetNull: All related rows will be set to DBNull as a result of the update action.

  - SetDefault: All of the related rows affected by the update action will be set to their default values as indicated by their DefaultValue property.

- The Accept/Reject Rule combo box contains the rule applied to the dataset when the AcceptChanges and RejectChanges methods are called. It can assume one of the following values: (Default), None, and Cascade.

After clicking the OK button, the relationship will be added to the XSD, and shown in the Dataset Designer (see Figure A-30).

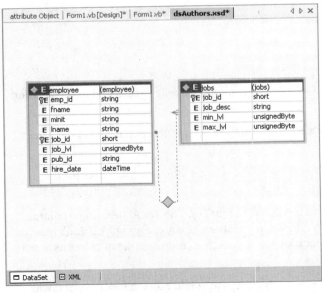

Figure A-30. *The typed dataset after specifying the relation*

Generating and Filling a Typed DataSet Object

Visual Studio .NET allows developers to generate a strongly typed `DataSet` class by right-clicking a `DataAdapter` component in the tray and selecting Generate Dataset. Visual Studio .NET will study the `SELECT` statement provided when creating the `DataAdapter` and will generate a new XSD schema file and a new source file containing the complete typed `DataSet` class.

In the following code, you can see the XML representation of the `DataSet`:

```
<xsd:schema id="dsEmployee"
 targetNamespace="http://www.tempuri.org/dsEmployee.xsd"
xmlns="http://www.tempuri.org/dsEmployee.xsd"
xmlns:xsd="http://www.w3.org/2001/XMLSchema"
xmlns:msdata="urn:schemas-microsoft-com:xml-msdata"
 attributeFormDefault="qualified" elementFormDefault="qualified">
 <xsd:element name="dsEmployee" msdata:IsDataSet="true">
  <xsd:complexType>
   <xsd:choice maxOccurs="unbounded">
    <xsd:element name="Employees">
     <xsd:complexType>
      <xsd:sequence>
       <xsd:element name="Title" type="xsd:string" minOccurs="0" />
       <xsd:element name="FirstName" type="xsd:string" />
       <xsd:element name="LastName" type="xsd:string" />
       <xsd:element name="HomePhone" type="xsd:string" minOccurs="0" />
       <xsd:element name="EmployeeID" msdata:ReadOnly="true"
             msdata:AutoIncrement="true" type="xsd:int" />
      </xsd:sequence>
     </xsd:complexType>
    </xsd:element>
   </xsd:choice>
  </xsd:complexType>
  <xsd:unique name="Constraint1" msdata:PrimaryKey="true">
   <xsd:selector xpath=".//Employees" />
   <xsd:field xpath="EmployeeID" />
  </xsd:unique>
 </xsd:element>
</xsd:schema>
```

Filling the `DataSet` object is really easy now that every `DataAdapter` component is declared in the code. Just call the `Fill` method of the `DataAdapter` object, specifying the `DataSet` object to fill.

```
' Fill the employee dataset
daEmployee.Fill(dsEmployee)
```

You can display the data contained in the dataset in various ways, such as using a data grid component, filling text fields, and saving the data using XML and then using an XML template to display the record. You will now go on to explore different ways of displaying a dataset using Visual Studio .NET.

Using the Techniques Acquired to Create a Web Service

For the purposes of this appendix, you will now create a web service using every data aspect that you have seen until this moment. Very briefly, a web service represents the biggest innovation introduced by the .NET Framework: allowing developers to call remote procedures and show results within their own applications.

The fictional BltAirlines company airline has a web service that lists all the flights that it organizes for the present day. The Apress Intranet Portal has a special section, useful for Apress employees, which displays all the BltAirlines flights retrieved using its web service. The employee can choose a flight then inform the related office, which will then book the selected flight. Naturally, the scenario could be extended to allow particular employees to book a flight directly, maybe by calling another remote procedure, but this is beyond the scope of this simple example, which just shows how to join together the data components you have studied.

Creating the Web Service

Let's start creating the web service. From the New Project menu in Visual Studio .NET, choose ASP.NET web service and call it `BltAirlinesWebService`. The project will contain a service that you will use to add a remote procedure that will return a dataset containing the flights list. Now you can create the database and the table that will contain every flight. You can choose the database you prefer—we chose Microsoft SQL Server—and use that to build the `Blt-AirlinesDB` database, specifying the following columns (see Figure A-31) in the `tabFlights` table (scripts for creation of the database are available in the download).

Figure A-31. *The* `tabFlights` *table design*

You can create a database connection within the Server Explorer window and drag the table onto an empty typed dataset, called `WebService`, that you have to add to the project.

So, now you need to create a `DataAdapter` to fill the DataSet with the data retrieved from the table. Drag the `SqlDataAdapter` data component from the Toolbox window onto the web service design page and use the wizard steps to create an object that only retrieves the records without inserting, updating, and deleting them. This is accomplished by clearing the Generate Insert, Update, and Delete Statements check box from the Advanced dialog box. We chose to create a stored procedure to retrieve the data, but you may need to choose another option if you have used another database.

The last operation you have to do consists of inserting a typed dataset data component pointing to the dataset you have added in the project. Now that the Visual Studio .NET tool has added all the code, you just have to define the web method that returns the dataset.

```
<WebMethod()> Public Function RetrieveFlights() As dsWebService
    da.Fill(ds)
    Return ds
End Function
```

Creating the Apress Portal Application

The Apress Intranet portal will allow employees to book a flight by retrieving the flights list directly from the BltAirlines site, as seen in Figure A-32 (of course, you remember that actually booking a flight online is beyond the scope of this appendix!).

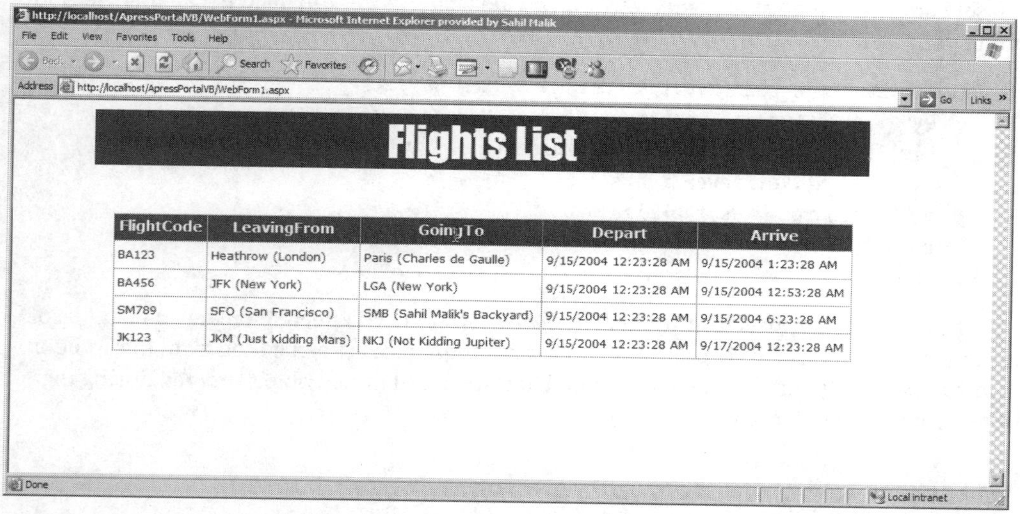

Figure A-32. *Results of the BltAirline web service in a* `DataGrid`

The first operation is adding a web reference to the web service. You can select the Add Web Reference... menu from the Project menu and add the URL where the web service is located, as illustrated in Figure A-33.

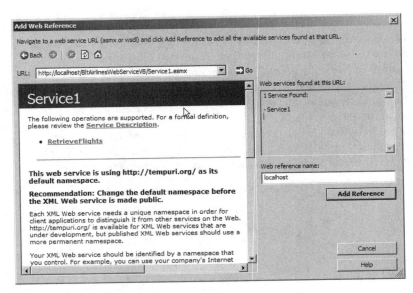

Figure A-33. *Adding a web reference of your web service to your project*

In Figure A-33, you can see the list of methods exposed by the Service1 web service. In this case, just one method is available: the RetrieveFlights procedure. This method returns a dataset containing the list of flights retrieved by the web service. You need to call this method within your code.

```
Private Sub Page_Load(ByVal sender As System.Object, _
    ByVal e As System.EventArgs) Handles MyBase.Load
    Dim flight As New localhost.Service1()
    ds = flight.RetrieveFlights()
    dg.DataSource = ds.tabFlights
    dg.DataBind()
End Sub
```

The method is exposed by the Service1 web service, so you need to create an instance of this object and then call it. The ds DataSet data component has been added from the Toolbox window, specifying that it is to create a typed dataset based on the object created during the web reference linking (see Figure A-34).

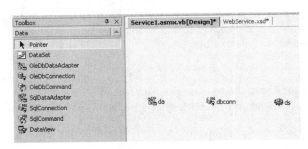

Figure A-34. *Various objects from the Data Toolbox in your project*

To accomplish this task, just drag the `DataSet` data component onto the Design service page and select the typed dataset contained in the project, as illustrated in Figure A-35.

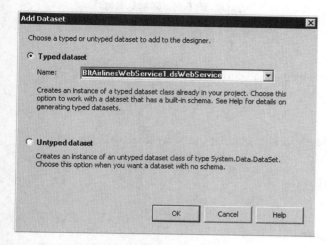

Figure A-35. *Adding a typed dataset to your project*

Now that the dataset is retrieved, you can choose a way to display its records. We chose the `DataGrid` web server control that you'll learn to use at the end of the appendix.

The DataView Data Component

The final data component that you'll look at is the `DataView`. The `DataView` enables developers to filter and sort data in a dataset.

In Visual Studio .NET, you can create a `DataView` object by dragging the icon from the toolbox to a form or other container, in the same way as you have done previously. In this section, you'll see how to create and use a `DataView` data component using the features of Visual Studio .NET.

Using the DataView to View Selected Rows

Usually, a `DataView` data component is added to the project to display a subset of the records in a `DataSet` or `DataTable`. Using a `DataView` data component, you can accomplish two kinds of filtering operation.

- Filter the dataset records using a filter expression—for example, all rows where `lastname` begins with B

- Filter the dataset records using their own row state—for example, all rows that have been changed, or all rows that have been marked for deletion

Note A typed dataset contains a `DataView` object accessible from the `DefaultView` property in the code. So, you do not need to add a `DataView` data component when you have a typed dataset in your code. However, you might choose to add one if you want to set the `DataView` properties at design time using Visual Studio .NET tools.

Let's list the main properties offered by the data component that are necessary for the correct execution of the application.

- `Name`: The object's name
- `AllowDelete`, `AllowEdit`, `AllowNew`: Specifies whether the `DataView` data component allows update operations
- `Table`: Specifies the underlying `DataTable`

Filtering Rows Using a Filter Expression

The `DataView` offers a `RowFilter` property, which you can use to provide a filter expression. You can set the filter expression in the Property field. Its syntax is similar to a SQL `WHERE` clause. Figure A-36 illustrates a filter that retrieves a specific row in the `tabFlights` table of the typed dataset called `ds`.

Figure A-36. `DataView` *properties in Visual Studio .NET*

Visual Studio .NET will generate the code that will filter the content of the dataset retrieving just the row having the value specified.

```
This.dvFlights.RowFilter = "FLIGHTCODE=\'BA101\'"
```

Filtering Rows on Row State

When a DataSet is filled from a data source, each record will be marked as Unchanged. When you use a DataAdapter to write changes back to a data source, it will only make database calls for rows that have changed in some way. So, when you delete a record from a dataset, you are really marking the row as deleted—the data remains in memory until you call the dataset's AcceptChanges method.

The DataView data component offers the RowStateFilter property just to filter the dataset records having a particular row state. By default, it will be set to CurrentRows, which displays Unchanged rows, New rows, and Current Modified rows. However, for your purposes, you'll need to check only Deleted (as shown in Figure A-37).

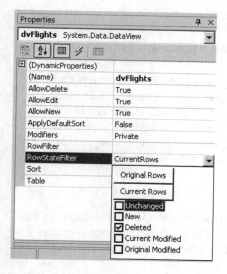

Figure A-37. *Changing the* RowStateFilter *of a* DataView *within Visual Studio .NET*

You can modify the state filter by changing the state of the check boxes in the Property pull-down. The tool will generate the related code to allow the DataView to retrieve filtered records.

```
dvFlights.RowStateFilter = System.Data.DataViewRowState.Deleted
```

This example will only display rows that are marked as deleted—useful if you want to tell the user what rows they are about to delete when they choose to update the data source.

In Figure A-38, a Windows Form shows two data grids: the first contains the current rows retrieved and stored in a typed dataset, while the second shows just the records removed from the typed dataset.

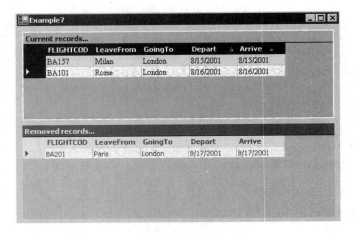

Figure A-38. *Showing the same data through a* DataSet *and a* DataView

Producing an application like this is simple. First, you need two DataView data components pointing to the same typed dataset. The first DataView shows the current records, while the second object is filtered to display only the removed records. At the beginning, the removed records data grid will not display any records, but it will be filled automatically as you select and remove records from the first data grid. This could be a good way to inform the user about every change made to the records before updating the data source.

Using the DataView to Sort Rows

Another useful feature offered by the DataView is sorting the dataset content for display. If you want to sort records by the date and time values contained in the Depart column, you can specify the column name in the Sort property, as illustrated in Figure A-39.

Figure A-39. DataView dvFlights *properties*

The syntax for the Sort property is similar to the SQL ORDER BY clause. You can specify a descending sort simply by putting the DESC instruction after the column name. In addition, you can sort data using more than one column, separating each column name with a comma.

The DataGrid Component

Visual Studio .NET provides an enhanced version of the DataGrid component already available in Visual Basic 6.0. The new features added to this new version are extremely useful. The first thing to note is that a new version of the component is provided, even for web applications. The web version is really powerful: it creates an HTML representation of the data contained in the data source to which it is bound. You can choose to create pages based on simple HTML that display in any browser, or to generate the code specifically for Internet Explorer so that some DHTML code is generated.

Tip The DataGrid class is located in the System.Web.UI.WebControls namespace.

In this final part of the appendix, you'll look at the data grid Web and Windows Form components. First, the Web Forms data grid.

DataGrid Web Component

The DataGrid web component is a web server control that generates an HTML table. The control can bind to a dataset, a data table, a data view, or an array. The DataGrid is read-only by default, but can be customized easily to accomplish updates, insertions, and deletions. Moreover, the DataGrid component enables the user to select a sort column, and adds particular events to manage the records.

To use the DataGrid component, simply drag it from the Web Forms tab within the toolbox onto the aspx page.

Binding the DataGrid Component to a Data Source

To use the DataGrid component correctly, you need to bind it to a data source. This data source could be a dataset, a data table, or a data view object—you use the DataSource and DataMember properties to make the selection (see Figure A-40).

Figure A-40. *Data binding the* DataGrid

In Figure A-40, the data grid is bound to a typed dataset called ds, and you are looking at the tabFlights table within that dataset. Also, you can set the DataKeyField property, which specifies the column that uniquely identifies a given row in this table. This value does not need to be displayed, but it is necessary to specify a DataKeyField if you wish to use the data grid to edit data.

After defining the data source, you need to add a few code instructions to populate the dataset and refresh the content of the data grid. Each time the data grid changes, you must call the DataBind method, in order to display data source changes. So, in the Page_Init event handler, after the component initialize phase, add the following instructions:

```
' Fill the dataset using the data adapter component
daFlights.Fill(dsFlights)

' Populate the data grid
dgFlights.DataBind()
```

The result in Figure A-41 looks unrefined, but is fully working.

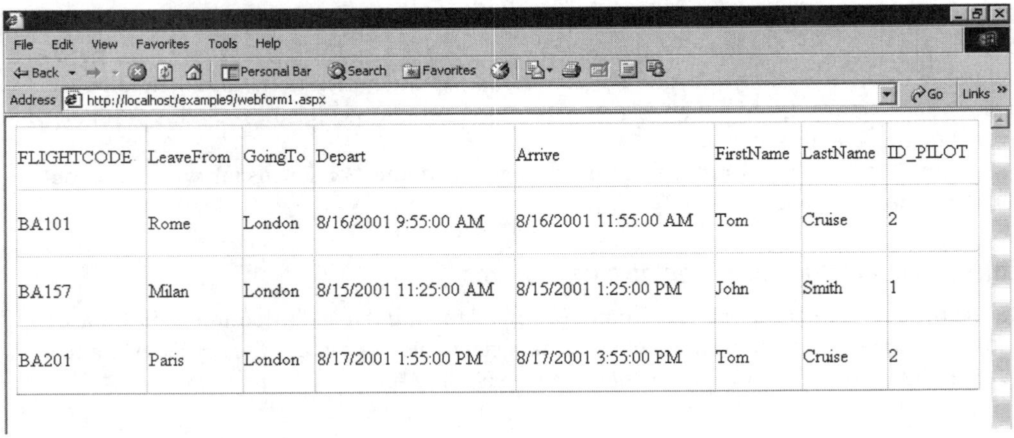

Figure A-41. *The* DataBound *data grid in action*

Formatting the DataGrid

As you can see in Figure A-41, the data grid's default properties make the table look rather sparse. However, Visual Studio .NET provides two ways to improve the component's appearance.

- The Auto Format wizard
- The Property Builder wizard

You can select these wizards by right-clicking on the DataGrid component and choosing the respective menu item.

The Auto Format wizard shows a list of templates to choose from, as shown in Figure A-42.

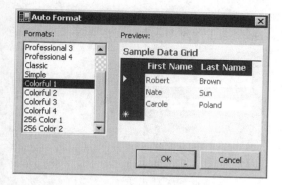

Figure A-42. *Autoformatting the* DataGrid

After clicking the OK button, the layout and the schema will be applied to the data grid immediately, as shown in Figure A-43.

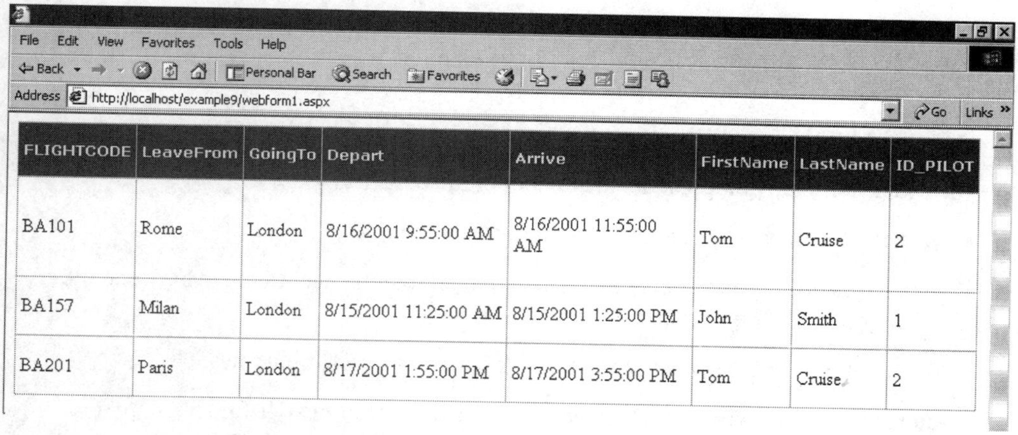

FLIGHTCODE	LeaveFrom	GoingTo	Depart	Arrive	FirstName	LastName	ID_PILOT
BA101	Rome	London	8/16/2001 9:55:00 AM	8/16/2001 11:55:00 AM	Tom	Cruise	2
BA157	Milan	London	8/15/2001 11:25:00 AM	8/15/2001 1:25:00 PM	John	Smith	1
BA201	Paris	London	8/17/2001 1:55:00 PM	8/17/2001 3:55:00 PM	Tom	Cruise	2

Figure A-43. *The* DataGrid *in Figure A-41 after autoformatting*

The Property Builder wizard allows developers to choose a style for each data grid section, such as Header and Footer (see Figure A-44). In this way, you have more options than with the Auto Format wizard.

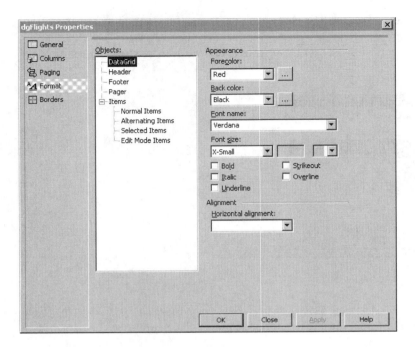

Figure A-44. *Specifying your own format styles for the* DataGrid

You can associate a style with each element contained in the Objects tree view, and preview the results using the Apply button. You can change the appearance of each of the following objects:

- DataGrid: This object represents the appearance of the whole data grid.

- Header: This object represents the header of the data grid.

- Footer: This object represents the footer of the data grid.

- Pager: This object represents the buttons that enable the user to move between different pages, when the data grid is divided into pages.

- Normal Items: This object represents the appearance of normal rows.

- Alternating Items: This object allows you to have a different style for alternate rows, which can help users to scan across a row because not all rows look identical.

- Selected Items: This object represents the style of the currently selected row.

- Edit Mode Items: This object represents the appearance of rows as they are being edited.

You can also configure the columns that will be displayed in the DataGrid component. By default, the columns are displayed automatically, retrieving their names from the data source. You can modify this and specify which columns to display, what to call them, and how to display them. To do this, select the Columns tab in the left pane of the Property Builder, which will display the dialog box shown in Figure A-45.

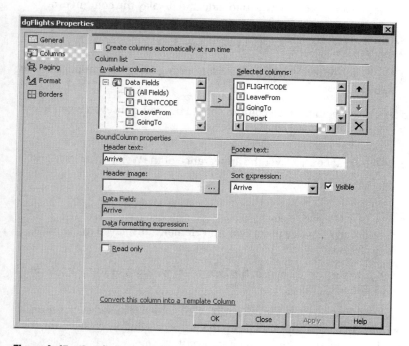

Figure A-45. *Configuring the columns for the* DataGrid

By default, Create Columns Automatically at Run Time is checked. Before setting up the columns manually, you have to uncheck it. After that, you can select and customize the columns that will be displayed in the data grid. Let's look at your options.

- The Available Columns tree view lists four items: *Data Fields* contains all the fields within the data source bound to the data grid component; *Button Column* allows you to add a button to each data grid's row to accomplish particular tasks (there are five buttons already defined to select a data grid's row, to edit, update, cancel an update, and delete a row); *HyperLink Column* allows you to define a URL link for the data grid's column value; *Template Column* allows you to add controls other than buttons to the data grid's rows.

- The Selected Columns list box enables you to change the order of the columns and remove the ones that you don't want to display.

- Header Text specifies the text that will appear as the title of the column.

- Footer Text specifies the text that will appear on the data grid column footer.

- Header Image specifies a path and a filename for an image file that you want use in the data grid column header. The image will replace the header text.

- Sort Expression contains the column that will be used to sort the grid.

- The Visible check box allows you to hide and to show a column. Making the column invisible, instead of removing it, will allow you to hide and display the column programmatically.

- Data Field is used to bind the column to a particular data field in your data source.

- Data Formatting Expression allows you to define a formatting expression applied to the column before it is shown.

- The Read Only check box specifies that a column should be read-only even when in Edit mode.

These properties give you great control over the appearance of the Web Form's data grid component.

Sorting DataGrid Records

The data grid component offers an easy way to sort column elements displayed in the page. There are three easy steps, as follows:

1. Set the AllowSorting property to true from the Properties window, or from the General tab in the Property Builder.

2. Add an event handler to the SortCommand data grid event, which is raised each time the user sorts the records. You can easily add it from the Property window by selecting the events list and double-clicking on the SortCommand event.

3. Add just a few code instructions to sort and to display the sorted column records.

The code to accomplish the sort operation is shown here.

```
Private Sub dgFlights_SortCommand(ByVal source As Object, _
    ByVal e As DataGridSortCommandEventArgs) _
    Handles dgFlights.SortCommand
  dvFlights.Sort = e.SortExpression
  dgFlights.DataBind()
End Sub
```

The DataGridSortCommandEventArgs object contains the element to which the sort has to be applied. The code applies the sort to a DataView object associated with the data source.

Selecting, Editing, Updating, and Deleting DataGrid Records

The DataGrid component offers some properties to allow users to edit data. By using these properties, we can

- Select a row, consequently changing the data grid's SelectIndex property

- Edit a data grid record, showing text fields where the data has changed

- Update the edited record
- Delete a data grid row

Selecting a DataGrid Row

Often, a data grid acts as a menu, allowing the user to select a particular row. For example, an e-commerce site might show a grid listing available items, and allow users to select what they want to buy. To create a data grid that does this, open the Property Builder and add a Select Button column. You can specify the column's header, the caption that should appear in each cell, and the command name.

In addition, you can choose a different style to be shown when the row is selected. From the Property Builder, change the selected tab to Format and specify a new style for the Selected Items object.

The last and most important operation is to retrieve the content of the selected row. To do this, add an event handler to the SelectedIndexChanged event and insert some instructions. The following code snippet shows how to add a confirmation message when a specific row is selected:

```
Private Sub dgFlights_SelectedIndexChanged(ByVal sender As Object, _
        ByVal e As System.EventArgs) _
     Handles dgFlights.SelectedIndexChanged
  Dim dgi As DataGridItem = CType(sender, DataGrid).SelectedItem

  outputText.InnerHtml = "The flight " & dgi.Cells(1).Text & _
     " has been booked"
End Sub
```

The sender object is the DataGrid component that raised the event. You retrieve the selected DataGridItem using the SelectedItem property. Then you can retrieve the data grid's cells using the Cells collection exposed by the object. The final result is shown in Figure A-46.

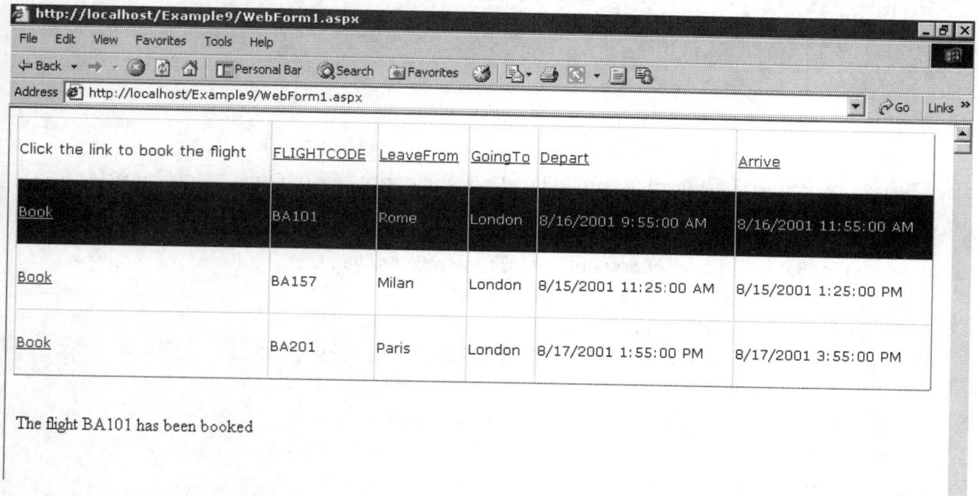

Figure A-46. *An interactive* DataGrid

Putting a DataGrid Row into Edit Mode

The DataGrid component offers an easy way for users to edit and modify its content. You can add an Edit button to each row that will put that row into Edit mode. In order to add the editing functionality, you need to add the Edit, Update, Cancel button column object. Optionally, you can specify the text that has to be shown on the buttons within the data grid. Then you have to add the EditCommand event handler, inserting the necessary code to put the chosen row into Edit mode. The following code manages the EditCommand event:

```
Private Sub dgFlights_EditCommand(ByVal source As Object, _
        ByVal e As DataGridCommandEventArgs) _
        Handles dgFlights.EditCommand
    dgFlights.EditItemIndex = e.Item.ItemIndex
    dgFlights.DataBind()
End Sub
```

The DataGridCommandEventArg object passed to the event handler contains the item index of the edited row, which you use to specify which row should be made editable.

Updating a DataGrid Row

After the editing operations, the user can select the Update button (which doesn't always look like a button, but you can see it in the left portion of the screenshot in Figure A-47) in order to reflect the changes back to the database. In Figure A-47, the user can change the quantity of goods ordered in a basket.

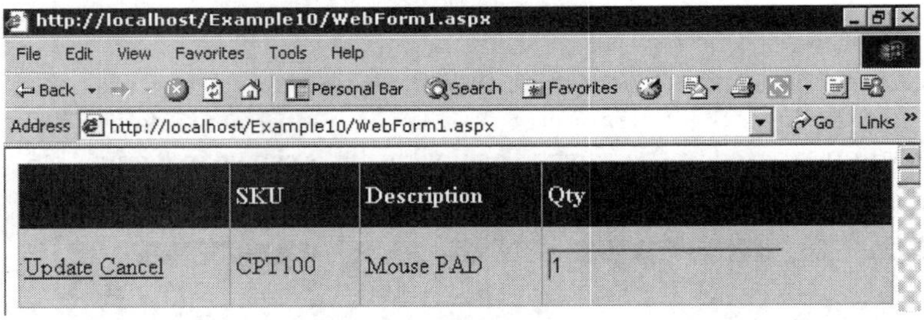

Figure A-47. *An editable* DataGrid

The Update button link will raise the UpdateCommand event, which you catch in order to update the data source with the new value.

```
Private Sub dgBasket_UpdateCommand(ByVal source As Object, _
        ByVal e As DataGridCommandEventArgs) _
        Handles dgBasket.UpdateCommand
    Dim strQTY As String = CType(e.Item.Cells(3).Controls(0), _
            TextBox).Text
    ds.Basket(0).Qty = System.Int16.Parse(strQTY)
    dgBasket.EditItemIndex = -1
    dgBasket.DataBind()
End Sub
```

Using the `Cells` collection exposed by the `DataGrid` component, you retrieve the text contained in the cell. If you didn't use a template for the column, the cell would always contain a single text field—so you only retrieve the first item in the `Controls` collection. If the cell contains multiple components, you can retrieve them one at a time using their index in the `Controls` collection.

The Cancel button cancels the update operation and returns to the normal view. You use the `CancelCommand` event to implement this behavior.

```
Private Sub dgBasket_CancelCommand(ByVal source As Object, _
      ByVal e As DataGridCommandEventArgs) _
      Handles dgBasket.CancelCommand
   dgBasket.EditItemIndex = -1
   dgBasket.DataBind()
End Sub
```

The first instruction puts all of the rows into normal mode without updating the data source, the second rebinds the data to the data grid.

Deleting a DataGrid Row

The data grid operation that you'll look at now is row deletion. To add this feature, follow these steps:

1. Insert a Delete button object into the data grid, using the Property Builder dialog box.

2. Add an event handler for the `DeleteCommand` event.

3. Add the code to update the data source.

The first two steps are very similar to operations you have already seen. The code required in the event handler could be the following:

```
Private Sub dgBasket_DeleteCommand(ByVal source As Object, _
      ByVal e As DataGridCommandEventArgs) _
      Handles dgBasket.DeleteCommand
   Dim row As dsBasket.BasketRow = _
         ds.Basket.FindBySKU(e.Item.Cells(1).Text)
   ds.Basket.RemoveBasketRow(row)

   dgBasket.DataBind()
End Sub
```

This handler, used the `FindBySKU` method to find the correct row in the dataset, is based on the primary key of the row that is being deleted. The `e.Item.Cells(1).Text` instruction retrieves the SKU value present on the selected item that is the primary key column for the template. Then, it removes that row from the dataset, and finally rebinds the data grid to the data.

Breaking a DataGrid into Pages

If a data grid contains a lot of records, it can be a good idea to display a limited number of rows per page, and allow users to move between pages. Usually, just ten rows are displayed for each page, but you can change this by setting the Page Size in the Paging sheet of the Properties Builder, as seen in Figure A-48.

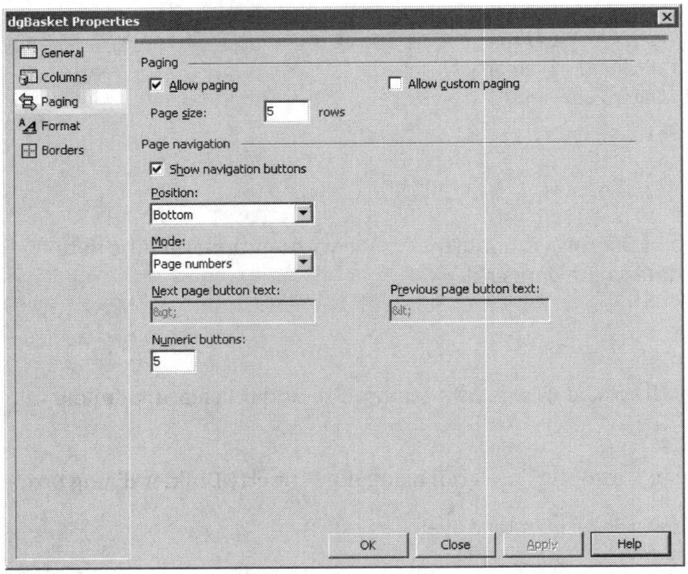

Figure A-48. *Specifying pagination properties for the* DataGrid

You also choose where to display the navigation buttons and whether to display navigation buttons as numbers or as Next/Previous buttons. To enable these settings, make sure Allow Paging is checked. This will cause the DataGrid to display a new Navigation bar, as shown in Figure A-49.

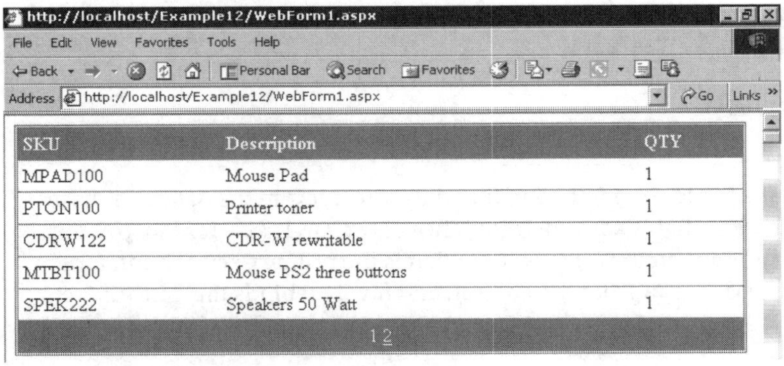

Figure A-49. *A paginated DataGrid*

You have to attach some code to the PageIndexChanged event handler in order to manage the navigation. The code is really simple, as follows:

```
dgBasket.CurrentPageIndex = e.NewPageIndex
dgBasket.DataBind()
```

This sets the CurrentPageIndex property of the data grid to the page index selected by the user.

DataGrid Window Component

The DataGrid window component offers similar features to the web control, but with more flexibility and power.

The big difference is how the data is managed. You no longer need to call the DataBind method repeatedly: the data source changes are reflected in the component immediately. Moreover, every data grid operation, such as removing or modifying a record, is managed by the DataGrid component automatically. Even the sort operation is executed by the component without the need to write event handler code.

The DataGrid window component provides features that you don't find in the web control, because they cannot be represented in an HTML page. One of these is record navigation, which allows users to navigate among related tables—passing from parent records to child records using buttons provided by the component.

Figure A-50 shows two tables that are related in a single dataset object. The DataGrid component allows the user to navigate between the tables.

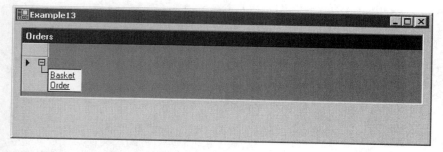

Figure A-50. *WinForms* DataGrid, *with two tables in it*

Setting the DataGrid's DataSource property to a DataView allows you to use the AllowEdit, AllowNew, and AllowDelete DataView properties to either enable or disable features in the DataGrid component. For example, setting the AllowNew property to False in the DataView prevents the DataGrid component from creating a new record in the data source. You can prevent the DataGrid from allowing modifications, regardless of whether the data source is a DataView object, by setting the DataGrid's ReadOnly property to True.

Summary

In this appendix, you have seen how you can use Visual Studio .NET to create ADO.NET applications quickly and easily. You have found easy ways to implement common database access features into your applications. Using Visual Studio .NET, and very little code, you have learned to

- Connect to a database

- Execute commands against a database

- Work with `DataAdapters`

- Create and use typed datasets

- Work with the `DataView` component

- Display data using the `DataGrid`

With this we end this book. Like anything else, ADO.NET in itself is a topic that can be dealt with any extent of depth; however, if you have read this book cover to cover, it would have lent you enough insight into a practical use of ADO.NET with a lot of other surrounding Microsoft technologies. The best approach to any problem is never a single black magic bullet, but an esoteric art gained over an experience of many years, which this book has attempted to shed some light upon. We certainly hope you enjoyed reading it as much as we enjoyed writing it. Now let's put this knowledge to good use!

Index

forums.apress.com

FOR PROFESSIONALS BY PROFESSIONALS™

JOIN THE APRESS FORUMS AND BE PART OF OUR COMMUNITY. You'll find discussions that cover topics of interest to IT professionals, programmers, and enthusiasts just like you. If you post a query to one of our forums, you can expect that some of the best minds in the business—especially Apress authors, who all write with *The Expert's Voice*™—will chime in to help you. Why not aim to become one of our most valuable participants (MVPs) and win cool stuff? Here's a sampling of what you'll find:

DATABASES
Data drives everything.

Share information, exchange ideas, and discuss any database programming or administration issues.

INTERNET TECHNOLOGIES AND NETWORKING
Try living without plumbing (and eventually IPv6).

Talk about networking topics including protocols, design, administration, wireless, wired, storage, backup, certifications, trends, and new technologies.

JAVA
We've come a long way from the old Oak tree.

Hang out and discuss Java in whatever flavor you choose: J2SE, J2EE, J2ME, Jakarta, and so on.

MAC OS X
All about the Zen of OS X.

OS X is both the present and the future for Mac apps. Make suggestions, offer up ideas, or boast about your new hardware.

OPEN SOURCE
Source code is good; understanding (open) source is better.

Discuss open source technologies and related topics such as PHP, MySQL, Linux, Perl, Apache, Python, and more.

PROGRAMMING/BUSINESS
Unfortunately, it is.

Talk about the Apress line of books that cover software methodology, best practices, and how programmers interact with the "suits."

WEB DEVELOPMENT/DESIGN
Ugly doesn't cut it anymore, and CGI is absurd.

Help is in sight for your site. Find design solutions for your projects and get ideas for building an interactive Web site.

SECURITY
Lots of bad guys out there—the good guys need help.

Discuss computer and network security issues here. Just don't let anyone else know the answers!

TECHNOLOGY IN ACTION
Cool things. Fun things.

It's after hours. It's time to play. Whether you're into LEGO® MINDSTORMS™ or turning an old PC into a DVR, this is where technology turns into fun.

WINDOWS
No defenestration here.

Ask questions about all aspects of Windows programming, get help on Microsoft technologies covered in Apress books, or provide feedback on any Apress Windows book.

HOW TO PARTICIPATE:
Go to the Apress Forums site at **http://forums.apress.com/**.
Click the New User link.